Computer Confluence

EXPLORING TOMORROW'S TECHNOLOGY

FOURTH EDITION

Computer Confluence

EXPLORING TOMORROW'S TECHNOLOGY

George Beekman

Oregon State University

Prentice
Hall

PRENTICE HALL

Upper Saddle River, New Jersey 07458

Editor-in-Chief:	Mickey Cox
Senior Developmental Editor:	Lena Buonanno
Managing Editor:	Melissa Whitaker
Editorial Assistant:	Maryann Broadnax
Director Strategic Marketing:	Nancy Evans
Assistant Editor:	Kerri Limpert
Media Project Manager:	Nancy Welcher
Production Editor:	Marc Oliver
Managing Editor/Production:	Sondra Greenfield
Production Manager:	Paul Smolenski
Associate Director/Manufacturing:	Vincent Scelta
Senior Designer:	Cheryl Asherman
Design Director:	Patricia Smythe
Interior Design:	Ox + Company
Photo Research Supervisor:	Beth Boyd
Image Permission Supervisor:	Kay Dellosa
Photo Researcher:	Abby Reip
Cover Design:	Ox + Company
Cover Photos:	Schlowsky Computer Imagery, Christopher Irion Photography, and Bruce Byers Photography © Workbook Stock Photography, Photo Montage by Robin Milecevic and Blair Brown
Production Service:	Carlisle Communications

Photo, screen capture, and text credits appear on pages 493–495.

Library of Congress Cataloging-in-Publication Data

Beekman, George.
   Computer confluence : exploring tomorrow's technology / George Beekman.—4th ed.
      p. cm.
   Includes bibliographical references and index.
   ISBN 0-13-088237-2
   1. Computers. 2. Information technology. I. Title.

   QA76.5.B3652 2001
   004—dc21

                                                        00-042794

Pearson Education Limited (UK)
Pearson Education Australia Pty Ltd
Prentice Hall Canada Ltd
Pearson Educación de Mexico, S.A. de C.V.
Pearson Education Japan KK
Pearson Education China Ltd
Pearson Education Asia Pte Ltd

10 9 8 7 6 5 4 3 2 1
ISBN 0-13-088237-2

To Sue, Ben, and Johanna
My inspiration...
yesterday, today, and tomorrow.

Computer Confluence Fourth Edition

More Than a Textbook

Computer Confluence is regarded by many as the best textbook available for introducing students to computers, the Internet, and the human impact of information technology. But *Computer Confluence* is much more than a textbook—it's an integrated teaching/learning system designed to meet the needs of students and instructors alike. In addition to this book, the Computer Confluence system includes the following components:

STUDENT CD-ROM Included free with every new copy of the book, this digital companion offers 2-D and 3-D animated illustrations and exercises, thought-provoking video clips, self-paced interactive tutorials, and self-assessment quizzes that can be printed out with text referenced pages.

The contents of the CD-ROM are tightly integrated with the book, expanding on and illustrating key concepts using state-of-the-art multimedia. Each chapter of the book opens with a list of CD-ROM highlights. CD-ROM icons throughout the chapters point to related multimedia material on the CD-ROM.

COMPANION WEBSITE (www.prenhall.com/beekman) This comprehensive on-line supplement offers a wealth of integrated material to expand on the contents of the text. For faculty, the Companion Website includes a Syllabus Manager that provides instructors with an easy, step-by-step process to create and revise syllabi with direct links into the Companion Website and additional on-line content. The site also includes faculty resources available for instant download. For students, the Companion Website includes a free on-line interactive study guide, on-line Internet exercises, and communication tools including chat rooms and bulletin boards. Both students and faculty appreciate the hundreds of tightly organized, clearly annotated, regularly updated links to related material on the Web. Each chapter of the book opens with a list of highlights on the Web for the chapter. Web icons throughout each chapter signal that additional content on subjects appear on the book's Web site.

INSTRUCTOR'S RESOURCE CD-ROM for Windows 95, 98, 2000, and NT. The Instructor's Resource CD-ROM contains the tools you need whether you do full-blown multimedia presentations and post self-assessment quizzes on the Web or teach with an overhead projector and test using paper-and-pencil quizzes. The CD-ROM includes the Instructor's Resource Manual, Computerized Test Bank, PowerPoint presentation, the Image Library of text art, and an HTML Reference Help File.

- The **Instructor's Resource Manual (IRM)**, prepared by Jerry Reed, is available both in a Microsoft Word and Adobe Acrobat format. The IRM includes chapter objectives, chapter overviews, key term definitions, class outlines, perspective notes to share with the students, technical notes to help elaborate on more complex issues, teaching tips on how to present material in a "new" way, quotes that are pertinent to the material at hand, and test bank and PowerPoint presentation references.

- **Test Item File,** prepared by Lucille Genduso of Nova University, includes thousands of high-quality test questions designed to test student knowledge and understanding. The test bank includes four types of questions: Multiple choice, True or false, Completion, and Essay. Each question is labeled with a level of difficulty and references the text section where the answer to the question can be found. This edition's test bank is greatly expanded and contains 50% new questions.

- **Computerized Test Bank** allows you to view and edit questions, create multiple versions of tests, easily search and arrange questions in the order you prefer, add or modify test bank questions, administer tests on a network, or convert your tests to HTML to post to the Web.

- **PowerPoint Presentation,** prepared by Glenda Frieson, includes images, animation, video, sound clips, and lecture outlines that allow you to present and discuss key images from the book.

- An **HTML Reference** help file includes all the commands in HTML 4.0, with examples of their use, and runs in your Web browser. This can be used as a supplement to *Compact Guide: Web Page Creation and Design,* Second Edition, by Linda Ericksen, which is packaged free with the student text.

VIDEO Prentice Hall and Computer Chronicles have joined forces to provide a video library that offers a variety of documentary and feature-style stories on computers and applications of information technology.

Computer Confluence Applications Bundles

Prentice Hall offers a full range of computer applications texts. All of these series are available as a custom bundle with *Computer Confluence.* The applications series are all supported by MOUS-certified (Microsoft Office User Specialist) interactive computer-based tutorials and skills-based assessment software. This outstanding product line includes the

- Learn Office Series,

- Ericksen Quick/Simple Series,

- Select Lab Series,

- Essentials Series,

- Duffy Office Series, and

- Grauer Exploring Office Series.

The MOUS Essentials Series and the Prentice Hall MOUS Test Prep Series are also available and focus specifically on MOUS exam preparation. Your Prentice Hall representative will be happy to work with you and your bookstore manager to provide the most current information on these products, outline the ordering process, and provide pricing, ISBN's, and delivery information.

Brief Contents

Contents

| **Chapter 3** | Hardware Basics: Peripherals | **52** |

Chapter 4 Software Basics: The Ghost in the Machine 82

Part Two USING COMPUTERS 119

Essential Applications

Chapter 5 Working with Words: Word Processing and Digital Publishing 120

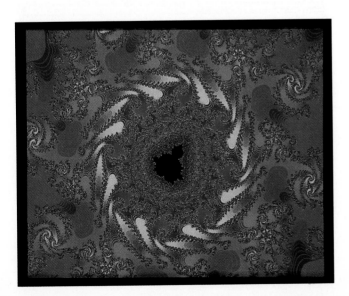

Chapter 6   Calculation, Visualization, and Simulation   150

Part Three

EXPLORING WITH COMPUTERS   237

Networks and Gateways

Chapter 9   Networking and Telecommunication   238

Chapter 10   From Internet to Information Infrastructure   262

Part Four

MASTERING COMPUTERS   301

Issues, Algorithms, and Intelligence

Chapter 11   ### Computer Security and Risks   302

Chapter 12   Systems Design and Development   332

Chapter 13   Is Artificial Intelligence Real?   364

Part Five   LIVING WITH COMPUTERS   391

Information Age Implications

Chapter 14   Computers at Work   392

Chapter 15   Computers at School and Home   418

Chapter 16   Inventing the Future   444

Preface

Confluence 1: a coming or flowing together, meeting, or gathering at one point (a happy confluence of weather and scenery); 2a: the flowing together of two or more streams; b: the place of meeting of two streams; c: the combined stream formed by conjunction

—Merriam Webster's Collegiate Dictionary, **Electronic Edition**

When powerful forces come together, change is inevitable. As we enter the 21st century, we're standing at the confluence of three powerful technological forces: computers, telecommunications, and electronic entertainment. The computer's digital technology is showing up in everything from telephones to televisions, and the lines that separate these machines are eroding. This digital convergence is rapidly—and radically—altering the world's economic landscape. Start-up companies and industries are emerging to ride the waves of change, while older organizations reorganize, regroup, and redefine themselves to keep from being washed away.

Smaller computers, faster processors, smarter software, larger networks, new communication media—in the world of information technology, it seems like change is the only constant. In less than a human lifetime, this technological cascade has transformed virtually every facet of our society—and the transformation is just beginning. As old technologies merge and new technologies emerge, far-fetched predictions routinely come true. This headlong rush into the high-tech future poses a formidable challenge for all of us: How can we extract the knowledge we need from the deluge of information? What must we understand about information technology to successfully navigate the waters of change that carry us into the future? *Computer Confluence: Exploring Tomorrow's Technology* is designed to aid travelers on their journey into that future.

What Is *Computer Confluence*?

Computer Confluence is more than a textbook; it's the confluence of three powerful information sources: an illustrated textbook, a multimedia CD-ROM, and a dynamic World Wide Web site. This integrated learning package takes advantage of the unique strengths of three media types:

► *Computer Confluence, the book.* In spite of the talk about a paperless future, a book's user interface still has many advantages: You can read it under a tree or on the subway, you can bend the corners and scribble in the margins, you can study the words and pictures for hours without suffering from eyestrain or backache. A well-written text can serve as a learning tool, a reference work, a study guide, and even a source of motivation and inspiration. A textbook is no substitute for a good teacher, but a good textbook can almost always make a good teacher better. This book, which started out as *Computer Currents* in 1994, has served as an information-age guidebook for hundreds of thousands of students through its first three editions.

► *Computer Confluence, the CD-ROM.* A CD-ROM may not be as warm and friendly as a good book, but it can deliver video, audio, animation, and other dynamic media that can't be printed on paper. A well-designed CD-ROM can encourage exploration through interactivity. The *Computer Confluence* CD-ROM supplements and reinforces the material in the book with state-of-the-art 3-D animation, audio, and video. Unlike many textbook CD-ROMs, this one was designed from the ground up to supplement and expand on the material in the book. The CD-ROM has a wealth of materials, including interactive explorations, video clips, practice quizzes with printable results, that make it easy to monitor student progress. Students find that it's easy and fun to explore the CD-ROM using its innovative 3-D user interface and its streamlined hypertext interface. The CD-ROM runs on almost all modern Windows and Macintosh machines, so students can use it on their own computers—even computers that aren't the same kind as they use in school labs. It runs without installing any files on the local hard disk, requiring only QuickTime for animations, so it can be used even in the most tightly controlled public labs.

► *Computer Confluence, the Web site* (www.prenhall.com/beekman). The information in computer books and CD-ROMs has a short shelf life. The Internet makes it possible to publish up-to-the-minute information and link that information to other sources around the world. The Internet can also serve as a communication conduit for on-line discussion and research. An extensive collection of timely, media-rich Web pages keeps the information in *Computer Confluence* current. The pages include multimedia tidbits, and links to the most important computer and information technology sites, all organized by chapter and topic. The Web site also includes discussion areas where students, instructors, and authors can meet online. Students can also to take practice quizzes and submit answers to on-line exercises.

    Students don't need to have access to CD-ROM drives and the World Wide Web to benefit from *Computer Confluence;* they can easily master the material in the book without using other media. But the additional material on the CD-ROM and the Web can make their learning experiences more interesting, exciting, and timely.

Computer Confluence presents computers and information technology on three levels:

► **Explanations:** *Computer Confluence* clearly explains what a computer is and what it can (and can't) do; it explains the basics of information technology, from multimedia PCs to the Internet, clearly and concisely.

► **Applications:** *Computer Confluence* illustrates how computers and networks can be used as practical tools to solve a wide variety of problems.

► **Implications:** *Computer Confluence* puts computers in a human context, illustrating how information technology affects our lives, our world, and our future.

Who Is *Computer Confluence* For?

Computer Confluence: Exploring Tomorrow's Technology is designed especially for the introductory computer class for both non-majors and majors. *Computer Confluence* is also appropriate for introductory computer science classes, discipline-specific computer courses offered through other departments, high school courses, and adult education courses. *Computer Confluence* can also serve as a self-study guide for anyone who's motivated to understand the changing technological landscape.

    Most introductory computer courses are divided into lecture and lab sections. In some courses the labs cover desktop applications such as Microsoft Office; in other courses the labs cover Internet tools such as electronic mail and the World Wide Web; a few courses include programming with langauges such as Visual BASIC, C, and Java. Since this book focuses on concepts rather than keystrokes, it can be used in courses that teach any combination of lab applications and tools.

Throughout Computer Confluence special focus boxes complement the text:

Throughout the book, icons indicate links to supplementary material on the CD-ROM and the World Wide Web.

Human Connection

Human Connection boxes at the beginning of all chapters feature stories of personalities who made an impact on the world of computing, and in some cases, people whose lives were transformed by computers and information technology.

How It Works

How It Works boxes are designed to provide additional technical material for courses and students who need it. How does the CPU execute a program? Why does a color image look different on the screen than on a printout? How does compression make files smaller? How can messeges be encrypted? Students will find answers to these kinds of questions in the How It Works boxes. For classes where this kind of technical detail isn't necessary, students can safely skip these boxes without missing any critical information. How It Works boxes are numbered to make it easy for instructors to create customized reading assignments by specifying which are required and which are optional.

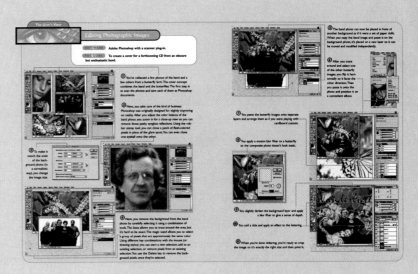

The User's View

The User's View boxes show the reader, through screens and text, what it's like to work with computer applications without getting bogged down in the details of button pushing. Featured applications are the latest versions of applications used by professionals, including Microsoft Office 2000, Quark xPress, and Adobe Photoshop. These applications are available in similar versions on both Windows and Macintosh platforms.

Rules of Thumb

Rules of Thumb boxes provide practical, nontechnical tips for avoiding the pitfalls and problems created by computer technology. How can you use graphics effectively and tastefully in a computer document? How can you minimize the health hazards of extended computer use? How can you protect your data from viruses and other software risks? What's the best way to communicate effectively with electronic mail? These are the types of questions that are answered in Rules of Thumb boxes.

Crosscurrents

Crosscurrents boxes at the end of each chapter provide thought-provoking, timely, and sometimes controversial essays and articles by respected writers, analysts, and industry insiders. How is this technology changing our lives? What have we given up in return for a high-tech future? Who stands to gain the most, and who stands to lose the most, as we move into an information-based economy? How will future generations experience you digital works of art and literature? Is personal privacy history? Are digital implants in our medical future? These and other questions are raised—and wrestled with—in Crosscurrents boxes.

How Is *Computer Confluence* Organized?

The book consists of 16 chapters organized into five broad sections:

1 Approaching Computers: Hardware and Software Fundamentals

2 Using Computers: Essential Applications

3 Exploring with Computers: Networks and Gateways

4 Mastering Computers: Issues, Algorithms, and Intelligence

5 Living with Computers: Information Age Implications

Part 1 provides the basics: a brief historical perspective, a nontechnical discussion of computer and Internet basics, and an overview of hardware and software options. These chapters quickly introduce key concepts that recur throughout the book, putting the student on solid ground for understanding future chapters. **Part 2** covers the most important and widely used computer applications, including word processing, desktop publishing, spreadsheets, graphics, multimedia tools, and databases. These applications, like those in Parts 3 and 4, are presented in terms of concepts and trends rather than keystrokes. **Part 3** explores the world of networks, from simple interoffice LANs to the massive global infrastructure that's evolving from the Internet. **Part 4** begins with a discussion of information technology risks and related ethical issues; it then explores the process and the problems of creating software, including the curious field of computer science known as artificial intelligence. **Part 5** explores the far-reaching impact of computers on our work, our schools, our homes, our society, and our future.

Throughout the five parts, the book's focus gradually flows from the concrete to the controversial and from the present to the future. Individual chapters have a similarly expanding focus. After a brief introduction, each chapter flows from concrete concepts that provide grounding for beginners toward abstract, future-oriented questions and ideas.

Each chapter includes **instructional aids** to help students master the material quickly. Key terms are highlighted in boldface blue type for quick reference; secondary terms are italicized blue. Terms are defined in context, in a glossary at the end of the text, and in the CD-ROM's hypertext glossary. Each chapter opens with a summary of the key content that can be found in the chapter, on the Web site, and on the CD, and a list of objectives. Each chapter ends with a chapter summary; a list of key terms; collections of review questions, discussion questions, and projects; and an annotated list of sources and resources for students who want more information or intellectual stimulation.

New to the Fourth Edition

Each edition of *Computer Confluence* is written, in part, by professors and students like you. We receive hundreds of email messages and Web responses commenting on the book, the CD-ROM, and the Web site, and the way they work—and don't work—together to provide an integrated learning experience. Your comments and suggestions are important to us; many have a direct impact on the content of future editions. For this edition, as with previous editions, we've systematically surveyed professors and incorporated many of their ideas in the new edition. This edition also reflects rapid and significant changes in the technological landscape brought on by the Internet explosion. Here's a chapter-by-chapter breakdown of major changes to this edition:

▶ Chapter 1, "Computer Currents: From Calculation to Communication," has been expanded so that it is, in essence, a survey and preview of the rest of the book. It's the "where are we going?" chapter. Most significant is the increase in Internet material. Chapter 1 now covers everything from Web browsers to Internet appliances. There's also more in this chapter—and throughout the book—on ethical and social implications of digital technology.

- Chapter 2, "Hardware Basics: Inside the Box," and Chapter 3, "Hardware Basics: Peripherals," have been updated with coverage of state-of-the-market hardware. There's a more practical emphasis on equipment that students will encounter in their day-to-day computing experience. A new section on expansion includes a survey of slots and ports found in standard "legacy" PCs, plus details about USB and IEEE 1394 (FireWire), modern I/O standards that are taking center stage in new machines.

- Chapter 4, "Software Basics: The Ghost in the Machine," features new coverage of Linux, the open-software phenomenon, along with other major OSs. The chapter opener features Linus Torvolds, the young father of Linux.

- Chapter 5, "Working with Words: Word Processing and Digital Publishing," includes expanded coverage of publishing for the Web and speech input for word processors.

- Chapter 6, "Calculation, Visualization, and Simulation," has updated examples and illustrations of number-crunching and modeling applications.

- Chapter 7, "Graphics, Hypermedia, and Multimedia," addresses the emergence of nonlinear video editing, digital video interfaces via IEEE 1394 (FireWire), MP3 music files, and multimedia Web publishing. It also includes a new Rules of Thumb box with tips for making powerful presentations.

- Chapter 8, "Database Applications and Implications," includes updated examples of Web database searching and expanded coverage of PDAs, multimedia databases, and Web databases.

- Chapter 9, "Networking and Telecommunication," introduces DSL, cable modems, and other broadband modem alternatives. (These are covered in depth in Chapter 10.) Ethical issues are more visible with a revised section entitled On-Line Issues: Reliability, Security, Privacy, and Humanity. New technologies such as GPS are now included. Connectivity options and bandwidth coverage, formerly in a How It Works box, have been streamlined into the main text.

- Chapter 10, "From Internet to Information Infrastructure," is significantly expanded to include three new major sections: (1) Internet Connections provides detailed coverage of DSL, cable modems, satellite dishes, and other broadband connection options. (2) Internet Issues: Ethical and Political Dilemmas discusses social problems related to the Net. (3) Internet Everywhere: The Invisible Information Infrastructure deals with the science-fiction future that's almost here, populated by Internet appliances that can talk to each other. Several sections from the previous edition have been updated. For example, the section on search engines, now called Searching the Web: Search Engines and Portals, has been updated and expanded to reflect the latest terminology and technology, including natural-language search engines and portals. The section called From Hypertext to Multimedia has been expanded to include clear explanations of streaming media, MP3, downloadable video and audio, real-time audio and video (Webcasts), and the most important plug-ins and helper applications. Coverage of Internet2, the next-generation academic/research Internet, has been expanded. The Web authoring section emphasizes the evolving Web with clear explanations of the role of HTML, JavaScript, Java, dynamic HTML, XML, VRML, and WML. A How It Works box on Internet addressing has been merged into the main text and covers new domain names. There's a new How It Works 10.1: The World Wide Web.

- Chapter 11, "Computer Security and Risks," has been updated with the latest data on computer crime and security. A new section called Virus Wars describes the ongoing race between new strains of viruses and antivirus tools, with clear implications for computer users. Recent examples of security breaches, including webjacking and denial of service (DOS) attacks, make the chapter more timely. There's more on security hardware, including UPS devices, RAID systems, and firewalls. There's more of an ethical emphasis in the expanded and updated section called Security, Privacy, Freedom, and Ethics: The Delicate Balance. The updated section on Security and Reliability includes an analysis of the lessons we can learn from the Y2K phenomenon. And a new Computer Ethics Rules of Thumb box presents a concise summary of the application of ethical principles to information technology.

► Chapter 12, "Systems Design and Development," has been updated for currency and reorganized so it flows more smoothly. There's also more on programming for the Web.

► Chapter 13, "Is Artificial Intelligence Real?" has been updated with recent examples of AI in action.

► Chapter 14, "Computers at Work," and Chapter 15, "Computers at School and Home," have been updated and streamlined. Examples and data throughout both chapters have been supplemented with the most current information available. There's more on telecommuting, Web-based commerce, distance education, and Web-based instruction. Chapter 15 has been streamlined so it can be read more quickly because many instructors assign it along with other chapters.

► Chapter 16, "Inventing the Future," is also downsized. Much of the material from the future chapter of the previous edition has migrated into other chapters. This chapter now emphasizes techniques for projecting today's trends into tomorrow and for predicting future trends. Since the short-term future of technology is explored throughout the book, this chapter looks further down the road, with discussions of optical computing, sensory computing, ubiquitous computing, microtechnology, nanotechnology, and biotechnology. As in previous editions, the chapter ends by giving this futuristic technology a human context; the final pages raise difficult questions and pose ethical challenges for all of us.

► Appendix. The ACM Code of Ethics is the most widely known code of conduct specifically for computer professionals. This appendix reprints the code, along with detailed annotations that link specific tenants to related ethics material throughout the text.

► Crosscurrents. Almost all of the Crosscurrents articles that close each chapter are new to this edition. They include some of the best short essays on our relationship to technology that have been published in the past year. Topics include the erosion of personal privacy, the abuse of intellectual property laws, software reliability, machine intelligence, and our future as borgs. Authors include Bill Joy, Carly Fiorina, Andy Grove, Steven Levy, Bruce Sterling, and others.

► The CD-ROM has been updated with new multimedia material, including timely video clips, engaging animated exercises, and interactive explorations. The CD-ROM has been thoroughly tested to ensure that it runs without installation on just about any Windows 95, Windows 98, Windows NT4, Windows 2000, or Macintosh system with Quicktime 4 (runs on Macintosh OS 7.5.3 or later). Prentice Hall's technical support team can help you if you have any problem with the CD or the Web site.

► The Web site (www.prenhall.com/beekman) is continually updated to reflect changes in the Web and the subject matter. New to the fourth edition is Prentice Hall Web support material, including a syllabus manager, student chat rooms, and self-assessment quizzes.

The *Computer Confluence* book, CD-ROM, and Web site, when combined with your guidance and instruction, can provide students with unprecedented resources for understanding the technologies that are shaping their future. Hopefully, many of those students will use their knowledge to take an active part in shaping that future.

A Word to Instructors

Even if you're on the right track, you'll get run over if you just sit on it.

—Pat Koppman

When *Computer Currents* was published in 1994, most introductory computer classes were taught using command-line software on hardware that couldn't support any form of multimedia. Few introductory books even mentioned the Internet, few students used email, and the World Wide Web was a well-kept secret. Today's computer user takes the graphical user interface for granted, new software is delivered on CD-ROMs or on line, and multimedia computers are the norm. The Internet is everywhere, email is part of daily life for many students, and Web addresses are commonplace on business cards and in television commercials.

The pace of change threatens to make even the most successful introductory computer classes irrelevant. How do we provide timely information on a subject about which last year's news seems remarkably old? How can we be sure that an Introduction to Computers class won't seem like a History of Computers class by the time students graduate? How do we design courses that provide students with practical, expansive, lasting knowledge about computers and information technology?

It's no longer enough to teach students the fundamentals of programming and call them "computer literate." Nor can we assume that students who know word processor and spreadsheet keystrokes are adequately equipped to survive and prosper in the information age. Even today's email programs and Web browsers will look like antiques in a few short years. In fact, any hands-on experience is likely to have a short useful life unless it's accompanied by material that provides a broader context.

Computer Confluence, Fourth Edition, is designed to provide that context. Like the first three editions, the book emphasizes big ideas, broad trends, and the human aspects of technology—the critical concepts that tend to remain constant even while hardware and software change. But even big ideas and broad trends change over time. For example, the past few years have seen the Internet and interactive multimedia move from the fringe to the center of our collective computer consciousness. *Computer Confluence* has been rewritten and restructured to reflect those changes.

A Word to the Student

If you're like most students, you aren't taking this course to read about computers—you want to use them. That's sensible. You can't really understand computers without some hands-on experience, and you'll be able to apply your computer skills to a wide variety of future projects. But it's a mistake to think that you're computer savvy just because you can use a PC to write term papers and surf the Internet. It's important to understand how people use and abuse computer technology, because that technology has a powerful and growing impact on your life. (If you can't imagine how your life would be different without computers, read the vignette called "Living without Computers" in Chapter 1.) Even if you have lots of computer experience, future trends are almost certain to make much of that experience obsolete—probably sooner than you think. In the next few years, computers are likely to take on entirely new forms and roles because of breakthroughs in artificial intelligence, voice recognition, virtual reality, interactive multimedia, networking, and cross-breeding with telephone and home entertainment technologies. If your knowledge of computers stops with a handful of PC and Internet applications, you may be standing still while the world changes around you.

When you're cascading through white water, you need to be able to use a paddle, but it's also important to know how to read a map, a compass, and the river. *Computer*

Confluence: Exploring Tomorrow's Technology is designed to serve as a map, compass, and book of river lore to help you ride the information waves into the future.

Computer Confluence will help you understand the important trends that will change the way you work with computers and the way computers work for you. This book discusses the promise and the problems of computer technology without overwhelming you with technobabble.

Computer Confluence is intentionally nontechnical and down to earth. Occasional mini-stories bring concepts and speculations to life. Illustrations and photos make abstract concepts concrete. Quotes add thought-provoking and humorous seasoning.

Whether you're a hard-core hacker or a confirmed computerphobe, there's something for you in *Computer Confluence.* Dive in!

George Beekman

Acknowledgments

Writing a book requires countless hours of working alone, but it isn't just solo work. This book is a team effort. I'm deeply grateful to all of the people who've helped bring *Computer Confluence* together. Their names may not be on the cover, but their high-quality work shows in every detail of this project.

I'll start by saying thanks again to the marvelous Benjamin/Cummings team that worked with me to put together the first edition. If it hadn't been for the vision, talent, and hard work of these folks, the original *Computer Currents* wouldn't have been such a big success, and there wouldn't be second, third, or fourth editions. I was doubly fortunate to have many of those same people back to help me turn *Computer Currents* into *Computer Confluence*.

When it moved east from Benjamin/Cummings California headquarters to the main Addison Wesley campus in Massachusetts, *Computer Confluence* inherited a new family. Personnel changes and deadlines made for some difficult adjustments, but the talented team came together and helped produce a third edition that exceeded just about everyone's expectations.

In publishing, as in technology, it seems that change is inevitable, and *Computer Confluence* has a new home again—this time under the banner of Prentice Hall in New Jersey. Transitions are never easy, especially when they disrupt tight schedules. But the Prentice Hall team, under direction of Editor-in-Chief Mickey Cox and Managing Editor Melissa Whitaker have done an admirable job under difficult circumstances.

I'm especially indebted to Developmental Editor Lena Buonanno, who worked closely with me on the development of this fourth edition. Lena's skill, professionalism, patience, and attention to detail helped me to stay the course during the most trying of times. The book is much better thanks to her.

Many others brought their considerable talents to *Computer Confluence*. Patricia Smythe, design manager, and Cheryl Asherman, senior designer, are the people most responsible for the beautiful design of the book. Marc Oliver and Sondra Greenfield worked on all aspects of production, helping ensure that the project could make all those nearly impossible deadlines. Assistant Editor Kerri Limpert focuses on the many supplements that make *Computer Confluence* a complete instructional package. Abby Reip's patient and persistent research uncovered most of the excellent photos in these pages. Melene Kubat, administrative assistant, had the big job of rounding up books for the Sources and Resources reviews. Gary Brent and Paul Thurrot contributed most of the original material for the How It Works boxes in earlier editions. For this edition Paul served as a valued technical advisor. Ben Beekman, Robert Rose, and Miriam Rose captured most of the screens in the book. Susan Beekman and Lena Buonanno helped research the Crosscurrents articles. Loretta Palagi's sharp eyes edited copy. Michael Jennings, Arik Ohnstad, and the staff at Carlisle Publishers Services produced the final book from all of the raw materials supplied by the others listed here.

The Computer Confluence CD-ROM was produced by a team of Oregon wizards headed by Mark Dinsmore and Dave Trenkel, two former students who morphed into multimedia professionals. Mark's technical expertise, design talent, problem-solving skills, insatiable curiosity, and endless energy made him indispensable. Dave's crystal-clear tutorials, imaginative 3-D animations, and intelligent electronic music rival the best in the business. Graphic designer Delores Dinsmore lent her unique set of talents to the team and the project. Back in New Jersey, the details of the CD-ROM and the Web site were skillfully coordinated by Nancy Welcher, media product manager. Content for the Web site is provided by Sherry Thorpe.

I owe a special thank you to my son Ben Beekman, who served as my able assistant throughout the project. As a college student, Ben is an ideal helper—he knows our readership from the inside. But Ben also knows the business of writing and the business of multimedia, and he's applied his expertise to every phase of this massive project—Web research, book research, information organization, screen shots, fact checking, Web-page editing, CD-ROM work, and more. I simply couldn't have completed *Computer Confluence,* Fourth Edition, without his help.

All of this effort would be wasted if *Computer Confluence* didn't reach its intended audience. Thankfully, Kris King, senior marketing manager, and her team have a strong track record for getting the good word out to the right people.

There are others who contributed to *Computer Confluence* in all kinds of ways, including critiquing chapters, answering technical questions, tracking down obscure references, guiding me through difficult decisions, and being there when I needed support. There's no room here to detail their contributions, but I want to thank the people who gave time, energy, talent, and support during the years that this book was under development, including Alex von Rosenberg, Peter Harris, Jan Dymond, Sherry Clark, Mike Johnson, Mike Quinn, Walter Rudd, Cherie Pancake, Bruce D'Ambrosio, Bernie Feyerham, Rajeev Pandey, Dave Stuve, Clay Cowgill, Keith Vertanen, Megan Slothover, Claudette Hastie-Baehrs, Shjoobedebop, Sujita, Isaiah Jones, Inner Strength, Oyaya, Breitenbush, Oregon Public Broadcasting, and KLCC. Thanks also to all the hardware and software companies whose cooperation made my work easier. And most of all, thanks to my family, whose patience, support, love, and sacrifice inspired me every day through all these years.

Computer Confluence Academic Advisors

A special thanks to the Computer Confluence Academic Advisors, a group of dedicated professors from all areas of the United States and Canada who were committed to providing valuable feedback and suggestions for all parts of this text. *Computer Confluence,* Third Edition, benefited tremendously from your honest and insightful analyses. Their comments are also reflected in the new Fourth Edition.

Warren Boe, University of Iowa; **David Bozak,** SUNY Oswego; **Nancy Cosgrove,** University of Central Florida; **Allen Dooley,** Pasadena City College; **Dwight Graham,** Prairie State College; **Margaret Guertin,** Boston University; **Lynne Hanrahan,** Salem State College; **Edward Kaplan,** Bentley College; **Linda Kieffer,** Eastern Washington University; **Larry Lagerstrom,** University of California, Berkeley; **Doug MacDormand,** Red Deer College; **Virginia Phillips,** Youngstown State University; **Paul Ryburn,** University of Memphis; **Susan Switzer,** Central Michigan University; **Dale Underwood,** Lexington Community College.

Academic Reviewers

Thanks to all of the dedicated educators who reviewed the manuscript at various stages of development; *Computer Confluence* and its accompanying CD-ROM are significantly more valuable educational tools as a result of your ideas, suggestions, and constructive criticism.

William Allen, University of Central Florida; **William Boroski,** Trident Technical College; **Frederick Bounds,** DeKalb College; **Gary Brent,** Scottsdale Community College; **Judy Cameron,** Spokane Community College; **Mark Ciampa,** Volunteer State Community College; **Daniel Combellick,** Scottsdale Community College; **Elaine Cousins,** University of Michigan at Ann

Arbor; **H. E. Dunsmore,** Purdue University; **Joseph Fahs,** Elmira College; **Pat Fenton,** West Valley College; **David Fickbohm,** Golden Gate University; **Blaine Garfolo,** San Francisco State University; **Wade Graves,** Grayson County College; **Ananda Gunawardena,** University of Houston–Downtown; **Dale Gust,** Central Michigan University; **Michael Hansen,** Midlands Technical College; **Sally Ann Hanson,** Mercer County Community College; **Shelly Hawkins,** Duquesne University; **Trevor Jones,** Duquesne University; **Fred Klappenberger,** Anne Arundel City College; **Robert Kuhn,** Muskingum Area Technical College; **Larry Lagerstrom,** University of California, Berkeley; **Deborah Ludford,** Glendale Community College; **Brenda Mathews,** University College of the Cariboo; **Pat Mattsen,** St. Cloud University; **Vicki McCullough,** Palomar College; **J. Michael McGrew,** Ball State University; **Doris McPherson,** Schoolcraft College; **Linda Wise Miller,** University of Idaho; **William Moates,** Indiana State University; **Sally Peterson,** University of Wisconsin at Madison; **Gerhard Plenert,** Brigham Young University; **Loreto Porte,** Hostos City College; **John Rezac,** Johnson County Community College; **Mike Quinn,** Oregon State University; **Jennifer Sedelmeyer,** Broome City College; **Margaret Sklar,** Northern Michigan University; **Raoul Smith,** Northeastern University; **Jayne Stasser,** Miami University; **Randy Stolze,** Marist College; **Tim Sylvester,** Maricopa City College; **John Telford,** Salem State College; **Dwight Watt,** Athens Area Technical Institute; **Patricia Wermers,** North Shore City College; **Alan Whitehurst,** Brigham Young University; **Melissa Wiggins,** Mississippi College; **Floyd Jay Winters,** Manatee City College; **Rich Yankosky,** Frederick City College

Student Reviewers

The interactive CD-ROM has benefited from student reviewers who provided clear and objective revision recommendations. Special thanks to these students in helping us create a stronger technology support package:

Janet Hwang, University of California at Berkeley; **Chun-Ying Frank Lin,** University of California at Berkeley; **Amanda C. McNeely,** Trident Technical College; **Jessica Strauss,** University of Wisconsin at Madison

Navigating Computer Confluence (Read Me First!)

Here are a few pointers for exploring *Computer Confluence*.

► *Know your boxes.* Text chapters include several types of boxes, each of which is designed to be read in a particular way.

The User's View boxes show you what it's like to be in the driver's seat with some of today's most popular software. Even if you have experience with the software, take a little time to look over these boxes. Some key concepts are introduced here. A **UV** in the main text means "This is a good time to look over *The User's View* box."

Rules of Thumb boxes provide practical tips on everything from designing a publication to protecting your privacy. They bring concepts down to earth with useful suggestions that can save you time, money, and peace of mind.

How It Works boxes are for those readers who want—or need—to know more about what's going on under the hood. These boxes use words and pictures to take you deeper into the inner workings without getting bogged down in technical detail. The CD-ROM includes multimedia versions of many of these boxes as well as bonus *How It Works* features that aren't in the text. If your course objectives or personal curiosity doesn't motivate you to learn *How It Works*, that's OK; you can skip every *How It Works* box and still understand the rest of *Computer Confluence*.

Crosscurrents boxes showcase diverse, timely, and often controversial points of view on the technology and its impact on our lives. These short essays, which close each chapter, offer perspectives from some of the most important writers and thinkers on information technology.

► *Watch for media roadsigns.* You don't need a CD-ROM drive and an Internet connection to explore *Computer Confluence*—you don't even need a computer. But these tools can make your journey more interesting. As you're reading the text, look for icons pointing you toward other media:

This icon means that the CD-ROM contains information related to this section of the book. It may be an animated illustration, a video clip, a software demonstration, or an interactive exercise. Use the CD-ROM's Multimedia Study Guide to find the chapter and section. The study guide is organized through a table of contents that matches the text; you can explore any subject by clicking on its name. If you're feeling more adventurous than hurried, you can explore the CD-ROM by navigating through the 3-D Virtual Computing Center.

This icon means that there's material in the *Computer Confluence* Companion Website (http://www.prenhall.com/beekman) related to this section of the book. The *Computer Confluence* Web site includes in-depth discussions on relevant topics, updates to time-sensitive material, multimedia illustrations, and links to hundreds of other interesting and useful Web sites. If you're in a hurry, exercise self-discipline; it's easy to spend hours following your curiosity around the Web.

► *Read it and read it again.* If possible, read each chapter twice: once for the big ideas and the second time for more detailed understanding. You may also find it helpful to survey each chapter's outline in the table of contents before reading the chapter for the first time.

► *Don't get stuck.* If a concept seems unclear on the first reading, make a note and move on. Sometimes ideas make more sense after you've seen the bigger picture. If you still don't understand the concept the second time through, check the CD-ROM and the Web site for further clarification. When in doubt, ask questions.

► *Remember that there's more than one way to learn.* Some of us learn best by reading, others learn best by exploring interactive examples, and still others learn best by discussing ideas with others, online or in person. *Computer Confluence* offers you the opportunity to learn in all of these ways. Use the learning tools that work best for you.

► *Don't try to memorize every term the first time through.* Throughout the text, key terms are introduced in **boldface blue**, and secondary terms are *italicized in blue*. Use the Key Terms list at the end of each chapter to review and the glossary to recall any forgotten terms. The CD-ROM contains an interactive cross-referenced version of the glossary to find any term quickly.

► *Don't overanalyze examples.* *Computer Confluence* is designed to help you understand concepts, not memorize keystrokes. You can learn the nuts and bolts of working with computers in labs. The examples in this text may not match the applications in your lab, but the concepts are similar.

► *Get your hands dirty.* Try the applications while you're reading about them. Your reading and lab work will reinforce each other and help solidify your newfound knowledge.

► *Study together.* There's plenty to discuss here, and discussion is a great way to learn.

► *In a hurry? Turn the page.* The next few pages will give you a quick start—just enough information so you can start using the CD-ROM, the Web site, and related computer applications right away.

Computer Confluence Quick Start

The first few chapters of this book will provide you with a broad orientation to computers, CD-ROMs, the Internet, and related technology. In the meantime this Quick Start provides the basics—without detailed explanations—so you can get started with the *Computer Confluence* CD-ROM and Web site right away.

Details vary from computer to computer, but the basics are generally the same. You'll probably need a few additional instructions for your lab's computers to supplement the steps in this Quick Start.

Exploring the Computer Confluence CD-ROM

1. Turn on the computer. The switch may be on the main system box, on the keyboard, or somewhere else. Check your lab-specific instructions or ask for help if necessary. After a minute or so the screen will show icons (small pictures) that represent disks and other computer resources. It may also show open windows that reveal the contents of these resources. A row of words will appear at the top of each window (or, if you're using a Macintosh, at the top of the screen). Each of these words represents a menu of choices that reveals itself when you point to the word and click on it with the mouse.

2. If you haven't used a mouse before, try moving the mouse around and watch the pointer on the screen move in the same motion. (If you run out of space on the mouse pad or table, you can lift the mouse and reposition it.) Point to an icon and click on it by clicking on the mouse button. (If there are two or more buttons, use the left button.) You'll click this way to select objects, press on-screen buttons, and navigate around the Web site and CD-ROM.

3. Insert the *Computer Confluence* CD-ROM in the CD-ROM drive. Once again, details vary between systems. Generally, the CD-ROM drive is part of the main system box. Press the drive's button to make the CD tray slide open. Place the CD, label side up, on the tray, being careful not to handle the other side. Close the CD tray by pressing the button again.

4. The next step depends on your operating system software. If you're not sure, ask.

WINDOWS 95, 98, 2000, AND NT

a. Point to the icon called "My Computer" and double-click on it (click twice in rapid succession with the left mouse button).

b. Double-click on the CD-ROM icon in the "My Computer" window.

c. Double-click on the icon named "CCWin.EXE."

MACINTOSH

Double-click on the "CCMac" icon in the "CCCD" window.

5. The *Computer Confluence* multimedia program is launched; it will take a few seconds to load into the computer's memory. The program requires Apple's Quick Time extension to play videos. The opening screen will tell you if you have Quick Time installed, and what version. If you need to install a new version of Quick Time, the CD has directions. If you don't need to install Quick Time, click on the button labeled "Next."

6. You should now see and hear a short video introduction from George Beekman, the author of *Computer Confluence*. You can stop or skip this video by clicking any time.

7. The simplest way to explore the CD-ROM is by using the Table of Contents. You will find a list of all the

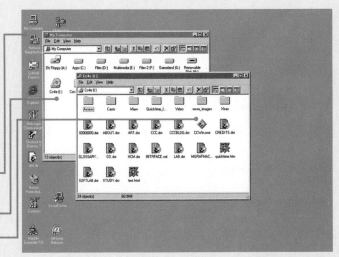

chapters on the left side of your screen. Click on Chapter 2, "Hardware Basics: Inside the Box".

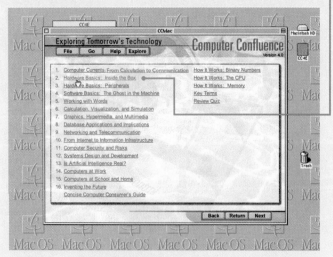

8. When a list of interactive options for that chapter appears, click on "How It Works: Binary Numbers."

9. To turn the "pages" in this example, click on the button labeled "next." To go back, click on the "back" button. Follow the on-screen instructions and you'll have a chance to play a simple binary number guessing game.

10. When you complete the example, press Return or Enter to go back to that chapter's contents.

11. To take a quiz on the contents of a chapter, click on "Review Quiz," select the number of questions you want to answer, and then start the quiz. Read each question and the answers carefully; then click on the correct answer. You'll be told at the bottom of the screen whether you answered the question correctly. At the end of the quiz you'll be given the option to view, print, or save your results, including the page numbers to review for the missed questions.

12. To explore the CD in another way, click on the "Explore" button at the top of your screen, and select "Building Directory Kiosk" from the pull-down menu. You are now entering a 3D Virtual Computing Center, with several rooms to explore. You will be standing at a kiosk listing the rooms in the Center. You can click on the room number or name to be transported to that room, or you can click outside the kiosk to walk down the hall and explore on your own.

13. You can also go directly to any of the rooms in the Center by selecting it from the "Explore" menu.

14. In the Virtual Computing Center, you navigate by clicking in the center of the screen to go forward and clicking on the eges to turn left or right. Anytime your cursor turns to an arrow, you can move or turn in that direction. Anytime your cursor turns to a finger, you can click on that object to trigger an activity.

15. When you're ready to leave the 3-D world, you can return to the kiosk and click on "Table of Contents," or you can select "Table of Contents" from the Go menu. You can also use the Go menu to go to the Glossary and Key Terms, or perform any of the Review Quizzes.

16. If you need help navigating the CD-ROM, select a topic from the HELP menu for more information. Also, if you have a Web browser installed on your computer, and are connected to the Internet, you can connect to the *Computer Confluence* Companion Website (http:// www.prenhall.com/beekman) by selecting it in the Help menu. This will automatically launch your browser and connect you to our site.

17. When you're done exploring the CD-ROM, select "Quit" from the File menu to exit the program.

EXPLORING THE COMPUTER CONFLUENCE WEB SITE

To explore the *Computer Confluence* Web site, you'll need a Web browser and an Internet link, through either a modem or a direct connection. Your computer probably includes Netscape Navigator, Netscape Communicator, Internet Explorer, or America Online's Web browser.

1. Locate the browser and double-click on its icon. If you can't find your computer's Web browser, or if you can't establish a connection, ask for help.

2. Point to the long rectangle at the top of the browser window. If the text in that window is black on a white background, double-click on it to highlight it. Then type "http://www.prenhall.com/beekman" to replace the highlighted text. (Depending on your browser, you may be able to get the same results by simply typing "computerconfluence.") Press Return or Enter.

3. If an error message appears, click on the OK button, check your typing carefully, correct any errors, and press Return or Enter again. When you type it correctly, you'll be taken to the Computer Confluence opening screen.

4. If you're using your own computer, you can mark this page so you can return by selecting it from a menu rather than retyping its name. If you're using Netscape Navigator or Communicator, select Add Bookmark from the Bookmark menu. If you're using Internet Explorer, select Add to Favorites from the Favorites menu.

5. Click on "Standard Edition."

6. Click on the drop down box to select a chapter, then click "Begin." This will take you to Objectives for that particular chapter.

7. There's plenty more to explore at the *Computer Confluence* Web site. You'll find study guide questions, internet explorations, CD-ROM help, and Software downloads on the left hand navigation bar. New features are added regularly, and the look may change as we add new functionality, so be sure to check back from time to time.

Approaching Computers

Hardware and Software Fundamentals

Chapter 1

Chapter

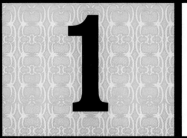

Computer Currents: From Calculation to Communication

The Analytical Engine has **no pretensions whatever** to originate anything. It can do whatever we know how **to order it** to perform.

— Augusta Ada King, **countess of Lovelace**

The Analytical Engine Lady Lovelace referred to was the first computer, conceived by Charles Babbage, a 19th-century mathematics professor at Cambridge University. Babbage was an eccentric genius. He calculated that they sapped him of 25% of his working power, and he strove to have them outlawed. But Babbage was more than a crank; his many inventions included the skeleton key, the speedometer, and . . . the computer.

Babbage's computer vision grew out of frustration with the tedious and error-prone process of creating mathematical tables. In 1823 he received a grant from the British government to develop a "difference engine"—a mechanical device for performing repeated additions. Two decades earlier Joseph-Marie Charles Jacquard, a French textile maker, had developed a loom that could automatically reproduce woven patterns by reading information encoded in patterns of holes punched in stiff paper cards. After learning of Jacquard's programmable loom, Babbage abandoned the difference engine for a more ambitious enterprise: an Analytical Engine that could be programmed with punched cards to carry out any calculation to 20 digits of accuracy. Babbage's design included the four basic components found in every modern computer: components for performing the basic functions of input, output, processing, and storage.

Augusta Ada King, countess of Lovelace (sometimes erroneously called "Ada Lovelace"), the daughter of poet Lord Byron, visited Babbage and the Analytical Engine. Ada corresponded regularly with him. She is often called the first computer programmer because she wrote a plan for using the Analytical Engine to calculate Bernoulli numbers. But programmer is probably the wrong term to describe her actual contribution. She was more of an interpreter and promoter of Babbage's visionary work.

Babbage was obsessed with completing the Analytical Engine. Eventually the government withdrew financial support; there simply wasn't enough public demand to justify the ever-increasing cost. The technology of the time was not sufficient to turn their ideas into reality. The world wasn't ready for computers, and it wouldn't be for another 100 years. ◼

Charles Babbage (1791–1871)

Analytical Engine

Augusta Ada King, countess of Lovelace (1815–1852)

Computers are so much a part of modern life that we hardly notice them. But computers are everywhere, and we'd certainly notice them if they suddenly stopped working. Imagine . . .

⬛—| Living Without Computers |

You wake up with the sun well above the horizon and realize your alarm clock hasn't gone off. You wonder if you've overslept. You have a big research project to finish today. The face of your digital wristwatch stares back at you blankly. The TV and radio are no help; you can't find a station on either one. You can't even get the time by telephone, because the telephone doesn't work either.

The morning newspaper is missing from your doorstep. You'll have to guess the weather forecast by looking out the window. No music to dress by this morning—your CD player refuses your requests. How about some breakfast? Your automatic coffeemaker refuses to be programmed; your microwave oven is on strike too.

You decide to go out for breakfast. Your car won't start. In fact, the only cars moving are at least 15 years old. The lines at the subway are unbelievable. People chatter nervously about the failure of the subway's computer-controlled scheduling device.

You duck into a coffee shop and find long lines of people waiting while cashiers handle transactions by hand. While you're waiting, you join the conversation that's going on around you. People seem more interested in talking to each other since all the usual tools of mass communication have failed.

You're down to a couple of dollars in cash, so you stop after breakfast at an automated teller machine. Why bother?

You return home to wait for the book you ordered by overnight mail. You soon realize that you're in for a long wait; planes aren't flying because air traffic control facilities aren't working. You head for the local library to see if the book is in stock. Of course, it's going to be tough to find since the book catalog is computerized.

Computer screens and television screens populate today's television control rooms. ▷

As you walk home, you speculate on the implications of a worldwide computer failure. How will people function in high-tech, high-rise office buildings that depend on computer systems to control everything from elevators to humidity? Will electric power plants be able to function without computer control? What will happen to patients in computerized medical facilities? What about satellites that are kept in orbit by computer-run control systems? Will the financial infrastructure collapse without computers to process and communicate transactions? Will the world be a safer place if all computer-controlled weapons are grounded?

Our story could go on, but the message should be clear enough by now. Computers are everywhere, and our lives are affected in all kinds of ways by their operation—and nonoperation. It's truly amazing that computers have infiltrated our lives so thoroughly in such a short time.

Computers in Perspective: An Evolving Idea

Consider the past and you shall know the future.

—Chinese Proverb

While the computer has been with us for only about half a century, its roots go back to a time long before Charles Babbage conceived of the Analytical Engine in 1823. This extraordinary machine is built on centuries of insight and intellectual effort.

Before Computers

Computers grew out of a human need to quantify. Early humans were content to count with fingers or rocks. As cultures became more complex, so did their counting tools. The abacus (a type of counting tool and calculator used by the Babylonians, the Chinese, and others for thousands of years) and the Hindu-Arabic number system are examples of early calculating concepts that had an immediate and profound effect on society. (Imagine trying to conduct business without a number system that allows for easy addition and subtraction.)

The Analytical Engine had little impact until a century after its invention, when it served as a blueprint for the first real programmable computer. Virtually every computer in use today follows the basic plan laid out by Babbage and Lovelace.

San Francisco's Bay Area Rapid Transit (BART) District (right) was one of the world's first automated train systems. An automatic fare collection system tracks entry and exit points, calculates fares, and takes tickets without human intervention. The centralized Operations Control Center is used to perform supervisory control of train operations and remote control of electrification, ventilation, and emergency response systems.

The Information-Processing Machine

Like the Analytical Engine, the computer is a machine that changes information from one form to another. All computers take in information (**input**) and give out information (**output**) as shown here.

| Input | Computer | Output |

Because information can take many forms, the computer is an incredibly versatile tool, capable of everything from computing federal income taxes to guiding the missiles those taxes buy. For calculating taxes, the input to the computer might be numbers representing wages, other income, deductions, exemptions, and tax tables, and the output might be the number representing the taxes owed. If the computer is deploying a missile, the input might be radio and radar signals for locating the missile and the target, and the output might be electrical signals to control the flight path of the missile. Amazingly enough, the same computer could be used to accomplish all of these tasks.

How can a machine be so versatile? The computer's flexibility isn't hidden in **hardware**—the physical parts of the computer system. The secret is **software**, or **programs**—the instructions that tell the hardware how to transform the input **data** (information in a form it can read) into the necessary output.

Whether a computer is doing a simple calculation or producing a complex animation, a program controls the process from beginning to end. In effect, changing programs can turn the computer into a different tool. Because it can be programmed to perform various tasks, the typical modern computer is a general-purpose tool.

The First Real Computers

First we shape our tools, thereafter they shape us.

—Marshall McLuhan

Although Ada Lovelace predicted that the Analytical Engine might someday compose music, the scientists and mathematicians who designed and built the first working computers a century later had more modest goals: to create machines capable of doing repetitive mathematical calculations. Here are some landmark examples:

▶ In 1939 a young German engineer named Konrad Zuse completed the first programmable, general-purpose digital computer—a machine he built from electric relays to automate the process of doing engineering calculations. "I was too lazy to calculate and so I invented the computer," Zuse recalls. In 1941 Zuse and a friend asked the German government for funds to build a faster electronic computer to help crack enemy codes. The Nazi military establishment turned him down, confident that their aircraft could quickly win the war without the aid of sophisticated calculating devices.

▶ At about the same time, the British government was assembling a top-secret team of mathematicians and engineers to crack Nazi military codes. In 1943 the team, led by mathematician Alan Turing and others, completed Colossus, considered by many to be the first electronic digital computer. This special-purpose computer successfully broke codes, allowing British military intelligence to eavesdrop on even the most secret German messages throughout most of the war.

▶ In 1939 Iowa State University professor John Atanasoff, seeking a tool to help his graduate students solve long, complex differential equations, developed what could have been the first electronic digital computer, the Atanasoff-Berry Computer (ABC). His university never bothered to patent Atanasoff's groundbreaking machine, and Atanasoff never managed to turn it into a fully operational product. The International Business Machines Corporation responded to his queries by telling him "IBM will never be interested in an electronic computing machine."

▶ Harvard professor Howard Aiken was more successful in financing the automatic general-purpose calculator he was developing. In 1944, with a million dollars from IBM, he completed the Mark I. This 51-foot-long, 8-foot-tall monster used noisy electromechanical relays to calculate five or six times faster than a person could, but it was far slower than a modern $5 pocket calculator.

▶ After consulting with Atanasoff and studying the ABC, John Mauchly teamed up with J. Presper Eckert to help the U.S. effort in World War II by constructing a machine to calculate trajectory tables for new guns. The machine was the ENIAC (Electronic Numerical Integrator and Computer), a 30-ton behemoth with 18,000 vacuum tubes that failed at an average of once every 7 minutes. When it was running, it could calculate 500 times faster than the existing electromechanical calculators—about as fast as a modern pocket calculator. Nevertheless, it failed in its first mission: It wasn't completed until two months after the end of the war. Still, it convinced its creators that large-scale computers were commercially feasible. After the war Mauchly and Eckert started a private company called Sperry and created UNIVAC I, the first general-purpose commercial computer. UNIVAC I went to work for the U.S. Census Bureau in 1951.

Evolution and Acceleration

Invention breeds invention.

—Ralph Waldo Emerson

Computer hardware evolved rapidly from those early days, with new technologies replacing old every few years. Historians marked major hardware changes in the first decades of the computer age by defining four generations of computers. UNIVAC I and other computers in the early 1950s were, according to this common classification scheme, first-generation computers. This was the era of machines built around vacuum tubes—light-bulb-sized glass tubes that housed switching circuitry. First-generation machines were big, expensive, and finicky. Only a big institution like a major bank or the U.S. government could afford a computer, not to mention the climate-controlled computer center needed to house it and the staff of technicians needed to program it and keep it running. But with all their faults, first-generation computers quickly became indispensable tools for scientists, engineers, and other professionals.

The **transistor,** invented in 1948, could perform the same function as a vacuum tube by transferring electricity across a tiny resistor. Transistors were first used in a computer in 1956, an event generally viewed as the beginning of the computer's second generation. Computers that used transistors were radically smaller, more reliable, and less expensive than tube-based computers. Because of improvements in software at about the

J. Presper Eckert (middle) and CBS News Correspondent Walter Cronkite (right) confer while UNIVAC I tallies votes in the 1952 presidential election. After counting 5% of the votes, UNIVAC correctly predicted that Eisenhower would win the election, but CBS cautiously chose to withhold the prediction until all votes were counted. Today networks commonly announce winners based on computer projections while many people are still voting.

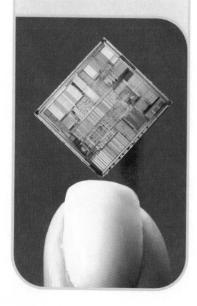

These three devices define the first three computer generations. The vacuum tube (left) housed a few switches in a space about the size of a light bulb. The transistor (middle) allowed engineers to pack the same circuitry in a semiconductor package that was smaller, cooler, and much more reliable. The first silicon chips packed several transistors' worth of circuitry into a speck much smaller than a single transistor.

Today a single chip the size of your fingernail can contain the equivalent of millions of transistors.

same time, these machines were also much easier and faster to program and use. As a result, computers became more widely used in business as well as in science and engineering.

But America's fledgling space program, determined to surpass the Soviet satellite successes of the 1950s, needed computers that were even smaller and more powerful than the second-generation machines, so researchers developed technology that allowed them to pack hundreds of transistors into a single integrated circuit on a tiny silicon chip. By the mid-1960s transistor-based computers were replaced by smaller, more powerful third-generation machines built around the new integrated circuits.

Integrated circuits rapidly replaced early transistors for the same reasons that transistors superseded vacuum tubes:

- ▶ *Reliability.* Machines built with integrated circuits were less prone to failure than their predecessors because the chips could be rigorously tested before installation.
- ▶ *Size.* Single chips could replace entire circuit boards containing hundreds or thousands of transistors, making it possible to build much smaller machines.
- ▶ *Speed.* Because electricity had shorter distances to travel, the smaller machines were markedly faster than their predecessors.
- ▶ *Efficiency.* Since chips were so small, they used less electrical power. As a result, they created less heat.
- ▶ *Cost.* Mass production techniques made it easy to manufacture inexpensive chips.

Just about every breakthrough in computer technology since the dawn of the computer age has presented similar advantages over the technology it replaced.

The relentless progress of the computer industry is illustrated by Moore's Law. In 1965 Gordon Moore, the chairman of Intel, predicted in jest that the power of a silicon chip of the same price would double about every 18 months for at least two decades. So far Moore's prediction has been uncannily accurate!

The Microcomputer Revolution

Computer cost effectiveness has risen 100 millionfold since the late 1950s—a 100,000-fold rise in power times a thousandfold drop in cost.

—George Gilder

The inventions of the vacuum tube, the transistor, and the silicon chip had impacts on society, which is why they're used as computer-generational boundaries by many historians. But none of these had a more profound effect than the invention in 1971 of the first microprocessor—the critical components of a complete computer housed on a tiny silicon chip. The development of the microprocessor by Intel engineers marked the beginning of the fourth generation of computers and the end of an era when it made sense to count computer generations. The microprocessor's invention caused immediate and radical changes in the appearance, capability, and availability of computers.

The research and development costs for the first microprocessor were tremendous. But once the assembly lines were in place, silicon computer chips could be mass produced cheaply. The raw materials were certainly cheap enough; silicon is the second most common element (behind oxygen) in the Earth's crust. It's the main ingredient in beach sand.

The microcomputer revolution didn't just increase the number of computers in offices; it opened up entirely new possibilities for computer habitats. This police officer (left) uses a computer to record case notes and track crime information. The marine biologist uses a laptop computer to record research notes and analyze data in the field.

American companies soon flooded the marketplace with watches and pocket calculators built around inexpensive microprocessors. The economic effect was immediate: Mechanical calculators and slide rules became obsolete overnight, electronic hobbyists became wealthy entrepreneurs, and California's San Jose area gained the nickname Silicon Valley when dozens of microprocessor manufacturing companies sprouted and grew there.

The microcomputer revolution began in the late 1970s when companies like Apple, Tandy, and Commodore introduced low-cost, typewriter-sized computers as powerful as many of the room-sized computers that had come before. Personal computers, or PCs, as microcomputers have come to be known, are now common in offices, factories, homes, schools, and just about everywhere else. Because chip manufacturers have been so successful at obeying Moore's Law, microcomputers have steadily increased in speed and power during the last two decades. At the same time, personal computers have taken over many tasks formerly performed by large computers, and every year people find new, innovative ways to harness these tiny workhorses.

The 1950s and 1960s represented an era of *institutional computing*. Corporations and government institutions used the large, expensive computers of the time to transform and streamline their operations, and the world changed as a result. Small computers had an even greater impact on society during the decades that followed—the *personal computer era*. Still, desktop computers haven't completely replaced big computers, which have also evolved. Today's world is populated with a variety of computers, each particularly well suited to specific tasks.

Computer-driven display systems are important fixtures in meeting rooms. It is getting harder to find a workplace that doesn't have at least one computer.

Computers Today: A Brief Taxonomy

There may still be plenty of stragglers who have yet to nuzzle up to computers, but there is

no one unaffected by the explosion of computer technology.

—Steven Levy, *technology writer*

People today work with mainframe computers, super-computers, workstations, notebook computers, hand-held computers, embedded computers, and, of course, PCs. Even though they're based on the same technology, these machines have important differences.

Mainframes and Supercomputers

Before the microcomputer revolution, most information processing was done on mainframe computers—room-sized machines with price tags that matched their size. Today large organizations such as banks and airlines still use mainframes for big computing jobs. Today's mainframes are smaller and cheaper than their ancestors; a typical mainframe today might be the size of a refrigerator and cost around a million U.S. dollars. These industrial-strength computers are largely invisible to the general public because they're hidden away in climate-controlled rooms.

But the fact that you can't see them doesn't mean you don't use them. When you make an airline reservation or deposit money in your bank account, a mainframe computer is involved in the transaction. Your travel agent and your bank teller communicate with a mainframe using a computer terminal—a combination keyboard and screen that transfers information to and from the computer. The computer might be in another room or another country.

A mainframe computer can communicate with several users simultaneously through a technique called timesharing. For example, a timesharing system allows travel agents all over the country to make reservations using the same computer and the same information at the same time.

Timesharing also makes it possible for users with diverse computing needs to share expensive computing equipment. Many research scientists and engineers, for example, need more mathematical computing power than they can get from personal computers. Their computing needs might require a powerful mainframe computer. A timesharing machine can simultaneously serve the needs of scientists and engineers in different departments working on a variety of projects.

Many researchers can't even get the computing power they need from a mainframe computer; traditional "big iron" simply isn't fast enough for their calculation-intensive work such as weather forecasting, telephone network design, oil exploration, and medical imaging. These power users need to have access to the fastest, most powerful computers made. Super fast, super powerful computers are called supercomputers or high-performance computers.

Until a few years ago people commonly referred to another class of multiuser machine called the *minicomputer*. According to traditional definitions minicomputers were smaller and less expensive than mainframes but larger and more powerful than

Terminals like the one in the photo to the right make it possible for ticket agents all over the world to send information to a single mainframe computer like the one shown to the left.

personal computers. But most of today's mainframes are no bigger than yesterday's minicomputers, and most desktop computers are more powerful than those early minis. By most accounts the minicomputer is history.

Workstations and PCs

For many applications the minicomputer has been replaced by a **server**—a computer designed to provide software and other resources to other computers over a network. Just about any computer can be used as a server, but some computers are specifically designed with this purpose in mind. (Networks and servers are discussed later in this chapter and in later chapters.) For other applications, such as large-scale scientific data analysis, the minicomputer has been replaced by the workstation—a high-end desktop computer with massive computing power at a fraction of the cost. **Workstations** are widely used by scientists, engineers, financial analysts, designers, and animators whose work involves intensive computations. Although many workstations are capable of supporting multiple users simultaneously, in practice they're typically used by only one person at a time.

The Blue Mountain supercomputer at the U.S. Department of Energy's Los Alamos National Laboratory can perform 1.6 trillion operations per second. The machine is used to simulate nuclear tests and perform intensive calculations for other research projects.

Of course, like many computer terms, *workstation* means different things to different people. Some people refer to all desktop computers and terminals as workstations. Those who reserve the term for the most powerful desktop machines admit that the line separating personal computers and workstations is fading. As workstations become less expensive and personal computers become more powerful, the line becomes as much a marketing distinction as a technical one. It's becoming harder and harder to find a definition for workstation that excludes the most powerful personal computers.

Most computer users don't need the power of a scientific workstation to do their day-to-day business. A modern personal computer (PC) has plenty of computing power for word processing, accounting, and other common applications. No surprise there— today's personal computers are far more powerful than the mainframes that dominated the world of computing a human generation ago. A personal computer, as the name implies, is almost always dedicated to serving a single user.

A word about terminology: The terms *personal computer* and *PC* occasionally generate confusion because in 1981 IBM named its desktop computer the IBM Personal Computer. That's why the terms *personal computer* and *PC* often are used to describe only IBM computers or machines compatible with IBM hardware. ("The office has a network of Macs and PCs.") But in another context, PC might describe any general-purpose single-user computer ("Every student needs a PC to connect to the Internet.")

Workstations are used for applications that demand more computing power than is available in typical personal computers. The Silicon Graphics workstation is popular with animators, graphic designers, and multimedia artists because of its state-of-the-art graphics capabilities.

Modern desktop PCs and workstations don't all look alike, but they generally have similar components. A typical desktop computer includes at least four separate pieces:

▶ A **system unit** containing the computer's microprocessor (CPU), memory, storage devices, and connecting circuitry. Storage devices typically include (but aren't limited to) a nonremovable hard disk for storage and retrieval of large quantities of information; a diskette drive for reading and writing smaller quantities of data on removable, transportable diskettes; and a CD-ROM or DVD-ROM drive for reading programs, data, audio, and video from pre-recorded optical disks.

▶ A **monitor** for displaying text, numbers, and pictures. On some computers, including Apple's popular iMac, the system unit is built into the monitor; these models are sometimes called *all-in-one computers.*

Personal computers today come in a variety of form factors. Apple's iMac includes the CPU, monitor, and storage devices in a stylish all-in-one box; only the keyboard and mouse are separate. The NEC Power Mate VT 300 is a more traditional design, with monitor separate from the system unit containing the CPU and storage.

▶ A keyboard for typing text and numerical data.

▶ A mouse or some other device for pointing to different areas on the screen.

We'll examine these components, along with other hardware devices, in Chapters 2 and 3.

Portable Computers

Two decades ago the terms *personal computer* and *desktop computer* were interchangeable; virtually all PCs were desktop computers. Today, however, one of the fastest growing segments of the PC market involves machines that aren't tied to the desktop—portable computers.

Of course, portability is a relative term. The first "portable" computers were 20-pound suitcases with fold-out keyboards and small TV-like screens. Today those "luggable" computers have been replaced by flat-screen, battery-powered laptop computers that are so light you can rest one on your lap while you work or carry it in a briefcase when it's closed.

Today's laptop, commonly called a notebook computer, weighs between 3 and 8 pounds. Heavier models compare favorably with powerful desktop PCs. Extra-light, stripped down notebooks are sometimes called *subnotebooks*. To keep size and weight down, manufacturers often leave out some components that would be standard equipment on desktop machines. For example, some laptops don't have built-in CD-ROM or diskette drives. Some have bays that allow these devices to be inserted one at a time. Most have ports that allow external drives to be attached with cables. A *docking station* allows a laptop to be quickly connected to external monitor, keyboard, mouse, and disk drives. Many mobile workers use docking stations to turn their laptops into full-featured desktop PCs when they return to their offices.

Handheld computers small enough to be tucked into a jacket pocket serve the needs of users who value mobility over a full-sized keyboard and screen. Many of these tiny devices are designed as much for communication as for computing. *Docks* for handheld computers allow them to share information with desktop and laptop PCs. Handheld computers are sometimes called palmtop computers, *personal digital assistants, PDAs,* or *personal communicators*.

Size notwithstanding, most portable computers in all their variations are general-purpose computers built around microprocessors similar to those that drive desktop models. But portability comes at a price—portable computers generally cost more than comparable desktop machines. They're also more difficult to upgrade when newer hardware components become available.

The portable computers shown here represent just a small sample of sizes and types available today. Apple's iBook (above left) applies a stylish design to the traditional laptop. The IBM Think Pad (below left) can be converted from a laptop to a desktop PC using the docking station shown here. The Palm V is a handheld computer designed to accept input from a stylus or from a communications link with a larger computer. The Hewlett-Packard Jornada is a handheld computer with a tiny keyboard.

Embedded Computers and Special-Purpose Computers

Not all computers are general-purpose machines. Many are special-purpose (dedicated) computers that perform specific tasks, ranging from controlling the temperature and humidity in a high-rise office building to monitoring your heart rate while you work out. Embedded computers enhance all kinds of consumer goods: wristwatches, toys, game machines, stereos, video cassette recorders, and ovens. In fact, 90% of the world's microprocessors are hidden inside common household and electronic devices. Because of embedded computers, a typical new car probably has more computing power than the salesperson's PC! Embedded computers are also used in industry, the military, and science for controlling a variety of hardware devices, including robots. Ninety percent of all microprocessors are embedded in some kind of consumer or electronic device other than a PC.

Most special-purpose computers are, at their core, similar to general-purpose personal computers. But unlike their desktop cousins, these special-purpose machines typically have their programs etched in silicon so they can't be altered. When a program is immortalized on a silicon chip, it becomes firmware—a hybrid of hardware and software.

Computer Connections: The Internet Revolution

All persons are caught in an inescapable network of mutuality, tied in a single garment of destiny. Whatever affects one directly, affects all indirectly. . . .

—Martin Luther King, Jr

Embedded computers are so common in today's world that they're all but invisible. This experimental children's doll is a robot in disguise. The Independence™ 3000 IBOT Transporter™ is an intelligent wheelchair that allows disabled people to climb and descend stairs, "stand up" on two wheels, and even stroll on the beach. This Sony digital video camera includes hardware and software for on-board video editing.

We've seen how breakthroughs in switching, storage, and processor technology have produced new types of computers. Each of these technological advances had an impact on our society as people found new ways to put computers to work. Most historians stopped counting computer generations after the microcomputer became commonplace; it was hard to imagine another breakthrough having as much impact as the tiny microprocessor. But while the world was still reeling from the impact of the microcomputer revolution, another information technology revolution was quietly building up steam: a network revolution. If current trends continue, we may look back on the 1990s as the beginning of the era of *interpersonal computing*.

The Emergence of Networks

The first computers were large, expensive, self-contained machines that could process only one job at a time. As demand for computing power grew, computer scientists searched for ways to make scarce computer resources more accessible. The invention of timesharing in the 1960s allowed multiple users to connect to a single mainframe computer through individual terminals. When personal computers started replacing terminals, many users found they had all the computing power they needed on their desktops. Still, there were advantages to linking some of these computers in local-area networks (LANs). When clusters of computers were networked, they could share scarce, expensive resources. For example, a single high-speed printer could meet the needs of an entire office if it was connected to a network. As a bonus, people could use computers to send and receive messages electronically through the networks.

The advantages of electronic communication and resource sharing were multiplied when smaller networks were joined to larger networks. Emerging telecommunication technology eventually allowed wide-area networks (WANs) to span continents and oceans. A remote computer could connect to a network through standard telephone lines by using a modem—an electronic device that could translate computer data into signals compatible with the telephone system. Banks, government agencies, and other large, geographically distributed institutions gradually built information-processing systems to take advantage of long-distance networking technology. But for most computer users outside of these organizations, networking was not the norm. People saw computers as tools for doing calculations, storing data, and producing paper documents—not as communication tools.

There were exceptions: A group of visionary computer scientists and engineers, with financial backing from the U.S. government, built an experimental network called ARPANET in 1969. This groundbreaking network would become the Internet—the global collection of networks that is radically transforming the way the world uses computers.

Computer Time Line

These *Time* covers symbolize changes in the way people saw and used computers as they evolved through the last half of this century. Notice that the beginning of each new "era" doesn't mean the end of the old ways of computing; today we live in a world of institutional, personal, and interpersonal computing.

1950   1975   1995

Institutional Computing Era
(Starting approximately 1950)

Characterized by a few large, expensive mainframe computers in climate-controlled rooms; controlled by experts and specialists; used mainly for data storage and calculation.

Personal Computing Era
(Starting approximately 1975)

Characterized by millions of small, inexpensive micro-computers on desktops in offices, schools, homes, factories, and almost everywhere else; controlled mostly by independent users; used mostly for document creation, data storage, and calculation.

Interpersonal Computing Era
(Starting approximately 1995)

Characterized by networks of interconnected computers in offices, homes, schools, vehicles, and almost everywhere else; controlled by users (clients) and network operators; used mostly for communication, document creation, data storage, and calculation.

In the early 1950s the first computers were changing the military and a few government agencies and big businesses. By 1980 the microcomputer revolution was transforming offices, schools, and some homes. In the early 21st century the network revolution is likely to have an even bigger impact on our society.

The Internet Explosion

In its early years the Internet was the domain of researchers, academics, and government officials. It wasn't designed for casual visitors; users had to know cryptic commands and codes that only a programmer could love. In the 1990s Internet software took giant leaps forward in usability.

Electronic mail (often abbreviated **email** or *e-mail*) was the application that lured many people to the Internet for the first time. Modern, easy-to-use programs made it possible for even casual computer users to send messages to each other without learning complex codes. Because an email message could be written, addressed, sent, delivered, and answered in a matter of minutes—even if the correspondents were on opposite sides of the globe—email quickly replaced air mail for rapid, routine communication in many organizations.

But the biggest changes came with the development of the **World Wide Web (WWW)**, a vast tract of the Internet accessible to just about anyone who could point to buttons on a computer screen. The **Web**, as it's often called, led the Internet's transformation from a text-only environment into a multimedia landscape incorporating pictures, animation, sounds, and video. Millions of people connect to the Web each day through **Web browsers**—easy-to-use software programs that, in effect, serve as windows into the Web's information space.

The World Wide Web is made up of millions of interlinked documents called **Web pages.** Some Web pages stand alone; others, like those that accompany this book, are grouped in related collections called **Web sites.** A typical Web site is organized around a home page that serves as an entry page and a stepping off point for

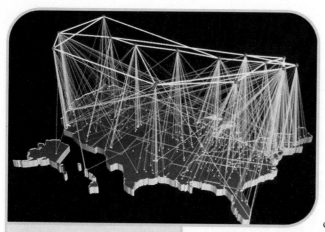

This computer-generated 3-D map represents major Internet connections in the United States.

other pages in the site. Each Web page has a unique address, technically referred to as a **URL** (uniform resource locator). For example, the URL for this book's home page is *www.prenhall.com/beekman*. You can visit the site by typing that URL into your Web browser. (If you're using Netscape Communicator or Internet Explorer as your browser you can just type computerconfluence and the browser will fill in the rest automatically.)

Once you're there, you can jump to different Web pages within the site by clicking on *hyperlinks*—on-screen pictures and highlighted text that act as buttons. Many hyperlinks at the *Computer Confluence* Web site will take you to pages on other Web sites. These off-site pages contain articles, illustrations, audio clips, video segments, and other resources created by others. They reside on servers of corporations, universities, libraries, institutions, and individuals around the world. The World Wide Web is the first successful mass publishing medium that encourages this kind of interlinking of documents across the planet.

In less than a decade the Web has become a massive global information storehouse. The biggest challenge for many Web users is extracting the useful information from the rest. Programs for locating information on the Web, called **search engines,** have become invaluable tools for researchers, shoppers, and browsers. Many search engines are located on Internet **portals**—Web sites designed as first-stop gateways for Internet explorers. Many portals, including Excite and Yahoo, allow users to create personalized home pages that greet them whenever they launch their Web browsers.

The Internet Culture

It is not proper to think of networks as connecting computers. Rather they connect people using computers to mediate. The great success of the Internet is not technical, but its human impact.

—**Dave Clark,** Internet pioneer, now a senior research scientist at MIT

Today the Internet is used by mom-and-pop businesses and multinational corporations who want to communicate with their customers, sell products, and track economic conditions; by kindergartners and college students doing research and exploration; by consumers and commuters who need access to timely information, goods, and services; and by families and friends who just want to stay in touch. All kinds of people are logging onto the Internet, and they're doing it in record numbers.

Why? Reasons vary, but most people connect to the Internet because it gives them the power to do things that they couldn't easily do otherwise. Using the Internet you can:

▶ Study material that's designed to supplement this book, including late-breaking news, interactive study aids, and multimedia simulations that can't be printed on paper.

▶ Send a message to 1 or 1,001 people, around town or around the world, and receive replies as quickly as the recipients can read the message and type a response.

▶ Quickly explore vast libraries of research material, ranging from classic scholarly works to contemporary reference works.

▶ Find instant answers to time-sensitive questions such as "What's the weather like in Boston right now?" or "What software do I need to make my new computer work with my new printer?" or "Who won this morning's Olympic high-diving competition?" or "What did the United Nations secretary general say on National Public Radio's *All Things Considered* last night?" or "Where in the world is the Federal Express package I sent yesterday?"

▶ Get medical advice from a wide variety of experts.

▶ Listen to live radio broadcasts from all around the world.

▶ Participate in discussions or play games with people all over the globe who share your interests; with the right equipment, you can set aside your keyboard and communicate through live audio-video links.

▶ Shop for obscure items like out-of-print books and CDs that you can't find elsewhere.

▶ Download free software or music clips from servers all over the world onto your computer.

▶ Order a custom-built computer, car, or condominium.

▶ Track hourly changes in the stock markets and buy and sell stocks based on those changes.

▶ Take a course for college credit from a school thousands of miles away.

▶ Publish your own writings, drawings, photos, and multimedia works so they can be viewed by Internet users all over the world.

▶ Start your own business and have a worldwide clientele.

It seems the Internet is everywhere these days. This beauty parlor offers Internet access along with haircuts and permanents.

The growth of the Internet has been nothing short of staggering. In 1994, 3 million people were connected; today, hundreds of millions are. Roughly one third of all American households were connected to the Internet by the end of 1999; by 2003 that number is expected to double. Before the first decade of the 21st century is over, 90% of U.S. households will likely be connected, making the Internet almost as universal as the television and the telephone. The United States leads the world in Internet activity, but the rest of the world is catching up. About one sixth of all Western European homes were on line in 1999—almost half of them new to the net.

Internet users tend to be younger, better educated, and wealthier than the rest of the population. But as the Internet's population grows, it will look more like the population at large. According to the U.S. Internet Council, the percentage of blacks, Hispanics, and women who use the Internet is rising rapidly. And while there are still some areas, even in the United States, with no Internet access, those are becoming harder to find. In just about any city on Earth you can rent time on a PC to check your e-mail or explore the Web.

Traffic on the Internet is doubling about every few months, with no end in sight. The Internet is growing faster than television, radio, or any other communication technology that came before it. This growth is in part fueled by the rapid expansion of commerce on the Web. The U.S. Internet economy generates hundreds of billions of dollars in revenues and millions of jobs each year. And this is only the beginning.

The Internet has become so pervasive that many organizations have rebuilt their entire information-processing systems around Internet technology. A growing number of companies are replacing their aging mainframe-and-PC-based systems with **intranets**—private intraorganizational networks based on Internet technology. Intranets mimic the Internet in the ways in which they allow people to transmit, share, and store information within an organization.

Many people believe we'll soon use computers mostly as gateways to intranets and the Internet. In fact, several companies, including IBM, Sun, and Hewlett Packard, are developing and marketing stripped-down computers designed to function mainly as

Network computers like this one provide fast access to company networks and the Internet without the high maintenance costs of traditional PCs.

network terminals. These companies don't all agree on exactly what these boxes should include, how much they should be able to do without the aid of a server, or even what they should be called. You might hear people referring to **network computers,** *NCs, thin clients, managed PCs, net PCs,* or *Windows terminals* when they talk about network-centric machines.

In spite of their different names and designs, all of these machines share two common characteristics: They cost less than typical PCs because they contain less hardware, and they are easier to maintain because much of the software can be stored on a central server. Like a TV, a network computer is designed to receive information from elsewhere. But unlike a TV, an NC allows you to send and receive information; it's a two-way connection to the wired world.

Network computers make economic sense in many workplaces, but most of them are not designed for use in homes. But many manufacturers now sell **information appliances** (or *Internet appliances*) that allow home as well as office users to connect to the Internet without a full-blown PC. (The terms *Internet appliance* and *information appliance* are used by some people to refer to network computers in offices as well as homes; the terminology is, at this point, as fluid as the technology.) For example, Internet telephones have screens and keyboards to allow easy access to email and the Web. **Set-top boxes,** including some game consoles, provide Internet access through television sets. Some handheld computers, like the popular Palm 7, provide wireless access to the Internet. Even a few cellular phones can display Internet data on tiny screens. Who knows? Future homes and businesses may have dozens of devices—computers, telephones, televisions, stereos, security systems, and even kitchen appliances—continually connected to the Internet, monitoring all kinds of data that can have an impact on our lives and our livelihoods. Whatever happens, it's clear that the Internet is going to play an increasing role in our future.

Millions of homes may soon be connecting to the Internet using televisions through set-top boxes like this Web TV box.

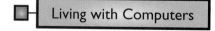 **Living with Computers**

Just as Michelangelo's contemporaries couldn't have foreseen abstract expressionism, we can't foresee how people will use the computing medium in the future.

—Clement Mok, in *Designing Business*

In less than a human lifetime, computers have evolved from massive, expensive, error-prone calculators like the Mark I and ENIAC into (mostly) dependable, versatile machines that have worked their way into just about every nook and cranny of modern society. The pioneers who created and marketed the first computers did not foresee these spectacular advances in computer technology.

Thomas Watson, Sr., the founding father of IBM, declared in 1953 that the world would not need more than five computers! And the early pioneers certainly couldn't have predicted the extraordinary social changes that resulted from the computer's rapid evolution. In the time of UNIVAC who could have imagined Sun workstations, Sony PlayStations, smart bombs, ATMs, or the World Wide Web?

Technological breakthroughs encourage further technological change, so we can expect the rate of change to continue to increase in coming decades. In other words, the technological and social transformations of the past five decades may be dwarfed by the changes that occur over the next half century! It's just a matter of time, and not very much time, before today's state-of-the-art computers look as primitive as ENIAC looks to us today. Similarly, today's high-tech society just hints at a future world that we haven't begun to imagine.

What do you really need to know about computers today? The remaining chapters of this book, along with the accompanying CD-ROM and Web site, provide answers to that question by looking at the technology on three levels: explanations, applications, and implications.

Explanations: Clarifying Technology

You don't need to be a computer scientist to coexist with computers. But your encounters with technology will make more sense if you understand a few basic computer concepts. Computers are evolving at an incredible pace, so many of the details of hardware and software change every few years. And the Internet is evolving even faster; it's often suggested that one normal year is equal to several "Internet years." But most of the underlying concepts remain constant as computers and networks evolve. If you understand the basics, you'll find that it's a lot easier to keep up with the changes.

Applications: Computers in Action

Many people define computer literacy as the ability to use computers. But because computers are so versatile, there's no one set of skills that you can learn to become computer literate in every situation. *Application programs*, also known simply as *applications*, are the software tools that allow a computer to be used for specific purposes. Many computer applications in science, government, business, and the arts are far too specialized and technical to be of use or of interest to people outside the field. On the other hand, some applications are so flexible that they can be used by anyone.

Regardless of your background or aspirations, you can almost certainly benefit from knowing a little about these applications.

▶ *Word processing and desktop publishing.* Word processing is a critical skill for anyone who communicates in writing. It's far and away the number one application used by students. Desktop publishing uses the personal computer to transform written words into polished, visually exciting publications.

▶ *Spreadsheets and other number-crunching applications.* In business the electronic spreadsheet is the personal computer application that pays the rent—or at least calculates it. If you work with numbers of any kind, spreadsheets and statistical software can help you turn those numbers into insights.

▶ *Databases.* If word processors and spreadsheets are the most popular PC applications, databases reign supreme in the world of mainframes. Of course, databases are widely used on PCs, too. As libraries, banks, and other institutions turn to databases for information storage, the average person has more reasons to learn the basics of databases. What's more, databases are at the heart of many modern Web sites on the Internet.

▶ *Computer graphics.* Today's computers are capable of producing all kinds of graphics, from the charts and graphs produced by spreadsheets to realistic 3-D animation. As graphics tools become more accessible, visual communication skills become more important for all of us.

11th century movable type, decimal number system, musical notation
12th century modern abacus
15th century Gutenberg's printing press
16th century algebraic symbols, lead pencil
17th century calculus, Pascal's calculator, probability, binary
arithmetic, newspapers, mailboxes
18th century typewriter, three-color printing, industrial revolution
19th century automated loom, Analytical Engine, telegraph,
vacuum tube, cathode-ray tube, telephone, color photograph,
Hollerith's data-processing machine, radio, sound recordings
Early 20th century assembly-line automated production, analog
computer, television, motion pictures, binary number theory

The floodgates are open, and
information technology ideas
are flowing faster all the time.

1939 Atanasoff creates the first digital computer
1939 Zuse completes first programmable, general-purpose computer
1943 Turing's Colossus computer breaks Nazi codes
1944 Aiken completes the Mark I
1945 Von Neumann proposes storing programs as data
1945 A. C. Clarke envisions geosynchronous communication satellites
1946 Mauchly and Eckert design ENIAC
1947 Shockley, Brittain, and Ardeen invent the transistor
1949 Orwell writes 1984, a novel about totalitarianism and computers
1951 Univac I is delivered to U.S. Census Bureau
1954 IBM makes first mass-produced computer
1955 Sony introduces portable transistor radio
1956 first computer operating system
1956 Bell labs build first transistorized computer
1956 computerized banking begins
1957 USSR launches Sputnik; United States responds by forming ARPA
1959 Jack Kilby and Robert Noyce develop the integrated circuit
1960 laser invented
1962 DEC introduces minicomputer
1962 first timesharing operating system
1963 Doug Engelbart patents mouse
1991 many PC makers launch multimedia products
1991 first war fought primarily from air with "smart" weapons
1992 several pen-based computers and handheld communications devices introduced
1993 computer companies, phone companies, and cable TV companies from alliances to create new interactive media
1994 Apple introduces Power Macintosh using CPU developed by IBM
1994 White House announces its World Wide Web page
1994 Intel replaces thousands of Pentium processors because of bugs
1995 Microsoft introduces Windows 95 with $200 million marketing campaign
1995 Disney/Pixar releases Toy Story, first all digital feature-length movie
1996 PCs outsell TVs in the United States for the first time
1997 Several companies introduce network computers for Internet access
1997 U.S. Supreme Court defends Internet free speech by striking down Communications Decency Act
1998 U.S. Justice Department sues Microsoft and Intel for separate antitrust violations
1998 Sharp introduces wristwatch PC
1998 Apple's iMac starts trend toward stylish designer computers
1999 Yugoslav hackers attack one of NATO's computer servers
1999 Internet stock explosion pushes Dow past 10,000
1999 free PCs offered to lure Internet subscribers for the first time
1999 Internet e-mail outpaces the post office
1999 Y2K millennium bug captures public attention, costs businesses billions
2000 Denial of service attacks cripple many of the largest commercial Web sites
2000 Hackers form a corporation to advise corporations on security
2000 Arizona holds first Internet primary election
2000 Love Bug email virus infiltrates millions of computers worldwide within hours of release
2000 Microsoft is found guilty of illegal monopolistic practices

► *Interactive multimedia.* Many of the computing industry's visionaries have their sights focused on this exciting new technology. Multimedia tools for PCs make it possible to combine audio and video with traditional text and graphics, adding new dimensions to computer communication. Unlike books, videos, and other linear media, which are designed to be experienced from beginning to end, interactive multimedia documents (including many Web sites) allow users to explore a variety of paths through media-rich information sources.

► *Telecommunication and networking.* A network connection is a door into a world of electronic mail, on-line discussion groups, Web publishing ventures, and database sharing. If current trends continue, telecommunication—long-distance communication—may soon be the single most important function of computers. The multipurpose global communication web known as the Internet may become as important in our lives as the telephone system, the postal service, and broadcast television are today.

► *Artificial intelligence.* Artificial intelligence is the branch of computer science that explores the use of computers in tasks that require intelligence, imagination, and insight—tasks that have traditionally been performed by people rather than machines. Until recently, artificial intelligence was mostly an academic discipline—a field of study reserved for researchers and philosophers. But that research is paying off today with commercial applications that exhibit intelligence, from basic speech recognition to sophisticated expert systems.

► *General problem solving.* People use computers to solve problems. Most people use software applications written by professional programmers. But some kinds of problems can't easily be solved with off-the-shelf applications; they require at least some custom programming. Programming languages aren't applications; they're tools that allow you to build and customize applications. Many computer users find their machines become more versatile, and valuable, when they learn a little about programming.

Implications: Social and Ethical Issues

True computer literacy is not just knowing how to make use of computers and computational ideas. It is knowing when it is appropriate to do so.

—**Seymour Papert**, in *Mindstorms*

Computers and networks are transforming the world rapidly and irreversibly. Jobs that existed for hundreds of years are eliminated by automation while new careers are built on emerging technology. Start-up businesses create multiple millionaires overnight, while older companies struggle to keep pace with "Internet time." Instant worldwide communication changes the way businesses work and challenges the role of governments. Computers routinely save lives in hospitals, keep space flights on course, and predict the weekend weather.

More than any other recent technology, the computer is responsible for profound changes in our society; we just need to imagine a world without computers to recognize their impact. Of course, computer scientists and computer engineers are not responsible for all of the technological turbulence. Developments in fields as diverse as telecommunications, genetic engineering, medicine, and atomic physics contribute to the ever-increasing rate of social change. But researchers in all of these fields depend on computers to produce their work.

The future is rushing toward you, and computer technology is a big part of it. It's exciting to consider the opportunities arising from advances in artificial intelligence, multimedia, robotics, and other cutting-edge technologies of the electronic revolution—opportunities in the workplace, the school, and the home. But it's just as important to pay attention to the potential risks. Here's a sampling of the kinds of issues we'll confront in this book:

▶ *The threat to personal privacy posed by large databases and computer networks.* When you use a credit card, buy an airline ticket, place a phone call, visit your doctor, send an e-mail message, or explore the World Wide Web, you are leaving a trail of personal information in one or more computers. Who owns that information? Is it OK for them to share that information with others or make it public? Do you have the right to check its accuracy and change it if it's wrong? Do laws protecting individual privacy rights place undue burdens on businesses and governments?

▶ *The hazards of high-tech crime and the difficulty of keeping data secure.* Even if you trust the institutions and businesses that collect data about you, you can't be sure that data will remain secure in their computer systems. Computer crime is at an all-time high, and law enforcement officials are having a difficult time keeping it under control. How can society protect itself from information thieves and high-tech vandals? How can lawmakers write laws about technology that they are just beginning to understand? What kinds of personal risk do you face as a result of computer crime?

▶ *The difficulty of defining and protecting intellectual property in an all-digital age.* Software programs, musical recordings, videos, and books can be difficult and expensive to create. But in our digital age, all of these can easily be copied. What rights do the creators of intellectual property have? Is a teenager who copies music files from the Web a computer criminal? What about a Chinese shopkeeper who sells pirated copies of Microsoft Office for $10? Or a student who posts a clip from *Star Wars* on his Web site? Or a musician who uses a two-second sample from a Michael Jackson song in an electronic composition?

▶ *The risks of failure of computer systems.* Computer software is difficult to write because it is incredibly complex. As a result, no computer system is completely fail-safe. Computer failures routinely cause communication problems, billing errors, lost data, and other inconveniences. But they also occasionally result in power blackouts, telephone system meltdowns, weapons failure, and other potentially deadly problems. Who is responsible for loss of income—or loss of life—caused by software errors? What rights do we have when buying and using software? How can we, as a society, protect ourselves from software disasters?

▶ *The threat of automation and the dehumanization of work.* Computers and the Internet fueled unprecedented economic growth in the last decade of the 20th century, producing plenty of new jobs for workers with the right skills. But the new information-based economy has cost many workers—especially older workers—their jobs and their dignity. And many workers today find that their jobs involve little more than tending to machines—and being monitored by bosses with high-tech surveillance devices. As machines replace people in the workplace, what rights do the displaced workers have? Does a worker's right to privacy outweigh an employer's right to read employee e-mail or monitor worker actions? What is the government's role in the protection of worker rights in the high-tech workplace?

▶ *The abuse of information as a tool of political and economic power.* The computer age has produced an explosion of information, and most of that information is concentrated in corporate and government computers. The emergence of low-cost personal computers and the Internet makes it possible for more people to have access to information and the power that comes with that information. But the majority of the people on the planet have never made a phone call, let alone used a computer. Will the information revolution leave them behind? Do information-rich people and countries have a responsibility to share technology and information with the information-poor?

This robot security guard protects this museum from vandals and thieves. But does it threaten the jobs of other guards?

▶ *The dangers of dependence on complex technology.* One of the biggest news stories of 1999 was the impending threat of massive problems caused by the Y2K bug—the failure of some software programs on January 1, 2000, because they represented the year with only two digits. Businesses and governments spent billions of dollars trying to repair and replace computer systems that might be affected by the problem. People stockpiled food and fuel, hid cash and jewels, made paper copies of all their critical records, and prepared for the possibility that the power grid would fail, leaving much of the world's population helpless and hungry. The Y2K scare reminded us how much we have come to depend on this far-from-foolproof technology. Are we, as a society, addicted to computer technology? Should we question new technological innovations before we embrace them? Can we build a future in which technology never takes precedence over humanity?

Today's technology raises fascinating and difficult questions. But these questions pale in comparison to the ones we'll have to deal with as the technology evolves in the coming years:

▶ *The death of privacy.* Governments and private companies alike are installing extensive video surveillance networks to monitor security and track lawbreakers. Computer databases are accumulating more information about you all the time, and networks are making it easier to transmit, share, and merge that information. Will these converging technologies destroy the last of our personal privacy, as some experts have suggested? Is there anything we can do about it?

▶ *The blurring of reality.* Virtual reality (VR) is widely used by scientific researchers and computer gamers alike. But if VR doesn't live up to its name, it does suggest a future technology in which artificial environments look and feel real. And rapid developments in Internet technology are likely to lead us to shared virtual environments ranging from shopping malls to gaming centers. We are already seeing people suffering from computer addiction and Internet addiction. Will these diseases become epidemics when VR feels like real life, only better? Will VR technology be abused by unscrupulous con artists? Should governments limit what's legal when just about anything is possible?

▶ *The evolution of intelligence.* Artificial intelligence research is responsible for many products, including software that can read books to the blind, understand spoken words, and play world-class chess. But tomorrow's machine intelligence will make today's smartest machines look stupid. What rights will human workers have when software can do their jobs better, faster, and smarter? What rights will smart machines have in a world run by humans? Will there come a time when humans aren't smart enough to maintain control of their creations?

What impact will computer technology have on traditional cultures that have evolved for thousands of years without computers?

▶ *The emergence of bio-digital technology.* Today thousands of people walk around with computer chips embedded in their bodies, helping them to overcome disabilities and lead normal lives. At the same time, researchers are making progress developing computers that use biology, rather than electronics, as their underlying technology. As the line between organism and machine blurs, what happens to our vision of ourselves? What are the limits of our creative powers, and what are our responsibilities in using those powers?

For better and for worse, we will be coexisting with computers until death do us part. As with any relationship, a little understanding can go a long way. The remaining chapters of this book will help you gain the understanding you need to survive and prosper in a world of computers.

In a 1965 article futurist Alvin Toffler described a condition called future shock—a condition that afflicts people who are overwhelmed by the rapid changes brought on by technology. His 1970 book Future Shock *predicted a world of ever-increasing change and raised questions about our ability to adapt to such rapid-fire changes. That's just one of the problems raised in this article by Peter McGrath for a special September 20, 1999 issue of* Newsweek *on the impact of the Internet on our lives.*

Tense about the future? You're not alone. High tech can create high anxiety.

Go on, admit it: you've wanted to smash that screen, haven't you? Or fry the keyboard in a manic deluge of diet cola. Or maybe tear your modem line out by its twisted copper roots. Sometimes you harbor dark suspicions of your computer: it wants to foul you up. Why else would it freeze just when you need it most, and send creepy messages like "This program has performed an illegal operation and will be shut down."

There's no escape. Networked digital devices set the pace of change today. As James Gleick notes in his new book, *Faster,* the truly breakneck technologies are the ones governed by Moore's Law, the prediction in 1965 by Intel cofounder Gordon Moore that microchip miniaturization would lead to a doubling of computer power every 18 months. He was right, as it turned out. The result is exuberance among researchers, a strange blend of triumphalism and paranoia among business people—and for many ordinary users of technology, a sense of dislocation and even fear.

The fear takes four forms.

▶ I can't make this thing work. It's a common anxiety. A recent survey of 6,000 PC users showed they wasted an average of 5.1 hours a week in sheer computer hassle. Another study, conducted over 43 months by psychologists Larry D. Rosen and Michelle M. Weil, found that about 60 percent of respondents could be called "hesitant" users of technology, joined by a much smaller number of active "resisters." In the American public overall, Rosen suspects, about 70 percent are at best uneasy about technological change, even as they are resigned to it. "People feel driven, like they have to keep up, or they'll be lost forever," says Rosen, who with Weil wrote the 1998 book *TechnoStress: Coping with Technology @WORK @HOME @PLAY.* "Software engineers have a hard time understanding what ordinary users will find hard or easy," says Yogen Dalal, a partner in the Mayfield Fund, a top Silicon Valley venture-capital firm.

▶ It's my fault. The current emphasis on anthropomorphic design—the idea that the computer should be "friendly" and show human qualities ("You've got mail")—seduces people into imagining the machine as a real partner in a social transaction. But, says Ben Shneiderman, the head of the Human–Computer Interaction Laboratory at the University of Maryland, the result can actually make us feel stupid. Error messages are accusatory: you "performed an illegal operation" or caused a "fatal exception." You compromised the "integrity" of the system files, as though system files had moral qualities. These terms "suggest the designer's condemnation of the user," says Shneiderman. Weil adds: "People compare themselves to the technology. . . . It seems so alive. It talks to you, it flashes lights in your face. . . . Users, especially the more hesitant ones, take the glitches personally, because of the perception that technology never fails." The other version of this syndrome is, The machine doesn't like me.

▶ You, too? Technology makes for external stress, like that of the Y2K survivalists with their bunker-down belief that Jan. 1, 2000, is a computer-decreed day of reckoning. Then there's the worry about personal privacy in a networked world, as people become aware of how invasive Web technologies can be. Also the job uncertainty found in survey after survey, despite the longest economic boom in living memory. And why not? As the science writer James Burke said in his book *The Pinball Effect,* the rate of technological change is becoming "so high that for humans to be qualified in a single discipline . . . will be as outdated as quill and parchment. Knowledge will be changing too fast for that. We will need to reskill ourselves constantly every decade just to keep a job."

▶ There's never enough time anymore. A decade ago, Alvin Toffler wrote that the next competition would not take place between East and West, nor North and South, but between "the fast and the slow"—the quick and the dead. Toffler had whole economies in mind, but his point holds at the personal level, too. The future belongs to those with nimble if not always careful minds. Microsoft, for example, is notorious for job interviews in which candidates are evaluated on their ability to solve in seconds mathematical puzzles and logical twists.

For better and for worse, we are stuck with speed. For better: in a global economy, technology companies will create untold wealth through sheer frenzies of creation. For worse: we will lose sight of the virtues of languor and deliberation. Some things can't be rushed, such as diplomacy and love. The techno-tycoons themselves know this: in the rush to be first-to-market, they cut corners and drive customers crazy with bug-ridden products (This program has performed an illegal operation and will be shut down), but they would never accept a similar lack of craftsmanship in their own golf clubs or yachts.

In the end, though, addressing techno-stress is a commercial imperative. The industry has exhausted the supply of buyers willing to put up with complex and alienating products. In fact, says Yogen Dalal, the realization is already underway, with devices like the Palm Pilot and technologists who are heeding "the needs of mass markets and understanding what people really want."

We'll see. In the meantime: don't smash that screen just yet.

DISCUSSION QUESTIONS

1. How do you feel about each of the problems listed here? Are you concerned? Why or why not?
2. Have you had any personal experiences that support or counter the author's arguments? Describe them.
3. Is there anything we can do to relieve techno-stress?

Summary

While the basic idea behind a computer goes back to Charles Babbage's 19th-century plan for an Analytical Engine, the first real computers were developed during the 1940s. Computers have evolved at an incredible pace since those early years, becoming consistently smaller, faster, more efficient, more reliable, and less expensive. At the same time, people have devised all kinds of interesting and useful ways to put computers to work to solve problems.

Computers today, like their ancestors, are information-processing machines designed to transform information from one form to another. When a computer operates, the hardware accepts input data from some outside source, transforms the data by following instructions called software, and produces output that can be read by a human or by another machine.

Computers today come in all shapes and sizes, with specific types being well suited for particular jobs. Mainframe computers and supercomputers provide more power and speed than smaller desktop machines, but they are expensive to purchase and operate. Timesharing makes it possible for many users to work simultaneously at terminals connected to these large computers. At the other end of the spectrum workstations, personal computers, and a variety of portable devices provide computing power for those of us who don't need a mainframe's capabilities. Microprocessors aren't just used in general-purpose computers; they're embedded in appliances, automobiles, and a rapidly growing list of other products.

Connecting to a network enhances the value and power of a computer—it can share resources with other computers and facilitate electronic communication with other computer users. Some networks are local to a particular building or business; others connect users at remote geographic locations. The Internet is an interconnected collection of networks that spans the globe. Businesses, public institutions, and individuals are rushing to connect their computers and other devices to the Internet, and people are finding new ways to take advantage of the global network every day. Electronic mail provides hundreds of millions of people with instant worldwide communication capabilities. With Web browsing software, those same Internet users have access to millions of Web pages on the World Wide Web. The Web is a distributed network of interlinked multimedia documents. Although it started out as a tool for researchers and scholars, the Web has quickly become a vital center for entertainment and commerce. As the Internet grows and changes, it will play an increasingly important role in our lives.

Computers and information technology have changed the world rapidly and irreversibly. We can easily list dozens of ways in which computers make our lives easier and more productive. Personal computer applications such as word processing, desktop publishing, spreadsheets, graphics, and databases continue to grow in popularity. Computer networks are emerging as important communication tools. Emerging technologies such as artificial intelligence offer promise for future applications. At the same time, computers threaten our privacy, our security, and perhaps our way of life. As we rush into the information age, our future depends on computers and on our ability to understand and use them in productive, positive ways.

Chapter Review

Key Terms

Analytical Engine, 3
application program (application), 19
data, 6
electronic mail (email), 15
embedded computer, 13
firmware, 13
handheld computer, 12
hardware, 6
high-performance computer, 10
input, 6
information appliance, 18
integrated circuit, 8
Internet, 14
intranet, 17
keyboard, 12
laptop computer, 12

mainframe computer, 10
microcomputer, 9
microcomputer revolution, 9
microprocessor, 8
Moore's Law, 8
network computer (NC), 12
network revolution, 14
notebook computer, 12
output, 6
personal computer (PC), 9
portable computer, 12
portal, 16
program, 6
search engine, 16
server, 11

set-top box, 18
silicon chip, 8
software, 6
special-purpose (dedicated) computer, 13
supercomputer, 10
terminal, 10
timesharing, 10
transistor, 7
URL (uniform resource locator), 16
Web browser, 15
Web page, 15
Web site, 15
workstation, 11
World Wide Web (WWW), 15

Review Questions

1. Provide a working definition of each of the key terms listed above. Check your answers in the glossary.
2. List several ways you interact with computers in your daily life.
3. Why was the Analytical Engine never completed during Charles Babbage's lifetime?
4. Outline the evolution of the computer from World War II to the present.
5. How are hardware and software related?
6. What is the most important difference between a computer and a calculator?
7. What is the difference between a mainframe and a microcomputer? What are the advantages and disadvantages of each?
8. What kinds of computer applications require the speed and power of a supercomputer? Give some examples.
9. What types of computers typically employ timesharing?
10. List several common personal computer applications.
11. Why is it important for people to know about and understand computers?
12. Describe some of the benefits and drawbacks of the computer revolution.
13. Take a practice quiz using the review questions on the CD-ROM and, if appropriate, e-mail the results to your instructor.
14. Do the Internet exercises on the Web pages for this chapter at www.prenhall.com/beekman.

Discussion Questions

1. What do people mean when they talk about the computer revolution? What is revolutionary about it?
2. How do you feel about computers? Examine your positive and negative feelings.
3. What major events before the 20th century influenced the development of the computer?
4. Suppose Charles Babbage and Ada Lovelace had been able to construct a working Analytical Engine and develop a factory for mass producing it. How do you think the world would have reacted? How would the history of the 20th century have been different as a result?
5. How would the world be different today if a wrinkle in time transported a modern desktop computer system, complete with software and manuals, onto the desk of Herbert Hoover? Adolf Hitler? Albert Einstein?
6. The automobile and the television set are two examples of technological inventions that changed our society drastically in ways that were not anticipated by their inventors. Outline several positive and negative effects of each of these two inventions. Do you think, on balance, that we are better off as a result of these machines? Why or why not? Now repeat this exercise for the computer.
7. Should all students be required to take at least one computer course? Why or why not? If so, what should that course cover?
8. Computerphobia—fear or anxiety related to computers—is a common malady among people today. What do you think causes it? What, if anything, should be done about it?
9. In your opinion what computer applications offer the most promise for making the world a better place? What computer applications pose the most significant threats to our future well-being?
10. Discuss one or more of the Internet exploration questions at the section for this chapter at www.prenhall.com/beekman.

Projects

1. Start a collection of news articles, cartoons, or television segments that deal with computers. Does your collection say anything about popular attitudes toward computers?
2. Trace computer-related articles through several years in the same magazine. Do you see any changes or trends?
3. Develop a questionnaire to try to determine people's attitudes about computers. Once you have people's answers to your questions, summarize your results.
4. Take an inventory of all the computers you encounter in a single day. Be sure to include embedded computers such as those in cars, appliances, entertainment equipment, and other machines.

Periodicals

Byte (general and technical); **PC**, **PC World**, **PC/Computing**, **Windows Magazine**, **Boot**, **Windows Sources** (Windows-compatible); **Macworld**, **MacAddict** (Macintosh); **Mobile Computing** & **Communication** (portable computers); **Pen Computing** (pen-based handheld computers). Because the world of personal computers changes so rapidly, computer users depend on magazines to keep them up to date on hardware and software developments. The average computer owner is interested mainly in information related to one type of machine, so most of these magazines target brand-specific audiences.

Computerworld and PC Week. These weekly newspapers provide up-to-the-week news on computers, emphasizing corporate applications.

Wired. This trend-setting monthly is billed as "the first consumer magazine for the digital generation to track technology's impact on all facets of the human condition." Some of the best writers and thinkers in the field contribute to this thought-provoking, influential magazine. *Wired* isn't for everybody, though. The ultra-hip style, controversial content, and bold design have led some to suggest that it should be called *Weird.*

Books

Microsoft Press Computer Dictionary, Third Edition (Redmond, WA: Microsoft Press, 1997). It sometimes seems like the computer industry makes three things: hardware, software, and jargon. Many computer terms are too new, too obscure, or too technical to appear in standard dictionaries. Fortunately, there are several good dictionaries that specialize in computer terminology. This is one of the most comprehensive and up to date. It covers PC, Macintosh, UNIX, and Internet terms, but the included CD-ROM only runs on Windows machines.

Crystal Fire: The Birth of the Information Age, by Michael Riordan and Lillian Hoddeson (New York: Norton, 1997). One of the defining moments of the information age occurred in 1947 when William Shockley and his colleagues invented the transistor. *Crystal Fire* tells the story of that earthshaking invention, clearly describing the technical and human dimensions of the story.

The Dream Machine: Exploring the Computer Age, by Jon Palfreman and Doren Swade (London: BBC Books, 1993). This book, designed to accompany a BBC TV documentary, is filled with photos and text describing the evolution of the computer from its earlier days.

Fire in the Valley: The Making of the Personal Computer Second Edition 1999, by Paul Freiberger and Michael Swaine (Berkeley, CA: Osborne/McGraw-Hill, 1984). This book chronicles the early years of the personal computer revolution. The text occasionally gets bogged down in details, but the photos and quotes from the early days are fascinating. The 1999 film **Pirates of Silicon Valley** is based loosely on this book.

Faster—The Acceleration of Just About Everything, by James Gleick (New York: Pantheon Books, 1999). The title says it all. In this age of ever-faster computers, electronic organizers, and Internet time, we're setting speed records at just about everything—but at what cost? Well worth reading if you have time.

Accidental Empires: How the Boys of Silicon Valley Make Their Millions, Battle Foreign Competition, and Still Can't Get a Date, Revised Edition, by Robert X. Cringely (New York, NY: Harper Business, 1996). Robert X. Cringely is the pen name for **InfoWorld's** computer-industry gossip columnist. In this opinionated, irreverent, and highly entertaining book Cringely discusses the past, present, and future of the volatile personal computer industry. When you read the humorous, colorful characterizations of the people who run this industry, you'll understand why Cringely didn't use his real name. **Triumph of the Nerds,** a 1996 PBS TV show and video based loosely on this book, lacks much of the humor and insight of the book, but includes some fascinating footage of the pioneers reminiscing about the early days.

The Difference Engine, by William Gibson and Bruce Sterling (New York: Spectra, 1992). How would the world of the 19th century be different if Charles and Ada had succeeded in constructing the Analytical Engine 150 years ago? This imaginative mystery novel takes place in a world where the computer revolution arrived a century early. Like other books by these two pioneers of the "cyberpunk" school of science fiction, *The Difference Engine* is dark, dense, detailed, and thought-provoking.

Dave Barry in Cyberspace, by Dave Barry, New York: Fawcett Columnbine, 1996). Dave Barry, the irreverent humor columnist, turns his irreverent wit loose on the information revolution in this hilarious little book. Here's a typical chapter title:"A Brief History of Computing from Cave Walls to Windows 95—Not That This Is Necessarily Progress." Whether you think computers are frustrating or funny, you'll probably find a few good laughs here.

World Wide Web Pages

Some of the best sources and resources on computers and information technology are on the Internet's World Wide Web. For example, the Boston Computer Museum's Web site (http://net.org) is a wonderful source of information about the past, present, and future of computers. But the Web is changing quickly, and new sites are appearing every day. *The Computer Confluence* Web pages include up-to-date links to many of the best computer-related resources on the Web. To find them, open your Web browsing software, enter the address www.prenhall.com/beekman, follow the on-screen buttons to the table of contents, select a chapter, and click on the links that interest you.

Chapter 2

Chapter

Hardware Basics: Inside the Box

AFTER YOU READ THIS CHAPTER YOU SHOULD BE ABLE TO:

Explain in general terms how computers store and manipulate information.

Describe the basic structure and organization of a computer.

Discuss the functions and interactions of a computer system's principal internal components.

Explain why a computer typically has different types of memory and storage devices.

In this chapter:

▶ Bits and bytes: the nature of digital information

▶ Inside the box: the computer's "brain" and memory

▶ How It Works features: visual explanations of the computer's inner workings

▶ Self-study questions and projects

▶ Mini-reviews of helpful resources for further study

. . . and more.

On the CD-ROM:

▶ An interactive binary arithmetic game

▶ Animated interactive tutorials explaining how CPU and memory work

▶ Instant access to glossary and key word references

▶ Interactive self-study quizzes

. . . and more.

On the Web:

www.prenhall.com/beekman

▶ Important documents describing and illustrating CPU and memory technology

▶ Links to Web sites of the most important computer hardware companies

▶ Self-study exercises

. . . and more.

There is no invention—**only discovery**.

—Thomas J. Watson, Sr.

As president or, as he has been called, the "emperor" of IBM, Thomas J. Watson, Sr. created a corporate culture that fostered both invention and discovery. In 1914 he joined the ailing Computing-Tabulating-Recording Company as a salesperson. The company specialized in counting devices that used punched cards to read and store information. Ten years later Watson took it over, renamed it International Business Machines, and turned it into the dominant force in the information industry.

Thomas Watson has been called autocratic. He demanded unquestioning allegiance from his employees and enforced a legendary dress code that forbade even a hint of color in a shirt. But in many ways Watson ran his company like a family, rewarding loyal employees with uncommon favors. During the Depression he refused to lay off workers, choosing instead to stockpile surplus machines. As if to prove that good deeds don't go unrewarded, the director of the newly formed Social Security Administration bought Watson's excess stock.

Watson's first involvement with computers was providing financial backing for Howard Aiken's Mark I, the pioneering electromechanical computer developed in the early 1940s at Harvard. But Watson stubbornly refused to develop a commercial computer, even as UNIVAC I achieved fame and commercial contracts for the fledgling Sperry company.

Shortly after Watson retired from the helm of IBM in 1949, his son, Thomas Watson, Jr., took over. The younger Watson led IBM into the computing field with a vengeance, eventually building a computing empire that dwarfed all competitors. When Watson Senior died of a heart attack in 1956 at the age of 82, he still held the title of chairman of IBM.

After decades of unchallenged dominance in the computer industry, IBM today struggles to maintain its reputation as the industry leader. The conservative giant has been slow to adjust to the rapid-fire changes in the computer industry, making it possible for smaller, more nimble companies such as Compaq, Dell, Sun, and Microsoft to seize emerging markets. Massive revenue losses forced IBM to reorganize, replace many of its leaders, and abandon the company's long-standing no-layoffs policy. (IBM also abandoned the legendary dress code, opting for a more casual image.) But in spite of recent difficulties, IBM maintains a position of dominance as a computer hardware company. ■

Thomas J. Watson, Sr. (1874—1956)

PCs are assembled in factories like this one at Dell Computer, Inc. In the next two chapters, we'll examine the components that make up the modern computer.

Computers schedule airline flights, predict the weather, play music, control space stations, and keep the world's economic wheels spinning. How can one kind of machine do so many things?

To understand what really makes computers tick you would need to devote considerable time and effort to studying computer science and computer engineering. Most of us don't need to understand every detail of a computer's inner workings, any more than a parent needs to explain wave and particle physics when a child asks why the sky is blue. We can be satisfied with simpler answers, even if those answers are only approximations of the technical truth. We'll spend the next three chapters exploring answers to the question, "How do computers do what they do?"

The main text of each of these chapters provides simple, nontechnical answers and basic information. *How It Works* boxes use text and graphics to dig deeper into the inner workings of the computer. Depending on your course, your learning style, and your level of curiosity, you may read these boxes as they appear in the text, read them after you've completed the basic material in the chapter, or (if you don't need the technical details) skip them altogether. You'll find interactive multimedia versions of many of these *How It Works* boxes on the *Computer Confluence* CD-ROM. Use the Sources and Resources section at each chapter's end for further explorations.

If you're interested in buying a computer, you'll find the information in the next three chapters helpful. More consumer information is available in the Concise Computer Consumer's Guide, an appendix to this book, and on the Computer Confluence CD-ROM and Web site.

What Computers Do

Stripped of its interfaces, a bare computer boils down to little more than a pocket calculator that can push its own buttons and remember what it has done.

—**Arnold Penzias**, in *Ideas and Information*

The simple truth is that computers perform only four basic functions:

1 *Receive input.* Computers accept information from the outside world.

2 *Process information.* Computers perform arithmetic or logical (decision-making) operations on information.

3 *Produce output.* Computers communicate information to the outside world.

4 *Store information.* Computers move and store information in memory.

Every computer system contains hardware components—physical parts—that specialize in each of these four functions:

▶ Input devices accept input from the outside world. The most common input device, of course, is the keyboard. But computers can accept input signals from a variety of other devices, including pointing devices such as mice and trackballs.

▶ Output devices send information to the outside world. Most computers use a TV-like video monitor as their main output device and a printer to produce paper printouts.

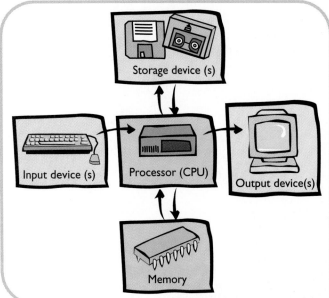

▸ A **processor**, or **central processing unit** (CPU), is, in effect, the computer's "brain." The CPU processes information, performing arithmetic calculations and making basic decisions by comparing information values.

▸ **Memory** and **storage devices** are both used to store information, but they serve different purposes. The computer's memory (sometimes called *primary storage*) is used to store programs and data that need to be instantly accessible to the CPU. Storage devices (sometimes called *secondary storage*), including disk and tape drives, serve as long-term repositories for data. A storage device such as a disk drive can be thought of as a combination input and output device because the computer sends information to the storage device (output) and later retrieves that information from it (input).

These four types of components, when combined, make up the hardware part of a computer system. Of course, the system isn't complete without software—the instructions that tell the hardware what to do. But for now we'll concentrate on hardware. In this chapter we'll focus on the central processing unit and the computer's memory; these components are at the center of all computing operations. In the next chapter we'll look at the input, output, and storage devices—that is, the **peripherals** of the computer system. Because every computer hardware component is designed either to transport or to transform information, we'll start with a little bit of information about information.

The basic components of every computer system include the central components (the CPU and memory, shown here in green) and peripherals (input, output, and storage devices, shown in orange and yellow).

A Bit About Bits

> Even the most sophisticated computer is really only a large, well-organized
> ## volume of bits.
>
> —**David Harel**, in *Algorithmics: The Spirit of Computing*

The term **information** is difficult to define because it has many meanings. According to many traditional definitions, information is communication that has value because it informs. People who subscribe to this definition say that computers turn raw *data,* which has no value in its current form, into *information,* which is valuable.

Many beginning textbooks use this model to emphasize the computer's role as a business data-processing machine. But in our modern interconnected world, where one computer's output might be another's input, it's difficult to draw a hard line between worthless data and valuable information.

In the language of communication and information theory, the term *information* can be applied to anything that can be communicated, whether it has value or not. By this definition, which is the one we'll be using in this book, information comes in many forms. The words, numbers, and pictures on these pages are symbols representing information. If you underline this sentence, you're adding new information to the page. The sounds and moving pictures that emanate from a television set are packed with information, too. (Remember, not all information has value.)

In the world of computers information is **digital**: It's made up of discrete units that can be counted, so it can be subdivided. In many situations people need to reduce

In the binary number system, every number is represented by a unique string of 0s and 1s. ▶

Decimal representation	Binary representation
0	0
1	1
2	10
3	11
4	100
5	101
6	110
7	111
8	1000
9	1001
10	1010
11	1011
12	1100
13	1101
14	1110
15	1111

information to simpler units to use it effectively. For example, a child trying to pronounce an unfamiliar word can sound out each letter individually before tackling the whole word.

A computer doesn't understand words, numbers, pictures, musical notes, or even letters of the alphabet. Like a young reader, a computer can't process information without dividing it into smaller units. In fact, computers can only digest information that has been broken into bits. A **bit** (*b*inary dig*it*) is the smallest unit of information. A bit can have one of two values. You can also think of these two values as yes and no, zero and one, on and off, black and white, or high and low.

If we think of the innards of a computer as a collection of microscopic on/off switches, it's easy to understand why computers process information bit by bit. Each switch can be used to store a tiny amount of information: a signal to turn on a light, for example, or the answer to a yes/no question. (In modern integrated circuits bits are represented by high and low electrical charges, but these circuits work the same as if they were really made up of tiny switches.)

Remember Paul Revere's famous midnight ride? His co-conspirators used a pair of lanterns to convey a choice between two messages, "One if by land, two if by sea"—a **binary** choice. It's theoretically possible to send a message like this with just one lantern. But "One if by land, zero if by sea" wouldn't have worked very well unless there was some way to know exactly when the message was being sent. With two lanterns the first lantern could say "Here is the message" when it was turned on. The second lantern communicated the critical bit's worth of information: land or sea. If the revolutionaries had wanted to send a more complex message, they could have used more lanterns ("Three if by subway!").

In much the same way, a computer can process larger chunks of information by treating groups of bits as units. For example, a collection of 8 bits, called a **byte**, can represent 256 different messages ($256 = 2^8$). If we think of each bit as a light that can be either on or off, then we can make different combinations of lights represent different messages. (Computer scientists usually speak in terms of 0 and 1 instead of on and off, but the concept is the same either way.) The computer has an advantage over Paul Revere in that it sees not just the number of lights turned on but also their order, so 01 (off–on) is different from 10 (on–off).

Building with Bits

What does a bit combination like 01100110 mean to the computer? There's no single answer to that question; it depends on context and convention. A string of bits can be interpreted as a number, a letter of the alphabet, or almost anything else.

Bits as Numbers

Because computers are built from switching devices that reduce all information to 0s and 1s, they represent numbers using the *binary number system*—a system that denotes all numbers with combinations of two digits. Like the 10-digit decimal system we use every day, the binary system has clear, consistent rules for every arithmetic operation.

The people who worked with early computers had to use binary arithmetic. But today's computers include software that converts decimal numbers into binary numbers automatically, and vice versa. As a result, the computer's binary number processing is completely hidden from the user.

Bits as Codes

Today's computers work as much with text as with numbers. To make words, sentences, and paragraphs fit into the computer's binary-only circuitry, programmers have devised codes that represent each letter, digit, and special character as a unique string of bits.

The most widely used code, ASCII (an abbreviation of American Standard Code for Information Interchange, pronounced "as-kee"), represents each character as a unique 8-bit code. Out of a string of 8 bits, 256 unique ordered patterns can be made—enough to make unique codes for 26 letters (upper- and lowercase), 10 digits, and a variety of special characters.

As the world shrinks and our information needs grow, ASCII's 256 unique characters simply aren't enough. ASCII is too limited to accommodate Greek, Hebrew, Japanese, Chinese, and other languages. To facilitate multilingual computing, the computer industry is embracing Unicode, a coding scheme that supports 65,000-unique characters—more than enough for all major world languages.

Of course, today's computers work with more than characters. A group of bits can also represent colors, sounds, quantitative measurements from the environment, or just about any other kind of information that's likely to be processed by a computer. We'll explore other types of information in later chapters.

Bits as Instructions in Programs

So far we've dealt with the ways bits can be used to represent *data*—information from some outside source that's processed by the computer. But another kind of information is just as important to the computer: the programs that tell the computer what to do with the data we give it. The computer stores programs as collections of bits, just as with data.

Program instructions, like characters, are represented in binary notation through the use of codes. For example, the code 01101010 might tell the computer to add two

Character	ASCII binary code
A	01000001
B	01000010
C	01000011
D	01000100
E	01000101
F	01000110
G	01000111
H	01001000
I	01001001
J	01001010
K	01001011
L	01001100
M	01001101
N	01001110
O	01001111
P	01010000
Q	01010001
R	01010010
S	01010011
T	01010100
U	01010101
V	01010110
W	01010111
X	01011000
Y	01011001
Z	01011010
0	00110000
1	00110001
2	00110010
3	00110011
4	00110100
5	00110101
6	00110110
7	00110111
8	00111000
9	00111001

The capital letters and numeric digits are represented in the ASCII character set by 36 unique patterns of 8 bits. (The remaining 92 ASCII bit patterns represent lowercase letters, punctuation characters, and special characters.)

How It Works 2.1

Binary Numbers

This is the first of many How It Works boxes you'll find in this book. How It Works boxes provide more technical detail than you'll find in the main text. Nothing in the How It Works boxes is critical for understanding the material in the rest of the book.

The MITS Altair, the first personal computer, came with no keyboard or monitor. It could only be programmed by using a bank of binary switches for input; binary patterns of lights provided the output.

In a computer, all information—program instructions, pictures, text, sounds, or mathematical values—is represented by patterns of microscopic switches. In most cases these groups of switches represent numbers or numerical codes.

The easiest kind of switch to manufacture is an on/off toggle switch: It has just two settings, on and off, like an ordinary light switch. That's the kind of switch that's used in every modern computer.

Binary arithmetic follows the same rules as ordinary decimal arithmetic. But with only two digits available for each position, you have to borrow and carry (manipulate digits in other positions) more often. Even adding 1 and 1 results in a two-digit number, 10. Multiplication, division, negative numbers, and fractions can also be represented in binary, but most people find them messy and complicated compared with decimal arithmetic.

1 The use of switches to represent numbers would be easy to understand if the switches each had 10 settings (0 through 9). The decimal number 67 might look like this:

numbers. Other groups of bits—instructions in the program—would contain codes that tell the computer where to find those numbers and where to store the result. You'll learn more about how these computer instructions work in later chapters.

Bits, Bytes, and Buzzwords

Trying to learn about computers by examining their operation at the bit level is a little like trying to learn about how people look or act by studying individual human cells; there's plenty of information there, but it's not the most efficient way to find out what

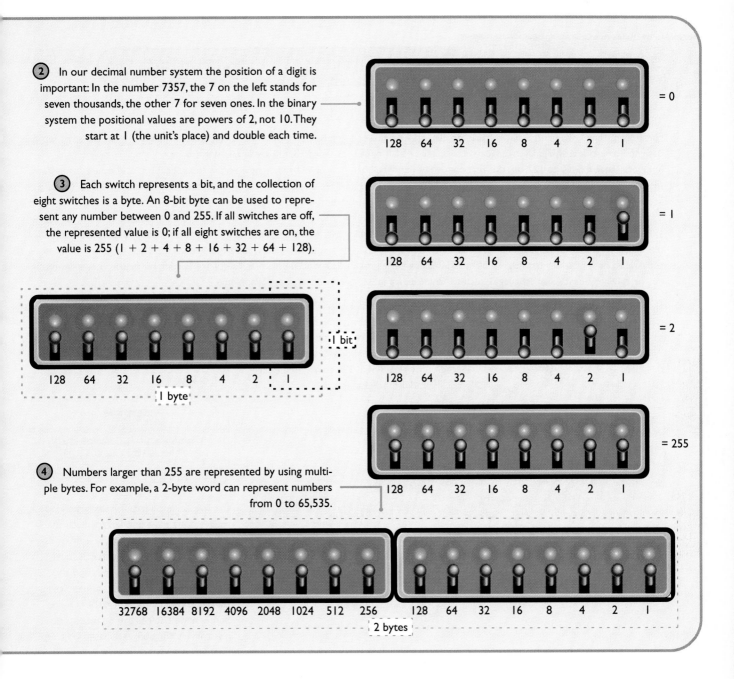

2 In our decimal number system the position of a digit is important: In the number 7357, the 7 on the left stands for seven thousands, the other 7 for seven ones. In the binary system the positional values are powers of 2, not 10. They start at 1 (the unit's place) and double each time.

3 Each switch represents a bit, and the collection of eight switches is a byte. An 8-bit byte can be used to represent any number between 0 and 255. If all switches are off, the represented value is 0; if all eight switches are on, the value is 255 (1 + 2 + 4 + 8 + 16 + 32 + 64 + 128).

4 Numbers larger than 255 are represented by using multiple bytes. For example, a 2-byte word can represent numbers from 0 to 65,535.

you need to know. Fortunately, people can use computers without thinking about bits. Some bit-related terminology does come up in day-to-day computer work, though. Most computer users need to have at least a basic understanding of the following terms for quantifying data:

Byte: A grouping of 8 bits. If you work mostly with words, you can think of a byte as one character of ASCII-encoded text.

K (kilobyte or *KB*): About 1,000 bytes of information. For example, about 5K of storage is necessary to hold 5000 characters of ASCII text. (Technically, 1K is 1,024 bytes because 1,024 is 2^{10}, which makes the arithmetic easier for binary-based computers. For those of us who don't think in binary, 1,000 is close enough.)

Representing the World's Languages

The United States has long been at the center of the computer revolution; that's why the ASCII character set was originally designed to include only English-language characters. ASCII code numbers range from 0 to 127, but this isn't enough to handle all of the characters used in the languages of Western Europe, including accents and other diacritical marks.

Both the ASCII and the Latin 1 character sets can use 8 bits—1 byte—to represent each character, but there's no room left for the characters used in languages such as Greek, Hebrew, Hindi, and Arabic, each of which has its own 50- to 150-character alphabet or syllabary. East Asian languages such as Chinese, Japanese,

and Korean present bigger challenges for computer users. Chinese alone has nearly 50,000 distinct characters, of which about 13,000 are in current use.

Most major new software applications and operating systems are designed to be transported to different languages. To make a software application work in different languages involves much more than translating the words. For example, some languages write from right to left or top to bottom. Pronunciation, currency symbols, dialects, and other variations often make it necessary to produce customized software for different regions even when the same language is spoken.

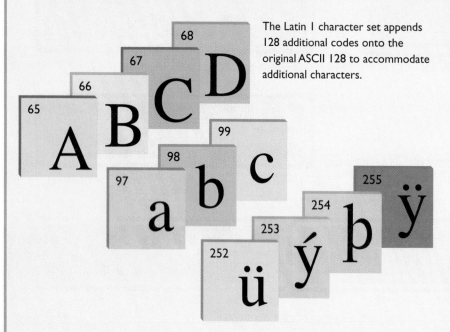

The Latin 1 character set appends 128 additional codes onto the original ASCII 128 to accommodate additional characters.

Computer keyboards for East Asian languages don't have one key for each character. Using phonetic input, a user types a pronunciation for a character using a Western-style keyboard and then chooses the character needed from a menu of characters that appears on the screen. Some menu choices can be made automatically by the software based on common language-usage patterns.

A character set that uses two bytes, or 16 bits, per character allows for 256 × 256 or 65,536 distinct codes—more than enough for all modern languages. The emerging international standard double-byte character set called Unicode is designed to facilitate multilingual computing. In Unicode the first 256 codes (0 through 255) are identical to the codes of the Latin 1 character set. The remaining codes are distributed among the writing systems of the world's other languages.

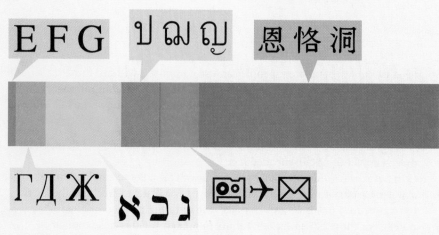

MB (megabyte or *meg*): Approximately 1,000K, or 1 million bytes.

GB (gigabyte or *gig*): Approximately 1,000MB.

TB (terabyte): Approximately 1 million megabytes. This astronomical unit of measurement applies to the largest storage devices commonly available today.

The abbreviations K, MB or meg, and GB or gig describe the capacity of memory and storage components. A computer might, for example, be described as having 128MB of memory and a hard disk as having a 20GB storage capacity. The same terms are used to quantify sizes of computer *files*. A file is an organized collection of information, such as a term paper or a set of names and addresses, stored in a computer-readable form. For example, the text for this chapter is stored in a file that occupies about 70K of space on a disk.

To add to the confusion, people often measure data transfer speed or memory size in *megabits (Mb)* rather than megabytes (MB). A megabit, as you might expect, is approximately 1,000 bits—one eighth the size of a megabyte. When you're talking in bits and bytes, a little detail like capitalization can make a significant difference.

The Computer's Core: The CPU and Memory

An IBM electronic calculator speeds through thousands of intricate computations so quickly that on many complex problems, it's just like having 150 extra engineers. . . .

—IBM ad showing dozens of slide-rule-toting engineers in *National Geographic*, February, 1952

It may seem strange to think of automated teller machines, video game consoles, and supercomputers as bit processors. But whatever it looks like to the user, a digital computer is at its core a collection of on/off switches designed to transform information from one form to another. The user provides the computer with patterns of bits—input—and the computer follows instructions to transform that input into a different pattern of bits—output—to return to the user.

The main circuit board of a typical PC contains the CPU, memory, and several other important chips and components.

The CPU: The Real Computer

The transformations of input into output are performed by the central processing unit (CPU), often called just the processor. Every computer has at least one CPU to interpret and execute the instructions in each program, to do arithmetic and logical data manipulations, and to communicate with all the other parts of the computer system indirectly through memory.

A modern CPU is an extraordinarily complex collection of electronic circuits. When all of those circuits are built into a single silicon chip, as they are in most computers today, that chip is referred to as a *microprocessor*. In a desktop computer, the CPU is housed along with other chips and electronic components on a circuit board. The circuit board that contains a computer's CPU is called the *motherboard* or *system board*.

Many different kinds of CPUs are in use today; when you choose a computer, the type of CPU in the computer is an important part of the decision. Although there are many variations in design among these chips, only two factors are important to a casual computer user: compatibility and speed.

Compatibility

Not all software is compatible with every CPU; that is, software written for one processor may not work with another. Every processor has a built-in *instruction set*—a vocabulary of instructions the processor can execute. CPUs in the same *family* are generally designed so newer processors can process all of the instructions handled by earlier models. For example, Intel's Pentium III chip is backward compatible with the Pentium II, Pentium Pro, Pentium, 486, 386, and 286 chips that preceded it, so it can run most software written for those older CPUs. But software written for the PowerPC family of processors used in Macintosh computers won't run on the Intel processors found in most IBM-compatible computers; the Intel processors can't understand programs written for the PowerPC CPUs. Similarly, the Macintosh Power PC processor can't generally run Windows software. (In Chapter 4 you'll see how *emulation* software can partially overcome incompatibility problems by translating instructions written for one CPU into instructions that can be executed by another.)

Speed

There's a tremendous variation in how fast different processors can handle information. Most computer applications, such as word processing, are more convenient to use on a faster machine. Many applications that use graphics or do computations, such as statistical programs, graphic design programs, and many computer games, *require* faster machines to produce satisfactory results.

The Intel Pentium III chip (left) contains intricate circuitry that looks like geometric colored patterns when magnified (right)

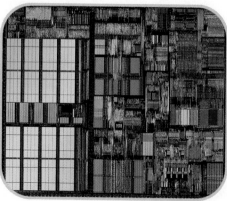

A computer's speed is determined in part by the speed of its internal *clock*—the timing device that produces electrical pulses to synchronize the computer's operations. A computer's clock speed is measured in units called *megahertz (MHz)*, for millions of clock cycles per second. Ads for new computer systems often emphasize megahertz ratings as a measure of speed. But these numbers can be misleading; judging a computer's speed by its megahertz rat-

POPULAR CPU FAMILIES AND WHERE TO FIND THEM

CPU Family	Word Size	Developer/Manufacturer	Where They Are Used
Itanium Family	64 bit	Developed by Intel	High-end workstations and servers
Pentium Family (including Celeron)	32 bit	Developed and manufactured by Intel; clones by AMD and others	Modern IBM-compatible computers (Pentium is used in mid- to high-end PCs and workstations; Celeron is used in less expensive computers; Xeon is used in high-end PCs and workstations)
x86 Family (386, 486)	16 and 32 bit	Developed and manufactured by Intel; clones by others	Older IBM-compatible computers
PowerPC family, including G3 and G4	32 bit	Developed by IBM, manufactured by IBM and Motorola	Modern Macintoshes, network computers, special-purpose devices
680x0 Family (68000, 68020, and others)	16 and 32 bit	Developed and manufactured by Motorola	Older Macintoshes, computer-controlled devices
Alpha	64 bit	Developed by Digital (now owned by Compaq), manufactured by Intel	Supercomputers, workstations, servers
MIPS	64 bit	Developed by Silicon Graphics, manufactured by many companies	Workstations, servers, network computers, video game machines, other devices
SPARC	64 bit	Sun	Workstations

ing alone is like measuring a car's speed by the engine's RPM (revolutions per minute). A 450-MHz Celeron system isn't necessarily faster than a 400-MHz Pentium II or a 400-MHz PowerPC G3 chip.

Clock speed by itself doesn't adequately describe how fast a computer can process words, numbers, or pictures. Speed is also determined by the architecture of the processor—the design that determines how individual components of the CPU are put together on the chip. For example, newer chips can manipulate more bits simultaneously than older chips, which makes them more efficient, and therefore faster, at performing most operations. The number of bits a CPU can process at one time—typically between 16 and 64—is sometimes called the CPU's *word size*. More often, though, people just use the number without a label, as in "The Itanium is Intel's first 64-bit processor."

Because speed is so important, engineers and computer scientists are constantly developing techniques for speeding up a computer's ability to manipulate and move bits. One common trick for improving a computer's performance is to put more than one processor in the computer. Many personal computers, for example, have

How It Works 2.3

The CPU

Most computer users don't know anything about what goes on inside the CPU; they just use it. Throughout most of this book we treat the CPU as a kind of black box that transforms information by following instructions. This *How It Works* box offers a peek inside that black box so you can get a feel for what makes your computer tick. Since the CPU functions as part of a larger collection of computer components, this *How It Works* box tells only part of the story; taken by itself, it may raise more questions than it answers. But *How It Works* boxes later in this chapter and in the next two chapters will fill in many of the missing details of the inner workings of the modern computer. Read these boxes if you want the inside story.

All computer programs are composed of instructions drawn from this tiny vocabulary. The typical computer program is composed of millions of instructions, and the CPU can execute millions of instructions every second. When a program runs, the rapid-fire execution of instructions creates an illusion of motion in the same way a movie simulates motion out of a sequence of still pictures.

The typical CPU is divided into several functional units: (1) control, (2) arithmetic, (3) decode, (4) bus, and (5) prefetch. These units work together like workers on an assembly line to complete the execution of program instructions.

The central processing unit (CPU) is the component that executes the steps in a program, performing math and moving data from one part of the system to another. The CPU contains the circuitry to perform a variety of simple tasks, called *instructions*. An individual instruction does only a tiny amount of work. A typical instruction might be "Read the contents of memory location x and add the number y to it." Most CPUs have a vocabulary of fewer than 1,000 distinct instructions.

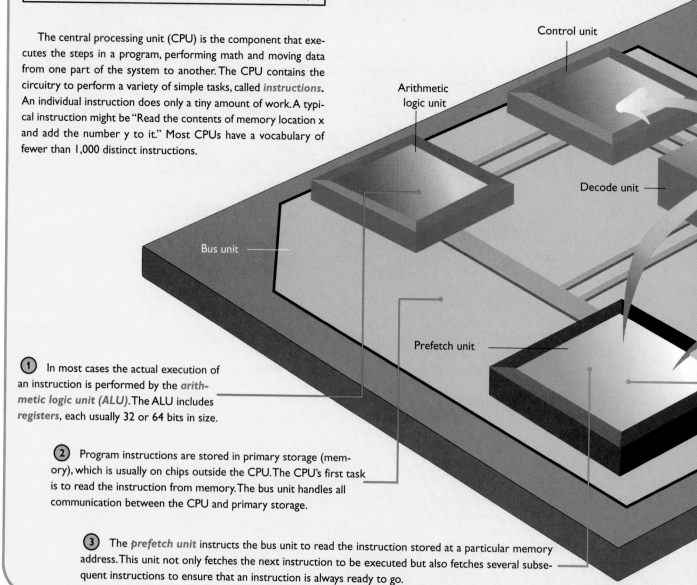

Control unit

Arithmetic logic unit

Decode unit

Bus unit

Prefetch unit

(1) In most cases the actual execution of an instruction is performed by the *arithmetic logic unit (ALU)*. The ALU includes *registers*, each usually 32 or 64 bits in size.

(2) Program instructions are stored in primary storage (memory), which is usually on chips outside the CPU. The CPU's first task is to read the instruction from memory. The bus unit handles all communication between the CPU and primary storage.

(3) The *prefetch unit* instructs the bus unit to read the instruction stored at a particular memory address. This unit not only fetches the next instruction to be executed but also fetches several subsequent instructions to ensure that an instruction is always ready to go.

④ The *decode unit* takes the instruction read by the prefetcher and translates it into a form suitable for the CPU's internal processing. It does this by "looking up" the steps required to complete an instruction in the control unit.

⑦ Most of today's computers have complex instruction sets that include instructions that are seldom, if ever, used. Research has shown that these *complex instruction set computer (CISC) processors* are slower and less efficient than processors designed to execute fewer instructions. Today many supercomputers and desktop computers use *reduced instruction set computer (RISC)* processors such as the Alpha processor developed by Digital Equipment Corporation. The most widely used type of RISC processor is the IBM/Motorola PowerPC processor used in Macintoshes, some workstations, and many consumer electronic devices. The Pentium processors from Intel, used in the overwhelming majority of PCs today, are based on CISC designs. But Intel engineers have incorporated other innovative speed-enhancing techniques into the Pentium family of processors. As a result, the speed differences between PowerPC and Pentium CPUs are, at this point, relatively small. Intel's 64-bit Itanium processor is based on CISC technology. Most RISC microprocessors and some advanced CISC processors use a *superscalar architecture*. This means that the CPU has multiple instruction *pipelines* and, as long as two sequential instructions don't depend on one another, can execute multiple instructions simultaneously.

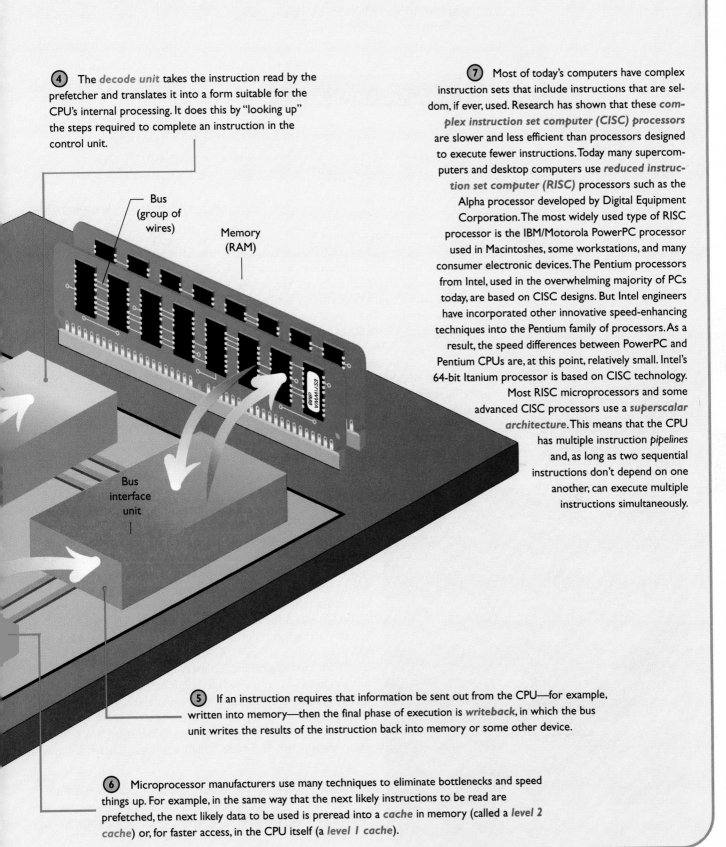

Bus
(group of
wires)

Memory
(RAM)

Bus
interface
unit

⑤ If an instruction requires that information be sent out from the CPU—for example, written into memory—then the final phase of execution is *writeback*, in which the bus unit writes the results of the instruction back into memory or some other device.

⑥ Microprocessor manufacturers use many techniques to eliminate bottlenecks and speed things up. For example, in the same way that the next likely instructions to be read are prefetched, the next likely data to be used is preread into a *cache* in memory (called a *level 2 cache*) or, for faster access, in the CPU itself (a *level 1 cache*).

specialized subsidiary processors that take care of mathematical calculations or graphics displays. Most supercomputers have multiple processors that can divide jobs into pieces and work in parallel on the pieces. This kind of processing, known as **parallel processing** or **multiprocessing**, is becoming more commonplace throughout the computing world.

The Computer's Memory

"What's one and one and one and one and one and one and one and one and one and one?" "I don't know," said Alice. "I lost count." "She can't do addition," said the Red Queen.

—**Lewis Carroll**, *in Through the Looking Glass*

The CPU's main job is to follow the instructions encoded in programs. But like Alice in *Through the Looking Glass,* the CPU can handle only one instruction and a few pieces of data at a time. The computer needs a place to store the rest of the program and data until the processor is ready for them. That's what RAM is for.

RAM *(random access memory)* is the most common type of primary storage, or computer memory. RAM chips contain circuits that store program instructions and data temporarily. Each RAM chip is divided by the computer into many equal-sized memory locations. Memory locations, like houses, have unique addresses so the computer can tell them apart when it is instructed to save or retrieve information. You can store a piece of information in any RAM location—you can pick one at random—and the computer can, if so instructed, quickly retrieve it. Hence the name *random access memory.*

The information stored in RAM is nothing more than a pattern of electrical current flowing through microscopic circuits in silicon chips. This means that when the power goes off the computer instantly forgets everything it was remembering in RAM. RAM is called **volatile memory** because information stored there is not held permanently.

This could be a serious problem if the computer didn't have another type of memory to store information that you don't want to lose. This **nonvolatile memory** is called **ROM** (**read-only memory**) because the computer can only read information from it; it can never write any new information on it. All modern computers include ROM that contains start-up instructions and other critical information. The information in ROM was etched in when the chip was manufactured, so it is available whenever the computer is operating, but it can't be changed except by replacing the ROM chip.

ROM isn't always hidden away on chips inside the computer's chassis. Many home video game machines use removable *ROM cartridges* as permanent storage devices for games and other programs.

Other types of memory are available; most are seldom used outside of engineering laboratories. There are two notable exceptions:

▶ *CMOS* (complementary metal oxide semiconductor) is a special low-energy kind of RAM that can store small amounts of data for long periods of time on battery power. CMOS RAM is used to store the date, time, and calendar in a PC. (CMOS RAM is called *parameter RAM* in Macintoshes.)

Slots and ports allow the CPU to communicate with the outside world via peripheral devices. Here a circuit board is being inserted into a slot. The panel holding the slot has been temporarily removed from the computer for easier viewing. The gray flat wire is a bus.

▶ *Flash memory* chips, like RAM chips, can be written and erased rapidly and repeatedly. But unlike RAM, flash memory is nonvolatile; it can keep its contents without a flow of electricity. Flash memory is used in cell phones, pagers, and some portable computers and handheld PDAs to store data that needs to be changed from time to time. It's also used in data flight recorders. Flash memory is still too expensive to replace RAM and other common storage media, but it may in the future replace disk drives as well as memory chips.

It takes time for the processor to retrieve data from memory—but not very much time. The *access time* for most memory is measured in *nanoseconds*—billionths of a second. Compare this to hard disk access time, which is measured in milliseconds—thousandths of a second. Memory speed (access time) is another factor that affects the computer's overall speed.

Buses, Ports, and Peripherals

In a desktop computer, the CPU and memory chips are attached to circuit boards along with other key components. Information travels between components through groups of wires called buses. Buses typically have 8, 16, or 32 wires, or data paths; a bus with 16 wires is called a *16-bit bus* because it can transmit 16 bits of information at once, twice as many as an 8-bit bus. Just as multilane freeways allow masses of automobiles to move faster than they could on single-lane roads, wider buses can transmit information faster than narrower buses. Newer, more powerful computers have wider buses so they can process information faster.

Buses connect to storage devices in bays—open areas in the system box for disk drives and other peripheral devices. Buses also connect to expansion slots (sometimes called just *slots*) inside the computer's housing. Users can customize their computers by inserting special-purpose circuit boards (called *cards*, *expansion cards*, or *boards*) into these slots. Buses also connect to external ports—sockets on the outside of the computer chassis. The back of a computer typically has a variety of ports to meet a variety of needs. Some of these ports—the keyboard and mouse ports, for example—are connected directly to the system board. Others, such as the monitor port, are generally attached to an expansion card. In fact, many expansion cards do little more than provide convenient ports for attaching particular types of peripherals. Macintosh computers generally have fewer expansion boards than their PC counterparts because their system boards include more components as standard equipment.

In portable computers, where size is critical, most common ports go directly to the system board. Because portable computers don't have room for full-sized cards, many have slots for PC cards—credit-card-sized cards that contain memory, miniature peripherals, and additional ports. (When these cards were first released, they were known as *PCMCIA cards*. One writer suggested that this stood for "People Can't Memorize Computer Industry Acronyms." Thankfully, the name was shortened to PC cards.)

A portable computer typically has one or more slots to accommodate credit-card-sized PC cards like this one.

Slots and ports make it easy to add external devices, or *peripherals*, to the computer system so the CPU can communicate with the outside world and store information for later use. Without peripherals, CPU and memory together are like a brain without a body. Some peripherals such as keyboards and printers serve as communication links between people and computers. Other peripherals link the computer to other machines. Still others provide long-term storage media. In the next chapter we'll explore a variety of input, output, and storage peripherals, and then revisit the slots and ports that connect those peripherals to the CPU and memory.

How It Works 2.4

Memory

Memory is the work area of the CPU. Think of memory as millions of tiny storage cells, each of which can contain a single byte of information. The information in memory could be program instructions, numbers for arithmetic, codes representing text characters, a part of a picture, or other kinds of data.

Each byte has an address that identifies it and helps the CPU keep track of where things are stored. A typical personal computer has from 16 to 64 million bytes (16 to 64 megabytes) of memory.

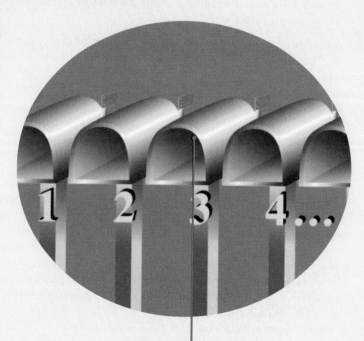

② Memory locations are like mailboxes. Each mailbox represents one address and holds 1 byte of information.

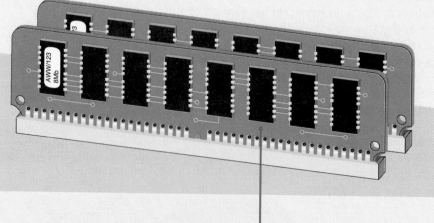

① Memory chips are usually grouped on small circuit boards called *SIMMs (single in-line memory modules)* and *DIMMs (dual in-line memory modules)* and are plugged into the main system board. This illustration represents a group of two SIMMs in a circuit board.

The CPU can only see into and access memory. Memory addresses make up the CPU's entire world, so any program that needs to be executed or data that needs to be modified must make its way into memory. Memory is composed of storage cells called bytes.

Most computer systems use *memory-mapped I/O*, where information for input and output is stored in special areas of memory. For example, information to be displayed on the monitor screen is written into a special range of memory addresses that is continually scanned by the video subsystem.

3 The executing instructions help the system start up and tell it how to load the operating system—copy it from disk into memory.

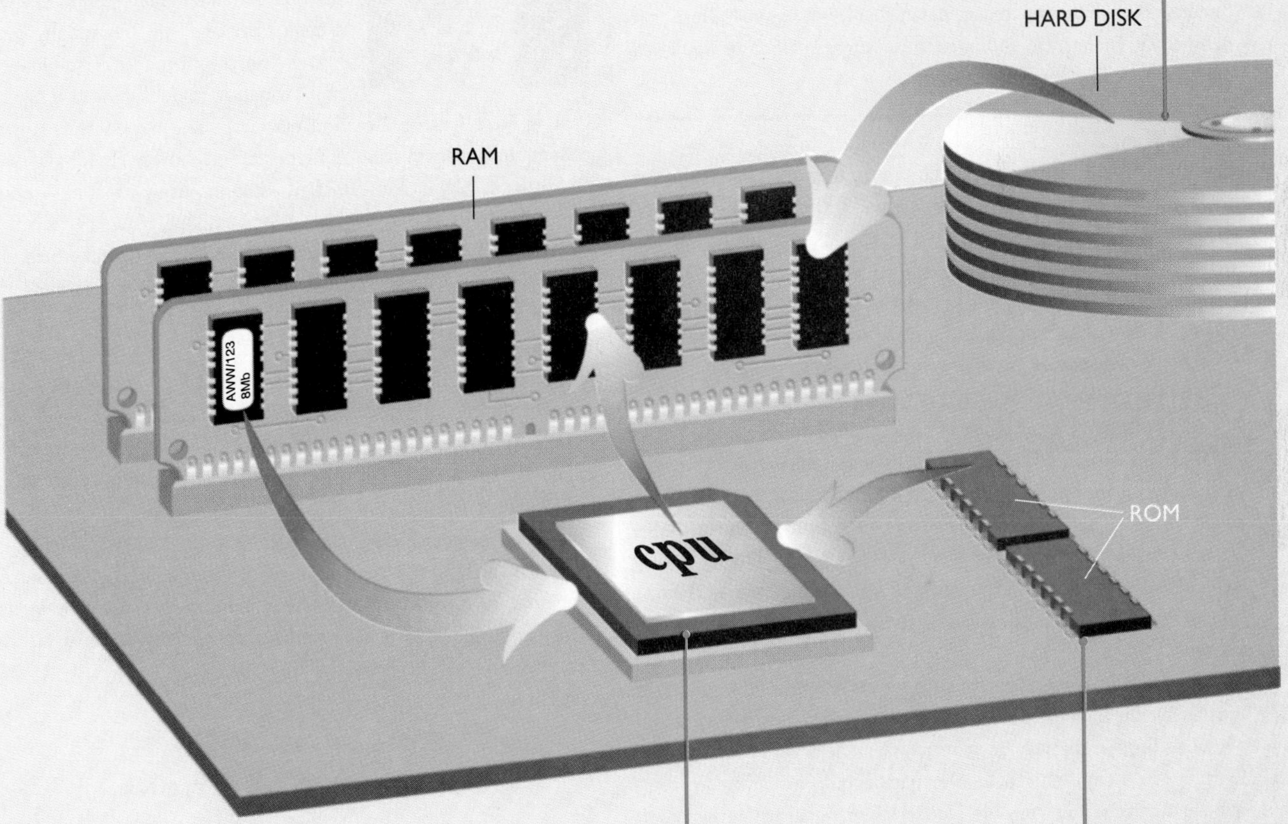

HARD DISK

RAM

cpu

ROM

4 Once executing instructions are loaded into memory, the CPU is able to execute them.

5 When you turn on the computer, the CPU automatically begins executing instructions stored in read-only memory (ROM). On most computer systems, ROM also contains parts of the operating system. The firmware programs in ROM are sometimes called the *BIOS* (basic input/output system).

CROSSCURRENTS

What Can Be Done, Will Be Done

Andy Grove

When he wrote this article Andrew S. Grove was the chairman and chief executive officer of Intel, the company that makes more than 85% of the microprocessors used in PCs today. He left his native Hungary in 1956 to escape Soviet repression and went on to help found one of the most successful companies of our time. His optimistic capitalist philosophy is expressed in his book, Only the Paranoid Survive. *In this article he quotes an expert on capitalism from an earlier era: economist Joseph Schumpeter. In his 1930s book,* Capitalism, Socialism, and Democracy, *Schumpeter expressed fear that democracy's future was threatened by "waves of creative destruction" that naturally arose from democracy. The article reprinted here suggests that technological advance is inevitable—and just what we need.*

I have a rule, one that was honed by more than thirty years in high tech. It is simple. "What can be done, will be done." Like a natural force, technology is impossible to hold back. It finds its way no matter what obstacles people put in its place.

The beauty of this rule is that it can be used to look into the future. All we need to do is remember what already can be done:

All information can be expressed digitally.

All information can be transported in digital form.

All information can be stored in digital form.

If all this can be done, the rule says, it will be. What this means is that digital creation and display of information will predominate over other forms of communication—telephony, broadcasting—at the workplace as well as in our personal lives. Digital display will also subsume all other forms of storing information—libraries (personal and public), professional records, photo albums.

There are many reasons to suggest we are headed in the right direction: Digital information is forever. It doesn't deteriorate and requires little in the way of material media. It is very much in sync with a world exploding with information, but with limited material resources. It is very low cost, and therefore lends itself extremely well to creation, transmission, and utilization of information. Digital information is without boundaries, fitting in with the trend toward a single, global community: It is instant, consistent with the rhythm of our times—fast, fast, and faster.

The movement toward this new digital medium will take place from the inside out. It started fifteen years ago inside the computer industry as mainframes—the paradigm of computing—were replaced by high-volume, low-cost PCs.

The movement toward this new digital medium has broken the boundaries of the computer industry and is now pounding at the communications industry. Here the transformation involves going from switched networks to packet-switched networks: low-cost, high-volume networks.

The first waves of change have hit upon the media industry and here the transformations will be equally profound. The creation and dissemination of information in publishing and broadcasting have been built upon elaborate and expensive printing presses and transmission equipment. This, however, will give way to low-cost, high-volume, instant—and intensely personal—communications.

The next stop may be health care where the digital world will also bring immediate expertise to people at a low cost and high volume. Likewise, digital information has the power to turn education upside down.

Change has been the way of the world, but what we are now facing is the digital world bringing positive feedback to the change process itself. As digital information becomes the medium for change, it speeds it up. Change feeds on itself; the process accelerates. The restructuring of the computer industry took fifteen years. The restructuring of the communications industry may take less than ten, and the restructuring of the media may be quicker than that. All this won't be easy: Schumpeter's creative destruction—on Internet time. But we have no choice. We must face it. For whatever can be done, will be done.

DISCUSSION QUESTIONS

1. Do you agree that "What can be done, will be done"?
2. Can you think of counterexamples—technologies that humankind has chosen not to pursue even though they're possible?
3. Are we, as Grove suggests, headed in the right direction?
4. Do you agree with Grove's predictions about the ways in which the movement toward the new digital medium will develop? Explain your answer.

Whether it's working with words, numbers, pictures, or sounds, a computer is manipulating patterns of bits—binary digits of information that can be stored in switching circuitry and represented by two symbols. Groups of bits can be treated as numbers for calculations using the binary number system. Bits can be grouped into coded messages that represent alphabetic characters, pictures, colors, sounds, or just about any other kind of information. Even the instructions computers follow—the software programs that tell the computer what to do—must be reduced to strings of bits before the computer accepts them. Byte, kilobyte, megabyte, and other common units for measuring bit quantities are used in descriptions of memory, storage, and file size.

The central processing unit (CPU) follows software instructions to perform the calculations and logical manipulations that transform input data into output. Not all CPUs are compatible with each other; each is capable of processing a particular set of instructions, so a program written for one family of processors can't be understood by a processor from another family. Engineers are constantly improving the clock speed and architecture of CPUs, making computers capable of processing information faster.

The CPU uses RAM (random access memory) as a temporary storage area—a scratch pad—for instructions and data. Another type of memory, ROM (read-only memory), contains unchangeable information that serves as reference material for the CPU as it executes program instructions.

The CPU and main memory are housed in silicon chips on one or more circuit boards inside the computer. Buses connect to slots and ports that allow the computer to communicate with peripherals.

Key Terms

architecture, 41
ASCII, 35
backward compatible, 40
bay, 45
binary, 34
bit, 34
bus, 45
byte, 37
central processing unit (CPU), 33
circuit board, 40
compatible, 40
digital, 33

expansions slot, 45
file, 39
GB (gigabyte), 39
information, 33
input device, 32
K (kilobyte), 37
MB (megabyte), 39
memory, 33
multiprocessing, 44
nonvolatile memory, 44
output device, 32

parallel processing, 44
PC card, 45
peripheral, 33
port, 45
processor, 33
RAM (random access memory), 44
ROM (read-only memory), 44
storage device, 33
TB (terabyte), 39
Unicode, 35
volatile memory, 44

Review Questions

1. Provide a working definition of each of the key words listed above. Check your answers in the glossary.
2. Draw a block diagram showing the major components of a computer and their relationship. Briefly describe the function of each component.
3. Think of this as computer input: 123.4. This might be read by the computer as a number or as a set of ASCII codes. Explain how these concepts differ.
4. Why is information stored in some kind of binary format in computers?
5. Why can't you normally run Macintosh software on a PC with an Intel Pentium II CPU?

6. Clock speed is only one factor in determining a CPU's processing speed. What is another?
7. How does a RISC processor differ from a CISC processor?
8. Explain how parallel processing can increase a computer's speed; use an example or a comparison with the way people work if you like.
9. What is the difference between RAM and ROM? What is the purpose of each?
10. What is the difference between primary and secondary storage?

Discussion Questions

1. Why are computer manufacturers constantly releasing faster computers? How do computer users benefit from the increased speed?

2. How is human memory similar to computer memory? How is it different?

Projects

1. Collect computer advertisements from newspapers, magazines, and other sources. Compare how the ads handle discussions of speed. Evaluate the usefulness of the information in the ads from a consumer's point of view.

2. Interview a salesperson in a computer store. Find out what kinds of questions people ask when buying a computer. Develop profiles for the most common types of computer buyers. What kinds of computers do these customers buy, and why?

Books

Building IBM: Shaping an Industry and Its Technology, by Emerson W. Pugh (Cambridge, MA: MIT Press, 1995). This book traces IBM's history from Herman Hollerith's invention of the punch card machine more than a century ago. This thoroughly researched and clearly written book is a valuable resource for anyone interested in understanding IBM's history.

ThinkPad: A Different Shade of Blue by Deboarh Dell and J. Gerry Purdy (Indianapolis: Sams, 2000). This is an insider's look at the making of IBM's wildly successful portable. Thomas Watson's philosophy inspired this product—a product that helped revive the company Watson founded.

How Computers Work: Millenium Edition, by Ron White (Indianapolis: Que, 1999). The first edition of *How Computers Work* launched a series and inspired many imitators. Like its predecessor, this revised and expanded edition clearly illustrates with beautiful pictures and accessible prose how each component of a modern personal computer system works. If you're interested in looking under the hood, this is a great place to start. The book was produced on a Macintosh, but the explanations and illustrations are based on Wintel (Windows/Intel) computers. Still, most of the concepts apply to computers in general. A Windows-only CD-ROM includes a multimedia tour of a computer.

How Macs Work: Bestseller Edition, by John Rizzo and K. Daniel Clark (Emeryville, CA: Ziff-Davis Press, 1997). This book covers the basics of Macintosh anatomy in the same style as *How Computers Work.*

The Soul of a New Machine, by Tracy Kidder (Modern Library, 1997). This award-winning book provides a journalist's inside look at the making of a new computer, including lots of insights into what makes computers (and computer people) tick.

Computer Sourcebook, by Alfred and Emily Glossbrenner (New York: Random House, 1997). This massive book is an eclectic collection of facts, figures, lists, and anecdotes related to PCs. Reading this book may give you the feeling that these two prolific authors are allowing you to rummage through their file cabinets.

Want to learn how to get free computer magazine subscriptions? How to get help when something goes wrong with your PC? How to choose a backup system? You're almost certain to find plenty of useful information here, along with quite a bit that's of little value.

Peter Norton's Inside the PC, Eighth Edition, by Peter Norton and John Goodman (Indianapolis: Sams, 1999). Norton's name is almost a household word among PC enthusiasts, many of whom consider Norton Utilities to be indispensable software. This book offers clear, detailed explanations of the inner workings of the PC, from CPU to peripherals, from hardware to software. You don't need to be a technical wizard to understand and learn from this book.

The Indispensable PC Hardware Handbook, Third Edition, by Hans-Peter Messmer (Reading, MA: Addison Wesley Longman, 1997). This book is more technically demanding than Norton's—it's packed with technical terminology and schematic diagrams. But if you want—or need—to delve deeply into a PC's innards, it's worth the effort.

World Wide Web Pages

Most computer hardware manufacturers have World Wide Web pages on the Internet. Use a Web browser such as Netscape Navigator or Microsoft Internet Explorer to visit some of these sites for information about the latest hardware from these companies. It's not hard to guess the Web addresses of computer companies; most follow the pattern suggested by these examples:

http://www.apple.com
http://www.compaq.com
http://www.dell.com
http://www.ibm.com

The Computer Confluence Web site www.prenhall.com/beekman, will guide you to these and other hardware pages of interest.

Chapter

3

Hardware Basics: Peripherals

AFTER YOU READ THIS CHAPTER YOU SHOULD BE ABLE TO:

List several examples of input devices and explain how they can make it easier to get different types of information into the computer.

List several examples of output devices and explain how they make computers more useful.

Explain why a typical computer has different types of storage devices.

Diagram how the components of a computer system fit together.

In this chapter:

- Why the letters on a keyboard are all mixed up
- Pointing, painting, typing, and talking to your computer
- Why on-screen pictures look different when you print them
- Getting pictures and sounds into and out of a computer
- How your PC can hurt your health, and how to protect yourself
- Self-study questions and projects
- Mini-reviews of helpful resources for further study

. . . and more.

On the CD-ROM:

- Interactive keyboard and mouse tutorials
- Animated interactive demonstrations that reveal the inner workings of computer monitors, printers, and disk drives
- Instant access to glossary and key word references
- Interactive self-study quizzes

. . . and more.

On the Web:

www.prenhall.com/beekman

- Important documents describing and illustrating a variety of state-of-the-art peripherals
- Links to Web sites of the most important computer peripheral companies
- Self-study exercises

. . . and more.

It's not like we were all smart enough to see a **revolution** coming. Back then, I thought there might be a revolution in opening your garage door, balancing your checkbook, keeping your recipes, that sort of thing. There are **a million people** who study markets and analyze economic trends, people who are more brilliant than I am, people who worked for companies like Digital Equipment and IBM and Hewlett-Packard. **None of them foresaw** what was going to happen, either.

—Steve Wozniak

What Steve Wozniak ("the Woz") and all those other people failed to foresee was the personal computer revolution—a revolution that he helped start. Wozniak, a brilliant engineer with an eye for detail, worked days as a calculator technician at Hewlett-Packard; he was refused an engineer's job because he lacked a college degree. At night he designed and constructed a scaled-down state-of-the-art computer system that would fit the home hobbyist's budget. When he completed the computer in 1975, he offered it to Hewlett-Packard, which turned it down.

Wozniak took his invention to the Homebrew Computer Club in Palo Alto, where it caught the imagination of another college dropout, Steven Jobs. A free-thinking visionary, Jobs persuaded Wozniak to quit his job in 1976 to form a company and market the machine, which they named the Apple I. Jobs raised $1,300 in seed capital by selling his Volkswagen, and Apple Computer, Inc., was born in Jobs's garage.

With the help and considerable financial backing of businessman A. C. Markkula, the two Steves turned Apple into a thriving business. Wozniak created the Apple II, a more refined machine for consumers and invented the first personal computer disk operating system so computers wouldn't be dependent on cassette tapes for storage. More interested in engineering than management, Wozniak allowed Jobs to assume the leadership role in the company.

Because it put computing power within everyone's reach, the Apple II became popular in businesses, homes, and especially schools. Apple became the first company in American history to join the Fortune 500 in less than 5 years. Still in his mid-twenties, Jobs was running a corporate giant. But troubled times were ahead for Apple.

When IBM introduced its PC in 1982, it quickly overshadowed Apple's presence in the business world, where people were accustomed to working with IBM mainframes. Other companies developed PC clones, treating the IBM PC as a standard—a standard that Apple refused to accept. Inspired by a visit to Xerox's Palo Alto Research Center (PARC), Jobs worked with a team of Apple engineers to develop the Macintosh, a futuristic computer he hoped would leapfrog IBM's advantage. When Jobs insisted on focusing most of Apple's resources on the Macintosh, Wozniak resigned to pursue other interests.

However, businesses failed to embrace the Mac, and Apple stockholders grew uneasy with Jobs's controversial management style. In 1985, a year and a half after the Macintosh was introduced, Jobs was ousted. He went on to form NeXT, a company that first produced workstations and then focused on software. He later bought Pixar, the computer animation company that captured the public's attention with *Toy Story*, the first computer-generated full-length motion picture.

After Apple's fortunes declined under a string of CEOs, the company bought NeXT in 1997 and invited an

Steve Wozniak and Steve Jobs.

older and wiser Jobs to—at least temporarily—retake the helm. He agreed to share his time between Pixar and Apple. Under his leadership, Apple has regained its innovative edge, releasing a flurry of successful products that combine high technology with high style. In 2000 Jobs removed "interim" from his title, to the delight of company shareholders. But Apple's rising market share is still small in a business world dominated by IBM-compatible PCs running Microsoft Windows. Still, the company retains an almost fanatically loyal customer base focused mainly in homes and creative markets, such as publishing, graphic design, multimedia, and education. While Jobs continues to lead Apple and Pixar, Woz is content to teach computing skills to kids in his community.

The Apple II's phenomenal success wasn't due to a powerful processor or massive memory; the machine had at its core a relatively primitive processor and only 16K of memory. The Apple II was more than a processor and memory; it included a keyboard, a monitor, and disk and tape drives for storage. While other companies sold computer kits to tinkerers, the two Steves delivered complete computer systems to hobbyists, schools, and businesses. They recognized that a computer wasn't complete without peripherals.

In this chapter we'll complete the tour of hardware we started in the last chapter. We've seen the CPU and memory at the heart of the system unit; now we'll explore the peripherals that radiate out from those central components. We'll start with input devices, then move on to output devices, and finish with a look at external storage devices. As usual, the main text provides the basic overview; if you want or need to know more about the inner workings, consult the *How It Works* boxes scattered throughout the chapter.

Input: From Person to Processor

We swim in a sea of information.

—Gary Snyder, **poet**

The nuts and bolts of information processing are usually hidden from the user, who sees only the input and output, or as the pros say, *I/O*. This wasn't always the case. Users of the first computers communicated one bit at a time by flipping switches on massive consoles or plugging wires into switchboards; they had to be intimately familiar with the inner workings of the machines before they could successfully communicate with them. In contrast, today's users have a choice of hundreds of input devices, which make it easy to enter data and commands into their machines. Of these input devices, the most familiar is the computer keyboard.

The Keyboard

Typing letters, numbers, and special characters with a computer keyboard is similar to typing on a standard typewriter keyboard. But unlike a typewriter, the computer responds by displaying the typed characters on the monitor screen at the position of the line or rectangle called the **cursor.** Some keys on the computer keyboard—*cursor (arrow) keys*, the *Delete key*, the *Enter key*, *function keys (f-keys)*, and others—send special commands to the computer. These keys may have different names or meanings on different computer systems. Some of the most important keys are shown in *The User's View* box. **UV**

The User's View

Working with a Keyboard

Keyboarding on a computer is like typing, except that certain keys send codes that have special meaning to the computer or terminal. This figure shows a typical keyboard on an IBM-compatible PC. Keyboards for Macintoshes and other types of systems have a few differences but operate on the same principles.

Function keys (f-keys), labeled F1, F2, and so on, send signals to the computer that have no inherent meaning. The function of these keys depends on the software being used. F1 might mean "Save file" to one program and "Delete file" to another. In other words function keys are programmable.

Backspace on a PC tells the computer to delete the character just typed (or the one to the left of the cursor on the screen, or the currently selected data).

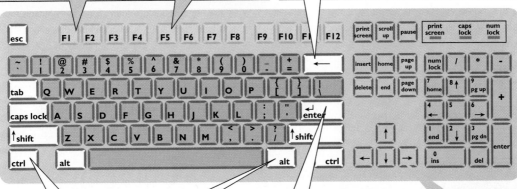

Control and Alt are modifier keys that cause nothing to happen by themselves but change the meaning of other keys. When you hold down a modifier key while pressing another key, the combination makes that other key behave differently. For example, typing S while holding down the Control key might send a command to save the current document.

Enter sends a signal telling the computer or terminal to move the cursor to the beginning of the next line on the screen. For many applications this key also "enters" the line just typed, telling the computer to process it.

Cursor (arrow) keys are used to move the cursor up, down, left, or right.

In spite of nearly universal acceptance as an input device, the QWERTY keyboard (named for the first row of letter keys) seems strangely out of place in a modern computer system. The original arrangement of the keys, chosen to reduce the likelihood of jammed keys on early typewriters, stays with us a century later, forcing millions of people to learn an awkward system just so they can enter text into their computers. Many alternatives to the QWERTY key arrangements have been shown to be superior and easier to learn. For example, on the Dvorak keyboard the most frequently typed letters are located closest to the fingers' resting positions. But technological traditions die hard, and the QWERTY keyboard is still standard equipment on virtually all PCs.

A standard keyboard sends signals to the computer through a coiled cable. A *wireless keyboard* can send infrared signals (similar to those of a TV remote control) so it isn't tethered to the rest of the system by a cable.

Pointing Devices

Computer users today use their keyboards mostly to enter text and numeric data. For other traditional keyboard functions such as sending commands and positioning the cursor, they use a *mouse*. The mouse is designed to move a pointer around the screen and point to specific characters or objects. The most common type of mouse has a ball on its underside that allows it to roll around on the desktop. Another type of mouse uses reflected light to detect movement. For either type of mouse, the pointer on the screen mimics the mouse's

---

The User's View

Working with a Mouse

As you slide the mouse across your desktop, a pointer echoes your movements on the screen. You can *click* the mouse—press the button while the mouse is stationary—or *drag* it—move it while holding the button down. On a two-button mouse, the left button is usually used for clicking and dragging. These two techniques can be used to perform a variety of operations.

Clicking the Mouse

If the pointer points to an on-screen button, clicking the mouse presses the button.

> **LView Pro 1.D2/32** ☒
>
> ❓ Image was changed, do you wish to save it?
>
> [Yes]   [No]   [Cancel]

If the pointer points to a picture of a tool or object on the screen, clicking the mouse selects the tool or object; for example, clicking on the pencil tool allows you to draw with the mouse.

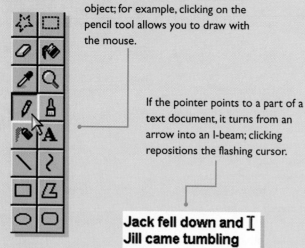

If the pointer points to a part of a text document, it turns from an arrow into an I-beam; clicking repositions the flashing cursor.

Jack fell down and I Jill came tumbling after.

Dragging the Mouse

If you hold the button down while you drag the mouse with a selected graphic tool (like a paintbrush), you can draw by remote control.

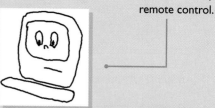

If you drag the mouse from one point in a text document to another, you select all the text between those two points so you can modify or move it. For example, you might select this movie title so you could italicize it.

The zany Duck Soup I captured the Marx Brothers at their peak.

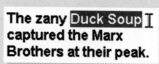

You can drag the mouse to select a command from a menu of choices. For example, this command would display files as large icons.

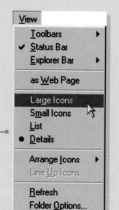

motion. The mouse has one or more buttons that can be used to send signals to the computer, conveying messages such as "Perform this command," "Activate the selected tool," and "Select all the text between these two points." Many modern PC mice include a scrolling wheel between the two standard buttons. **UV**

It's virtually impossible to find a new computer today that doesn't come with a mouse as standard equipment, but there is one exception: The mouse is impractical as a pointing device on portable computers because these machines are often used where there's no room for a mouse to roam across a desktop. Portable computer manufacturers provide a variety of alternatives to the mouse as a general-purpose pointing device:

▶ The **trackball** is like an upside-down mouse. It remains stationary while the user moves the protruding ball to control the pointer on the screen. (Trackballs are also available as space-saving mouse alternatives for desktop machines.)

▶ The **touch pad** (sometimes called *trackpad*) is a small flat panel thats's sensitive to light pressure. The user moves the pointer by dragging a finger across the pad.

▶ The **track point** is a tiny handle that sits in the center of the keyboard, responding to finger pressure by moving the pointer in the direction in which it's pushed. It's like a miniature embedded joystick (see below).

Other pointing devices offer advantages for specific types of computer work (and play). Here are some examples:

▶ The **joystick** is a gearshift-like device that's a favorite controller for arcade-style computer games.

This Apple PowerBook (upper left), like many portable computers, includes a built-in-trackpad as a pointing device. The IBM ThinkPad (lower left) has a tiny track point embedded in its keyboard (above the B key) for positioning the cursor on the screen. Some portable computers and many video game machines use trackballs (center) for pointing devices. Joysticks (upper right) are the chief weapons of the arcade army. Touch-screen monitors are ideal for kiosks like this one (lower right).

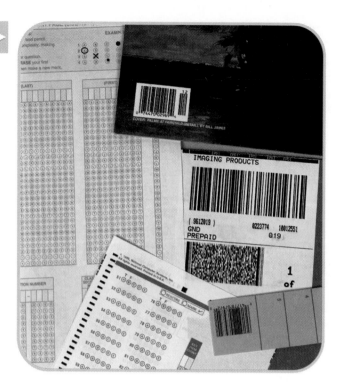

▶ The graphics tablet is popular with artists and designers. Most touch tablets are pressure sensitive, so they can send different signals depending on how hard the user presses on the tablet with a stylus.

▶ The touch screen responds when the user points to or touches different screen regions. Computers with touch screens are frequently used in public libraries, airports, and shopping malls where many users are unfamiliar with computers.

Reading Tools

In spite of their versatility, pointing devices are woefully inadequate for the input of text and numbers into computers, which is why the mouse hasn't replaced the keyboard on the standard personal computer. Still, there are alternatives to typing large quantities of data. Some input devices provide the computer with limited ability to "read" directly from paper, converting printed information into bit patterns that can be processed by the computer. Some reading devices are uniquely qualified for specific everyday tasks:

▶ Optical-mark readers use reflected light to determine the location of pencil marks on standardized test answer sheets and similar forms.

▶ Magnetic-ink character readers read those odd-shaped numbers printed with magnetic ink on checks.

▶ Bar-code readers use light to read *universal product codes (UPCs)*, inventory codes, and other codes created from patterns of variable-width bars.

▶ In many stores bar-code readers are attached to point-of-sale (POS) terminals. These terminals send scanned information to a mainframe computer. The computer determines the item's price, calculates taxes and totals, and records the transaction for future use in inventory, accounting, and other areas. When wand readers are used to recognize words and numbers at a POS terminal, the computer is performing.

▶ *Pen scanners* look like highlighters, but they're actually wireless scanners that can perform optical character recognition (OCR). When you drag a pen scanner across

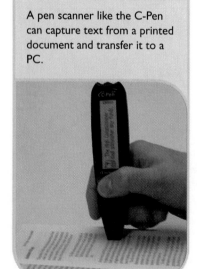

A pen scanner like the C-Pen can capture text from a printed document and transfer it to a PC.

a line of printed text, it creates a text file in its built-in memory, where it's stored until you transfer it into your computer's memory through a cable or infrared beam. A wireless pen scanner actually contains a small computer which interprets the black and white scanned patterns as letters and numbers. This kind of optical character recognition isn't 100 percent foolproof, but it's getting better all the time.

Handwriting recognition is even more difficult, but it's critical in a **pen-based computer**. This keyboardless machine accepts input from a stylus applied directly to a flat-panel screen. The computer electronically simulates a pen and pad of paper. **Handwriting recognition software** translates the user's handwritten forms into ASCII characters. Most such systems require users to modify their handwriting so that it's consistent and unambiguous enough for the software to decipher reliably. As OCR technology improves, pen-based systems are becoming popular with information workers who spend lots of time filling out forms and with people who lack typing skills. *Personal digital assistants (PDAs)* are pen computers that serve as pocket-sized organizers, notebooks, appointment books, and communication devices.(OCR and handwriting recognition are covered in more detail in later chapters.)

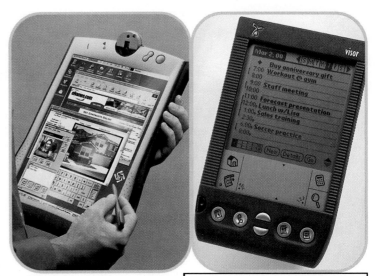

Pen input is used in handheld computers such as this Handspring Visor (above right). The Palm OS software can recognize hand-drawn characters, but only if they're printed according to the rules of the Graffiti system (above). The much larger Qbe (above left) is a full-featured Windows computer designed to accept pen input.

Digitizing the Real World

Before a computer can recognize handwriting or printed text, it must first **digitize** the information—convert it into a digital form that can be stored in the computer's memory. Because real-world information comes in so many forms, a variety of input devices have been designed for capturing and digitizing information.

A **scanner** is an input device that can create a digital representation of any printed image. Scanners are available in several sizes and shapes. The most common models today are *flatbed scanners*, which look and work like photocopy machines, except that they create computer files instead of paper copies. Inexpensive flatbed scanners are designed for home and small business use. More expensive models used by graphics professionals are capable of producing higher quality reproductions, and, with attachments, scan photographic negatives and slides. *Drum scanners* are larger and more expensive than flatbeds; they're used in publishing applications where image quality is critical. At the other end of the spectrum, *sheet-fed scanners* are small, portable, and inexpensive. Regardless of its type or capabilities, however, a scanner converts photographs, drawings, charts, and other printed information into bit patterns that can be stored and manipulated in a computer's memory using graphics software.

In the same way, a **digital camera** can be used to capture snapshots of the real world as digital images. Unlike a scanner, a digital camera isn't limited to capturing flat printed images; it can record anything that a normal camera can. A digital camera looks like a normal camera. But instead of capturing images on film, a digital camera stores bit patterns on disks or other digital storage media.

A *video digitizer* is a collection of circuits that can capture input from a video camera, video cassette recorder, television, or other video source and convert it to a digital signal that can be stored in memory and displayed on computer screens. *Digital video cameras* can send video signals directly into computers without video digitizers, because they capture images in digital form. Digital video input makes it possible for professionals and hobbyists to edit videos with a computer. Digital video is also used for multimedia applications such as Web page and CD-ROM

Flatbed scanners capture and digitize images from external paper sources.

Digitizing the Real World

We live in an analog world, where we can perceive smooth, continuous changes in color and sound. Modern digital computers store all information as discrete binary numbers. To store analog information, such as an analog sound or image, in a computer we must digitize it—convert it from analog to digital form.

Scanners

A typical desktop scanner contains a camera similar to the kind found in many video camcorders. The scanner camera moves back and forth across an original image, recording for each sample the intensities of red, green, and blue light at that point. (Human eyes have receptors for red, green, and blue light; all colors are perceived as combinations of these three.) A single byte is commonly used to represent the intensity of each color component; a 3-byte (24-bit) code represents the color for each sample. The scanner sends each digital code to the computer, where it can be stored and manipulated.

development. And a growing number of businesses use video cameras and PCs for desktop videoconferencing. With videoconferencing software and hardware, people in diverse locations can see and hear each other while they conduct long-distance meetings; their video images are transmitted through networks. These video applications are discussed in more detail in later chapters.

Audio digitizers contain circuitry to digitize sounds from microphones and other audio devices. Digitized sounds can be stored in a computer's memory and modified with software. Of course, audio digitizers can capture spoken words as well as music and sound effects. But digitizing spoken input isn't the same thing as converting speech into text. Like scanned text input, digitized *voice input* requires artificial intelligence software to be correctly interpreted by the computer as words. *Speech recognition software* has been available for PCs and Macintoshes for years, but until recently it wasn't reliable enough to be of practical use for most people. The latest products are still too limited to replace keyboards for most people. They generally must be trained to recognize individual voices, they typically require the speaker to carefully articulate each word, and they

Digitizing involves using an input device, such as a desktop scanner or audio board, to take millions of tiny samples of the original. A sample of an image might be one pinpoint-sized area of the image; each sample from an audio source is like a brief recording of the sound at a particular instant.

The value of a sample can be represented numerically and therefore stored on a computer. A representation of the original image or sound can be reconstructed by assembling all the samples in sequence.

Audio Digitizers

Digital audio is commonplace today; the CD player is really a computer system designed to translate digital information on a compact disc into analog signals that can be amplified and sent to speakers. In digital audio recording using a personal computer, sound waves vibrate the diaphragm of a microphone connected to the computer, usually through a sound card. The position of the microphone diaphragm is sampled frequently—as much as 44,000 times each second—and its level is stored as a number. The faster the sampling frequency, the better the sound recording. Better sound is also achieved by using more storage to represent finer gradations of the sound level. An 8-bit sample can represent 256 distinct levels; a 16-bit sample can represent 65,536 levels. Whether digitizing sounds or images, attempts to increase fidelity to the original will usually increase storage requirements.

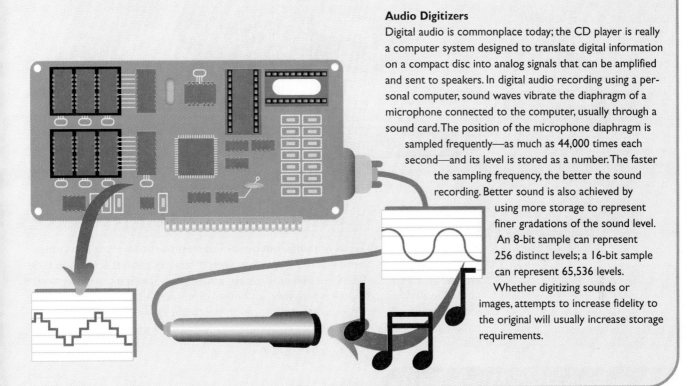

often work with limited vocabularies. Still, they're invaluable for people with disabilities and others who can't use their hands while they work. The promise and problems of automated speech recognition will be explored in later chapters.

Sensing devices designed to monitor temperature, humidity, pressure, and other physical quantities provide data used in robotics, environmental climate control, weather forecasting, medical monitoring, biofeedback, scientific research, and hundreds of other applications. Even our sense of smell can be simulated with sensors. Cyranose from Cyrano Sciences has sensors with polymers that swell when exposed to vapors; it might soon be used to detect spoiled foods, land mines, chemical spills, or even halitosis.

Computers can accept input from a variety of other sources, including manufacturing equipment, telephones, communication networks, and other computers. New input devices are being developed all the time as technologies evolve and human needs change. By stretching the computer's capabilities, these devices stretch our imaginations to develop new ways of using computers. We'll consider some of the more interesting and exotic technologies later; for now we turn our attention to the output end of the process.

Consumer cameras like the Epson shown here (top left) sell for under $1,000; professional models like the Nikon (top center) cost much more. Digital video cameras like this Sony model (bottom left) can deliver video data directly a PC or Macintosh. The Kritter (bottom right) is an example of a video camera designed to attach permanently to the computer. Video digitizers like the CapSure (top right) allows a computer to convert video images from an older analog video source into a digital form.

Output: From Pulses to People

There's a runaway market for bits.

—**Russell Schweickart**, *astronaut*

A computer can do all kinds of things, but none of them is worth anything to us unless we have a way to get the results out of the box. Output devices convert the computer's internal bit patterns into a form that humans can understand. The first computers were limited to flashing lights, teletypewriters, and other primitive communication devices. Most computers today produce output through two main types of devices: monitor screens for immediate visual output and printers for permanent paper output.

This doctor used voice input to record spoken notes on his PC.

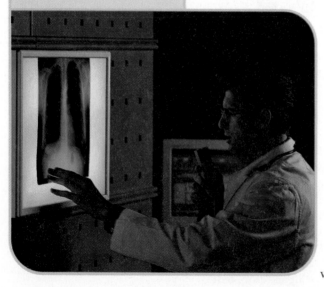

Screen Output

The **monitor**, or **video display terminal (VDT)**, is the most common PC output device; it serves as a one-way window between the computer user and the machine. Early computer monitors were designed to display characters—text, numbers, and tiny graphic symbols. Today's monitors are as likely to display graphics, photographic images, animation, and video as they are to display text and numbers. Because of the monitor's ever-expanding role as a graphical output device, computer users need to know a bit about the factors that control image size and quality.

Monitor size, like television size, is measured as the length of a diagonal line across the screen; a typical desktop monitor today measures from 15 to 21 inches diagonally, but the actual viewable area is usually smaller. Images on a monitor are composed of tiny dots, called **pixels** (for picture elements). A square inch of an image on a typical monitor is a grid of dots about 72 pixels on each side. Such a monitor has a **resolution** of 72 dots per inch (dpi). The higher the resolution, the closer together the dots and the clearer the image. Another way to describe *resolution* is to refer to the total number of pixels displayed on the screen. Assuming that two monitors are the same size, the one that displays the dots closest together displays more pixels—and has a sharper, clearer display. When describing resolution in this way, people usually indicate the number of columns and rows of pixels rather than the total number of pixels. For example, a 1,024 _ 768 image is composed of 1,024 columns by 768 rows of pixels, for a total of 786,432 pixels. The most common monitor resolution today is 800 × 600, but higher resolution monitors are quickly becoming the norm.

Resolution isn't the only factor that determines image quality. Computer monitors are limited by *color depth*—the number of different colors they can display at the same time. Color depth is sometimes called *bit depth* because a wider range of colors per pixel takes up more bits of space in video memory. If each pixel is allotted 8 bits of memory, the resulting image can have up to 256 different colors on screen at a time. (There are 256 unique combinations of 8 bits to use as color codes.) In other words, 8-bit color, common in older PCs, has a color depth of 256. Most graphics professionals use 24-bit color, or *true color,* because it allows more than 16 million color choices per pixel—more than enough for photorealistic images. *Monochrome monitors* can display only monochrome images. *Gray-scale monitors* (which can display black, white, and shades of gray but no other colors) and *color monitors* (which can display a range of colors) have greater color depth. A modern PC or Macintosh can display different combinations of resolution and color depth on the same monitor.

The monitor is connected to the computer by way of the *video adapter*, which is a circuit board installed in a slot inside the main system unit. An image on the monitor

The Cyranose is one of the first devices to digitize smells so they can be processed as data by computers.

These four images show the same photograph displayed in four different bit depths: 1, 4, 8, and 16 bits.

Color Video

The colors in some CRT video images glow because the monitor is a luminous source of light using *additive color synthesis*—colors are formed by adding different amounts of red, green, and blue light.

Like television sets, computer monitors *refresh* or update their images many times per second. If a monitor refreshes its image fewer than 70 times per second (70 hertz), the flicker may be enough to cause eye strain, headaches, and nausea. Many monitors slow down their refresh rates if the resolution is increased, so if you're shopping for a monitor, buy one with a refresh rate of more than 70 Hz at the maximum resolution you expect to be using.

Another factor that should figure into your purchasing decision is the monitor's dot pitch—the measurement of how close the holes in the grid are to each other. The smaller the dot pitch, the closer the holes and the sharper the image.

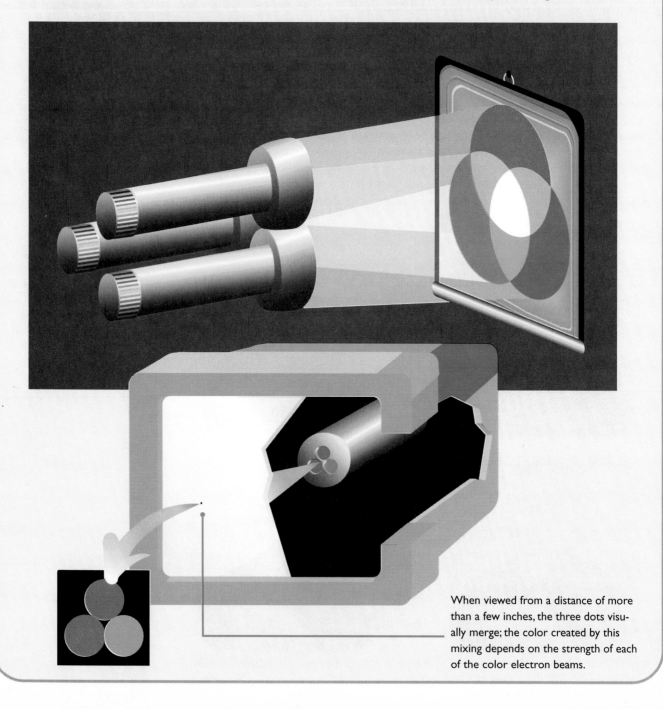

When viewed from a distance of more than a few inches, the three dots visually merge; the color created by this mixing depends on the strength of each of the color electron beams.

exists inside the computer in *video memory*, or *VRAM*, a special portion of RAM dedicated to holding video images. The amount of VRAM determines the maximum resolution and color depth that can be displayed by a computer system. The more video memory a computer has, the more detail it can present in a picture.

Most monitors fall into one of two classes: television-style **CRT (cathode-ray tube) monitors** and flat-panel **LCD (liquid crystal display) monitors**. Because of their clarity, speedy response time, and low cost, CRTs still dominate desktops. Lighter, more compact LCDs are used primarily in portable computers. But they're also used in *overhead projection panels* and *video projectors* to project computer screen images for meetings and classes. As LCDs improve in quality and come down in price, they are turning up on more and more desktops; many experts predict they'll eventually replace bulky CRTs on most desks.

Most desktop computers use CRT monitors because they're inexpensive and they produce high-quality images. But lightweight, flat-screen LCD monitors are becoming more popular on desktops as their prices come down and their image quality improves (left). LCDs are also used in projectors that allow computer screen images to be projected for large viewing audiences (right).

Paper Output

Output displayed on a monitor is immediate but temporary. A **printer** can produce a hard copy on paper of any information that can be displayed on the computer's screen. Printers come in several varieties, but they all fit into two basic groups: *impact printers* and *nonimpact printers*.

Impact printers include line printers and dot-matrix printers. Printers of this type share one common characteristic: They form images by physically striking paper, ribbon, and print hammer together, the way a typewriter does. **Line printers** are used by mainframes to produce massive printouts; these speedy, noisy beasts hammer out thousands of lines of text per minute. You've undoubtedly seen form letters from banks and stores, bills from utility companies, and report cards from schools that were printed with line printers. Because they're limited to printing characters, line printers are inadequate for applications such as desktop publishing, where graphics are essential.

Dot-matrix printers print text and graphics with equal ease. Instead of printing each character as a solid object, a dot-matrix printer uses pinpoint-sized hammers to transfer ink to the page. The printed page is a matrix of tiny dots, some white and some black (or, for color printers, other colors). It's almost as if the computer were hammering bits directly on the page. The final printout might be a picture, text, or a combination of the two. A typical dot-matrix printer produces printouts with a resolution—relative closeness of dots—of less than 100 dots per inch (dpi), so the dots that make up characters and pictures are obvious to even casual readers.

Except for those applications, such as billing, where multipart forms need to be printed, **nonimpact printers** are gradually replacing impact printers in most offices. The two main types of nonimpact printers are *laser printers* and *inkjet printers*. **Laser printers** use the same technology as photocopy machines: A laser beam creates patterns of electrical charges on a rotating drum; those charged patterns attract black toner and

Color Printing

Printed colors can't be as vivid as video colors because printed images don't produce light like a video monitor does; they only reflect light. Most color printers use *subtractive synthesis* to produce colors: Various amounts of cyan (light blue), magenta (reddish purple), yellow, and black pigments are mixed to create a color.

Most printers, like monitors, are *raster* devices—they form images from little dots. The resolution of raster printers is normally measured in dots per inch (dpi). Typical laser printers have resolutions of between 300 and 1,200 dpi. More expensive printers have resolutions of 1,200 to 5,000 dpi.

Matching on-screen color with printed color is difficult because monitors use additive color synthesis to obtain the color, whereas printers use subtractive synthesis. Monitors are able to display more colors than printers, though printers can display a few colors that monitors can't. But the range of colors that humans can perceive extends beyond either technology.

You can demonstrate subtractive synthesis by painting overlapping areas of cyan, magenta, and yellow ink. The combination of all three is black; combinations of pairs produce red, green, and blue, which are secondary colors of the subtractive system.

transfer it to paper as the drum rotates. Color laser printers can print multicolor images by mixing different toner shades, but they're still too expensive to be widely used.

People who work in color tend to favor **inkjet printers**, which spray ink directly onto paper to produce printed text and graphic images. Inkjets generally print fewer pages per minute than laser printers. But high-quality color inkjet printers cost far less than color laser printers—many are less expensive than the cheapest black-and-white laser printers. Inkjet printers are also typically smaller and lighter than laser printers; portable inkjet printers designed to travel with laptops weigh only a couple of pounds each.

Both laser and inkjet printers produce output with much higher resolution—usually 600 or more dots per inch—than is possible with dot-matrix models. At these resolutions it's hard to tell with the naked eye that characters are, in fact, composed of dots. The best color printers can reproduce photographs with striking accuracy. Because of their ability to print high-resolution text and pictures, nonimpact printers dominate the printer market today.

For certain scientific and engineering applications, a **plotter** is more appropriate than a printer for producing hard copy. A plotter is an automated drawing tool that can produce large, finely scaled drawings, engineering blueprints, and maps by moving the pen and/or the paper in response to computer commands.

Output You Can Hear

Most modern PCs include sound cards. A **sound card** allows the PC to accept microphone input, play music and other sound through speakers or headphones, and process

Dot-matrix printer (top left), desktop and portable inkjet printers, (bottom left and bottom right), laser printer (middle), and plotter (top right). All provide different forms of hard copy output.

sound in a variety of ways. (All Macintoshes and some PC shave audio circuitry integrated with the rest of the system so they don't need separate sound cards.) With a sound card, a PC can play digital recordings of all kinds of sounds, from personal recordings made with the PC and a microphone to music downloaded from the Internet.

Most sound cards also include *synthesizers*—specialized circuitry designed to generate sounds electronically. These synthesizers can be used to produce music, noise, or anything in between. A computer also can be connected to a stand-alone music synthesizer so the computer has complete control of the instrument. Computers can also generate synthesized speech with the right software. Of course, to produce any kind of sound, the computer needs to include or be attached to speakers or headphones.

The Chemical Brothers, like many modern musicians, use computers and electronic synthesizers extensively for composing and performing music.

Controlling Other Machines

In the same way that many input devices convert real-world sights and sounds into digital pulses, many output devices work in the other direction, taking bit patterns and turning them into nondigital movements or measurements. Robot arms, telephone switchboards, transportation devices, automated factory equipment, spacecraft, and a host of other machines and systems accept their orders from computers.

In one example familiar to computer gamers, output is delivered through an enhanced input device. The force feedback joystick can receive signals from a computer and give tactile feedback—jolts, scrapes, and bumps—that match the visual output of the game or simulation. Many video arcades take the

Ergonomics and Health

Along with the benefits of computer technology comes the potential for unwelcome side effects. For people who work long hours with computers, the side effects include risks to health and safety due to radiation emissions, repetitive-stress injuries, or other computer-related health problems. Inconclusive evidence suggests that low-level radiation emitted by video display terminals (VDTs) and other equipment might cause health problems, including miscarriages in pregnant women and leukemia. The scientific jury is still out, but the mixed research results so far have led many computer users and manufacturers to err on the side of caution.

More concrete evidence relates keyboarding to occurrences of repetitive-stress injuries such as *carpal tunnel syndrome*, a painful affliction of the wrist and hand that results from repeating the same movements over long periods. Prolonged computer use also increases the likelihood of headaches, eyestrain, fatigue, and other symptoms of "techno-stress."

Ergonomics (sometimes called human engineering) is the science of designing work environments that allow people and things to interact efficiently and safely. Ergonomic studies suggest preventive measures you can take to protect your health as you work with computers:

▶ *Choose equipment that's ergonomically designed.* When you're buying computer equipment, look beyond functionality. Use magazine reviews, manufacturer's information, and personal research to check on health-related factors, such as monitor radiation and glare, disk-drive noise levels, and keyboard layout. A growing number of computer products, such as split, angled keyboards, are specifically designed to reduce the risk of equipment-related injuries.

Ergonomic keyboards like this one allow you to type without placing your wrists at unnatural angles.

▶ *Create a healthy workspace.* Keep the paper copy of your work at close to the same height as your screen. Position your monitor and lights to minimize glare. Sit at arm's length from your monitor to minimize radiation risks.

▶ *Build flexibility into your work environment.* Whenever possible work with an adjustable chair, an adjustable table, an adjustable monitor, and a removable keyboard. Change your work position frequently.

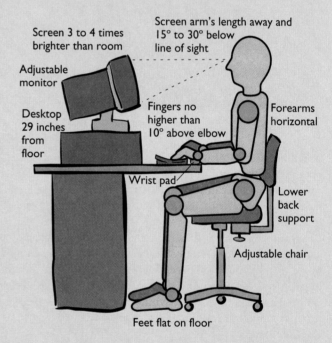

Screen 3 to 4 times brighter than room

Screen arm's length away and 15° to 30° below line of sight

Adjustable monitor

Desktop 29 inches from floor

Fingers no higher than 10° above elbow

Forearms horizontal

Wrist pad

Lower back support

Adjustable chair

Feet flat on floor

▶ *Rest your eyes.* Look up from the screen periodically and focus on a far-away object or scene. Blink frequently. Take a 15-minute break from using a VDT every 2 hours.

▶ *Stretch.* While you're taking your rest break, do some simple stretches to loosen tight muscles. Occasional stretching of the muscles in your arms, hands, wrists, back, shoulders, and lower body can make hours of computer work more comfortable and less harmful.

▶ *Listen to your body.* If you feel uncomfortable, your body is telling you to change something or take a break. Don't ignore it. Ergonomic keyboards like the split, angled keyboard allow computer users to hold their hands and arms in more natural positions while typing to reduce the risk of repetitive-stress injuries.

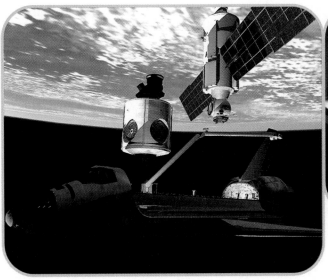

Computers control the movements of spacecrafts and virtual reality arcade games using output devices that operate on similar principles.

concept farther by having the computer shake, rattle, and roll the gamer's chair while displaying on-screen movements that match the action.

Of course, computers can send information directly to other computers, bypassing human interaction altogether. The possibilities for computer output are limited only by the technology and the human imagination, both of which are stretching further all the time.

Storage Devices: Input Meets Output

A retentive memory may be a good thing, but **the ability to forget** is the true token of greatness.

—Elbert Hubbard

Some computer peripherals are capable of performing both input and output functions. These devices, which include tape and disk drives, are the computer's *storage devices*. They're sometimes referred to as *secondary storage* devices, because the computer's memory is its *primary storage*. Unlike RAM, which forgets everything whenever the computer is turned off, and ROM, which can't learn anything new, secondary storage devices allow the computer to record information semipermanently so it can be read later by the same computer or by another computer.

Tape cartridges similar to this one have replaced spinning tape reels as backup storage devices.

Magnetic Tape

Tape drives are common storage devices on most mainframe computers and some personal computers. A tape drive can write data onto, and read data off of, a magnetically coated ribbon of tape. The reason for the widespread use of **magnetic tape** as a storage medium is clear: A magnetic tape can store massive amounts of information in a small space at a relatively low cost. The spinning tape reels that symbolized computers in so many old science fiction movies have for the most part been replaced by tape cartridges.

Whether it is inside the main system box or in a separate case, a hard drive looks like this on the inside.

Magnetic tape has one clear limitation: Tape is a **sequential access** medium. Whether a tape holds music or computer data, the computer must zip through information in the order in which it was recorded. Retrieving information from the middle of a tape is far too time consuming for most modern computer applications because people expect immediate response to their commands. As a result, magnetic tape is used today primarily for backup of data and a few other operations that aren't time sensitive.

Magnetic Disks

Like magnetic tape, a **magnetic disk** has a magnetically coated surface that can store encoded information; a *disk drive* writes data onto the disk's surface and reads data from the surface. But unlike a tape drive, a **disk drive** can rapidly retrieve information from any part of a magnetic disk without regard for the order in which the information was recorded, in the same way you can quickly select any track on an audio compact disc (CD). Because of their **random access** capability, disks are the most popular media for everyday storage needs.

Most computer users are familiar with the 3.5-inch **diskette** (or **floppy disk**)—a small, magnetically sensitive, flexible plastic wafer housed in a plastic case. The diskette is commonly used for transferring small data files between machines because just about every PC includes a disk drive that can read and write on these inexpensive disks. The most notable exception: Macintoshes no longer include diskette drives as standard equipment, because diskettes are too slow and limited for modern multimedia applications. A typical diskette has a capacity of less than 2MB—enough space to hold the words for half of this book, but not enough for even one large detailed photograph.

Virtually all PCs include hard disks as their primary storage devices. A **hard disk** is a rigid, magnetically sensitive disk that spins rapidly and continuously inside the computer chassis or in a separate box connected to the computer housing. This type of hard disk is never removed by the user. Information can be transferred to and from a hard disk *much* faster than with a diskette. A hard disk might hold several gigabytes (thousands of megabytes) of information—more than enough room for every word and picture in this book.

To fill the gap between low-capacity, slow diskettes and nonremovable, fast hard disks, manufacturers have developed high-capacity transportable storage solutions. There are many choices beyond diskettes in **removable media**. The most popular are listed here:

▶ *Zip Disks*, developed by Iomega. A Zip disk looks like a thicker version of a standard diskette. The most common Zip disks can hold up to 100 megabytes of data; a newer variety can hold up to 250 MB. Zip drives cannot read or write standard floppy disks, even though they use a similar technology. Zip drives are popular add-ons for PCs and Macintoshes; they're even installed as standard equipment on some models. Their popularity makes Zip disks useful for exchanging large data files between machines.

▶ *SuperDisks*, developed by Imation. A SuperDisk looks similar to a standard diskette, but it is capable of holding 120 megabytes of data—roughly 80 times as much as a typical diskette. The SuperDisk drive can't read or write data as fast as some other removable storage devices, but it has one big advantage: It can also read and write standard diskettes, so it can replace a standard floppy disk drive in a computer system. (Sony offers a similar but less widely used device called a HiFD drive; Caleb technology offers another called the it drive.)

▶ *Jaz Disks*, also developed by Iomega. Jaz disks, unlike Zip and SuperDisks, are based on hard disk technology. As a result, they have a much higher capacity (1 to 2 gigabytes) and faster read/write speeds. Jaz disks are, in effect, removable hard disk cartridges. They're ideal for storing and transporting large multimedia files.

▶ *Magneto-optical (MO) disks* use a combination of magnetic disk technology and optical disk technology to store and retrieve information. They're not as fast as hard disks, and they're expensive, but they're extremely reliable and they can hold hundreds of megabytes of data.

Iomega's Zip and Jaz disks are high capacity removable storage media.

Optical Disks

As multimedia applications become more commonplace, even the large storage capacity of a hard disk can be quickly gobbled up by sounds, color pictures, video sequences, and other storage-intensive items. For these applications, **optical disks** provide a viable storage alternative. An **optical disk drive** uses laser beams rather than magnets to read and write bits of information on the disk surface. While they aren't as fast as magnetic hard disks, optical disks have massive storage capacity and high reliability.

CD-ROM (compact disc—read-only memory) drives are optical drives that read CD-ROMs—data disks that are physically identical to musical compact discs. The similarity of audio and data CDs is no accident; it makes it possible for CD-ROM drives to play music CDs under computer control. A CD-ROM can hold the contents of an encyclopedia, including pictures, with room to spare for sounds and video clips. One secretary typing 90 words per minute, 8 hours per day, would take more than 8 years to type enough text to fill a single CD-ROM. But because CD-ROM drives are read-only

	Sequential access devices	**Random access devices**
Music	Cassette	Compact disc
Data	Magnetic tape cartridge	Floppy disk Hard disk

Most stereo systems include sequential access devices—cassette decks—and random access devices—compact disc players. The advantages of random access are the same for stereos as for computers.

How It Works 3.4

Disk Storage

Over the history of computing many devices have been invented to permanently store data. Magnetic and optical disks are two of the most important types of devices in use today.

Hard disks spin much faster than floppy disks and have a higher storage density (number of bytes per square inch). The *read/write head* of a hard disk glides on a thin cushion of air above the disk and never actually touches the disk.

Magnetic Disks

Both hard disks and floppy disks are coated with a *magnetic oxide* similar to the material used to coat cassette tapes and videotapes. The read/write head of a disk drive is similar to the record/play head on a tape recorder; it magnetizes parts of the surface to record information. The difference is that a disk is a digital medium—binary numbers are read and written. The typical hard disk consists of several *platters*, each accessed via a read/write

head on a movable *armature*. The magnetic signals on the disk are organized into concentric *tracks;* the tracks in turn are divided into *sectors*. This is the traditional scheme used to construct addresses for data on the disk.

CD-ROM

A personal computer's CD-ROM drive contains a small laser that shines on the surface of the disk, "reading" the reflections. Ordinary audio CDs and computer CD-ROMs have similar formats. (That's why you can play an audio CD with a CD-ROM drive.) In each case information is represented optically—the bottom surface of the CD, under a protective layer of plastic, is coated with a reflective metal film. A laser burns unreflective pits into the film to record data bits. Once a pit is burned, it can't be smoothed over and made shiny again; that's why ordinary CD-ROMs are read-only.

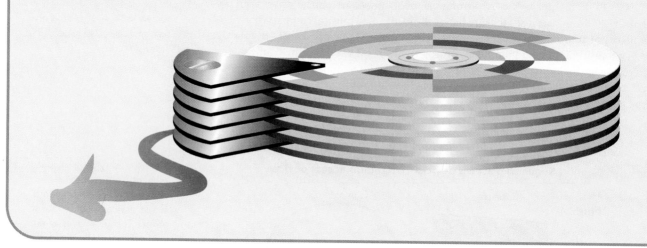

devices, they can't be used as secondary storage devices; instead, they're widely used to read commercially pressed CD-ROMs containing everything from business applications to multimedia games and reference libraries. In fact, most packaged commercial software today is stored on CD-ROMs.

The *Computer Confluence* CD-ROM illustrates the quantity and variety of information that can be packed onto a single disk: It contains hundreds of self-testing exercises, the complete glossary in an instant-access format, a wide variety of interactive animated tutorials, about an hour's worth of video clips, and several demonstration software packages.

Drives capable of writing on a blank CD have come down in price in recent years, making it possible for small organizations and individuals to produce their own CD-ROMs. These CD-R (compact disc-recordable) drives are a type of *WORM* (write-once, read-many) drive. They write digital information onto blank (or partially filled) optical disks, but they can't erase the information once it's burned in. A CD-ROM created on a CD-R drive can be read with a standard CD-ROM drive. Organizations and individuals use these drives to make archival copies of large data files. The drives are also useful for

DVD-ROM

A DVD-ROM drive works on the same principle as a CD-ROM drive; the main difference is that the pits are packed much closer together on a DVD, so about 7 times as many can fit on the disk surface. (To read these tightly packed bits, the DVD-ROM uses a narrower laser beam.) A DVD can hold even more data—up to 8.5 gigabytes—if it has a second layer of data. On a layered DVD the top layer is semireflective, allowing a second readback laser to penetrate to the layer below. The laser can "see through" the top layer, just as you can see through a picket fence when you look at it from just the right angle. For truly massive storage jobs, a DVD can have data on both sides—up to 17 gigabytes. Two-sided DVDs usually have to be turned over for the reader to read both sides; future drives may use additional readback lasers to read the second side without flipping the disk.

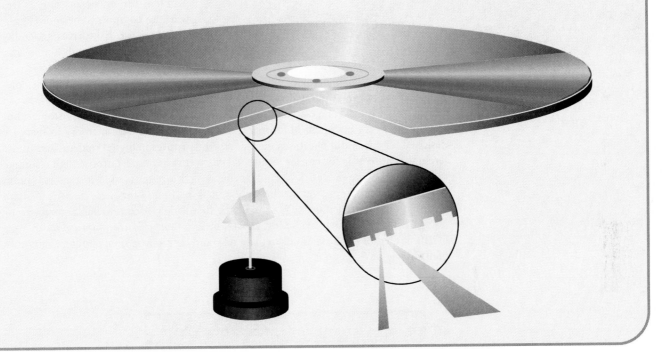

creating master copies of CD-ROMs and audio CDs for duplication and distribution. Newer **CD-RW** (compact disc-rewritable) drives can write, erase, and rewrite CDs, eliminating the read-only limitation from the CD format.

While the CD-ROM drive has become standard equipment in modern multimedia computers, a new device may soon replace the traditional CD-ROM drive. The **DVD** is the same size as a standard CD-ROM, but can hold between 3.8 and 17 gigabytes of information, depending on how the information is stored. DVD originally stood for digital video disk because the disks were designed to replace VHS tapes in video stores. Today DVD players are marketed as devices for playing movies in home entertainment systems, and many movies are available in DVD format. But because these disks are used for a variety of computer-based applications, they're more accurately described as *digital versatile disks*. **DVD-ROM** drives (which can also read standard CD-ROMs) are replacing CD-ROM drives on many PCs. A DVD-ROM drive can read standard CD-ROMs and audio CDs, but it can also read DVDs containing computer data or full-length movies. DVD-ROM drives might soon be overshadowed by **DVD-RAM** drives, which can read, erase, and write data on multi-gigabyte disks.

Sony's Memory Stick, front and center in this picture, is a solid-state storage medium that can be used by all of the devices shown here.

Solid-state Storage Devices

Until recently, disk drives were the only realistic random-access storage devices for most computer applications. In spite of their popularity, disk drives present problems for today's computer users. The moving parts in disk drives are more likely to fail than other computer components. For airline travelers and others who must depend on battery power for long periods of time, spinning disk drives consume too much energy. Disk drives can be noisy—a problem for musicians and others who use computers for audio applications. And disk drives are bulky when compared with computer memory.

Flash memory is a type of erasable memory chip that can serve as a reliable, low-energy, quiet, compact alternative to disk storage. Until recently, flash memory was too expensive for most storage applications. It's still more expensive than disk storage, but flash memory is now practical for many applications. Some flash memory formats are designed for specific applications, such as storing pictures in digital cameras and transferring them to PCs for editing. Sony's *memory stick* is an all-purpose digital storage card about the size of a stick of gum. Memory stick storage is used in cameras, audio devices, video equipment, and computers, making it easy for these devices to share information. Flash memory may soon be the first widely-used rewritable storage technology with no moving parts. Most experts believe that *solid state storage* technology like flash memory will eventually replace disk and tape storage in computers and other digital devices.

Computer Systems: The Sum of Its Parts

The computer is by all odds the most extraordinary of the technological clothing ever devised by man, since it is an extension of our central nervous system. Beside it

the wheel is a mere hula hoop.....

—Marshall McLuhan, in *War and Peace in the Global Village*

Most personal computers fall into one of four basic design classes:

1. Tall, narrow boxes that can be placed under or on top of desks. These *tower systems* generally have more expansion slots and bays than other designs.

2. Flat "pizza box" systems (sometimes ambiguously referred to as *desktop systems*) designed to sit under the monitor like a platform.

3. *All-in-one systems* (like the iMac) that combine monitor and system unit into a single housing.

4. Portable computers that include all the essential components, including keyboard and pointing device, in one compact box.

Whatever the design, a PC must allow for attachment of input, output, and storage peripherals. That's where slots, ports, and bays figure in. Now that we've explored the peripherals landscape, we can look again at the ways of hooking those peripherals into the system.

Ports and Slots Revisited

The system board, or motherboard, of a computer system generally includes several ports. The most common ports on system boards are also among the oldest—they've been standard on PCs for years and include the following:

▶ A *serial port* for attaching a modem or other device that can send and receive messages one bit at a time

▶ A *parallel port* for attaching a printer or other device that communicates by sending or receiving bits in groups, rather than sequentially

▶ *Keyboard/mouse ports* for attaching a keyboard and a mouse.

Other ports are typically included on expansion boards rather than the system board:

▶ A *video port* for plugging a color monitor into the video board

▶ Microphone, speaker, headphone, and MIDI (musical instrument digital interface) ports for attaching sound equipment to the sound board.

This rear view of a tower system unit shows several ports, including some (below) that are included in add-on-boards in slots.

All of these ports follow interface standards agreed on by the industry so that devices made by one manufacturer can be attached to systems made by other companies. The downside of industry standards is that they can sometimes hold back progress. For example, today's fastest modems outpace the classic serial port, and today's color printers are kept waiting by the pokey parallel port.

Computer manufacturers and owners use expansion cards to get around the limitations of these standard ports. For example, most modern computers include an *internal modem* in an expansion slot; this modem card adds a standard phone jack as a communication port. For faster connection to a local-area network (LAN), many modern PCs include a *network card* that adds a LAN port. For faster communication with peripherals like disk drives and scanners, a PC or Macintosh might include a SCSI (Small Computer Systems Interface, pronounced "scuzzy") card that adds a SCSI port to the back of the system box. (SCSI ports are standard on older Macintoshes.) The SCSI interface design allows several peripherals to be strung together (daisy-chained) and attached to a single port.

Internal and External Drives

Disk drives generally reside in *bays* inside the system unit. A new PC almost always has a floppy disk drive in one bay, a hard drive in another, and some kind of CD or DVD drive in a third bay. Some PCs have extra bays for additional hard drives or removable media. Tall tower models generally have more expansion bays than flat systems designed to sit under monitors. Disk drives that are housed in the system box are called *internal drives. External drives* are housed in their own boxes and connected to the system through ports like the SCSI port. A computer can have just about any combination of internal and external drives.

Most portable computers are too small to include three drive bays. But some models have bays that allow drives to be swapped. For example, you might remove the CD-ROM drive from a laptop and insert a floppy disk drive so you can save a backup copy of your work. Some models allow you to *hot swap* devices—remove and replace them

The portable computer shown here has a removable storage bay, allowing the user to swap a DVD-ROM drive with a Zip drive or other peripheral. This tower system has its side panel removed so you can see the storage bays containing disk drives (top right) and the expansion boards inserted into slots (top left).

without powering down. Most portables allow you to attach external peripherals through ports. Some portables can be plugged into docking stations that contain, or are attached to, all the necessary peripherals. When docked, a portable can function like a desktop computer, complete with large-screen monitor, full-sized keyboard, mouse, sound system, and a variety of other peripherals.

Expansion Made Easy: Emerging Interfaces

It's clear that the *open architecture* of the PC—the design that allows expansion cards and peripherals to be added—gives it flexibility and longevity that it wouldn't have otherwise. Many hobbyists have been using the same computer system for years; they just swap in new cards, drives, and even CPUs and motherboards to keep their systems up to current standards. But most computer users today prefer to keep their computers sealed; they like to use them, not take them apart. Fortunately, new interface standards are emerging that will allow a casual computer user to add the latest and greatest devices to their systems without cracking the box.

A USB, or universal serial bus, can transmit data at approximately 11 megabits—roughly 100 times faster than the PC serial port, and a newer, faster version is in the works. Up to 126 devices, including keyboards, mice, digital cameras, scanners, and storage devices—can be chained together from a single USB port. USB devices can be hot swapped, so the system instantly recognizes the presence of a new device when it is plugged in. And USB, like SCSI, is *platform independent*, so USB devices work on both PCs and Macintoshes. In fact, this paragraph is being typed on a keyboard that's shared by a PC and a Mac through a USB hub. All new PCs and Macintoshes include at least one USB port. In time, computer manufacturers may phase out other ports made unnecessary by USB's presence. Some, including Compaq, already have started producing *legacy-free PCs* that cost less because they use USB ports instead of older serial, parallel, keyboard, mouse, and SCSI ports.

Another interface standard that shows promise is *Firewire*, an extremely high-speed connection standard developed by Apple. Most PC makers refer to Firewire by the designation assigned by the Institute of Electrical and Electronic Engineers when they approved it as a standard: *IEEE 1394*. (Sony calls their version iLink.) Firewire can move data between devices at 400 or more megabits per second—far faster than most peripheral devices can handle it. This high speed makes it ideal for data-intensive work like digital video. Most modern digital video cameras have Firewire ports, so they can be connected directly to 1394-equipped PCs. Like USB, Firewire allows multiple devices to be connected to the same port and to be hot swapped. Firewire can also supply power to peripherals so they don't need an external power supply. While 1394 isn't standard equipment on all PCs yet, its growing acceptance suggests that it may be someday.

Putting It All Together

A typical computer system might have several different input, output, and storage peripherals. From the computer's point of view it doesn't matter which of these devices is used at any given time. Each input device is just another source of electrical signals; each output device is just another place to send signals; each storage device is one or the other, depending on what the program calls for. Read from here, write to there—the CPU doesn't care; it dutifully follows instructions. Like a stereo receiver, the computer is oblivious to which input and output devices are attached and operational, as long as they're compatible.

A typical desktop computer system includes a computer and several peripheral devices.

Networks: Systems Without Boundaries

Unlike a stereo system, which has clearly defined boundaries, a computer system can be part of a network that blurs the boundaries between computers. When computers are connected in a network, one computer can, in effect, serve as an input device for another computer, which serves as an output device for the first computer. Networks can include hundreds of different computers, each of which might have access to all of the peripherals on the system. Many public and private networks span the globe by taking advantage of satellites, fiber optic cables, and other communication technologies. Using a peripheral called a *modem,* a computer can connect to a network through an ordinary phone line, or (if it's a *cable modem*) a television cable. The rise in computer networks is making it more difficult to draw lines between individual computer systems. If you're connected to the Internet, your computer is, in effect, just a tiny part of a global system of interconnected networks.

Software: The Missing Piece

In the span of a few pages we've surveyed a mind-boggling array of computer hardware, but, in truth, we've barely scratched the surface. Nonetheless, all this hardware is worthless without software to drive it. In the next chapter we'll take a look at the software that makes a computer system come to life.

So Astounding We Hardly Notice It

Stephen Manes

Computer hardware breakthroughs happen with such regularity that we tend to take them for granted. Software is another matter. Stephen Manes is a PC World *editor and cohost of PBS's* Digital Duo. *In this article he contrasts hard-to-believe hardware with hard-to-depend-on software. He uses as examples drivers—those programs that communicate directly with hardware devices. Drivers are specialized parts of the operating system, the software that takes care of hundreds of routine tasks to keep the computer running smoothly. Unfortunately, today's software doesn't quite deliver what it promises.*

Our capacity for astonishment has all but disappeared. Digital wonders have become so routine, we take their magic for granted. The electronic devices we use every day—not just personal computers, but cell phones, CD and DVD players, pocket organizers, and game consoles—are astoundingly complex. But for some reason we firmly refuse to let such things astound us.

This thought came to me after an evening at home looking at DVD movies on a 5-foot-wide screen illuminated by a $3000 InFocus digital projector. It uses an amazing Texas Instruments technology known as Digital Light Processing.

Doing It With Mirrors

I don't use the term amazing lightly. The InFocus system is built around a chip with half a million minuscule mirrors that flip back and forth thousands of times a second. The image reflected off them and onto the screen gets its color from light shining through a rotating wheel segmented into red, blue, and green. And since the mirrors can only be on or off, gradations come from time-multiplexing; for each color within each image, the mirrors switch on for longer or shorter passages of time, which the eye and brain interpret as brighter or darker. Yet despite its complexity, the precision ballet of mirrors delivers an extraordinarily stable picture.

This technology looks particularly magical because of its micromechanical aspect, but others we take for granted are every bit as striking. Modern processors not only make educated guesses about which way a program is headed, but they manage to do it at ever-increasing speeds and ever-decreasing prices. We blithely toss off the phrase "500-megahertz processor" the way our parents might have said "350-horsepower engine," never stopping to think what 500 MHz means: unimaginably tiny circuits in the chip handling hundreds of millions of operations every second.

The continued improvement in disk storage is another form of magic. In the early 1980s, my first outboard unit held a whopping 10 megabytes in a box half the size of my entire IBM PC. Today my three-pound laptop holds more than 4 gigabytes. Just when it seems hardware engineers have run out of tricks, they come up with technology that makes things better, cheaper, faster.

Blinded by Software

Notice that I said hardware engineers. That's because there's often a single barrier between hardware and magic: software. In the systems we use today, there are magical devices that we can't yet take for granted, because we can't figure out how to make them work. Consider the infrared port. It's been part of virtually every notebook PC for years, but almost no one uses it. Getting two machines' IR ports to acknowledge each other is easy; getting them to do something useful like exchanging files is damnably hard. The culprit: software.

A colleague with a file I needed was recently sitting next to me during a boring presentation. We had virtually identical subnotebook machines with us, and mine was already set up to transfer files via IR. But installing and configuring the Windows plumbing on my colleague's machine took several reboots and about 20 minutes, and that was only because I'd done it before.

The IR port isn't the only cool hardware that bad software—much of it Microsoft's—has managed to sabotage or delay. Microsoft was supposedly a big booster of CD-ROM in the mid-1980s, but in those days of limited memory resources its driver was about as big as the rest of the operating system. And until recently, the USB ports built into most desktops were largely unusable, thanks to lackluster OS support.

Microsoft's hardly the only culprit. Vendors of otherwise wonderful video cards often shoot themselves in the foot by delivering drivers that just plain don't do their job. And DVD-ROM decoding software has been a constant annoyance.

But when this stuff works, it does so in ways most of us can't begin to fathom. That engineers have made the astonishing routine may well be their most astounding trick of all.

DISCUSSION QUESTIONS

1. What recent technology has seemed most "amazing" to you. Why?
2. What recent technology has most disappointed you because of unreliability or difficulty of operation?

A computer with just a CPU and internal memory is of limited value; peripherals allow that computer to communicate with the outside world and store information for later use. Some peripherals are strictly input devices. Others are output devices. Some are external storage devices that accept information from and send information to the CPU.

The most common input devices today are the keyboard and the mouse. But a variety of other input devices can be connected to the computer. Trackballs, touch-sensitive pads, touch screens, and joysticks provide alternatives to the mouse as a pointing device. Bar-code readers, optical-mark readers, and magnetic-ink readers are designed to recognize and translate specially printed patterns and characters. Scanners and digital cameras convert photographs, drawings, and other analog images into digital files that can be processed by the computer. Sound digitizers do the same thing to audio information. All input devices are designed to do one thing: Convert information signals from an outside source into a pattern of bits that can be processed by the computer.

Output devices perform just the opposite function: They accept strings of bits from the computer and transform them into a form that is useful or meaningful outside the computer. Video monitors, including CRTs and LCDs, are almost universally used to display information continually as the computer functions. A variety of printers are used for producing paper output. Sound output from the computer, including music and synthesized speech, is delivered through audio speakers. Output devices also allow computers to control other machines.

Unlike most input and output peripherals, storage devices such as disk drives and tape drives are capable of two-way communication with the computer. Because of their high-speed random access capability, magnetic disks—high-capacity hard disks, inexpensive diskettes, and a variety of removable media—are the most common forms of storage on modern computers. Sequential access tape devices are generally used only to archive information that doesn't need to be accessed often. Although optical disks today are used mostly as high-capacity read-only media, they may become the preferred interactive storage medium as the technology improves and the associated costs go down. Further into the future solid-state storage technology will probably replace disks and tapes for most applications.

The hardware for a complete computer system generally includes at least one processor, main memory, one or more secondary storage devices, and several I/O peripherals for communicating with the outside world. Network connections make it possible for computers to communicate with one another directly. Networks blur the boundaries between individual computer systems. With the hardware components in place a computer system is ready to receive and follow instructions encoded in software.

Key Terms

bar-code reader, 58	impact printer, 65	pixel, 63
CD-R, 72	inkjet printer, 66	plotter, 66
CD-ROM, 71	interface standards, 75	point-of-sale (POS) terminal, 58
CD-RW, 73	joystick, 57	printer, 65
click, 56	keyboard, 54	random access, 70
CRT (cathode-ray tube) monitor, 65	laser printer, 65	removable media, 70
cursor, 54	LCD (liquid crystal display) monitor, 65	repetitive-stress injuries, 68
digital camera, 59	line printer, 65	resolution, 63
digitize, 59	magnetic disk, 70	scanner, 59
disk drive, 70	magnetic-ink character reader, 58	sensing device, 61
diskette (floppy disk), 70	magnetic tape, 69	sequential access, 70
dot-matrix printer, 65	monitor, 62	sound card, 66
dragDVD, 56	mouse, 56	tape drive, 69
DVD-RAM, 74	nonimpact printer, 65	touch pad (trackpad), 57
DVD-ROM, 73	optical character recognition (OCR), 58	touch screen, 58
ergonomics, 68	optical disk, 71	track point, 57
flash memory, 74	optical disk drive, 71	trackball, 57
graphics tablet, 58	optical-mark reader, 58	USB (universal serial bus), 76
Handwriting recognition software, 59	pen-based computer, 59	video display terminal (VDT), 62
hard disk, 70	pen scanners, 58	

Review Questions

1. Provide a working definition for each of the key terms listed on the previous page. Check your answers in the glossary.
2. List five input devices and three output devices that might be attached to a personal computer. Describe a typical use for each.
3. Name and describe three special-purpose input devices that are commonly used by people in public places, such as stores, banks, and libraries.
4. The mouse is impractical for use as a pointing device on a laptop computer. Describe at least three alternatives that are more appropriate.
5. What are the advantages of CRT monitors over LCDs?
6. Name at least two hardware devices that use LCDs because using a CRT would be impractical.
7. What are the advantages of nonimpact printers such as laser printers over impact printers? Are there any disadvantages?
8. Some commonly used peripherals can be described as both input and output devices. Explain.
9. What is the difference between sequential access and random access storage devices? What are the major uses of each?
10. What is the main advantage of CD-ROM as a storage medium when compared with magnetic disks? What is the main disadvantage?

Discussion Questions

1. If we think of the human brain as a computer, what are the input devices? What are the output devices? What are the storage devices?
2. What kinds of new input and output devices do you think future computers might have? Why?

Projects

1. The keyboard is the main input device for computers today. If you don't know how to touch-type, you're effectively handicapped in a world of computers. Fortunately, many personal computer software programs are designed to teach keyboarding. If you need to learn to type, try to find one of these programs, and use it regularly until you are a fluent typist.
2. Using the inventory of computers you developed in Project 4 in Chapter 1, determine the major components of each (input devices, output devices, storage, and so on).
3. Visit a bank, store, office, or laboratory. List all the computer peripherals you see, categorizing them as input, output, and storage devices.
4. Using computer advertisements in magazines, newspapers, and catalogs, try to break down the cost of a computer to determine, on the average, what percentage of the cost is for the system unit (including CPU, memory, and disk drives), what percentage is for input and output devices, and what percentage is for software. How do the percentages change as the price of the system goes up?

Sources & Resources

Books

Apple: The Inside Story of Intrigue, Egomania, and Business Blunders, by Jim Carlton (New York: Times Books, 1997). During the 1980s Apple developed and marketed many technologies that were years ahead of anything the competition could offer. So why didn't it become the dominant player in the PC marketplace? This revealing book has some fascinating answers.

Disclosure, by Michael Crichton. (New York: Ballantine Books, 1977). This book-turned-movie provides an inside look at a fictional Seattle corporation that manufactures computer peripherals. Even though the author has clearly tampered with credibility for the sake of a suspenseful plot, the story provides insights into the roles money and power play in today's high-stakes computer industry.

How Computers Work: Millennium Edition, by Ron White (Indianapolis: Que, 1999) This book, described at the end of Chapter 2, provides clear explanations of the inner workings of most commonly used personal computer peripherals.

Upgrading PCs: Visual Quickstart Guide, by Bart G. Farkas and Jeff Govier (Berkeley, CA: Peachpit Press, 1999). There are basically two ways to keep up with the rapid-fire changes in PC technology: buy a new computer system every two or three years, or upgrade individual components regularly. This book is designed for people who'd like to be in the upgrade crowd but don't know much about electronic technology. Like other Visual Quickstart books, it clearly and concisely explains procedures with lots of pictures and a minimum of technobabble. If you're comfortable with a screwdriver, you'll probably be comfortable with this book.

Build Your Own Pentium III PC, by Aubrey Pilgrim (New York: McGraw-Hill, 2000). Building your own PC isn't as hard as it sounds-especially if you have a good guide. This book is designed to guide you step-by-step through the process—even if you're not an engineer. In today's competitive PC market, you may not save a lot of money by building your own, but you'll learn a lot-and hopefully have fun along the way.

Troubleshooting, Maintaining, and Repairing PCs, Millennium Edition, by Stephen J. Bigelow (New York: McGraw-Hill, 2000), and ***Bigelow's Drive and Memory Troubleshooting Pocket Reference,*** by Stephen J. Bigelow (New York: McGraw-Hill, 2000). PCs today are relatively easy to use-as long as nothing goes wrong. When trouble arises, or when it's time to upgrade a component, a PC can be frustrating and bewildering. If you want to-or need to-get inside your PC or its peripherals, Bigelow's hardbound PC reference may help you find your way around. The drive and memory pocket reference has a narrower focus, but a similar style. (In spite of its name, it probably won't fit in your pocket.) Some of the material in these books is highly technical, but that goes with the territory.

Upgrading and Troubleshooting Your Mac, by Gene Steinberg (Berkeley, CA: Osborne/McGraw-Hill, 2000). Macintoshes are generally easier to troubleshoot and repair than other PCs; from the beginning, they've been designed that way. This easy-to-read book is full of answers about making Macs and their peripherals work together.

Mac Answers, Second Edition, by Bob Levitus and Shelly Brisbin (Berkeley, CA: Osborne/McGraw-Hill, 2000). This book offers a wealth of information on Macintoshes and their peripherals in a question-and-answer format. The writing style is clear and friendly.

Scanning the Professional Way, by Sybil Ihrig and Emil Ihrig (Berkeley, CA: Osborne McGraw-Hill, 1995) and ***Real World Scanning and Halftones,*** by David Blatner and Steve Roth (Berkeley, CA: Peachpit Press, 1998). It's easy to use a scanner, but it isn't always easy to get high-quality scans. These two illustrated books cover scanner use from the basics to advanced tips and techniques. Start with a ***Digital Camera: A Guide to Using Digital Cameras to Create High-Quality Graphics,*** by John Odam (Berkeley, CA: Peachpit Press, 1999). This lavishly illustrated book provides an excellent overview of the world of digital photography. Technological issues, aesthetics, and practical shooting tips are all covered.

Zap! How Your Computer Can Hurt You—And What You Can Do about It, by Don Sellers (Berkeley, CA: Peachpit Press, 1994), and ***25 Steps to Safe Computing,*** by Don Sellers (Berkeley, CA: Peachpit Press, 1995). If you do much computer work (or play), you owe it to yourself to learn about the inherent dangers. These books can help you understand the health hazards of computing. Zap! provides clear descriptions of a wide range of medical problems that might result from improper computer use and suggests a variety of treatments and preventive measures. If you don't think you'll bother to read Zap!'s 150 illustrated pages, try 25 Steps to Safe Computing by the same author; it presents the essential tips in condensed form.

Periodicals

E-media. This slick trade monthly focuses on storage technologies, including CD-RW and DVD.

Computer Shopper. This massive monthly typically includes a few consumer-oriented articles, but most people read it for the ads—hundreds each month, complete with an index.

World Wide Web Pages

Most computer peripheral manufacturers have World Wide Web pages. The Computer Confluence Web site will guide you to many of the most interesting pages.

Chapter

4

Software Basics: The Ghost in the Machine

AFTER YOU READ THIS CHAPTER YOU SHOULD BE ABLE TO:

Describe three fundamental categories of software and their relationship.

Explain the relationship of algorithms to software.

Discuss the factors that make a computer application a useful tool.

Describe the role of the operating system in a modern computer system.

Outline the evolution of user interfaces from early machine-language programming to futuristic virtual reality interfaces.

Compare character-based user interfaces with graphical user interfaces and explain the trade-offs involved in choosing a user interface.

In this chapter:

▶ How programs happen
▶ Why software warranties don't promise much
▶ What the operating system does
▶ How user interfaces change the way we use computers
▶ A concise computer consumer's guide
▶ Self-study questions and projects
▶ Mini-reviews of helpful resources for further study
...and more.

On the CD-ROM:

▶ Animated close-up looks at an operating system booting and a program executing
▶ User interface design video clip
▶ Hardware and software buyer's guide
▶ Instant access to glossary and key word references
▶ Interactive self-study quizzes
...and more.

On the Web:

www.prenhall.com/beekman
▶ Sources for free software
▶ Software-related Web sites
▶ Links to Web sites of many important software companies
▶ Self-study exercises
...and more.

I had no idea what I was doing. I knew I was the

best programmer in the world.

Every 21-year-old programmer knows

that. "How hard can it be,

it's just an operating system?"

—Linus Torvalds

Linus Torvalds

When Linus Torvalds bought his first PC in 1991, he never dreamed it would be a critical weapon in a software liberation war. He just wanted to avoid waiting in line to get a terminal to connect to his university's mainframe.

Torvalds, a 21-year-old student at the University of Helsinki in Finland, had avoided buying a PC because he didn't like the standard PC's "crummy architecture with this crummy MS-DOS operating system." The operating system is the basic set of programs that tells the computer what to do; MS-DOS (Microsoft Disk Operating System) was the operating system on most PCs in 1991. But Torvalds had been studying operating systems, and he decided to try to build something on his own.

He based his work on Minix, a scaled-down textbook version of the powerful UNIX operating system. Little by little he cobbled together pieces of a *kernel,* the part of the system where the real processing and control work is done.

When he mentioned his project on an Internet discussion group, a member offered him space to post it on a university server. Others copied it from the server, tinkered with it, and sent the changes back to Torvalds. The communal work-in-progress became known as Linux (usually pronounced "Linn-uks"). Within a couple of years, it was good enough to release as a product.

Instead of copyrighting and selling Linux, Torvald made it freely available under General Public License (GPL) developed by the Free Software Foundation. According to the GPL, anyone could give away, modify, or even sell Linux, as long as the source code—the program instructions—remain freely available for others to improve. Linux is the best known example of open source software; it spearheads the popular open source software movement.

Thousands of programmers around the world have worked on Linux, writing routines, fixing errors, and making improvements, with Torvalds at the center of the activity. Some do it because they believe there should be alternatives to expensive corporate software products; others do it because they can customize the software to meet their special needs; still others do it just for the fun of it. As a result of all of their efforts, Linux has matured into a powerful, versatile product with millions of satisfied users in business, government, education, and homes.

Linux powers Web servers, film and animation workstations (as used in *Titanic*), desktop PCs, and scientific supercomputers. It's been ported to the tiny Palm Pilot handheld computer. It's even starting to show up in Internet-savvy appliances like refrigerators. Linux is especially popular among people who do heavy-duty computing on a tight budget. And since it can be freely copied, it's widely used in debt-ridden Third World countries.

The success of Linux has inspired Netscape, Apple, Sun, Hewlett-Packard, and other software companies to release products with open source code. Even the mighty

Microsoft is paying attention as this upstart operating system grows in popularity.

Today Torvalds is an Internet folk hero. Web pages pay homage to him, his creation, and the stuffed penguin that has become the Linux mascot. In 1996 he completed his master's degree in computer science and went to work for Transmeta Corp., a chip design company in Silicon Valley. He still spends hours every week on line with the Linux legions, improving the operating system that belongs to everybody—and nobody. ◻

Chapters 2 and 3 told only part of the story of how computers do what they do. Here's a synopsis of our story so far:

On one side we have a person—you, me, or somebody else; it hardly matters. We all have problems to solve—problems involving work, communication, transportation, finances, and more. Many of these problems cry out for computer solutions.

On the other side we have a computer—an incredibly sophisticated bundle of hardware capable of performing all kinds of technological wizardry. Unfortunately, the computer *recognizes only zeros and ones.*

A great chasm separates the person who has a collection of vague problems from the stark, rigidly bounded world of the computer. How can humans bridge the gap to communicate with the computer?

That's where software comes in. Software allows people to communicate certain kinds of problems to computers and makes it possible for computers to communicate solutions back to those people.

Modern computer software didn't just materialize out of the atmosphere; it evolved from the plug boards and patch cords and other hardware devices that were used to program early computers like the Eniac. Mathematician John von Neumann, working with Eniac's creators, J. Presper Eckert and John Mauchly, wrote a 1945 paper suggesting that program instructions could be stored with the data in memory. Every computer created since has been based on the *stored-program concept* described in that paper. That idea established the software industry and liberated programmers from the tyranny of hardware.

Instead of flipping switches and patching wires, today's programmers write *programs*—sets of computer instructions designed to solve problems—and feed them into the computer's memory through input devices such as keyboards and mice. These programs are the computer's software. Because software is stored in memory, a computer can switch from one task to another and then back to the first without a single hardware modification. For instance, the computer that serves as a word processor for writing this book can, at the click of a mouse, turn into an e-mail terminal, a window into the World Wide Web, a reference library, an

The communication gap....

accounting spreadsheet, a drawing table, a video editing workstation, a musical instrument, or a game machine.

What is software, and how can it transform a mass of circuits into an electronic chameleon? This chapter provides some general answers to that question along with details about each of the three major categories of software:

▶ *Compilers and other translator programs*, which allow programmers to create other software

▶ *Software applications*, which serve as productivity tools to help computer users solve problems

▶ *System software*, which coordinates hardware operations and does behind-the-scenes work the computer user seldom sees.

Processing with Programs

Leonardo da Vinci called music "the shaping of the invisible," and his phrase is even more apt as a description of software.

—**Alan Kay, developer of the concept of the personal computer**

Software is invisible and complex. To make the basic concepts clear, we start our exploration of software with a down-to-earth analogy.

Food for Thought

Think of the hardware in a computer system as the kitchen in a short-order restaurant: It's equipped to produce whatever output a customer (user) requests, but it sits idle until an order (command) is placed. Robert, the computerized chef in our imaginary kitchen, serves as the CPU, waiting for requests from the users/customers. When somebody provides an input command—say, an order for a plate of French toast—Robert responds by following the instructions in the appropriate recipe.

As you may have guessed, the recipe is the software. It provides instructions telling the hardware what to do to produce the output desired by the user. If the recipe is correct, clear, and precise, the chef turns the input data—eggs, bread, and other ingredients—into the desired output—French toast. If the instructions are unclear or if the software has **bugs**, or errors, the output may not be what the user wanted.

For example, suppose Robert has this recipe for "Suzanne's French Toast Fantastique."

This seemingly foolproof recipe has several trouble spots. Since step 1 doesn't say otherwise, Robert might include the shells in the "slightly beaten eggs." Step 2 says nothing

---

Suzanne's French Toast Fantastique

1. Combine 2 slightly beaten eggs with 1 teaspoon vanilla extract, ½ teaspoon cinnamon, and ⅔ cup milk.
2. Dip 6 slices of bread in mixture.
3. Fry in small amount of butter until golden brown.
4. Serve bread with maple syrup, sugar, or tart jelly.

Suzanne's French Toast Fantastique: The Recipe

about separating the six slices of bread before dipping them in the batter; Robert would be within the letter of the instruction if he dipped all six at once. Step 3 has at least two potential bugs. Since it doesn't specify *what* to fry in butter, Robert might conclude that the *mixture*, not the bread, should be fried. Even if Robert decides to fry the bread, he may let it overcook waiting for the *butter* to turn golden brown, or he may wait patiently for the top of the toast to brown while the bottom quietly blackens. Robert, like any good computer, just follows instructions.

A Fast, Stupid Machine

The most useful word in any computer language is "oops."

—**David Lubar**, in *It's Not a Bug, It's a Feature*

Our imaginary automated chef may not seem very bright, but he's considerably more intelligent than a typical computer's CPU. Computers are commonly called "smart machines" or "intelligent machines." In truth, a typical computer is incredibly limited, capable of doing only the most basic arithmetic operations (such as $7 + 3$ and $15 - 8$) and a few simple logical comparisons ("Is this number less than that number?" "Are these two values identical?").

Computers *seem* smart because they can perform these arithmetic operations and comparisons quickly and accurately. A typical desktop computer can do thousands of calculations in the time it takes you to pull your pen out of your pocket. A well-crafted program can tell the computer to perform a sequence of simple operations that, when taken as a whole, print a term paper, organize the student records for your school, or simulate a space flight. Amazingly, everything you've ever seen a computer do is the result of a sequence of extremely simple arithmetic and logical operations done very quickly. The challenge for software developers is to devise instructions that put those simple operations together in ways that are useful and appropriate.

Suzanne's recipe for French toast isn't a computer program; it's not written in a language that a computer can understand. But it could be considered an **algorithm**—a set of step-by-step procedures for accomplishing a task. A computer program generally

---

Suzanne's French Toast
Fantastique: The Algorithm ▷

Suzanne's French Toast Fantastique

1. Prepare the batter by following these instructions:
    - **1a.**   Crack 2 eggs so whites and yolks drop in bowl; discard shells.
    - **1b.**   Beat eggs slightly with wire whip, fork, or mixer.
    - **1c.**   Mix in 1 teaspoon vanilla extract, ½ teaspoon cinnamon, and ⅔ cup milk.
2. Place small amount of butter in frying pan and place on medium heat.
3. For each of 6 pieces of bread, follow these steps:
    - **3a.**   Dip slice of bread in mixture.
    - **3b.**   For each of the two sides of the bread do the following steps:
        - **3b1.**   Place the slice of bread in the frying pan with this (uncooked) side down.
        - **3b2.**   Wait 1 minute and then peek at underside of bread; if lighter than golden brown, repeat this step.
    - **3c.**   Remove bread from fry pan and place on plate.
4. Serve bread with maple syrup, sugar, or tart jelly.

starts as an algorithm written in English or some other human language. Like Suzanne's recipe, the initial algorithm is likely to contain generalities, ambiguities, and errors.

The programmer's job is to turn the algorithm into a program by adding details, hammering out rough spots, testing procedures, and correcting errors. For example, if we were turning Suzanne's recipe into a program for our electronic-brained short-order cook, we might start by rewriting it like the recipe shown here.

We've eliminated much of the ambiguity from the original recipe. Ambiguity, while tolerable (and sometimes useful) in conversations between humans, is a source of errors for computers. In its current form the recipe contains far more detail than any human chef would want but not nearly enough for a computer. If we were programming a computer (assuming we had one with input hardware capable of recognizing golden brown French toast and output devices capable of flipping the bread), we'd need to go into excruciating detail, translating every step of the process into a series of absolutely unambiguous instructions that could be interpreted and executed by a machine with a vocabulary smaller than that of a 2-year-old child!

The Language of Computers

The programmer, like the poet, works only slightly removed from
pure thought-stuff. He builds castles in the air,
creating by exertion of the imagination. Yet the program construct,
unlike the poet's words, is real in the sense that **it moves and works**,
producing visible outputs separate from the construct itself.

—**Frederick P. Brooks, Jr., in *The Mythical Man Month***

Every computer processes instructions in a native **machine language**. Machine language uses numeric codes to represent the most basic computer operations—adding numbers, subtracting numbers, comparing numbers, moving numbers, repeating instructions, and so on. Early programmers were forced to write every program in a machine language, tediously translating each instruction into binary code. This process was an invitation to insanity; imagine trying to find a single mistyped character in a page full of zeros and ones! Today most programmers use programming languages such as Visual BASIC, C++, and Java that fall somewhere between natural human languages and precise machine languages. These languages, referred to as **high-level languages**, make it possible for scientists, engineers, and businesspeople to solve problems using familiar terminology and notation rather than cryptic machine instructions. For a computer to understand a program written in one of these languages, it must use a translator program to convert the English-like instructions to the zeros and ones of machine language.

To clarify the translation process, let's go back to the kitchen. Imagine a recipe translator that allows our computer chef to look up phrases like "fry until golden brown." Like a reference book for beginning cooks, this translator fills in all of the details of testing and flipping foods in the frying pan, so Robert understands what to do whenever he encounters "fry until golden brown" in any recipe. As long as our computer cook is equipped with the translator, we don't need to include so many details in each recipe. We can communicate at a higher level. The more sophisticated the translator, the easier the job of the programmer. The most common type of translator program is called a **compiler** because it compiles a complete translation of the program in a high-level computer language before the program is run for the first time. The compiled program can be run again and again; it doesn't need to be recompiled unless instructions need to be changed.

Programming languages have steadily evolved during the last few decades. Each new generation of languages makes the programming process easier by taking on, and hiding from the programmer, more of the detail work. The computer's unrelenting

Executing a Program

Most programs are composed of millions of simple instructions. Here we'll observe the execution of a tiny part of a running program: a series of instructions that performs some arithmetic. The machine instructions are similar to those in actual programs, but the details have been omitted. The computer has already loaded (copied) the program from disk into main memory so that the CPU can see it.

The CPU automatically fetches and executes instructions in sequence—from a series of consecutive memory addresses—unless it's told to "jump" somewhere else. The CPU is about to read the next instruction from memory location 100. This instruction and the ones that follow (in locations 101, 102, and 103) tell the CPU to read a couple of numbers from memory (locations 2000 and 2001), add them, and store the result back into memory (location 2002). Translated into English, the instructions look like this:

(100) Get (read) the number at memory address 2000 (not the number 2000, but the number stored in location 2000) and place it in register A.

(101) Get the number at memory address 2001 and place it in register B.

(102) Add the contents of registers A and B, placing the result in register C.

(103) Write (copy) the number in register C to memory address 2002.

For this example, let's suppose that memory location 2000 contains the number 7 and memory location 2001 contains 9.

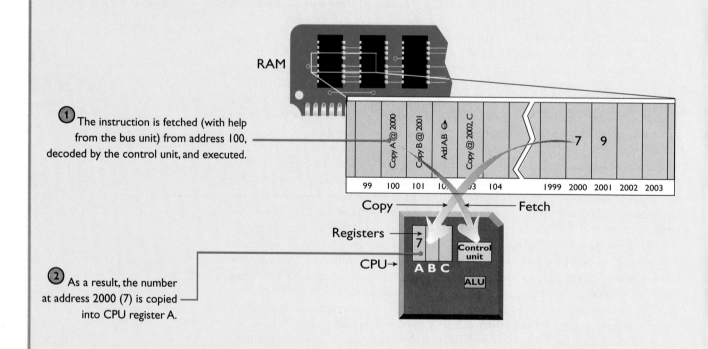

RAM

① The instruction is fetched (with help from the bus unit) from address 100, decoded by the control unit, and executed.

Copy A @ 2000 | Copy B @ 2001 | Add AB → | Copy @ 2002, C

7 | 9

99 100 101 102 103 104 1999 2000 2001 2002 2003

Copy → ← Fetch

Registers

Control unit

CPU → A B C

ALU

② As a result, the number at address 2000 (7) is copied into CPU register A.

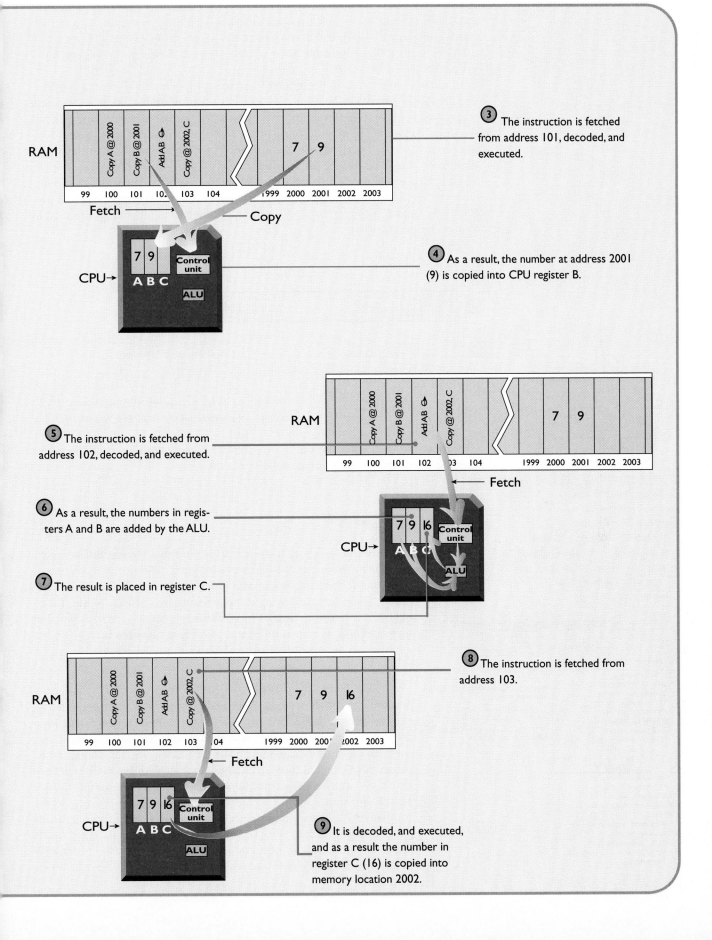

3 The instruction is fetched from address 101, decoded, and executed.

RAM

Fetch ⟶ — Copy

CPU →

4 As a result, the number at address 2001 (9) is copied into CPU register B.

5 The instruction is fetched from address 102, decoded, and executed.

RAM

— Fetch

6 As a result, the numbers in registers A and B are added by the ALU.

CPU →

7 The result is placed in register C.

8 The instruction is fetched from address 103.

RAM

— Fetch

CPU →

9 It is decoded, and executed, and as a result the number in register C (16) is copied into memory location 2002.

demands for technical details haven't gone away; they're just handled automatically by translation software. As a result, programming is easier and less error prone. As translators become more sophisticated, programmers can communicate in computer languages that more closely resemble natural languages—the languages people speak and write every day.

Even with state-of-the-art computer languages, programming requires a considerable investment of time and brain power. (You'll see why when we take a closer look at programming in Chapter 12.) Fortunately, most tasks that required programming two decades ago can now be accomplished with easy-to-use software applications—tools such as word processors, spreadsheets, and graphics programs. Programming languages are still used to solve problems that can't be handled with off-the-shelf software applications, but most computer users manage to do their work without programming. Programming today is done mainly by professional software developers, who use programming languages to create and refine the applications and other programs used by computer users every day.

Software Applications: Tools for Users

The computer is only a fast idiot, it has no imagination;
it cannot originate action. It is, and will remain, only a tool to man.

**—American Library Association reaction to the UNIVAC
computer exhibit at the 1964 New York World's Fair**

Software applications allow users to control computers without thinking like programmers. We now turn our attention to applications.

Most modern computer software provides some kind of on-line help on demand. Microsoft Windows provides context-sensitive help—help windows whose contents depend on what else is currently on the screen.

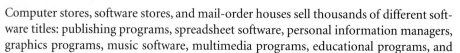

Consumer Applications

Computer stores, software stores, and mail-order houses sell thousands of different software titles: publishing programs, spreadsheet software, personal information managers, graphics programs, music software, multimedia programs, educational programs, and others. The process of buying computer software is similar to the process of buying music software (CDs or cassettes) to play on a stereo system. But there are some important differences; we'll touch on a few here.

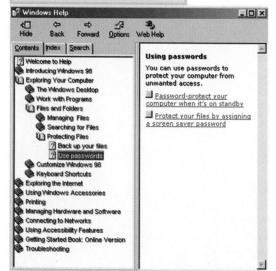

Documentation

A computer software package generally includes printed documentation with instructions for installing the software on a computer's hard disk. Many software packages also include tutorial manuals and reference manuals that explain how to use the software. Some software companies have replaced these printed documents with tutorials, reference materials, and *help files* that appear on-screen at the user's request. Most help files are supplemented and updated with *on-line help* at the company's Web site. Many programs today are so easy to use that it's possible to put them to work without reading the manuals or on-screen documentation. But most programs include advanced features that may not be obvious to users who haven't spent some time reading the documentation.

Upgrading

Most software companies continually work to improve their products by removing bugs and adding new features. As a result, new *versions* of most popular programs are released every year or two. To distinguish between versions, program names are generally followed by version numbers, such as 5.0 in FileMaker 5.0. Most companies use decimals to indicate minor revisions and whole numbers to indicate major revisions. For example, Adobe Premiere 5.1, a video editing program, includes only a few more features than Premiere 5.0, but Premiere 5.0 is significantly different than version 4.0. Not all software follows this logical convention. For example, the last four versions of Microsoft's consumer operating system have been labeled Microsoft Windows 3.1, Windows 95, Windows 98, and Windows Millennium Edition (Windows ME). When you buy a software program, you generally buy the current version. When a new version is released, you can **upgrade** your program to the new version by paying an upgrade fee to the software manufacturer.

Compatibility

A computer software buyer must be concerned with **compatibility**. When you buy a music cassette, you don't need to specify the brand of your cassette player because all manufacturers adhere to common industry standards. But no complete, universal software standards exist in the computer world, so a program written for one type of computer system may not work on another. Software packages contain labels with statements such as "Requires Windows 9x with 32MB of RAM and CD-ROM." (An x in a version specification generally means "substitute any number" so "Windows 9x" means "Windows ninety-*something*.") These demands should not be taken lightly; without compatible hardware and software most software programs are worthless.

Disclaimers

According to the warranties printed on many software packages, the applications might be worthless even if you have compatible hardware and software. Here's the first paragraph from a typical "limited warranty":

> This program is provided "as is" without warranty of any kind. The entire risk as to the result and performance of the program is assumed by you. Should the program prove defective, you—and not the manufacturer or its dealers—assume the entire cost of all necessary servicing, repair, or correction. Further, the manufacturer does not warrant, guarantee, or make any representations regarding the use of, or the result of the use of, the program in terms of correctness, accuracy, reliability, currentness, or otherwise, and you rely on the program and its results solely at your own risk.

Software companies hide behind disclaimers because nobody's figured out how to write error-free software. Remember our problems providing Robert with a foolproof set of instructions for producing French toast? Programmers who write applications such as word processing programs must try to anticipate and respond to all combinations of commands and actions performed by users under any conditions. Given the difficulty of this task, most programs work amazingly well—but not perfectly.

Licensing

When you buy a typical computer software package, you're not actually buying the software. Instead, you're buying a **software license** to use the program on a single machine. While licensing agreements vary from company to company, most include limitations on your right to copy disks, install software on hard drives, and transfer information to other users. Many companies offer *site licenses*—special licenses for

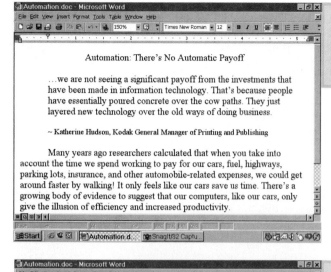

A word processor is based on the metaphor of a typewriter; the screen displays the type-written characters.

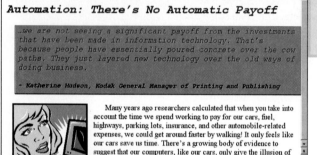

The word processor makes it easy to rearrange and change the appearance of the text—even add a picture—before printing the final document.

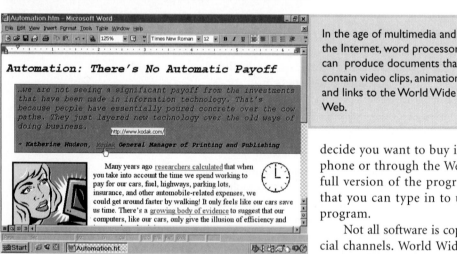

In the age of multimedia and the Internet, word processors can produce documents that contain video clips, animation, and links to the World Wide Web.

entire companies, schools, or government institutions. A few companies now *rent* software to corporate and government clients.

Virtually all commercially marketed software is copyrighted so it can't be *legally* duplicated for distribution to others; some disks (mostly games) are physically copy protected so they can't be copied *at all*. A more common type of copy protection prevents a newly installed program from running until the user types in his or her name and a product serial number. Because programming is so difficult, software development is expensive. Most software developers use copyrights and copy protection to ensure that they sell enough copies of their products to recover their investments and stay in business to write more programs.

Distribution

Software is distributed through direct sales forces to corporations and other institutions. Software is sold to consumers in computer stores, software specialty stores, book and record stores, and other retail outlets. Much software is sold through mail-order catalogs and Web sites. Web distribution makes it possible for some companies to offer software without packaging or disks. For example, you might download (copy) a *demo* version of a commercial program from a company's Web site or some other source; the demo program is identical to the commercial version, but with some key features disabled. After you try the program and decide you want to buy it, you can contact the company (by phone or through the Web site), pay (by credit card) for the full version of the program, and receive (by e-mail) a code that you can type in to unlock the disabled features of the program.

Not all software is copyrighted and sold through commercial channels. World Wide Web sites, user groups, and other sources commonly offer public domain software (free for the taking) and shareware (free for the trying, with a send-payment-if-you-keep-it honor system) along with demonstration versions of commercial programs. Public domain software, shareware, and demo software can be legally copied and shared. The same can't be said of copyrighted commercial software, which is easily the most common type of software in use today.

It may seem strange that anyone would pay several hundred dollars for a product that comes with no warranty and dozens of legal restrictions about how you can use it. In fact, the rapidly growing software industry has spawned dozens of programs that have sold millions of copies. Why do so many people buy and use these hit programs? Of course, the answer varies from person to person and from product to product. But in general most successful software products share two important characteristics:

1 Most *successful software applications are built around visual metaphors of real-world tools.* Word processors and drawing programs turn part of the screen into a sheet of paper; desktop publishing programs make the screen look like a designer's drafting table; spreadsheets resemble an accountant's ledger sheets. But if these programs merely mimicked their real-world counterparts, people would have no compelling reason to use them.

2 Most *popular computer applications are successful because they extend human capabilities in some way, allowing users to do things that can't be done easily, or at all, with conventional tools.* Word processors allow writers to edit and format documents in ways that aren't possible with a typewriter or pencil. An artist using a graphics program can easily add an otherworldly effect to a drawing and just as easily remove it if it doesn't look right. Spreadsheet programs allow managers to project future revenues based on best guesses and then instantly recalculate the bottom line with a different set of assumptions. And programs in all of these categories can now display multimedia material and links to Web sites around the world. Software applications that extend human capabilities are the driving force behind the computer revolution.

Appleworks is an integrated application program that combines several popular applications in an easy-to-use package.

Integrated Applications and Suites: Software Bundles

While most software packages specialize in a particular application such as word processing or photographic editing, low-priced integrated software packages include several applications designed to work well together. Popular integrated packages, such as AppleWorks and Microsoft Works, generally include word processing, database, spreadsheet, graphics, telecommunication, and personal information management (PIM) modules.

The parts of an integrated package may not have all the features of their separately packaged counterparts, but integrated packages still offer advantages. They apply a similar look and feel to all of their applications so users don't need to memorize different commands and techniques for doing different tasks. The best integrated programs blur the lines between applications so, for example, you can create a table full of calculations right in the middle of a typed letter without explicitly switching from a word processor to a spreadsheet. *Interapplication communication* allows quick, easy, and sometimes automatic transfer of data among applications so, for example, changes in a financial spreadsheet are automatically reflected in a graphic table embedded in a word-processed memo.

These advantages aren't unique to integrated packages. Many software companies offer application suites—bundles containing several application programs that are also sold as separate programs. The best selling suite, Microsoft Office, comes in several different versions designed for different types of users. All versions of Microsoft Office include Microsoft Word (a word processor), Excel (a spreadsheet program), PowerPoint (a presentation graphics program), Outlook (a personal information manager), and Internet Explorer (a Web browser). Windows versions of Microsoft Office

StarOffice is a popular freeware office suite from Sun Microsystems. StarOffice is available for many operating systems.

Vertical market software helps this researcher track geographic information.

packages also include Access (a database program) and other programs. Microsoft has designed these applications so they have similar command structures and easy interapplication communication. The price of a suite like Microsoft Office is less than the total price of its applications purchased separately, but more than the cost of an integrated package like Microsoft Works. Suites have more features than integrated programs but also make greater demands on system memory, disk storage, and the CPU. Many older computers simply aren't powerful enough to run a modern application suite. Still, Microsoft Office is the most widely used application package on newer PCs and Macintoshes.

Vertical-Market and Custom Software

Because of their flexibility, word processors, spreadsheets, databases, and graphics programs are used in homes, schools, government offices, and all kinds of businesses. But many computer applications are so job specific that they're of little interest or use to anybody outside a given profession. Medical billing software, library cataloging software, legal reference software, restaurant management software, and other applications designed specifically for a particular business or industry are called vertical-market or custom applications.

Vertical-market applications tend to cost far more than mass-market applications because companies that develop the software have very few potential customers through which to recover their development costs. In fact, some custom applications are programmed specifically for single clients. For example, the software used to control the space shuttle was developed with a single customer—NASA—in mind.

System Software: The Hardware–Software Connection

Originally, operating systems were envisioned as a way to handle one of the most complex input/output operations: communicating with a variety of disk drives. But, the operating system quickly evolved into an all-encompassing bridge between your PC and the software you run on it.

—Ron White, in *How Computers Work*

When you're typing a paper or writing a program, you don't need to concern yourself with the parts of the computer's memory that hold your document, the segments of the word processing software currently in the computer's memory, or the output instructions sent by the computer to the printer. These details, and hundreds of others, are handled behind the scenes by system software, a class of software that includes the *operating system* and *utility programs*.

What the Operating System Does

Virtually every general-purpose computer today, whether a timesharing supercomputer or laptop PC, depends on an operating system (OS) to keep hardware running efficiently and to make the process of communication with that hardware easier. Operating system software runs continuously whenever the computer is on, even when users are working with software applications. The operating system provides an additional layer of insulation between the user and the bits-and-bytes world of computer hardware. Because the operating system stands between the software application and the hardware, application compatibility is often defined by the operating system as well as the hardware.

The operating system, as the name implies, is a system of programs that performs a variety of technical operations, from basic communication with peripherals to complex networking and security tasks.

Communicating with Peripherals

Some of the most complex tasks performed by a computer involve communicating with screens, printers, disk drives, and other peripheral devices. A computer's operating system includes programs that transparently communicate with peripherals.

The user's view: When a person uses an application, whether a game or an accounting program, the person doesn't communicate directly with the computer hardware. Instead, the user interacts with the application, which depends on the operating system to manage and control hardware.

Coordinating Concurrent Processing of Jobs

Large, multiuser computers often work on several jobs at the same time—a technique known as concurrent processing. State-of-the-art parallel processing machines use multiple CPUs to process jobs simultaneously. But a typical computer has only one CPU, so it must work on several projects by rapidly switching back and forth between projects. The computer takes advantage of idle time in one process (for example, waiting for input) by working on another program. (Our computerized chef, Robert, might practice concurrent processing by slicing fruit while he waits for the toast to brown.) A timesharing computer practices **concurrent processing** whenever multiple users are connected to the system. The computer quickly moves from terminal to terminal, checking for input and processing each user's data in turn. If a PC has **multitasking** capabilities, the user can issue a command that initiates a process (for example, to print this chapter) and continue working with other applications while the computer executes the command.

Memory Management

When several jobs are being processed concurrently, the operating system must keep track of how the computer's memory is being used and make sure that no job encroaches on another's territory.

Memory management is accomplished in a variety of ways, from simple schemes that subdivide the available memory between jobs to elaborate schemes that temporarily swap information between the computer's memory and external storage devices. One common technique for dealing with memory shortages is to set aside part of a hard disk as **virtual memory**. Thanks to the operating system, this chunk of disk space looks just like internal memory to the CPU, even though access time is slower.

Resource Monitoring, Accounting, and Security

Many multiuser computer systems are designed to charge users for the resources they consume. These systems keep track of each user's time, storage demands, and pages printed so accounting programs can calculate and print accurate bills. Each user generally has a unique identification name and password, so the system can track and bill for individual resource usage. Even in environments where billing isn't an issue, the operating system should monitor resources to ensure the privacy and security of each user's data.

Program and Data Management

In addition to serving as a traffic cop, a security guard, and an accountant, the operating system acts as a librarian, locating and accessing files and programs requested by the user and by other programs.

How It Works 4.2

The Operating System

Most of what you see on screen when you use an application program and most of the common tasks you have the program perform such as saving and opening files are being performed by the operating system at the application's request.

When a computer is turned off, there's nothing in RAM, and the CPU isn't doing anything. The operating system (OS) programs must be in memory and running on the CPU before the system can function. When you turn on the computer, the CPU automatically begins executing instructions stored in ROM. These instructions help the system boot, and the operating system is loaded from disk into part of the system's memory.

Using the mouse, you "ask" the operating system to load a word processing application program into memory so it can run.

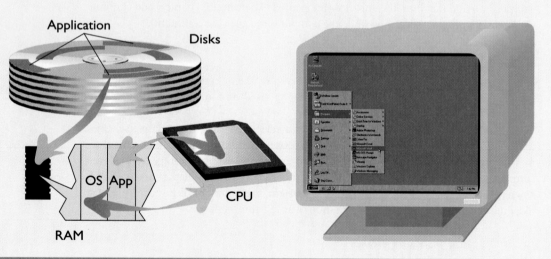

Coordinating Network Communications

Until recently, network communications weren't handled by the typical operating system; they were coordinated by specialized network operating systems. But many modern operating systems are designed to serve as gateways to networks, from the inner office to the Internet. These network communication functions are described in detail in later chapters.

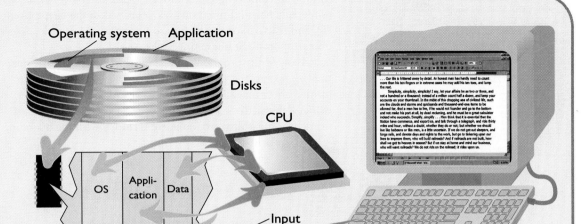

The loaded application occupies a portion of memory, leaving that much less for other programs and data. The OS remains in memory so it can provide services to the application program, helping it to display on-screen menus, communicate with the printer, and perform other common actions. Because the OS and application are in constant communication, control—the location in memory where the CPU is reading program instructions—jumps all around. If the application calls the OS to help display a menu, the application tells the CPU, "Go follow the menu display instructions at address x in the operating system area; when you're done, return here and pick up where you left off."

To avoid losing your data file when the system is turned off, you save it to the disk—write it into a file on the disk for later use. The OS handles communication between the CPU and the disk drive, ensuring that your file doesn't overwrite other information. (Later, when you reopen the file, the OS locates it on the disk and copies it into memory so the CPU—and therefore any program—can see it and work with it.)

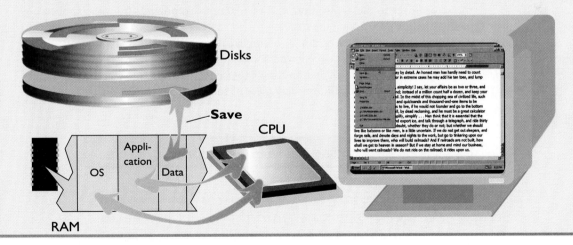

Utility Programs

Even the best operating systems leave some housekeeping tasks to other programs and to the user. Utility programs serve as tools for doing system maintenance and repairs that aren't automatically handled by the operating system. Utilities make it easier for users to copy files between storage devices, to repair damaged data files, to translate files

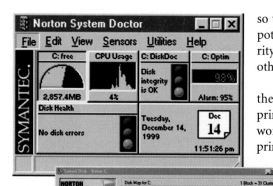

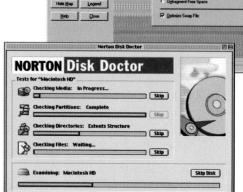

Norton Utilities (from Symantec) is a popular utility package that includes software tools for recovering damaged files, repairing damaged disks, and improving disk performance. (Screens from the Windows and Macintosh versions are shown here.)

so that different programs can read them, to guard against viruses and other potentially harmful programs (as described in the chapter on computer security and risks), to compress files so they take up less disk space, and to perform other important, if unexciting, tasks.

Many utility programs can be invoked directly by the operating system, so they appear to the user to be part of the operating system. For example, a printer driver that allows a computer to communicate with a particular printer works behind the scenes whenever the user requests that a document be printed. Some utility programs are included with the operating system; others are sold as separate products.

Where the Operating System Lives

Some computers—mostly game machines and special-purpose computers—store their operating systems permanently in ROM (read-only memory) so they can begin working immediately at start-up time. But since ROM is unchangeable, these machines can't have their operating systems modified or upgraded without hardware transplants. Most computers include only part of the operating system in ROM—the remainder of the operating system is loaded into memory in a process called **booting**, which occurs when you turn on the computer. (The term *booting* is used because the computer seems to pull itself up by its own bootstraps.)

Most of the time the operating system works behind the scenes, taking care of business without the knowledge or intervention of the user. But occasionally it's necessary for a user to communicate directly with the operating system. For example, when you boot a personal computer, the operating system takes over the screen, waiting until you tell it—with the mouse, the keyboard, or some other input device—what to do. If you tell it to open a graphics application, the operating system locates the program, copies it from disk into memory, turns the screen over to the application, and then accepts commands from the application while you draw pictures on the screen.

Interacting with the operating system, like interacting with an application, can be intuitive or challenging. It depends on something called the *user interface*. Because of its profound impact on the computing experience, the user interface is a critically important component of almost every piece of software.

◻ The User Interface: The Human–Machine Connection

> The anthropologist Claude Levi-Strauss has called human beings
> ## tool makers and symbol makers. The user interface is
> potentially the most sophisticated of these constructions, one in which the
> ## distinction between tool and symbol is blurred.
>
> —**Aaron Marcus and Andries van Dam**, **user interface experts**

Early computer users had to spend tedious hours writing and debugging machine-language instructions. Later users programmed in languages that were easier to understand but still technically challenging. Today users spend much of their time working with preprogrammed applications like word processors that simulate and amplify the capabilities of real-world tools. As software evolves, so does the user interface—the look and feel of the computing experience from a human point of view.

Probably the easiest way to understand the importance of user interfaces is to see how we might accomplish a simple task using different user interfaces. We'll look at the user interface of three widely used operating systems for desktop computers:

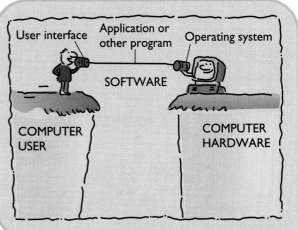

The user's view revisited: The user interface is the part of the computer system that the user sees. A well-designed user interface hides the bothersome details of computing from the user.

▶ MS-DOS—the operating system that's standard equipment in millions of older *IBM-compatible computers* (computers that are functionally identical to an IBM personal computer and therefore capable of running IBM-compatible software)

▶ Apple's Macintosh—the most popular alternative to IBM-compatible computers

▶ Microsoft Windows—software that provides a graphical user interface for newer IBM-compatible computers.

In all three examples we'll use the word processing application Corel® WordPerfect® (from the Corel WordPerfect Suite) to print a term paper we created in an earlier session. This term paper, stored as a file on the hard disk, is a Corel WordPerfect document. In general, a **document** is a file created with an application. For each example we'll perform a series of steps:

1 Locate either the WordPerfect application or the document on the hard disk.

2 **Open** (or *load*) the application (copy it from disk into memory so we can use it), and open the document.

3 Print the document.

4 Close the application.

5 Delete the document file from the hard disk.

Before we begin, a reminder and a disclaimer:

The reminder: The User's View examples are designed to give you a *feel* for the software, not to provide how-to instructions. If you want to learn how to use the software, refer to your lab manuals or to other books on the subject, some of which are listed in "Sources and Resources" at the ends of chapters in this book.

The disclaimer: This comparison is intended to compare different types of interfaces—not to establish a favorite. The brand of software in a particular *User's View* box isn't as important as the general concepts built into that software. One of the best things about computers is that they offer lots of different ways to do things. These examples, and others throughout the book, are designed to expose you to some of those possibilities.

Character-Based User Interfaces: MS-DOS

MS-DOS (Microsoft Disk Operating System, sometimes called just DOS) is the most widely used general-purpose operating system in the world. When IBM chose DOS as the operating system for its first personal computer in 1981, almost all computer displays were defined in terms of characters. A typical computer monitor displayed twenty-four 80-column lines of text, numbers, and/or symbols. The computer sent messages to the monitor telling it which character to display in each location on the screen. To comply with this hardware arrangement, MS-DOS was designed with a **character-based interface**—a user interface based on characters rather than graphics.

When communicating with MS-DOS (to start up an application, for example), the user carries on a dialog through the MS-DOS **command-line interface**. With a command-line interface the user types commands, and the computer responds. Some MS-DOS-compatible applications have a command-line interface, but it's more common for applications to have a **menu-driven interface** that allows users to

The User's View

Using Character-Based Interfaces

SOFTWARE **MS-DOS and Corel® WordPerfect®.**

THE GOAL **To open a term paper created with a word processor, print it, and delete it from the hard disk. (The other goal: to experience command-line and menu-driven character-based interfaces.)**

(1) When you turn on the computer, the MS-DOS operating system displays a prompt (C:\) and a flashing cursor and waits for you to type a command. You type dir /w to see a list of items in drive C's directory.

(2) MS-DOS displays a list of items on the hard disk, including files and subdirectories—collections of files that have been grouped together—followed by another C:\ prompt saying the operating system is waiting for another command.

(3) To open the paper you must first open the application program that created it: Corel WordPerfect. The application is stored in the subdirectory wp61, so you type cd wp61 to change to that directory.

(4) You type wp and then press Enter to open Corel WordPerfect.

```
C:\>dir /w

Volume in drive C is WIN95
Volume Serial Number is 6207-9FC6
Directory of C:\

COMMAND.COM    [CIRRUS]      WIN386.SWP     [EXCHANGE]     [PQMAGIC]
[PROGRAMF]     [TEMP]        [WINDOWS]      AUTOEXEC.BAT   CONFIG.SYS
[CDD]          [WP61]        WINZIP.LOG     [INTERNET]     [UTILS]
[PERSONAL]     [PROJECT]     [WPDOCS]
      5 file(s)          93,648 bytes
     13 dir(s)       32,391,168 bytes free

C:\>cd wp61
C:\WP61>wp
```

(5) Corel WordPerfect lets you choose commands from menus hidden in a menu bar at the top of the screen. The words in the menu bar—File, Edit, and the rest—are the names of the menus. You can use the mouse or keyboard to show menu choices and select commands.

(6) You select the Open command from the File menu and choose the file called privacy.wp6.

(8) You select the Print command to print the term paper.

(9) You select the Exit command to close the word processing application and return to the MS-DOS prompt.

(7) The file is loaded from disk into the computer's memory, and the first part of the term paper appears on the screen.

(11) The operating system doesn't recognize the command, so it responds with "Bad command or file-name"—an error message telling you you've done something wrong.

(10) To delete the file you just printed, you enter the command DEL followed by the file name. You accidentally mistype a character.

(12) You type the command correctly; the file is deleted.

```
C:\WP61>de c:\wp61\files\privacy.wp6
Bad command or file name

C:\WP61>del c:\wp61\files\privacy.wp6

C:\WP61>
```

choose commands from on-screen lists called **menus.** *The User's View* box on page 100 illustrates two different character-based interfaces: the command-line interface of MS-DOS and the menu-driven interface of Corel WordPerfect, a popular word processing application. **UV**

Graphical User Interface Operating Systems: Macintosh and Windows

In the years since the introduction of the IBM-PC, hardware advances have made it possible for low-cost computers to include graphic displays. A computer with a graphic display is not limited to displaying rows and columns of characters; it can individually control every dot on the screen. When the Apple Macintosh was introduced in 1984, it was the first low-cost computer whose operating system was designed with a graphic display in mind. The Macintosh operating system (Mac OS) sports a graphical user interface—abbreviated GUI, pronounced "gooey."

Instead of reading typed commands and file names from a command line, the Macintosh operating system determines what the user wants by monitoring movements of the mouse. With the mouse the user points to icons (pictures) that represent files, **folders** (collections of files), and disks. Documents are displayed in windows—framed areas that can be opened, closed, and rearranged with the mouse. The user selects commands from **pull-down menus** at the top of the screen. *The User's View* box on pages 102 and 103 shows a simple Macintosh session. **UV**

The difference between the Macintosh and MS-DOS sessions has less to do with hardware than software. Ironically, the Macintosh has been overshadowed in the GUI operating system market by a product from Microsoft, the company that produces MS-DOS. Originally, Microsoft Windows (commonly called *Windows*, or just *Win*) was a type of program, known as a shell, that put a graphical face on MS-DOS. The Windows shell stood between the user and the operating system, translating mouse movements and other user input into commands that could be recognized by MS-DOS. Windows 3.1 and its predecessors don't completely hide their command-line MS-DOS roots, but they do shield users from most of the details of DOS. With the introduction of Windows 95 in 1995, Microsoft completed the transition of Windows from an operating system shell into an operating system that seldom shows its MS-DOS roots. Windows today is similar in many ways to the Mac OS. Compare the Windows 98 session shown in *The User's View* box on pages 104 and 105 with the earlier MS-DOS and Macintosh sessions. **UV**

Why WIMP Won

> The first principle of human interface design, whether for a doorknob or a computer,
>
> is to keep in mind the human being who wants to use it.
>
> ## The technology is subservient to that goal.
>
> —Donald Norman, in *The Art of Human-Computer Interface Design*

In the three *User's View* examples on the following pages, we did the same job with different versions of the same application and produced the same output. In the case of MS-DOS and Windows we even used the same hardware platform. But from the user's point of view the Macintosh and Windows sessions have more in common, even though they involve different hardware. The critical difference between these sessions and the DOS session is in the user interfaces. This is more than just a difference between working with pictures and working with words. Graphical user interfaces with *w*indows, *i*cons, *m*enus, and *p*ointing devices (collectively known as *WIMP*) offer several clear advantages from the user's point of view:

The User's View

Using a Macintosh GUI

SOFTWARE Macintosh OS 9 and Corel® WordPerfect® (part of the Corel® WordPerfect® Suite).

THE GOAL To print and delete a term paper file, this time with a graphical user interface—a GUI.

① When you turn on the Macintosh, you see a visual representation of a desktop with a menu bar at the top.

② An open window shows the contents of the hard disk called Macintosh HD.

③ Icons in the window represent folders containing other files.

④ The term paper document is in a folder called School Work. You move the mouse so that the pointer points to the School Work icon and click the mouse button. It darkens to indicate that it has been selected.

⑤ When you hold the mouse button down while pointing to the File menu, a pull-down menu appears like a window shade. To open the selected folder, you drag the mouse down until the pointer points to the Open command and release the button to choose that command.

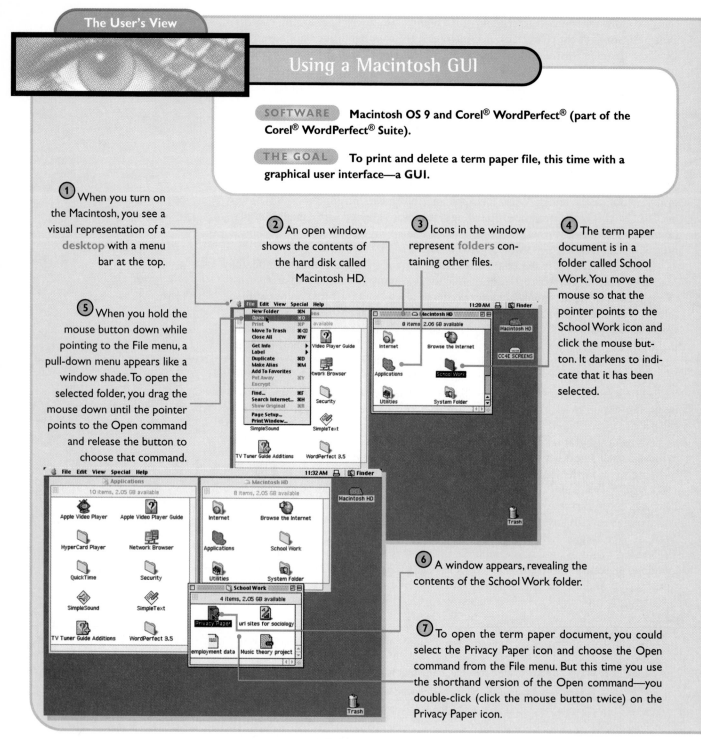

⑥ A window appears, revealing the contents of the School Work folder.

⑦ To open the term paper document, you could select the Privacy Paper icon and choose the Open command from the File menu. But this time you use the shorthand version of the Open command—you double-click (click the mouse button twice) on the Privacy Paper icon.

▶ *They're intuitive.* Visual metaphors like trash cans and folders are easier for people to understand and learn than typed commands. Users feel safe learning by trial and error because it's usually easy to predict the results of each action.

▶ *They're consistent.* GUI applications have the same user interface as their operating systems, so users don't need to learn new ways of doing things whenever they switch applications. Many Macintosh and Windows users have mastered dozens of applications without ever consulting a manual.

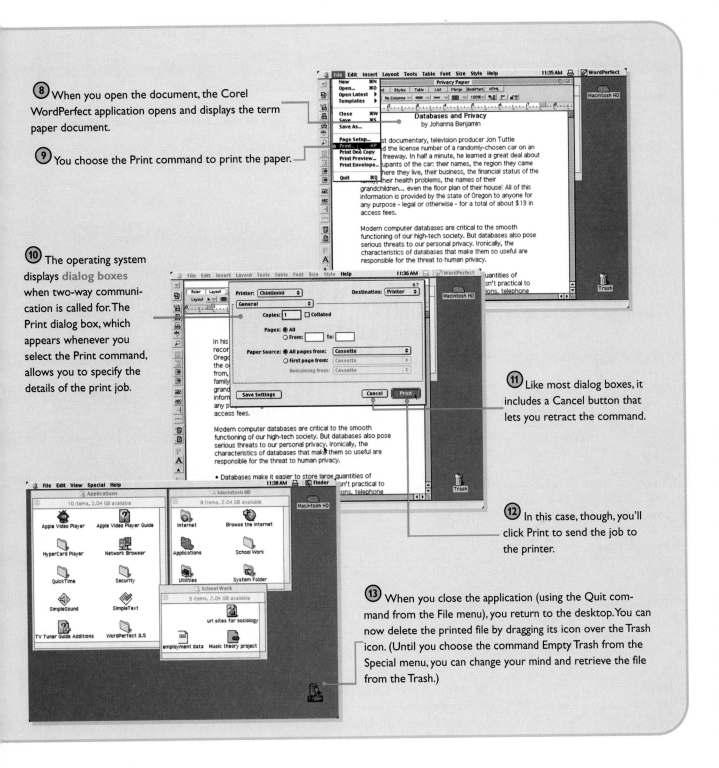

8 When you open the document, the Corel WordPerfect application opens and displays the term paper document.

9 You choose the Print command to print the paper.

10 The operating system displays dialog boxes when two-way communication is called for. The Print dialog box, which appears whenever you select the Print command, allows you to specify the details of the print job.

11 Like most dialog boxes, it includes a Cancel button that lets you retract the command.

12 In this case, though, you'll click Print to send the job to the printer.

13 When you close the application (using the Quit command from the File menu), you return to the desktop. You can now delete the printed file by dragging its icon over the Trash icon. (Until you choose the command Empty Trash from the Special menu, you can change your mind and retrieve the file from the Trash.)

▶ *They're forgiving.* Almost every dialog box includes a Cancel button, allowing the user to say, in effect, "Never mind." The Undo command can almost always take back the last command, restoring everything the way it was before the current command was issued.

▶ *They're protective.* When you're about to do something that may have unpleasant consequences (such as replacing the revised version of your term paper with an older version), the software opens a dialog box, reminding you to make sure you're doing what you want before you proceed.

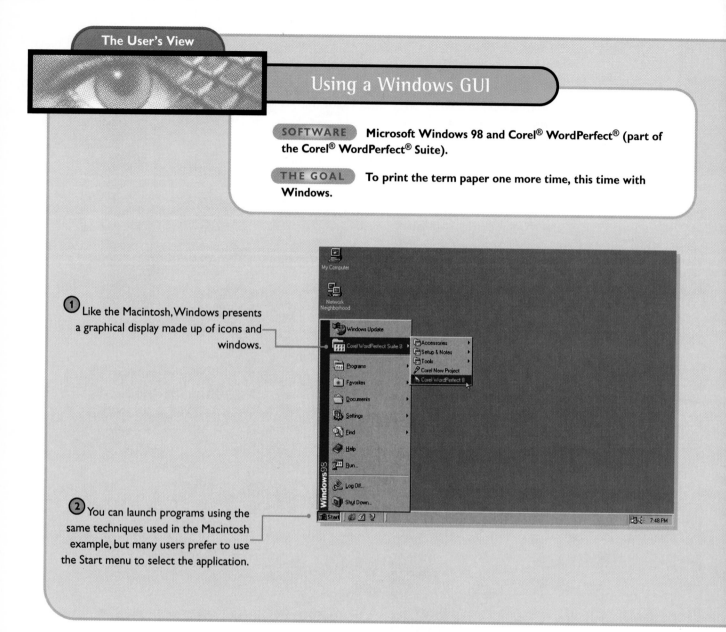

The User's View

Using a Windows GUI

SOFTWARE   Microsoft Windows 98 and Corel® WordPerfect® (part of the Corel® WordPerfect® Suite).

THE GOAL   To print the term paper one more time, this time with Windows.

1. Like the Macintosh, Windows presents a graphical display made up of icons and windows.

2. You can launch programs using the same techniques used in the Macintosh example, but many users prefer to use the Start menu to select the application.

▶ *They're flexible.* Users who prefer to keep their hands on the keyboard can use keyboard shortcuts instead of mouse movements to invoke most commands. Most actions can be accomplished in several different ways; each user can, in effect, customize the user interface.

Of course, all of this user-friendliness doesn't come free. Graphical user interfaces and friendly operating systems require more expensive graphics display systems, more memory, more disk space, faster processors, and more complex software. Character-based operating systems have minimal hardware requirements when compared with just about any GUI operating system or shell. But steadily falling hardware prices have made even the least expensive PCs powerful enough to handle GUIs.

Character-based interfaces aren't dead. They're still common in VCRs, cell phones, microwave ovens, stereos, and other consumer devices with limited memory and limited options for users. They're also widely used in applications built on older computer

③ After Corel WordPerfect opens, you can use the Open command in the File menu to locate and open the document. In Windows the menu bar is inside the window rather than across the top of the screen. When you point to File in the menu bar and press the mouse button, the menu appears. You move the pointer down the menu to the Open command and click to choose that command.

④ Once the document is open, the process of printing is almost identical to the Macintosh printing process.

⑤ After the document is printed, you quit Corel WordPerfect with the Exit command and return to the desktop. To delete the term paper file, you drag its icon to the recycle bin—the Windows equivalent to the Macintosh trash can. (In older Windows versions you need to launch the File Manager program, locate the file in the graphical directory, select it, and choose the Delete command.)

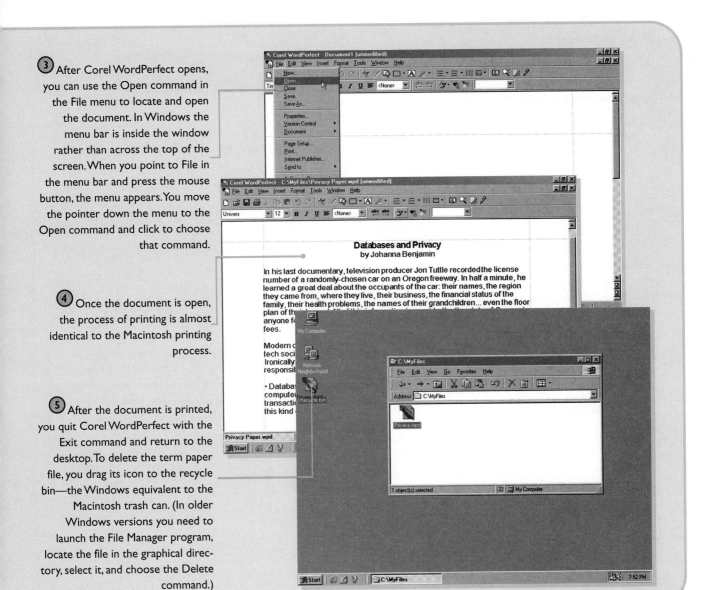

Many consumer devices today, including VCRs, cell phones, and pagers, use character-based user interfaces.

systems and in applications that involve transmitting data through networks. In fact, the explosive growth of the Internet has fueled growth in popularity of several versions of UNIX, a character-based OS that is older than any of the three we've looked at so far.

Multiple User Operating Systems: UNIX and Linux

Because of its historical ties to academic and government research sites, the Internet is heavily populated with computers running the UNIX operating system. UNIX, developed at Bell Labs in the time before PCs, allows a timesharing computer to communicate with several other computers or terminals at once. UNIX has long been the operating system of choice for workstations and mainframes in research and academic

The User's View

Connecting to a Multiuser UNIX System

SOFTWARE UNIX operating system.

THE GOAL To log into your school's UNIX mainframe from a terminal.

(1) When you press Return UNIX displays a system message to indicate that it's waiting for you to log in, that is, to provide an ID and password.

(2) You type your login name—the one-word name assigned to your computer account (in this example sanchez) and press Enter or Return.

(4) After you press Return, UNIX displays a system message to indicate that you've successfully logged in.

(3) The program then prompts you to enter your password so the host computer can verify your identity. When you type your password, it isn't echoed on the screen.

```
UNIX(r) System V Release 4.0

login: sanchez
Password:
AFS (R) 3.4 Login

==============================================================
=Welcome to node ai.asu.edu - Sparc 20 1000 running Solaris 2.3=
      =This system is only for use authorized by ASU=
==============================================================

You have mail.
Terminal type is vt100
Erase is Backspace
type 'menu' without quotes and press the enter key for our menu

ai > ls
AppleVolumes      Mail            dead.letter
Backup            Work            mbox
School            Reports         News
booklist          saved.notes     readme
ai > pine
```

(5) This UNIX system assumes you're using a VT-100 terminal (or at least a terminal that can emulate, or imitate, a VT-100)—the default type. When you press return without typing anything else, you're saying that the VT-100 default settings will work with your terminal.

(6) On this particular UNIX system you can launch a menu program that allows you to access common commands through menus. But you'll stick with the command-line interface for this example.

(7) This UNIX system responds to commands typed after the ai prompt.

(8) You type LS to list the files in your current directory.

settings. In recent years it has taken root in many business environments. In spite of competition from Microsoft, UNIX is still the most widely available multiuser operating system today. Some form of UNIX is available for personal computers, workstations, servers, mainframes, and supercomputers.

Unlike the other operating systems listed here, UNIX isn't owned and controlled by a single company. Many commercial brands of UNIX are available, including Sun's Solaris, Hewlett Packard's HP-UX, and IBM's AIX. Linux, described at the beginning of this chapter, is widely distributed for free and supported without cost by a devoted, technically savvy group of users.

At its heart, in all its versions, UNIX is a command-line, character-based operating system. The command-line interface is similar to that of MS-DOS, although the commands aren't the same. For most tasks the UNIX command-line interface feels like a single-user system, even when many users are *logged in,* that is, connected to and using the system. Until recently, some knowledge of UNIX commands was necessary for taking advantage of most Internet services. The character-based UNIX interface is still widely used on Internet hosts. *The User's View* box on page 106 shows how you might use a command-line interface to connect to a multiuser mainframe UNIX system from a terminal.   **UV**

Today's UNIX systems don't just work with typed commands. Several companies, including Sun and IBM, market UNIX variations and shells with graphical interfaces. *The User's View* box on the next page shows a short Linux session with a GUI shell that looks like a cross between Microsoft Windows and the Macintosh OS. Once again we'll use Corel® WordPerfect®, a word processor that is available in versions for most popular operating systems.   **UV**

Hardware and Software Platforms

In most electronic devices the operating system operates invisibly and anonymously. But some operating systems, especially those in PCs, are recognized by name and reputation. The most well-known operating system platforms include:

▶ *Microsoft Windows Millennium Edition, or Windows ME* is Microsoft's current "consumer" operating system. Previous versions of this OS include Windows 98, Windows 95, and Windows 3.1; all three are still widely used. The current version of this line is installed in the overwhelming majority of PCs sold today.

▶ *Microsoft Windows 2000* (formerly *Windows NT*) is a variant of the Windows operating system aimed at networked computers that need features not found in the consumer version of Windows. Windows 2000's multitasking capabilities and security controls make it a popular operating system for *servers*—computer systems that serve data and programs to networked PCs. (One version of Windows 2000 is designed specifically for servers.) In spite of its stiff hardware requirements Win 2000 is replacing other versions of Windows on many corporate desktops.

▶ Microsoft *Windows CE* occupies the opposite end of the spectrum from Windows 2000. This stripped-down Windows variant is designed mostly for handheld computers. Other versions of Win CE have been embedded into car accessories, televisions, and other electronic devices. Several other companies make operating systems for consumer devices and PDAs. But unlike Windows CE, most of these are designed

Compatibility issues: Hardware platforms and software environments. Most personal computers today are built on what's sometimes called the Wintel platform: Some form of the Windows OS running on an Intel (or compatible) CPU. The Macintosh platform—Mac OS software running on PowerPC processors—makes up a much smaller segment of the market. The Linux OS can run on many hardware platforms, including Intel and PowerPC processors, but different versions of Linux aren't necessarily compatible. Other hardware and software platforms represent smaller shares of the market.

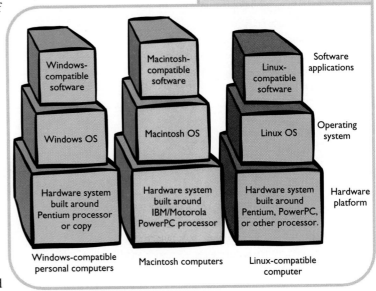

The User's View

Using a Linux GUI

SOFTWARE   **KDE Linux and Corel® WordPerfect® (part of the Corel® WordPerfect® Suite).**

THE GOAL   **To open and print that term paper again, this time with KDE Linux, one of many popular brands of the operating system. You'll start with a Linux GUI and then, for the sake of comparison, repeat part of the process with a command-line interface.**

① KDE Linux has a customizable graphical user interface; here it's configured with familiar features of Windows and the Macintosh OS. You select WordPerfect from the personal pop-up menu that resembles the Windows Start menu.

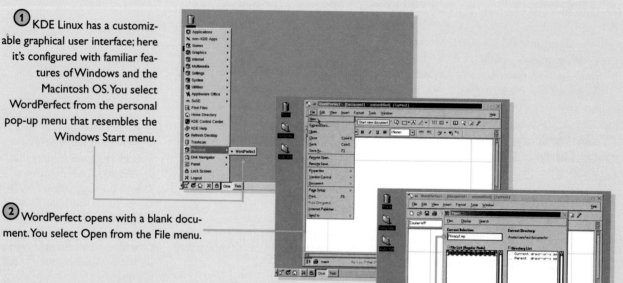

② WordPerfect opens with a blank document. You select Open from the File menu.

③ You select the Privacy1 document in the dialog box.

④ When the document opens, you select Print from the File menu, respond to the dialog box, close WordPerfect, and wait for your printout. You'd be done now, except . . .

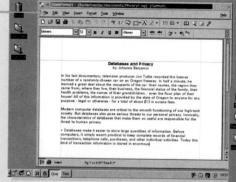

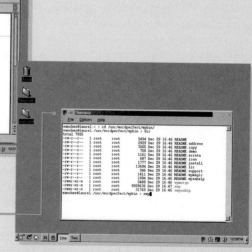

⑤ You decide to test your Linux literacy by launching the program again, but this time using the operating system's command-line interface. You use a terminal program to connect to a server called Laurel; you type commands to locate the directory and launch WordPerfect.

to work on specific devices rather than whole classes of devices. In response to sluggish sales of CE devices, Microsoft recently released a simpler version to be used in devices called Pocket PCs.

▶ 3-Com's *Palm OS* is probably the main reason for Win CE's lack of consumer acceptance. This OS, originally developed for the Palm Pilot, is now used in handheld devices manufactured by many companies, including Sony, IBM, and Handspring. Its pen-based user interface is intuitive and convenient to use. The Palm OS has communication capabilities that make it easy to transfer data between a handheld device and a desktop PC or Mac.

▶ Mac *OS 9* is the latest in a long line of Apple-developed operating systems for the Mac. OS 9 and its predecessors run only on Macs.

▶ Mac *OS X* is a completely new operating system for the Mac. Like Windows 2000, OS X was originally developed for servers and other high-powered computers. On the surface OS X sports a stylish, animated user interface that looks strikingly different than OS 9. Underneath its friendly exterior OS X is built on UNIX, the powerful OS known for security and stability rather than simplicity.

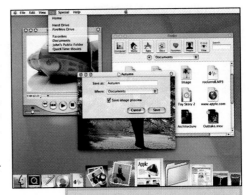

Apple's OS X is, at its core, a variation of UNIX, an OS that's been around for decades. But the OS X user interface has a strikingly modern look.

▶ *Linux, Sun's Solaris,* and other UNIX variations can be found on PCs, Macs, workstations, supercomputers, mainframes, and a variety of other devices. Linux is especially popular because it is free—and freely supported by its partisans. Since Linux doesn't offer as many applications programs as Windows, some people use *dual-boot PCs* that can switch back and forth between Windows and Linux by simply rebooting.

▶ IBM's *OS/2* can run most applications developed for both DOS and Windows. Originally designed in partnership with Microsoft, OS/2 has been losing market share since IBM took over sole control of the product. OS/2 is now only being updated for existing corporate customers and is no longer in active development. In the operating system wars, even Big Blue has trouble competing with the marketing power of Microsoft.

▶ *BeOS* is a relatively new operating system designed with multimedia and high-speed telecommunications in mind. Even though it offers technical advantages over older operating systems, its popularity is (so far) limited by a shortage of useful applications.

Operating systems by themselves aren't very helpful to people. They need application software so they can do useful work. But application software can't exist by itself; it needs to be built on some kind of platform. People often use the term **platform** to describe the combination of hardware and operating system software on which application software is built.

The trends are unmistakable. In the early days of the personal computer revolution there were dozens of different platforms—machines from Apple, Commodore, Tandy, Texas Instruments, Atari, Coleco, and other companies. All of these products have vanished from the marketplace, sometimes taking their parent companies with them. Today's market for new PC hardware and software is dominated by three general platforms: Windows in all its variations, the Mac OS, and various versions of UNIX. UNIX isn't often found in desktop PCs; it's mostly used in servers and high-end workstations. While the Mac commands a hefty share of specialized markets like graphic design, publishing, music, multimedia, and education, it runs far behind Windows in the massive corporate desktop market.

Emulation software allows software written for one computer platform to be used on another. For example, this Macintosh can run Macintosh and Windows programs simultaneously—and transfer data back and forth between them—using virtual PC from Connectrix.

To compete in a Windows-dominated world, Apple works with other companies to offer emulation options to make Windows and DOS software run on Macintoshes. One technique involves *software emulation*; a software program creates a *simulated* Windows machine in the Mac, translating all Windows-related instructions into signals the Mac's operating system and

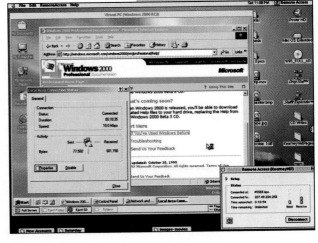

Rules of Thumb

Computer Consumer Concepts

The best computer for your specific needs is the one that will come on the market immediately after you actually purchase some other model.

—**Dave Barry**, humorist

This book's appendix, CD-ROM, and Internet Web site contain specific information about the nuts and bolts of buying hardware and software to make your own computer system. Of course, any brand-specific advice on choosing computer equipment is likely to be outdated within a few months of publication. Still, some general principles remain constant while the technology races forward. Here are nine consumer criteria worth considering, even if you have no intention of buying your own computer.

▶ *Cost.* Buy what you can afford, but be sure to allow for extra memory, extended warranties, peripherals (printer, extra storage devices, modem, cables, speakers, and so on), and software. If you join a user group or connect to an on-line shareware site, you'll be able to meet some of your software needs at low (or no) cost. But you'll almost certainly need some commercial software, too. Don't be tempted to copy copyrighted software from your friends or public labs; software piracy is theft, prosecutable under

federal laws. (Choosing software isn't easy, but many of the periodicals listed at the end of Chapter 1 publish regular reviews to help you sort out the best programs.)

▶ *Capability.* Is it the right tool for the job? Buy a computer that's powerful enough to meet your needs. Make sure the processor is fast enough to handle your demands. If you want to take advantage of state-of-the-art multimedia programs, consider only machines that meet the latest standards. If you want to create state-of-the-art multimedia programs, you'll need a powerful computer that can handle audio and video input as well as output—IEEE 1394 (FireWire) if you'll be using a digital video camera. Be sure the machine you buy can do the job you need it to do, now and in the foreseeable future.

▶ *Capacity.* If you plan to do graphic design, publishing, or multimedia authoring, make sure your machine has enough memory and disk storage to support the resource-intensive applications you'll need. Consider adding removable media drives for backup and transport of large files.

▶ *Customizability.* Computers are versatile, but they don't all handle all jobs with equal ease. If you'll be using word processors, spreadsheets, and other mainstream software packages, just about any computer will do. If you have off-the-beaten-path needs (video editing, instrument monitoring, and so on), choose a system with enough slots and ports to allow it to be extended for your work.

CPU can understand. But translation takes time, so software emulation isn't adequate when speed is critical. The other solution, *hardware emulation*, involves adding a circuit board containing an Intel-compatible CPU and additional PC hardware. This board effectively puts a second computer in the Mac's system unit. Emulation technology isn't unique to the Macintosh; there are emulation programs, for example, that allow Windows and Mac programs to run on UNIX-based Sun workstations. Emulation blurs the lines between platforms and allows users to avoid having to choose a single OS and user interface.

Tomorrow's User Interfaces

I hate computers. Telepathy would be better.

—**John Perry Barlow**, writer and cofounder of the Electronic Frontier Foundation

As attractive and popular as today's graphical user interfaces are, they're not likely to reign forever. Future user interfaces will be built around technologies that are still in development today. Here are some likely candidates:

▶ *The end of applications.* As more programs take advantage of interapplication communication, the boundaries between individual applications are likely to blur.

▶ *Compatibility.* Will the software you plan to use run on the computer you're considering? Most popular computers have a good selection of compatible software, but if you have specific needs, such as being able to take your software home to run on Mom's computer, study the compatibility issue carefully. Total compatibility isn't always possible or necessary. A typical Windows-compatible computer, for example, probably won't run every "Windows-compatible" program, but it will almost certainly run the mainstream applications that most users need. Many people don't care if all their programs will run on another kind of computer; they just need data compatibility—the ability to move documents back and forth between systems on disk or through a network connection. It's common, for example, for Windows users and Macintosh users to share documents over a network.

▶ *Connectivity.* In today's networked world it's shortsighted to see your computer as a self-contained information appliance. Make sure you include a high-speed modem and/or network connection in your system so you can take full advantage of the communication capabilities of your computer.

▶ *Convenience.* Just about any computer can do most common jobs, but which is the most convenient for you? Do you value portability over having all the peripherals permanently connected? Is it important to you to have a machine that's easy to install and maintain so you can take care of it yourself? Or do you want to choose the same kind of machine as the people around you so you can get help easily when you need it? Which user interface makes the kind of work you'll be doing easiest?

▶ *Company.* If you try to save money by buying an off-brand computer, you may find yourself the owner of an orphan computer. High-tech companies can vanish overnight. Make sure you'll be able to get service and parts down the road.

▶ *Curve.* Most models of personal computers seem to have a useful life span of just a few years—if they survive the first year or two. If you want to minimize financial risk, avoid buying a computer during the first year of a model's life, when it hasn't been tested on the open market. Also avoid buying a computer that's over the hill; you'll know it because most software developers will have abandoned this model for greener CPUs. In the words of Alexander Pope, "Be not the first by whom the new are tried, nor yet the last to lay the old aside."

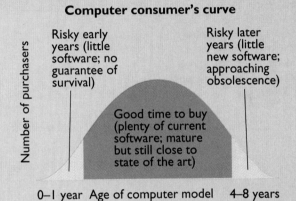

Computer consumer's curve

Future computer users may not think in terms of word processors, spreadsheets, and such; they'll just use their computers like we use pencils today—as all-purpose tools.

▶ *Network applications.* With the growing importance of the Internet and other networks, future applications may be more tied to networks than to desktop computer platforms. As the World Wide Web matures, computer users spend less time on their desktops and more time on the Web. This trend is sure to continue as network software tools improve. Many programmers today write programs in Java, a platform-neutral computer language developed by Sun Microsystems for use on multiplatform networks. Programs written in Java can run on computers running Windows, Macintosh, UNIX, and other operating systems, provided those computers have *Java virtual machine* software installed. Java *applets*—miniature application pieces designed to work with other applications or applets—are routinely included in World Wide Web pages today to add animation and interactivity. As this technology matures, it may make it possible for computer users to do their work without knowing—or caring—where in the world their software is.

▶ *Natural-language interfaces.* It's just a matter of time before we'll be able to communicate with computers in English, Spanish, Russian, Japanese, or some other natural language. Today many computers can reliably read subsets of the English language or can be trained to understand spoken English commands and text. Tomorrow's

Virtual reality is used for work and for play; here are two examples. The researcher uses a headset to view a VR image of a fetus derived from ultrasound scans. A computer shows this pool player how to hit the best shot through this VR headset.

machines should be able to handle much day-to-day work through a natural-language interface, written or spoken. Natural-language processing is discussed in more depth in later chapters.

▶ *Agents.* Artificial intelligence research will lead to intelligent *agents* that "live" in our computers and act as digital secretaries, anticipating our requests, filling in details in our work, searching networks for critical information, and adjusting the computerized workspace to fit our needs. Today's software agents, like the Microsoft Office help agent, only begin to suggest future possibilities. The last chapter of this book describes tomorrow's agents and other futuristic user interface technologies, including the technology of virtual reality.

▶ *Virtual realities.* Further into the future many experts predict that user interfaces will become so sophisticated that we'll be hard-pressed to detect the difference between the real world outside the computer and the **virtual reality** created by the computer, except that the virtual reality will allow us to do things that can't be done on the physical plane. Some computer games today provide surprisingly convincing simulations of the experience of driving a car or flying a plane. These games represent the tip of a gigantic iceberg of research into virtual reality software. More sophisticated virtual reality interfaces can be achieved today with specially designed hardware—for input, a glove or body suit equipped with motion sensors, and for output, a helmet with eye-sized screens whose views change as the helmet moves. This equipment, when coupled with appropriate software, allows the user to explore an artificial world of data as if it were three-dimensional physical space. Today's clumsy VR technology is a long way from living up to its name; virtual reality illusions are interesting, but they're poor substitutes for reality. Still, VR has practical applications: Virtual walkthroughs are used by architects and engineers to preview buildings and mechanical assemblies, VR models are used for education and simulations, and virtual worlds are popping up in amusement parks and arcades.

The best known example of the kind of virtual reality researchers are working toward is the Holodeck on TV's *Star Trek*. The Holodeck can create absolutely convincing simulations of anything from a Sherlock Holmes detective story to a 24th-century antimatter generator. No keyboards or screens are in sight; the user interface is a three-dimensional artificial world full of people, places, and things—real or imaginary—that can be seen, touched, talked to, and controlled by one or more "users." Far-fetched? Absolutely. Possible? Maybe. When? Don't sell your keyboard yet....

Why is UCITA Important?

Ed Foster

"It's all about money in government, and software and hardware companies have spent millions of dollars using hired guns to lobby state and federal legislators to support their cause—even if it's bad for their own customers," wrote InfoWorld's Micahel Vizard in August, 1999. The National Conference of Commissioners for Uniform State Law had just passed UCITA, a controversial legal package that would become law in any state that ratified it. According to Vizard, "Linux should now be looking better and better to IT organizations. The reason is that open-source software won't be affected by this legislation." Vizard was concerned about several controversial UCITA provisions, including one that allows a software vendor to remotely disable software installed on its customers' computers without customer knowledge or permission. Vizard was in good company; UCITA was opposed by consumer advocates, legal experts, and even some software developers. One of UCITA's most vocal opponents, Ed Foster, wrote this piece for InfoWorld's Web site.

I'm not interested in the law, and I'm not terribly political. So why have I spent so much time over the past four years tracking the progress of what is now called UCITA, the Uniform Computer Information Transactions Act?

In my role as InfoWorld's "reader advocate" and Gripe Line columnist, a big part of my job is to listen to the problems and difficulties InfoWorld readers have in dealing with software companies. For a long time now, I've felt there is a real problem in the way the software industry treats its customers. In what other industry will a company take your money for a product that doesn't actually exist yet, or charge you $2 per minute to report a flaw in its product, or tell you that its product comes with no guarantee that it even works?

The reason I first got involved with Article 2B, UCITA's predecessor, was in response to readers' complaints about the "known bug" syndrome—the common experience of discovering that a problem you've spent hours, days, or weeks trying to overcome is due to a bug or conflict that the software publisher knew about all along but chose not to make public. It's strange to think there'd even be an argument about it—why shouldn't a software publisher have some form of legal responsibility for the damage caused by a bug they chose to keep secret? But that's not the way the industry wants to play the game.

Far from rectifying the imbalance between software publisher and software customer, UCITA will reinforce the software industry in its worst practices. One of the few checks on companies who are willing to risk their customers' well-being with poorly tested and poorly debugged products has been the uncertainty of whether the terms of their shrinkwrap licenses would actually protect them in court. Article 2B would remove that uncertainty, and in the opinion of legal experts representing consumer organizations, would allow publishers in most circumstances to hide behind their standard disclaimers of all warranties, mandatory arbitration clauses, exclusion of damage awards, etc.

I don't mean to say that software companies are fundamentally evil organizations out to rob their customers at every turn. The great majority of people who work in the industry want to produce quality software products, want to support their customers properly, and strive to do so. But software companies are businesses, and businesses will naturally try to get away with anything the traffic will bear. And the software business, for a variety of reasons, is one where the traffic has learned to bear a lot.

Anyone familiar with the history of the software industry knows that the software developer with the best product isn't the one that wins in the marketplace. A company that puts the extra time and resources into making sure its product is sufficiently tested and has all the promised features will frequently lose out to the company that decides to ship now and take care of the bugs later. We all share some of the blame for that, but the question is: How we can change things for the better?

One way or another, the fight over UCITA is going to mark a watershed in the software industry's development. It will either lead to the day when the software industry fully accepts the responsibilities it has to its customers or the day when it finally rejects those responsibilities. If the latter occurs, I fear for what it will mean to the health of the American software industry down the road, because the piper will be paid sooner or later.

It's already become something of a cliche, but the parallels between the software industry in this country today and the American automobile industry's dominance in the 50s are remarkable. Back then, an industry where the marketing and distribution clout of the big players meant more than quality control, service, safety, and recognizing the customer's real needs failed to see the writing on the wall until it was too late. Foreign competitors with higher-quality products started eating the domestic giants' lunch, while the lawsuits, recalls, and new government regulations came in waves. If the software industry doesn't get its wake-up call soon, it will happen again.

If there's going to be a wake-up call, it has to happen very soon. That's why I think UCITA is important. The process of enactment for uniform state laws is not the best battleground for this fight—in fact, it's hard to imagine a worse one. But although we can't always pick and choose where we fight our battles, we at least had better recognize that we're in one.

DISCUSSION QUESTIONS

1. Do you think the software industry deserves the protection offered by UCITA?
2. UCITA would reinforce the legality of shrink-wrap licenses—stickers on shrink-wrap packaging that say "By opening this package you are agreeing to the following terms. . . ." Do you think this kind of agreement should be legally binding?
3. What do you think of the author's comparison of the software industry with the automobile industry?

Summary | Chapter Review

Software provides the communication link between humans and their computers. Because software is soft—stored in memory rather than hard-wired into the circuitry—it can easily be modified to meet the needs of the computer user. By changing software, you can change a computer from one kind of tool into another.

Most software falls into one of three broad categories: compilers and other translator programs, software applications, and system software. A compiler is a software tool that allows programs written in English-like languages such as BASIC and C to be translated into the zeros and ones of the machine language the computer understands. A compiler frees the programmer from the tedium of machine-language programming, making it easier to write quality programs with fewer bugs. But even with the best translators, programming is a little like communicating with an alien species. It's a demanding process, which requires more time and mental energy than most people are willing or able to invest.

Fortunately, software applications make it easy for most computer users today to communicate their needs to the computer without learning programming. Applications simulate and extend the properties of familiar real-world tools like typewriters, paintbrushes, and file cabinets, making it possible for people to do things with computers that would be difficult or impossible otherwise. Integrated software packages combine several applications in a single unified package, making it easy to switch between tools. For situations when a general commercial program won't do the job, programmers for businesses and public institutions develop vertical-market and custom packages.

Whether you're writing programs or simply using them, the computer's operating system is functioning behind the scenes, translating your software's instructions into messages that the hardware can understand. An operating system serves as the computer's business manager, taking care of the hundreds of details that need to be handled to keep the computer functioning. A timesharing operating system has the particularly challenging job of serving multiple users concurrently, monitoring the machine's resources, keeping track of each user's account, and protecting the security of the system and each user's data. Many of those system-related problems that the operating system can't solve directly can be handled by utility programs. Popular operating systems today include several versions of Microsoft Windows, the Mac OS, and several versions of UNIX.

Applications, utilities, programming languages, and operating systems all must, to varying degrees, communicate with the user. A program's user interface is a critical factor in that communication. User interfaces have evolved over the years to the point where sophisticated software packages can be operated by people who know little about the inner workings of the computer. A well-designed user interface shields the user from the bits and bytes, creating an on-screen façade or shell that makes sense to the user. Today the computer industry has moved away from the tried-and-true command-line interfaces toward a friendlier graphical user interface that uses windows, icons, mice, and pull-down menus in an intuitive, consistent environment. Tomorrow's user interfaces are likely to depend more on voice, three-dimensional graphics, and animation to create an artificial reality.

Summary | **Chapter Review**

Key Terms

algorithm, 86
application suite (office suite), 93
booting, 98
bug, 85
character-based interface, 99
command-line interface, 99
compatibility, 91
compiler, 87
concurrent processing, 95
copy-protected software, 92
copyrighted software, 92
custom application, 94
desktop, 102
dialog box, 103
document, 99
documentation, 90
emulation, 109
error message, 100

folder, 101
graphical user interface (GUI), 101
high-level language, 87
icon, 101
integrated software, 93
Java, 101
Linux, 83
machine language, 87
Macintosh operating system
    (Mac OS), 101
menu, 101
menu bar, 100
menu-driven interface, 99
Microsoft Windows, 101
MS-DOS, 99
multitasking, 95
natural language, 90
open, 99

open source software, 83
operating system (OS), 94
platform, 109
prompt, 100
public domain software, 92
pull-down menu, 101
shareware, 92
shell, 101
software license, 91
system software, 94
UNIX, 105
upgrade, 91
user interface, 98
utility program, 97
vertical-market application, 94
virtual memory, 95
virtual reality, 112
window, 101

Review Questions

1. Define or describe each of the key terms listed above. Check your answers in the glossary.
2. What is the relationship between a program and an algorithm?
3. Most computer software falls into one of three categories: compilers and other translator programs, software applications, and system software. Describe and give examples of each.
4. Which must be loaded first into the computer's memory, the operating system or software applications? Why?
5. Write an algorithm for changing a flat tire. Check your algorithm carefully for errors and ambiguities. Then have a classmate or your instructor check it. How did your results compare?
6. Describe several functions of a single-user operating system. Describe several additional functions of a multiuser operating system.
7. What does it mean when software is called *IBM-compatible* or *Macintosh-compatible?* What does this have to do with the operating system?
8. Why is the user interface such an important part of software?
9. What is a graphical user interface? How does it differ from a character-based interface? What are the advantages of each?
10. In what important ways does UNIX differ from the Macintosh and Windows operating systems?

Discussion Questions

1. In what way is writing instructions for a computer more difficult than writing instructions for a person? In what way is it easier?
2. How would using a computer be different if it had no operating system? How would programming be different?
3. Speculate about the user interface of a typical computer in the year 2010. How would this user interface differ from those used in today's computers?
4. If you had the resources to design a computer with a brand new user interface, what would your priorities be? Make a rank-ordered list of the qualities you'd like to have in your user interface.
5. How do you feel about the open software movement? Would you be willing to volunteer your time to write software or help users for free?

Projects

1. Write a report about available computer applications in your field of study or in your chosen profession.
2. Take an inventory of computer applications available in your computer lab. Describe the major uses for each application.

Books

The Little Windows 98 Book, by Alan Simpson (Berkeley, CA: Peachpit Press, 1998), **The Little Mac Book,** Sixth Edition, by Robin Williams (Berkeley, CA: Peachpit Press, 1999), and **The Little Palm Book,** by Corbin Collins (Berkeley, CA: Peachpit Press, 1999). These popular guides succinctly and clearly introduce first-time users to the Macintosh, Windows, and Palm operating systems. They're ideal for people who don't want to spend a lot of time reading long manuals. If you can't find one of these, there are dozens of other beginner books for learning the basics of working with operating systems.

The PC Bible, by Robert Lauriston (Berkeley, CA: Peachpit Press, 1999), **The Windows 98 Bible,** by Fred Davis and Kip Crosby (Berkeley, CA: Peachpit Press, 1998), and **The Macintosh Bible,** Seventh Edition, by Sharon Zardetto Aker (Berkeley, CA: Peachpit Press, 1998). At the other end of the spectrum from the "Little" books, these massive bibles contain enough information to keep you reading and learning for weeks. The PC and Mac bibles cover a variety of software products; the Windows 98 book focuses on the operating system itself. If these books don't meet your needs, you'll find similar offerings from other publishers.

Windows for Mac Users, by Cynthia Barron and Robin Williams (Berkeley, CA: Peachpit Press, 1998) If you're a Macintosh user, this book will get you up to speed on Windows machines without forcing you to sit through the basics again. Chapters walk you through the nuts and bolts of the Windows world with a friendly, conversational style.

Crossing Platforms: A Macintosh/Windows Phrasebook, by Adam Engst and David Pogue (Sebastapol, CA: O'Reilly, 1999). Windows and Macintosh computers are just different enough to be confusing to people who occasionally have to switch platforms. Example: An alias on the Macintosh is roughly speaking, the equivalent of a Windows shortcut, but what are the differences? This book includes two A-to-Z translation guides—one for Mac-to-Win translation, one for Win-to-Mac. The writing is clear, concise, and clever. Highly recommended.

Windows 98 Annoyances, by David A. Karp (Cambridge, MA: O'Reilly & Associates, 1998). Microsoft Windows is the most widely used operating system, but that doesn't mean it's loved by everyone. The Windows Annoyances Web site has been visited by millions of Windows users who are frustrated with the user interface and design of various flavors of Windows. Karp's book takes many of the best tips for customizing Windows so it works more like you want it to. The book assumes you already know the basics.

UNIX: Visual QuickStart Guide, by Deboarh S. Ray and Eric J. Ray (Berkeley, CA: Peachpit Press, 1998). Many UNIX books assume that you speak fluent techno-jargon and that you want to know all about the operating system and how it works. This book is designed for people who want to (or need to) use UNIX but don't particularly want to read a massive volume of UNIX lore. No book can make mastering UNIX simple, but this one at least makes getting started with UNIX simpler.

Red Hat Linux 6: Visual QuickPro Guide, by Harold Davis (Berkeley, CA: Peachpit Press, 1999). If you have a spare PC laying around and want to find out what the fuss is about Linux, or if you just want an alternative to Microsoft software, this book is a great place to start. It covers the basics, from installation to applications. The built-in CD contains a complete Copy of Red Hat Linux (without technical support).

Linux: The Complete Reference, by Richard Petersen (Berkeley, CA: Osborne/McGraw-Hill, 1999), and **UNIX: The Complete Reference,** by Kenneth Rosen, Douglas Host, James Farber, and Richard Rosinski (Berkeley, CA: Osborne/McGraw-Hill, 1999). These massive books will probably tell you more than you need to know about Linux and other UNIX variants. They're well organized and clearly written.

PalmPilot: The Ultimate Guide, Second Edition, by David Pogue (Sebastapol, CA: O'Reilly, 1999). The Palm OS is far and away the most popular operating system for handheld computers. In this book David Pogue offers a wealth of information for Palm owners and users. Pogue is a great writer and a Palm expert. The accompanying CD allows you to download software from your Windows, Mac, or Linux computer into your handheld machine.

Special Edition: Using StarOffice, by Michael Koch and Sarah Murray, with Werner Roth (Indianapolis: Que, 1999). There are dozens of books on Microsoft Office and other commercial PC applications, but very few on freeware apps. This book can serve as an introduction and a valuable reference for anyone wanting to use the powerful, free StarOffice Suite on Windows or Linux.

The Cathedral and the Bazaar: Musings on Linux and Open Source by an Accidental Revolutionary, by Eric S. Raymond (Sebastapol, CA: O'Reilly, 2000). This widely praised book is an expanded version of the original manifesto for the open-source software movement—the movement that threatens to revolutionize the software industry. Tom Peters calls it "wonderful, witty, and, ultimately, wise."

The Art of Human–Computer Interface Design, edited by Brenda Laurel (Reading, MA: Addison-Wesley, 1990). This entertaining, provocative, and highly informative book is filled with essays by the experts on what makes a user interface work or not work. Chapters cover everything from menus and icons to virtual reality.

Things That Make Us Smart: Defending Human Attributes in the Age of the Machine, by Donald A. Norman (Reading, MA: Addison-Wesley, 1993). Norman left his position as the founding Chair of the Department of Cognitive Science at the University of California, San Diego, to work in the computer industry. His research on the relationship between technology and the human cognitive system is especially relevant in an industry where user interface decisions affect millions of users every day. This book, like Norman's others, is informative, thought provoking, and enjoyable. His argument for a more human-centered technology should be required reading for all software designers.

Designing the User Interface: Strategies for Effective Human–Computer Interaction, Third Edition, by Ben Schneiderman (Reading, MA: Addison-Wesley, 1998). This book thoroughly explores the issues that face anyone designing a user interface, whether it's a simple application program, a complex hypermedia document, or a virtual reality environment. In a style that's both academic and approachable, Schneiderman discusses everything from input and output hardware to the ultimate social impact of the technology.

A Guide to Usability: Human Factors in Computing, edited by Jenny Preece (Reading, MA: Addison-Wesley, 1993). User interface design is part psychology and part technology. This little book clearly and concisely outlines many of the most important issues in this rapidly growing field.

The Inmates Are Running the Asylum: Why High-Tech Products Drive Us Crazy and How to Restore the Sanity, by Alan Cooper (Indianapolis: Sams, 1999). User interface issues aren't just about computers. The same questions apply to all kinds of devices. Cooper clearly lays out the issues in this call-to-arms for friendlier technology.

World Wide Web Pages

Software companies, like hardware companies, have established their presence on the Net. Most of the companies use addresses that follow the formula http://www.companyname.com. Examples include http://www.microsoft.com, http://www.apple.com, and http://www.corel.com. Content varies from company to company; you might find technical support, product descriptions, demo software, software updates, and user tips on a typical software home page. For more software information check the home pages of publishers that specialize in computer books. For example, Peachpit Press (*http://www.peachpit.com),* McGraw Hill (http://www.books.mcgraw-hill.com/), and other publishers include sample chapters from software books on their Web sites. As usual, www.computerconfluence.com provides up-to-date links to a variety of valuable Web resources.

Using Computers

Essential Applications

Chapter 5

Chapter

Working with Words: Word Processing and Digital Publishing

This **newfangled writing machine** has several virtues. It piles an **awful stack** of words on one page. It don't muss things or scatter ink blots around. Of course it **saves paper.**

—Mark Twain

In 1874 Mark Twain bought a Remington Type-Writer for $125. One year later he became the first author in history to submit a typewritten manuscript: *The Adventures of Tom Sawyer.*

Twain later invested almost $200,000 (the equivalent of $1.5 million today) in the promising new Paige typesetting technology. He wrote, "All the other wonderful inventions of the human brain sink pretty nearly into commonplaces contrasted with this awful mechanical miracle. Telephones, telegraphs, locomotives, cotton gins, sewing machines, Babbage calculators, Jacquard looms, perfecting presses, all mere toys, simplicities! The Paige Compositor marches alone and far in the land of human inventions," and on a more down-to-earth level, "This typesetter does not get drunk."

The Paige might very well have transformed book and magazine publishing, as Twain predicted, had not Ottmar Mergenthaler invented the Linotype casting machine in 1886. The Linotype set and cast type in properly spaced leaden lines. An operator would produce the type by pressing keys on a board similar to the keyboard of a typewriter. The Linotype was adopted by major newspapers around the world. Because of the Linotype, Twain's promising publishing machine was obsolete at its inception, and Twain was forced into bankruptcy.

Linotypes dominated the publishing industry until the 1960s, when electronic typesetting with mainframe computers took over. Now mainframe publishing systems are being displaced by personal computers. From simple word processors to professional desktop publishing systems, small computers are rapidly and radically transforming the entire publishing process. ◼

Mark Twain (1835–1910)

Early computers were no threat to typewriters; they were too unfriendly, inconvenient, inflexible, and expensive to be used by anyone but highly skilled experts. Special-purpose "word processing machines" used by clerical workers in the 1960s represented a step forward, but they were a far cry from the word processing programs on modern personal computers.

The entire writing process has been transformed by modern word processing software. Instead of suffering through the painful and disjointed process of typing and retyping in pursuit of a "clean" draft, a writer can focus on developing ideas and let the machine take care of the details of laying out the words neatly on the page. Today's word processing technology makes it possible for just about any literate person to communicate effectively in writing. More than any other software application, word processing is a tool for everybody.

In this chapter we take a brief writer's tour of word processing, from the first stages of entering text right on through to printing the final document. We consider software tools for working with words, from outliners to sophisticated reference tools. We look at how desktop publishing technology has transformed the publishing process and provided more people with the power to communicate in print. Finally, we look at how cutting-edge technologies will soon change writing and publishing in even more profound ways.

The Word Processing Process

I...cannot imagine now that I ever wrote with a typewriter.

—**Arthur C. Clarke, author and scientist**

Working with any word processor (a common way of referring to word processing software) involves several steps:

▶ Entering text

▶ Editing text

▶ Formatting the document

▶ Proofreading the document

▶ Saving the document on disk

▶ Printing the document.

Early word processing systems generally forced users to follow these steps in a strict order. Some systems still in use today—mainly on mainframes and other timesharing systems—segregate these processes into steps that can't easily be mixed. But modern word processing systems provide all of the necessary tools in a single, seamless program. Most writers today switch freely between editing and formatting, in some cases doing both at the same time. Still, for our discussion it makes sense to consider these as separate processes.

Entering Text

Entering text using a word processor is similar to using a typewriter but simpler. As you type on the computer keyboard, your text is displayed on the screen and stored in the computer's RAM. Since random access memory is not a permanent storage medium, it's important to regularly save your document—that is, create a disk file containing your work in progress. If the power fails, or the computer fails, or you accidentally erase part of the text, you can restart the machine (if necessary) and *open* the saved version of your document— copy it back from a floppy or hard disk into the computer's memory. If you save your work on a diskette, you can take a break and later return to your computer (or another one like it at a different location), open your document, and start where you left off.

The User's View box shows a sample of entering text with Microsoft Word, the most popular word processing program in use today. Like most of the applications featured in this book, Microsoft Word is available for both Macintosh and Windows-compatible computers. **UV**

The User's View

Entering Text

SOFTWARE **Microsoft Word.**

THE GOAL **To produce a copy of a classic work to be read in an English class presentation.**

① A word processing document starts as an empty window.

② A flashing cursor (sometimes called an insertion bar) indicates your location in the document. As you type, the cursor moves to the right, leaving a trail of text in its wake. At the same time, those characters are stored in the computer's memory. If you mistype a character or string of characters, you can press Delete or Back Space to eliminate the typos.

③ Because of a feature called word wrap, the word processor automatically transports any words that won't fit on the current line to the next line along with the cursor. The only time you need to press Return or Enter is when you want to force the program to begin a new line—such as at the end of a paragraph.

④ As you type, the topmost lines scroll out of view to make room on the screen for the new ones. The text you've entered is still in memory, even though you can't see it on the screen.

⑤ You can retrieve it anytime by scrolling backward through the text. In this respect a word processor document is like a modern version of ancient paper scrolls.

⑥ Every few minutes you select the Save command to save your document in a disk file containing your work so far. This provides insurance against accidental erasure of the text you've entered.

To be continued. . . .

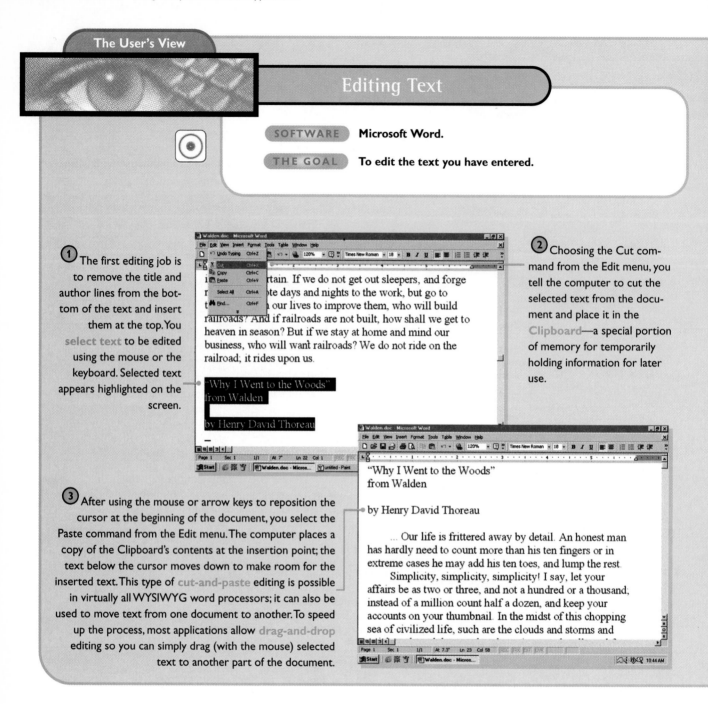

The User's View

Editing Text

SOFTWARE **Microsoft Word.**

THE GOAL **To edit the text you have entered.**

① The first editing job is to remove the title and author lines from the bottom of the text and insert them at the top. You select text to be edited using the mouse or the keyboard. Selected text appears highlighted on the screen.

② Choosing the Cut command from the Edit menu, you tell the computer to cut the selected text from the document and place it in the Clipboard—a special portion of memory for temporarily holding information for later use.

③ After using the mouse or arrow keys to reposition the cursor at the beginning of the document, you select the Paste command from the Edit menu. The computer places a copy of the Clipboard's contents at the insertion point; the text below the cursor moves down to make room for the inserted text. This type of cut-and-paste editing is possible in virtually all WYSIWYG word processors; it can also be used to move text from one document to another. To speed up the process, most applications allow drag-and-drop editing so you can simply drag (with the mouse) selected text to another part of the document.

Editing Text

All word processors allow you to edit text—to write and refine a document on screen until it's good enough to commit to paper. If you're working with a modern WYSIWYG (short for "what you see is what you get" and pronounced "wizzy-wig") word processor, the arrangement of the words on the screen represents a close approximation to the arrangement of the words on the printed page.

With a word processor you can easily

- ▶ Navigate to different parts of the document by scrolling or by using a Find command to locate a particular word or phrase

- ▶ Insert text at any point in the document

- ▶ Delete text from any part of the document

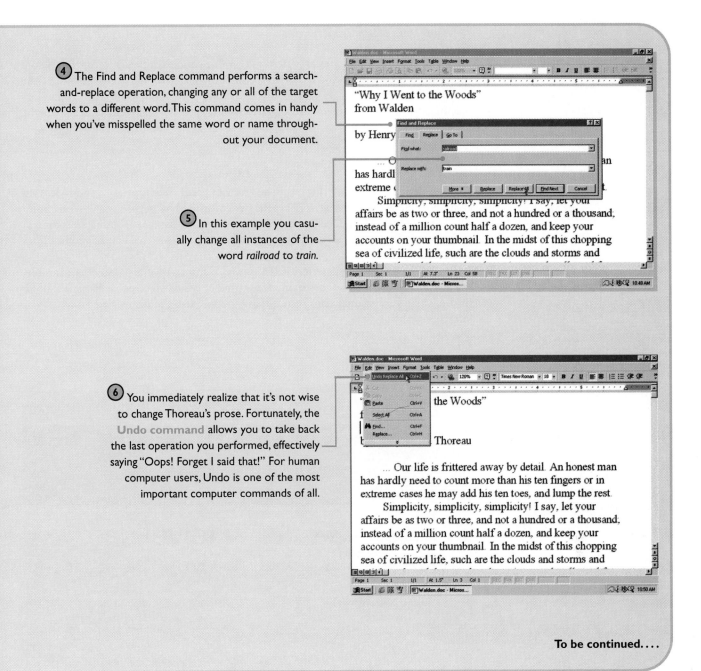

④ The Find and Replace command performs a search-and-replace operation, changing any or all of the target words to a different word. This command comes in handy when you've misspelled the same word or name throughout your document.

⑤ In this example you casually change all instances of the word *railroad* to *train*.

⑥ You immediately realize that it's not wise to change Thoreau's prose. Fortunately, the Undo command allows you to take back the last operation you performed, effectively saying "Oops! Forget I said that!" For human computer users, Undo is one of the most important computer commands of all.

To be continued....

▶ Move text from one part of the document to another section of the same document or to another document

▶ Copy text from one part of a document and duplicate it in another section of the document or in a different document

▶ Find and replace selected words or phrases throughout a document (sometimes called *search and replace*).

Most modern word processing programs contain sophisticated variations of these basic editing features. But even with this basic set of features, you can eliminate much of the drudgery that plagued writers in the precomputer era.

This *User's View* box shows a brief editing session. Of course, real-world editing often involves several sessions of writing and rewriting. **UV**

Formatting Text

When you're editing text, you only need to concern yourself with the words. But before you print your document, you'll need to consider the *format* of the document—how the words will look on the page. **Text formatting** commands allow you to control the format and style of the document. Most modern word processors allow users to control the formats of individual characters and paragraphs, as well as complete documents.

Formatting Characters

Most modern printers can print text in a variety of point sizes, typefaces, and styles that aren't possible with typewriters. Characters are measured by **point size**, with one point equal to 1/72 inch. Most documents, including this book, use smaller point sizes for text to fit more information on each page and larger point sizes to make titles and headings stand out.

In the language of typesetters a **font** is a size and style of **typeface**. For example, the Helvetica typeface includes many fonts, one of which is 12-point Helvetica bold. In the world of personal computing many people use the terms *font* and *typeface* interchangeably.

These fonts represent just a few of the hundreds of typefaces available for personal computers and printers today. The two symbol fonts given, Symbol and Zapf Dingbats, provide special characters not available with other fonts.

Examples of	12-point size	24-point size
Serif fonts	Times Courier	Times Courier
Sans-serif fonts	Helvetica Avant Garde	Helvetica Avant Garde
Script fonts	Zapf Chancery Kuenstler Script	Zapf Chancery Kuenstler Script
Display fonts	Regular Joe Birch Remedy	Regular Joe Birch Remedy
Symbol fonts (Symbol and Zapf Dingbats)	Σψμβολ ✳❀☐❅ ♣❄■	Σψμβολ ✳❀☐❅ ♣❄■

Font Technology

When a computer displays a character on a monitor or prints it on a laser, inkjet, or dot-matrix printer, the character is nothing more than a collection of dots in an invisible grid. Bit-mapped fonts store characters in this way, with each pixel represented as a black or white bit in a matrix. A bit-mapped font usually looks fine on screen in the intended point size but doesn't look smooth when printed on a high-resolution printer or enlarged on screen.

A bit-mapped font suffers from pixel-lization when enlarged.

Most computer systems now use scalable outline fonts to represent type in memory until it is displayed or printed. A scalable font repre-

This outline for a lowercase letter "a" retains its original shape at any size or resolution.

sents each character as an outline that can be scaled—increased or decreased in size without distortion. Curves and lines are smooth and don't have stair-stepped, jagged edges when they're resized. The outline is stored inside the computer or printer as a series of mathematical statements about the position of points and the shape of the lines connecting those points.

Downloadable fonts (soft fonts) are stored in the computer system (not the printer) and downloaded to the printer only when needed. These fonts usually have matching screen fonts and are easily moved to different computer systems. Most importantly, you can use the same downloadable font on many printer models.

Laser printers are really dedicated computer systems that contain their own CPU, RAM, ROM, and specialized operating system. Printer fonts are stored in the printer's ROM and are always available for use with that printer, but you may not be able to achieve WYSI-WYG if your computer doesn't have a screen font to match your printer font. And if you move your document to a different computer and printer, the same printer font may not be available on the new system.

Fonts are most commonly available in two scalable outline forms: Adobe PostScript and Apple/Microsoft TrueType. Because Apple and Microsoft supply TrueType downloadable fonts with their operating systems, TrueType fonts are more popular among general computer users. PostScript fonts usually require additional software but are the standard among many graphics professionals. PostScript is actually a complete page description language particularly well suited to the demands of professional publishers.

For the past few years Adobe and Microsoft have been codeveloping OpenType, a universal font format that combines TrueType and PostScript technology. OpenType allows character shapes to travel with documents in compressed forms so that a document transmitted electronically or displayed on the World Wide Web will look like the original even if the viewer's system doesn't include the original document's fonts.

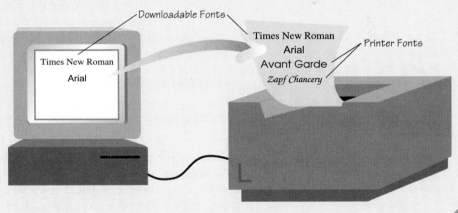

Whatever you call them, you have hundreds of choices of typefaces for most modern computers. **Serif fonts**, like those in the Times family, are embellished with serifs—fine lines at the ends of the main strokes of each character. **Sans-serif fonts**, like those in the Helvetica family, have plainer, cleaner lines. **Monospaced fonts** that mimic typewriters, like those in the Courier family, produce characters that always take up the same amount of space, no matter how skinny or fat the characters are. In contrast, **proportionally spaced fonts** allow more room for wide characters like *w*'s than for narrow characters like *i*'s. (See the font table on the previous page for examples.)

Most word processors provide four different options for justifying text. ▷

This text illustrates centered justification. For centered text both margins are ragged. Centered text is often used for titles.

This text illustrates left justification. For left-justified text the left margin is smooth and the right margin is ragged.

This text illustrates right justification. For right-justified text the right margin is smooth and the left margin is ragged.

This text illustrates full justification. For fully justified text, spaces between words are adjusted to make both m a r g i n s smooth.

Formatting Paragraphs

Many formatting commands apply to paragraphs rather than characters: those commands that control margins, space between lines, indents, tab stops, and justification. Justification refers to the alignment of text on a line. Four justification choices are commonly available: *left justification* (with a smooth left margin and ragged right margin), *right justification*, *full justification* (both margins are smooth), and *centered justification*.

Formatting the Document

Some formatting commands are applied to entire documents. For example, Word's Page Setup command allows you to control the margins that apply throughout the document. Other commands allow you to specify the content, size, and style of headers and footers—blocks that appear at the top and bottom of every page, displaying repetitive information, such as chapter titles, author names, and automatically calculated page numbers. *The User's View* box demonstrates some basic text formatting operations using Microsoft Word. **UV**

Most modern word processing programs provide a great deal of formatting flexibility. Here are some examples of what you can do:

▶ Define style sheets containing custom styles for each of the common elements in a document. (For example, you can define a style called "subhead" as a paragraph that's left-justified in a boldface, 12-point Helvetica font with standard margins and then apply that style to every subhead in the document without reselecting all three of these commands for each new subhead. If you decide later to change the subheads to 14-point Futura, your changes in the subhead style are automatically reflected throughout the document.)

▶ Define alternate headers, footers, and margins so that left- and right-facing pages can have different margins, headers, and footers.

▶ Create documents with variable-width multiple columns.

▶ Create, edit, and format multicolumn tables.

▶ Incorporate graphics created with other applications.

▶ Use automatic footnoting to save you from having to place footnotes and endnotes; the program automatically places them where they belong on the page.

▶ Use automatic hyphenation to divide long words that fall at the ends of lines.

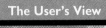

The User's View

Formatting Text

SOFTWARE   **Microsoft Word.**

THE GOAL   **To change the look of the text you've entered and edited. Most applications today allow you to do common tasks using either menu commands or on-screen buttons. This example illustrates both techniques.**

① To italicize the title Walden, you select the characters to be changed ...

② ....choose the Font command from the Format menu ...

③ ....and then select the Italic font style in the Font dialog box.

④ You can center text by selecting the text ...

⑤ ....and clicking the Center button.

⑥ You can see a miniature picture of your final output by selecting the Print Preview command from the File menu.

⑦ If it looks right, you can select the Print command or click on the printer icon to produce a hard copy.

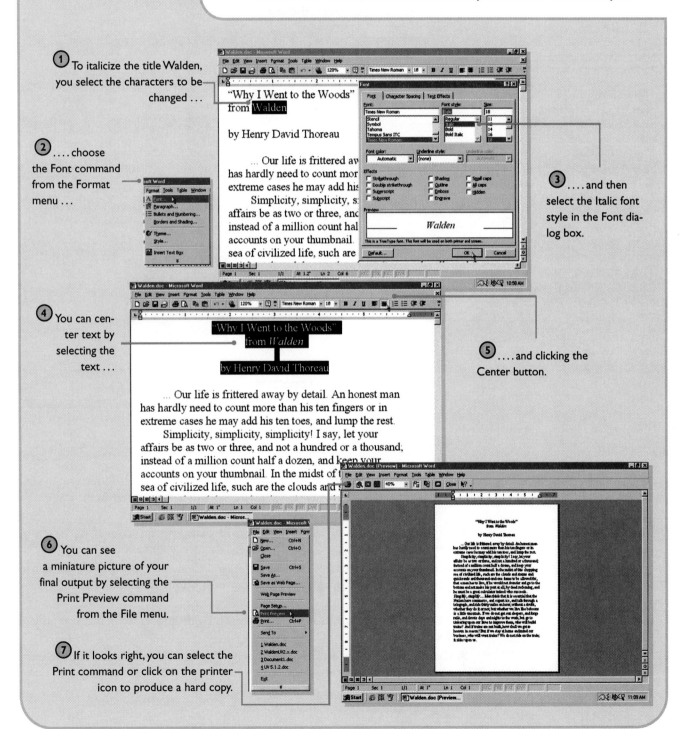

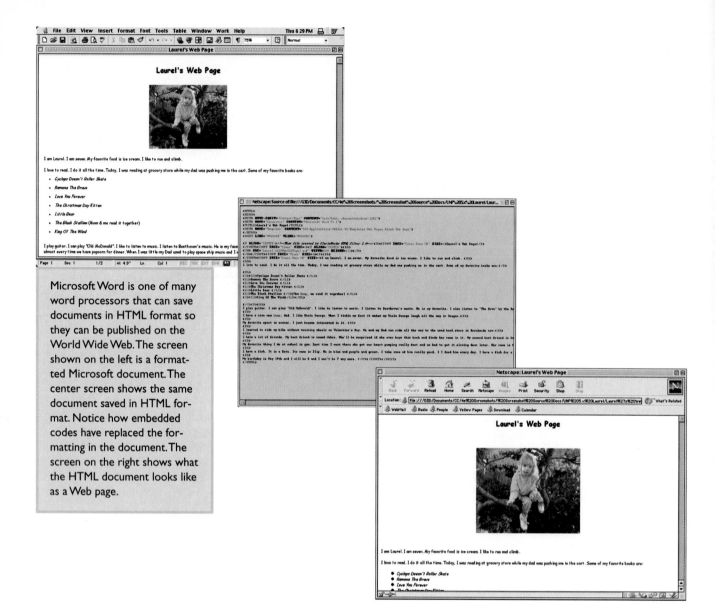

Microsoft Word is one of many word processors that can save documents in HTML format so they can be published on the World Wide Web. The screen shown on the left is a formatted Microsoft document. The center screen shows the same document saved in HTML format. Notice how embedded codes have replaced the formatting in the document. The screen on the right shows what the HTML document looks like as a Web page.

▶ Use **automatic formatting (autoformat)** to automatically apply formatting to your text. For example, to automatically number lists (like the exercises at the end of this chapter) and apply proper indentation to those lists.

▶ Use **automatic correction (autocorrect)** to catch and correct common typing errors. For example, if you type *THe* or *Teh*, the software will automatically change it to *The.*

▶ Generate tables of contents and indexes for books and other long works (with human help for making judgments about which words belong in the index and how they should be arranged).

▶ Attach hidden comments that can be seen without showing up in the final printed document.

▶ Use coaching or help features (sometimes called **wizards**) to walk you through complex document formatting procedures.

▶ Convert formatted documents to *HTML (hypertext markup language)* so they can be easily published on the World Wide Web.

Word Processing Is Not Typing

If you're already a touch typist, your typing skills will help you become proficient at word processing quickly. (If you're not a touch typist, see Project 1, Chapter 3.) Unfortunately, a few typing skills are counterproductive on a modern word processor. Here's a short list of new word processing habits that should replace outmoded typing habits:

▶ Use the Return or Enter key only when you must. Let the computer's automatic word wrap handle routine end-of-line business.

▶ Use tabs and margin guides, not the spacebar, to align columns. WYSIWYG is a matter of degree, and text that looks perfectly aligned on screen may not line up on paper if you depend on your eyes and the spacebar.

▶ *Don't underline.* Use italics and boldface for emphasis. Italicize book and journal titles.

▶ Use only one space after a period. Most type experts agree that proportionally spaced fonts look better if you avoid double spaces.

▶ Take advantage of special characters. Bullets (•), em dashes (—), curly quotes (" "), and other nontypewriter characters make your work look more professional, and they don't cost a thing.

The Wordsmith's Toolbox

When you had to carve things in stone, you got the Ten Commandments. When things had to be written with a goose quill and you had to boil blood or whatever to make ink, you got Shakespeare. When you went over to the steel pen and manufactured inks, you got Henry James. You get to the typewriter, you get Jack Kerouac. When you get down to the wordprocessor—you get me. So improvement in the technology of writing hasn't improved writing itself, as far as I can tell.

—P. J. O'Rourke, **Humorist**

In addition to basic editing and formatting functions, a typical word processor might include a built-in *outliner*, *spelling checker*, and *thesaurus*. But even word processors that don't include those features can be enhanced with stand-alone programs specifically designed to accomplish the same things. We examine a few of these tools next.

Outliners and Idea Processors

If any man wishes to write in a clear style, let him first be clear in his thoughts.

—Johann W. von Goethe

For many of us the hardest part of the writing process is collecting and organizing our thoughts. Traditional English-class techniques, including outlines and 3×5 note cards, involve additional work. But when computer technology is applied to these time-honored techniques, they're transformed into high-powered tools for extending our minds and streamlining the process of turning vague thoughts into solid prose.

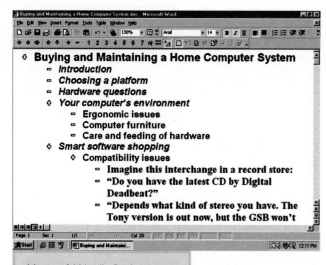

Microsoft Word's Outline view allows you to examine and restructure the overall organization of the document, while showing each topic in as much detail as you need. When you move headlines, the attached subheads and paragraphs follow automatically.

Outliners like the one in Microsoft Word are, in effect, **idea processors**. Outliners are particularly effective at performing three functions:

- ▶ Arranging information into hierarchies or levels so that each heading can be fleshed out with more detailed subheads, which can then be broken into smaller pieces

- ▶ Rearranging ideas and levels so that sub-ideas are automatically moved with their parent ideas

- ▶ Hiding and revealing levels of detail as needed so that you can examine the forest, the trees, or an individual leaf of your project.

For a project that requires research, an outliner can be used as a replacement for note cards. Ideas can be collected, composed, refined, rearranged, and reorganized much more efficiently when they're stored in an outline. When the time comes to turn research into a research paper, the notes don't need to be retyped; they can be polished with standard text-editing techniques. If the outliner is built into the word processor, the line between notes and finished product blurs to the point where it almost disappears.

Synonym Finders

The difference between the right word and the almost-right word is the difference between the lightning and the lightning-bug.

—Mark Twain

The classic synonym finder, or **thesaurus**, is an invaluable tool for finding just the right word, but it's not particularly user-friendly. A computerized thesaurus is another matter altogether. With a good on-screen thesaurus, it's a simple matter to select a word and issue a command for a synonym search. The computerized thesaurus provides almost instant gratification, displaying all kinds of possible replacements for the word in question. If you find a good substitute in the list, you can indicate your preference with a click or a keystroke; the software even makes the substitution for you. It couldn't be much simpler.

Digital References

Microsoft Word's on-line thesaurus puts synonyms at your fingertips. In this case, the computer is providing synonyms for the word improve.

Writers rely on dictionaries, quotation books, encyclopedias, atlases, almanacs, and other references. Just about all of these resources are now available in digital form, both on CD-ROM and on the World Wide Web.

The biggest advantage of digital references is speed; searching for subjects or words by computer is usually faster than thumbing through a book. Even Web searches that *seem* to take a long time can produce results in a fraction of the time it would take you to locate sources in a library. Well-designed electronic references make it easy to jump between related topics in search of elusive facts. In addition, copying quotes electronically takes a fraction of the time it takes to retype information from a book. Of course, this kind of quick copying makes plagiarism easier than ever and may tempt more writers to violate copyright laws.

Some references lose meaning or clarity in the translation to electronic form. Because pictures, maps, and drawings take up so much disk space (and Internet trans-

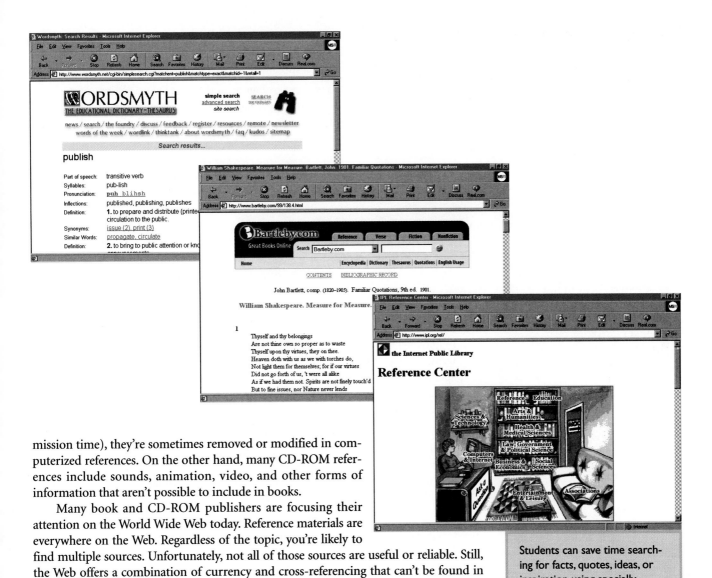

Students can save time searching for facts, quotes, ideas, or inspiration using specially-designed Web reference sites.

mission time), they're sometimes removed or modified in computerized references. On the other hand, many CD-ROM references include sounds, animation, video, and other forms of information that aren't possible to include in books.

Many book and CD-ROM publishers are focusing their attention on the World Wide Web today. Reference materials are everywhere on the Web. Regardless of the topic, you're likely to find multiple sources. Unfortunately, not all of those sources are useful or reliable. Still, the Web offers a combination of currency and cross-referencing that can't be found in any other reference source. We'll revisit Web references in later chapters.

Spelling Checkers

It's a darn poor mind that can only think of one way to spell a word.

—Andrew Jackson

While many of us sympathize with Jackson's point of view, the fact remains that correct spelling is an important part of most written communication. That's why most word processors include a built-in spelling checker. A spelling checker compares the words in your document with words in a disk-based dictionary. Every word that's not in the dictionary is flagged as a suspect word—a potential misspelling. In many cases, the spelling checker suggests the corrected spelling and offers to replace the suspect word. Ultimately, though, it's up to you to decide whether the flagged word is, in fact, spelled incorrectly.

Most spelling checkers offer several choices for each suspect word:

▸ Replace the word with the suggested alternative.

▸ Replace the word with another alternative typed by the user.

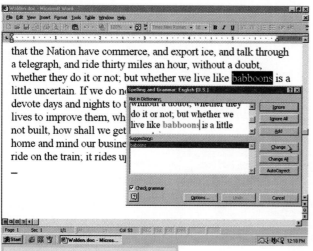

Most spell checkers offer a user several choices for handling words that aren't in the dictionary (Software: Microsoft Word.)

▶ Leave the word alone (used when the word is spelled correctly, but it's not in the dictionary because it's an obscure word, a specialized term, or a proper name).

▶ Leave the word alone and add it to the dictionary so that it won't be flagged next time (used when the word is spelled correctly, it's not in the dictionary, and it's a regular part of the user's written vocabulary).

A *batch spelling checker* checks all of the words in your document in a batch when you issue the appropriate command. An *interactive spelling checker* checks each word as it's typed; a typical interactive spelling checker might mark each mistyped word with a distinct underlining. Some spelling checkers, like the one in Microsoft Word, can operate in either batch or interactive mode.

While spelling checkers are wonderful aids, they can't replace careful proofreading by alert human eyes. When you're using a spelling checker, it's important to keep two potential problems in mind:

1 *Dictionary limitations and errors.* No dictionary includes every word, so you have to know what to do with unlisted words—proper names, obscure words, technical terms, foreign terms, colloquialisms, and other oddities. If you add words to your spelling checker's dictionary, you run the risk of adding an incorrectly spelled word, making future occurrences of that misspelling invisible to the spelling checker and to you.

2 *Errors of context.* The biggest limitation of today's spelling checkers is their lack of intelligence in dealing with a word's context. The fact that a word appears in a dictionary does not guarantee that it is correctly spelled in the context of the sentence. The following passage, for example, contains eight spelling errors, none of which would be detected by a spelling checker:

> I wood never have guest that my spelling checker would super seed my editor as my mane source of feed back. I no longer prophet from the presents of an editor while I right.

Grammar-and-style-checking software flags possible errors and makes suggestions about how they might be fixed. (Software: Microsoft Word.)

Grammar and Style Checkers

The errors in the preceding quote would have slipped by a spelling checker, but many of them would have been detected by a **grammar and style checker**. In addition to checking spelling, grammar-and-style-checking software analyzes each word in context, checking for errors of context ("I wood never have guest"), common grammatical errors ("Ben and me went to Boston"), and stylistic foibles ("Suddenly the door was opened by Bethany."). In addition to pointing out possible errors and suggesting improvements, it can analyze prose complexity using measurements such as sentence length and paragraph length. This kind of analysis is useful for determining whether your writing style is appropriate for your target audience.

Grammar-and-style-checking software is, at best, imperfect. A typical program misses many true errors, while flagging correct passages. Still, it can be a valuable writing aid, especially for students who are mastering the complexities of a language for the first time. But software is no substitute for practice, revision, editing, and a good English teacher.

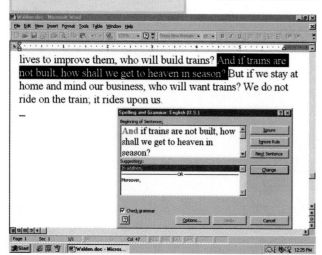

Form Letter Generators

Congratulations, Mr. <lastname>. You may
already have won!

Most word processors today have **mail merge** capabilities for producing personalized form letters. When used with a database containing a list of names and addresses, a word processor can quickly generate individually addressed letters and mailing labels. Many programs can incorporate custom paragraphs based on the recipient's personal data, making each letter look as if it were individually written. This kind of technology was exploited by direct-mail marketing companies for years before it became available in inexpensive PC software.

Microsoft Word's Track Changes feature allows several writers and editors to contribute to the same document and see each other's changes.

Collaborative Writing Tools

Writing only leads to more writing.

—Colette

Most large writing projects, including this one, involve groups of people working together. Computer networks make it easy for writers and editors to share documents, but it's not always easy for one person to know how a document has been changed by others. **Groupware**—software designed to be used by a workgroup—can keep track of a document's history as it's passed among group members and make sure that all changes are incorporated into a single master document. Using groupware, each writer can monitor and make suggestions concerning the work of any other writer on the team. Editors can "blue pencil" corrections and attach notes directly to the electronic manuscript. The notes can be read by any or all of the writers—even those who are on the other side of the continent.

This kind of collaborative writing and editing doesn't require specialized software anymore; it can be done with many word processing and publishing programs. For example, Microsoft Word's Track Changes option can record and display contributions of several writers and editors; it can also compare document versions and highlight differences between versions.

A typical desktop publishing system includes a personal computer, a high-resolution printer, a scanner, and a variety of software programs.

The Desktop Publishing Story

Freedom of the press
belongs to the person who owns one.

—A. J. Liebling, the late media critic for *The New Yorker*

Just as word processing changed the writer's craft in the 1970s, the world of publishing was radically transformed in the 1980s when Apple introduced its first LaserWriter printer and a new company named Aldus introduced a Macintosh program called PageMaker that could take advantage of that printer's high-resolution output capabilities. Publishing—traditionally an

expensive, time-consuming, error-prone process—instantly became an enterprise that just about anyone with a computer and a little cash could undertake.

What Is Desktop Publishing?

The process of producing a book, magazine, or other publication includes several steps:

1 Writing text.

2 Editing text.

3 Producing drawings, photographs, and other graphics to accompany the text.

4 Designing a basic format for the publication.

5 Typesetting text.

6 Arranging text and graphics on pages.

7 Typesetting and printing pages.

8 Binding pages into a finished publication.

In traditional publishing, many of these steps required expensive equipment, highly trained specialists to operate the equipment, and lots of time.

With modern **desktop publishing (DTP)** technology, the bulk of the production process can be accomplished with tools that are small, affordable, and easy to use. A desktop publishing system generally includes one or more Macs or PCs, a scanner, a high-resolution printer, and software. It's now possible for a single person with a modest equipment investment to do all the writing, editing, graphic production, design, page-layout, and typesetting for a desktop publication. Of course, few individuals have the skills to handle all of these tasks, so most publications are still the work of teams that include writers, editors, designers, artists, and supervisors. But even if the titles remain the same, each of these jobs is changing because of desktop publishing technology.

The first steps in the publishing process involve producing **source documents**— articles, chapters, drawings, maps, charts, and photographs that are to appear in the

Source documents are merged in a publication document, which can be printed on a laser or inkjet printer, printed on a high-resolution phototypesetter, or even published on the World Wide Web.

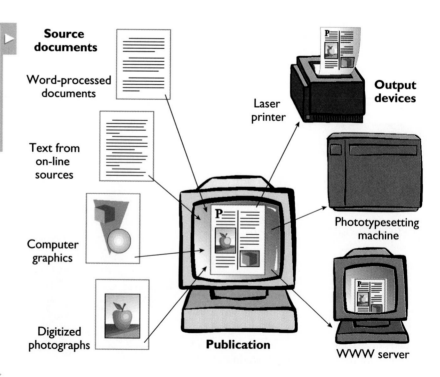

Source documents

Word-processed documents

Text from on-line sources

Computer graphics

Digitized photographs

Publication

Laser printer

Output devices

Phototypesetting machine

WWW server

Rules of Thumb

Beyond Desktop Tacky!

Many first-time users of WYSIWYG word processors and desktop publishing systems become intoxicated with the power at their fingertips. It's easy to get carried away with all those fonts, styles, and sizes and to create a document that makes supermarket tabloids look tasteful. While there's no substitute for a good education in the principles of design, it's easy to avoid tacky-looking documents if you follow a few simple guidelines:

▶ *Plan before you publish.* Design (or select) a simple, visually pleasing format for your document, and use that format throughout the document.

▶ *Use appropriate fonts.* Limit your choices to one or two fonts and sizes per page, and be consistent throughout your document. Serif fonts like the one used in the main text of this book generally are good choices for paragraphs of text; the serifs gently guide the reader's eye from letter to letter. Sans-serif fonts, like the one used in the box you are reading, work well for boxed text, tables, headings, and titles. It's generally better to use only one sans-serif font in a document. Make sure all your chosen fonts work properly with your printer.

▶ *Don't go style-crazy.* Avoid overusing italics, boldface, ALL CAPS, underlines, and other styles for emphasis. When in doubt, leave it out.

▶ *Look at your document through your readers' eyes.* Make every picture say something. Don't try to cram too much information on a page. Don't be afraid of white space. Use a format that speaks clearly to your readers. Make sure the main points of your document stand out. Whatever you do, do it for the reader.

▶ *Learn from the masters.* Study the designs of successful publications. What makes them work? Use design books, articles, and classes to develop your aesthetic skills along with your technical skills. With or without a computer, publishing is an art.

▶ *Know your limitations.* Desktop publishing technology makes it possible for anyone to produce high-quality documents with a minimal investment of time and money. But your equipment and skills may not be up to the job at hand. For many applications, personal desktop publishing is no match for a professional design artist or typesetter. If you need the best, work with a pro.

▶ *Remember the message.* Fancy fonts, tasteful graphics, and meticulous design can't turn shoddy ideas into words of wisdom, or lies into the truth. The purpose of publishing is communication; don't try to use technology to disguise the lack of something to communicate.

publication. Desktop publishers generally use standard word processors and graphics programs to produce most source documents. Scanners with image editing software are used to transform photographs and hand-drawn images into computer-readable documents. Page-layout software, such as Quark Xpress, PageMaker, or InDesign, is used to combine the various source documents into a coherent, visually appealing publication. Pages are generally laid out one at a time on screen, although most programs have options for automating multiple-page document layout.

Page-layout software provides graphic designers with control over virtually every element of the design, right down to the spacing between each pair of letters (*kerning*) and the spacing between lines of text (*leading*). Today's word processing programs include basic page-layout capabilities, too; they're sufficient for producing many types of books and periodicals, complete with graphics. For users without background in layout and design, most page-layout and word processing programs include **templates**— professionally designed "empty" documents that can easily be adapted to specific user needs. Even without templates, it's possible for beginners to create professional-quality publications with a modest investment of money and time.

Desktop publishing becomes more complicated when color is introduced. *Spot color*—the use of a single color (or sometimes two) to add interest—is relatively easy. But *full-color* desktop publishing, including color photos, drawings, and paintings, requires you to deal with the inconsistencies of different color output devices. Because printers and monitors use different types of color-mixing technologies (as described in the *How It Works* boxes in Chapter 3), what you see on the screen isn't always what you get when you print it. It's even difficult to get two monitors (or two printers) to produce images with exactly the same color balance. Still, color desktop publishing is big busi-

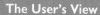

Desktop Publishing

SOFTWARE Adobe® PhotoShop® with Umax VistaScan plug-in, QuarkXPress page-layout software.

THE GOAL To create a publication that includes a collection of class projects and presentations with graphic illustrations.

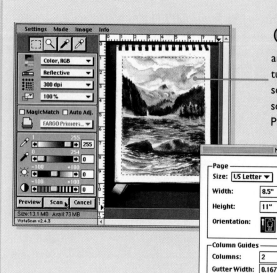

(1) The first step is to create and collect source documents. The articles are all word processor files, so they're ready to go. The pictures are a mixture of computer graphics files and hand-drawn images. You start by using a scanner to convert these drawings and paintings into graphics files. Your scanner comes with software that adds scanner controls to Adobe Photoshop, your image-editing program.

(2) After the source documents are ready, you open QuarkXPress to design and lay out the pages. You create a new document and specify the size of the pages, the margin sizes, and the number of columns per page. These measurements apply to all of the pages in the document; they become part of the **master pages** that control the general layout of the document. You can add page numbers, graphical elements, additional guides, and other embellishments to the master pages, and they'll automatically apply to all left- and right-facing pages.

(3) Next, choose View Master Page, and add a horizontal guide so it's easy to see the exact center of each page.

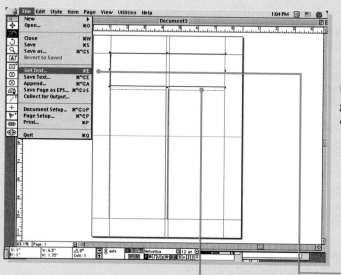

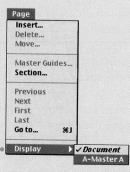

(4) On the first page, you use the text box tool to draw boxes to contain text from the Walden document you created earlier. The box for the title spans both columns; the boxes for text fill the remainder of the two columns.

(5) You place the cursor in the horizontal text box and choose the Get Text command.

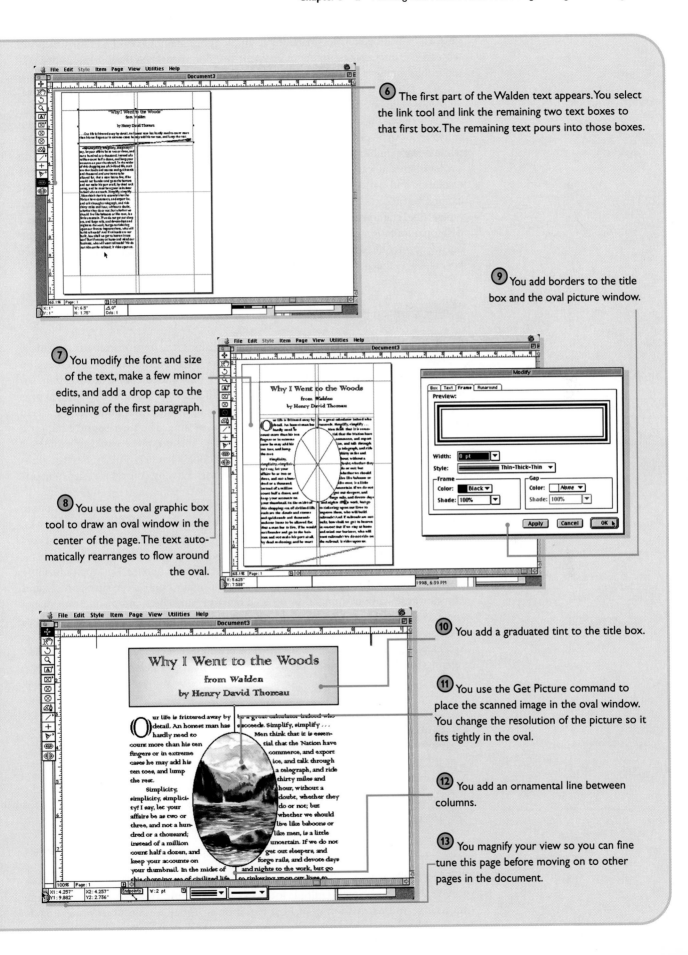

6 The first part of the Walden text appears. You select the link tool and link the remaining two text boxes to that first box. The remaining text pours into those boxes.

9 You add borders to the title box and the oval picture window.

7 You modify the font and size of the text, make a few minor edits, and add a drop cap to the beginning of the first paragraph.

8 You use the oval graphic box tool to draw an oval window in the center of the page. The text automatically rearranges to flow around the oval.

10 You add a graduated tint to the title box.

11 You use the Get Picture command to place the scanned image in the oval window. You change the resolution of the picture so it fits tightly in the oval.

12 You add an ornamental line between columns.

13 You magnify your view so you can fine tune this page before moving on to other pages in the document.

ness, and advances in color-matching technology are making it easier all the time. And with an ever-increasing number of inexpensive color printers on the market, color desktop publishing is rapidly becoming the norm.

The User's View box on the previous pages shows how a simple publication is created with page-layout software.   **UV**

Whether a document is created with a word processor or professional page-layout software, it can be printed on a variety of high-resolution output devices. Most black-and-white desktop publications are printed on laser printers capable of producing output with a resolution of at least 600 dots per inch (dpi). The number of dots per inch influences the resolution and clarity of the image. Output of 600 dpi is sufficiently sharp for most applications, but it's less than the 1,200 dpi that is the traditional minimum for professional typesetting. High-priced devices, called *phototypesetting machines* or *imagesetters*, allow desktop publications to be printed at 1,200 dpi or higher. Many desktop publishers rely on outside service bureaus with phototypesetting machines to print their final camera-ready pages—pages that are ready to be photographed and printed.

Why Desktop Publishing?

More than any other application, desktop publishing was responsible for the initial acceptance by large corporations of computers with graphical user interfaces. Desktop publishing offers several advantages for businesses. First and foremost, desktop publishing saves money. Publications that used to cost hundreds or thousands of dollars to produce through outside publishing services can now be produced in-house for a fraction of their former cost. Desktop publishing also saves time. The turnaround time for a publication done on the desktop can be a few days instead of the weeks or months it might take to publish the same thing using traditional channels. Finally, desktop publishing can reduce the quantity of publication errors. Quality control is easier to maintain when documents are produced in-house.

The real winners in the desktop publishing revolution might turn out to be not big businesses but everyday people with something to say. With commercial TV networks, newspapers, magazines, and book publishers increasingly controlled by a few giant corporations, many media experts worry that the free press guaranteed by our First Amendment is seriously threatened by *de facto* media monopolies. Desktop publishing technology offers new hope for every individual's right to publish. Writers, artists, and editors whose work is shunned or ignored by large publishers and mainstream media now have affordable publishing alternatives. The number of small presses and alternative, low-circulation periodicals is steadily increasing as publishing costs go down. If, as A. J. Liebling suggested, freedom of the press belongs to the person who owns one, that precious freedom is now accessible to more people than ever before.

Tomorrow's Word Tools

Paper, often underrated as a communication medium, will not be eliminated by the growth of electronic media. It remains inexpensive, extremely portable, and capable of carrying very high-resolution images.

—Mark Duchesne, **Vice President, AM Multigraphics**

The first books were so difficult to produce that they were considered priceless. They were kept in cabinets with multiple locks so that they couldn't be removed without the knowledge and permission of at least two monks. Today we can print professional-quality publications in short order using equipment that costs less than a used car. But the technological revolution in publishing revolution isn't over yet. Based on current trends and research, several trends are clear.

Paperless Publishing and the Web

> At the [*San Jose*] *Mercury News,* we spend $60 million per year for newsprint. *Nothing* on the Internet costs $60 million.
>
> —**Robert Ingle**, **vice president for new media at Knight Ridder**

A common prediction is that desktop publishing—and paper publishing in general—will be replaced by paperless electronic media. Paper still offers advantages for countless communication tasks. Reading printed words on pages is easier on the eyes than reading from a screen. Paper documents can be read and scribbled on almost anywhere, with or without electricity. And there's no electronic equivalent for the aesthetics of a beautifully designed, finely crafted book. Predictions aside, the printed word isn't likely to go away anytime soon.

Still, digital media *are* likely to eclipse paper for many applications. Electronic mail messages now outnumber post office deliveries of letters. CD-ROM encyclopedias briskly outsell their overweight paper counterparts. Adobe's **PDF (Portable Document Format)** allows documents of all types to be stored, viewed, or modified on any Windows or Macintosh computer, making it possible for many organizations to reduce paper flow. And the World Wide Web offers unprecedented mass publishing possibilities to millions of Internet users.

Programs as diverse as Microsoft Word, AppleWorks, and PageMaker can save documents in HTML formats so they can be published on the World Wide Web. Other programs, specifically designed for Web publishing, offer advanced capabilities for graphics, animation, and multimedia publishing. (We'll explore some of these tools in Chapters 7 and 11 when we discuss multimedia and the Web in greater depth.)

Never before has a communication medium made it so easy or inexpensive for an individual to reach such a wide audience. For a few dollars a month—or for free, in many cases—an Internet service provider can provide you with space to publish your essays, stories, reviews, and musings. It doesn't matter whether you're a student, a poet, an artist, a government official, a labor organizer, or a corporate president—on the Web all URLs are created equal.

Of course, the most popular commercial Web sites cost their owners more than a few dollars a month. A typical Web storefront costs a million dollars just to build. And one of the biggest challenges in Web publishing is attracting people to your site once it's on-line. Copyright protection is another problem for Web publishers; anything that's published on the Web for all of the world to see is also available for all of the world to copy. How can writers and editors be paid fairly for their labors if their works are so easy to duplicate?

Still, the Web is far more accessible to small-budget writers and publishers than any other mass medium. And many experts predict that Web technology will eventually include some kind of mechanism for automatic payment to authors whose works are downloaded. In any case, the free flow of ideas may be more significant than the flow of money. In the words

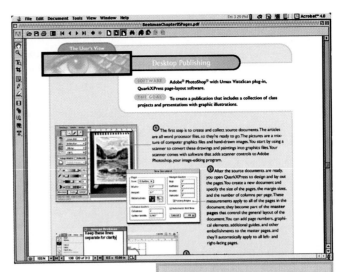

Adobe Acrobat is a cross-platform software program that allows PDF documents to be shared electronically, eliminating the need for paper in many publishing projects.

Many popular magazines, from *Newsweek* to *Rolling Stone,* publish electronic versions on the Web. *Salon* is an example of a popular magazine that publishes exclusively on the Web.

of writer Howard Rheingold, the World Wide Web "might be important in the same way that the printing press was important. By expanding the number of people who have the power to transmit knowledge, the Web might trigger a power shift that changes everything."

Electronic Books

The worth of a book
is to be measured by what you can carry away from it.

—James Bryce

Science fiction writers have long predicted the electronic book—a handheld device that can contain anything from today's top news stories to an annotated edition of *War and Peace*. Until recently, these types of devices have been commercial failures for two reasons: (1) The screens were hard to read and (2) content for them was not easily accessible.

LCD technology has made great strides in recent years, and screens are brighter and easier to read than ever before. Recent advances in font technologies from Microsoft and Adobe should help, too. Microsoft's ClearType enhances the clarity of text on flat-panel LCD screens, reducing pixel "blockiness." Adobe has developed a similar technology called Precision Graphics. Easy-on-the-eyes electronic books are likely to take advantage of these technologies soon.

To make it easier for electronic book owners to find content—books, periodicals, and other software to download into their devices—Everybook, Bertelsmann, HarperCollins, Microsoft Press, Time-Warner Books, and other companies are cooperating to develop an Open eBook standard. Once industry-wide standards are in place, electronic book publishing will be more practical—and popular. Future students may download texts rather than carrying them out of bookstores. Everybook CEO Daniel Munyan predicts that college freshmen will load their e-books with their notes and texts for the next 4 years and receive future updates via the Internet.

Word Processing Without a Keyboard

I think that the primary means of communication
with computers in the next millennium will be speech.

—Nicholas Negroponte, director of MIT's Media Lab

Changes in output devices—graphic screens and high-resolution printers—have had a tremendous impact on writing and publishing software in the last decade. As a result, the major bottlenecks in most modern desktop publishing systems occur on the input side. Many experts predict that the next big advances will occur as a result of emerging input devices.

In today's computers the mouse has taken over many of the functions of the keyboard. For a small but growing population, pen-based systems provide an alternative tool for entering text. Handwriting recognition doesn't come easy to computers; it requires sophisticated software that can interpret pen movements as characters and words. The diversity in handwriting makes it impossible for today's programs to translate all of our scribbles into text. Popular pen-based systems like the Palm devices work reliably because they require users to print characters using a carefully defined system that minimizes errors. Future pen devices will undoubtedly be more flexible, learning how their users write rather than requiring that their users learn new ways to write.

Ultimately, though, most writers long for a computer that can accept and reliably process *speech* input—a talkwriter. With such a system, a user can *tell* the computer what to type—and how to type it—by simply talking into a microphone. The user's speech enters the computer as a digital audio signal. Speech-recognition software looks for patterns in the sound waves and interprets sounds by locating familiar patterns, segmenting input sound patterns into words, separating commands from the text, and passing those commands on to the word processing software.

Speech-recognition software systems have been around for many years, but until recently, most were severely limited. It takes a great deal of intelligence to understand the complexities of human language speech. Most current commercial systems need to be trained to recognize a particular person's voice before they can function reliably. Even then, many systems require that the user speak slowly in a quiet environment and use a small, predefined vocabulary. Otherwise the machine might interpret, say, "recognize speech" as "wreck a nice beach." Research in speech recognition today focuses on overcoming these limitations and producing systems that can accomplish the following tasks:

▶ Recognize words without being trained to an individual speaker, an ability known as *speaker independence*.

▶ Handle speech without limiting vocabulary.

▶ Handle continuous speech—natural speech in which words run together at normal speed.

Researchers are making great strides toward these goals. Companies like IBM, Philips, and Lernout and Hauspie have developed programs that can achieve two of these goals. No one has yet developed a system that consistently achieves all three goals, the human body excepted.

While it's not yet trouble free or error free, PC speech-recognition software is growing in popularity, especially for people who can't use keyboards because of physical disabilities or job restrictions. As the technology improves, the microphone may become the preferred input device for PC users. Future pocket-sized personal digital assistants may become digital dictation machines.

Intelligent Word Processors

The real technology—behind all of our other technologies—is language. It actually creates the world our consciousness lives in.

—Norman Fischer, **Abbot, Green Gulch Farm Zen Center**

Speech recognition is just one aspect of artificial intelligence research that's likely to end up in future word processors. Many experts foresee word processors that are able to anticipate the writer's needs, acting as an electronic editor or coauthor. Today's grammar and style checkers are primitive forerunners of the kinds of electronic writing consultants that might appear in a few years. Microsoft Word's Help system includes a software agent that can watch what you do and make simple suggestions.

Here are some possibilities:

▶ As you're typing a story, your word processor reminds you (via a pop-up message on the screen or an auditory message) that you've used the word *delicious* three times in the last two paragraphs and suggests that you choose an alternative from the list shown on the screen.

What would you like to do?

- ◉ Check spelling and grammar
- ◉ Ways to check spelling and grammar
- ◉ Check the spelling and grammar of text in another language
- ◉ AutoCorrect doesn't automatically correct typos or spelling errors.
- ◉ Automatically correct typos and spelling errors
- ▼ See more...

check my spelling

[Options]   [Search]

Microsoft Office's automated help used primitive artificial intelligence techniques to answer basic user questions.

▶ Your word processor continuously analyzes your style as you type, determines your writing habits and patterns, and learns from its analysis. If your writing tends to be technical and formal, the software modifies its thesaurus, dictionary, and other tools so they're more appropriate for that style.

▶ You're writing a manual for a large organization whose documentation has specific style guidelines. Your word processor modifies your writing as you type so that it conforms to the organizational style.

▶ You need some current figures to support your argument on the depletion of the ozone layer. You issue a command, and the computer does a quick search of the literature on the Web and quickly reports back to you with several relevant facts.

All of these examples are technically possible now. The trend toward intelligent word processors is clear. Nevertheless, you're in for a long wait if you're eager to buy a system with commands such as Clever Quote, Humorous Anecdote, and Term Paper.

Where the eBooks Are

Hans Hansen

In March 2000, Stephen King's novella Riding the Bullet *was published on the Internet. 400,000 readers downloaded the digital book within 24 hours. Are paper books headed for extinction? In this article from the February 2000 issue of* Publish, *Hans Hansen, a developer of rare books in electronic formats at Octavo Corporation and the author of* The iMac Way *(a paper book), discusses the state of electronic books.*

Whenever two industries collide, there's confusion as corporations and startups try to stake out a niche for themselves. The print publishing industry is watching the Internet undermine their booksellers and periodicals while the price of paper escalates. The computer industry is vying for yet another opportunity to grow, adding one more digital stranglehold on traditional media. Out of this hope and despair has emerged the eBook. But can the eBook satisfy a consumer craving while serving the needs of the publishing and computer industries?

Hardware eBooks today seem more akin to Apple's now defunct Newton than a revolution in access to electronic content. Adobe and Microsoft are tripping over each other in a rush to standardize the format of electronic texts; Adobe has begun to refer to PDF as ePaper, and Microsoft is once again bullying the marketplace by advertising its less-than-original electronic reader technology ClearType. Meanwhile, publishing mega-corporations are already cornering these outlets before consumers are even demonstrating any interest. In other words, there's a whole lot of nothing going on out there.

Perhaps one reason the eBook market seems to be so chaotic is that there are so many competing notions of what an eBook is. Is it simply electronic text that's readable on any computer system, independent of specific hardware? Or is it a hardware device specifically tailored for easy reading of electronic documents, books, periodicals, and even Web pages? Most likely, an eBook is a combination of both. Technology developers and media publishers alike are struggling with this balance, trying to create an open definition so that a market can grow, while carefully positioning themselves in such a way that if their technology wins they'll be able to close the market and limit further innovation.

The Open eBook Initiative (www.openebook.org) is an attempt to solve the eBook definition dilemma by creating a forum for both the technology and publishing industries that allows them to direct their efforts toward a standard. This certainly sounds sensible if we are ever to enjoy the dream of global access to robust digital libraries. So far, the organization has published a specification for an electronic text format that is compatible with a wide variety of reading devices and platforms. Partners and contributors to this specification include just about everyone related to and interested in participating in both the consumer electronics industry and the media publishing industry. This specification is quickly developing as an HTML derivative—fast and easy to process but limited in its layout and typography controls.

This is no PDF. Clearly, trying to make a robust standard is tricky, especially one that allows for the most simple devices.

Setting aside the tradition of book design and typography, hardware developers want to build technological devices that consumers will buy. But notions of the best form for an electronic book reader vary greatly. For many, a small portable device that is easy to take everywhere seems sensible—akin to a paperback. But a small device may also mean fewer features—at least given today's technology. While a sharp high-quality display with good contrast and the ability to render both text and images seems a given, some devices seem headed toward small screens that can only display black-and-white pixels. Others are headed toward larger high-resolution full-color displays: Developer Everybook Inc. is building devices with two large screens side by side to emulate the form of a traditional book—a noble but costly approach. How much text an eBook should hold is also a source of debate—should it incorporate several novel-length books or an entire library of hundreds of volumes? Other technical concerns include user controls (push-button or touch-screen), battery life, and PC and Internet data connectivity.

And all this technology comes at a steep price, which ranges from $200 for the most meager device to over $2,000 for the most robust. Because of this wide array of options, there will continue to be a multitude of devices, all at varying prices and supporting different book formats—certainly not a simple consumer market like the one for DVDs or CDs.

Publishers and book sellers are also pushing and pulling on the eBook paradigm, signing exclusive partnerships with individual hardware and software developers while attempting to build new publicity and marketing opportunities. After all, whether the eBook revolution comes now or in another hundred years, it will come, and it will likely change the way books are authored, printed, published, and sold. And as with any multibillion-dollar industry, there's a lot of money to be gained or lost in the process.

Clearly this whole boondoggle will depend on the consumer. And until eBooks demonstrate an obvious advantage, technically or spiritually—and certainly at an economic scale that is accessible to more than the Silicon Valley elite—they will continue to float in the limbo between the computer and publishing industries. In the end all I care about is having something thought-provoking to read, whether it appears on a computer screen, a piece of paper, or even a stone tablet.

DISCUSSION QUESTIONS

1. Do electronic books threaten paper books? Explain your answer.
2. What features would an electronic textbook have to have for you to choose it over a paper textbook?

Even though the computer was originally designed to work with numbers, it quickly became an important tool for processing text. Today the word processor has all but replaced the typewriter as the tool of choice for committing words to paper.

Word processing is far more than typing text into a computer. Word processing software allows the writer to use commands to edit text on the screen, eliminating the chore of retyping pages until the message is right. Other commands allow the writer to control the format of the document: typefaces, spacing, justification, margins, columns, headers, footers, and other visual components. WYSIWYG word processors make it possible to see the formatted pages on the screen before printing them on paper. Most professional word processing programs automate footnoting, hyphenation, and other processes that are particularly troublesome to traditional typists.

Many advanced word processing functions are available as part of modern word processing programs or as stand-alone special-purpose applications. Outlining software turns the familiar outline into a powerful, dynamic organizational tool. Spelling checkers and grammar and style checkers partially automate the proofreading process, although they leave the more difficult parts of the job to literate humans. On-line thesauruses, dictionaries, and other computer-based references automate reference work. Production of specialized documents such as personalized form letters and full-length illustrated books can be simplified with other word processing tools.

As word processors become more powerful, they take on many of the features previously found only in desktop publishing software. Still, many publishers use word processors and graphics programs to create source documents that can be used as input for page-layout programs. The combination of the graphical user interface (GUI), desktop publishing software, and the high-resolution printer has revolutionized the publishing process by allowing publishers and would-be publishers to produce professional-quality text-and-graphics documents at a reasonable cost. Amateur and professional publishers everywhere use desktop publishing technology to produce everything from comic books to reference books.

The near-overnight success of desktop publishing may foreshadow other changes in the way we communicate with words as new technologies emerge. Computer networks in general and the World Wide Web in particular have made it possible for potential publishers to reach mass audiences without the problems associated with printing and distributing paper documents. Typing may no longer be a necessary part of the writing process as handwriting and speech-recognition technologies improve, and word processing software that incorporates other artificial intelligence technologies may become as much a coach as a tool for future writers.

Summary · **Chapter Review**

Key Terms

automatic correction (autocorrect), 130
automatic footnoting, 128
automatic formatting (autoformat), 130
automatic hyphenation, 128
camera-ready, 140
Clipboard, 124
copying text, 125
cursor, 123
cut-and-paste, 124
deleting text, 124
desktop publishing (DTP), 136
drag-and-drop, 124
editing text, 124
find command, 124
find and replace (search and replace), 125
font, 126

footer, 128
grammar and style checker, 134
groupware, 135
header, 128
idea processor, 132
inserting text, 124
insertion bar, 123
justification, 128
mail merge, 135
master pages, 138
monospaced font, 127
moving text, 125
navigating, 124
outlining, 132
page-layout software, 137
PDF (portable document format), 141
point size, 126
proportionally spaced font, 127

sans-serif font, 127
saving a document, 122
scrolling, 124
selecting text, 124
serif font, 127
service bureau, 140
source document, 136
spelling checker (batch or interactive), 133
style sheet, 128
template, 137
text formatting, 126
thesaurus, 132
typeface, 126
undo command, 125
wizard, 130
word wrap, 124
WYSIWYG, 124

Review Questions

1. Define or describe each of the key terms listed on the previous page. Check your answers in the glossary.
2. How is word processing different from typing?
3. What happens to your document when you turn the computer off? What should you do if you want to work on the document later?
4. Explain the difference between text editing and text formatting. Give several examples of each.
5. What is scrolling, and how is it useful?
6. When do you use the Enter or Return key in word processing?
7. How many different ways can a paragraph or line of text be justified? When might each be appropriate?
8. How is working with an outliner (or idea processor) different from working with a word processor?
9. What is a font, and how is it used in word processing and desktop publishing?
10. Describe three different ways a spelling checker might be fooled.
11. How does desktop publishing differ from word processing?
12. List several advantages of desktop publishing over traditional publishing methods.
13. What are the most important components of a desktop publishing system?
14. Is it possible to have a computer publishing system that is not WYSIWYG? Explain.
15. An automated speech-recognition system might have trouble telling the difference between a "common denominator" and a "comedy nominator." What must the speaker do to avoid confusion? What other limitations plague automated speech-recognition systems today?

Discussion Questions

1. Which of the word processing features and software categories described in this chapter would be the most useful to you as a student? How do you think you would use them?
2. What do you think of the arguments that word processing reduces the quality of writing because (1) it makes it easy to write hurriedly and carelessly and (2) it puts the emphasis on the way a document looks rather than on what it says?
3. Many experts fear that desktop publishing technology will result in a glut of unprofessional, tacky-looking publications. Others fear that it will result in a glut of slick-looking documents full of shoddy ideas and dangerous lies. How do you feel about each of these fears?
4. Like Gutenberg's development of the movable-type printing press more than 500 years ago, the development of desktop publishing puts powerful communication tools in the hands of more people. What impact will desktop publishing technology have on the free press and the free exchange of ideas guaranteed in the United States Constitution? What impact will the same technology have on free expression in other countries?
5. Discuss Question 4, substituting Web publishing for desktop publishing.

Projects

1. Using advertisements, hands-on demonstrations, and personal experience, compare the features of two or more popular word processing programs. (You may include the word processing modules of integrated software packages like ClarisWorks in your comparison.) What are the advantages and disadvantages of each program from a student's point of view?
2. Research one or more of your favorite local or national publications to find out how computers are used in their production.
3. Use a word processing system or a desktop publishing system to produce a newsletter, brochure, or flyer in support of an organization or cause that is important to you.

Sources & Resources

Books

Most word processing and desktop publishing books are hardware- and software-specific, that is, they're designed to be used with a specific version of a specific program on a specific machine running a specific operating system. If you need a book to get you started, choose one that fits your system. Make sure the book is an introductory tutorial, not a reference manual or a collection of "power user" tips. If possible, browse before you buy.

The Non-Designer's Design Book, by Robin Williams (Berkeley, CA: Peachpit Press, 1994). In this popular book, Robin Williams provides a friendly introduction to the basics of design and page layout in her popular, down-to-earth style. The first half of the book illustrates the four basic design principles (proximity, alignment, repetition, and contrast). The second half focuses on using type as a design element. This book is highly recommended for anyone new to graphic design.

The Non-Designer's Type Book, by Robin Williams (Berkeley, CA: Peachpit Press, 1998). This followup to *The Non-Designer's Design Book* focuses on fonts and typography. It uses lots of examples and conversational prose to clearly illustrate many ways type can be used to enhance publications.

The Non-Designer's Scan and Print Book, by Sandee Cohen and Robin Williams (Berkeley, CA: Peachpit Press, 1999). Desktop publishers must wear at least two hats, because publishing involves both design and production. This book focuses on the production part of the process. It's packed with information and tips on paper, printers, scanners, color, file formats, fonts, and more. Like the other *Non-Designer* books, it's easy to read, beautifully designed, and informative.

Looking Good in Print, Fourth Edition, by Roger C. Parker and Patrick Berry (Scottsdale, AZ: Coriolis, 1998). This book covers the non-technical side of desktop publishing. Now that you know the mechanics, how can you make your work look good? Parker and Berry clearly describe the basic design tools and techniques and then apply them in sample documents ranging from brochures to books.

The Official Adobe Print Publishing Guide: The Essential Resource for Print Publishing (San Jose: Adobe Press, 1998). This colorful book covers the entire publication process, from design and construction to proofing and printing. It can be a valuable reference tool for anyone serious about desktop publishing.

The Official Adobe Electronic Publishing Guide: The Essential Resource for Electronic Publishing (San Jose: Adobe Press, 1998). This companion to *The Official Adobe Print Publishing Guide* focuses on the "brave new world" of paperless publishing. Like the print guide, this book uses rich color illustrations and clear, concise explanations to illuminate the entire publishing process.

Adobe PDF with Acrobat 4 Visual Quickstart Guide, by Ted Alspach. Adobe's PDF has become a standard for platform-neutral publishing in print and on screen. This little book shows you how to work with PDF using Acrobat, a tool for creating, editing, and viewing PDF files.

Stop Stealing Sheep and Find Out How Type Works, by Eric Spiekermann and E. M. Ginger (Mountain View, CA: Adobe Press, 1993). This beautiful little book isn't so much a how-to text as a celebration of type as an art form. You'll see printed text differently after you read this book, and you'll have a deeper understanding of how to use it to communicate.

A Blip in the Continuum, Macintosh Version, by Robin Williams (Berkeley, CA: Peachpit Press, 1995), and *A Blip in the Continuum, Windows Version,* by Robin Williams (Berkeley, CA: Peachpit Press, 1996). Once you've learned the design basics from one or more of the books listed above, you might want to spend some time in this bold little book. Williams demonstrates how it sometimes pays to break time-honored rules by using contemporary "grunge" fonts to create bold, in-your-face layouts. A Macintosh- or Windows-compatible disk of fonts is included.

Bugs in Writing, by Lynn Dupre (Reading, MA: Addison-Wesley, 1998). This entertaining little book is designed to help computer science and computer information systems students—who presumably already know how to debug their programs—debug their prose. It's a friendly, readable tutorial that can help almost anybody to be a better writer.

The Elements of Style, Fourth Edition, by William Strunk, Jr., and E. B. White (Needham Heights, MA: Allyn & Bacon, 1999). If you want to improve your writing, this book is a classic.

Wired Style: Principles of English Usage in the Digital Age, by Constance Hale and Jessie Scanlon (San Francisco: Broadway Books, 2000). Should an e-mail address be italicized when it's included in a paragraph of text? For that matter, is it E-mail, e-mail, or email? Do you back up files or backup files? When you write about IBM should you use its unabbreviated name? Digital communication changes our language quickly, and the classic grammar and style manuals don't always have the answers. In this sometimes controversial guidebook the editors of *Wired* answer these questions, explain their writing and editing philosophies, and provide tips for writing about rapidly evolving technologies and ideas. If you like the informal future-focused style of *Wired,* you'll appreciate this book.

The Microsoft Manual of Style for Technical Publications, Second Edition (Redmond, WA: Microsoft Press, 1998). This style guide isn't as much fun to read as *Wired's,* and it doesn't offer much in the way of guidance or philosophy. But it's a useful alphabetical reference when you need to write about computer hardware and software.

Periodicals

Publish! This monthly provides cover-to-cover desktop publishing coverage. (The brand-specific magazines like *PC* and *Macworld* mentioned at the end of Chapter 1 also regularly discuss word processing and desktop publishing.)

World Wide Web Pages

The Web is full of fascinating resources for publishers, writers, and page designers. Some, like http://www.adobe.com, are obvious; others are harder to find but no less useful. Check the Computer Confluence web site for links to the best pages.

Chapter

6

Calculation, Visualization, and Simulation

Chapter 6

AFTER YOU READ THIS CHAPTER YOU SHOULD BE ABLE TO:

Describe the basic functions and applications of spreadsheet programs.

Explain how computers can be used to answer "what if?" questions.

Show how spreadsheet graphics can be used and misused as communication tools.

Describe other software tools for processing numbers and symbols on personal computers, workstations, and mainframes.

Explain how computers are used as tools for simulating mechanical, biological, and social systems.

In this chapter:

▶ Why spreadsheet programs opened the office door for PCs
▶ How spreadsheet software can answer "what if" questions
▶ How charts and graphs can illuminate—or hide—the truth
▶ Computer simulations: good news, bad news
... and more.

On the CD-ROM:

▶ Creating a spreadsheet and a chart: interactive walk-throughs
▶ Video clips of virtual reality visualizations
▶ An interactive fractal geometry game
▶ Instant access to glossary and key word references
▶ Interactive self-study quizzes
... and more.

On the Web:

www.prenhall.com/beekman
▶ Links to resources for working with numbers, charts, and graphs
▶ On-line simulation games and visualization tools
▶ Examples of state-of-the-art scientific simulations and visualizations
▶ Self-study exercises
... and more.

In terms of the success of VisiCalc, I don't feel I have
to repeat it. But it is nice to be able to realize

you've done something very worthwhile.

—Dan Bricklin

In 1978 Harvard graduate student Dan Bricklin watched his professor continually erase and recalculate rows and columns of numbers on a blackboard during classroom exercises in corporate financial planning. He envisioned a computer program that would do the calculations and recalculations automatically on the screen of his Apple II. With the help of his friend Bob Frankston, an MIT student, he developed VisiCalc, the first computer spreadsheet program. Almost overnight this revolutionary software changed the world of personal computing. Before VisiCalc personal computers were used mostly to mimic the functions of mainframes. But VisiCalc was a unique tool—one that provided managers with capabilities they never had before. Financial projections, budgetary reports, and other documents that might have taken days before could be created in minutes, and just as quickly modified if the results weren't satisfactory. VisiCalc was responsible for the early success of the Apple II, and the desktop computer in general, in the business world. Because of VisiCalc, managers and executives could see the value and power of those early machines.

After IBM introduced the IBM PC in 1981, many VisiCalc-inspired spreadsheet programs were competing

Dan Bricklin.

Mitch Kapor

for the software dollars of businesses. One of those programs was developed by Mitch Kapor, an idealistic young entrepreneur who had worked for a VisiCalc distributor and tested a release of VisiCalc. In 1983 Kapor's start-up company, Lotus, released a powerful, easy-to-use integrated spreadsheet/graphics package called 1-2-3 that quickly established itself as the standard spreadsheet on IBM-compatible computers. By backing a solid software product with an expensive marketing campaign and a support program that made it easier for non-technical corporate users to get training and help, Lotus established new standards for software success. Lotus 1-2-3 quickly became the most successful software product the computer industry had ever seen.

Today 1-2-3 has been eclipsed by Microsoft Excel, a graphical spreadsheet program originally developed for the Macintosh. The original VisiCalc program was purchased by Lotus and discontinued. After an unsuccessful trade-secret-theft lawsuit against Lotus, VisiCalc's parent company faded into obscurity. In 1995 IBM purchased Lotus and began bundling Lotus products with its computers.

What happened to Bricklin and Kapor? Both left their original companies for other computer ventures. Bricklin still develops innovative software, including pen-based systems and multimedia authoring tools. Kapor became the cofounder of and spokesperson for the Electronic Frontier Foundation, an organization dedicated to protecting human rights and the free flow of information on the Internet.

Computers were originally created to calculate, and today's machines are still widely used for numeric computations. Numbers are at the heart of applications ranging from accounting to statistical analysis. The most popular number-crunching application is the spreadsheet, conceived by Bricklin and institutionalized by Lotus. Executives, engineers, scientists, and others use the spreadsheet for the same reason: It allows them to create and work with simulations of real-world situations.

A well-designed simulation, whether constructed with a spreadsheet or with another software application, can help people achieve a better understanding of the world outside the computer. Computer simulations have their limitations and risks, too. In this chapter we explore the world of number manipulation and computer simulation, starting with the spreadsheet.

The Spreadsheet: Software for Simulation and Speculation

Compare the expansion of business today to the conquering of the continent in the nineteenth century. The spreadsheet in that comparison is like the transcontinental railroad. It accelerated the movement, made it possible, and changed the course of the nation.

—Mitch Kapor

More than any other type of personal computer software, the spreadsheet has changed the way people do business. In the same way a word processor can give a computer user control over words, spreadsheet software allows the user to take control of numbers, manipulating them in ways that would be difficult or impossible otherwise. A spreadsheet program can make short work of tasks that involve repetitive calculations: budgeting, investment management, business projections, grade books, scientific simulations, checkbooks, and so on. A spreadsheet can also reveal hidden relationships between numbers, taking much of the guesswork out of financial planning and speculation.

The Malleable Matrix

The goal was that it had to be better than the back of an envelope.

—Dan Bricklin

Almost all spreadsheet programs are based on a simple concept: the malleable matrix. A spreadsheet document, called a worksheet, typically appears on the screen as a grid of numbered rows and alphabetically lettered columns. The box representing the intersection of a row and a column is called a cell. Every cell in this grid has a unique address made up of a row number and column letter. For example, the cell in the upper-left corner of the grid is called cell A1 (column A, row 1). All the cells are empty in a new worksheet; it's up to the user to fill them. Each cell can contain a numeric value, an alphabetic label, or a formula representing a relationship between numbers in other cells.

Values (numbers) are the raw material used by the spreadsheet software to perform calculations. Numbers in worksheet cells can represent wages, test scores, weather data, polling results, or just about anything that can be quantified.

To make it easier for people to understand the numbers, most worksheets include labels at the tops of columns and at the edges of rows, such as "Monthly Wages," "Midterm Exam 1," "Average Wind Speed," or "Final Approval Rating." To the computer, these labels are meaningless strings of characters. The label "Total Points" doesn't tell the

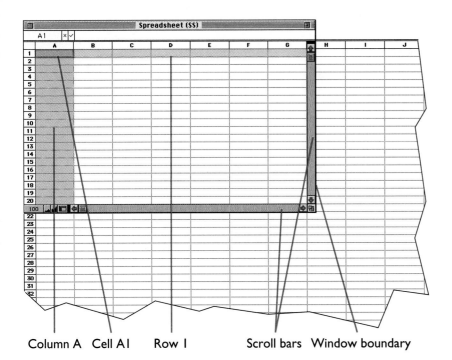

Column A   Cell A1   Row 1   Scroll bars   Window boundary

The worksheet may be bigger than what appears on your screen. The program allows you to scroll horizontally and vertically to view the larger matrix. (After Z, columns are labeled with double letters: AA, AB, and so on.)

computer to calculate the total and display it in an adjacent cell; it's just a road sign for human readers.

To calculate the total points (or the average wind speed or the final approval rating), the worksheet must include a **formula**—a step-by-step procedure for calculating the desired number. The simplest spreadsheet formulas are arithmetic expressions using $+$, $-$, $*$, and $/$ to represent addition, subtraction, multiplication, and division, respectively. For example, cell B5 might contain the formula $=(B2+B3)/2$. This formula tells the computer to add the numbers in cells B2 and B3, divide the result by 2, and display the final result in the cell containing the formula, cell B5. You don't see the formula in cell B5; you just see its effect. It doesn't matter whether the numbers represent test scores, dollars, or nothing at all; the computer obediently calculates their average and displays the results. If either number in cell B2 or B3 changes, the number displayed in B5 automatically changes, too. *The User's View* illustrates how you might create a simple worksheet. **UV**

Different brands of spreadsheets, such as Lotus 1-2-3 and Microsoft Excel, are distinguished by their features and their user interfaces. In spite of their differences, all popular spreadsheet programs work in much the same way and share most of these features:

▶ *Automatic replication of values, labels, and formulas.* Most worksheets contain repetition: Budgetary amounts remain constant from month to month; exam scores are calculated the same way for every student in the class; a scheduling program refers to the same seven days each week. Many spreadsheet commands streamline entry of repetitive data, labels, and formulas. **Replication** commands are, in essence, flexible extensions of the basic copy-and-paste functions found in other software. The most commonly used replication commands are the Fill Down and Fill Right commands illustrated in *The User's View* example. Formulas can be constructed with *relative references* to other cells, as in the example, so they refer to different cells when replicated in other locations, or as *absolute references* that don't change when copied elsewhere.

▶ *Automatic recalculation.* **Automatic recalculation** is one of the spreadsheet's most important capabilities. It not only allows for the easy correction of errors, but also makes it easy to try out different values while searching for solutions. For large, complicated worksheets, recalculation can be painfully slow, so most spreadsheets allow you to turn off the automatic recalculation feature and recalculate the worksheet only when you need it.

Creating a Simple Worksheet

SOFTWARE   **Microsoft Excel.**

THE GOAL   **To create a computerized version of a worksheet showing projected expenses for one college student's fall term. The design of the worksheet is based on this hand-drawn planning version.**

① The first step is to type descriptive labels for the worksheet title and to label the rows and columns. Typing appears in the current or active cell—the cell containing the cursor—and in the long window above the worksheet, called the console or formula bar. You move from cell to cell by clicking with the mouse or by navigating with the keyboard.

② To make room for row labels, you widen the first column by dragging its border to the right.

③ After typing the labels, you type numeric values to represent dollar values for each category in each month.

④ To change cell formats so numbers are displayed with dollar signs, you select the range (rectangular block) of cells by dragging between cells B3 and F11, two opposite corners of the rectangle.

⑤ Choose the Cells command from the Format menu . . .

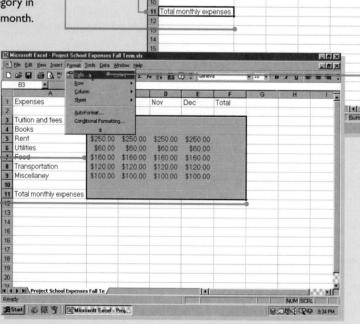

6 ...and then select the Currency format to change the appearance of all values in the range.

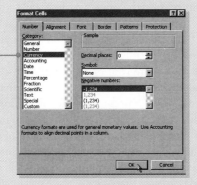

7 You enter a formula to calculate the total expenses for September in cell B11: =sum(B3:B9). When you press Enter, the formula in the cell is replaced by the calculated value—the sum of the numbers in cells B3 through B9. (The formula is still visible in the formula bar whenever cell B11 is active.)

8 You don't need to repeat this process for the other columns in the worksheet; instead you can replicate this formula in cells C11 through F11. When you select the range of cells from B11 to F11 and apply the Fill Right command, each cell in the block gets a version of this formula automatically adjusted to calculate the total for that cell's column.

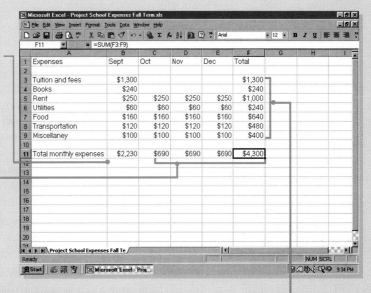

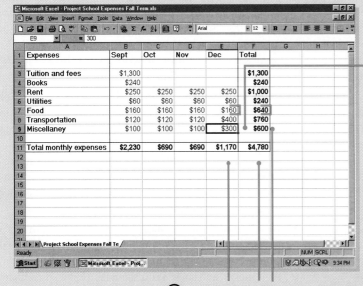

9 A similar process (using the Fill Down command) calculates the totals in column F.

10 After you change the format of some cells to make the worksheet more readable, you decide to change numbers in two of December's cells to allow for holiday gifts and travel.

11 The spreadsheet software automatically recalculates all formulas to reflect the revised input data.

▶ *Predefined functions.* The first calculators made computing a square root a tedious and error-prone series of steps. On today's calculators a single press of the square-root button tells the calculator to do all of the necessary calculations to produce the square root. Spreadsheet programs contain built-in functions that work like the calculator's square-root button. A function in a formula instructs the computer to perform some predefined set of calculations. For example, the formula =SQRT(C5) calculates the square root of the number in cell C5. Modern spreadsheet applications have large libraries of predefined functions. Many, like SUM, AVERAGE (or AVG), MIN, and MAX, represent simple calculations that are performed often in all kinds of worksheets. Others automate complex financial, mathematical, and statistical calculations that would be extremely difficult to do manually. The IF function allows the worksheet to decide what to do based on the contents of other cells, giving the worksheet logical decision-making capability. (For example: If the number of hours worked is greater than 40, calculate pay using the overtime schedule.) Like the calculator's square-root button, these functions can save time and reduce the likelihood of errors.

▶ *Macros.* A spreadsheet's menu of functions, like the menu in a fast-food restaurant, is limited to the most popular selections. For situations where the built-in functions don't fill the bill, most spreadsheets allow the user to capture sequences of steps as reusable macros—custom-designed procedures that you can add to the existing menu of options. Some programs insist that you type macros using a special macro language; others allow you to turn on a macro recorder that captures every move you make with the keyboard and mouse, recording those actions in a macro transcript. Later you can ask the computer to carry out the instructions in that macro. Suppose, for example, you use the same set of calculations every month when preparing a statistical analysis of environmental data. Without macros you'd have to repeat the same sequence of keystrokes, mouse clicks, and commands each time you created the monthly report. But by creating a macro called, for instance, Monthstats, you can effectively say, "Do it again!" by issuing the Monthstats command.

▶ *Formatting.* Most modern spreadsheets allow you to control typefaces, text styles, cell dimensions, and cell borders. They also allow you to include pictures and other graphic embellishments in documents.

▶ *Templates.* Even with functions and macros, the process of creating a complex worksheet from scratch can be intimidating. Many users take advantage of worksheet templates that contain labels and formulas but no data values. These reusable templates produce instant answers when you fill in the blanks. Some common templates are packaged with spreadsheet software; others are marketed separately. When templates aren't available, users can create their own or commission programmers to write them. Whatever its origin, a well-designed template can save considerable time, effort, and anguish.

▶ *Linking.* Sometimes a change in one worksheet produces changes in another. For example, a master sales summary worksheet for a business should reflect changes in each department's sales summary worksheet. Most spreadsheet programs allow you to create automatic links between worksheets so when values change in one, all linked worksheets are updated automatically. Some programs can create three-dimensional worksheets by stacking and linking several two-dimensional sheets. Some spreadsheet programs allow you to create links to Web pages so data can be downloaded and updated automatically.

▶ *Database capabilities.* Many spreadsheet programs can perform basic database functions: storage and retrieval of information, searching, sorting, report generation, mail merge, and such. With these features a spreadsheet can serve users whose database needs are modest. For those who require a full-featured database management system, spreadsheet software might still be helpful; many spreadsheet programs support automatic two-way communication with database software.

All of these worksheets are linked together into a single 3-D worksheet.

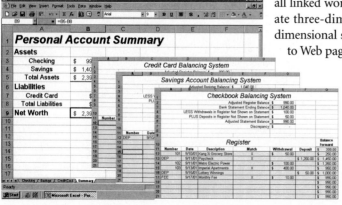

Avoiding Spreadsheet Pitfalls

Spreadsheet errors are easy to make and easy to overlook. When creating a worksheet, you can minimize errors by following a few basic guidelines:

▶ *Plan the worksheet before you start entering values and formulas.* Think about your goals, and design the worksheet to meet those goals.

▶ *Make your assumptions as accurate as possible.* Answers produced by a worksheet are only as good as the assumptions built into the data values and formulas. A worksheet that compares the operating costs of a gas guzzler and a gas miser must make assumptions about future trips, repair costs, and, above all, gasoline prices. The accuracy of the worksheet is tied to all kinds of unknowns, including the future of Middle East politics. The more accurate the assumptions, the more accurate the predictions.

▶ *Double-check every formula and value.* Values and formulas are input for worksheets, and input determines output. Computer professionals often describe the dark side of this important relationship with the letters *GIGO—garbage in, garbage out*. One highly publicized spreadsheet transcription error for Fidelity Investments resulted in a $2.6 billion miscalculation because of a single missing minus sign! You may not be working with values this big, but it's still important to proofread your work carefully.

▶ *Make formulas readable.* If your software allows you to attach names to cell ranges, use meaningful names in formulas. It's easier to create and debug formulas when you can use readily understandable language like payrate*40+1.5*payrate*(hoursworked–40) instead of a string of characters like C2*40+1.5*C2*(D2-40).

▶ *Check your output against other systems.* Use another program, a calculator, or pencil and paper to verify the accuracy of a sampling of your calculations.

▶ *Build in cross-checks.* Compare the sum of row totals with the sum of column totals. Does everything add up?

▶ *Change the input data values and study the results.* If small input adjustments produce massive output changes, or if major input adjustments result in little or no output changes, something may be wrong.

▶ *Take advantage of preprogrammed functions, templates, and macros.* Why reinvent the wheel when you can buy a professionally designed vehicle?

▶ *Use a spreadsheet as a decision-making aid, not a decision maker.* Some errors aren't obvious; others don't show up immediately. Stay alert and skeptical.

"What If?" Questions

The purpose of computation is not numbers but insight.

—R. W. Hamming

A spreadsheet program is a versatile tool, but it's especially valuable for answering "what if?" questions: "What if I don't complete the third assignment? How will that affect my chances for getting an A?" "What if I put my savings in a high-yield, tax-sheltered IRA account with a withdrawal penalty? Will I be better off than if I leave it in a low-yield passbook account with no penalty?" "What if I buy a car that gets only 10 miles per gallon instead of a car that gets 40? How much more will I pay altogether for fuel over the next four years?" Because it allows you to change numbers and instantly see the effects of those changes, spreadsheet software streamlines the process of searching for answers to these questions.

Some spreadsheet programs include equation solvers that turn "what if?" questions around. Instead of forcing you to manipulate data values until formulas give you the numbers you're looking for, an equation solver allows you to define an equation, enter your target value, and watch while the computer determines the necessary data values. For example, an investor might use an equation solver to

This worksheet compares two different car loans for total interest expense: a 5-year loan at 7.61% and a 4-year loan at 9.15%. The cells whose contents appear in color (blue or red) contain formulas that compute results based on the contents of the worksheet. The 4-year loan, even though it has a higher interest rate, is a slightly better choice.

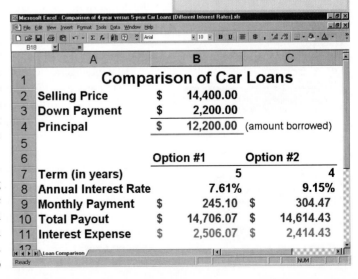

	A	B	C
1	**Comparison of Car Loans**		
2	**Selling Price**	$ 14,400.00	
3	**Down Payment**	$ 2,200.00	
4	**Principal**	$ 12,200.00	(amount borrowed)
5			
6		Option #1	Option #2
7	**Term (in years)**	5	4
8	**Annual Interest Rate**	7.61%	9.15%
9	**Monthly Payment**	$ 245.10	$ 304.47
10	**Total Payout**	$ 14,706.07	$ 14,614.43
11	**Interest Expense**	$ 2,506.07	$ 2,414.43

answer the question "What is the *best* mix of these three stocks for minimizing risk while producing a 10 percent return on my investment?"

Spreadsheet Graphics: From Digits to Drawings

Our work . . . is to present things that are
as they are.

—Frederick II (1194–1250), **King of Sicily**

Most spreadsheet programs include charting commands that can turn worksheet numbers into charts and graphs automatically. Stand-alone charting programs create charts from any collection of numbers, whether stored in a worksheet or not. The process of creating a chart is usually as simple as filling in a few blanks in a dialog box.

The growth in election campaign spending seems more real as a line shooting toward the top of a graph than as a collection of big numbers on a page. The federal budget makes more (or less?) sense as a sliced-up dollar pie than as a list of percentages. The correct chart can make a set of stale figures come to life, awakening our eyes and brains to trends and relationships that we might not have otherwise seen.

Most spreadsheet and charting programs offer a variety of basic chart types and options for embellishing charts. The differences among these chart types are more than aesthetic; each chart type is well suited for communicating particular types of information. **UV**

Pie charts show the relative proportions of the parts to a whole. Line charts are most often used to show trends or relationships over time or to show relative distribution of one variable through another. (The classic bell-shaped normal curve is a line chart.) Bar charts are similar to line charts, but they're more appropriate when data falls into a few categories. Bars can be stacked in a stack chart that shows how proportions of a whole change over time; the effect is similar to a series of pie charts. Scatter charts are used to discover, rather than display, a relationship between two variables. A well-designed chart can convey a wealth of information, just as a poorly designed chart can confuse or mislead.

Microsoft Office's Help system attempts to answer questions written in English, but the answers aren't always relevant.

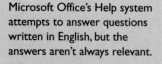

- Total the numbers in a row or column
- Referencing cells in a table
- Calculate the average
- Perform calculations in a table
- Field codes: = (Formula) field
- ▼ See more...

How can I calculate the average monthly temperature?

Options   Search

Tomorrow's Spreadsheet?

As revolutionary as VisiCalc was when it was introduced in 1979, it simply couldn't meet the demands of today's spreadsheet user. Even the original 1-2-3 looks primitive next to modern graphic spreadsheets. It's unlikely that spreadsheets have reached the end of their evolutionary path. What's next?

Microsoft Excel, Lotus 1-2-3, and other spreadsheets are beginning to incorporate artificial intelligence to guide users through complex procedures. (The wizard shown in the charting *User's View* box is a very simple example.) To help users check complex worksheets for consistency of entries and formula logic, future spreadsheets are likely to include *validators*—the equivalent of spelling and grammar checkers for spreadsheets.

Further down the road, spreadsheets may disappear into the background along with other applications. Today's feature-laden spreadsheets may be replaced by smaller software tools that can be combined into custom applications. Users will work with words, numbers, and other types of data without having to think about separate word processors, spreadsheets, and other applications. The program components, like the data they use in their calculations, might be spread across a network—or the entire Internet. From the user's point of view the focus will be more on the problem solution than on tools.

The User's View

Charting with a Spreadsheet

SOFTWARE **Microsoft Excel.**

THE GOAL **To create a chart to bring your budget into focus.**

① To chart the breakdown totals from your budget, you'll use two ranges of cells: One contains the column of totals (F3 through F9) ...

② and another contains the category names for those totals (A3 through A9).

③ After selecting both ranges, you click on the Chart Wizard icon on the button bar. Chart Wizard walks you through the process of creating a chart by presenting a series of dialog boxes.

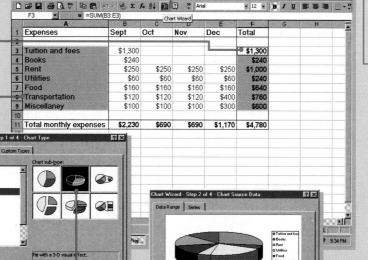

Expenses	Sept	Oct	Nov	Dec	Total
Tuition and fees	$1,300				$1,300
Books	$240				$240
Rent	$250	$250	$250	$250	$1,000
Utilities	$60	$60	$60	$60	$240
Food	$160	$160	$160	$160	$640
Transportation	$120	$120	$120	$400	$760
Miscellaney	$100	$100	$100	$300	$600
Total monthly expenses	$2,230	$690	$690	$1,170	$4,780

④ You select the 3-D Pie chart type.

⑤ Step 2 lets you verify the data range and specify that the data is in columns, not rows.

⑥ Step 3 allows you to add a title and, if necessary, other information.

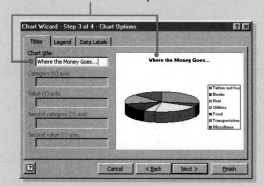

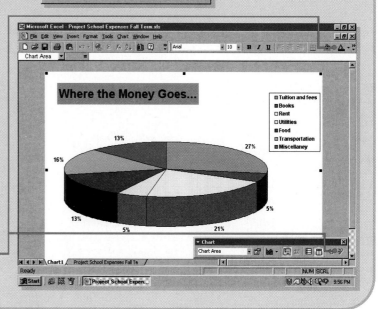

⑦ You can use the program's graphics tools to fine-tune the chart's appearance.

Statistical Software: Beyond Spreadsheets

Science is what we understand well enough to explain to a computer;
art is everything else.

—Donald Knuth, **author of** *The Art of Computer Programming*

Spreadsheet software is remarkably versatile, but no program is perfect for every task. Other types of number-manipulation software are available for those situations in which spreadsheets don't quite fit the job.

Money Managers

Spreadsheet software has its roots in the accountant's ledger sheets, but spreadsheets today are seldom used for accounting and bookkeeping. Accounting is a complex concoction of rules, formulas, laws, and traditions, and creating a worksheet to handle the details of the process is difficult and time consuming. Instead of relying on

Line charts and bar charts (below) can be used to show trends over time or distribution over categories. Scatter charts (right) are used to see relationships between variables.

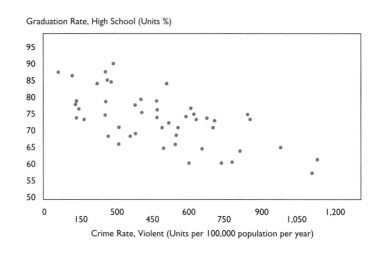

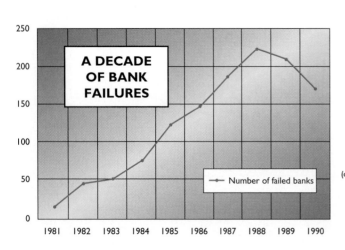

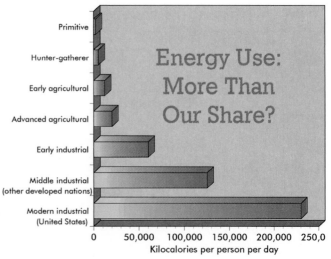

Making Smart Charts

A chart can be a powerful communication tool if it's designed intelligently. If it's not, the message may miss the mark. Here are some guidelines for creating charts that are easy to read and understand.

▶ *Choose the right chart for the job.* Think about the message you're trying to convey. Pie charts, bar charts, line charts, and scatter charts are not interchangeable.

▶ *Keep it simple, familiar, and understandable.* Use charts in magazines, books, and newspapers as models.

▶ *Strive to reveal the truth, not hide it.* Whether accidentally or intentionally, many computer users create charts that convey misinformation. Changes in the scale or dimensions of a chart can completely transform the message, turning information into propaganda.

These charts are based on identical data; only the values on the vertical axes have been changed to distort the facts.

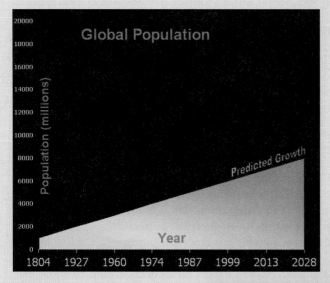

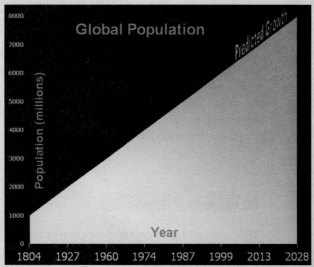

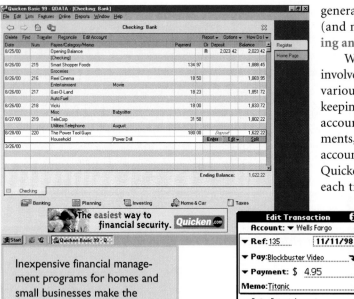

general-purpose spreadsheets for accounting, most businesses (and many households) use professionally designed **accounting and financial management software**.

Whether practiced at home or at the office, accounting involves setting up **accounts**—monetary categories to represent various types of income, expenses, assets, and liabilities—and keeping track of the flow of money between those accounts. An accountant routinely records *transactions*—checks, cash payments, charges, and other activities—that move money from one account to another. Accounting software, such as Intuit's popular Quicken, automatically adjusts the balance in every account after each transaction. What's more, it records every transaction so that the history of each account can be retraced, step by step. This *audit trail* is a necessary part of business financial records, and it's one reason accountants use special-purpose accounting packages rather than spreadsheet programs.

In addition to keeping records, financial management software can automate check writing, bill paying, budgeting, and other routine money matters. Periodic reports and charts can provide detailed answers to questions such as "Where does the money go?" and "How are we doing compared to last year?"

Inexpensive financial management programs for homes and small businesses make the accounting process easier to understand by simulating checks and other familiar documents on the screen. Quicken allows you to track cash, check, and credit card transactions, and use the data in a variety of ways. Pocket Quicken allows you to record transactions on a handheld computer when you're away from your desk and upload those transactions into your desktop machine later.

The Internet has made it possible for programs like Quicken to expand beyond the boundaries of the PC. Through an Internet connection, a home accounting program can recommend investments based on up-to-the-hour performance statistics, track investment portfolios, comparison shop for insurance and mortgages, and link to specialized on-line calculators and advisors. Hundreds of financial institutions now offer on-line banking services, making it possible to pay bills, check account balances, and transfer funds using software.

Most accounting and financial management programs don't calculate income taxes, but they *can* export records to programs that do. **Tax preparation software** works like a prefabricated worksheet. As you enter numbers into the blanks in on-screen forms, other blanks are filled automatically by the program. Every time a number is entered or changed, the bottom line is recalculated automatically. When the forms are completed, they're ready to print, sign, and mail to the Internal Revenue Service. Some taxpayers bypass paper forms altogether by sending the completed forms electronically to the IRS.

Automatic Mathematics

An abstract mathematical relationship is easier to understand when turned into a visible object with high-level mathematical software. (Software: Mathematica.)

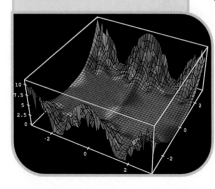

Most of us seldom do math more complicated than filling out our tax forms. But higher mathematics is an essential part of the work of many scientists, researchers, engineers, architects, economists, financial analysts, teachers, and other professionals. Mathematics is a universal language for defining and understanding natural phenomena as well as a tool used to create all kinds of products and structures. Whether or not we work with it directly, our lives are constantly being shaped by mathematics.

Many professionals and students whose mathematical needs go beyond the capabilities of spreadsheets depend on symbolic **mathematics processing software** to grapple with complex equations and calculations. Mathematics processors make it easier for mathematicians to create, manipulate, and solve equations, in much the same way word processors help writers. Features vary from program to program, but a typical mathematics processor can do polynomial factoring, symbolic and

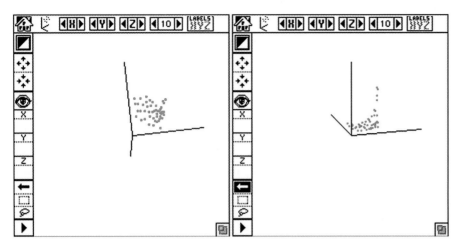

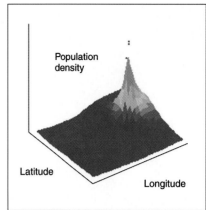

These 3-D scatter charts show the relationship among three variables: latitude, longitude, and population density in the United States. In (A), the relationship isn't clear. But when the "structure" is rotated and viewed from a different angle, as in (B), it makes more sense. The final picture (C) spells out the pattern by adding a surface. It is clear from this plot that the population is spread unevenly across the country.

numeric calculus, real and complex trigonometry, matrix and linear algebra, and three-dimensional graphics.

Mathematics processors generally include an interactive question-and-answer mode, a programming language, and tools for creating interactive documents that combine text, numerical expressions, and graphics. Although mathematics processors have only been available for a few years, they've already changed the way professionals use mathematics and the way students learn it. By handling the mechanics of mathematics, these programs allow people to concentrate on the content and implications of their work.

Statistics and Data Analysis

Yet to calculate is not in itself to analyze.

—Edgar Allan Poe, 1841

One branch of applied mathematics that has become more important in the computer age is **statistics**—the science of collecting and analyzing data. Modern computer technology provides us with mountains of data—census data, political data, consumer data, economic data, sports data, weather data, scientific data, and more. We often refer to the data as statistics ("The government released unemployment statistics today"), but the numbers by themselves tell only part of the story. The analysis of those numbers—the search for patterns and relationships among them—can provide meaning for the data. ("Analysts note that the rise in unemployment is confined to cities most heavily impacted by the freeze on government contracts.") Statisticians in government, business, and science depend on computers to make sense of raw data.

Do people who live near nuclear power plants run a higher cancer risk? Does the current weather pattern suggest the formation of a tropical storm? Are rural voters more likely to support small-town candidates? These questions can't be answered with absolute certainty; the element of chance is at the heart of statistical analysis. But **statistical analysis software** can suggest answers to questions such as these by testing the strength of data relationships. Statistical software can also produce graphs showing how two or more variables relate to each other. Statisticians can often uncover trends by browsing through two- and three-dimensional graphs of their data, looking for unusual patterns in the dots and lines that appear on the screen. This kind of visual exploration of data is an example of a type of application known as *scientific visualization*.

Inside two simulated molecules in Argonne National Laboratory's Cave Automatic Virtual Environment, computer scientist David Levine investigates how one molecule "docks" into another. His research uses advanced computers to understand how proteins form string-like molecules that are related to Alzheimer's disease and rheumatoid arthritis.

Scientific Visualization

The wind blows over the lake and stirs the surface of the water. Thus, visible effects of the invisible are manifested.

—The I Ching

Scientific visualization software uses shape, location in space, color, brightness, and motion to help us understand relationships that are invisible to us. Like mathematical and statistical software, scientific visualization software is no longer confined to mainframes and supercomputers; some of the most innovative programs have been developed for use on high-end personal computers and workstations, working alone or in conjunction with more powerful computers.

Scientific visualization takes many forms, all of which involve graphical representation of numerical data. The numbers can be the result of abstract equations, or they can be data gleaned from the real world. Either way, turning the numbers into pictures allows researchers and students to see the unseeable, and sometimes, as a result, to know what was previously unknowable. Here are two examples:

▶ Astronomer Margaret Geller of Harvard University created a three-dimensional map of the cosmos from data on the locations of known galaxies. While using her computer to "fly through" this three-dimensional model, she saw something that no one had seen before: the mysterious clustering of galaxies along the edges of invisible bubbles.

▶ Dr. Mark Ellisman of the University of California, San Diego, School of Medicine used a 30-foot electron microscope to collect data from cells of the brain and enter it into a supercomputer, which rendered a 3-D representation of the brain cell. When Ellisman's team displayed the data on a graphic workstation, they saw several previously undiscovered aberrations in brains of patients who had Alzheimer's disease—aberrations that may turn out to be clues for discovering the cause and cure for this disease.

In these examples and hundreds of others like them, visualization helps researchers see relationships that might have been obscure or even impossible to grasp without computer-aided visualization tools.

Calculated Risks: Computer Modeling and Simulation

We have the ability to model—to prototype—faster, better, and cheaper than ever before. The old back-of-the-envelope is becoming supercomputer driven louver!

—Michael Schrage, author of Serious Play

Whether part of a simple worksheet or a complex set of equations, numbers often symbolize real-world phenomena. Computer modeling—the use of computers to create abstract models of objects, organisms, organizations, and processes—can be done with spreadsheets, mathematical applications, or standard programming languages. Most of the applications discussed in this chapter are examples of computer modeling. A business executive who creates a worksheet to project quarterly profits and losses is trying to model the economic world that affects the company. An engineer who uses a mathematics processor to test the stress capacity of a bridge is modeling the bridge mathemati-

How It Works 6.1

Scientific Computing

Computers have long been used to analyze and visualize scientific data collected through experiments and observation. A computer can also serve as a virtual laboratory that simulates a physical process without real-world experiments. Of course, an inaccurate simulation can give incorrect results.

The problem of accurate simulation helped initiate the study of chaos and fractals. Chaos is now a vast field of study with applications in many disciplines.

The "Chaos Game" illustrates how computers can quickly complete repetitive tasks in experiments that would otherwise be impractical or impossible. You could perform the first few steps of such an experiment with pencil, paper, and ruler, like this:

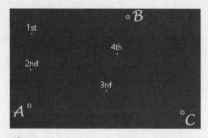

1 Draw three widely separated points on the paper to form a triangle; label the points A, B, and C. Draw a random starting point anywhere on the paper. This will be the first "current" point.

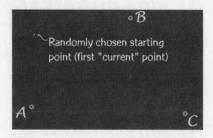

2 Repeat the following process four times: randomly choose from among points A, B, and C, and draw a new point halfway (on an imaginary straight line) between the current point and the chosen point. The newly drawn point then becomes the new current point.

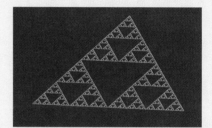

3 If you use a simple computer program to plot 100,000 repeats of step 2 (excluding the first few points from the drawing), you'll see a pattern emerge rather than a solid mass of dots. This pattern, called a Sierpinski gasket, is a fractal—an object in which pieces are miniatures of the whole figure. You will see a pattern like this.

Because some fractal formulas mimic the patterns of natural objects, such as coastlines and mountains, chaos has found applications in computer-generated scenery and special effects for movies and television shows.

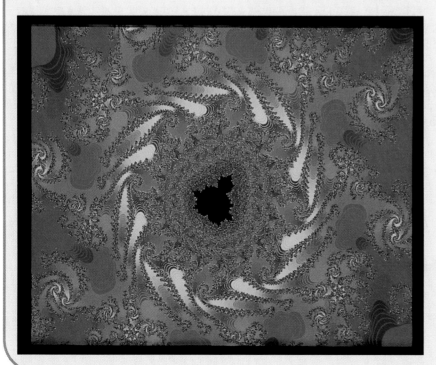

The Mandelbrot set, discovered by the mathematician Benoit Mandelbrot (who coined the term *fractal*) while he was working at IBM's Thomas J. Watson Research Facility, is one of the most famous fractals to emerge from the theory of chaos.

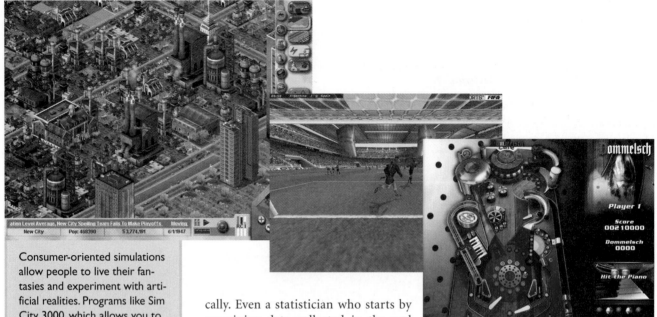

Consumer-oriented simulations allow people to live their fantasies and experiment with artificial realities. Programs like Sim City 3000, which allows you to control the development of a city, combine education with entertainment. Recreational and sports simulations such as FIFA Soccer and Dommelsch, a pinball game, and are popular in homes and video arcades.

cally. Even a statistician who starts by examining data collected in the real world creates statistical models to describe the data.

Computer models aren't always serious; most computer games are models. Chess boards, pinball games, battlefields, sports arenas, ant colonies, cities, medieval dungeons, interplanetary cultures, mythological societies—they've all been modeled in computer games. Students use computer models to travel the Oregon Trail, explore nuclear power plants, invest in the stock market, and dissect digital frogs.

Whether it's created for work, education, or play, a computer model is an *abstraction*—a set of concepts and ideas designed to mimic some kind of system. But a computer model isn't static; it can be put to work in a computer **simulation** to see how the model operates under certain conditions. A well-designed model should behave like the system it imitates.

Suppose, for example, an engineer constructs a computer model of a new type of airplane to test how the plane will respond to human commands. In a typical flight simulation the "pilot" controls the plane's thrust and elevator angle by feeding input data to the model plane. The model responds by adjusting air speed and angle of ascent or descent, just as a real plane would. The pilot responds to the new state of the aircraft by adjusting one or more of the controls, which causes the system to respond by revising the aircraft's state again. This **feedback loop**, where plane and pilot react to data from each other, continues throughout the simulation.

A flight simulator might have a graphical user interface that makes the computer screen look and act like the instrument panel of a real plane so that it can be run interactively by human pilots. Or it might display nothing more than numbers representing input and output values, and the input values might be generated by a simulated pilot—another computer model! Either way, it can deliver a wealth of information about the behavior of the plane, provided the model is accurate.

Computer Simulations: The Rewards

We are reaching the stage where problems that we must solve

are going to become insolvable without computers.

I do not fear computers; I fear the lack of them.

—Isaac Asimov, **scientist and science fiction writer**

Computer simulations are widely used for research in the physical, biological, and social sciences and in engineering. Schools, businesses, and the military also use simulations for training. There are many reasons:

▶ *Safety.* While it's safer to learn piloting skills sitting in front of a computer than actually flying in the air, it's still possible to learn to fly without a computer simulation. Some activities, however, are so dangerous that they aren't ethically possible without computer simulations. How, for example, can scientists study the effects of a nuclear power plant meltdown on the surrounding environment? Until a meltdown occurs, there's only one practical answer: computer simulation.

▶ *Economy.* It's far less expensive for an automobile manufacturer to produce a digital model of a nonexistent car than to build a prototype out of steel. The computer model can be tested for strength, handling, and efficiency in a series of simulations before the company builds and tests a physical prototype. The cost of the computer model is small when compared with the possible expense of producing a defective car.

▶ *Projection.* Without computers it could take decades for biologists to determine whether the rising deer population on an island threatens other species, and by the time they discover the answer, it would be too late to do anything about it. A computer model of the island's ecosystem would speed up natural biological processes so their effects over several generations could be measured in a matter of minutes. A computer simulation can, in effect, serve as a time machine for exploring one or more possible futures.

▶ *Visualization.* Computer models make visualization possible, and visualization allows researchers and students to see and understand relationships that might otherwise go unnoticed. Computer models can speed time up or slow it down; they can make subatomic particles big and the universe small.

▶ *Replication.* In the real world it can be difficult or impossible to repeat a research project with slightly different conditions. But this kind of repetition is an important part of serious research. An engineer needs to fine-tune dimensions and angles to achieve peak performance. A scientist studies the results of one experiment and develops a new hypothesis that calls for further testing. An executive needs to test a business plan under a variety of economic scenarios. If the research is conducted on a computer model, replication is just a matter of changing input values and running a new simulation.

Flight simulator games for home computers like A–10 X-Plane are simplified versions of flight simulators used to train military pilots. Both varieties allow users to test their wings without risking their necks.

> **Computer Simulations: The Risks**

All information is imperfect.

—Jacob Bronowski

The downside of computer simulation can be summed up in three words: Simulation isn't reality. The real world is a subtle and complex place, and capturing even a fraction of that subtlety and complexity in a computer simulation is a tremendous challenge.

GIGO Revisited

The accuracy of a simulation depends on how closely its mathematical model corresponds to the system being simulated. Mathematical models are built on assumptions, many of which are difficult or impossible to verify. Some models suffer from faulty assumptions; others contain hidden assumptions that may not even be obvious to their creators; still others go astray simply because of clerical or human errors.

The daily weather report is the result of a complex computer model. Our atmosphere is far too complex to capture exactly in a computer model; that's why the weather forecast is wrong so often. Occasionally simulation errors produce disastrous results. Faulty computer models have been responsible for deadly flooding of the Colorado River, the collapse of the roof of a Salt Lake City shopping mall, and the crash of a test plane on its first flight. These kinds of disasters are rare. It's much more common for computer models to help avert tragedies by pointing out design flaws. In fact, sometimes things go wrong because people ignore the results of accurate simulations—the trouble-plagued baggage control system in the Denver, Colorado, airport is an example. Still, *garbage in, garbage out* is a basic rule of simulation.

Making Reality Fit the Machine

Simulations are computation intensive. Today's personal computers can run modest simulations, but they're hopelessly underpowered for medium to large simulations. Most scientists and engineers who work extensively with mathematical models depend on workstations, mainframes, or supercomputers to run simulations.

Some simulations are so complex that researchers need to simplify models and streamline calculations to get them to run on the best hardware available. Even when there's plenty of computing power available, researchers face a constant temptation to reshape reality for the convenience of the simulation. In one classic example a U.S. Forest Service computer model reduced complex old-growth forests to "accumulated capital." Aesthetics, ecological diversity, and other hard-to-quantify factors didn't exist in this model.

Sometimes this simplification of reality is deliberate; more often it's unconscious. Either way, information can be lost, and the loss may compromise the integrity of the simulation and call the results into question.

The Illusion of Infallibility

Risks can be magnified because people take computers seriously. For many people, information takes on an air of respectability if it comes from a computer. Computer-generated reports tend to be emphasized, often at the expense of other sources of knowledge. Executives use worksheets to make decisions involving hundreds of jobs and millions of dollars. Politicians decide the fate of military weapons and endangered species based on summaries of computer simulations. Doctors use computer models to make life-and-death decisions involving new drugs and treatments. All of these people, in some sense, are placing their trust in computer simulations. Many of them trust the data precisely *because* it was generated by a computer.

A computer simulation, whether generated by a PC spreadsheet or churned out by a supercomputer, can be an invaluable decision-making aid. The risk is that the people who make decisions with computers will turn over too much of their decision-making power to the computer. The Jedi Master in *Star Wars* understood the danger when he encouraged Luke Skywalker in the heat of battle to turn off his computer simulation rather than let it overpower his judgment. His admonition was simple: "Trust your feelings."

As If

Char Davies

Most of the simulation tools in this chapter, from spreadsheets to flight simulators, are designed to be "experienced" on computer screens. But what happens when simulations become environments that can surround us and flood our senses? Char Davies is an artist living in Montreal and a founder of the software graphics company Softimage. In this article, originally published in the October 4, 1999 Issue of Forbes ASAP, she writes about her experiences creating—and exploring—virtual environments. Her words suggest a future in which the lines between simulations and reality are fuzzy.

I make virtual environments. About being in nature. For almost 20 years, in a variety of media, I've worked to communicate how extraordinary it is to be alive, conscious, and embodied in the flow of life through space and time.

The medium of immersive virtual environments offers a unique means of expressing this sensibility. You can't step into the space of a painting because it's two-dimensional, but you can do that in an immersive virtual environment because of its enveloping quality. Just as the invention of film extended the stillness of painting into the flow of time, the technology associated with virtual environments extends painting and film into three-dimensional space. In such a place, the artist can construct animated, conceptual models of the world that can be explored by others through real-time interaction. The viewer becomes a participant within the artist's visionary world.

I write this essay in a clearing in a forest on the slope of a mountain in southern Quebec. Surrounding me are a sea of summer greens, the rush of wind through leaves, and apples growing in June warmth. Nearby, a creek flows over rock. I have been coming to this land for five years, seeking an antidote for the high tech world I customarily inhabit. This land is my comfort, my muse.

Since 1994 I've created two virtual environments, Osmose and Ephemere, drawing on the natural world for inspiration. To enter these works, you wear a head-mounted display, enabling you to see 3D computer graphics and hear sounds generated in real time by an SGI supercomputer. Every person's journey is different—what you experience depends on your behavior and location within the work. Your breath and balance are tracked by an interface vest. Breathing in causes you to rise; exhaling causes you to slowly fall. Leaning gently lets you change direction. Thus, it is possible to float, gravity free, through these places—visually and aurally enveloped in an unreal world.

In both works you can travel through forest clearings, into moving water, or down through the earth. In these realms everything is semitransparent and immaterial. You can see and pass through everything as if you've left your physical body behind. In Ephemere, the ebb and flow of day and night, spring, summer, and fall highlight the metaphor of time. Seeds sprout when gazed upon; staring at boulders reveals other worlds hidden inside, visible but inaccessible. Both works end gently after 15 minutes.

Many of the more than 10,000 people who have been immersed in these two installations reported feeling as if they were dreaming. Others felt like angels and said they were no longer afraid of death. Some expressed feelings of euphoria and wonder, while a few wept upon emerging.

Thirty-five years ago, in The Poetics of Space, the philosopher Gaston Bachelard wrote: "By leaving the space of one's usual sensibilities, one enters into communication with a space that is psychically innovating. . . . For we do not change place, we change our nature." At the time, he was speaking about the potential of places such as the desert and the deep sea—spaces unlike the environments with which most of us are familiar—to transform us psychologically.

Full-body immersion in Osmose and Ephemere triggers shifts in mental awareness—it feels real but it's not. It feels real because of the three-dimensionality of the space and because you're navigating via your own breath. It's not real because of the semitransparent graphics and the feeling of floating. This is the paradox of immersive virtual space.

Those who enter the dreamy landscapes of Osmose and Ephemere are released from their everyday perceptions. These kinds of immersive environments, capable of evoking feelings ranging from euphoria to loss, are a potent means of reminding people how extraordinary it is to be conscious and embodied in the living world.

DISCUSSION QUESTIONS

1. What is your reaction to the author's descriptions of immersive environments? Do you think you would enjoy experiencing them?
2. Do you think we're likely to see immersive environments like the Holodecks on TV's Star Trek? When?
3. Is there a down side to this kind of technology? Explain.

Spreadsheet programs, first developed to simulate and automate the accountant's ledger, are widely used today in business, science, engineering, and education. Spreadsheet software can be used for tracking financial transactions, calculating grades, forecasting economic conditions, recording scientific data—just about any task that involves repetitive numeric calculations. Spreadsheet documents, called worksheets, are grids with individual cells containing alphabetic labels, numbers, and formulas. Changes in numeric values can cause the spreadsheet to update any related formulas automatically. The responsiveness and flexibility of spreadsheet software make it particularly well suited for providing answers to "what if?" questions.

Most spreadsheet programs include charting commands to turn worksheet numbers into a variety of graphs and charts. The process of creating a chart from a spreadsheet is automated to the point where human drawing isn't necessary; the user simply provides instructions concerning the type of

chart and the details to be included in the chart, and the computer does the rest.

Number crunching often goes beyond spreadsheets. Specialized accounting and tax preparation software packages perform specific business functions without the aid of spreadsheets. Symbolic mathematics processors can handle a variety of higher mathematics functions involving numbers, symbols, equations, and graphics. Statistical analysis software is used for data collection and analysis. Scientific visualization can be done with math processors, statistical packages, graphics programs, or specialized programs designed for visualization.

Modeling and simulation are at the heart of most applications involving numbers. When people create computer models, they use numbers to represent real-world objects and phenomena. Simulations built on these models can provide insights that might be difficult or impossible to obtain otherwise, provided that the models reflect reality accurately. If used wisely, computer simulation can be a powerful tool to help people understand their world and make better decisions.

Key Terms

account, 162
accounting and financial management software, 162
active cell, 154
address, 152
automatic link, 156
automatic recalculation, 153
bar chart, 158
cell, 152
column, 152
console, 154
equation solvers, 157
feedback loop, 153

formula, 153
formula bar, 154
function, 156
label, 152
line chart, 158
macro, 156
mathematics processing software, 162
modeling, 164
pie chart, 158
range, 154
replication, 153
row, 158

scatter chart, 158
scientific visualization software, 164
simulation, 166
spreadsheet software, 152
stack chart, 158
statistical analysis software, 163
statistics, 163
tax preparation software, 162
template, 156
value, 152
"what if?" question, 157
worksheet, 152

Review Questions

1. Define or describe each of the key terms listed above. Check your answers using the glossary.
2. In what ways are word processors and spreadsheet programs similar?
3. What are some advantages of using a spreadsheet over using a calculator to maintain a budget? Are there any disadvantages?
4. If you enter =B2+C2 in cell B1 of a worksheet, the formula is replaced by the number 125 when you press the Enter key. What happened?
5. Using the worksheet from Question 4, you change the number in cell B2 from 55 to 65. What happens to the number in cell B1? Why?

6. Explain the difference between a numeric value and a formula.
7. What is a spreadsheet function, and how is it useful?
8. What is the difference between a spreadsheet program and a financial management program?
9. Describe or draw examples of several different types of charts, and explain how they're typically used.
10. Describe several software tools used for numeric applications too complex to be handled by spreadsheets. Give an example of an application of each.
11. List several advantages and disadvantages of using computer simulations for decision making.

Discussion Questions

1. Spreadsheets are sometimes credited with legitimizing the personal computer as a business tool. Why do you think they had such an impact?
2. Why do you think errors in spreadsheet models go undetected? What can you do to minimize the risk of spreadsheet errors?
3. The statement "Computers don't make mistakes, people do" is often used to support the reliability of computer output. Is the statement true? Is it relevant?
4. Are computer simulations misused? Give some examples, and explain your answer.
5. Before spreadsheets people who wanted to use computers for financial modeling had to write programs in complex computer languages to do the job. Today spreadsheets have replaced those programs for many financial applications. Do you think spreadsheets will be replaced by some easier-to-use software tool in the future? If so, try to imagine what it will be like.
6. Discuss the advantages and disadvantages of computer simulation as a tool for research and education.

Projects

1. Use a spreadsheet or a financial management program to develop a personal budget. Try to keep track of all your income and outgo for the next month or two, and record the transactions with your program. At the end of that time evaluate the accuracy of your budget, and discuss your reactions to the process.
2. Use a spreadsheet to search for answers to a "what if" question that's important to you. Possible questions: What if I lease a car instead of buying it—am I better off? What if I borrow money for school—how much does it cost me in the long run?
3. Develop a multiple-choice questionnaire for determining public attitudes on an issue that's important to you.

Use a computer to analyze, summarize, and graphically represent the results, trying to be as fair and accurate in your summary as you can.
4. Use a spreadsheet to track your grades in this (or another) class. Apply weightings from the course syllabus to your individual scores, calculating a point total based on those weightings.
5. Choose a controversial issue—environmental, economic, or other—and locate numeric data related to the issue. Develop a set of charts and graphs that argues effectively for one point of view. Using the same data, create visuals to support the other point of view. Compare audience reactions (and your reactions) to both presentations.

Books

Books covering basic spreadsheet operations number in the hundreds—far too many to review here. Almost all of these books are software and hardware specific. Some are intended to be used as reference manuals; some are collections of tips, hints, and shortcuts; others are collections of sample documents that can be used as templates; still others are overviews or hands-on tutorials for beginners. If you're new to spreadsheets, start with a book in the last category. Look for one that fits your system and that's readable and easy to understand.

How to Lie with Statistics, by Darrell Huff (New York: Norton, 1954). This 45-year-old book has more relevance in today's computer age than it did when it was written.

Designing Infographics, by Eric K. Meyer (Indianapolis: Hayden Books, 1997). This book provides an excellent overview of the theory and the practice of designing graphs, charts, and other informative illustrations. It covers tools, techniques, forms, and applications of quantitative and informative graphics; there's even a section on statistical ethics.

The Visual Display of Quantitative Information, Envisioning Information, and *Visual Explanations: Images and Quantities, Evidence and Narrative,* by Edward R. Tufte (Cheshire, CT: Graphics Press, 1987, 1990, and 1997, respectively). These three beautiful books make a powerful case for intelligent design of charts, graphics, and other visual aids. Many of the examples in these books show how graphs and charts can be both creative and informative.

Elements of Graph Design, by Stephen M. Kosslyn (New York: W. H. Freeman and Company, 1993). This handy book is smaller, more affordable, and more accessible than the Tufte books. It's packed with useful tips for designing charts and graphs that communicate clearly, with plenty of examples comparing charts done the wrong way with charts done correctly.

Serious Play: How the World's Best Companies Simulate to Innovate, by Michael Schrage (Cambridge, MA: Harvard Business School Press, 1999). "When talented innovators innovate, you don't listen to the specs they quote. You look at the models they've created," says Michael Schrage, MIT Media Lab fellow and *Fortune* Magazine columnist. In this book Scrage looks at the kind of "serious play" being done at innovative companies such as Disney, 3M, Sony, and Hewlett Packard.

World Wide Web Pages

The Internet was created as a tool for scientific researchers and engineers. Today the Web is filled with sites that deal with mathematics, statistics, scientific visualization, and simulation. The Computer Confluence Web pages include links to many of the best sites in government, education, and private corporations.

Chapter

7

Graphics, Hypermedia, and Multimedia

AFTER YOU READ THIS CHAPTER YOU SHOULD BE ABLE TO:

Compare and contrast several types of computer graphics software programs used by artists and non-artists alike.

Explain how computers are changing the way professionals and amateurs work with video, animation, audio, and music.

Describe several ways that computers are used to create multimedia materials in the arts, entertainment, education, and business.

Explain the relationship between hypermedia and multimedia, describing applications of each.

Describe several present and future applications for multimedia technology.

In this chapter:

▶ Computer graphics, from illustration to digital photography
▶ Dynamic digital media: animation, video, and audio
▶ Hypermedia and multimedia: emerging art forms
▶ Data compression, how and why
...and more.

On the CD-ROM:

▶ Doug Engelbart's history-making Augment presentation
▶ Creating a graphical presentation: an interactive walk-through
▶ Animated illustrations of compression technology
▶ Dynamic computer art and animation examples
▶ Video demo of photoediting and drawing software
▶ Instant access to glossary and key word references
▶ Interactive self-study quizzes
...and more.

On the Web:

www.prenhall.com/beekman

▶ More on Doug Engelbart's groundbreaking work
▶ Links to outstanding art, animation, video, and audio Web sites
▶ Resources for creating your own audio, video, graphic, and multimedia works
▶ Self-study exercises
...and more.

If you **look out in the future,**
you can see how best to
make right choices.

—Doug Engelbart

On a December day in 1950 Doug Engelbart looked into the future and saw what no one had seen before. Engelbart had been thinking about the growing complexity and urgency of the world's problems and wondering how he could help solve those problems. In his vision of the future Engelbart saw computer technology augmenting and magnifying human mental abilities, providing people with new powers to cope with the urgency and complexity of life.

Doug Engelbart

Engelbart decided to dedicate his life to turning his vision into reality. Unfortunately, the rest of the world wasn't ready for Engelbart's vision. His farsighted approach didn't match the prevailing ideas of the time, and most of the research community denounced or ignored Engelbart's work. In 1951 there were only about a dozen computers in the world, and those spent most of their time doing military calculations. It was hard to imagine ordinary people using computers to augment their personal productivity. So Engelbart put together the Augmentation Research Center at the Stanford Research Institute to create working models of his visionary tools.

In 1968 he demonstrated his Augment system to an auditorium full of astonished computer professionals and changed forever the way people think about computers. A large screen showed a cascade of computer graphics, text, and video images, controlled by Engelbart and a coworker several miles away. "It was like magic," recalls Alan Kay, one of the young computer scientists in the audience. Augment introduced the mouse, video display editing (the forerunner to word processing), mixed text and graphics, windowing, outlining, shared-screen video conferencing, computer conferencing, groupware, and hypermedia. Although Engelbart used a large computer, he was really demonstrating a futuristic "personal" computer—an interactive multimedia workstation for enhancing individual abilities.

Today many of Engelbart's inventions and ideas have become commonplace. He is widely recognized for one small part of his vision: the mouse. But Engelbart hasn't stopped looking into the future. He now heads the Bootstrap Institute at Stanford University, a nonprofit think tank dedicated to helping organizations make decisions with the future in mind. In a world where automation can dehumanize and eliminate jobs, Engelbart is still committed to replacing automation with augmentation. But now he focuses more on the human side of the equation, helping people chart a course into the future guided by intelligent, positive vision. He talks about turning organizations into "networked improvement communities" and demonstrates ways to "improve the improvement process." If anyone understands how to build the future from a vision, Doug Engelbart does. ■

By combining live-action video with long-distance text editing and idea processing, Doug Engelbart showed that the computer could be a multiple-media communication tool with fantastic potential. Today the personal computer is living up to that potential. Graphics programs allow artists, designers, engineers, publishers, and others to create and edit visual images. Hypermedia documents guide users through information along uniquely personal trails rather than traditional start-to-finish paths. Interactive multimedia tools combine text, graphics, animation, video, and sound in computer-controlled packages. In this chapter we look into these cutting-edge technologies and see how they can augment human abilities.

Focus on Computer Graphics

Mastering technology is only part of what it means to be an artist in the twenty-first century. The other hurdle is mastering creative expression, so that art has something substantial to say. Expression has been the one constant among artists from the Stone Age until now. The only thing that has changed is the technology.

—Steven Holtzman, **author of *Digital Mantras***

The last chapter demonstrated how spreadsheet programs, statistical programs, and other mathematical software create *quantitative* graphics—charts and graphs generated from numbers. These programs help businesspeople, scientists, and engineers who lack the time or talent to create high-quality drawings by hand. But computer graphics today go far beyond pie charts and line graphs. In this section we explore a variety of graphical applications, from simple drawing and painting tools to complex programs used by professional artists and designers.

Painting: Bitmapped Graphics

Everything you imagine is real.

—Pablo Picasso

When it's used with compatible software, a pen on a pressure-sensitive tablet can simulate the feel of a paintbrush on paper. As the artist presses harder on the tablet, the line becomes thicker and denser on the screen.

An image on a computer screen is made of a matrix of pixels—tiny dots of white, black, or color arranged in rows. The words, numbers, and pictures we see are nothing more than patterns of pixels created by software. Most of the time the user doesn't directly control those pixel patterns; software creates the patterns automatically in response to commands. For example, when you press the "e" key while word processing, software constructs a pattern that appears on the screen as an "e." Similarly, when you issue a command to create a bar chart from a spreadsheet, software automatically constructs a pixel pattern that looks like a bar chart. Automatic graphics are convenient, but they can also be restrictive. When you need more control over the details of the screen display, another type of graphics software might be more appropriate.

Painting software allows you to "paint" pixels on the screen with a pointing device. A typical painting program accepts input from a mouse, joystick, trackball, touch pad, or pen, translating the pointer movements into lines and patterns on screen. A professional artist might prefer to work with a pen on a pressure-

sensitive tablet because it can, with the right software, simulate a traditional paintbrush more accurately than other pointing devices.

A painting program typically offers a **palette** of tools on screen. Some tools mimic real-world painting tools, while others can do things that are difficult, even impossible, on paper or canvas.

Painting programs create **bitmapped graphics** (or, as they're sometimes called, **raster graphics**)—pictures that are, to the computer, simple maps showing how the pixels on the screen should be represented. For the simplest bitmapped graphics, a single bit of computer memory represents each pixel. Since a bit can contain one of two possible values, 0 or 1, each pixel can display one of two possible colors, usually black or white.

Higher-quality pictures can be produced by allocating more memory per pixel so each pixel can display more possible colors or shades. *Gray-scale graphics* allow each pixel to appear as black, white, or one of several shades of gray. A program that assigns 8 bits per pixel allows up to 256 different shades of gray to appear on the screen—more than the human eye can distinguish.

Realistic color graphics require even more memory. Many older computers have hardware to support 8-bit color, allowing 256 possible colors to be displayed on the screen at a time—enough to display rich images, but not enough to exactly reproduce most photographs. Photorealistic color requires hardware that can display millions of colors at a time—24 or 32 bits of memory for each pixel on the screen.

The number of bits devoted to each pixel—called **color depth** or **bit depth**—is one of two technological factors limiting an artist's ability to create realistic on-screen images with a bitmapped graphics program. The other factor is **resolution**—the density of the pixels, usually described in *dots per inch*, or *dpi*. Not surprisingly, these are also the two main factors controlling image quality in monitors, as described in Chapter 3. But some graphics images are destined for the printer after being displayed on screen, so the printer's resolution comes into play, too. When displayed on a 72-dpi computer screen—on a Web page, for example—a 72-dpi picture looks fine. But when printed on paper, that same image lacks the fine-grain clarity of a photograph. Diagonal lines, curves, and text characters have tiny "jaggies"—jagged, stair-step-like bumps that advertise the image's identity as a collection of pixels.

Painting programs get around the jaggies by allowing you to store an image at 300 dots per inch or higher, even though the computer screen can't display every pixel at that resolution and normal magnification. Of course, high-resolution pictures demand more memory and disk space. But for printed images the results are worth the added cost. The higher the resolution, the harder it is for the human eye to detect individual pixels on the printed page.

Practically speaking, resolution and bit-depth limitations are easy to overcome with today's hardware and software. Artists are able to use paint programs to produce works that convincingly simulate watercolors, oils, and other natural media, and transcend the limits of those media. Similarly, bitmapped image-editing software can be used to edit photographic images.

> Professional painting programs like Syntetik's Studio Artist allow artists and non-artists alike to use tools that work like real-world painting tools.

Digital Image Processing: Photographic Editing by Computer

> The aim of every artist is to **arrest motion**, which is life, by artificial means
> and hold it fixed so that a hundred years later, when a stranger looks at it,
> **it moves again** since it is life.
>
> —**William Faulkner**

Like a picture created with a high-resolution paint program, a digitized photograph or a photograph captured with a digital camera is a bitmapped image. **Digital image processing**

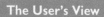

Editing Photographic Images

SOFTWARE Adobe Photoshop with a scanner plug-in.

THE GOAL To create a cover for a forthcoming CD from an obscure but enthusiastic band.

① You've collected a few photos of the band and a few others from a butterfly farm. The cover concept combines the band and the butterflies. The first step is to scan the photos and save each of them as Photoshop documents.

② Next, you take care of the kind of business Photoshop was originally designed for: slightly improving on reality. After you adjust the color balance of the band photo, you zoom in for a close-up view so you can remove those pesky eyeglass reflections. Using the rubber stamp tool, you can clone a patch of flesh-colored pixels in place of the glare spots. You can even clone one eyeball onto the other.

③ To make it match the scale of the background photo (in a surrealistic way), you change the image size.

④ Next, you remove the background from the band photo by carefully selecting it using a combination of tools. The lasso allows you to trace around the area, but it's hard to be exact. The magic wand allows you to select a group of pixels that are approximately the same color. Using different key combinations with the mouse (or drawing stylus) you can start a new selection, add to an existing selection, or remove pixels from an existing selection. You use the Delete key to remove the background pixels once they're selected.

⑤ The band photo can now be placed in front of another background as if it were a set of paper dolls. When you copy the band image and paste it on the background photo, it's placed on a new layer so it can be moved and modified independently.

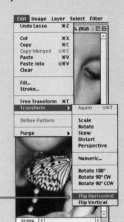

⑥ After you trace around and select one of the other butterfly images, you flip it horizontally so it faces the other direction. Then you paste it onto the photo and position it on a convenient elbow.

⑦ You paste the butterfly images onto separate layers and arrange them as if you were playing with cardboard cutouts.

⑧ You apply a motion blur filter to a butterfly so the composite photo doesn't look static.

⑨ You slightly darken the background layer and apply a blur filter to give a sense of depth.

⑩ You add a title and apply an effect to the lettering.

⑪ When you're done tinkering, you're ready to crop the image so it's exactly the right size and then print it.

This image served as the cover art for a Herbie Hancock album called *Dis is de Drum.* Photographer Sanjay Kothari created the image through the process of digital photographic manipulation. Several of the photographs used in the final photo-collage are shown along the right side of the larger image. The three small images at the bottom of the screen show several of the steps in the process of combining the images using Adobe's Photoshop.

software allows the user to manipulate photographs and other high-resolution images with tools similar to those found in paint programs. Digital image processing software like Adobe Photoshop is in many ways similar to professional paint software like Painter—both are tools for editing high-resolution bitmapped images.

Digital image processing software makes it easier for photographers to remove unwanted reflections, eliminate "red eye," and brush away facial blemishes—to perform the kinds of editing tasks that were routinely done with magnifying glasses and tiny brushes before photographs could be digitized. But digital photographic editing is far more powerful than traditional photo-retouching techniques. With image processing software it's possible to distort and combine photographs, creating fabricated images that show no evidence of tampering. Supermarket gossip tabloids routinely use these tools to create sensationalistic cover photos. Many experts question whether photographs should be allowed as evidence in the courtroom now that they can be doctored so convincingly. See *The User's View* box on the previous page. **UV**

Drawing: Object-Oriented Graphics

Actually, a root word of technology, techne, originally meant "art." The ancient Greeks never separated art from manufacture in their minds, and so never developed separate words for them.

—**Robert Pirsig, in *Zen and the Art of Motorcycle Maintenance***

Because high-resolution paint images and photographs are stored as bit maps, they can make heavy storage and memory demands. Another type of graphics program can economically store pictures with virtually *infinite* resolution, limited only by the capabilities of the output device. Drawing software stores a picture not as a collection of dots, but as a collection of lines and shapes. When you draw a line with a drawing program, the software doesn't record changes in a pixel map. Instead, it calculates and remembers a mathematical formula for the line. A drawing program stores shapes as shape formulas and text as text. Because pictures are collections of lines, shapes, and other objects, this approach is often called object-oriented graphics or vector graphics. In effect, the computer is remembering "a blue line segment goes here and a red circle goes here and a chunk of text goes here" instead of "this pixel is blue and this one is red and this one is white. . . ."

Many drawing tools—line, shape, and text tools—are similar to painting tools in bitmapped programs. But the user can manipulate objects and edit text without affecting neighboring objects, even if the neighboring objects overlap. On screen, an object-oriented drawing looks similar to a bitmapped painting. But when it's printed, a drawing appears as smooth as the printer's resolution allows. (Of course, not all drawings are designed to be printed. You may, for example, use a drawing program to create images for

The User's View

Drawing with a Computer

SOFTWARE   **Macromedia Freehand.**

THE GOAL   **To find the best way to fit your furniture into the space available in your new room. Your furniture is heavy, but you can easily create digital scale models that weigh nothing. It's easier to drag these drawings around a floor plan than to move their real-world counterparts.**

① After creating a new Freehand document, you turn on the Page Rulers option so you can scale your drawing at 2 feet per inch.

② Using the rectangle tool from the toolbox, you drag diagonally to draw a rectangle representing the room's floor. Square handles allow you to adjust the shape of this rectangle until it's exactly right.

③ You tell Freehand to display a faint rectangular grid so it's easy to judge sizes and align objects anywhere on the page.

④ Freehand includes a color mixer so you can create custom colors. For this project it's easier to use colors from a standard color palette—in this case a palette of colors normally used for Web graphics. You choose to display all 216 color chips without names so you can easily drag the colors you need onto the objects you draw.

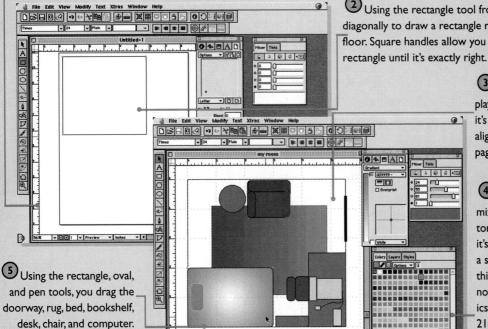

⑤ Using the rectangle, oval, and pen tools, you drag the doorway, rug, bed, bookshelf, desk, chair, and computer.

⑥ The Group command allows you to group several objects so you can manipulate them as a single object. You group the desk, chair, and computer into a single object so you can rotate it and move it around in the room.

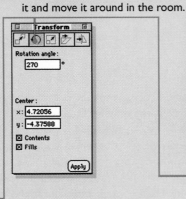

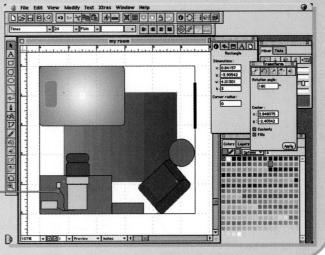

Pixels versus Objects
How do you edit a picture? It depends on what you're doing and how the picture is stored.

The task . . .	Using bit-mapped graphics	Using object-oriented graphics
Moving and removing parts of pictures	Easier to work with regions rather than objects (note), especially if those objects overlap	Easier to work with individual objects or groups of objects, even if they overlap
Working with shapes	Shapes stored as pixel patterns can be edited with eraser and drawing tools	Shapes stored as math formulas can be trans-formed mathematically
Magnification	Magnifies pixels for fine detail editing	Magnifies objects, not pixels
Text handling	Text "dries" and can't be edited, but can be moved as a block of pixels	Text can always be edited
	When paint text "dries" it can't be edited like other text	Draw text always can be changed
Printing	Resolution of printout can't exceed the pixel resolution of the stored picture	Resolution is limited only by the output device
Working within the limits of the hardware	Photographic quality is possible but requires considerable memory and disk storage	Complex drawings require considerable computational power for reasonable speed

publication on a Web page. Because most Web browsers recognize only bitmapped images, you'll probably convert the drawings to bit maps before they're displayed.) See *The User's View* box on the previous page. **UV**

Many professional drawing programs, including Adobe Illustrator and Macromedia Freehand, store images using **PostScript**—a standard **page-description language** for describing text fonts, illustrations, and other elements of the printed page. PostScript is built into many laser printers and other high-end output devices, so those devices can understand and follow PostScript instructions. PostScript-based drawing software constructs a PostScript program as the user draws. This program provides a complete set of instructions for reconstructing the picture at the printer. When the user

Rules of Thumb

Creating Smart Art

Modern graphics software isn't just for professional artists. Just about anybody can use it to create pictures and presentations. Here are some guidelines to help you make the most of the computer as a graphic tool:

▶ *Overcome art anxiety.* For many of us the hardest part is getting started. We are all programmed by messages we received in our childhood, which for many of us included "You aren't creative" and "You can't draw." Fortunately, a computer can help us overcome this early programming and find the artist that's locked within us. Most drawing and painting programs are flexible, forgiving, and fun. Allow yourself to experiment; you'll be surprised at what you can create if you're patient and playful.

▶ *Choose the right tool for the job.* Is your artwork to be displayed on the computer screen or printed? Does your output device support color? Would color enhance the finished work? Your answers to these questions will help you determine which software and hardware tools are most appropriate. As you're thinking about options, don't rule out low-tech tools. The best approach may not involve a computer, or it may involve some combination of computer and nonelectronic tools.

▶ *Borrow from the best.* Art supply stores sell **clip art**—predrawn images that artists can legally cut out and paste into their own pictures or posters. Computer artists have hundreds of digital clip art collections to choose from, with a difference: Computer clip art images can be cut, pasted, and edited electronically. Some computer clip art collections are in the public domain (that is, they are free); others can be licensed for a small fee. Computer clip art comes in a variety of formats, and it ranges from simple line drawings to scanned color photographs. If you have access to a scanner, you can create your own digitized clip art from traditional photos and drawings.

▶ *Don't borrow without permission.* Computers, scanners, and digital cameras make it all too easy to create unauthorized copies of copyrighted photographs, drawings, and other images. There's a clear legal and ethical line between using public domain or licensed clip art and pirating copyrighted material. If you use somebody else's creative work, make sure you have written permission from the owner.

▶ *Protect you own work.* Copyright laws aren't just to protect other people's work. If you've created something that's marketable, consider copyrighting it. The process is easy and inexpensive, and it might help you to get credit (and payment) where credit is due.

issues a Print command, the computer sends PostScript instructions to the printer, which uses those instructions to construct the grid of microscopic pixels that will be printed on each page. Most desktop publishing software uses PostScript in the same way.

Object-oriented drawing and bitmapped painting each offer advantages for certain applications. Bitmapped image-editing programs give artists and photo editors unsurpassed control over textures, shading, and fine detail; they're widely used for creating screen displays (for example, in video games, multimedia presentations, and Web pages), for simulating natural paint media, and for embellishing photographic images. Object-oriented drawing and illustration programs are a better choice for creating printed graphs, charts, and illustrations with clean lines and smooth shapes. Some integrated programs like Corel Draw and AppleWorks include both drawing and painting modules, allowing you to choose the right tool for each job. A growing number of programs merge features of both in a single application, blurring the distinction and offering new possibilities for amateur and professional illustrators.

3-D Modeling Software

Working with a pencil, an artist can draw a three-dimensional scene on a two-dimensional page. Similarly, an artist can use a drawing or painting program to create a scene that

This personal computer system from the *Computer Confluence* CD-ROM is a 3-D model created on a Macintosh using Strata Studio Pro 3-D modeling software. The images are shown in wireframe view; the ones on the right have been fully rendered to add surface textures.

appears to have depth on a two-dimensional computer screen. But in either case the drawing lacks true depth; it's just a flat representation of a scene. With **3-D modeling software graphic** designers can create three-dimensional objects with tools similar to those found in conventional drawing software. You can't touch a 3-D computer model; it's no more real than a square, a circle, or a letter created with a drawing program. But a 3-D computer model can be rotated, stretched, and combined with other model objects to create complex 3-D scenes.

Illustrators who use 3-D software appreciate its flexibility. A designer can create a 3-D model of an object, rotate it, view it from a variety of angles, and take two-dimensional "snapshots" of the best views for inclusion in final printouts. Similarly, it's possible to "walk through" a 3-D environment that exists only in the computer's memory, printing snapshots that show the simulated space from many points of view. For many applications the goal is not a printout but an animated presentation on a computer screen or videotape. Animation software, presentation graphics software, and multimedia authoring software (all described later in this chapter) can display sequences of screens showing 3-D objects being rotated, explored, and transformed. Many modern television and movie special effects involve combinations of live action and simulated 3-D animation. Techniques pioneered in films like *Jurassic Park* make it almost impossible for audiences to tell clay and plastic models from computer models.

This abstract image is actually a computer-aided design, created by the designer shown below the image.

CAD/CAM: Turning Pictures into Products

Three-dimensional graphics also play an important role in the branch of engineering known as **computer-aided design (CAD)**—the use of computers to design products. CAD software allows engineers, designers, and architects to create designs on screen for products ranging from computer chips to public buildings. Today's software goes far beyond basic drafting and object-oriented graphics. It allows users to create three-dimensional "solid" models with physical characteristics like weight, volume, and center of gravity. These models can be rotated and viewed from any angle. The computer can evaluate the structural performance of any part of the model by applying imaginary force to the object. Using CAD, an engineer can crash-test a new model of an automobile before it ever leaves the computer screen. CAD tends to be cheaper, faster, and more accurate than traditional design-by-hand techniques. What's more, the forgiving nature of the computer makes it easy to alter a design to meet the goals of a project.

In this motion capture studio at Industrial Light and Magic, 3-D animated figures are modeled using sensors attached to human 3-D models and mannequins.

Computer-aided design is often linked to computer-aided manufacturing (CAM). When the design of a product is completed, the numbers are fed to a program that controls the manufacturing of parts. For electronic parts, the design translates directly into a template for etching circuits onto chips. The emergence of CAD/CAM has streamlined many design and manufacturing processes. The combination of CAD and CAM is often called computer-integrated manufacturing (CIM); it's a major step toward a fully automated factory.

Presentation Graphics: Bringing Lectures to Life

One common application for computer graphics today is the creation of visual aids—slides, transparencies, graphics displays, and handouts—to enhance presentations. While drawing and painting programs can create these aids, they aren't as useful as programs designed with presentations in mind.

Presentation graphics software helps to automate the creation of visual aids for lectures, training sessions, sales demonstrations, and other presentations. Presentation graphics programs are most commonly used for creating and displaying a series of on-screen "slides" to serve as visual aids for presentations. Slides might include photographs, drawings, spreadsheet-style charts, or tables. These different graphical elements are usually integrated into a series of bullet charts that list the main points of a presentation. Slides can be output as 35mm color slides, overhead transparencies, or handouts. Presentation graphics programs can also display "slide shows" directly on computer monitors or LCD projectors, including animation and video clips along with still images. Some can convert presentations into Web pages automatically. **UV**

Because they can be used to create and display on-screen presentations with animated visual effects and video clips, presentation graphics programs like Microsoft's PowerPoint are sometimes called *multimedia presentation tools*. These programs *do* make it easy for non-artists to combine text, graphics, and other media in simple multimedia presentations. But as you'll see, true *multimedia authoring tools* are more flexible and powerful than are basic slide presentation programs.

We now turn our attention to several types of media that go beyond the limitations of the printed page or the static screen; then we look at how multimedia authoring software can combine these diverse media types to produce dynamic, interactive documents.

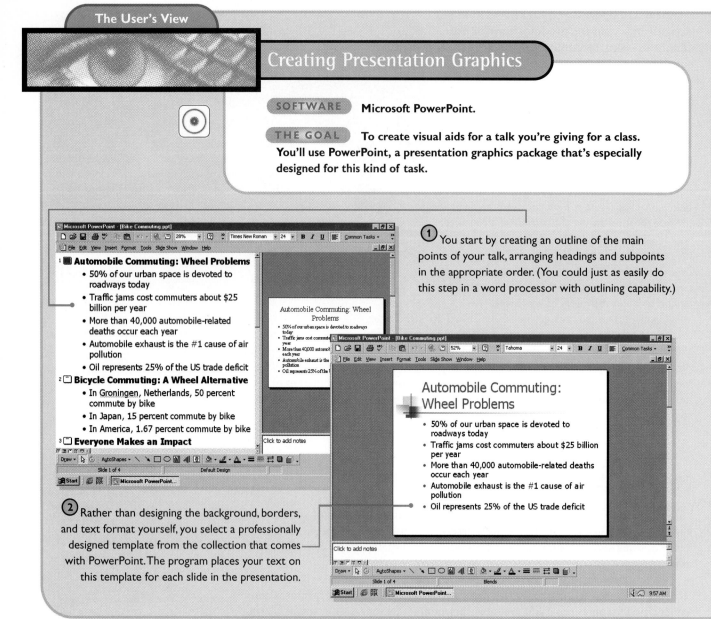

The User's View

Creating Presentation Graphics

SOFTWARE Microsoft PowerPoint.

THE GOAL To create visual aids for a talk you're giving for a class. You'll use PowerPoint, a presentation graphics package that's especially designed for this kind of task.

① You start by creating an outline of the main points of your talk, arranging headings and subpoints in the appropriate order. (You could just as easily do this step in a word processor with outlining capability.)

② Rather than designing the background, borders, and text format yourself, you select a professionally designed template from the collection that comes with PowerPoint. The program places your text on this template for each slide in the presentation.

Dynamic Media: Beyond the Printed Page

The world is complex, dynamic, multidimensional;
the paper is static, flat. How are we to represent the rich visual world
of experience and measurement on mere flatland?

—Edward R. Tufte, in *Envisioning Information*

Most personal computer applications—painting and drawing programs, word processors, desktop publishers, and so on—are designed to produce paper documents. But many types of modern media can't be reduced to pixels on printouts because they contain *dynamic* information—information that changes over time or in response to user input. Today's multimedia computers allow us to create and edit animated sequences, video clips, sound, and music along with text and graphics. Just as words and pictures serve as the raw materials for desktop publishing, dynamic media like animation, video, audio, and hypertext are important components of interactive multimedia projects.

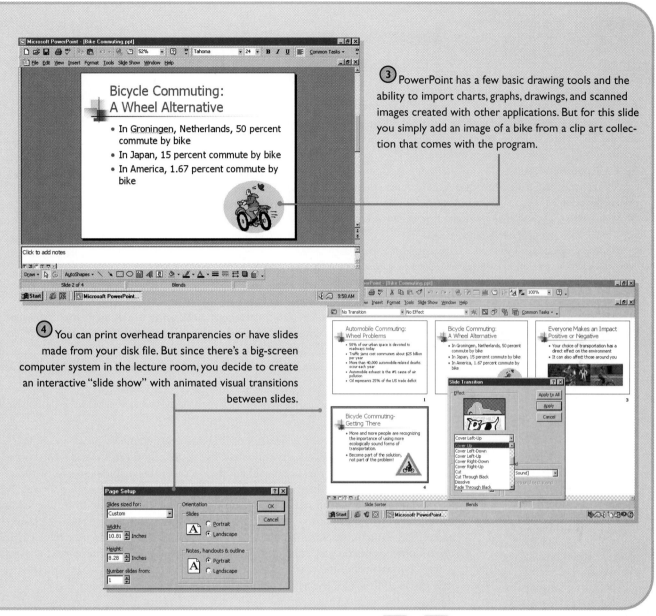

③ PowerPoint has a few basic drawing tools and the ability to import charts, graphs, drawings, and scanned images created with other applications. But for this slide you simply add an image of a bike from a clip art collection that comes with the program.

④ You can print overhead tranparencies or have slides made from your disk file. But since there's a big-screen computer system in the lecture room, you decide to create an interactive "slide show" with animated visual transitions between slides.

Animation: Graphics in Time

We're on the threshold of a moment in cinematic history that is unparalleled. Anything you can imagine can be done. If you can draw it, if you can describe it, we can do it. It's just a matter of cost.

—James Cameron, **Filmmaker**

Creating motion from still pictures—this illusion is at the heart of all **animation**. Before computers, animated films were hand-drawn one still picture, or **frame**, at a time. Modern computer graphics technology has transformed both amateur and professional animation by allowing many of the most tedious aspects of the animation process to be automated.

In its simplest form computer-based animation is similar to traditional frame-by-frame animation techniques—each frame is a computer-drawn picture, and the computer displays those frames in rapid succession. But computer animation programs, even the low-priced packages aimed at the home market, contain software tools that can do much more than flip pages. They can take much of the tedium out of animation by

Making Powerful Presentations

Presentation graphics programs like PowerPoint make it easy to create dynamic, lively presentations. They also make it easy to create ugly, boring presentations. These suggestions will help you to ensure that your presentations aren't snoozers.

▶ *Remember your goal.* Know what you're trying to communicate . Keep your goal in mind throughout the process of creating the presentation.

▶ *Remember your audience.* How much do they know about your topic? Do key terms need to be defined?

▶ *Outline your ideas.* If you can't express your plan in a clear, concise outline, you probably won't be able to create a clear, concise presentation. Once your outline is done, you can import it into your presentation graphics software and massage it into a presentation.

▶ *Be stingy with words.* Avoid big words, long sentences, complex lists, and tiny type. Keep your prose lively and to the point.

▶ *Keep it simple.* Avoid useless decorations and distractions. Avoid fancy borders and backgrounds.

▶ *Use a consistent design.* Make sure all of your slides look like they belong together. Use the same fonts, backgrounds, and colors throughout your presentation. If you don't trust your design skills, use predesigned templates.

▶ *Be smart with art.* Don't clutter your presentation with random clip art. Make sure each illustration contributes to your message. Use simple data graphs if they can support your main points. When you do use clip art or illustrations, make sure they coordinate with the colors and design of the rest of the presentation.

▶ *Keep each slide focused.* Each screen should convey one idea clearly, possibly with a few concise supporting points.

▶ *Tell them what you're going to tell them, then tell them, then tell them what you told them.* It's the speechmaker's fundamental rule, and it applies to presentations, too.

---

automating repetitive processes. Instead of drawing every frame by hand, an animator can create key frames and objects and use software to help fill in the gaps—a process known as *tweening*. The most powerful animation programs include tools for working with animated objects in three dimensions, adding depth to the scene on the screen.

Computer animation has become commonplace in everything from television commercials to feature films. Sometimes computer animation is combined with live-action film; James Cameron's *Titanic* and George Lucas's *Phantom Menace* rely heavily on computer animation to "enhance" reality. Other films, including *Toy Story, Antz,* and *A Bug's Life,* use computer animation to create every character, scene, and event, leaving only the soundtrack for live actors and musicians to create.

Macromedia's Director is a popular multimedia program with powerful animation capabilities. The frames in the Cast window (below) show several different views of an object as it moves through the timeline shown in the Score window (below).

Desktop Video: Computers, Film, and TV

Digital technology is the same revolution as adding sound to pictures and the same revolution as adding color to pictures. Nothing more and nothing less.

—George Lucas, **Filmmaker**

There's more to the **digital video** revolution than computer animation. Computers can be used to edit video, splice scenes, add transitions, create titles, and do other tasks in a fraction of the time—and at a fraction of the cost—of precomputer techniques. The only requirement is that the video be in a digital form so the computer can treat it as data.

Analog and Digital Video

Conventional television and video images are stored and broadcast as analog (smooth) electronic waves. A **video digitizer** can convert analog video signals from a television broadcast or videotape into digital data. Most video digitizers must be installed as add-on cards or external devices that plug into serial or USB ports. Broadcast-quality digitizers are relatively expensive; low-cost models are available for hobbyists who can settle for less-than-perfect images.

Many video digitizers can import signals from televisions, videotapes, video cameras, and other sources and display them on the computer's screen in *real time*—at the same time they're created or imported. The computer screen can serve as a television screen or, with a network connection, a viewing screen for a live video teleconference. For many applications, it's not important to display digitized images in real time; the goal

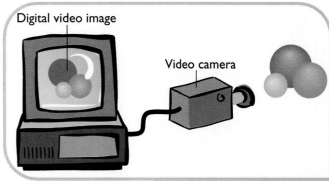

Digital video image

Video camera

Video can be easily transferred from a tape in a video camera to a computer's memory. If the camcorder is digital, the video data can be copied through Firewire cable. If the camcorder is analog, the tape signals must be converted to digital data by a digitizer.

Nonliner editing software like Apple's Final Cut Pro (above) turns a desktop computer into a powerful video editing workstation. Adobe's After Effects (below) is used by professional video editors and animators to create special effects like this flying shark.

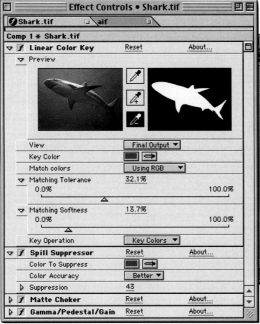

In Steven Speilberg's Survivors: Testimonies of the Holocaust, four Holocaust survivors tell their stories in illustrated video presentations that emphasize the importance of tolerance in everyday life.

is to capture entire video sequences and convert them into digital "movies" that can be stored, edited, and played on computer screens without external video equipment.

Video professionals and hobbyists who use *digital video cameras* don't need to digitize their video footage before working with it in a computer, because it's already in digital form. Digital video cameras capture and store all video footage as digital data. Most digital video cameras have IEEE 1394 "FireWire" ports (see Chapter 3) that can be used to copy raw video footage from tape to a computer (even an inexpensive iMac) and later copy the edited video back from computer to tape. Because digital video can be reduced to a series of numbers, it can be copied, edited, stored, and played back without any loss of quality. Digital video will soon replace analog video for most applications.

Video Production Goes Digital

A typical video project starts with an outline and a simple *storyboard* describing the action, dialog, and music in each scene. The storyboard serves as a guide for shooting and editing scenes.

Today most video editing is done using *nonlinear editing* technology. For nonlinear editing, video and audio clips are stored in digital form on a computer's hard disk. These digital clips can be organized, rearranged, enhanced, and combined using on-screen tools and commands. Nonlinear editing is faster and easier than older editing techniques, and it allows filmmakers to do things that aren't possible without computers. Video editing makes massive storage and memory demands on a computer. Until recently, nonlinear editing technology was only available to professionals. But falling hardware prices and technological advances make it possible for hobbyists to edit video with inexpensive desktop machines.

Video editing software (such as Adobe Premiere, Adobe After Effects, and Apple Final Cut Pro) makes it easy to eliminate extraneous footage, combine clips from multiple takes into coherent scenes, splice together scenes, insert visual transitions, superimpose titles, synchronize a soundtrack, and create special effects. Editing software can combine live action with computer animation. Software can also create **morphs**—video clips in which one image metamorphoses into another. Photoshop-style tools allow artists to, for example, paint one or two frames with a green polka-dotted sky and then have those painting effects automatically applied to the other frames.

After it's edited, the video clip can be "printed" on a videotape. The process is simplest and most effective in an all-digital system using FireWire and a digital camcorder. Systems that use inexpensive digitizers may not be able to produce satisfactory videotapes.

Edited video doesn't need to be exported to tape. Many digital clips end up in multimedia presentations. On-screen digital movies can add realism and excitement to educational, training, presentation, and entertainment software. Video clips are also common on the Web. System extensions like Apple's cross-platform QuickTime make it possible for any multimedia-capable computer to display digital video clips without additional hardware.

Data Compression

Digital movies can make heavy hardware demands; even a short full-screen video clip can quickly fill a large hard disk or CD-ROM. To save storage space and to allow the processor to keep up with the quickly changing frames, digital movies designed for the Web or CD-ROM are often displayed in small windows with fewer than the standard video rate of 30 frames per second. In addition, **data compression** software and hardware are used to squeeze data out of movies so they can be stored in smaller spaces, usually with a slight loss of image quality. General data compression software can be used to reduce the size of almost any kind of data file; specialized *image compression software* is generally used to compress graphics and video files. System extensions like QuickTime include several common software compression schemes. But the best compression schemes involve specialized hardware as well as software.

Even highly compressed video clips gobble up storage space quickly. As compression and storage technologies continue to improve, digital movies will become larger, longer, smoother, and more common in everyday computing applications. In fact, compression hardware may soon become standard equipment in multimedia computers.

Professionals in the motion picture, television, and video industries create their products using graphics workstations that cost hundreds of thousands of dollars. Today it's possible to put together a Windows- or Macintosh-based system that can perform most of the same functions for a fraction of the cost. These systems might not meet all of Stephen Spielberg's needs, but they satisfy thousands of individuals, schools, and small businesses with smaller budgets. If current trends continue, low-cost systems will transform the film and video industry in the same way that desktop publishing has revolutionized the world of the printed word.

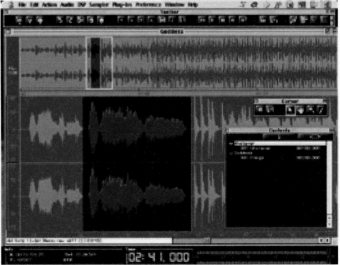

The MP3 format (discussed on page 195) allows music recordings to be compressed so they can be stored in small, portable storage devices. The software shown here allows owners of the Rio portable MP3 player to convert CD tracks to MP3 and download those tracks into the player.

The Synthetic Musician: Computers and Audio

It's easy to play any musical instrument: all you have to do is touch the right key at the right time and the instrument will play itself.

—J. S. Bach

Sound and music can turn a visual presentation into an activity that involves the ears, the eyes, and the whole brain. For many applications, sound puts the *multi* in *multimedia*. Computer sounds can be digitized—digitally recorded—or **synthesized**—synthetically generated. PCs (using *sound cards;* see Chapter 3) and Macintoshes (which have sound hardware already built in) can produce sounds that go far beyond the basic beeps of early computers; most of them can also digitize sounds.

Digitized Sounds as Computer Data

Any sound that can be recorded can be captured with an **audio digitizer** and stored as a data file on a disk. Digitized sound data, like other computer data, can be loaded into the computer's memory and manipulated by software. Sound-editing software can change a sound's volume and pitch, add special effects such as echoes, remove extraneous noises, and even rearrange musical passages. Sound data is sometimes called *waveform audio* because this kind of editing often involves manipulating a visual image of the sound's waveform. To play a digitized sound, the computer must load the data file into memory, convert it to an analog sound, and play it through a speaker.

Waveform audio files can be edited in a variety of ways using software tools such as Peak, from Bias, Inc. Here a section of a muscial recording has been selected so that it can be copied and pasted elsewhere in the recording.

How It Works 7.1

Data Compression

A full-screen 256-color photograph or painting takes about a megabyte of storage—the same as the complete text from a typical paperback book! Graphic images, digital video, and sound files can consume massive amounts of storage space on disk and in memory; they can also be slow to transmit over computer networks. Data compression technology allows large files to be temporarily squeezed so they take less storage space and network transmission time. Before they can be used, compressed files must be decompressed. (In the physical world many companies "compress" goods to save storage and transportation costs: When you "just add water" to a can of concentrated orange juice, you're "decompressing" the juice.)

All forms of compression involve removing bits; the trick is to remove bits that can be replaced when the file can be restored. Different compression techniques work best for different types of data.

Suppose you want to store or transmit a large text file. Your text compression software might follow steps similar to those shown here:

① Each character in the uncompressed ASCII file occupies 8 bits; a seven-character word—invoice, for example—requires 56 bits of storage.

invoice (space) payable

② A 2-byte binary number can contain code values ranging from 0 to 65,535—enough codes to stand for every commonly used word in English. This partial code dictionary shows the code values for a few words, including invoice and payable.

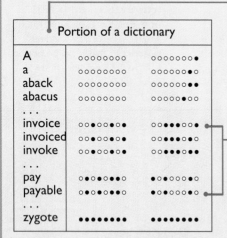

Portion of a dictionary		
A	○○○○○○○○	○○○○○○○●
a	○○○○○○○○	○○○○○○●○
aback	○○○○○○○○	○○○○○○●●
abacus	○○○○○○○○	○○○○○●○○
. . .		
invoice	○○●○○●○●	○○●●●○○●
invoiced	○○●○○●○●	○○●●●○●○
invoke	○○●○○●○●	○○●●●○●●
. . .		
pay	○●○○●○●○	●○●○○○●○
payable	○●○○●○●○	●○●○○○●○
. . .		
zygote	●●●●●●●○	●●●●●●●○

③ To compress a file using a code dictionary, the computer looks up every word in the original file, in this example, invoice and payable. It replaces each word with its 2-byte code value. In this example they are % 9 and V ú. The seven-character word now takes up only 16 bits—less than one-third of its original size.

④ In a compressed file, these 2-byte code values would be used to store or transmit the information for invoice and payable, using fewer bits of information either to increase storage capacity or to decrease transmission time.

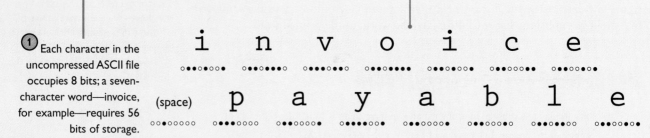

% 9 V ú

To reverse the process of compression, the same dictionary (or an identical one on another computer) is used to decompress the file, creating an exact copy of the original. All the tedious dictionary lookup is performed quickly by a computer program.

Most modern compression programs usually work on patterns of bits rather than English words. For example, one type of digital video compression stores values for pixels that change from one frame to the next; there's no need to repeatedly store values for pixels that are the same in every frame.

For example, the only pixels that change in these two pictures are the ones that represent the unicycle and the shadows. In general, compression works because most raw data files contain redundancy that can be "squeezed out."

Lossless compression systems allow a file to be compressed and later decompressed without any loss of data; the decompressed file will be an identical copy of the original file. Popular lossless compression systems include ZIP/PKZIP (DOS/ Windows), Stufflt (Macintosh), tar (UNIX), and GIF (general graphics). A *lossy compression* system can usually achieve better compression than a lossless one but may lose some information in the process; the decompressed file isn't always identical to the original. This is tolerable in many types of sound, graphics, and video files but not for most program and data files. JPEG is a popular lossy compression system for graphics files.

MPEG is a popular compression system for digital video. An MPEG file takes just a fraction of the space of an uncompressed video file. Because decompression programs demand time and processing power, playback of compressed video files can sometimes be jerky or slow. Some computers get around the problem with MPEG hardware boards that specialize in compression and decompression, leaving the CPU free for other. *Hardware compression* is likely to be built into most computers as multimedia becomes more commonplace.

The original photographic image (above) is clear with an uncompressed size of 725 KB. The image on the right shows the visible lossy effect of aggressive JPEG compression. But the size of the compressed file is only 19 KB.

Computers can generate sound using waveform digital audio, CD audio, or MIDI audio.

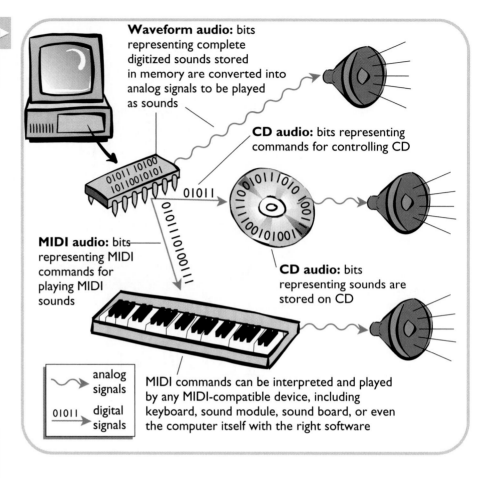

Waveform audio: bits representing complete digitized sounds stored in memory are converted into analog signals to be played as sounds

CD audio: bits representing commands for controlling CD

MIDI audio: bits representing MIDI commands for playing MIDI sounds

CD audio: bits representing sounds are stored on CD

| ∿ | analog signals |
| 01011 | digital signals |

MIDI commands can be interpreted and played by any MIDI-compatible device, including keyboard, sound module, sound board, or even the computer itself with the right software

Sequencing software is like a cross between a multitrack tape recorder and a word processor. A sequencer allows a single person to compose, edit, and combine several MIDI parts into a complete instrumental composition. Amateur and professional musicians use sequencing software for composition, recording, and performance. Cakewalk, the most popular PC sequencer, can combine digital audio tracks with MIDI sequences, allowing your computer to serve as a complete recording studio.

Recorded sound can consume massive amounts of space on disk and in memory. As you might expect, higher quality sound reproduction generally requires more memory. The difference is due in part to differences in *sampling rate*—the number of sound "snapshots" the recording equipment takes each second. A higher sampling rate produces more realistic digital sounds in the same way that higher resolution produces more realistic digital photographs—it allows for more accurate modeling of the analog source. The quality of the sound is also affected by the number of bits per sample, usually 8 or 16; this is similar to a digital photograph's bit depth.

Music is digitized on audio CDs at a high sampling rate and bit depth—high enough that it's hard to tell the difference between the original analog sound and the final digital recording. But CD audio is memory intensive; a 3-minute song takes about 30 megabytes of space on a compact disc. Files that large are expensive to store and slow to transmit through networks. That's why most computer sound files are recorded at a lower sampling rate and bit depth—and therefore don't have the sound quality of an audio CD recording. Sound data compression, like image compression, can make a file even smaller, but may further compromise quality.

Until recently, high-quality sounds required large files, and compact files compromised quality. But a relatively new method of compression called **MP3** (for MPEG Audio Layer 3) can squeeze a music file to a fraction of its original CD-file size with only a slight loss of quality. MP3 makes it practical to transmit songs and other recordings through the Internet, store them on hard disks, and play them on pocket-sized devices without disk or tape. MP3 files are available for free on hundreds of Web sites. Many are contributed by undiscovered musicians who want exposure; others are copied from copyrighted CDs and distributed illegally. Ethical and legal issues raised by MP3 will be discussed in more detail in Chapter 11.

In the modern music studio computer keyboards and music keyboards often sit side by side.

CD Audio and MIDI: Sounds on Command

A computer can also play sounds from standard audio CDs using a CD-ROM or DVD-ROM drive connected to headphones or amplified speakers. Sounds are stored on CDs, not in the computer's memory. When the sounds are stored on CDs, software needs to contain only *commands* telling the drive what to play and when to play it.

Multimedia computers can also control a variety of electronic musical instruments and sound sources using **MIDI** (Musical Instrument Digital Interface)—a standard interface that allows electronic instruments and computers, regardless of type or brand, to communicate with each other and work together. In the same way that PostScript is the common language of desktop publishing hardware, MIDI is the universal language of electronic music hardware. MIDI is used to send commands to instruments and sound sources—commands that, in effect, say "play this sound at this pitch and this volume for this amount of time. . . ."

MIDI commands can be interpreted by a variety of music *synthesizers* (electronic instruments that synthesize sounds using mathematical formulas), *samplers* (instruments that can digitize, or sample, audio sounds, turn them into notes, and play them back at any pitch), and hybrid instruments that play sounds that are part sampled and part synthesized. But most multimedia PCs can also interpret and execute MIDI commands using sounds built into their sound cards or stored in software form. Whether the sounds are played back on external instruments or internal devices, the computer doesn't need to store the entire recording in memory or on disk; it just has to store commands to play the notes in the proper sequence. A MIDI file containing the MIDI messages for a song or soundtrack requires just a few kilobytes of memory.

Non-musicians can use ready-to-play *clip music* MIDI files for multimedia productions. But anyone with even marginal piano-playing skills and sequencing software can create MIDI music files. **Sequencing software** turns a computer into a musical composition, recording, and editing machine. The computer records MIDI signals as a musician plays each part on a keyboard. The musician can use the computer to layer instrumental tracks, substitute instrument sounds, edit notes, cut and paste passages, transpose keys, and change tempos, listening to each

Music publishing software can turn a MIDI file into a musical score ready for publishing. For many musicians and publishers this kind of software has eliminated the tedious and error-prone process of transcribing musical scores by hand. (Software: Overture from Cakewalk.)

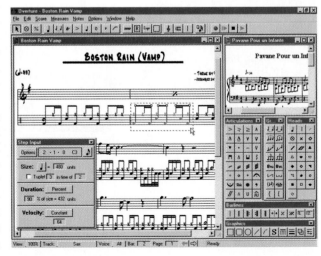

Some music applications allow non-musicians to exercise their musical creativity. Mixman Studio simulates DJ turntables, allowing users to create real-time dance music from digital samples.

change as it's made. The finished composition can be played by the sequencing software or exported to any other MIDI-compatible software, including a variety of multimedia applications.

With the appropriate software a computer can be used as an aid for composing, recording, performing, music publishing, and music education. Just as computer graphics technology has changed the way many artists work, electronic music technology has transformed the world of the musician. What's more, computer music technology has the power to unleash the musician in the rest of us.

Hypertext and Hypermedia

The future of writing is in space, not in time.

—**William S. Burroughs, writer**

Word processors, drawing programs, and most other applications today are WYSIWYG—*what you see* (on the screen) *is what you get* (on the printed page). But as Doug Engelbart has demonstrated for decades, WYSIWYG isn't always necessary or desirable. If a document doesn't need to be printed, it doesn't need to be structured like a paper document. If we want to focus on the relationship of ideas rather than the layout of the page, we may be better off with another kind of document—a dynamic, cross-referenced super document that takes full advantage of the computer's interactive capabilities.

Since 1945 when President Roosevelt's science advisor, Vannevar Bush, first wrote about such an interactive cross-referenced system, computer pioneers like Doug

While you're reading about Mark Twain, you might become curious about his hometown in Missouri, his novels, or the river that inspired those novels. Your explorations of 19th-century Hannibal, Missouri, might lead you to explore other Mississippi River towns of the time, or they might inspire you to learn more about Midwestern geography. Hypertext puts you in control.

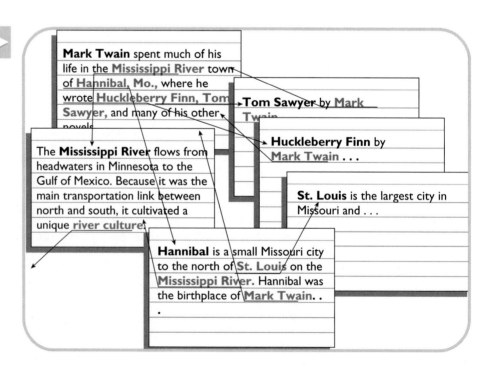

Mark Twain spent much of his life in the Mississippi River town of Hannibal, Mo., where he wrote Huckleberry Finn, Tom Sawyer, and many of his other novels.

Tom Sawyer by Mark Twain.

Huckleberry Finn by Mark Twain . . .

The Mississippi River flows from headwaters in Minnesota to the Gulf of Mexico. Because it was the main transportation link between north and south, it cultivated a unique river culture.

St. Louis is the largest city in Missouri and . . .

Hannibal is a small Missouri city to the north of St. Louis on the Mississippi River. Hannibal was the birthplace of Mark Twain . . .

Engelbart and Ted Nelson (who coined the term "hypertext") have pushed the technology toward that vision. Early efforts were called **hypertext** because they allowed textual information to be linked in *nonsequential* ways. Conventional text media like books are linear, or *sequential*: They are designed to be read from beginning to end. A hypertext document contains *links* that can lead readers quickly to other parts of the document or to other related documents. Hypertext invites readers to cut their own personal trails through information.

If this book were a hypertext document, you might click on the name Doug Engelbart in the previous paragraph to learn more about Engelbart. You would be transported to the profile at the beginning of this chapter that describes Engelbart's visionary work. After reading that profile, you might want to return to this section and continue reading about hypertext. On the other hand you might want to learn more about Alan Kay, the computer scientist quoted in Engelbart's profile. Clicking on Kay's name would transport you to the profile at the beginning of the final chapter. From that point you could continue to explore topics related to Alan Kay or return here to learn more about hypertext. With a comprehensive, well-designed hypertext reference you could follow your curiosity just about anywhere by pointing and clicking.

Hypertext first gained widespread public attention in 1987, when Apple introduced HyperCard, a **hypermedia** system that could combine text, numbers, graphics, animation, sound effects, music, and other media in hyperlinked documents. (Depending on how it's used, the term *hypermedia* might be synonymous with *interactive multimedia*.) Today millions of Windows and Macintosh users routinely use hypertext whenever they consult on-line Help files. But the biggest hotbed of hypertext/hypermedia activity is the World Wide Web. Hypertext on the Web allows readers to jump between documents all over the Internet. The Web has spawned countless hypermedia documents, many of them created by educators, students, and hobbyists.

But in spite of its popularity hypertext isn't likely to replace paper books any time soon. Web users and others who use hypertext have several legitimate complaints:

▶ Hypermedia documents can be disorienting and leave readers wondering what they've missed. When you're reading a book, you always know where you are and where you've been in the text. That's not necessarily true in hypermedia.

▶ Hypermedia documents don't always have the links readers want. Hypermedia authors can't build every possible connection into their documents, so some readers are frustrated because they can't easily get "there" from "here."

▶ Hypermedia documents don't encourage scribbled margin notes, highlighting, or turned page corners for marking key passages. Some hypermedia documents provide buttons for making "bookmarks" and text fields to add personal notes, but they aren't as friendly and flexible as traditional paper markup tools.

▶ Hypermedia hardware can be hard on humans. Most people find that reading a computer screen is more tiring than reading printed pages. Many complain that extended periods of screen-gazing cause eyestrain, headache, backache, and other ailments. It's not always easy to stretch out under a tree or curl up in an easy chair with a Web-linked computer.

▶ The art of hypermedia is still in its infancy. Every new art form takes time to develop. How can writers develop effective plot lines if they don't know what path their readers will choose through their stories? This is just one of the hundreds of questions with which hypermedia authors are struggling.

Still, hypermedia is not all hype. As the art matures, advances in software and hardware design will take care of many of these problems. Even today hypermedia documents provide extensive cross-referencing, flexibility, and instant keyword searches that simply aren't possible with paper media.

Interactivity and multiplicity: the two dimensions of multimedia.

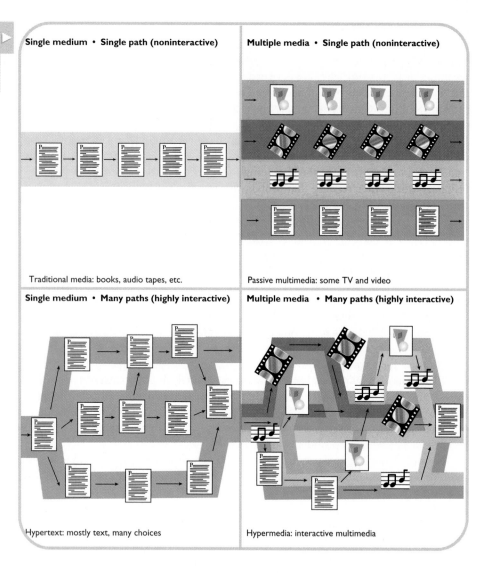

Single medium • Single path (noninteractive)

Traditional media: books, audio tapes, etc.

Multiple media • Single path (noninteractive)

Passive multimedia: some TV and video

Single medium • Many paths (highly interactive)

Hypertext: mostly text, many choices

Multiple media • Many paths (highly interactive)

Hypermedia: interactive multimedia

Interactive Multimedia: Eye, Ear, Hand, and Mind

The hybrid or the meeting of two media is a moment of truth and revelation from which a new form is born.

—Marshall McLuhan, in *Understanding Media; The Extensions of Man*

We live in a world rich in sensory experience. Information comes to us in a variety of forms: pictures, text, moving images, music, voice, and more. As information-processing machines, computers are capable of delivering information to our senses in many forms. Until recently, computer users could work with only one or two forms of information at a time. Today's multimedia computers allow users to work with information-rich documents that intermix a variety of audiovisual media.

Interactive Multimedia: What Is It?

The term multimedia generally means using some combination of text, graphics, animation, video, music, voice, and sound effects to communicate. By this defini-

tion an episode of *Sesame Street* or the evening news might be considered multimedia. In fact, computer-based multimedia tools are used heavily in the production of *Sesame Street,* the evening news, and hundreds of other television programs. Entertainment industry professionals use computers to create animated sequences, display titles, construct special video effects, synthesize music, edit sound tracks, coordinate communication, and perform dozens of other tasks crucial to the production of modern television programs and motion pictures.

So when you watch a typical TV program, you're experiencing a multimedia product. With each second that passes, you are bombarded with millions of bits of information. But television and video are *passive media*—they pour information into our eyes and ears while we sit and take it all in. We have no control over the information flow. Modern computer technology allows information to move in both directions, turning multimedia into interactive multimedia. Unlike TV, radio, and video, interactive multimedia allow the viewer/listener to take an active part in the experience. The best interactive multimedia software puts the user in charge, allowing that person to control the information flow.

Interactive multimedia software is delivered to consumers on a variety of platforms. Multimedia computers—Macintosh and Windows machines with fast processors, large memories, CD-ROM or DVD-ROM drives, speakers, and sound cards—are everywhere. Thousands of education and entertainment multimedia programs are available on CD-ROM and DVD-ROM for these machines. Many more multimedia software titles are designed to be used with television sets and controlled by game machines and other *set-top boxes* from Nintendo, Sega, Sony, and other companies. Many multimedia documents are created for use in kiosks in stores, museums, and other public places. A typical multimedia kiosk is a PC-in-a-box with a touch screen instead of a keyboard and mouse for input.

Interactive multimedia materials are all over the Web, too. But multimedia on the Web today is full of compromises, because today's Web pipelines can't deliver large media files quickly enough. Still, Web technology is improving rapidly, making many experts wonder whether disk-based multimedia will eventually be unnecessary.

A children's book with animated pictures that can read aloud to the child in multiple languages while words light up on the screen; an interactive exploration of the universe that turns a personal computer into a virtual planetarium; and in an interactive version of the world's most popular encyclopedia—are just three of the thousands of interactive multimedia programs available today. (Software: Dr. Seuss's *The Cat in the Hat* from Living Books; *Starry Night Backyard* from Sienna; and *Encyclopaedia Britannica DVD 2000*.)

Making Interactive Multimedia Work

Whether you're creating a simple presentation or a full-blown multimedia extravaganza, your finished product will communicate more effectively if you follow a few simple guidelines:

▶ *Be consistent.* Group similar controls together, and keep a consistent visual appearance throughout the presentation.

▶ *Make it intuitive.* Use graphical metaphors to guide viewers, and make your controls do what they look like they should do.

▶ *Strive for simplicity.* A clean, uncluttered screen is more inviting than a crowded one—and easier to understand, too.

▶ *Keep it lively.* If your presentation doesn't include motion, sound, and user interaction, it probably should be printed and distributed as a paper.

▶ *The message is more important than the media.* Your goal is to communicate information, not saturate with sensations. Don't let the bells and whistles get in the way of your message.

▶ *Put the user in the driver's seat.* Include controls for turning down sound, bypassing repetitive animation, and turning off annoying features. Provide navigation aids, search tools, bookmarks, on-line help, and "Where am I?" feedback. Never tell the user "You can't get there from here."

▶ *Let real people test your presentation.* The best way to find out if your presentation works is to test it on people who aren't familiar with the subject. If they get lost or bored, find out why, and fix it.

Multimedia Authoring: Making Mixed Media

Style used to be an interaction between the human soul and tools that were limiting. In the digital era, it will have to come from the soul alone.

—Jaron Lanier, **virtual reality pioneer**

Multimedia authoring software is used to create and edit multimedia documents. Like desktop publishing, interactive multimedia authoring involves combining source documents—including graphics, text files, video clips, and sounds—in an aesthetically pleasing format that communicates with the user. Multimedia authoring software, like page layout software, serves as glue that binds documents created and captured with other applications. But since a multimedia document can change in response to user input, authoring involves specifying not just *what?* and *where?* but also *when?* and *why?* Some authoring programs are designed for professionals. Others are designed for children. Many are used by both.

Some authoring programs, including HyperStudio and MetaCard, use the card-and-stack user interface originally introduced with Apple's HyperCard. According to this metaphor, a multimedia document is a stack of cards. Each screen, called a card, can contain graphics, text, and **buttons**—"hot spots" that respond to mouse clicks. Buttons can be programmed to transport the user to another card, play music, open dialog boxes, launch other applications, rearrange information, perform menu operations, send messages to hardware devices, or do other things. Some authoring programs, including ToolBook, use a similar user interface with a book-and-page metaphor: A book replaces the stack and a page replaces the card. The World Wide Web uses metaphorical pages to represent screens of information; many authoring tools are designed specifically to create Web pages. The most widely used professional multimedia authoring tool, Macromedia's Director, has a different kind of user interface. A Director document is a *movie* rather than a stack of cards or a book of pages. A button can transport a user to another frame of a movie rather than another card or page. Some authoring tools, such as Authorware, use flowcharts as tools for constructing documents.

The authoring tool's interface metaphor is important to the person creating the multimedia document, but not to the person viewing the finished document, who sees

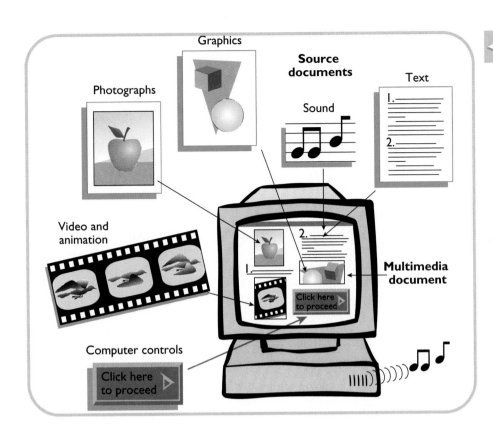

Multimedia authoring software glues together media captured and created with other applications.

Multimedia authoring involves programming objects on the screen to react, or behave, in particular ways under particular circumstances. Macromedia's Director, the most popular cross-platform multimedia authoring tool, includes prewritten behaviors that can be attached to buttons, images, or other on-screen objects. These behaviors make it possible to create sophisticated multimedia documents without actually writing scripts or programs.

only the user interface that was built into the document by the author. When you're using a well-designed multimedia document, you can't tell whether it was created by Director, Authorware, ToolBook, or another authoring tool.

With the growing interest in the Internet, many people expect the World Wide Web to replace CD-ROMs for most multimedia delivery. Most multimedia authoring tools can create Web-ready multimedia documents. For example, documents created by Authorware and Director can be converted into Web documents using Macromedia's Shockwave technology. Shockwave software compresses multimedia documents so they can appear and respond more quickly on the Web. But even with compression, the Internet isn't fast enough to deliver the high-quality audio and video that's possible with CD-ROM and DVD-ROM. On the other hand, the contents of a disk are static; they can't be continually updated like a Web site. And CD-ROMs don't offer opportunities for communication with other people the way a Web site can. Many multimedia manufacturers today produce *hybrid disks*—media-rich CD-ROMs and DVD-ROMs that automatically draw content and communication from the Web. Hybrid disks hint at the types of multimedia experiences that will be possible without disks through tomorrow's faster Internet.

Multimedia authoring software today puts a great deal of power into the hands of computer users, but it doesn't solve all of the technical problems in this new art form. Many of the problems with hypertext and hypermedia outlined earlier are even more serious when multiple media are involved. What's more, current technology hasn't lived up to the hype; multimedia consumers spend far too much time installing, loading, and waiting, and the results often aren't worth the wait. Still, the best multimedia productions transcend these problems and show the promise of this emerging technology.

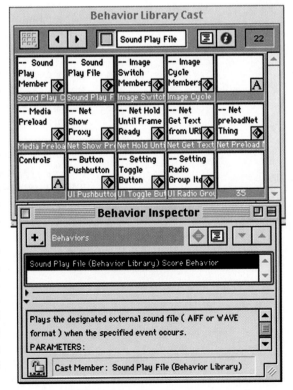

Interactive Media: Visions of the Future

For most of recorded history, the interactions of humans with their media have been primarily passive in the sense that marks on paper, paint on walls, even motion pictures and television, do not change in response to the viewer's wishes. [But computers can] respond to queries and experiments—so that the message may involve the learner in a two-way conversation.

—Alan Kay

For hundreds of thousands of years, two-way interactive communication was the norm: One person talked, another responded. Today television, radio, newspapers, magazines, and books pour information into billions of passive people every day. For many people one-way passive communication has become more common than interactive discourse.

According to many experts, interactive multimedia technology offers new hope for turning communication back into a participation sport. With interactive multimedia software the audience is a part of the show. Interactive multimedia tools can give people control over the media—control traditionally reserved for professional artists, filmmakers, and musicians. The possibilities are far reaching, especially when telecommunication enters the picture. Consider these snapshots from a not-too-distant future:

▶ Instead of watching your biology professor flip through overhead transparencies, you control a self-paced interactive presentation complete with video footage illustrating key concepts.

▶ In your electronic mailbox you find a "letter" from your sister. The letter shows her performing all of the instrumental parts for a song she composed, followed by a request for you to add a vocal line.

▶ Your favorite TV show is an interactive thriller that allows you to control the plot twists and work with the main characters to solve mysteries.

▶ You share your concerns about a proposed factory in your hometown at the televised electronic town meeting. Thousands of others respond to questions from the mayor by pressing buttons on their remote control panels. The overwhelming citizen response forces the city council to reconsider the proposal.

Of course, the future of interactive multimedia may not be all sunshine and roses. Many experts fear that these exciting new media possibilities will further remove us from books, other people, and the natural world around us. If television today can mesmerize so many people, will tomorrow's interactive multimedia TVs cause even more serious addiction problems? Or will interactive communication breathe new life into the media and the people who use them? Will interactive electronic media make it easier for abusers of power to influence and control unwary citizens, or will the power of the push button create a new kind of digital democracy? Will interactive digital technology just turn "sound bites" into "sound bytes," or will it unleash the creative potential in the people who use it? For answers, stay tuned.

CROSSCURRENTS:

Digital Revolution in Retrospect

Bruce Sterling

Bruce Sterling is well known for his dark, thoughtful science fiction works about the impact of technology and bureaucracy on our future. But Sterling is more than a cyberpunk writer. In this essay, written for the 50th anniversary of the Association for Computing Machinery, and published in the anniversary issue of Communications of the ACM, *Sterling points out one of the hidden problems of modern computer and multimedia technology. If we're putting our creative works in digital form on the Web and CD-ROMs, how can we be sure that anyone will be able to experience them in the future?*

After 50 years of the ACM, it's clear that computers have become history. We now live in the Information Age. This is a lovely situation, but it won't last. We're extremely good at transforming "ages" into mere history now—the Radio Age, the Aviation Age, the Atomic Age, the Space Age . . . all of these so called "ages"— are history. Soon our much-trumpeted "Information Age" will have that same archaic ring.

The Information Age has accomplished great work during its span on the historical stage, dissolving jobs, transforming industries, frenetically building and destroying great fortunes. Computers have revolutionized the working lives of doctors and artists and clerks, generals and engineers, and politicians. It's delightful to look back and realize how little harm has been done by this transformative tide of computers. By comparison to other ages, we've been lucky. After 50 years of development of the Aviation Age, the Luftwaffe had blitzed London, and Dresden was a giant firestorm. For its part, the so-called Atomic Age never even began to live up to its hype (thank goodness). The Information Age has been much gentler with us. We may dare to hope that trend continues.

The Information Age doesn't always keep its promises—what age ever does?—but computers do change things. The extent and the rate of this quiet immolation have been enormous. The victims of obsolescence are sadly little recognized. In fact, many victims don't even know yet that they're victims. The World-Wide Web has become the great pop hit of late '90s global culture, but there are no formal archives anywhere for the Web. In five years,

there will probably be no way to access a contemporary Web page, and in 50 years, the very idea of a "Web page" will seem as arcane as a magic-lantern slide.

There are few archives for computer-generated texts, programs, computer art, or computer-generated cultural activity of any kind. Almost every manifestation of what we call "new media" would be much better described as "temporary media." None of it has any place to hide, no zone of safety from the searing pace of innovation. Everything done by, through, or with a computer is desperately vulnerable.

Computers swallow whatever they can touch, and everything they swallow is forced to become as unstable as they are. With the soaring and brutal progress of Moore's Law, computer systems have become a series of ever-faster, ever more complex, and ever more elaborate coffins.

In the 1990s, we produce computers that are high-tech sarcophagi with the working life span of hamsters. The contemporary computer industry has the production values, and the promotional values, and even the investment structure of the couture industry. This may be why computers are the first truly arcane technology that has become deeply and genuinely glamorous.

We are very glamorous now, but we are building on sand, and the quicker we build, the quicker that sand becomes. In 50 years, however, we will have gotten over this. We'll have put it behind us. We'll have developed other obsessions and other problems. And then perhaps we will really know the full extent of the price we have paid for the revolution.

DISCUSSION QUESTIONS

1. Do you agree with the author's statement that "computer systems have become a series of ever-faster, ever more complex, and ever more elaborate coffins"?

2. Are we creating artistic and intellectual works that will be lost to future generations because of their digital nature?

3. What do you think the author means by "[c]omputers swallow whatever they can touch, and everything they swallow is forced to become as unstable as they are"?

Computer graphics today encompass more than quantitative charts and graphs generated by spreadsheets. Bitmapped painting programs allow users to "paint" the screen with a mouse, pen, or other pointing device. The software stores the results in a pixel map, with each pixel having an assigned color. The more possible colors there are and the higher the resolution (pixel density) is, the more the images can approach photorealism. Object-oriented drawing programs also allow users to draw on the screen with a pointing device, with the results stored as collections of geometric objects rather than as maps of computer bits.

Bitmapped graphics and object-oriented graphics each offer advantages in particular situations; trade-offs involve storage, printing, editing, and ease of use. Both types of graphics have applications outside the art world. Bitmapped graphics are used in high-resolution digital image processing software for on-screen photo editing. Object-oriented graphics are at the heart of 3-D modeling software and computer-aided design (CAD) software used by architects, designers, and engineers. Presentation graphics software, which may include either or both graphics types, automates the process of creating slides, transparencies, handouts, and computer-based presentations, making it easy for non-artists to create visually attractive presentations.

Computers today aren't limited to working with static images; they're widely used to create and edit documents in media that change over time or in response to user interaction. For animation and digital video work PCs mimic many of the features of expensive professional workstations at a fraction of the cost. Similarly, today's personal computers can perform a variety of sound and music editing tasks that used to require expensive equipment and numerous musicians.

The interactive nature of the personal computer makes it possible to create nonlinear documents that allow users to take individual paths through information. Early nonlinear documents were called hypertext because they could contain only text. Today we can create or explore hypermedia documents—interactive documents that mix text, graphics, sounds, and moving images with on-screen navigation buttons—on disk and on the World Wide Web.

Multimedia computer systems make a new kind of software possible—software that uses text, graphics, animation, video, music, voice, and sound effects to communicate. Interactive multimedia documents are available for desktop computers, video game machines, set-top boxes connected to televisions, and networks. Regardless of the hardware, interactive multimedia software allows the user to control the presentation rather than just watch or listen passively. Only time will tell whether these new media will live up to their potential for enhancing education, training, entertainment, and cultural enrichment.

Key Terms

animation, 187
audio digitizer, 191
bitmapped (raster) graphics, 177
bullet chart, 185
button, 200
clip art, 183
color depth (bit depth), 177
computer-aided design (CAD), 184
computer-aided manufacturing (CAM), 185
computer-integrated manufacturing (CIM), 185
data compression, 190

digital image processing software, 177
digital video, 188
drawing software, 180
frame, 187
hypermedia, 197
hypertext, 197
interactive multimedia, 199
MIDI, 195
morph, 190
MP3, 195
multimedia, 198
multimedia authoring software, 200
object-oriented (vector) graphics, 180

page-description language, 182
painting software, 176
palette, 177
pixel, 176
PostScript, 182
presentation graphics software, 185
resolution, 177
sequencing software, 195
synthesized sound, 191
3-D modeling software, 184
video digitizer, 188
video editing software, 190
WYSIWYG, 196

Review Questions

1. Define or describe each of the key terms listed above. Check your answers using the glossary.
2. What is the difference between bitmapped graphics and object-oriented graphics? What are the advantages and disadvantages of each?

3. What two technological factors limit the realism of a bitmapped image? How are these related to storage of that image in the computer?
4. How is digital image processing of photographs related to bitmapped painting?

5. Describe several practical applications for 3-D modeling and CAD software.
6. Why is image compression an important part of digital video technology?
7. Describe three different technologies for adding music or other sounds to a multimedia presentation. Describe a practical application of each sound source.
8. How do hypertext and other hypermedia differ from linear media?
9. Describe several practical applications for hypermedia.
10. What are the main disadvantages of hypermedia when compared with conventional media such as books and videos?
11. Is it possible to have hypermedia without multimedia? Is it possible to have multimedia without hypermedia? Explain your answers.
12. How does presentation graphics software differ from multimedia authoring software? Give an example of a practical application of each.

Discussion Questions

1. How does modern digital image processing technology affect the reliability of photographic evidence? How does digital audio technology affect the reliability of sound recordings as evidence? How should our legal system respond to this technology?
2. Scanners, video digitizers, and audio digitizers make it easier than ever for people to violate copyright laws. What, if anything, should be done to protect intellectual property rights of the people who create pictures, videos, and music? Under what circumstances do you think it's acceptable to copy sounds or images for use in your own work?
3. Do you think hypermedia documents will eclipse certain kinds of books and other media? If so, which ones and why?
4. Thanks to modern electronic music technology, one or two people can make a record that would have required dozens of musicians 20 years ago. What impact will electronic music technology ultimately have on the music profession?
5. Try to answer each of the questions posed at the end of the section called "Interactive Media: Visions of the Future."

Projects

1. Draw a familiar object or scene using a bitmapped painting program. Draw the same object or scene with an object-oriented drawing program. Describe how the process changed using different software.
2. Create visual aids for a speech or lecture using presentation graphics software. In what ways did the software make the job easier? What limitations did you find?
3. Create an interactive hypermedia document using HyperCard, ToolBook, or some other authoring tool.
Test your document on several people and describe the results.
4. Compose an original music composition using a synthesizer, a computer, and a sequencer. Describe the experience.
5. Review several interactive multimedia titles. Discuss their strengths and weaknesses as communication tools. In what ways did their interactivity enhance their usefulness? (*Extra challenge:* Make your review interactive.)

Books and CD-ROMs

Most of the best graphics, video, music, and multimedia applications books are software specific. When you decide on a software application, choose books based on your chosen software and on the type of information you need. If you want quick answers with a minimum of verbiage, you'll probably be delighted with a book from Peachpit's Visual Quickstart series. Most of the titles listed below aren't keyed to specific applications.

Information Illustration, by Dale Glasgow (Reading, MA: Addison-Wesley, 1994). A professional illustrator shows you, through a series of real-world projects, how he uses his computer to create graphic illustrations that communicate clearly.

The New Drawing on the Right Side of the Brain: A Course in Enhancing Creativity and Artistic Confidence, by Betty Edwards (Los Angeles: J. P. Tarcher, 1999). If you're convinced you have no artistic ability, give this book a try; you might surprise yourself.

VizAbility, by Kristina Hooper Woolsey, Scott Kim, and Gayle Curtis (Boston: PWS Publishing Co., 1996). Is it a book that comes with a CD-ROM or a CD-ROM that comes with a book? In the case of this package it's hard to say. VizAbility is a multimedia package designed to help you see and think in more artistic, creative ways. Chapters and software modules have names like "Seeing," "Drawing," and "Imagining." The authors have been working with interactive multimedia since the early days of the field; in VizAbility they have created a tool that can open your eyes . . . and your mind.

Graphic Communications Dictionary, by Daniel J. Lyons (Upper Saddle River, NJ: Prentice Hall, 2000). This is an excellent alphabetic reference for anyone wrestling with the terminology of graphic design.

Real World Digital Photography: Industrial Strength Techniques, by Deke McClelland and Katrin Eismann (Berkeley, CA: Peachpit Press, 1999). This book covers everything from shopping for a digital camera to creating immersive virtual reality environments with QuickTime VR. The authors have lots of experience and they communicate clearly.

Visual Quickstart Guide: Photoshop 5.5 for Windows and Macintosh, by Elaine Weinmann and Peter Lourekas (Berkeley, CA: Peachpit Press, 1999). Peachpit's Visual Quickstart Guides are popular because they provide maximum instruction for a minimal investment of time. This Photoshop guide is exemplary. Using lots of pictures and few words, it unlocks the secrets of the program that is the industry standard for professional photo and bitmap editing software.

Step by Step Electronic Design Techniques, edited by Talitha Harper and Sara Booth (Berkeley, CA: Peachpit Press, 1998). This collection of articles from *Step by Step Electronic Design* allows you to look over the shoulders of the pros as they develop projects with Painter, Freehand, PageMaker, PhotoShop, Xpress, Illustrator, and Ray Dream. Once you've learned the basics of some of these programs, this book will show you tips and techniques that can make your work stand out.

Designing Web Graphics.2, by Lynda Weinman (Indianapolis: New Riders Publishing, 1997). Weinman is a well-respected expert on Web design and graphic design; this lavish book explores tools, techniques, and issues of graphic design for the Web.

Looking Good in Presentations: Third Edition, by Molly W. Joss (Scottsdale, AZ: Coriolis Group, 1999) Programs like PowerPoint can help non-designers create stylish presentations, but they're not foolproof. (How many ugly, boring computer-enhanced presentations have you had to sit through?) This is a great book for anyone creating presentations, from simple slide shows to full-featured multimedia extravaganzas. Starting with "How To Not Be Boring" in Chapter 1, you'll find plenty of tips to make your presentations shine.

Animation on the Web, by Sean Wagstaff (Berkeley, CA: Peachpit Press, 1999). From simple scrolling banners to 3-D digital video, animation is everywhere on the Web. This "Guide to Webtop Publishing" is a great resource for beginners who want to learn the basics of animation and for experienced animators who want to learn about the technology that can put their works on the Web.

Animation Tips and Tricks for Windows and Mac, by Don and Melora Foley (Berkeley, CA: Peachpit Press, 1997). This colorful book is a great resource for learning about 3-D graphics and animation. It includes a portfolio of stunning examples by pros, an overview of software and hardware tools, a collection of useful tips that aren't platform specific, and a CD-ROM full of textures, models, and sound files that you can use in your 3-D projects.

QuickTime Pro 4 for Macintosh and Windows Visual Quickstart Guide, by Judith Stern and Robert Letteieri (Berkeley, CA: Peachpit Press, 1999). QuickTime is a cross-platform multimedia standard for digital video, but it's also a good tool for working with audio, interactive media, virtual reality, and more. This book is a good introduction to this powerful software technology.

Digital Video for Dummies, by Martin Doucette (Foster City, CA: IDG Books, 1999). This book covers the basics of digital video, from shooting and capturing to editing and producing final footage. It includes a Windows-only CD-ROM containing sample software.

Digital Guerrilla Video: A Grassroots Guide to the Revolution, by Avi Hoffer (San Francisco: Miller Freeman Books, 1999). Digital video technology is spawning a revolution—for the first time in history, small-budget operations can produce big-time video productions. This book is as much about the creative process of creating video as it is about the technology. After you learn the basics, this book can provide professional advice and a creative kick.

Producing Great Sound for Digital Video, by Jay Rose (San Francisco: Miller Freeman Books, 1999). The soundtrack is often the difference between a good video and a great one. This book provides a wealth of information and advice on capturing, creating, and using sound in your video and multimedia projects.

Audio on the Web: The Official IUMA Guide, by Jeff Patterson and Ryan Melcher (Berkeley, CA: Peachpit Press, 1998). This book is an excellent resource for learning the basics of digital audio and its applications on the Web. It includes easy-to-understand explanations of technology and techniques, plus a cross-platform CD-ROM.

The Complete Idiot's Guide to MP3: Music on the Internet, by Rod Underhill and Nat Gertler (Indianapolis, IN: Que, 2000). This book is part of the Complete Idiot's Guide series, Que's response to IDG's wildly popular Dummy's series. Even if you're not an idiot, you'll find this guide has lots of helpful information about the MP3 phenomenon. Technical, legal, ethical, and aesthetic dimensions of MP3 are covered in this book, which comes with a Windows CD-ROM containing music and MP3 players.

The Desktop Musician: Creating Music on Your Computer, by David M. Rubin (Berkeley, CA: Osborne McGraw-Hill, 1995). This book is a good but somewhat dated introduction to MIDI and digital audio, written from a musician's perspective.

The Computer Music Tutorial, by Curtis Roads (Cambridge, MA: The MIT Press, 1996). Not for the fainthearted, this highly technical 1,200+ page book covers nearly every aspect of creating music on the computer. The focus is on the mathematics and algorithms behind various computer synthesis techniques.

The Dictionary of Multimedia: Terms and Acronyms, by Brad Hansen (Chicago: Fitzroy Dearborn Publishers, 1999). If you want to keep a book handy for those times when you need to know the difference between MPC-1 and MPC-2, or what JPEG stands for, this is a good choice. It includes appendices on HTML standards organizations and (surprisingly) DOS commands.

Theoretical Foundations of Multimedia, by Robert S. Tannenbaum (New York: W.H. Freeman, 1998). Multimedia is an ideal profession for a modern Renaissance person. To be truly multimedia literate, a person needs to understand concepts from fields as diverse as computer science, physics, design, law, psychology, and communication. This introductory text/CD-ROM surveys each of these fields from the multimedia perspective, providing valuable conceptual background with practical value.

Understanding Media: The Extensions of Man, by Marshall McLuhan (Cambridge, MA: MIT Press, 1994.) This classic, originally published in 1964, explores the relationship of mass media to the masses. The new introduction in this 30th Anniversary reissue reevaluates McLuhan's visionary work 30 years later.

Audio CD

Wired Music Futurists (Rhino). Digital technology doesn't just make it easier for musicians to do what they've always done; it makes it possible for them to do things that haven't been done before. This CD from *Wired* offers a wide variety of examples of new music for a digital culture, with tracks from Sun Ra, Steve Reich, Laurie Anderson, Brian Eno, Beck, Sonic Youth, DJ Spooky, and others.

Periodicals

Step by Step Electronic Design, Step by Step Graphics, and *Dynamic Graphics.* These publications are aimed at graphic designers and artists who use computers in their work. There are lots of tips, techniques, and tutorials for a variety of applications.

DV and *AV Video & Multimedia Producer.* These days video producers have to pay attention to the world of computers and multimedia. These two publications provide current coverage of the converging worlds of video and multimedia.

Keyboard and *Electronic Musician.* These two magazines are among the best sources for up-to-date information on computers and music synthesis.

Artbyte. This stylish magazine explores the world and culture of digital design.

World Wide Web Pages

The Web is known as the multimedia part of the Internet, and there are plenty of Web sites for learning about—and experiencing first hand—a variety of mixed media. The *Computer Confluence* Web pages will link you to multimedia hardware and software companies and pages that demonstrate state-of-the-art multimedia on the Web.

Chapter

8

Database Applications and Implications

AFTER YOU READ THIS CHAPTER YOU SHOULD BE ABLE TO:

Explain what a database is and describe its basic structure.

Identify the kinds of problems that can be best solved with database software.

Describe different kinds of database software, from simple file managers to complex relational databases.

Describe database operations for storing, sorting, updating, querying, and summarizing information.

Explain how databases threaten our privacy.

In this chapter:

▶ The basics of databases
▶ Database applications large and small
▶ The future of database technology
▶ How databases threaten your privacy
... and more.

On the CD-ROM:

▶ An interactive game based on database logic
▶ Videoclip of Bill Gates
▶ Instant access to glossary and key word references
▶ Interactive self-study quizzes
... and more.

On the Web:

www.prenhall.com/beekman
▶ Links to major database companies
▶ Resources for database users
▶ Resources to help you protect your personal privacy
▶ Self-study exercises
... and more.

The goal is **information at your fingertips.**

—Bill Gates

In the early days of the personal computer revolution Bill Gates and Paul Allen formed a company called Microsoft to produce and market a version of the BASIC programming language for microcomputers. Microsoft BASIC quickly became the standard language installed in virtually every desktop computer on the market.

BASIC was important, but Microsoft's biggest break came when IBM went shopping for an operating system for its new personal computer. Gates purchased an operating system from a small company, reworked it to meet IBM's specifications, named it MS-DOS (for Microsoft Disk Operating System), and offered it to IBM. The IBM PC became an industry standard, and Microsoft found itself owning the operating system that kept most of the PCs in the world running.

Bill Gates and Paul Allen as students.

Today Bill Gates and Microsoft dominate the personal computer software industry, selling operating systems, programming languages, and applications programs for desktop computers. Microsoft is a $70 billion company with about 33,000 employees and about $20 billion in annual revenues. Software has made Gates the richest man on earth.

Microsoft's desktop dominion was threatened in the mid-1990s by the Internet explosion. For many computer users, desktop software was becoming irrelevant; their computers were little more than portals into the Internet. Microsoft may have owned Windows and MS Office, but it didn't own the World Wide Web. Recognizing the threat to his PC supremacy, Gates turned the massive company around in short order, making the Internet a critical part of its software strategy. Today Microsoft's Internet Explorer Web browser is being redefined as a central component of the Windows operating system; Microsoft desktop applications have links to the Internet, and Microsoft has partnerships with dozens of Web-related businesses worldwide.

According to writer Steven Levy, Gates "has the obsessive drive of a hacker working on a tough technical dilemma, yet has an uncanny grasp of the marketplace, as well as a firm conviction of what the future will be like and what he should do about it." The future, says Gates, will be digital. Even the pictures on our walls will be high-definition digital reproductions of paintings and photographs that can be changed at the touch of a button. The walls of the $40 million Gates mansion are already decorated with his collection of digital art.

To prepare for this all-digital future, Microsoft is extending its tentacles beyond software into all kinds of information-related business ventures, from on-line banking and shopping to the MS-NBC cable TV network. Microsoft has even bought the electronic rights to hundreds of works of literature, art, and cinema so that it can profit every time anyone views a digital reproduction on line or on TV.

Bill Gates's success is not without controversy. Critics insist that he uses unethical business practices to ruthlessly—and sometimes illegally—stomp out competition. Many of Microsoft's biggest customers and partners confide

The Gates mansion.

that they mistrust Gates and fear a Microsoft monopoly. The Federal Trade Commission has repeatedly investigated the company's practices for possible violations of monopoly laws. In 1997 the U.S. Department of Justice investigated Microsoft for a variety of antitrust violations. The government claimed that, among other things, Microsoft forced computer manufacturers to include only one Web browser—Microsoft Internet Explorer—on all Windows computers. The company's arrogant response triggered a tidal wave of anti-Microsoft sentiment. In 1998 twenty states joined the federal government in a widely-publicized lawsuit against Microsoft's anti-competitive practices.

In March, 2000, a Federal Judge ruled that Microsoft had, indeed, operated as an illegal monopoly, and that Microsoft's crimes had hurt consumers as well as other businesses. The ultimate impact of the ruling is uncertain, but it's clear that Microsoft's legal troubles are far from over.

The stakes in these legal battles extend far beyond market share. According to Michael Moritz, a California venture capitalist, "It's difficult to think of a company in the history of the world that's positioned to influence so many aspects of life as Microsoft...." In short, Bill Gates is poised to become one of the most powerful people on Earth, with more practical influence on our lives than most elected officials. In early 2000, Gates stepped aside as CEO of Microsoft to become Chief Software Architect for the company. But few doubt that Gates, who is still Microsoft's Chairman, is the power behind the company. Whether you admire or despise him, you probably won't be able to ignore Bill Gates as his digital empire expands. In a future where we have all kinds of "information at our fingertips," Microsoft wants to be the source of that information. ◼

We live in an information age. We're bombarded with information by television, radio, newspapers, magazines, books, and computers. It's easy to be overwhelmed by the sheer quantity of information we're expected to deal with each day. Computer applications like word processors and spreadsheets can aggravate the problem by making it easier for people to generate more documents full of information.

A *database program* is a data manager that can help alleviate information overload. Databases make it possible for people to store, organize, retrieve, communicate, and manage information in ways that wouldn't be possible without computers. To control the flood of information, people use databases of all sizes and shapes—from massive mainframe database managers that keep airlines filled with passengers to computerized appointment calendars on palmtop computers and public database kiosks in shopping malls.

First the good news: "Information at your fingertips" can make your life richer and more efficient in a multitude of ways. Ready cash from street-corner ATMs, instant airline reservations from any telephone, catalog shopping with overnight mail-order delivery, exhaustive Web searches in seconds—none of these conveniences would be possible without databases.

Now the bad news: Much of the information stored in databases is your data, and you have little or no control over who has it and how they use it. Ironically, the database technology that liberates us in our day-to-day lives is, at the same time, chipping away at our privacy. We explore both sides of this important technology in this chapter.

The Electronic File Cabinet: Database Basics

The next best thing to knowing something is knowing where to find it.

—Samuel Johnson

We start by looking at the basics of databases. Like word processors, spreadsheets, and graphics programs, database programs are applications—programs for turning computers into productive tools. If a word processor is a computerized typewriter and a spreadsheet is a computerized ledger, we can think of a database program as a computerized file cabinet.

While word processors and spreadsheets generally are used to create printed documents, database programs are designed to maintain *databases*—collections of information stored on computer disks. A database can be an electronic version of a phone book, a recipe file, a library's card catalog, an inventory file stored in an office file cabinet, a school's student grade records, a card index containing the names and addresses of business contacts, or a catalog of your compact disc collection. Just about any collection of information can be turned into a database.

What Good Is a Database?

Why do people use computers for information-handling tasks that can be done with index cards, three-ring binders, or file folders? Computerized databases offer several advantages over their paper-and-pencil counterparts:

▶ *Databases make it easier to store large quantities of information.* If you have only 20 or 30 compact discs, it makes sense to catalog them in a notebook. If you have 2,000 or 3,000, your notebook may become as unwieldy as your CD collection. With a computerized database, your complete CD catalog can be stored on a single diskette. The larger the mass of information, the bigger the benefit of using a database.

▶ *Databases make it easier to retrieve information quickly and flexibly.* While it might take a minute or more to look up a phone number in a card file or telephone directory, the same job can be done in seconds with a database. If you look up 200 numbers every week, the advantage of a database is obvious. That advantage is even greater when your search doesn't match your file's organization. For example, suppose you have a phone number on a scrap of paper and you want to find the name and address of the person with that number. That kind of search may take hours if your information is stored in a large address book or file alphabetized by name, but the same search is almost instantaneous with a computerized database.

▶ *Databases make it easy to organize and reorganize information.* Paper filing systems force you to arrange information in one particular way. Should your book catalog be organized by author, by title, by publication date, or by subject? There's a lot riding on your decision because if you decide to rearrange everything later, you will waste a lot of time. With a database you can instantly switch between these organizational schemes as often as you like; there's no penalty for flexibility.

▶ *Databases make it easy to print and distribute information in a variety of ways.* Suppose you want to send letters to hundreds of friends inviting them to your postgraduation party. You'll need to include directions to your place for out-of-towners but not for home-towners. A database, when used with a word processor, can print personalized form letters, including extra directions for those who need them, and print preaddressed envelopes or mailing labels in a fraction of the time it would take you to do it by hand and with less likelihood of error. You can even print a report listing invitees sorted by zip code so you can suggest possible car pools. (If you want to bill those who attend the party, your database can help with that, too.)

Databases
are made up of

Books

Files
which are made up of

Records
which are made up of

Lubar, Steven
INFOCULTURE
1993/Houghton Mifflin
Boston
0-395-57042-5

Fields

0-395-57042-5

Database Anatomy

As you might expect, a specialized vocabulary is associated with databases. Unfortunately, some terms take on different meanings depending on their context, and different people use these words in different ways. We'll begin by charting a course through marketing hype and technical terminology to find our way to the definitions most people use today.

For our purposes, a database is a collection of information stored in an organized form in a computer, and a database program is a software tool for organizing storage and retrieval of that information. A variety of programs fit this broad definition, ranging from simple address book programs to massive inventory-tracking systems. We explore the differences between types of database programs later in the chapter, but for now we treat them as if they are more or less alike.

Many terms that describe the components of database systems grew out of the file cabinet terminology of the office. A database is composed of one or more files. A file is a collection of related information; it keeps that information together the way a drawer in a file cabinet does. If a database is used to record sales information for a company, separate files might contain the relevant sales data for each year. For an address database, separate files might hold personal and business contacts. It's up to the designer of the database to determine whether or not information in different categories is stored in separate files on the computer's disk.

The term *file* sometimes causes confusion because of its multiple meanings. A disk can contain application programs, system programs, utility programs, and documents, all of which are, from the computer's point of view, files. But for database users, the term *file* usually means a file that is part of a database—a specific kind of file. In this chapter *file* refers specifically to a data file created by a database program.

A database file is a collection of records. A record is the information relating to one person, product, or event. In the library's card catalog database a record is equivalent to one card. In an address book database a record contains information about one person. A compact disc catalog database would have one record per CD.

Each discrete chunk of information in a record is called a field. A record in the library's card catalog database would contain fields for author, title, publisher, address, date, and title code number. Your CD database could break records into fields by title, artist, and so on.

The type of information a field can hold is determined by its *field type*. For example, the author field in the library database would be defined as a text field, so it could contain text. The field specifying the number of copies of a book would be defined as a *numeric field*, so it could contain only numbers—numbers that can be used to calculate totals and other arithmetic formulas, if necessary. A date-of-purchase field might be a *date field* that could contain only dates. In addition to these standard field types, many database programs allow fields to contain graphics, digitized photographs, sounds, or even video clips. Computed fields contain formulas similar to spreadsheet formulas; they display values calculated from values in other numeric fields. For example, a computed field called GPA might contain a formula for calculating a student's grade point average using the grades stored in other fields.

Most database programs provide you with more than one way to view the data, including *form views*, which show one record at a time, and *list views*, which display several records in lists similar to a spreadsheet. In any view, fields can be rearranged without changing the underlying data.   **UV**

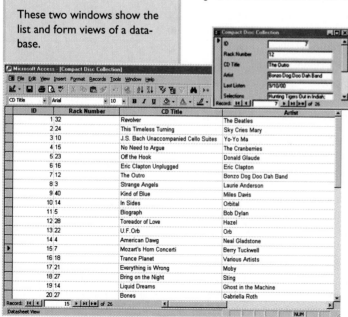

These two windows show the list and form views of a database.

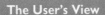
The User's View

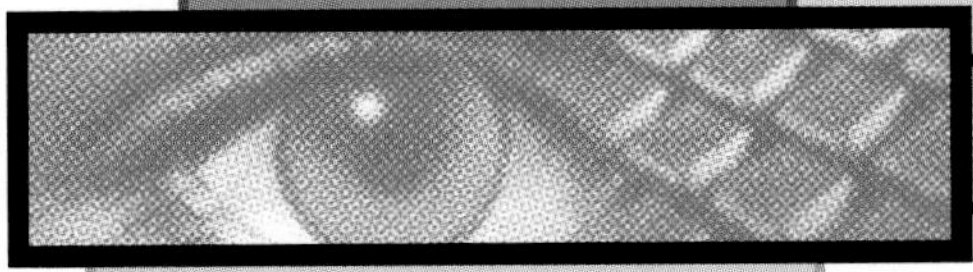

Building a Database

SOFTWARE   **FileMaker Pro.**

THE GOAL   **To create an Addresses database file to replace your tattered address book, the bundle of business cards in your desk drawer, and the scribbled list of numbers posted by your phone.**

① To create a new Addresses database file, you must first define fields by typing a name and specifying a field type for each one. In addition to including text fields for last name, first name, and other information, you add two date fields: one for birthday and one that will automatically display the most recent modification date for each record. You also include a picture field and two value lists—restricted fields that can only contain values from lists specified by you.

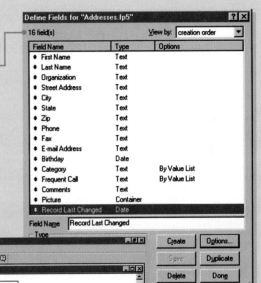

② The program creates a standard form-style layout for data entry, but it could be easier to use.

③ You modify the layout by rearranging fields and labels and changing their formats.

④ You type information into the first record of the reformatted layout, using the Tab key to move from field to field.

⑤ The Category and Frequent Call fields use mouse clicks to select the appropriate values.

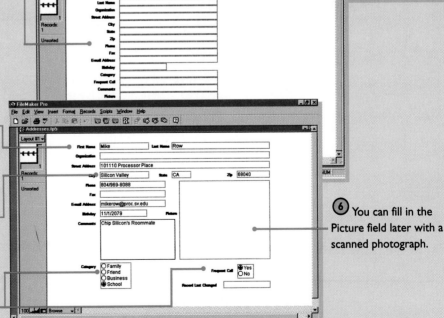

⑥ You can fill in the Picture field later with a scanned photograph.

⑦ When you're through, you use the New Record command to store this record in the data file and replace it on the screen with a new empty record.

To be continued . . .

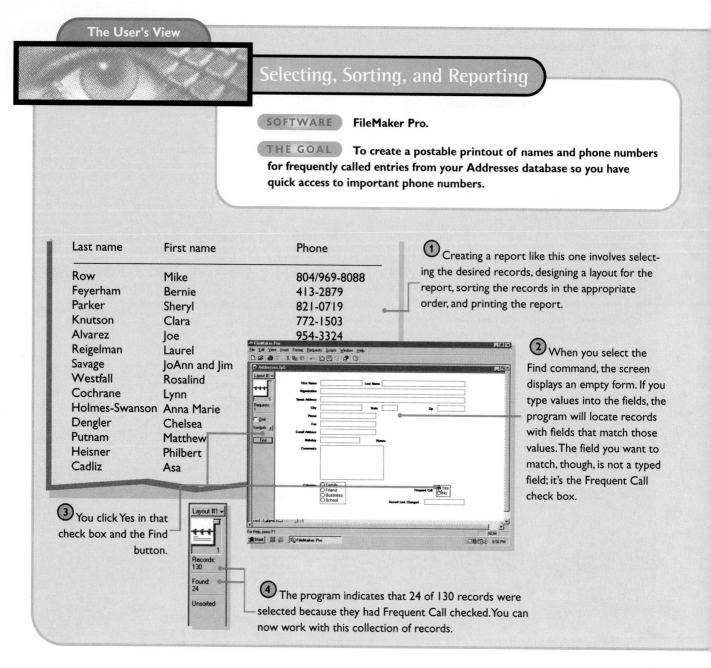

The User's View

Selecting, Sorting, and Reporting

SOFTWARE   FileMaker Pro.

THE GOAL   **To create a postable printout of names and phone numbers for frequently called entries from your Addresses database so you have quick access to important phone numbers.**

Last name	First name	Phone
Row	Mike	804/969-8088
Feyerham	Bernie	413-2879
Parker	Sheryl	821-0719
Knutson	Clara	772-1503
Alvarez	Joe	954-3324
Reigelman	Laurel	
Savage	JoAnn and Jim	
Westfall	Rosalind	
Cochrane	Lynn	
Holmes-Swanson	Anna Marie	
Dengler	Chelsea	
Putnam	Matthew	
Heisner	Philbert	
Cadliz	Asa	

1 Creating a report like this one involves selecting the desired records, designing a layout for the report, sorting the records in the appropriate order, and printing the report.

2 When you select the Find command, the screen displays an empty form. If you type values into the fields, the program will locate records with fields that match those values. The field you want to match, though, is not a typed field; it's the Frequent Call check box.

3 You click Yes in that check box and the Find button.

4 The program indicates that 24 of 130 records were selected because they had Frequent Call checked. You can now work with this collection of records.

Database Operations

Information has value, but it is as perishable as fresh fruit.

—Nicholas Negroponte, founder and director of the MIT Media Lab

Once the structure of a database is defined, it's easy to get information in; it's just a matter of typing. Typing may not even be necessary if the data already exists in some computer-readable form. Most database programs can easily import or receive data in the form of text files created with word processors, spreadsheets, or other databases. When information changes or errors are detected, records can be modified, added, or deleted.

Browsing

The challenging part of using a database is retrieving information in a timely and appropriate manner. Information is of little value if it's not accessible. One way to find informa-

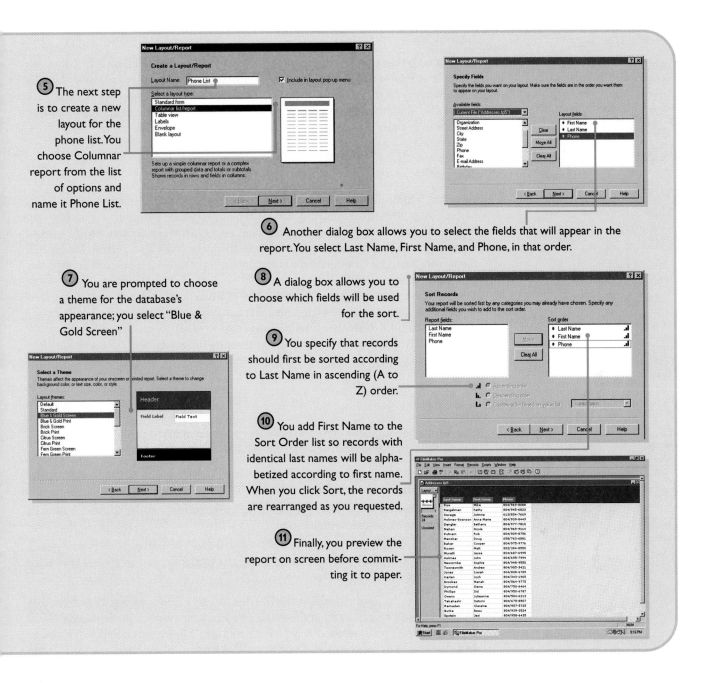

⑤ The next step is to create a new layout for the phone list. You choose Columnar report from the list of options and name it Phone List.

⑥ Another dialog box allows you to select the fields that will appear in the report. You select Last Name, First Name, and Phone, in that order.

⑦ You are prompted to choose a theme for the database's appearance; you select "Blue & Gold Screen"

⑧ A dialog box allows you to choose which fields will be used for the sort.

⑨ You specify that records should first be sorted according to Last Name in ascending (A to Z) order.

⑩ You add First Name to the Sort Order list so records with identical last names will be alphabetized according to first name. When you click Sort, the records are rearranged as you requested.

⑪ Finally, you preview the report on screen before committing it to paper.

tion is to browse through the records of the database file just as you would if they were paper forms in a notebook. Most database programs provide keyboard commands, on-screen buttons, and other tools for navigating quickly through records. But this kind of electronic page turning offers no particular advantage over paper, and it's painfully ineffi-cient for large files. Fortunately, most database programs include a variety of commands and capabilities that make it easy to get the information you need when you need it.

Database Queries

The alternative to browsing is to ask the database for specific information. In database terminology an information request is called a query. A query may be a simple search for a specific record (say, one containing information on Abraham Lincoln) or a request to select *all* the records that match a set of criteria (for example, records for all U.S. pres-idents who served more than one term). Once you've selected a group of records, you can browse through it, produce a printout, or do just about anything else you might do with the complete file.

Sorting Data

Sometimes it's necessary to rearrange records to make the most efficient use of data. For example, a mail-order company's customer file might be arranged alphabetically by name for easy reference, but it must be rearranged in order by zip code to qualify for postal discounts on catalog mailings. A sort command allows you to arrange records in alphabetic or numeric order based on values in one or more fields.

Printing Reports, Labels, and Form Letters

In addition to displaying information on the screen, database programs can produce a variety of printouts. The most common type of database printout is a report—an ordered list of selected records and fields in an easy-to-read format. Most business reports arrange data in tables with rows for individual records and columns for selected fields; they often include summary lines containing calculated totals and averages for groups of records.

Database programs can also be used to produce mailing labels and customized form letters. Many database programs don't actually print letters; they simply export data or transmit the necessary records and fields to word processors with mail merge capabilities, which then take on the task of printing the letters. See *The User's View* box on the previous pages.   **UV**

Complex Queries

Queries may be simple or complex, but either way they must be precise and unambiguous. With appropriate databases, queries could be constructed to find:

▶ In a hospital's patient database, the names and locations of all of the patients on the hospital's fifth and sixth floors

▶ In a database of airline flight schedules, the least expensive way to fly from Boston to San Francisco on Tuesday afternoon

▶ In a politician's database, all voters who contributed more than $1,000 to last year's legislative campaign and who wrote to express concern over gun control laws since the election.

These may be legitimate targets for queries, but they aren't expressed in a form that most database programs can understand. The exact method for performing a query depends on the user interface of the database software. Most programs allow the user to specify the rules of the search by filling in a dialog box or a blank on-screen form. Some require the user to type the request using a special query language that's more precise than English. For example, to view the records for males between 18 and 35, you might type

```
Select * From Population Where
Sex = M and Age = 18 and Age = 35
```

Many database programs include programming languages so queries can be included in programs and performed automatically when the programs are executed. While the details of the process vary, the underlying logic is consistent from program to program.

Most modern database management programs support a standard language for programming complex queries called SQL (from *Structured Query Language*). Because SQL is available for many different database management systems, programmers and sophisticated users don't need to learn new languages when they work with different hardware and software systems. Users are usually insulated from the complexities of the query language by graphical user interfaces that allow point-and-click queries.   **UV**

The User's View

Querying a Web Search Database

SOFTWARE   **Internet Explorer.**

THE GOAL   **To search current news articles for stories about a new method for recycling laser printer toner cartridges. You'll use your Web browser to search newspapers, wires and transcripts on the Northern Lights Web search engine database.**

① You don't want to search for anything on the Web about recycling toner cartridges; you're just interested in tracking down a recent news story, so you select "Newspapers, Wires, and Transcripts."

② You want to search for two key words, so you type *recycle* OR *toner* to indicate that you want to locate all records that have either of those two key words in their subject field; then you click Search.

③ In a few seconds the search reveals that 12,159 records contain at least one of your two target words in the subject field. Your search strategy was flawed. Most of the articles listed for recycle probably have nothing to do with toner cartridges, so you've selected a large collection of mostly irrelevant titles.

④ You replace the OR with AND in the Search field and click Search again to request records that contain both recycle AND toner.

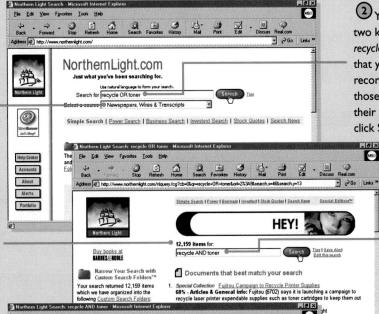

⑤ The search reveals 69 records that contain both words in the subject field, driving home the importance of choosing every word carefully when defining a database query.

⑥ You can now browse through the abstracts for relevant articles. Of course, there's no guarantee that you've found all the references on these subjects: you can only be sure that you've found all the articles that had both words listed in their subject fields. If you don't find what you're looking for in this list, you might need to try different search strategies or different databases.

How It Works 8.1

The Language of Database Queries

Years ago the number of incompatible database languages made it difficult for people using different applications to access the same database. In the mid-1970s IBM's E. F. Codd proposed a standardized Structured English Query Language, which evolved into SQL. With SQL, users and programmers can employ the same language to access databases from a wide variety of vendors.

SQL combines the familiar database concepts of tables, rows (records), and columns (fields) and the mathematical idea of a set. Here we illustrate a simple SQL command using the Rental Vehicles database from Clem's Transportation Rental ("If it moves, we rent it."). Here's a complete listing of the database records:

Vehicle_ID	Vehicle_Type	Transport_Mode	Num_Passengers	Cargo_Capacity	Rental_Price
1062	Helicopter	Air	6	500	$1,250.00
1955	Canoe	Water	2	30	$5.00
2784	Automobile	Land	4	250	$45.00
0213	Unicycle	Land	1	0	$10.00
0019	Minibus	Land	8	375	$130.00
3747	Balloon	Air	3	120	$340.00
7288	HangGlider	Air	1	5	$17.00
9430	Sailboat	Water	8	200	$275.00
8714	Powerboat	Water	4	175	$210.00
0441	Bicycle	Land	1	10	$12.00
4759	Jet	Air	9	2300	$2,900.00

Special-Purpose Database Programs

The best way to organize information is **the way that reveals** what we want to communicate.

—**Richard Saul Wurman**, **author of** *Information Anxiety*

Specialized database software is preprogrammed for specific data storage and retrieval purposes. The CD-ROM databases used in many libraries are examples of special-purpose database programs. Users of special-purpose databases don't generally need to define file structures or design forms because these details have been taken care of by the designers of the software. In fact, some special-purpose database programs are not even sold as databases; they have names that more accurately reflect their purposes.

Directories and Geographic Information Systems

For example, an *electronic phone directory* can pack millions of names and phone numbers onto a single CD-ROM or Web site. Using an electronic phone directory for the United States, you can track down phone numbers of people and businesses all over the

A typical SQL statement filters the records of a database, capturing only those that meet the specific criteria. For example, suppose you wanted to list the ID numbers and types of the vehicles that travel on land and cost less than $20.00 per day. The SQL statement to perform this task would look like this:

```
SELECT Vehicle_ID, Vehicle_Type
FROM Rental_Vehicles
WHERE Transport_Mode = 'Land' AND
Rental_Price 20.00 ;
```

In English this SQL statement says "Show me (from the Rental Vehicles database) the vehicle IDs and vehicle types for those vehicles that travel by land and cost less than $20.00 per day to rent."

Two rows in the database meet these criteria, the unicycle and bicycle:

```
0213 Unicycle
0441 Bicycle
```

The selection rules for SQL are consistent and understandable whether queries are simple or complex. This simple example is designed to give you an idea of how they work.

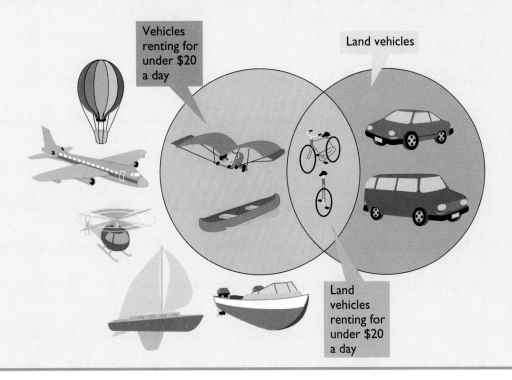

Vehicles renting for under $20 a day

Land vehicles

Land vehicles renting for under $20 a day

country—even if you don't know where they are. You can look up a person's name if you have the phone number or street address. You can generate a list of every dentist in town—any town. Then using another type of specialized database, an *electronic street atlas*, you can pinpoint each of your finds on a freshly printed map.

Geographical information systems (GISs) go beyond simple mapping programs. A GIS allows a business to combine tables of data such as customer sales lists with demographic information from the U.S. Census Bureau and other sources. The right combination can reveal valuable strategic information. For example, a stock brokerage can pinpoint the best locations for branch offices based on average incomes and other neighborhood data; a cable TV company can locate potential customers who live close to existing lines. Because they can display geographic and demographic data on maps, they allow users to see data relationships that might be invisible in table form.

Personal Information Managers

One broad category of specialized database program goes by a number of names, including **personal information managers (PIMs)** and **electronic organizers**. This type of program can automate some or all of these functions:

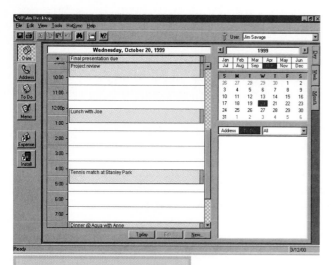

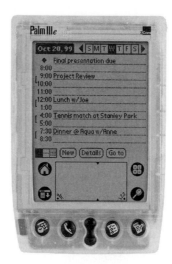

Personal information management software can help you keep track of appointments, phone numbers, and to-do lists. The information is readily accessible as long as your computer is nearby or you can find a way to carry the data with you. Handheld computers like this Palm III can share information with PC and Macintosh programs, so you can carry the essentials with you as you move through your day.

▶ *Address/phone book.* Software address books provide options for quickly displaying specific records and printing mailing labels, address books, and reports. Some include automatic phone-dialing options and fields for recording phone notes.

▶ *Appointment calendar.* A typical PIM calendar allows you to enter appointments and events and display or print them in a variety of formats, ranging from one day at a time to a monthly overview. Many include built-in alarms for last-minute reminders.

▶ *To-do list.* Most PIMs allow users to enter and organize ongoing lists of things to do and archive lists of completed tasks.

▶ *Miscellaneous notes.* Some PIMs accept diary entries, personal notes, and other hard-to-categorize tidbits of information.

PIMs have long been popular among people with busy schedules and countless contacts. They're easier to understand and use than general-purpose database programs, and they're faster and more flexible than their leather-bound paper counterparts. For people on the go, PIMs work especially well with notebook computers or handheld computers. In fact, the market for PIM software has been eclipsed by an even larger market for handheld computers and personal digital assistants with built-in PIM software. For example, software that's built into the Palm OS allows a pocket-sized device to be hot-synched, at the touch of a button, to the PIM software on a desktop PC or Mac. This instant data linking makes it easy to keep up-to-date personal information both in and out of the office.

In many organizations, PIMs have been replaced by enterprise information systems such as Microsoft Outlook. These systems allow networked coworkers to easily share calendars and contacts. The Web offers another alternative: Several Web sites provide free PIM software that can be accessed from any Web-accessible computer; many of these allow for workgroups to share calendars and other information.

Beyond the Basics: Database Management Systems

When we try to pick out anything,
we find it hitched to everything else in the universe.

—John Muir, **first director of the National Park Service**

So far we've used simple examples to illustrate concepts common to most database programs. This oversimplification is useful for understanding the basics, but it's not the whole story. In truth database programs range from simple mailing label programs to massive financial information systems, and it's important to know a little about what makes them different as well as what makes them alike.

From File Managers to Database Management Systems

Technically speaking, many consumer databases and personal information manager programs aren't really database managers at all; they're file managers. A file manager is a program that allows users to work with one file at a time. A true database management system (DBMS) is a program or system of programs that can manipulate data in a large collection of files—the database—cross-referencing between files as needed. A database management system can be used interactively, or it can be controlled directly by other programs. A file manager is sufficient for mailing lists and other common data management applications. But for many large, complex jobs there's no substitute for a true database management system.

Consider, for example, the problem of managing student information at a college. It's easy to see how databases might be used to store this information: a file containing one record for each student, with fields for name, student ID number, address, phone, and so on. But a typical student generates far too much information to store practically in a single data file.

Most schools choose to keep several files containing student information: one for financial records, one for course enrollment and grade transcripts, and so on. Each of these files has a single record for each student. In addition, a school must maintain class enrollment files with one record for each class and fields for information on each student enrolled in the class. Three of these files might be organized like this:

> Student information is duplicated in several different files of this inefficient, error-prone database.

Transcript file	Financial info file	Class list file
Student ID	Student ID	Course Number
Name	Name	Department
Local Street Address	Local Street Address	Section Number
Apartment No.	Apartment No.	Instructor
City	City	Time
State	State	Location
Zip	Zip	Number of Students
Permanent Street Address	Permanent Street Address	
Apartment No.	Apartment No.	(Student 1 Information)
City	City	Student ID
State	State	Name
Zip	Zip	Class Standing
Sex	Sex	Major
Citizenship	Citizenship	
Year Admitted	Year Admitted	(Student 2 Information)
Class Standing	Class Standing	Student ID
Major	Major	Name
GPA	GPA	Class Standing
		Major
(Course 1 information)	Tuition	
Department	Deposits	
Number	Registration Fees	
Credits	Parking Fees	
Grade	Housing Fees	
Date	Lab Fees	
(Course 2 information)		
Department		

In the database on the previous page, each of the three separate files contains basic information about every student. This redundant data not only occupies expensive storage space, but also makes it difficult to ensure that student information is accurate and up to date. If a student moves to a different address, several files must be updated to reflect this change. The more changes, the greater the likelihood of a data-entry error.

With a database management system there's no need to store all of this information in every file. The database can include a basic student file containing demographic information—information that's unique for each student. Because the demographic information is stored in a separate file, it doesn't need to be included in the financial information file, the transcript file, the class list file, or any other file. The student ID number, included in each file, serves as a *key field*; it unlocks the relevant student information in the student file when it's needed elsewhere. The student ID field is, in effect, shared by all files that use data from this file. If the student moves, the change of address need only be recorded in one place. Databases organized in this way are called *relational databases*.

The Student file serves as a reference when grade reports and class lists are created. The Student ID fields in the Transcript file and the Class List file are used as a key for locating the necessary student information in the Student file.

What Makes a Database Relational?

To most users a relational database program is one that allows files to be related to each other so that changes in one file are reflected in other files automatically. To computer scientists the term *relational database* has a technical definition related to the underlying structure of the data and the rules specifying how that data can be manipulated.

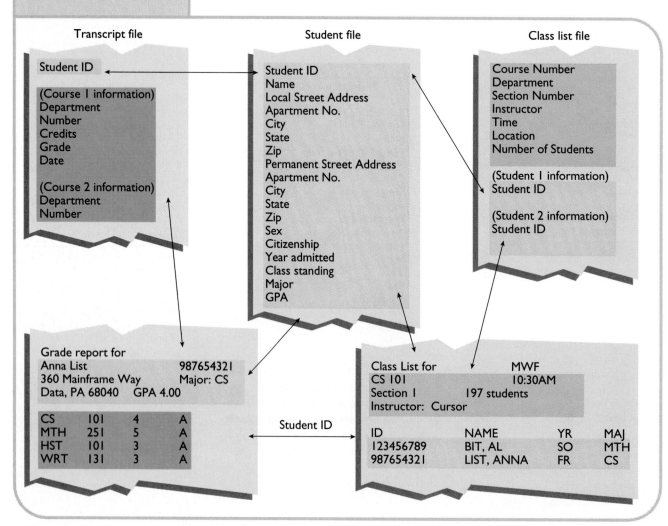

Clerk's view

Video rental view used by clerks to access renter information, scan bar codes on videos, and print rental invoices

Video store database

Manager's view

• Inventory-tracking view used by managers to check on rental history and inventory for individual movies

• Policy view used by managers to change pricing, membership, and other policies

Technician/programmer's view

Technical view used by programmer to create other user interfaces and custom queries

The structure of a relational database is based on the relational model—a mathematical model that combines data in tables. Other kinds of database management systems are based on different theoretical models, with different technical advantages and disadvantages. But the majority of DBMSs in use today, including virtually all PC-based database management systems, use the relational model. So from the average computer user's point of view, the distinction between the popular and technical definitions of relational is academic.

The Many Faces of Databases

Large databases can contain hundreds of interrelated files. This maze of information could be overwhelming to users if they were forced to deal with it directly. Fortunately, a database management system can shield users from the complex inner workings of the system, providing them with only the information and commands they need to get their jobs done. In fact, a well-designed database puts on different faces for different classes of users.

Retail clerks don't need to be able to access every piece of information in the store's database; they just need to enter sales transactions on point-of-sale terminals. Databases designed for retail outlets generally include simple, straightforward terminal interfaces that give the clerks only the information, and the power, they need to process transactions. Managers, accountants, data processing specialists, and customers see the database from different points of view because they need to work with the data in different ways.

Clerks, managers, programmers, and customers see different views of a video rental store's database. Customers can browse through listings and reviews of available movies using a touch-screen kiosk. The clerk's view allows only for simple data-entry and check-out procedures. The manager, working with the same database, has control over pricing, policies, and inventory but can't change the structure or user interface of the database. The programmer can work "under the hood" to fine-tune and customize the database so it can better meet the needs of other employees and customers.

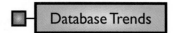

Database Trends

It is better to ask some of the questions
than to know all of the answers.

—James Thurber, in *Fables for Our Time*

Database technology isn't static. Advances in the last two decades have changed the way most organizations deal with data, and current trends suggest even bigger changes in the near future.

Real-Time Computing

The earliest file management programs could do only batch processing, which required users to accumulate transactions and feed them into computers in large batches. These batch systems weren't able to provide the kind of immediate feedback we expect today. Questions like "What's the balance in my checking account?" or "Are there any open flights to Denver next Tuesday?" were likely to be answered "Those records will be updated tonight, so we'll let you know tomorrow."

Today, disk drives, inexpensive memory, and sophisticated software have allowed interactive processing to replace batch processing for most applications. Users can now interact with data through terminals, viewing and changing values on line in real time. Batch processing is still used for printing periodic bills, invoices, and reports and for making backup copies of data files—jobs for which it makes sense to do a lot of transactions at once. But for applications that demand immediacy, such as airline reservations, banking transactions, and the like, interactive, multiuser database systems have taken over.

This trend toward real-time computing is accelerated by the Internet, which makes it possible to have almost instant access to information anywhere on Earth, inside or outside the boundaries of the enterprise.

Downsizing and Decentralizing

In the pre-PC days, most databases were housed in mainframe computers accessible only to information-processing personnel. But the traditional hard-to-access centralized database on a mainframe system is no longer the norm.

Today many businesses use a *client/server* approach: *Client* programs in desktop (or laptop) computers send information requests through a network to server databases on mainframes, minicomputers, or desktop computers; the *servers* process queries and send the requested data back to the client. A client/server system allows users to take advantage of the PC's simple user interface and convenience, while still having access to data stored on large server systems.

Some corporations keep copies of all corporate data in integrated data warehouses. In some respects, data warehouses are similar to old-style systems: they're large, relatively expensive, and centralized. But unlike older centralized systems, data warehouses give users more direct access to enterprise data. Data warehouses are most commonly found in large corporations and government departments.

Some companies use distributed databases, where data is strewn across networks on several different computers rather than stored in one central site. Many organizations have both data warehouses and distributed databases. From the user's point of view the differences between these approaches may not be apparent. Connectivity software, sometimes called *middleware*, links the client and server machines, hiding the complexity of the

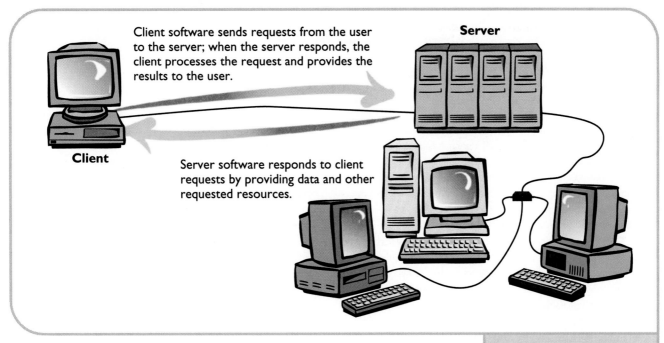

Client software sends requests from the user to the server; when the server responds, the client processes the request and provides the results to the user.

Server

Client

Server software responds to client requests by providing data and other requested resources.

Client/server computing involves two-way communication between client and server programs.

interaction between those machines. Wherever the data is stored, the goal is to provide quick and easy access to important information.

Data Mining

Today's technology makes it easy for a business to accumulate masses of information in a database. Many organizations are content to retrieve information using the queries, searches, and reports. But others are finding that there's gold hidden in their large databases—gold that can only be extracted using a new technology called data mining. Data mining is the discovery and extraction of hidden predictive information from large databases. It uses statistical methods and artificial intelligence technology to locate trends and patterns in data that would have been overlooked by normal database queries. For example, a grocery chain used data mining to discover differences between male and female shopping patterns so they could create gender-specific marketing campaigns. (In an industry ad they announced that some men habitually buy beer and diapers every Friday!) In effect, data-mining technology allows users to "drill down" through masses of data to find valuable veins of information.

Databases and the Web

Many businesses are retooling to take advantage of Internet technology on their internal networks. These *intranets* allow employees to access corporate databases using the same Web browsers and search engines they use to access information outside the company networks. As Internet tools rapidly evolve, database access should become easier and more transparent.

HTML, the language used to construct most Web pages, wasn't designed to build database queries. But a newer, more powerful language called *XML* is designed with industrial-strength database access in mind. Database manufacturers are currently retooling their products so they can process data requests in XML. Because XML can serve as both a query language and a Web page construction tool, it's likely to open up all kinds of databases to the World Wide Web, making it easy for us to request and receive information.

Rules of Thumb

Dealing with Databases

Whether you're creating an address file with a simple file manager or retrieving data from a full-blown relational database management system, you can save yourself a great deal of time and grief if you follow a few commonsense rules:

▶ **Choose the right tool for the job.** Don't invest time and money in a programmable relational database to computerize your address book, and don't try to run the affairs of your multinational corporation with a $99 file manager.

▶ **Think about how you'll get the information out before you put it in.** What kinds of files, records, and fields will you need to create to make it easy to find things quickly and print things the way you'll want them? For example, use separate fields for first and last name if you want to sort names alphabetically by last name and print first names first.

▶ **Start with a plan, and be prepared to change your plan.** It's a good idea to do a trial run with a small amount of data to make sure everything works the way you think it should.

▶ **Make your data consistent.** Inconsistencies can mess up sorting and make searching difficult. For example, if a database includes residents of Minnesota, Minn., and MN, it's hard to group people by state.

▶ **Databases are only as good as their data.** When entering data, take advantage of the data-checking capability of your data-

base software. Does the first name field contain nonalphabetic characters? Is the birth date within a reasonable range? Automatic data checking is important, but it's no substitute for human proofreading or for a bit of skepticism when using the database.

▶ **Query with care.** In the words of Aldous Huxley, "People always get what they ask for; the only trouble is that they never know, until they get it, what it actually is that they have asked for." Here's a real example: A student searching a database of classic rock albums requested all records containing the string "Dylan," and the database program obediently displayed the names of several Bob Dylan albums . . . plus one by Jimi Hendrix called Electric Ladyland. Why? Because dylan is in Ladyland! Unwanted records can go unnoticed in large database selections, so it's important to define selection rules very carefully.

▶ **If at first you don't suceed, try another approach.** If your search doesn't turn up the answers you were looking for, it doesn't mean the answers aren't there; they may just be wearing a disguise. For example, if you search a standard library database for "Vietnam War" references, you might not find any. Why? Because the government officially classifies the Vietnam War as a conflict, so references are stored under the subject "Viet Nam Conflict." Technology meets bureaucracy!

Object-Oriented Databases

Some of the biggest changes in database technology in the next few years may take place under the surface, where they may not be apparent to most users. For example, many computer scientists believe that the relational data model will be supplanted in the next decade by an object-oriented data model and that most future databases will be object-oriented databases rather than relational databases. Instead of storing records in tables and hierarchies, object-oriented databases store software *objects* that contain procedures (or instructions) along with data. Object-oriented databases often are used in conjunction with object-oriented programming languages, which are discussed in Chapter 12. Experts suggest that object technology will make construction and manipulation of complex databases easier and less time consuming. Users will find databases more flexible and responsive as object technology becomes more widespread, even if they aren't aware of the underlying technological reasons for these improvements. Today many companies are experimenting with databases that combine relational and object concepts into hybrid systems.

Multimedia Databases

Today's databases can efficiently store all kinds of text and numeric data. But today's computers are multimedia machines that routinely deal with pictures, sounds, animation, and video clips. Multimedia databases can handle graphical and dynamic data along with text and numbers. Multimedia professionals use databases to catalog art, photographs, maps, video clips, sound files, and other types of media files. Media files aren't generally stored in databases because they're too large. Instead, a multimedia database serves as an index to all of the separately stored files. Multimedia capability will probably find its way into all kinds of databases—even personal information managers—in the near future.

Natural Language Databases

Ultimately, database technology will all but disappear from *The User's View* as interfaces become simpler, more powerful, and more intelligent. Future databases will undoubtedly incorporate more artificial intelligence technology. We're already seeing databases and data mining software that can respond to simple *natural language* queries—queries in English or some other human language. Today's natural-language technology is far from perfect, but it's getting better quickly. It won't be long before we'll be able to ask for data using the same language we'd use when addressing a human being.

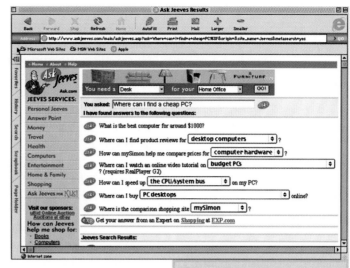

Ask Jeeves allows users to search the Web by stating their queries in plain English.

No Secrets: Computers and Privacy

Advanced technology has created new opportunities for America as a nation, but it has also created the possibility for new abuses of the individual American citizen. Adequate safeguards must always stand watch so that man remains master and never the victim of the computer.

—**Richard Nixon, 37th president of the United States, Feb. 23, 1974**

Instant airline reservations, all-night automated banking, overnight mail, instant library searches—databases provide us with conveniences that were unthinkable a generation ago. But convenience isn't free. In the case of databases the price we pay is our privacy.

The Privacy Problem

We live in an information age, and data is one of the currencies of our time. Businesses and government agencies spend billions of dollars every year to collect and exchange information about you and me. More than 15,000 specialized marketing databases contain 2 billion consumer names, along with a surprising amount of personal information. The typical American consumer is on 25 marketing lists. Many of these lists are organized by characteristics like age, income, religion, political affiliation, and even sexual preference—and they're bought and sold every day.

The Internal Revenue Service workers shown here enter taxpayers' personal financial information into massive computer databases. When you shop by phone, respond to a survey, or fill out a warranty card, it's likely that a clerk somewhere will enter that data into a computer.

Marketing databases are only the tip of the iceberg. Credit and banking information, tax records, health data, insurance records, political contributions, voter registration, credit card purchases, warranty registrations, magazine and newsletter subscriptions, phone calls, passport registration, airline reservations, automobile registrations, arrests, Internet explorations—they're all recorded in computers, and we have little or no control over what happens to most of those records once they're collected.

For most of us this data is out of sight and out of mind. But lives are changed because of these databases. Here are three representative stories:

▶ When members of Congress investigated ties between President Jimmy Carter's brother Billy and the government of Libya, they produced a report that detailed, among other things, the exact time and location of phone calls placed by Billy Carter in three different states. The phone records, which revealed a great deal about Billy Carter's activities, were obtained from AT&T's massive network of data-collecting computers. Similar information is available on every phone company customer.

▶ When a credit bureau mistakenly placed a bankruptcy filing in the file of a St. Louis couple, banks responded by shutting off loans for their struggling construction business, forcing them into real bankruptcy. They sued but lost because credit bureaus are protected by law from financial responsibility for "honest" mistakes!

▶ A Los Angeles thief stole a wallet and used its contents to establish an artificial identity. When the thief was arrested for a robbery involving murder, the crime was recorded under the wallet owner's name in police databases. The legitimate owner of the wallet was arrested five times in the following 14 months and spent several days in jail before a protracted court battle resulted in the deletion of the record.

▶ In a more recent, more typical example of *identity theft*, an imposter had the mail of an innocent individual temporarily forwarded to a post office box so he could easily collect credit card numbers and other personal data. By the time the victim discovered an overdue Visa bill, the thief had racked up $42,000 in bogus charges. The victim wasn't liable for the charges, but it took the better part of a year to correct all of the credit bureau errors.

Privacy violations aren't new, and they don't always involve computers. The German Nazis, the Chinese Communists, and even Richard Nixon's 1972 campaign committee practiced surveillance without computers. But the privacy problem takes on a whole new dimension in the age of high-speed computers and databases. The same characteristics that make databases more efficient than other information storage methods—storage capacity, retrieval speed, organizational flexibility, and ease of distribution of information—also make them a threat to our privacy.

Big Brother and Big Business

> If all records told the same tale,
> then the lie passed into history and became truth.
>
> —George Orwell, in *1984*

In George Orwell's *1984,* information about every citizen was stored in a massive database controlled by the ever-vigilant Big Brother. Today's data warehouses in many ways resemble Big Brother's database. Data-mining techniques can be used to extract information about individuals and groups without their knowledge or consent. And databases can be easily sold or used for purposes other than those for which they were collected. Most of the time this kind of activity goes unnoticed by the public. Here are three examples where public knowledge changed privacy policy:

▶ In 1998 CVS drug stores contracted with Elensys, a Massachusetts direct marketing company, to send reminders to customers who had not renewed their prescriptions. While some customers undoubtedly appreciated the reminders, others objected to this commercial use of their private medical records. CVS terminated the practice as a result of protests.

▶ In many states driver's license information is considered public record, available to anyone for a fee. In 1998 Florida's legislature voted to make driver's license photographs available on the same basis. But after a public outcry, Florida, along with several other states, ended its practice of selling driver's license photos to private companies.

▶ In 1999 Amazon.com introduced "Purchase Circles"—a feature that allowed customers to see which books, CDs, tapes, and videos are most popular within particular companies, schools, government organizations, and cities. Amazon didn't make individual purchase information available to the public, but it used that information to create customer profiles for groups. Using these Purchase Circle profiles, Amazon's Web site might tell you the most popular books and videos among Microsoft employees, Stephens College students, or residents of Hays, Kansas, for example. In response to protests, Amazon decided to give customers the option of being excluded from Purchase Circles.

▶ In 1999 online advertising agency DoubleClick acquired a direct marketing firm along its database of 90 million households. The company intended to combine supposedly anonymous data on Web user activity with personal information from the massive consumer database, creating data files rich with personal data about consumers. In March, 2000, in response to outcries from consumers and privacy watchdog groups, DoubleClick backed away from the data-matching plan, calling it a "big mistake" to try to match information in that way before government or industry standards could be put into place.

Centralized data warehouses aren't necessary for producing computerized dossiers of private citizens. With networked computers it's easy to compile profiles by combining information from different database files. As long as the files share a single unique field, like Social Security number, record matching is trivial and quick. And when database information is combined, the whole is often far greater than the sum of its parts.

Sometimes the results are beneficial. Record matching is used by government enforcement agencies to locate criminals ranging from tax evaders to mass murderers. Because credit bureaus collect data about us, we can use credit cards to borrow money wherever we go. But these benefits come with at least three problems:

▶ *Data errors are common.* A study of 1,500 reports from the three big credit bureaus found errors in 43% of the files.

▶ *Data can become nearly immortal.* Because files are commonly sold and copied, it's impossible to delete or correct erroneous records with absolute certainty.

▶ *Data isn't secure.* A *Business Week* reporter demonstrated this in 1989 by using his computer to obtain then Vice President Dan Quayle's credit report. Had he been a skilled criminal, he might have been able to change that report.

Protection against invasion of privacy is not explicitly guaranteed by the U.S. Constitution. Legal scholars agree that the right to privacy—freedom from interference in the private sphere of a person's affairs—is implied by other constitutional guarantees, although debates rage about what this means. Federal and state laws provide forms of privacy protection, but most of those laws were written years ago. Most European countries have had strong privacy protection laws for years. The 1998 European Data Protection Directive guarantees that all countries in the European Union will guarantee a basic set of privacy rights to citizens—rights that go far beyond those of American citizens. The directive allows citizens to have access to all personal data, to know where that

Rules of Thumb

Your Private Rights

Sometimes computer-aided privacy violations are nuisances; sometimes they're threats to life, liberty, and the pursuit of happiness. Here are a few tips for protecting your right to privacy.

▶ **Your Social Security number is yours—don't give it away.** Since your SSN is a unique identifier, it can be used to gather information about you without your permission or knowledge. For example, you could be denied a job or insurance because of something you once put on a medical form. Never write it (or your driver's license number or phone number, for that matter) on a check or credit card receipt. Don't give your SSN to anyone unless they have a legitimate reason to ask for it.

▶ **Don't give away information about yourself.** Don't answer questions about yourself just because a questionnaire or company representative asks you to. When you fill out any form—coupon, warranty registration card, survey, sweepstakes entry, or whatever—think about whether you want the information stored in somebody else's computer.

▶ **Say no to direct mail and phone solicitations.** Businesses and political organizations pay for your data so they can target you for mail campaigns and phone solicitations. You can remove yourself from many lists using forms from the Direct Mail Marketing Association (www.the-dma.org). If this doesn't stop the flow, you might want to try a more direct approach. Send back unwanted letters along with "Take me off your list" requests in the postage-paid envelopes that come with them. When you receive an unsolicited phone marketing call, tell the caller "I never purchase or donate anything as a result of phone solicitations," and ask to be removed from the list. If they call within 12 months of being specifically told not to, you can sue and recover up to $500 per call according to the Telephone Consumer Protection Act of 1991. Unfortunately, there's no comparable federal law to protect you against junk email yet, so you should be especially careful about giving out your email address if you don't like receiving unsolicited email.

▶ **Say no to sharing your personal information.** If you open a private Internet account, tell your Internet service provider that your personal data is not for sale. If you don't want your state's Department of Motor Vehicles selling information about you, notify them. A relatively new federal law gives you more control over DMV use of personal data. If you don't want credit agencies sharing personal information, let them know. The Federal Trade Commission's Privacy Web site (www.ftc.gov/privacy) includes clear guidelines and forms for contacting your DMV and credit agencies.

▶ **Say no to pollsters.** Our political system has been radically transformed by polling; most of our "leaders" check the polls before they offer opinions on controversial issues. If you and I don't tell the pollsters what we're thinking, then politicians will be more likely to tell us what *they're* thinking.

▶ **If you think there's incorrect or damaging information about you in a file, find out.** The Freedom of Information Act of 1966 requires that most records of U.S. government agencies be made available to the public on demand. The Privacy Act of 1974 requires federal agencies to provide you with information in your files relating to you and to amend incorrect records. The Fair Credit Reporting Act of 1970 allows you to see your credit ratings—for free if you have been denied credit—and correct any errors. The three big credit bureaus are Equifax (www.equifax.com), Trans Union (www.tuc.com), and Experian (www.experian.com).

▶ **To maximize your privacy, minimize your profile.** If you don't want a financial transaction recorded, use cash. If you don't want your phone number to be public information, use an unlisted number. If you don't want your mailing address known, use a post office box.

▶ **Know your electronic rights.** Privacy protection laws in the United States lag far behind those of other high-tech nations, but they are beginning to appear. For example, the 1986 Electronic Communications Privacy Act provides the same protection that covers mail and telephone communication to some—but not all—electronic communication. The 1988 Computer Matching and Privacy Protection Act regulates the use of government data in determining eligibility for federal benefits.

▶ **Support organizations that fight for privacy rights.** If you value privacy rights, let your representatives know how you feel, and support the American Civil Liberties Union, Computer Professionals for Social Responsibility, the Electronic Frontier Foundation, Electronic Privacy Information Center, Private Citizen, and other organizations that fight for those rights.

data originated, to have inaccurate data rectified, to seek recourse in the event of unlawful processing, and to withhold permission to use their data for direct marketing. The American legislature has refused to pass similar laws because of intense lobbying by business interests. When it comes to privacy violation in America, technology is far ahead of the law.

Database technology clearly poses a threat to personal privacy, but other information technologies amplify that threat. Networking technology, described in the next two chapters, makes it possible for personal data to be transmitted almost anywhere instantly. The Internet is particularly fertile ground for collecting personal information about you. And the Web makes it alarmingly easy for anyone with a connected computer to examine your personal information. Workplace monitoring technology, described in Chapter 14, allows managers to learn more than ever before about the work habits and patterns of workers. Smart cards and other intelligent personal devices, discussed in the last three chapters of this book, allow us to trade personal privacy for convenience.

In George Orwell's *1984* personal privacy was the victim of a centralized Communist police state controlled by Big Brother. Today our privacy is threatened by *many* Big Brothers—with new threats emerging almost every day. As Simson Garfinkel says in *Database Nation,* "Over the next 50 years, we will see new kinds of threats to privacy that don't find their roots in totalitarianism, but in capitalism, the free market, advanced technology, and the unbridled exchange of electronic information."

Democracy depends on the free flow of information, but it also depends on the protection of individual rights. Maintaining a balance is not easy, especially when new information technologies are being developed at such a rapid pace. With information at our fingertips it's tempting to think that more information is the answer. But in the timeless words of populist philosopher Will Rogers, "It's not the things we don't know that get us into trouble, it's the things we do know that ain't so."

The Spies in Your Pocket

Jane Bryant Quinn

Our privacy is threatened by technology on multiple fronts: health data, legal data, communications, travel, and more. In this edited August 16, 1999 article, Newsweek *writer Jane Bryant Quinn (with reporter Temma Ehrenfeld) sounds a cautionary alarm concerning the misuse of our financial data.*

When we worry about who might be spying on our private lives, we usually think about the Feds. But the private sector outdoes the government every time. It's our banks, not the IRS, that pass our private financial data to telemarketing firms.

To call this "betrayal of trust" would be hopelessly out of date. Betrayal was rethought years ago, and emerged as a viable business model for the Information Age.

Consumer activists are pressing Congress for better privacy laws without much result so far. The legislators lean toward letting businesspeople track our financial habits virtually at will.

As an example of what's going on, consider U.S. Bancorp, which was recently sued for deceptive practices by the state of Minnesota. According to the lawsuit, the bank supplied a telemarketer called MemberWorks with sensitive customer data such as names, phone numbers, bank-account and credit-card numbers, Social Security numbers, account balances and credit limits.

With these customer lists in hand, MemberWorks started dialing for dollars—selling dental plans, videogames, computer software and other products and services. Customers who accepted a "free trial offer" had 30 days to cancel. If the deadline passed, they were charged automatically through their bank or credit-card accounts. U.S. Bancorp collected a share of the revenues.

Customers were doubly deceived, the lawsuit claims. They didn't know that the bank was giving account numbers to MemberWorks. And if customers asked, they were led to think the answer was no.

The state sued MemberWorks separately for deceptive selling. The company denies that it did anything wrong. For its part, U.S. Bancorp settled without admitting any mistakes. But it agreed to stop exposing its customers to nonfinancial products flogged by outside firms. A few top banks, including Wells Fargo and Bank of America, decided to do the same. Many other banks will still do business with MemberWorks and similar firms.

And banks will still be mining data from your account in order to sell you financial products, including things of little value, such as credit insurance and credit-card protection plans.

You have almost no protection from businesses that use your personal accounts for profit. For example:

▶ *No federal law shields "transaction and experience" information*—mainly, the details of your bank and credit-card accounts. Your bank can freely disclose them to telemarketers or other commercial users, says Amy Friend, assistant chief counsel at the Office of the Comptroller of the Currency. They don't even have to tell you that your personal data was sold. (A few states provide some protection, but usually not much.)

▶ *Social Security numbers are for sale by private firms.* They've generally agreed not to sell to the public (that's you and me). But to businesses, the numbers are an open book. You shouldn't keep your own number in your wallet lest it be stolen and used to get credit in your name. But it's sloshing around in the river of commerce and there's nothing you can do.

▶ *Self-regulation doesn't work.* A firm might publish a privacy-protection policy, but who enforces it? How can you even be sure that it means what it appears to say. As an example, take U.S. Bancorp again. Customers were told, in writing, that "all personal information you supply to us will be considered confidential." Then it sold your data to MemberWorks. The bank even claims that it doesn't "sell" your data at all. It merely "shares" it and reaps a profit. Now you know.

▶ *The next frontier will be the data held by states.* Personal stuff from driving records is already sold by many departments of motor vehicles. Marketers also have access to your property-tax assessments or the price of your new house.

Businesses are now pressing for individual wage information collected for state employment files. So far, four states provide it: Iowa, Minnesota, Texas and North Carolina. Pennsylvania and California backed off after public outcries.

Selling wage information isn't as bad as it sounds, at least under current rules. The states release it only to verify what you've said on a credit application, which could also be checked with your boss. But the states hold many other records that are truly public, such as wills and divorce agreements. Is it OK to publish them on the Net? Could they be compiled, mixed with your financial data and sold for marketing purposes? That's going to happen, unless consumers start shouting about privacy fast.

▶ *No law protects your activity on the Net.* Most Web sites openly (or surreptitiously) collect data about what you view and buy.

Congress is close to transforming the financial world by allowing banks, insurers and brokerage firms to merge. If privacy rights aren't granted now, it will be hard for consumers to win them later, says Marc Rotenberg, director of the Electronic Privacy Information Center in Washington, D.C. But the Senate bill ignores privacy, and the House offers only window dressing. At the very least, you should be able to opt out of mailing and data-sharing lists you don't want to be on.

Currently, your opt-out rights are few.

And that's about it. Your video-rental records are better protected than your financial life. Tell Congress there oughta be a law.

DISCUSSION QUESTIONS

1. Why do you think Americans have fewer legal privacy protections than Europeans have?
2. Do you agree that "there oughta be a law"? If so, what should that law say?

Database programs allow users to quickly and efficiently store, organize, retrieve, communicate, and manage large amounts of information. Each database file is a collection of records, and each record is made up of fields containing text strings, numbers, and other chunks of information. Database programs allow users to view data in a variety of ways, sort records in any order, and print reports, mailing labels, and other custom printouts. A user can search for an individual record or select a group of records with a query.

While most database programs are general-purpose tools that can be used to create custom databases for any purpose, some are special-purpose tools programmed to do a particular set of tasks. Geographical information systems, for example, combine maps and demographic information with data tables to provide new ways to look at data. Personal information managers provide automated address books, appointment calendars, to-do lists, and notebooks for busy individuals.

Many database programs are, technically speaking, file managers because they work with only one file at a time. But technically, a true database is a collection of files. Database management systems (DBMSs) can work with several files at once, cross-referencing information among files when appropriate. A DBMS can provide an efficient way to store and manage large quantities of information by eliminating the need for redundant information in different files. A well-designed database provides different views of the data to different classes of users so each user sees and manipulates only the information necessary for the job at hand.

The trend today is clearly away from large, centralized databases accessible only to data processing staff. Instead, most organizations are moving toward a client/server approach that allows users to have access to data stored in servers throughout the organization's network.

The accumulation of data by government agencies and businesses is a growing threat to our right to privacy. Massive amounts of information about private citizens are collected and exchanged for a variety of purposes. Today's technology makes it easy to combine information from different databases, producing detailed profiles of individual citizens. While there are many legitimate uses for these procedures, there's also a great potential for abuse.

Key Terms

batch processing, 224
browse, 215
centralized database, 224
client/server database, 224
computed field, 212
data mining, 225
data warehouse, 224
database, 212
database management system (DBMS), 221
database program, 212
distributed database, 224
electronic organizer, 219

export data, 216
field, 212
file, 212
file manager, 221
geographical information system (GIS), 219
import data, 214
interactive processing, 224
mail merge, 216
object-oriented database, 226
personal information manager (PIM), 219

query, 215
query language, 216
real time, 224
record, 212
record matching, 230
relational database, 222
report, 216
right to privacy, 229
search, 215
select (records), 216
sort, 216
SQL, 216

Review Questions

1. Define or describe each of the key words listed above. Check your answers in the glossary.
2. What is the difference between a file manager and a database management system? How are they similar?
3. Describe the structure of a simple database. Use the terms *file*, *record*, and *field* in your description.
4. What is a query? Give examples of the kinds of questions that might be answered with a query.
5. What steps are involved in producing a standard multi-column business report from a database?

6. What are the advantages of personal information management software over paper notebook organizers? What are the disadvantages?
7. What does it mean to sort a data file?
8. How can a database be designed to reduce the likelihood of data-entry errors?
9. Describe how record matching is used to obtain information about you. Give examples.
10. Do we have a legal right to privacy? On what grounds?
11. Why are computers important in discussions of invasion of privacy?

Discussion Questions

1. Grade books, checkbooks, and other information collections can be managed with either a database program or a spreadsheet program. How would you decide which type of application is most appropriate for a given job?
2. What have you done this week that directly or indirectly involved a database? How would your week have been different in a world without databases?
3. "The computer is a great humanizing factor because it makes the individual more important. The more information we have on each individual, the more each individual counts." Do you agree with this statement by science fiction writer Isaac Asimov? Why or why not?
4. Suppose you have been incorrectly billed for $100 by a mail-order house. Your protestations are ignored by the company, which is now threatening to report you to a collection agency. What do you do?
5. What advantages and disadvantages does a computerized law enforcement system have for law-abiding citizens?
6. In what ways were George Orwell's "predictions" in the novel *1984* accurate? In what ways were they wrong?

Projects

1. Design a database for your own use. Create several records, sort the data, and print a report.
2. Find out as much as you can about someone (for example, yourself or a public figure) from public records like tax records, court records, voter registration lists, and motor vehicle files. How much of this information were you able to get directly from the Web? How much was available for free?
3. Find out as much as you can about your own credit rating.
4. The next time you order something by mail or phone, try encoding your name with a unique middle initial so you can recognize when the company sells your name and address to other companies. Use several different spellings for different orders if you want to do some comparative research.
5. Determine what information about you is stored in your school computers. What information are you allowed to see? What information are others allowed to see? Exactly who may access your files? Can you find out who sees your files? How long is the information retained after you leave?
6. Keep track of your purchases for a few weeks. If other people had access to this information, what conclusions might they be able to draw about you?

Books

Like word processors, spreadsheet software, and multimedia programs, databases have inspired hundreds of how-to tutorials, user's guides, and reference books. If you're working with a popular program, you should have no trouble finding a book to help you develop your skills.

Database Design for Mere Mortals, by Michael J. Hernandez (Reading, MA: Addison-Wesley, 1997). This book can save time, money, and headaches for anyone who's involved in designing and building a relational database. After defining all of the critical concepts, the author clearly outlines the design process using case studies to illustrate important points.

The Practical SQL Handbook: Using Structured Query Language, Third Edition, by Judith S. Bowman, Sandra L. Emerson, and Marcy Darnovsky (Reading, MA: Addison-Wesley, 1996). If you want to learn to communicate with relational databases using the standard database query language, this book can help you learn the language.

Object Technology: A Manager's Guide, Second Edition, by David A. Taylor (Reading, MA: Addison-Wesley, 1998). This book clearly explains the basics of object technology in non-technical terms. The author explores object-oriented databases, object-oriented programs, and object-oriented software on networks.

Database Publishing on the Web with Filemaker Pro, by Maria Langer (Berkeley, CA: Peachpit Press, 1998). Many enterprising businesses, organizations, and individuals are making their Web pages more dynamic by linking them to databases. The marriage of database technology and Web technology makes it possible for anyone with a Web browser (and, if necessary, a password) to easily view (and, in many cases, modify) data without mastering SQL or other technical languages. Langer's book is a clear, non-technical introduction to database Web publishing using Filemaker Pro on Windows and Macintosh systems.

Data Smog: Surviving the Information Glut, by David Shenk (New York: HarperEdge, 1997). It's possible to have too much "information at your fingertips." David Shenk's book clearly describes the hazards to individuals and society of all this information.

Database Nation: The Death of Privacy in the 21st Century, by Simson Garfinkel (Cambridge, MA: O'Reilly, 2000). This is a frightening, sobering account of the erosion of our personal privacy as a result of misuse of technology—databases, on-the-job monitoring, data networks, biometric devices, video surveillance, and more. Simson skillfully mixes chilling true stories and futuristic scenarios with practical advice for reclaiming our individual and collective rights to privacy. Highly recommended.

The Transparent Society: Will Technology Force Us to Choose Between Freedom and Privacy?, by David Brin (Cambridge, MA: Perseus Press, 1998). Brin, a mathematician and award-winning science fiction writer, presents a compelling case that personal privacy is doomed by technology. He argues that our best hope is to provide equal access to all information, rather than let the biggest brothers have the only windows into our lives. Compelling reading.

You'll find several other books that deal with privacy issues listed in later chapters of this book.

Videos

Many popular films and television shows, from ***Clear and Present Danger*** to ***The X Files,*** deal directly or indirectly with issues related to privacy and technology. One recent action film, ***Enemy of the State,*** used those issues as central themes. There's plenty of fantasy in this non-stop thriller about a man on the run and a government that can watch his every move. But there's a good deal of truth here, too.

Periodical

The Privacy Journal, P.O. Box 28577, Providence, RI 02908, 401/274-7861, 0005101719@mcimail.com. This widely quoted monthly newsletter covers all issues related to personal privacy.

Organizations

Computer Professionals for Social Responsibility, P.O. Box 717, Palo Alto, CA 94302, 650/322-3778, cpsr@cpsr.org. CPSR provides the public and policy makers with realistic assessments of the power, promise, and problems of information technology. Much of their work deals with privacy-related issues. Their newsletter is a good source of information.

The Electronic Frontier Foundation, 1550 Bryant Street, Suite 725, San Francisco, CA 94103-4832, 415/436-9333, ask@eff.org. EFF strives to protect civil rights, including the right to privacy, on emerging communcation networks.

Electronic Privacy Information Center, 666 Pennsylvania Ave., SE, Suite 301, Washington, DC 90003, 202/544-9240, info@epic.org. EPIC serves as a watchdog on government efforts to build surveillance capabilities into the emerging information infrastructure.

Private Citizen, P.O. Box 233, Naperville, IL 60566. This organization can help keep you off junk phone lists—for a price.

World Wide Web Pages

Check the *Computer Confluence* Web site for links to many of the organizations listed above, along with links to other database and privacy-related sites.

Exploring with Computers

Networks and Gateways

Chapter 9

Networking and Telecommunication

1. If an elderly but distinguished scientist says that something is possible he is almost certainly right, but if he says that it is impossible he is **very probably wrong.**

2. The only way to find the **limits of the possible** is to go beyond them into the impossible.

3. Any sufficiently advanced technology is **indistinguishable from magic.**

—Clarke's Three Laws

Arthur C. Clarke

Besides coining Clarke's laws, British writer Arthur C. Clarke has written more than 100 works of science fiction and nonfiction. His most famous work was the monumental 1968 film *2001: A Space Odyssey*, in which he collaborated with movie director Stanley Kubrick. The film's villain, a faceless English-speaking computer with a lust for power, sparked many public debates about the nature and risks of artificial intelligence.

HAL, the rebellious computer in the movie *2001: A Space Odyssey*

But Clarke's most visionary work may be a paper published in 1945 in which he predicted the use of *geostationary* **communications satellites**—satellites that match the Earth's rotation so they can hang in a stationary position relative to the spinning planet below. Clarke's paper pinpointed the exact height of the orbit required to match the movement of the satellite with the planetary rotation. He also suggested that these satellites could replace many telephone cables and radio towers, allowing electronic signals to be beamed across oceans, deserts, and mountain ranges, linking the people of the world with a single communications network.

A decade after Clarke's paper appeared, powerful rockets and sensitive radio receiving equipment made communications satellites realistic. In 1964 the first synchronous TV satellite was launched, marking the beginning of a billion-dollar industry that has changed the way people communicate.

Today Clarke is often referred to as the father of satellite communications. He lives in Sri Lanka, where he continues his work as a writer, but now he uses a personal computer and beams his words around the globe to editors using the satellites he envisioned half a century ago. ◻

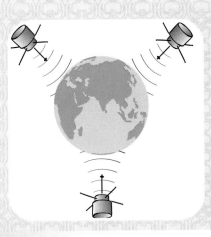

The Battle of New Orleans, the bloodiest battle of the War of 1812, was fought two weeks after the war officially ended; it took that long for the cease-fire message to travel from Washington, D.C., to the front line. In 1991, 179 years later, six hard-line Soviet communists staged a coup to turn back the tide of democratic and economic reforms that were sweeping the U.S.S.R. Within hours messages zipped between the Soviet Union and Western nations on telephone and computer networks. Cable television and computer conferences provided up-to-the-minute analyses of events—analyses that were beamed to computer bulletin boards inside the Soviet Union. Networks carried messages among the resistors, allowing them to stay steps ahead of the coup leaders and the Soviet military machine. People toppled the coup and ultimately the Soviet Union—not with guns, but with courage, will, and timely information.

Telecommunication technology—the technology of long-distance communication—has come a long way since the War of 1812, and the world has changed dramatically as a result. After Samuel Morse invented the telegraph in 1844, people could, for the first time, send long-distance messages instantaneously. Alexander Bell's invention of the telephone in 1876 extended this capability to the spoken voice. Today systems of linked computers allow us to send data and software across the room or around the world. The technological transformation has changed the popular definition of the word *telecommunication*, which today means long-distance electronic communication in a variety of forms.

In this chapter we look at the computer as part of a network rather than as a self-contained appliance, and we discuss ways in which such linked computers are used for communication and information gathering. We also consider how networks are changing the way we live and work. In the next chapter we'll explore the Internet—the global computer network at the heart of the next telecommunication revolution.

Linking Up: Network Basics

The grand irony of our times is that **the era of computers is over.** All the major consequences of standalone computers have already taken place. Computers have **speeded up our lives a bit**, and that's it. In contrast, all the most promising technologies making their debut now are chiefly due to communication between computers—that is, to connections rather than to computations. And since **communication is the basis of culture**, fiddling at this level is indeed momentous.

—**Kevin Kelly,** *Wired* **Executive Editor**

A student uses a terminal in the library to connect with an on-line information source.

A computer network is any system of two or more computers that are linked together. Why is networking important? The answers to this question revolve around the three essential components of every computer system:

▶ *Hardware.* Networks allow people to share computer hardware, reducing costs and making it possible for more people to take advantage of powerful computer equipment.

▶ *Software.* Networks allow people to share data and software programs, increasing efficiency and productivity.

▶ *People.* Networks allow people to work together in ways that are otherwise difficult or impossible.

Important information is hidden in these three statements. But before we examine them in more detail, we need to look at the hardware and software that make computer networks possible.

Basic Network Anatomy

The most desirable interaction with a network is one in which
the network itself is invisible and unnoticeable.
Planners often forget that people do not want to use systems at all—easy or not.
What people want is to delegate a task and not to worry about how it is done.

—**Nicholas Negroponte, director of MIT's Media Lab**

In Chapter 2 we saw how information travels among the CPU, memory, and other components within a computer as electrical impulses that move along collections of parallel wires called buses. A network extends the range of these information pulses, allowing them to travel to other computers. A computer may have a direct connection to a network—for example, it might be one of many machines linked together in an office—or it might have remote access to a network through a phone line, a television cable system, or a satellite link. Either way, the computer will need some specialized hardware to complete the connection. To connect directly, the computer needs a network interface card; for a remote connection it generally needs a modem or similar device.

The Network Interface

Chapter 2 described personal computer ports—sockets that allow information to pass in and out. *Parallel ports*, commonly used to connect older printers to a computer, allow bits to pass through in groups of 8, 16, or 32. *Serial ports*, on the other hand, require bits to pass through one at a time. Most PCs have at least one of each. Macintoshes don't have built-in parallel ports. Older Macs have multipurpose serial ports for connecting to printers, modems, and some networks. The standard serial port on an IBM-compatible computer is designed to attach peripherals such as modems—not to connect directly to networks. Modern Macs and PCs have *USB ports* that are much faster and more flexible than traditional serial and parallel ports.

A network interface card (NIC) adds an additional serial port to the computer—one that's especially designed for a direct network connection. The network interface card controls the flow of data between the computer's RAM and the network cable. At the same time it converts the computer's internal low-power signals into more powerful signals that can be transmitted through the network. The type of card depends on the type of network connection needed. The most common types of networks today require some kind of Ethernet card in each computer. Ethernet is a popular networking architecture developed in 1976 at Xerox. (Most Macintoshes and some PCs include an Ethernet port on the main circuit board and don't need an additional card to connect to an Ethernet network.) Details vary—and there are *many* details—but the same general principles apply to all common network connections.

In the simplest networks two or more computers are linked by cables. But direct connection is impractical for computers that are miles or oceans apart. For computers to communicate over long distances, they need to transmit information through other paths.

A network interface card allows a PC to connect to a network.

Communication á la Modem

The world is outfitted with plenty of electronic communication paths: An intricate network of cables, radio transmitters, and satellites allows people to talk by telephone between just about any two places on the planet. The telephone network is ideal for connecting remote computers, too, except it was designed to carry sound waves, not streams of bits. Before a digital signal—a stream of bits—can be transmitted over a standard phone line, it must be

An external modem (left) connects to the computer's serial port. An internal modem (right) is installed inside the computer's chassis.

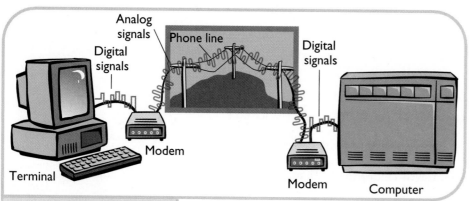

Analog signals

Digital signals

Phone line

Digital signals

Modem

Terminal

Modem   Computer

A modem converts digital signals from a computer or terminal into analog signals. The analog waves are transmitted through telephone lines to another modem, which converts them back into digital signals.

converted to an analog signal—a continuous wave. At the receiving end the analog signal first must be converted back into the bits representing the original digital message. Each of these tasks is performed by a modem (short for modulator/demodulator)—a hardware device that connects a computer's serial port to a telephone line.

An internal modem is installed on a circuit board inside the computer's chassis. An external modem sits in a box linked to a serial port. Both types use phone cables to connect to the telephone network through standard modular phone jacks. Modems differ in their transmission speeds, measured in bits per second (bps). Many people use the term *baud rate* instead of bps, but bps is technically more accurate for high-speed modems. Modems today commonly transmit at 28,800 bps to 56.6K (56,600) bps over standard phone lines. In general, communication by modem is slower than communication between computers that are directly connected on a network. High-speed transmission isn't usually critical for small text messages, but it can make a huge difference when the data being transmitted includes graphics, sound, video, and other multimedia elements—the kinds of data commonly found on the World Wide Web.

Faster Modem Alternatives

For faster remote connections, many businesses and homes bypass standard modems. Three competing technologies are available to computer users in many areas: DSL, cable modems, and satellite modems.

▶ *DSL* uses standard phone lines and is provided by phone companies in many cities.

▶ *Cable modems* provide fast network connections through cable television networks in many areas.

▶ *Satellite dishes* can deliver fast computer network connections as well as television programs.

These technologies are discussed in more detail later in the next chapter.

Networks Near and Far

Imagine how useful an office would be without a door.

—Doug Engelbart, **on the importance of network connections**

Computer networks come in all shapes and sizes, but most can be categorized as either local-area networks or wide-area networks.

A local-area network (LAN) is a network in which the computers are physically close to each other, usually in the same building. A typical local-area network includes a collection of computers and peripherals; each computer and shared peripheral is an individual *node* on the network. Nodes are directly connected by cables, which serve as pathways for transporting data between machines. Some LAN cables, known as *twisted pair*, resemble the copper wires in standard telephone cables. Another type of cable, *coaxial cable,* is the same type of cable used to transport television signals. Some networks, mostly in homes, use existing household electrical or telephone wiring to transmit data.

In a wireless network each node has a tiny radio or infrared transmitter connected to its network port so it can send and receive data through the air rather than through cables. Wireless network connections are especially convenient for workers who are constantly on the move. They're also used for creating small networks in homes because they can be installed without digging or drilling.

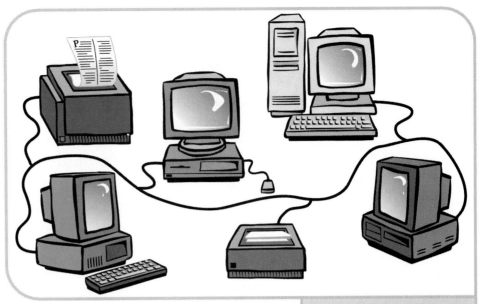

A local-area network can contain a variety of computers and peripherals that are connected.

All computers on a LAN do not have to be the same brand or use the same operating system. For example, a single network might include Macintoshes, Windows PCs, and UNIX workstations. The computers can be connected in many different ways, and many rules and industry-defined *standards* dictate what will and won't work. Most organizations depend on network administrators to take care of the behind-the-scenes details so others can focus on using the network.

A wide-area network (WAN), as the name implies, is a network that extends over a long distance. In a WAN each network site is a node on the network. Data is transmitted long-distance between networks on a collection of common pathways known as a *backbone*. Large WANs are possible because of the web of telephone lines, microwave relay towers, and satellites that span the globe. Most WANs are private operations designed to link geographically dispersed corporate or government offices.

Wide-area networks are often made up of LANs linked by phone lines, microwave towers, and communication satellites.

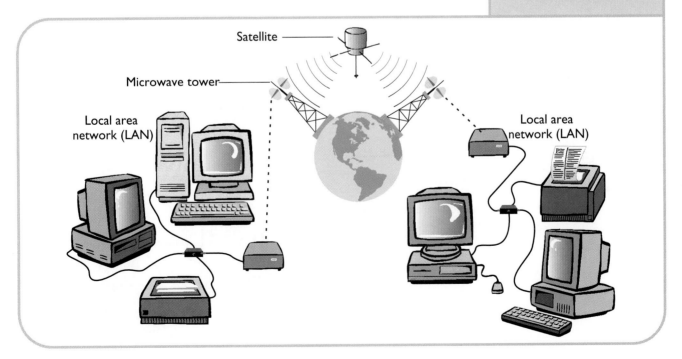

Satellite

Microwave tower

Local area network (LAN)

Local area network (LAN)

In today's internetworked world, communication frequently happens between LANs and WANs. *Bridges, routers,* and *gateways* are hardware devices that can pass messages between networks and, in some cases, translate messages so they can be understood by networks that obey different software protocols.

Communication Software

Pretty soon you'll have no more idea of
what computer you're using
than you have an idea of where your electricity comes from.

—**Danny Hillis, developer of the Thinking Machines supercomputer**

Whether connected by cables, radio waves, or a combination of modems and telephone lines, computers need some kind of communication software to interact. To communicate with each other, two machines must follow the same protocol—a set of rules for the exchange of data between a terminal and a computer or between two computers. One such protocol is transmission speed: If one machine is "talking" at 56,600 bps and the other is "listening" at 28,800 bps, the message doesn't get through. (Most modems can avoid this particular problem by adjusting their speeds to match each other.) Protocols include prearranged codes for messages such as "Are you ready?" "I am about to start sending a data file," and "Did you receive that file?" For two computers to understand each other, the software on both machines must be set to follow the same protocols. Communication software establishes a protocol that is followed by the computer's hardware.

Communication software can take a variety of forms. For users who work exclusively on a local-area network, many communication tasks are taken care of by a network operating system (NOS) such as Novell's Netware or Microsoft's Windows 2000 Server. Just as a personal computer's operating system shields the user from most of the nuts and bolts of the computer's operation, a network operating system shields the user from the hardware and software details of routine communication between machines. But unlike a PC operating system, the NOS must respond to requests from many workstations and must coordinate communication throughout the network. Today many organizations are replacing their specialized PC-based network operating systems with *intranet* systems—systems built around the open standards and protocols of the Internet, as described in more detail in the next chapter.

Client/server computing involves two-way communication between client and server programs.

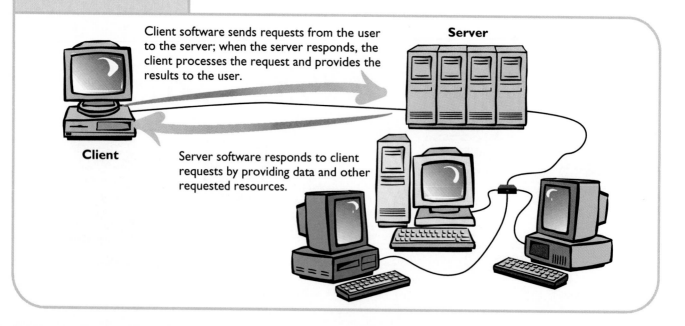

Client software sends requests from the user to the server; when the server responds, the client processes the request and provides the results to the user.

Server

Client

Server software responds to client requests by providing data and other requested resources.

The function and location of the network operating system depend in part on the *LAN model*. Some LANs are set up according to the client/server model, a hierarchical model in which one or more computers act as dedicated servers and all the remaining computers act as clients. Each server is a high-speed, high-capacity computer containing data and other resources to be shared with client computers. Using NOS server software, the server fulfills requests from clients for data and other resources. In a client/server network the bulk of the NOS resides on the server, but each client has NOS client software for sending requests to servers.

Many small networks are designed using the peer-to-peer model, which allows every computer on the network to be both client and server. In this kind of network every user can make files publicly available to other users on the network. Some desktop operating systems, including many versions of Windows and the Macintosh OS, include all the software necessary to operate a peer-to-peer network without an additional NOS. In practice many networks are hybrids, combining features of the client/server and peer-to-peer models.

The server on the right provides software and data for client workstations throughout this factory.

Outside of a LAN one of the most common types of communication software is the terminal program, which allows a personal computer to function as a character-based terminal. This kind of program (sometimes called a *terminal emulator*) handles phone dialing, protocol management, and the miscellaneous details necessary for making a personal computer and a modem work together. With terminal software and a modem, a personal computer can communicate through phone lines with another PC, a network of computers, or, more commonly, a large multiuser computer. The Windows operating system package includes a basic terminal emulation program. Many integrated packages, including AppleWorks for the Macintosh, contain terminal emulation communication modules.

These basic terminal emulators are fine for bare-bones computer-to-computer connections, but their character-based user interfaces can be confusing to people who are used to the friendlier graphical user interfaces of Windows and the Macintosh. What's more, they can't be used to explore media-rich on-line destinations on or off the World Wide Web. That's why most on-line explorers today use Web browsers and other specialized graphical client software instead of generic terminal programs.

At the other end of the line the communication software is usually built into the multiuser operating system of the host system—the computer that provides services to multiple users. This software allows a timesharing computer to communicate with several other computers or terminals at once. The most widely used host operating system today is UNIX, the 30-year old OS that has many variants, including the noncommercial Linux OS discussed in Chapter 4.

The Network Advantage

A network becomes more valuable as
it reaches more users.

—Metcalf's Law, by Bob Metcalf, inventor of Ethernet

With this background in mind let's reconsider the three reasons people use networks:

▶ *Networks allow people to share computer hardware, reducing costs and making it possible for more people to take advantage of powerful computer equipment.*

When computers and peripherals are connected in a local-area network, computer users can share expensive peripherals. Before LANs the typical office had a printer connected to each computer. Today it's more common to find a small number of high-quality printers shared by a larger group of computers and users. In a client/server network each printer may be connected to a print server—a server that accepts, prioritizes, and processes print jobs.

While it may not make much sense for users to try to share a printer on a wide-area network, WAN users often share other hardware resources. Many WANs include powerful mainframes and supercomputers that can be accessed by authorized users at remote sites.

▶ *Networks allow people to share data and software programs, increasing efficiency and productivity.*

In offices without networks people often transmit data and software by *sneakernet*—that is, by carrying diskettes between computers. In a LAN one or more computers can be used as **file servers**—storehouses for software and data that are shared by several users. With client software a user can get software and data from any server on the LAN without taking a step. A large file server is typically a dedicated computer that does nothing but serve files. But a peer-to-peer approach, allowing any computer to be both client and server, can be an efficient, inexpensive way to share files on small networks.

Of course, sharing computer software on a network can violate *software licenses* (see Chapter 4) if not done with care. Many, but not all, licenses allow the software to be installed on a file server as long as the number of simultaneous users never exceeds the number of licensed copies. Some companies offer **site licenses** or **network licenses**, which reduce costs for multiple copies or remove restrictions on software copying and use at a network site. (Software copying is discussed in more detail in Chapter 11.)

Networks don't eliminate compatibility differences between different computer operating systems, but they can simplify data communication between machines. Users of Windows-compatible computers, for example, can't run Macintosh applications just because they're available on a file server. But they can, in many cases, use data files and documents created on a Macintosh and stored on the server. For example, a poster created with Adobe Illustrator on a Macintosh could be stored on a file server so it can be opened, edited, and printed by users of Illustrator on Windows PCs. But file sharing isn't always that easy. If users of different systems use programs with incompatible file formats, they need to use *data translation software* to read and modify each other's files.

On wide-area networks the transfer of data and software can save more than shoe leather; it can save time. There's no need to send diskettes by overnight mail between two sites if both sites are connected to the same network. Typically, data can be sent electronically between sites in a matter of minutes.

▶ *Networks allow people to work together in ways that are difficult or impossible without network technology.*

Some software applications can be classified as **groupware**—programs designed to allow several networked users to work on the same documents at the same time. Groupware programs include multiuser appointment calendars, project management software, database management systems, and software for group editing of text-and-graphics documents. Many groupware programs today are built on Internet protocols, so group members can communicate and share information using Web browsers and other standard Internet software tools. Workgroups can benefit from networks without groupware packages like Notes. Most groupware features—email, message posting, calendars, and the rest—are generally available through Web and

---

Lotus Notes, the most widely used groupware application, combines distributed databases, electronic mail, and document management to facilitate information sharing and workgroup collaboration. Lotus Notes is a client/server application that works on all major operating systems. Notes is compatible with many Internet protocols and services. (Lotus Notes® is a registered trademark of Lotus Development Corporation.)

PC applications. Still, for large organizations a full-featured groupware package can be easier to manage than a collection of separate programs.

For many LAN and WAN users, network communication is limited to sending and receiving messages. As simple as this might sound, electronic messaging profoundly changes the way people and organizations work. In the next section we take a close look at the advantages and implications of interpersonal communication with computers.

Electronic Mail, Teleconferences, and Instant Messages: Interpersonal Computing

What interests me about it . . . is that it's a form of communication unlike any other and yet the second you start doing it you understand it.

—Nora Ephron, **Director of** *You've Got Mail*

Whether you're connected to a local-area network, a wide-area network, a timesharing mainframe, or the Internet, you probably have access to some kind of **electronic mail (email)** system. Electronic mail systems allow users to send messages (mail) from one computer to another. Details and user interfaces vary, but the basic concepts of email are the same for almost all systems. Each user has a *mailbox*—a storage area for messages. Any user can send a mail message to the mailbox of any other user, whether or not the recipient is currently logged into the system. Only the owner of the mailbox (and the system administrator) can read the mail in that box. Most email messages are plain ASCII text, without the kinds of formatting found in printed documents. Newer email programs can send, receive, edit, and display email messages formatted in HTML, the formatting language used in most Web pages. HTML email messages can include multiple typeface sizes and styles, and the text can be formatted in a variety of ways. The email client software hides the HTML from the sender and the recipient; they just see the formatted message. If the recipient views a formatted message with a mail program that doesn't recognize HTML, the formatting doesn't appear. Messages can carry formatted documents, pictures, multimedia files, and other computer files as **attachments**. **UV**

A variation of electronic mail is the **teleconference**—an on-line meeting between two or more people. Many teleconferencing systems allow users to communicate in real time, just as they would by telephone. In a typical **real-time teleconference** each participant sits at a computer or terminal, watching the messages appear on the screen as they're typed by other participants and typing comments for others to see immediately. Because of their give-and-take, informal nature, public real-time teleconferences are often called **chat rooms**. Whatever they're called, they tend to be chaotic, and typing responses can seem painfully slow to participants watching the process on the screen. Still, many people enjoy the immediacy of real-time communication. **Instant messaging** adds spontaneity by allowing an on-line user to create a "buddy list" to determine who on the list is logged on at any given time, and start an instant conversation with anyone who's available from the list.

In an **asynchronous teleconference** (sometimes called a *delayed teleconference*), participants type, post, and read messages at their convenience. In effect, participants in a delayed teleconference share an electronic mailbox for messages related to the group's purposes. The Internet's Usenet *newsgroups*, discussed in the next chapter, are popular examples of asynchronous teleconferences.

Email, teleconferencing, and other types of on-line communication can replace many memos, letters, phone calls, and face-to-face meetings, making organizations more productive and efficient.

The User's View

Communicating with Electronic Mail

SOFTWARE **America Online.**

THE GOAL **To catch up on your mail. Using a PC, a modem, and America Online software, you're about to connect to America Online, an information service that serves as your electronic post office.**

② You select your login name or, as it's known in AOL, *screen name*—the one-word name you've chosen to identify yourself on the screen.

① When you double-click on the America Online (AOL) icon, the application opens and displays a dialog box so you can identify yourself and sign in.

③ Then you type your password—a string of letters and numbers known only by you and the AOL computer—so that AOL can verify your identity. As you type your password, only asterisks appear on the screen, so there's no risk of anyone reading it over your shoulder.

④ When you click the Sign On button, the software passes the necessary commands on to the modem along with the network phone number and other information. You hear the dial tone, the touch-tone dialing signals, a high whistle, and a hiss as the modem dials and establishes the connection.

You've Got Mail

⑤ When a connection is made, AOL locates your screen name in its billing database and checks your password. If you typed the password correctly, you're greeted by an AOL headline screen and a digitized voice telling you that you have mail. You're now on line (sometimes spelled online)—connected to the computer system and ready to communicate. You click on the You've Got Mail icon to get your mail.

The Postal Alternative

The number of email messages now exceeds the number of letters sent through the U.S. postal service each year. Most experts expect electronic mail to take an even bigger chunk of the post office's business in coming years. Here's why:

▶ *Email is fast.* A typical electronic mail message takes no more than a few minutes from the time it's conceived until it reaches its destination—across the office or across the ocean. Electronic mail users often refer to traditional mail as "snail mail."

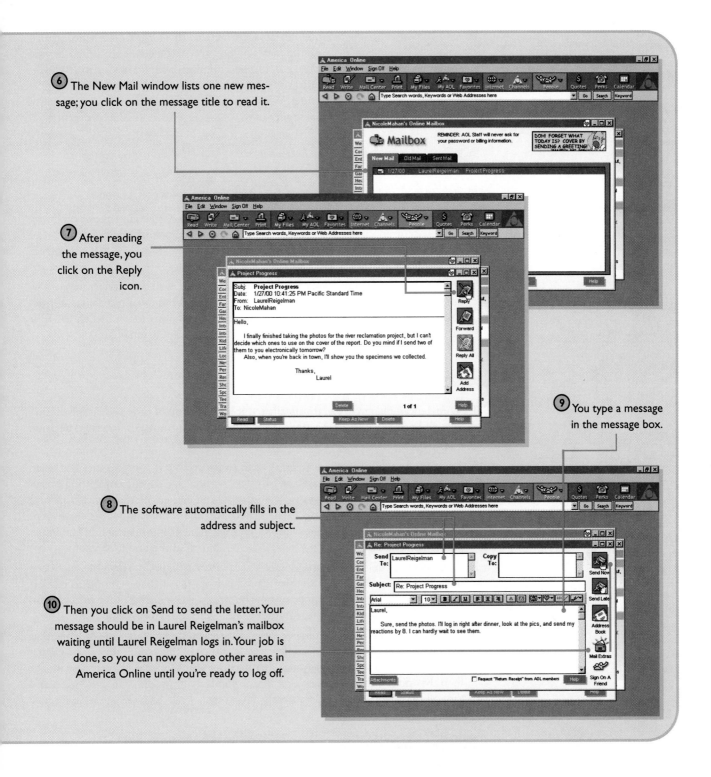

⑥ The New Mail window lists one new message; you click on the message title to read it.

⑦ After reading the message, you click on the Reply icon.

⑨ You type a message in the message box.

⑧ The software automatically fills in the address and subject.

⑩ Then you click on Send to send the letter. Your message should be in Laurel Reigelman's mailbox waiting until Laurel Reigelman logs in. Your job is done, so you can now explore other areas in America Online until you're ready to log off.

▶ *Email doesn't depend on location.* If you send someone an electronic message, that person can log in and read it from a computer at home, at the office, or anywhere in the world.

▶ *Email facilitates group communication.* In most email systems it's no harder and no more expensive to send a message to several people than to send it to one person. Most systems allow groups to have named distribution lists (sometimes called *aliases*) so a mail message addressed to an alias name (like faculty, office, or sales) is sent automatically to everyone in the group.

▶ *Email messages are digital data that can be edited and combined with other computer-generated documents.* Because the messages you receive by email are stored in your computer electronically, you can edit text and numbers without having to retype the entire document and without wasting paper. You can easily add text from other documents stored on your computer. When you're finished, you can forward the edited document back to the original sender or to somebody else for further processing.

Bypassing the Telephone

Electronic mail and teleconferencing also offer advantages over telephones:

▶ *On-line communication is less intrusive than the telephone.* A ringing phone can interrupt concentration, disrupt a meeting, and bring just about any kind of activity to a standstill. Instead of shouting "Answer me now!" an email message waits patiently in the mailbox until the recipient has the time to handle it.

▶ *On-line communication allows time shifting.* Electronic mail users aren't plagued by busy signals, unanswered rings, and message machines. You can receive email messages when you're busy, away, or asleep, and they'll be waiting for you when you have the time to pick them up. Time zones are largely irrelevant to email users.

Minimizing Meetings

Teleconferences and email can drastically reduce the amount of time people spend traveling to and participating in meetings. They offer several advantages for group decision making:

▶ *Teleconferences and email allow decisions to evolve over time.* A group can discuss an issue electronically for hours, days, or weeks without the urgency of getting everything settled in a single session. New information can circulate when it's current rather than at the next meeting. Participants have time to think about each statement before responding. When organizations use teleconferences for discussion and information dissemination, meetings tend to be infrequent, short, and to the point.

▶ *Teleconferences and email make long-distance meetings possible.* Teleconferences can include people from all over the world, and nobody needs to leave home to participate. In fact, a growing number of programmers, writers, and other information workers literally work at home, communicating with colleagues by modem.

▶ *Teleconferences and email emphasize the message over the messenger.* In companies that rely on electronic mail and teleconferences for much of their communication, factors like appearance, race, gender, voice, mannerisms, and title tend to carry less weight than they do in other organizations. Status points go to people with good ideas and the ability to express those ideas clearly in writing.

On-Line Issues: Reliability, Security, Privacy, and Humanity

Networks aren't made of printed circuits, but of people....
My terminal is a door to countless, intricate pathways, leading to untold numbers of neighbors. Thousands of people trust each other enough to tie their systems together.

—**Cliff Stoll**, in *The Cuckoo's Egg*

Any new technology introduces new problems, and on-line communication is no exception. Here are some of the most important:

▶ *Email and teleconferencing are vulnerable to machine failures, network glitches, human errors, and security breaches.* A system failure can cripple an organization that depends on the system for critical communications. One 1996 system error left 6 million America Online subscribers without email access for 19 hours. In 1998 Lockheed's email system crashed for 6 hours after an employee sent 60,000 coworkers an email announcing a prayer day. Other Internet users have experienced email blackouts caused by power outages, satellite failures, and other technological breakdowns. Email attachment viruses like 2000's Love Bug have caused billions of dollars worth of damage worldwide (See Chapter 11 for more on viruses.)

▶ *Email can pose a threat to privacy.* The U.S. Postal Service has a centuries-old tradition of safeguarding the privacy of first-class mail. Electronic communication is not grounded in that tradition. While most email messages are secure and private, there's always a potential for eavesdropping by an organization's system administrators and crafty system snoopers. In 1999 an on-line bookseller was found guilty of intercepting competitor's email to gain market advantage. That same year users of Microsoft's popular HotMail service learned that their private email messages and address books could be easily accessed by anyone with a basic knowledge of how Web addresses work. Microsoft quickly corrected the problem, but questions of email security remain.

▶ *Email can be faked.* Email forgery can be a serious threat on a surprising number of email systems. Some systems have safeguards against sending mail using someone else's ID, but none completely eliminates the threat. In time, it's likely that a digital signature will be encoded into every email message (using cryptography technology described in Chapter 11). Until then, forgery is a problem.

▶ *Email works only if everybody plays.* Just as the postal system depends on each of us checking our mailboxes daily, an email system can work only if all subscribers regularly log in and check their mail. Most people develop the habit quickly if they know important information is only available on line.

▶ *Email can be overwhelming.* Many people find themselves receiving hundreds of messages a day—many of them unsolicited. Sifting through all those messages can consume hours of time that could have been used in other ways.

▶ *Email and teleconferencing filter out many "human" components of communication.* When Bell invented the telephone, the public reaction was cool and critical. Businesspeople were reluctant to communicate through a device that didn't allow them to look each other in the eye and shake hands. While this reaction might seem strange today, it's worth a second look. When people communicate, part of the message is hidden in body language, eye contact, voice inflections, and other nonverbal signals. The telephone strips visual cues out of a message, and this can lead to misunderstandings. Most on-line communication systems peel away the sounds as well as the sights, leaving only plain words on a screen—words that might be misread if they aren't chosen carefully. What's more, email and teleconferences seldom replace casual "water cooler conversations"—those chance meetings that result in important communications and connections.

Problems notwithstanding, email and electronic messaging have become fixtures in businesses, schools, and government offices everywhere.

Converging Communication Technologies: From Messages to Money

Never in history has distance meant less.

—**Alvin Toffler, in** *Future Shock*

The Internet is at the heart of the telecommunications explosion that's going on today. But before we focus on the Internet in the next chapter, we'll survey a variety of telecommunication services and technologies that aren't dependent on the Internet. Many people regularly use fax machines, voice mail, video teleconferencing, and ATMs without even thinking about the fact that they're using digital computer technology to communicate. But each of these applications *is* built around computer technology. And the boundaries that separates these devices from personal computers are growing fuzzy as communication technologies converge.

On-line Information Services

A decade ago, when the Internet was the domain of researchers, thousands of electronic *bulletin board systems (BBS)* served as modem destinations for on-line explorers. Most BBSs were small operations operated out of homes. Visitors could post messages and read messages left by others with similar interests, send and receive email, and share software. Today most BBSs have been replaced by Web sites that offer the same services, and more, via the Internet. The same fate has befallen most *on-line databases.* Customers who used to connect directly to the Database services like Dow Jones News Retrieval Service now retrieve the same information through Web sites on the Internet.

Commercial on-line services—America Online and Prodigy—can still be accessed without venturing onto the Internet. Subscribers have access to a variety of services: news, research tools, shopping, banking, games, chat rooms, bulletin boards, email, instant messaging, software libraries. Subscribers can download software—copy it from the host computer to their computers—and upload software—post it on the host system so it's available for others. (Software sharing is part of the community spirit networks, but it's not without problems. Two of these problems, software piracy and viruses, are discussed in Chapter 11.)

The explosive growth of the Internet has forced on-line services to change the way they do business. Users who used to be content within the confines of a particular service now want to have access to the World Wide Web. Many information services have responded to the Web's popularity by becoming part of it. Before the Web, CompuServe was the largest on-line information service. In 1997, after several consecutive years of declining enrollment, it converted to a fee-based subscription outpost on the World Wide Web. Not long afterward it was purchased by America Online (AOL), now the largest private on line service.

America Online's customers use special client software rather than a Web browser to connect and use its services. But the AOL client software includes a Web browser so AOL users can explore the entire Web—not just the offerings inside AOL. AOL also provides space for customers to build and display personal Web pages. By including Internet email and Web services in its package, AOL has become the largest Internet service provider.

Many experts question whether everything-under-one-roof services like America Online can successfully compete with the free-for-all World Wide Web. Others believe there'll always be a place for services that can simplify the on-line experience. One thing is certain: The Internet will continue to bring changes to these services, and the changes will come rapidly.

Fax Machines and Fax Modems

A facsimile (fax) machine is a fast and convenient tool for transmission of information stored in paper documents, such as typed letters, handwritten notes, photographs, drawings, book pages, and news articles. When you send a fax of a paper document, the sending

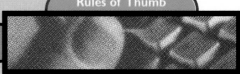

On-Line Survival Tips

Rules of Thumb

Whether you log into a BBS, an information service, or the Internet, you're using a relatively new communication medium with new rules. Here are some suggestions for successful on-line communication:

▶ *If you don't have to be on line, go off line.* Even if you're not paying by the minute for connect time, you may be consuming network resources and possibly slowing things down for other users. Do your homework before you log in so you don't have to look things up while the meter is running. Compose, edit, and address messages before you log on. Plan your strategy before you connect.

▶ *Avoid peak hours.* On-line traffic comes in waves. If you avoid the peaks, you'll save time and aggravation.

▶ *Let your system do as much of the work as possible.* If your email program can sort mail, filter mail, or automatically append a signature file to your mail, take advantage of those features. If you send similar messages over and over, store them, and recycle the relevant text. If you find yourself sending messages to the same group of people repeatedly, create an alias that includes all of those people—a distribution list that can save you the trouble of typing or selecting all those names each time. If you can automate repetitive processes like logging in and downloading mail, do it; the time you invest will be paid back over and over.

▶ *Store names and addresses in an on-line address book.* Email addresses aren't always easy to remember and type correctly. If you mistype even a single character, your message will probably either go to the wrong person or *bounce*—come back to you with some kind of "undeliverable mail" message. An on-line address book allows you to select addresses without typing them each time you use them.

▶ *Protect your privacy.* Miss Manners said it well in a 1998 *Wired* interview: "For email, the old postcard rule applies. Nobody else is supposed to read your postcards, but you'd be a fool if you wrote anything private on one."

▶ *Cross-check on-line information sources.* Don't assume that every information nugget you see on line is valid, accurate, and timely. If you "hear" something on line, treat it with the same degree of skepticism that you would if you heard it in a cafeteria or coffee shop.

▶ *Be aware and awake.* It's easy to lose track of yourself and your time on line. In his book *Virtual Community,* Howard Rheingold advises, "Rule Number One is to pay attention. Rule Number Two might be: Attention is a limited resource, so pay attention to where you pay attention."

▶ *Avoid information overload.* When it comes to information, more is not necessarily better. Search selectively. Don't waste time and energy trying to process mountains of on-line information. Information is not knowledge, and knowledge is not wisdom.

---

fax machine scans each page, converting the scanned image into a series of electric pulses and sending those signals over phone lines to another fax machine. The receiving fax machine uses the signals to construct and print black-and-white facsimiles or copies of the original pages. In a sense the two fax machines and the telephone line serve as a long-distance photocopy machine.

A computer can send on-screen documents through a fax modem to a receiving fax machine. The fax modem translates the document into signals that can be sent over phone wires and decoded by the receiving fax machine. In effect, the receiving fax machine acts like a remote printer for the document. A computer can also use a fax modem to receive transmissions from fax machines, treating the sending fax machine as a kind of remote scanner. A faxed letter can be displayed on screen or printed to paper, but it can't be immediately edited with a word processor the way an electronic mail message can. Like a scanned document, the digital facsimile is nothing more than a collection of

A fax modem (left) allows a personal computer to communicate with a fax machine (right).

black-and-white dots to the computer. Before a faxed document can be edited, it must be processed by optical character recognition (OCR) software.

Voice Mail and Computer Telephony

"Hi. This is Anita Chen. I'm either away from my desk or on another line. Please leave your name, number, and a message. If you prefer to talk to a receptionist, press zero." The voice mail system that delivers this recorded message is more than an answering device; it's a voice messaging system with many of the features of an electronic mail system.

Your response is recorded in Anita's voice mailbox. When she dials the system number from any telephone and enters her ID number or password on the phone's keypad, she can listen to her messages, respond to them, forward copies to others, and delete unneeded messages. She can do just about anything she could do with an electronic mail message except edit messages electronically and attach computer documents.

In spite of its growing popularity, voice mail has detractors. Many people resent taking orders from a machine rather than being able to talk to a human operator. Many callers are frustrated by having to wade through endless voice menus before they can speak to a real person. Office workers often complain about the time-consuming processes of recording and listening to messages.

Many personal computers have telephony software and hardware that allow them to serve as speakerphones, answering machines, and complete voice mail systems. A typical computer telephony system connects to a standard phone line through a modem capable of handling voice conversations. But it's also possible to send voice signals through a LAN, a WAN, or the Internet, bypassing the phone companies (and their charges) altogether. So far this kind of network telephony isn't as simple or reliable as commercial phone services, but it may soon pose a threat to phone company profits.

At the same time the PC is taking on telephone functions and features, phones are encroaching on the computer's turf. Many cell phones and other portable phones now can be connected to the Internet and other computer networks so they can upload and download short email messages, stock quotes, and other news nuggets. Personal communicators like the Palm VII (sometimes referred to as *personal digital assistants*, or *PDAs*) combine wireless communication with handheld computer capability. These devices are designed using a new *wireless application protocol (WAP)* that allows them to connect to the Internet anytime, anywhere (or, at least, anywhere the wireless service is supported). The computer and telephone industries recently developed *Bluetooth*, a set of standards for short-range wireless communication between mobile phones, computers, and personal digital assistants. Bluetooth technology allows phones and computers to share information, taking on functions of pagers, fax machines and other communication devices.

This Earthmate GPS Receiver serves as an input device for the laptop computer, displaying current location information on the on-screen map. (Software: DeLorme Street Atlas USA)

Global Positioning System

The U.S. Department of Defense Global Positioning System (GPS) includes 24 satellites that circle the Earth, carefully spaced so that they can pinpoint any location on the planet. The satellites are positioned so that from any point on the planet, at any time, four satellites will be above the horizon. Each satellite contains a computer, an atomic clock, and a radio. On the ground, a *GPS receiver* can use signals broadcast by three or four visible satellites to determine its position. Handheld GPS receivers can display locations, maps, and directions on small screens; GPS receivers can also be embedded in automobile navigation systems or connected to laptop computers. Members of the U.S. military use GPS receivers to keep track of where they are, but so do scientists, engineers, motorists, hikers, boaters, and others. The only difference between the military and civilian receivers is accuracy; signals are intentionally scrambled so that nonmilitary receivers are slightly less accurate than military models.

Video Teleconferencing

A video teleconference allows people to communicate face to face over long distances by combining video and computer technology. In its simplest form video teleconferencing is like two-way television. Each participant sits in a room equipped with video cameras, microphones, and television monitors. Video signals are beamed between sites so that every participant can see and hear every other participant on television monitors. Video teleconferencing is mainly practiced in special conference rooms by groups that meet too often to travel. But some businesses now use video telephones that transmit pictures as well as words through phone lines.

With the addition of a video camera, an interface, and a high-speed network connection, a telephone-capable desktop computer can be used for video teleconferencing. These systems allow callers to see each other on their computer screens while they carry on phone conversations over high-speed computer networks, including the Internet. Some allow them to view and edit shared documents while they talk. Today most PC-based video teleconferencing systems suffer from erratic video transmission, but the technology is getting better quickly.

Video conferencing hardware and software make this long-distance business meeting possible.

E-Money

Every day stock traders move billions of dollars in funds electronically through world markets.

When you strip away the emotional trappings, money is just another form of information. Dollars, yen, pounds, and rubles are all just symbols that make it easy for people to exchange goods and services. Money can be just about anything, provided people agree to its value. During the last few centuries paper replaced metal as the major form of money. Today paper is being replaced by digital patterns stored in computer media. Most major financial transactions take place inside computers, and most money is stored on computer disks and tapes instead of in wallets and safe deposit boxes.

Money, like other digital information, can be transmitted through computer networks. That's why it's possible to withdraw cash from your checking account using an *automated teller machine (ATM)* at a bank, airport, or shopping mall thousands of miles from your home bank. An ATM (not to be confused with the communication protocol with the same initials) is a specialized terminal linked to a bank's main computer through a commercial banking network. An ATM can handle routine banking transactions 24 hours a day, providing the kind of instant service that wouldn't be possible without computer networks.

An ATM isn't necessary for *electronic funds transfer* to take place. Many people have paychecks deposited automatically in checking or savings accounts and have bills paid automatically out of those accounts. These automatic transfers don't involve cash or checks; they're done inside computer networks. Many banks allow you to use your home computer or your touch-tone phone to transfer money between accounts, check balances, and pay bills.

Electronic funds transfer is one component of electronic commerce, or e-commerce—commercial activity that takes place through networked computers. But today e-commerce isn't limited to transaction processing on private banking networks. Recent years have seen rapid growth of e-commerce on the Internet. Even though the Internet is a shared public network, security procedures have been developed to make Internet financial transactions private and secure. (E-commerce and security will be discussed in more detail in later chapters.)

Different types of networks are built with different physical media; the media play critical roles in determining network performance. The two most important performance variables on the physical layer are bandwidth—the amount of information that can be transmitted in a given amount of time—and maximum operating distance.

Building Bandwidth

... after more than a century of electric technology, we have extended our central nervous system itself in a global embrace, abolishing both space and time as far as our planet is concerned.

—Marshall McLuhan, in *Understanding Media*

Networks Are Built on Physical Media

Type		Principal Uses	Bandwidth (megabits per second)	Maximum Operating Distance (without amplification)	Cost
Twisted pair (Category 5)		Small LANs	5–15	300 feet	Low
Twisted pair (Traditional)		Large LANs	100	300 feet	High
Coaxial cable		Large LANs	10–100	600–2,500 feet	Medium
Fiber optic		Network backbones; WANs	100	1–25 miles	High
Wireless/ infrared		LANs	2–11	300–1,000 feet	Medium
Wireless/ radio		Connecting things that move	1.25–5	Varies considerably	High

Computer networks transmit text, numbers, pictures, sounds, speech, music, video, and money as digital signals. The World Wide Web is fertile ground for mixing of these diverse media. Video on demand, pay-by-the-song music shopping, interactive multiplayer games, real-time auctions, picture phones, customized news feeds, and more are available on the Web—if you don't mind putting up with small, jerky videos, grainy images, and (especially) long waits.

The cause of most of these problems on the Internet and other networks is a lack of bandwidth at some point in the path between the sending computer and the receiving computer. The word has a technical definition, but in the world of computer networks bandwidth generally refers to the quantity of information that can be transmitted through a communication medium in a given amount of time. In general, increased bandwidth means faster transmission speeds. Bandwidth is typically measured in megabits (millions of bits) per second. (Since a byte is 8 bits, a megabit is 1/8 of a megabyte. The text of this chapter is about 1/16 megabyte, or a half megabit of information. A physical medium capable of transmitting 100 megabits per second could theoretically transmit this chapter's text 200 times in one second.) Bandwidth can be affected by many factors, including the physical media that make up the network, the amount of network traffic, the software protocols of the network, and the type of network connection.

Some people find it easier to visualize bandwidth by thinking of a network cable as a highway. One way to increase bandwidth in a cable is to increase the number of parallel wires in that cable—the equivalent of adding more lanes to a freeway. Another way is to increase the speed with which information passes through the cable; this is the same as increasing the speed of the vehicles on the freeway. Of course, it's easier and safer to increase highway speed limits if you have a traffic flow system that minimizes the chance of collisions and accidents; in the same way, more efficient, reliable software can increase network bandwidth. But increasing a highway's throughput doesn't help much if cars pile up at the entry and exit ramps; in the same way, a high-bandwidth network seems like a low-bandwidth network if you're connected through a slow modem.

Coaxial cables, copper telephone lines, and satellite connections are competing for the fast-Internet connection market today, but even faster access is on the horizon. Telephone companies worldwide are gradually converting their phone services from analog to digital. At the same time they're replacing aging copper lines with high-capacity fiber optic cables. Fiber optic cables use light waves to carry information at blinding speeds. A single fiber optic cable can transmit half a gigabit (500 *million* bits) per second, replacing 10,000 standard telephone cables! Fiber optic cables are already used in many telephone systems, and more miles of cable are laid every year.

All-digital fiber optic networks improve the sound quality of phone calls and the speed of long-distance phone response while cutting costs for callers. But, more importantly, a digital system can transmit email, computer data, fax, real-time video, and other messages more accurately and reliably.

Digital Communication Comes Home

High-speed digital networks are already having a huge impact on the world of work, where people depend on communication technology to get their business done. But integrated digital communication lines will eventually find their way into our homes, radically changing our lives in the process. Telephone industry predictions suggest that 90% of American homes may have high-bandwidth fiber optic cables installed by the year 2026. These cables will provide two-way links to the outside world for our phones, televisions, radios, computers, and a variety of other devices.

Multi-person video phone conversations, universal electronic mail, customized digital newspapers, automatic utility metering, and almost unlimited entertainment options may come to pass through these glass cables in the not-too-distant future. The lines that separate the telephone industry, the computer industry, and the home entertainment industry will blur as voices, data, and pictures flow back and forth on light waves. Many services we take for granted today—video rentals, cable TV, newspapers, and magazines, for example—may be transformed or replaced by digital delivery systems of the future. Whatever happens, it's clear that communication tomorrow will be radically different from communication today. We'll explore these ideas further in the next chapter as we focus on the Internet—the network of networks at the center of the communication revolution.

Before we do, let's step back and put electronic communication in a larger perspective. As futurist Stewart Brand reminded us in his groundbreaking book, *The Media Lab:*

> We can be grateful for the vast dispersed populations of peasant and tribal cultures in the world who have never used a telephone or a TV, who walk where they're going, who live by local subsistence skills honed over millennia. You need to go on foot in Africa, Asia, South America to realize how many of these people there are and how sound they are. If the world city goes smash, they'll pick up the pieces, as they've done before. Whatever happens, they are a reminder that electronic communication may be essential to one kind of living, but it is superfluous to another.

The Other Divide

James Fallows

Is the Internet widening the gap between the haves and the have-nots in our society? In this article, edited from the January 3, 2000 issue of The Industry Standard, *James Fallows argues that there is a more serious digital divide than the one politicians are talking about.*

The Internet's innate optimism comes through even when it is choosing things to worry about. In late 1999, the shape of the next perceived "menace" of the Net—the digital divide—was becoming clear. But the problem now being defined as the new Net challenge will actually be easier to deal with than one that nobody really wants to talk about yet.

Until recently, the big "danger" of the Net appeared to be that people would use it too much. Youngsters would loiter in chat rooms and be lured away to child porn sites. Teens would find terrorist or Nazi sites and learn how to blow up their schools. Adults would join Net-based millennial sects and wait to be levitated to the stars. It was only three years ago that the mass suicide of several dozen Heaven's Gate members provoked widespread theorizing that the Internet was responsible for the deaths.

Now, as the Net has become more mainstream, the grounds for concern are reversed. The perceived danger is no longer that isolated cultural minorities will use the Net too much. Instead it is that racial minorities, and others at an economic disadvantage, will not use the Net enough.

Thus the "digital divide," the fear that the benefits brought by the Net will intensify, rather than ease, the existing splits in society.

What's so optimistic about this concern? Simply that if the digital divide is defined as unequal access to the Net and its wonders, then the problem will very likely cure itself.

"Access" to the Net means two different things: whether people can make a connection to the Net, and whether they actually choose to do so. Access in the first sense is clearly a matter of basic social fairness. As telephone networks, electricity, water and sewage systems, and other elements of modernity came into service, most societies quickly decided that they should be distributed as widely as possible, rather than limited to those who could pay.

Regulators have set basic telephone and electricity rates low enough that almost everyone can afford them; 95 percent of U.S. households now have phones. By comparison, just under half of U.S. households have a computer, and only about half of those have modems. When Net connections and devices become as cheap as basic phones are now, there will be similar demands for universal service. Until then, the most important "equal access" step is to ensure that schools and libraries across the country offer connections to those who can't afford them at home.

And if the digital divide means that people who could afford to use the Net have, for now, chosen not to . . . well, if only all our national crises were this trivial. Yes, there are countless studies (many available on DigitalDivide.gov) showing that today's patterns of Net use mirror existing patterns of privilege. The richer, the better educated, and the whiter you are, the more likely you are to say you like to spend time online. But one thing we know about the Net is that people spend time there when it offers something they find valuable, mostly starting with good old e-mail. And the Net's ecology, with tens of millions of competitors scheming for ways to attract attention, guarantees that sooner or later it will cater to every conceivable taste.

So if market forces, Moore's Law, and regulation together will solve the U.S. digital divide as it's currently defined, is there any other divide to fret about? Indeed there is: the more persistent, wider gulf between economic haves and have-nots created by the Net.

Let's consider two tiers of Net beneficiaries: the thin, top layer of entrepreneurs whose startup gambles have paid off, and the much larger cadre of skilled engineers, designers, marketers and dreamers who keep the companies growing.

Those in the first group have created—and shared in—the most rapid accumulation of wealth in history. Those in the second group have average earnings about twice as high as the norm for the U.S.

These citizens of the Net economy differ from the rest of the U.S. in distinct ways. They're better educated. A higher proportion are male. And their racial makeup is very different from the U.S. norm; fewer of them are white.

As a study from the California Institute of Public Policy pointed out, immigrants from India and China alone were responsible for 29 percent of Silicon Valley startups between 1995 and 1998, and were running a quarter of all tech firms—not counting U.S. citizens of Asian ancestry. And essentially none of the members of the new, rising class are African Americans and Hispanics.

What makes this pattern intriguing is that it can't be traced to "normal" racism. Net companies are filled with dark-skinned people; they just don't happen to come from the U.S. It also can't be a matter of pure old-school connections. Friendships and informal networks still matter in the Net world, like when you need to staff up. But a Net company won't survive unless it ultimately judges its people on their ability to produce the code and make the sale.

This pattern has to reflect long imbalances in technical preparation and education within the U.S.—which means the debates we've had for generations about education and equity will soon extend to the Net. And there's nothing in today's market dynamics to suggest that, unlike the other kind of digital divide, this one will cure itself.

Bill Gates may have pointed to one solution, with his Millennium Scholars program to train African-American and Hispanic technologists. He won't be the only one expected to have an answer.

DISCUSSION QUESTIONS

1. Do you agree that the "digital divide" will naturally disappear? Explain.
2. Do you agree that the "other divide" is a more serious problem? Explain.

Networking is one of the most important trends in computing today. Computer networks are growing in popularity because they (1) allow computers to share hardware, (2) allow computers to send software and data back and forth, and (3) allow people to work together in ways that would be difficult or impossible without networks.

Local-area networks (LANs) are made up of computers that are close enough to be directly connected with cables or wireless radio transmitters/receivers. Most LANs include shared printers and file servers. Wide-area networks (WANs) are made up of computers separated by considerable distance. The computers are connected to each other through the telephone network, which includes cables, microwave transmission towers, and communication satellites. Before it can be transmitted on a phone network, a computer's digital signal is converted to an analog signal using a modem.

Communication software takes care of the details of communication between machines—details like protocols that determine how signals will be sent and received. Network operating systems typically handle the mechanics of LAN communication. Terminal programs allow personal computers to function as character-based terminals when connected to other PCs or to timesharing computers. Other types of specialized client programs have graphical user interfaces and additional functionality. Timesharing operating systems allow multiuser computers to communicate with several terminals at a time.

Electronic mail and teleconferencing are the two most common forms of communication between people on computer networks. Email and teleconferencing offer many advantages over traditional mail and telephone communication and can shorten or eliminate many meetings. But because of several important limitations email and teleconferencing cannot completely replace older communication media.

A modem can link a computer to a variety of systems, including bulletin board systems (BBSs), database services, and consumer-oriented on-line services. These services offer shopping, banking, teleconferencing, software downloading, electronic mail, games, and other features. But BBSs and information services are being overshadowed by the Internet, the global network that provides the same services and many more.

Other kinds of telecommunication, including fax, voice mail, GPS, video teleconferencing, and electronic funds transfer, are built on computer technology. The conversion of the global phone network to fiber optic cables with digital switching makes it possible for phone lines to transmit all kinds of digital data along with phone calls. Increased bandwidth increases communication options on and off the Internet. The lines that separate the telephone, computer, and home entertainment industries will blur as new communication options blossom.

Key Terms

analog signal, 242
asynchronous teleconference, 247
attachment, 247
bandwidth, 256
bits per second (bps), 242
chat room, 247
client/server model, 244
communication software, 244
communications satellite, 239
digital signal, 241
direct connection, 241
download, 252
electronic commerce (e-commerce), 256
electronic mail (email), 247
Ethernet, 241
facsimile (fax) machine, 252
fax modem, 253

fiber optic cable, 257
file server, 246
Global Positioning System (GPS), 254
groupware, 246
host system, 245
instant messaging, 247
local-area network (LAN), 242
login name, 248
modem, 242
network, 240
network interface card (NIC), 241
network license, 246
network operating system (NOS), 244
on line (online), 248
on-line service, 252
password, 248
peer-to-peer model, 245

peer-to-peer network, 245
personal communicator, 254
port, 241
protocol, 244
real-time teleconference, 247
remote access, 241
server, 245
site license, 246
telecommunication, 240
teleconference, 247
telephony, 254
terminal program, 245
upload, 252
video teleconference, 255
voice mail, 254
wide-area network (WAN), 243
wireless network, 243

Review Questions

1. Define or describe each of the key terms listed above. Check your answers using the glossary.
2. Give three general reasons for the importance of computer networking. (*Hint:* Each reason is related to one of the three essential components of every computer system.)
3. How do the three general reasons listed in Question 2 relate specifically to LANs?
4. How do the three general reasons listed in Question 2 relate specifically to WANs?
5. Under what circumstances is a modem necessary for connecting computers in networks? What does the modem do?
6. Describe at least two different kinds of communication software.
7. How could a file server be used in a student computer lab? What software licensing issues would be raised by using a file server in a student lab?
8. What are the differences among electronic mail, real-time teleconferencing, and delayed teleconferencing?
9. Describe some things you can do with electronic mail that can't be done with regular mail.
10. Describe several potential problems associated with electronic mail and teleconferencing.
11. "Money is just another form of information." Explain this statement, and describe how it relates to automated teller machines and electronic funds transfer.

Discussion Questions

1. Suppose you have an important message to send to a friend in another city, and you can use the telephone, electronic mail, real-time teleconference, fax, or overnight mail service. Discuss the advantages and disadvantages of each. See if you can think of a situation for each of the five options in which that particular option is the most appropriate choice.
2. Some people choose to spend several hours every day on line. Do you see potential hazards in this kind of heavy modem use? Explain your answer.
3. In the quote at the end of the chapter, Stewart Brand points out that electronic communication is essential for some of the world's people and irrelevant to others. What distinguishes these two groups? What advantages and disadvantages does each have?

Projects

1. Find out about your school's computer networks. Are there many LANs? How are they connected? Who has access to them? What are they used for?
2. Spend a few hours exploring an on-line service like America Online. Describe the problems you encounter in the process. Which parts of the service are the most useful and interesting?

Sources & Resources

Books

If you're interested in using an on-line service like America Online, a service-specific guidebook can save you time on line. Choose a recent book that's written in a style that appeals to you. Make sure it has a quick reference section or, at the very least, an index. The resources listed here aren't specific to any particular service.

The Communications Miracle: The Telecommunication Pioneers from Morse to the Information Superhighway, by John Bray (New York: Plenum, 1995). This book gives the communication revolution a historical perspective by mixing technical explanations with human stories.

How Networks Work, Fourth Edition, by Frank J. Derfler, Jr., and Les Freed (Indianapolis, IN: Que, 1998), follows the model popularized with the *How Computers Work* series. It uses a mix of text and graphics to illuminate the nuts and bolts of PC networks.

Teach Yourself Networking Visually, by MaranGraphics (Foster City, CA: IDG Books, 1997). This book, like others in the "Teach Yourself Visually" series, includes a 3-D drawing for just about every explanatory paragraph. It covers the basics of networks.

The Little Network Book, by Lon Poole and John Rizzo (Berkeley, CA: Peachpit Press, 1999). Networking isn't just for professionals anymore. Today's operating systems and network hardware make it (almost) easy to set up a network in a home or small business. This little book clearly explains options, techniques, and technology for setting up and using a network of PCs, Macs, or both.

Home Networking Bible, by Sue Plumley (Foster City, CA: IDG Books, 1999). This 680-page book provides clear explanations and instructions for building and troubleshooting Windows-based computer networks at home.

Networking: A Beginner's Guide, by Bruce Hallberg (Berkeley, CA: Osborne McGraw-Hill, 2000). This book is written for people who know a fair amount about bits and bytes inside a computer but want to learn the ins-and-outs of transmitting those bits and bytes between computers. It's clearly written, but probably too technical for *true* beginners.

Networking Essentials, Second Edition (Redmond, WA: Microsoft Press, 1997). This self-study tutorial is designed to teach the fundamentals of network technology. The lessons in the book are supplemented by demos and simulations on CD-ROM. It's a relatively expensive, but thorough, introduction to networking.

Computer Networks and Internets, Second Edition, by Douglas E. Comer, CD-ROM by Ralph Droms (Upper Saddle River, NJ: Prentice Hall, 1999). This text answers the question, "how do computer networks and internets operate?" Coverage includes LANs, WANs, Internet packets, digital telephony, protocols, client-server interaction, network security, and the underpinnings of the World Wide Web. A CD-ROM and a companion Web site supplement the text.

Telecommunications Systems and Technology, by Michael Khader and William E. Barnes (Upper Saddle River, NJ: Prentice Hall, 2000). This text is a technical overview of telecommunications systems, with in-depth discussions of modems, telephony systems, multimedia communication, TCP/IP, and many other topics.

Encyclopedia of Networking: Electronic Edition, by Tom Sheldon (Berkeley, CA: Osborne/McGraw-Hill, 1998). This massive reference book includes thousands of alphabetical entries covering a variety of network operating systems. A Windows CD-ROM contains a hypertext version of the book.

Cyber Speak: An Online Dictionary, by Andy Ihnatko (New York: Random House, 1997). Ihnatko, the outspoken columnist for the now defunct *MacUser* magazine, provides a dictionary of computer, network, and Internet jargon that's both useful and entertaining. Technical terms are clearly defined, on-line jargon is explained, and many products and entities are lampooned in short order.

Jargon Watch: A Pocket Dictionary for the Jitterati, as overheard by Gareth Branwin (San Francisco: HardWired, 1997). Hard-core computer networkers speak a language all their own—a language rich with opaque acronyms and shorthand descriptors for complex concepts. This tiny book leaves the technical definitions for other references. It focuses instead on "geek speak, exec lingo, and memo slang." If you have any doubt that computers are changing our language, you'll be convinced by reading this collection of colorful, often hilarious phrases.

New Community Networks: Wired for Change, by Douglas Schuler (Reading, MA: Addison-Wesley, 1996). Networks don't just connect computers—they connect people. This book, by the chair of Computer Professionals for Social Responsibility, surveys the many ways computer networks can be used to build on-line communities. Education, community health, political activism, grassroots democracy, and economic opportunity—success stories abound here, along with specifics for making technology work for your community concerns.

F2f, by Phillip Finch (New York: Bantam, 1997). As communities form on computer networks, they bring with them many of the problems found in other communities. This suspense thriller captures some of the potential risks of on-line communities in an exciting, tightly written story.

Film

You've Got Mail. This light comedy, named for AOL's ubiquitous greeting, and points out the power of electronic communication to build strong emotional bonds.

Periodicals

Network Magazine focuses on networks with a business perspective.

Computer Telephony and *CTI* are two magazines that cover the rapidly changing territory where computers and telephones meet. Both periodicals are aimed at professionals and include a fair amount of technical material.

World Wide Web Pages

Computer networking technology is changing faster than publishers can print books and periodicals about it. The Computer Confluence Web site can connect you to up-to-date networking information all over the Internet.

10

From Internet to Information Infrastructure

AFTER YOU READ THIS CHAPTER YOU SHOULD BE ABLE TO:

Describe the nature of the Internet and the variety of functions it performs.

Discuss several software tools for navigating and using the Internet.

Describe the evolution of the World Wide Web into a multifaceted tool for entertainment, education, communication, collaboration, and commerce.

Explain how the Internet and other telecommunication technologies are evolving into an all-encompassing information infrastructure.

Discuss the future of the Internet in particular and cyberspace in general.

In this chapter:

▶ The roots of the Internet
▶ Why nobody controls the Internet
▶ How the Internet works
▶ The World Wide Web and other Internet tools
▶ Publishing pages on the Web
▶ The next generation Internet and beyond
... and more.

On the CD-ROM:

▶ A 3-D model of a global information network
▶ Animated demonstration showing how a Web browser works
▶ Important access to glossary and key word references
▶ Interactive self-study quizzes
... and more.

On the Web:

www.prenhall.com/beekman
▶ Articles and books on the Internet's history, structure, and use
▶ Tools for exploring the Internet
▶ Resources for building and publishing multimedia Web pages
▶ Self-study exercises
... and more.

It's a bit like **climbing a mountain**.
You don't know how far you've come until you
stop and look back.

—Vint Cerf, **ARPANET pioneer and first president
of the Internet Society**

In the 1960s the world of computers was a technological Tower of Babel—most computers couldn't communicate with each other. When people needed to move data from one computer to another, they carried or mailed a magnetic tape or a deck of punch cards. While most of the world viewed computers only as giant number crunchers, J. C. R. Licklider, Robert Taylor, and a small group of visionary computer scientists saw the computer's potential as a communication device. They envisioned a network that would allow researchers to share computing resources and ideas.

U.S. military strategists during those Cold War years had a vision, too: They foresaw an enemy attack crippling the U.S. government's ability to communicate. The Department of Defense wanted a network that could function even if some connections were destroyed. They provided a million dollars to Taylor and other scientists and engineers to build a small experimental network. The groundbreaking result, launched in 1969, was called ARPANET, for Advanced Research Projects Agency NETwork. When a half dozen researchers sent the first historic message from UCLA to Doug Engelbart's lab at the Stanford Research Institute, no one even thought to take a picture.

ARPANET was built on two unorthodox assumptions: (1) The network itself was unreliable, so it had to be able to overcome its own unreliability, and (2) all computers on the network would be equal in their ability to communicate with other network computers. In ARPANET there was no central authority because that would make the entire network vulnerable to attack. Messages were contained in software "packets" that could travel independently by any number of different paths, through all kinds of computers, toward their destinations.

ARPANET grew quickly into an international network with hundreds of military and university sites. In addition to carrying research data, ARPANET channeled debates over the Viet Nam War and intense discussions about Space War, an early computer game. ARPANET's peer-to-peer networking philosophy and protocols were copied in other networks in the 1980s. Vint Cerf and Bob Kahn, two of the original researchers, developed the protocols that became the standard computer communication language, allowing different computer networks to be linked.

In 1990 ARPANET was disbanded, having fulfilled its research mission and spawned the Internet. In a recent interview Cerf said about the network he helped create, "It was supposed to be a highly robust technology for supporting military command and control. It did that in the Persian Gulf War. But, along the way, it became a major research support infrastructure and now has become the best example of global information infrastructure that we have."

The ARPANET pioneers have gone on to work on dozens of other significant projects and products. In the words of Bob Kahn, "Those were very exciting days, but there are new frontiers in every direction I can look these days." □

The team that built the Internet included, from front to back: Bob Taylor, Vint Cerf, Frank Heart, Larry Roberts, Len Kleinrock, Bob Kahn, Wes Clark, Doug Engelbart, Barry Wessler, Dave Walden, Severo Ornstein, Truett Thach, Roger Scantlebury, Charlie Herzfeld, Ben Barker, Jon Postel, Steve Crocker, Bill Naylor, and Roland Bryan.

The team that designed ARPANET suspected they were building something new and important. They couldn't have guessed, though, that they were laying the groundwork for a system that would become a universal research tool, a hotbed of business activity, a virtual shopping mall, a popular social hangout, a publisher's clearinghouse of up-to-the-minute information, and one of the most talked about institutions of our time.

The Internet is a technology, a tool, and a culture. It was originally designed by computer scientists for computer scientists, and other scientists and engineers are continually adding new features. Consequently, the vocabulary of the Internet often seems like a flurry of technobabble to newcomers. But you don't need to understand every acronym and protocol to make sense of the Internet; you just need to know a little bit of netspeak to understand the basics. In this chapter we explore the many faces of the Internet without getting too deep into the technical details. If you want to know more, you can explore the resources listed at the end of the chapter.

The Internet is changing at a phenomenal pace. It's almost impossible to tell from week to week how it will evolve. Still, some trends are unmistakable. With those in mind, we close the chapter by looking at the future of the Internet as it evolves into an all-encompassing information infrastructure.

The Internet: A Network of Networks

No LAN is an island.

—Karyl Scott, *InfoWorld* writer

The Internet (or just Net) is an interconnected network of thousands of networks linking academic, research, government, and commercial institutions and other organizations and individuals. The Internet includes dozens of national, statewide, and regional networks, hundreds of networks within colleges and research labs, and thousands of commercial sites. Most sites are in the United States, but the Internet has connections in almost every country in the world. Mainframes, workstations, servers, and microcomputers of almost every type are connected to the Internet.

The Internet provides millions of people with a multitude of services, including electronic mail, network newsgroups, instant messaging, Web publishing, shopping, banking, and research.

Many of these services are similar to those provided by America Online and other on-line services. But the Internet is far bigger than any single network or on-line service. America Online is, in essence, a members-only club that occupies a tiny corner of the always-open-to-anybody Internet. (America Online members use their AOL accounts to explore the rest of the Web as well as the private AOL areas.) More importantly, the Internet is not centrally controlled by any one government, corporation, individual, or legal system. Several international advisory organizations develop standards and protocols for the evolving Internet, but no one has the power control the Net's operation or evolution. The Internet is, in a sense, a massive anarchy unlike any other organization the world has ever seen.

Counting Connections

In its early days, the Internet connected only a few dozen computers at U.S. universities and

Cyber cafes around the world allow travelers to stay connected to their homes—and the rest of the world. Customers pay by the minute to log into their home servers, keep up with email, and explore the Web.

government research centers, and the U.S. government paid most of the cost of building and operating it. Today it connects millions of computers in almost every country in the world, and costs are shared by thousands of connected organizations. It's impossible to pin down the exact size of the Internet for several reasons:

▶ *The Internet is growing too fast to track.* Recent public interest in the Internet has triggered explosive growth. Millions of new users connect to the Internet every year in the United States alone, and the rest of the world is adding new connections by the minute.

▶ *The Internet is too decentralized to quantify.* There's no Internet Central that keeps track of user activity or network connections. To make matters worse for Internet counters, some parts of the Internet can't be accessed by the general public; they're sealed off to protect private information.

▶ *The Internet doesn't have hard boundaries.* There are several ways to connect to the Internet (described later in this chapter); these different types of connections offer different classes of services and different degrees of interactivity. As choices proliferate, it's becoming harder and harder to know exactly what it means to "belong to the Internet."

This last point is worth a closer look because of the growing availability of Internet services to consumers. It's easier to understand the different types of Internet access if you know a little bit about the protocols that make the Internet work.

Internet Protocols

The most important quality of the Internet is that it lends itself to
radical reinvention.... In another 10 years,
the only part of the Internet as we know it now that will have survived will be
bits and pieces of the underlying Internet protocol....

—**Paul Saffo, director of the Institute for the Future**

The protocols at the heart of the Internet are called TCP/IP (Transmission Control Protocol/Internet Protocol). They were developed as an experiment in internetworking—connecting different types of networks and computer systems. The TCP/IP specifications were published as open standards, not owned by any company. As a result TCP/IP became the "language" of the Internet, allowing cross-network communication for almost every type of computer and network. These protocols are generally invisible to users; they're hidden deep in software that takes care of communication details behind the scenes. They define how information can be transferred between machines and how machines on the network can be identified with unique addresses.

The TCP protocols define a system similar in many ways to the postal system. When a message is sent on the Internet, it is broken into *packets,* in the same way you might pack your belongings in several individually addressed boxes before you ship them to a new location. Each packet has all the information it needs to travel independently from network to network toward its destination. Different packets might take different routes, just as different parcels might be routed through different cities by the postal system. (The host systems that use software to decide how to route Internet transmissions are called *routers,* although sometimes the same routing work can be done by faster, less flexible hardware *switches.*) Regardless of the route they follow, the packets eventually reach their destination, where they are reassembled into the original message. This packet-switching model is flexible and robust, allowing messages to get through even when part of the network is down.

The other part of TCP/IP—the IP part—defines the addressing system of the Internet. Every host computer on the Internet has a unique *IP address*: a string of four numbers separated by periods, or, as they say in netspeak, dots. A typical IP address

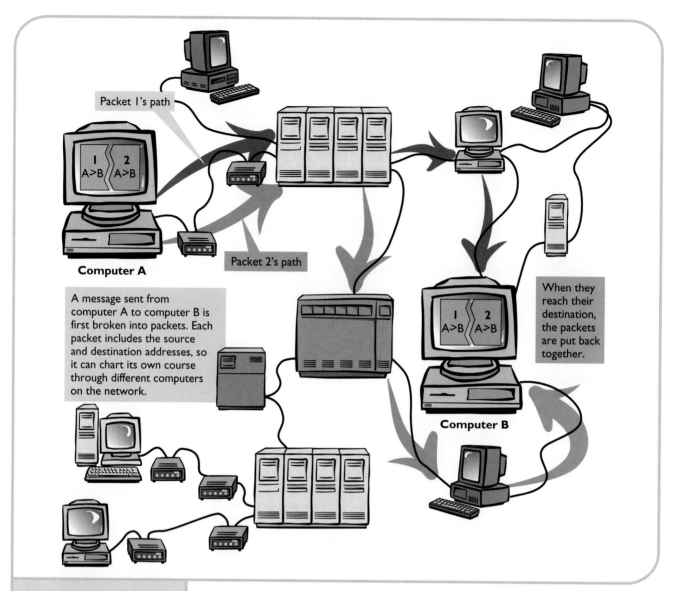

Packet 1's path

Packet 2's path

A message sent from computer A to computer B is first broken into packets. Each packet includes the source and destination addresses, so it can chart its own course through different computers on the network.

When they reach their destination, the packets are put back together.

Computer A

Computer B

Packet switching gets the message through.

might look like this: 123.23.168.22 ("123 dot 23 dot 168 dot 22"). Every packet includes the IP address of the sending computer and the receiving computer.

Many Internet programs and protocols were originally developed on computers that used the UNIX operating system. Even today, most Internet servers run some form of UNIX, and a few Internet services require UNIX knowledge. But UNIX isn't part of the protocols that define the Internet. Today's Internet is made up of a tremendous number of computers and operating systems communicating with each other using TCP/IP protocols.

Internet Access Options

The grand design keeps getting grander.
A global computer is taking shape, and we're all connected to it.

Stewart Brand, in *The Media Lab*

Internet *host computers*—the ones that provide services—are able to speak TCP/IP and have an IP address. Computers are connected to the Internet through three basic types of connections: direct connections, dial-up connections through modems, and broadband connections through high-speed alternatives to modems.

Direct Connections

In many schools and businesses the computers have a direct (dedicated) connection to the Internet through a LAN and have their own IP addresses. A direct connection offers several advantages: You can take full advantage of Internet services without dialing in; your files are stored on your computer, not on a remote host; and response time is much faster, making it possible to transfer large files (like multimedia documents) quickly. Direct connect digital lines come in many varieties, including *T1* connections, which can transmit voice, data, and video at roughly 1.5Mbps, and *T3*, which is even faster. (On some continents a technology called E1 is used instead of T1.)

Dial-up Connections

If your computer isn't directly connected to the Internet, you can temporarily connect to an Internet host through a dial-up connection—a connection using a modem and standard telephone lines. The time-honored method—one that works even with ancient equipment and questionable phone lines—is called *dial-up terminal emulation*. *Terminal emulation software* makes your computer act as a *dumb terminal*—an input/output device that allows you to send commands to and view information on the host computer. Email messages and other files are stored on the host computer, not yours; if you want to save them on your computer, you need to download them. Many Internet services, including most of the World Wide Web, are off limits with this kind of serial line connection because of the character-based, command-line interface. Graphics and multimedia files must be specially encoded before they can be transmitted or received.

Software that uses *PPP* (point-to-point protocol) or the older SLIP (serial line interface protocol) allows a computer connected via modem and phone line to temporarily have full Internet access and an IP address. *Full-access dial-up connections* offer most of the advantages of direct connection, including full Web access, but response time is limited by the modem's speed. A typical connection through a modem and *POTS* (plain old telephone service) is much slower (and often less reliable) than a direct Internet connection. While modern modems are theoretically capable of delivering data at 56Kb, they're usually much slower when connected to typical noisy phone lines.

Broadband Connections

Until a few years ago, a slow dial-up connection was the only alternative to direct Internet for most users. But today millions of Internet users connect via DSL, cable modems, and satellites. These modem alternatives are often called broadband connections because they have much higher bandwidth than standard modem connections. In some cases, broadband connections offer data transmission speeds comparable to direct connection speeds. Many broadband services offer another big advantage to users: they can be continually connected. The user of always-on broadband services doesn't need to log into their Internet service; it's instantly available anytime. The three most common broadband alternatives are based on different technologies:

▶ *DSL.* Many phone companies offer DSL (digital subscriber line) services to customers within geographical range of their service hubs. (*Jargon alert:* There are several variants of DSL, including IDSL and HDSL. The term *xDSL* is sometimes used to refer to any and all forms of DSL. DSL is newer, faster, and cheaper than *ISDN*, a digital service offered by phone companies in the 1990s. Most experts believe DSL and other newer technologies will soon make ISDN obsolete.) DSL transmission speeds vary, but they're far faster than conventional modem, sometimes approaching T1 speeds. A graphics-heavy Web page that takes minutes to download through a conventional modem will load in seconds through a DSL connection. Unlike a standard modem transmission, a DSL signal can share a standard telephone line with voice traffic. DSL connections aren't available everywhere, and installation can be complicated and expensive. But DSL's ultra-high-speed, always-connected signal brings the advantages of a direct Internet connection to homes and small businesses.

▶ *Cable modem connections.* Some cable TV companies offer ultra-high-speed Internet connections through cable modems. Cable modems allow Internet connections using the same network of coaxial cables that delivers television signals to millions of households. Like DSL, cable modem service isn't available everywhere. Cable modem speeds can exceed DSL speeds. But because a single cable is shared by an entire neighborhood, transmission speeds can go down when the number of users goes up. For many homes, cable modems offer the fastest possible Internet connections.

▶ *Satellite connections.* The same DirecTV satellite dishes that provide hundreds of television channels to viewers in outlying areas can be used to download Web pages, email, and other Internet data via a service called DirecPC. *Downstream traffic*—information from the Internet to the subscriber—is much faster than conventional modem traffic, if not quite as fast as DSL or cable modems. Unfortunately, *upstream traffic*—messages and other data travelling from the home computer to the Internet—goes through standard phone lines at standard modem rates. But satellite connections are, for many homes and businesses outside of urban centers, the only high-speed Internet access options available.

None of these broadband technologies is universally available, but each is rapidly expanding its area of coverage. In the future, many homes and small businesses may have direct connection to the Internet via fiber optic cables. But for now, most Internet users must settle for modem speeds or choose from broadband services available in their areas.

Internet Service Providers

Internet service providers (ISPs) generally offer several connection options at different prices. *Local ISPs* are local businesses with permanent connections to the Internet; they provide connections to their customers, usually through local telephone lines, along with other services. For example, an ISP might provide an email address, a server for customers to post Web pages, and technical help as part of a service package. *National ISPs* such as EarthLink and the Microsoft Network offer similar services on a nationwide scale. National ISPs have local telephone numbers in most major cities so travelers can dial into the Net on the road without paying long-distance charges. In some cities inexpensive or free access to the Internet is available through a *freenet*—a local bulletin board system designed to provide community access to on-line forums, announcements, and services.

Many private networks and on-line services (including America Online, CompuServe, and Prodigy) provide Internet access through gateways. A gateway is a computer connected to two networks—in this context the Internet and an outside network—that translates communication protocols and transfers information between the two.

Intranets and Extranets

Our customers are moving at Internet speed.
They need us to respond at Internet speed.

—Laurie Tucker, **Federal Express vice president**

For many organizations, Internet protocols and software are more important than the Net itself. Members of these organizations communicate through intranets—self-contained intraorganizational networks that are designed using the same technology as the Internet. A typical intranet offers email, newsgroups, file transfer, Web publishing, and other Internet-like services, but not all of these services are available to people outside the organization. For example, an intranet Web document might be accessible only to users within the organization—not to the entire Internet community. If an intranet has a gateway connection to the Internet, the gateway probably has some kind of *firewall* to prevent unauthorized communication and to secure sensitive internal data.

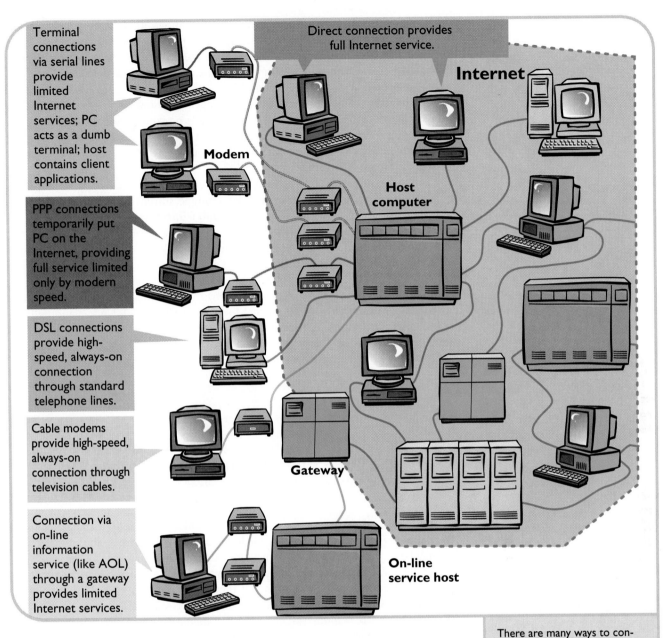

Terminal connections via serial lines provide limited Internet services; PC acts as a dumb terminal; host contains client applications.

PPP connections temporarily put PC on the Internet, providing full service limited only by modem speed.

DSL connections provide high-speed, always-on connection through standard telephone lines.

Cable modems provide high-speed, always-on connection through television cables.

Connection via on-line information service (like AOL) through a gateway provides limited Internet services.

Direct connection provides full Internet service.

Internet

Modem

Host computer

Gateway

On-line service host

There are many ways to connect a PC to the Internet.

Some private TCP/IP networks are designed for outside use by customers, clients, and business partners of the organization. These networks, often called extranets, are typically for electronic commerce—business transactions through electronic networks. Most use *electronic data interchange (EDI)*—a decade-old set of specifications for ordering, billing, and paying for parts and services over private networks. Some extranets are *virtual private networks* that use *encryption software* (described in the next chapter) to create secure "tunnels" through the public Internet. Others use their own lines or lease lines that aren't subject to the traffic and security problems of the public Internet. (Security issues are discussed in detail in the next chapter.)

Internet Applications: Communication and Connection

No other medium gives every participant the capability to communicate instantly with thousands and thousands of people.

—Tracy LaQuey, in *The Internet Companion*

Internet applications, like personal computer applications, are software tools for users. But working with Internet applications is different from working with word processors or spreadsheets because of the distributed nature of the Internet and the client/server model used by most Internet applications. In the client/server model a client program asks for information, and a server program fields the request and provides the requested information from databases and documents. Depending on the type of connection and the application you're using, the client might reside on your personal computer or the host computer, and the server might reside on that same host computer or another host computer elsewhere on the network. The client's user interface hides the details of the network and the server from the user.

Two different users might access the same server using completely different client applications with different user interfaces. For example, consider three users accessing the same information on the same server. A user with a direct connection might be using a Web browser with a point-and-click graphical user interface to explore a particular server, while another user with a dial-up terminal connection might be typing UNIX commands and seeing only text on screen. A third user might be viewing the same data, a few words at a time, on the tiny screen of a handheld personal communicator or digital telephone.

Even though most people think of the World Wide Web as the Internet, important Internet applications existed long before the Web was invented. Understanding those applications makes it easier to make sense of the Web, because key concepts behind those applications have been assimilated into Web applications. We'll survey those applications before diving deeper into the Web.

Internet Addresses

Each person on the "Internet" has a unique e-mail "address" created by
having a squirrel run across a computer keyboard. . . .

—Dave Barry, **humorist**

The most popular Internet application is one of the oldest—electronic mail. Thanks to the interconnected Internet, you don't need to limit your mail to people on the same network. Whether you're connected to the Internet directly or through a gateway, you can send messages to anyone with an Internet link, provided you know his or her Internet address.

Internet addresses look strange, but they're easy to decipher if you know how they're made. A person's email address is made up of two parts separated by an at sign (@): the person's *user name* (login name) and the *host name*—the name of the host computer or network where the user receives mail. Here's the basic form:

```
username@hostname
```

The host is named using what's called the *domain name system (DNS)*—a system that translates the computer's numerical IP address into something that's easier for humans to read and remember. The DNS uses a string of names separated by dots to specify the exact Internet location of the host computer.

Internet addresses are classified by *domains*. In the United States the most widely used top-level domains are general categories that describe types of organizations:

edu	Educational sites
com	Commercial sites
gov	Government sites
mil	Military sites
net	Network administration sites
org	Nonprofit organizations

To accommodate recent growth, the Internet Ad Hoc Committee recently created seven additional top-level domain names:

arts	Arts and cultural entities
firm	Businesses
info	Information services
nom	Individuals and families
rec	Network administration sites
store	Merchants and stores
web	Web-related organizations

Outside (and occasionally inside) the United States top-level domains are two-letter country codes, such as jp for Japan, th for Thailand, au for Australia, uk for United Kingdom, and us for United States.

The top-level domain name is the last part of the address. The other parts of the address, when read in reverse, provide information that narrows down the exact location on the network. The words in the domain name, like the lines in a post office address, are arranged hierarchically from little to big. They might include the name of the organization, the name of the department or network within the organization, and the name of the host computer. The illustration dissects a typical email address so that you can see what each part means.

Anatomy of an email address.

benjamin@cs.orst.edu

benjamin is the login name of the user.

cs is the name of benjamin's host network in the Computer Science Department.

orst is the domain name for Oregon State University's LAN, which includes the cs LAN.

edu is the name of the top-level domain containing Internet educational sites.

Here are some other examples of email addresses and how to read them:

president@whitehouse.gov	user *president* whose mail is stored on the host *whitehouse* in the government domain
hazel_filbert@lane.k12.or.us	User *hazel_filbert* (the underscore character is sometimes used as a substitute for a space because spaces can't be embedded in email addresses) at the server for the Lane County, Oregon, k-12 school district server
crabbyabby@AOL.com	the user called *crabbyabby* whose mail is handled by America Online (AOL), a commercial service provider connected to the Internet via a gateway

As you can see, no one email addressing scheme applies to everybody. (When you think about it, the same can be said of postal addresses.) The domain naming scheme allows you to make educated guesses about email addresses, but it doesn't provide a sure-fire formula for determining an address if you don't know it. Many Web sites, including Yahoo!, Excite, and search.com, offer free email search services. Most email software allows users to keep personal Internet address books.

Email on the Internet

Because the Internet is made up of all kinds of computers on diverse networks, there's no single way to send and receive mail. What you see on the screen depends on the type of Internet connection you have and the mail program you use. If you have a dial-up connection to a UNIX-based host, you might send and receive mail using a UNIX mail program like Pine. Pine, developed at the University of Washington, is character-based, but it has an easy-to-use menu system, an online address book, and a full-screen text editor that works like a word processor. It works with almost any kind of Internet connection. Users with full Internet connections have many more mail software options, including graphical programs like Microsoft Outlook Express, Qualcom, Eudora, and Netscape Communicator. These programs allow PCs to download and handle mail locally rather than depending on a host as a post office.

Many commercial Web sites offer *free email* accounts. Sometimes these free email services are subsidized by advertisers; sometimes they're provided to attract Web site visitors. Free email services are popular with users of public computers (for example, in libraries), people who don't receive email from their ISPs, people who want multiple email addresses not associated with their workplace, and travelers who want to check email on the road without lugging a laptop. Some free email programs have less than

Internet email programs have many faces. Shown here are Qualcomm's Eudora and Pine.

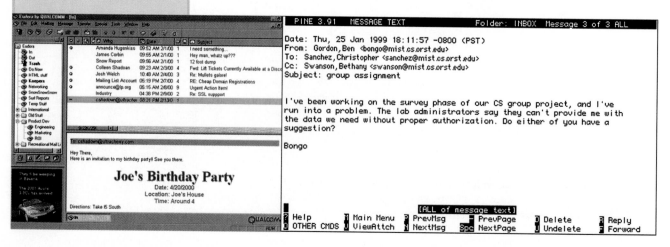

perfect security records; as noted in the last chapter, the accounts of 40 million users of HotMail were easy prey for snoopers before Microsoft plugged a security leak. Still, free email services are growing in popularity every day.

Standard Internet mail messages are plain ASCII text. Plain text messages can be viewed with any mail client program, including those built into pocket communicators and email-capable phones. Modern email programs that support *MIME (multipurpose Internet mail extensions)* can also send and receive documents formatted with *HTML*— the language used to create most Web pages. HTML messages can include text formatting, pictures, and links to Web pages, none of which are visible with text-only mail programs. That's why most email users send formatted word processor documents, pictures, and other multimedia files as attachments to text messages. Attachments need to be temporarily converted to ASCII using some kind of encoding scheme before they can be sent through Internet mail. Programs like Eudora, Outlook, Communicator, and Pine take care of the encoding and decoding automatically; some mail programs require extra steps. If you're sending mail to or from a network that doesn't support MIME, you may not be able to attach files. Of course, all this is changing as newer software tools become available.

Email appliances like MailStation provide access to email without a PC.

Mailing Lists

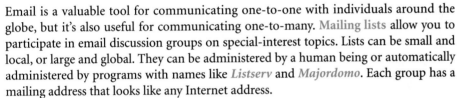

Email is a valuable tool for communicating one-to-one with individuals around the globe, but it's also useful for communicating one-to-many. Mailing lists allow you to participate in email discussion groups on special-interest topics. Lists can be small and local, or large and global. They can be administered by a human being or automatically administered by programs with names like *Listserv* and *Majordomo*. Each group has a mailing address that looks like any Internet address.

You might belong to one student group that's set up by your instructor to carry on discussions outside of class, another group that includes people all over the world who use Macromedia Director to create multimedia, a third that's dedicated to saving endangered species in your state, a fourth for customers of an on-line bookstore, and a fifth that's made up of African music fans. When you send a message to a mailing list address, every subscriber receives a copy. And, of course, you receive a copy of every mail message sent by everyone else to those lists.

Subscribing to a busy list might mean receiving hundreds of messages each day. To avoid being overwhelmed by incoming mail, many list members sign up to receive them in daily *digest* form; instead of receiving many individual messages each day, they receive one message that includes all postings. But digest messages can still contain lots of repetitive, silly, and annoying messages. Some lists are *moderated* to ensure that the quality of the discussion remains high. In a moderated group, a designated moderator acts as an editor, filtering out irrelevant and inappropriate messages and posting the rest.

Network News

You can participate in special-interest discussions and debates without overloading your mailbox by taking advantage of the hundreds of Usenet newsgroups. These are public discussions that you can check into and out of whenever you want; all messages are posted on virtual bulletin boards for anyone to read. There are groups for every interest and taste . . . and a few for the tasteless. Newsgroups are organized hierarchically, with dot names like rec.music.makers.percussion and soc.culture.french.

To explore network newsgroups, you need a client program that can serve as a **newsreader.** Most UNIX-based computers have text-only newsreaders, but graphical newsreaders are common; they're even built into Internet Explorer and Netscape Communicator. You can use a newsreader or an email program to *post* messages to newsgroups.

Many Usenet newsgroups contain the same kind of free-flowing discussions you'll find in Internet mailing lists, but there are two important differences:

1 Listserv mail messages are delivered automatically to your mailbox, but you have to seek out information in Usenet groups. Practically speaking, this makes a mailing list slightly more convenient, but only if you want to make sure you never miss anything. Many people prefer newsgroups because they don't want to receive all those messages.

2 Mailing list messages are sent to a specific group of people, whereas newsgroup messages are available for anyone to see. You may not personally know all of the subscribers to a mailing list, but you can usually find out something about them if you need to. But a newsgroup message is as public as an ad in the newspaper; there's no way to know who'll read it.

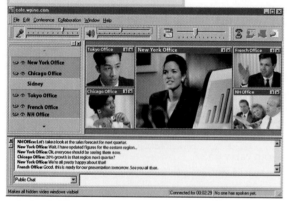

CU-SeeMe allows real-time audio/visual communication over the Internet.

Many Internet old-timers complain that newsgroups have become almost unusable now that millions of people use the Internet. Discussions get bogged down by repetitive questions from newcomers, childish rants, off-topic trivia, and other counterproductive messages. *Moderated newsgroups* contain only messages that have been filtered by designated moderators. The moderator discards inappropriate messages, making it easier for others to find the information they're looking for.

Real-Time Communication

For time is the longest distance between two points.

—Tennessee Williams

Mailing lists and newsgroups are delayed or **asynchronous communication** because the sender and the recipients don't have to be logged in at the same time. The Internet offers programs for **real-time communication**, too. **Instant messaging** has been possible since the days of text-only Internet access. Internet relay chat (IRC) and Talk allow UNIX users to type and send instant messages to their on-line friends and co-workers. But newer, easier to use messaging systems from AOL/Netscape, Microsoft, Yahoo, ICQ, and others have turned instant messaging into one of the most popular Internet activities.

These instant messaging systems are similar to on-line service chat rooms, except that participants aren't limited to members of a particular on-line service. Instant messaging programs allow users to create buddy lists, check for "buddies" who are logged in, and exchanged typed messages and files with those who are. Most of these programs are available for free. Unfortunately, most instant messaging programs (so far) limit conversations to people using the same messaging software.

Many multi-user games and chat rooms today are populated by avatars representing participants. These avatars are attending an historic on-line wedding in which two of their human counterparts are actually being married.

The Web makes it possible for chat rooms and multi-player games to use computer graphics to simulate real-world environments. Participants can represent themselves with *avatars*—graphical "bodies" that might look like simple cartoon sketches, elaborate 3-D figures, or exotic abstract icons.

Emerging multimedia technology is making it possible for Internet communication to move beyond text and avatars. Many programs allow you to use a computer's microphone and speaker to turn the Internet into a toll-free long-distance telephone service. Most **Internet telephony** programs work only when both parties are running the same program at the same time, and they're not nearly as trouble-free as traditional long-distance service. Still, many experts predict that this kind of technology will soon pose a serious competitive threat to the current telephone infrastructure.

Internet messaging systems aren't limited to voice. Several programs make it possible to carry on two-way *video teleconferences*—provided you have a video camera and a high-speed Internet connection for each computer. With high-powered hardware, it's even possible to have multi-person videoconferences through the Web. The video images may be small, grainy, and jerky, but they're bound to get better as the technology matures.

Telnet and FTP

To find and retrieve information located on remote sites, Net explorers have long used two software tools: *remote login* and *file transfer*. **Remote login** allows users to connect to hosts all over the world from just about anywhere. It also allows travelers to connect to their home servers—for example, to check email, from just about anywhere. The protocol that makes remote login possible is called *telnet*. Telnet is also the name of the UNIX command for remote login and the name of a program that executes the telnet command from directly connected PCs and Macs.

In the pre-Web days telnet was the best way to find and explore on-line archives of software and data files. Today anyone with a Web browser can explore those software archives using mouse clicks rather than typed commands. The Internet's **file transfer protocol (FTP)** allows users to *download* files from remote sites to their computers— and to *upload* files they want to share from their computers to these archives. Several programs, including popular Web browsers, put a friendly face on FTP, allowing you to

Telnet lets you log in to a computer almost anywhere on the Internet just as if you were using a terminal directly connected to the computer.

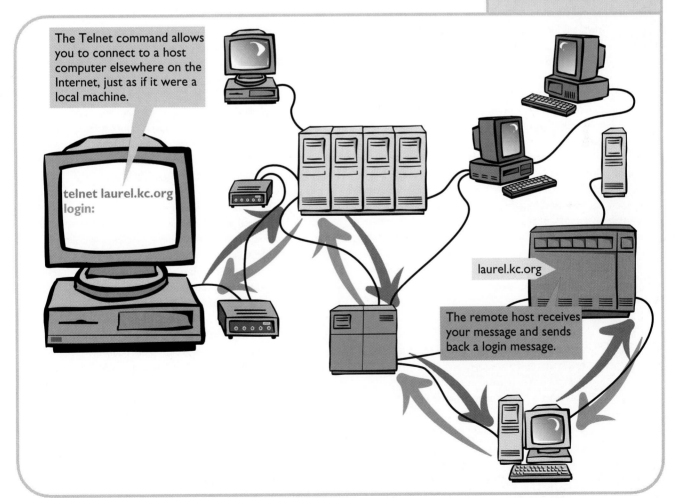

The Telnet command allows you to connect to a host computer elsewhere on the Internet, just as if it were a local machine.

telnet laurel.kc.org
login:

laurel.kc.org

The remote host receives your message and sends back a login message.

Netiquette

The Internet is a new type of community that uses new forms of communication. Like any society the Net has rules and guidelines of acceptable behavior. If you follow these rules of netiquette, you'll be doing your part to make life on the Net easier for everybody—especially yourself.

▶ *Say what you mean, and say it with care.* Once you send something electronically, there's no way to call it back. Compose each message carefully, and make sure it means what you intend it to mean. If you're replying to a message, double-check the heading to make sure your reply is going only to those people you intend to send it to. Even if you took only a few seconds to write your message, it may be broadcast far and wide and be preserved forever in on-line archives.

▶ *Keep it short and to the point.* Include a descriptive subject line, and limit the body to a screen or two. If you're replying to a long message, include a copy of the relevant part of the message—but not the whole message. Remember that many people receive hundreds of email messages each day and they're more likely to read and respond to short ones.

▶ *Proofread your messages.* A famous *New Yorker* cartoon by Peter Steiner shows one dog telling another, "On the Internet no one knows you're a dog." You may not be judged by the color of your hair or the clothes you wear when you're posting messages, but that doesn't mean appearances aren't important. Other people will judge your intelligence and education by the spelling, grammar, punctuation, and clarity of your messages. If you want your messages to be taken seriously, present your best face.

▶ *Learn the "nonverbal" language of the Net.* A simple phrase like "Nice job!" can have very different meanings depending on the tone of voice and body language behind it. Since body language and tone of voice can't easily be stuffed into a modem, on-line communities have developed text-based substitutes, sometimes called emoticons. Here are a few:

:-)	These three characters represent a smiling face. (To see why, look at them with this page rotated 90° to the right.) "Smilie" suggests the previous remark should not be taken seriously. (The dash is optional.)
;-)	This winking smilie usually means the previous remark was flirtatious or sarcastic.
:-(	This frowning character suggests something is bothering the author—probably the previous statement in the message.
:-I	This character represents indifference.
:->	This usually follows an extremely biting sarcastic remark.
:-P	This one is sticking its tongue out as if to say, "I'm grossed out!"
<g>	People who don't like smilies use this to say "grin."
ROTFL	This is short for "rolling on the floor laughing"; it's one of hundreds of keystroke-saving acronyms.

BTW	This one means "by the way."
IMHO	This one says "in my humble opinion."
Flame on	This statement, inspired by a comic book hero, warns readers that the following statements are inflammatory.
Flame off	This means the tirade is over.
<rant>	The angle brackets make this emoticon look like HTML, the page description language of the Web; this one means "beginning of rant."
</rant>	Using the HTML convention, this means "end of rant."

▶ *Keep your cool.* Many otherwise timid people turn into raging bulls when they're on line. The facelessness of Internet communication makes it all too easy to shoot from the hip, over state arguments, and get caught up in a digital lynch-mob mentality. Emotional responses are fine as long as they don't cause hurt feelings or spread half-truths. On line or off, freedom of speech is a right that carries responsibility.

▶ *Don't be a source of spam.* Internet junk mail is known as spam because it can be just as annoying and repetitive as this list of menu choices recited by a waitress in a skit by Monty Python's Flying Circus: "Well there's egg and bacon; egg, sausage and bacon; egg and spam; bacon and spam; egg, bacon, sausage and spam; spam, bacon, sausage and spam; spam, egg, spam, spam, bacon and spam; spam, spam, spam, egg and spam; spam, spam, spam, spam, spam, spam, baked beans, spam, spam, spam and spam; or lobster thermidor aux crevettes with a mornay sauce garnished with truffle paté, brandy and a fried egg on top of spam." It's so easy to send multiple copies of electronic mail that many networkers generate mountains of email and newsgroup postings. Target your messages carefully; if you're trying to sell tickets to a local concert, don't broadcast the message worldwide.

▶ *Lurk before you leap.* People who silently monitor mailing lists and newsgroups without posting messages are called lurkers. There's no shame in lurking, especially if you're new to a group—it can help you to figure out what's appropriate. After you've learned the culture and conventions of a group, you'll be better able to contribute constructively and wisely.

▶ *Check your FAQs.* Many newsgroups and mailing lists have FAQs (pronounced "facks")—posted lists of frequently asked questions. These lists keep groups from being cluttered with the same old questions and answers, but only if members take advantage of them.

▶ *Give something back.* The Internet is populated with volunteers who answer beginner questions, archive files, moderate newgroups, maintain public servers, and provide other helpful services that make the internet valuable and fun for the rest of us. If you appreciate the work these volunteers do, tell them in words, and show them in actions—do your part to help the Internet community.

locate and transfer files without typing commands. When you click on a Web link that downloads a file, you're probably using FTP.

Most files in Net archives are *compressed*—made smaller using special encoding schemes. File **compression** saves storage space on disk and saves transmission time when files are transferred through networks. (See Chapter 7 for more on compression.) Once files are downloaded to a PC, they have to be decompressed before they can be used. You don't need to know how compression works to take advantage of it; software makes the process automatic and transparent.

Inside the World Wide Web

Tim Berners-Lee, inventor of the World Wide Web, is now at MIT, where he heads the World Wide Web Consortium (W3C), a standards-setting organization dedicated to helping the Web evolve in positive directions rather than disintegrating into incompatible factions.

The dream behind the Web is of a common information space in which we communicate by sharing information.

—Tim Berners-Lee, **creator of the World Wide Web**

The **World Wide Web (WWW)** is a distributed browsing and searching system originally developed at CERN (European Laboratory for Particle Physics) by research scientist Tim Berners-Lee. The Internet had been around for years, but it wasn't easy for people to share the information on all of those networked computers. Berners-Lee wanted to create a system that would allow one-click access to documents stored on remote computers. He designed a system for giving Internet documents unique addresses, wrote the HTML language for encoding and displaying documents, and built a software browser for viewing those documents from remote locations. Rather than trying to "own" these inventions, he made them freely available to the public.

Since it was introduced in 1993, the Web has become phenomenally popular as a system for exploring, viewing, and publishing multimedia documents on the Net. When he created the Web, Tim Berners-Lee turned the Internet into a mass medium.

Browsing the Web

The web was built by millions of people simply because they wanted it, without need, greed, fear, hierarchy, authority figures, ethnic identification, advertising, or any form of manipulation. Nothing like this ever happened before in history. We can be blasé about it now, but it is what we will be remembered for. We have been made aware of a new dimension of human potential.

—Jaron Lanier, **virtual reality pioneer**

Science and art belong to the whole world, and before them vanish the barriers of nationality.

—Johann Wolfgang von Goethe

At the heart of the Web is the concept of **hypertext**. A Web document, called a **Web page**, is typically made up of text and images, like a page in a book. A collection of related pages stored on the same **Web server** is called a **Web site**; the main entry page to

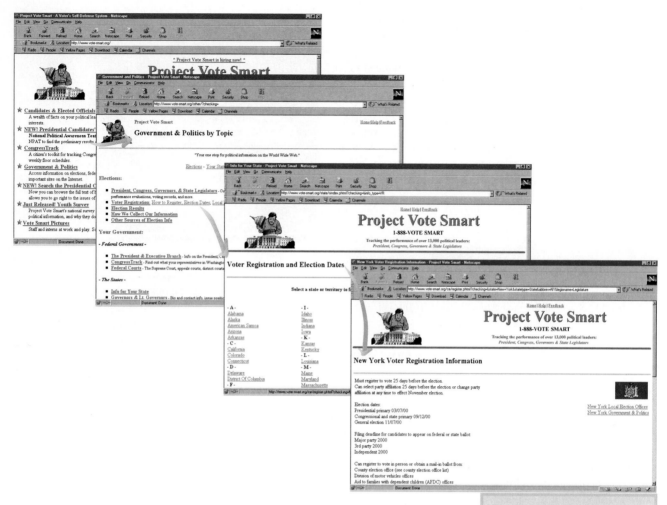

Hypertext links make it easy to jump from one Web page to another until you find the information you need.

a Web site is called the site's home page. The best way to navigate and view Web pages is with a Web browser—a client program like Netscape Communicator or Internet Explorer—which allows you to explore the Web by clicking on hyperlinks—words or pictures that act as buttons, allowing you to explore with mouse clicks. Text links are typically, but not always, underlined and displayed in a different color than standard text on the page. The World Wide Web is like a giant, constantly changing hypermedia document created by thousands of unrelated authors and scattered about in computers all over the world.

You can explore an amazing variety of Web pages by clicking on links. But this kind of random jumping isn't without frustrations. Many links lead to cobwebs—Web pages that haven't been kept up to date by their owners—and dead-ends—pages that have been removed or moved. It can also be frustrating to try to find your way back to pages you've seen on the Web. That's why browsers have *Back* and *Forward buttons*; you can retrace your steps and re-retrace your steps as often as you like. These buttons won't help, though, if you're trying to find an important page from an earlier session. Most browsers include tools for keeping personal lists of memorable sites, called *bookmarks* or *favorites*. When you run across a page worth revisiting, you can mark it with a Bookmark or Favorite command. Then you can revisit that site anytime by selecting it from the list.

Web Addresses

The Web is built around a naming scheme that allows every information resource on the Internet to be referred to using a uniform resource locator or, as it's more commonly

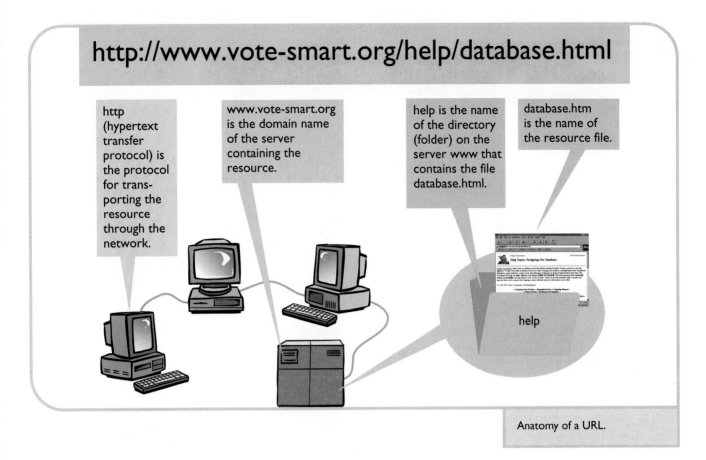

http://www.vote-smart.org/help/database.html

http (hypertext transfer protocol) is the protocol for trans-porting the resource through the network.

www.vote-smart.org is the domain name of the server containing the resource.

help is the name of the directory (folder) on the server www that contains the file database.html.

database.htm is the name of the resource file.

help

Anatomy of a URL.

known, URL. Like email addresses, URLs look strange, but they're not hard to read once you understand the general scheme. Here's a typical URL:

```
http://www.prenhall.com/beekman/help/
```

The first part of this URL refers to the protocol that must be used to access information; it might be FTP, news, or something else. It's most commonly *http*, for *hypertext trans-fer protocol*, the protocol used to transfer Web pages across the net. The second part (the part following the //) is the address of the host containing the resource; it uses the same domain-naming scheme used for email addresses. The third part, following the dot address, describes the path to the particular resource on the host—the hierarchical nesting of directories (folders) that contain the resource.

Even if you don't understand the details of how URLs are constructed, they're easy enough to use; you just type the exact URL and let your Web browser do the rest. Of course, once you've reached the requested site, there's nothing to stop you from clicking on links that take you to other interesting-looking sites. . . .

Searching the Web: Search Engines and Portals

> The ability to ask the right question is more than half the battle of finding the answer.
>
> —Thomas J. Watson

With its vast storehouses of useful information, the Web is like a huge library. Unfortunately, the Web is a poorly organized library; you might find information on a particular topic almost anywhere. (What can you expect from a library where nobody's in charge?)

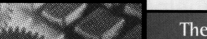

The World Wide Web

① When you type a URL into the location box of your Web browser, the browser sends a message through the Internet to the server with the specified domain name www.requestfiles.com. The message requests a particular file from the server: request file.

www.xyz123.com

② The server responds by sending the specified file to the client browser. The file is an HTML file containing the text contents of the requested Web page along with HTML codes for formatting and adding other elements to the page. Because HTML files are all text, they're small and easy to transmit through the Internet.

<H1> xyz123 </H1> <IMG

③ The browser reads the HTML file and interprets the HTML commands, called *tags*, embedded in angle brackets <like this>. It uses the formatting tags to determine the look and layout of the text on the page. For example, <H1> indicates a level-one heading to be displayed in large text; <I> indicates italics, and so on.

Server

④ The HTML file doesn't contain pictures; it's a text file. But it does contain a tag specifying where a picture file is stored and where in the page it is to be displayed. The server responds to this tag by sending the requested graphics files.

Server

⑤ The HTML file also contains a tag indicating a hyperlink to another document with a URL on another server. When the user clicks on that link, a message is sent to the new server, and the process of building a Web page in the browser window starts anew.

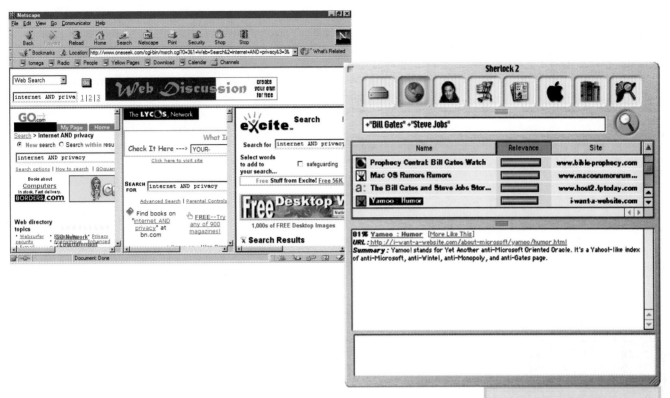

Search Engines

If you're looking for a specific information resource, but you don't know where it is located on the Web, you might be able to find it using a **search engine**. A search engine is built around a database that catalogs Web locations based on content. Most search engines use *software agents*, sometimes called *spiders, software robots*, or just *bots*, to explore the Web, retrieve information, and add it to the database. For some search engines, researchers organize and evaluate Web sites in databases; other search engines are almost completely automated. The quality and usefulness of a search engine depends in part on the information in its database. But it also depends on the search engine's user interface. The Web offers a variety of search engines with different kinds of user interfaces for extracting information from their databases.

To find information with a typical search engine, you type a query using keywords, just as you might locate information in other types of databases. (Recall *The User's View* example in Chapter 8.) You can construct complex queries using *Boolean logic* (for example, American AND Indian BUT NOT Cleveland), quotations, and other tools for refining queries. A search engine can easily produce a list of hundreds or thousands of *hits*—pages that contain requested keywords or match a query. Most search engines attempt to list pages in order from best to worst, but these automatic rankings aren't always reliable.

Another popular way to use a search engine is to repeatedly narrow the search using a *directory* or *subject tree*—a hierarchical catalog of Web sites compiled by researchers. The search engine at Yahoo! is probably the best-known example. A screen presents you with a menu of subject choices. When you click on a subject—say, Government—you narrow your search to that subject, and you're presented with a menu of subcategories within that subject—Military, Politics, Law, Taxes, and so on. You can continue to narrow your search by proceeding through subject menus until you reach a list of selected Web sites related to the final subject. The sites are usually rank-ordered by researchers based on their value. The list of Web sites on a given index page is not usually exhaustive—there may be hundreds of pages related to the subject that aren't included in any directory. It's simply not possible to keep a complete index of all the pages on the ever-changing Web.

Meta-search engines like OneSeek and Sherlock coordinate searches using multiple search engines and directories.

Natural language search engines allow users to ask for what they want in plain English—or some other human language. For example, Ask Jeeves accepts typed questions on almost any subject and does a surprisingly good job of finding Web sites with relevant information.

There are at least a dozen major search engine sites, and each is particularly well suited for certain types of tasks. A page might go undetected by one search engine and appear at the top of a list on another. That's why many researchers use *meta-search engines* like MetaCrawler and OneSeek—software tools that conduct parallel searches using several different search engines and directories. The Windows and Macintosh operating systems contain meta-search engines that scan the Web without opening a browser.

Portals

Many Web sites that started out as search engines have evolved into **portals**—Web entry stations that offer quick and easy access to a variety of services. Popular general-interest portals include Yahoo!, Excite, Lycos, Alta-Vista, Netscape Netcenter, and Snap. A typical *consumer portal* might include a search engine, an email service, chat rooms, references such as maps and encyclopedias, news and sports headlines, shopping malls, other services, and advertisements—many of the same things found in on-line services like AOL. Many portals can be personalized so they automatically display local weather conditions, sports scores for favorite teams, current prices for particular stocks, news headlines related to particular subjects, horoscopes, and ads targeted toward the user's interests. Many Web users use portals as their home base whenever they're on the Web. Most browsers allow users to choose a home page that opens by default whenever the browser is launched; portals are designed with this feature in mind.

In addition to these general interest portals, the Web has a growing population of specialized portals. *Corporate portals* on intranets serve the employees of particular corporations. *Vertical portals*, or *vortals*, like vertical market software (Chapter 3), are targeted at members of a particular industry or economic sector. For example, *webmd* is a portal for medically-minded consumers and health-care professionals. In coming years you're likely to see all kinds of specialized portals competing to be your browser's home page.

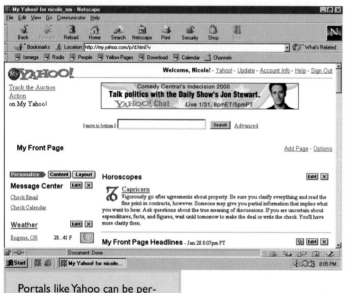

Portals like Yahoo can be personalized to highlight weather, news, sports, and financial headlines specified by the user.

From Hypertext to Multimedia

We are still a multimedia organism. If we want to push the envelope of complexity further, we have to use all of our devices for accessing information—not all of which are rational.

—Psychologist Mihaly Csikszentmihalyi

Way back in the early 1990s (!) the first World Wide Web pages were straight hypertext. Within a couple of years graphics were common, and a few cutting-edge Web pages allowed browsers to download scratchy video and audio clips to their hard disks. Today color graphics and simple animation are everywhere, and a typical Web page can contain any or all of these:

▶ *Tables* whose rows and columns contain neatly laid out text and graphical elements.

▶ *Frames* that divide a Web browser's viewing area into smaller areas, allowing you to scroll and view different parts of a page—or even multiple pages—simultaneously.

▶ *Forms* that can be filled in by page visitors who want to order goods and services, respond to questionnaires, enter contests, express opinions, or add comments to ongoing discussions.

▶ *Downloadable audio* in the form of sound and music clips that must be downloaded onto your computer's hard disk before they can be played by the browser or some other application. Web sound files are compressed so they'll download in a reasonable amount of time. (See Chapter 7.) Some types of audio compression cause significant sound quality degradation. But MP3 compression produces music files that are near CD quality. MP3 downloads are popular with music lovers in search of new sounds and musicians looking for new fans. Companies have responded to the demand by creating everything from jukebox-style MP3 player software to portable MP3 players. There's a downside to the MP3 phenomenon though: Many MP3 files on the Web are illegal copies of copyrighted recordings, making potential criminals of everyone from the Web site owners to the people downloading the music. (Copyrights are discussed in more detail in the next chapter.)

▶ *Downloadable video* clips are also available for viewing on your computer. Many are small, short, and jerky, but quality is rapidly improving as new video compression technologies mature. These raise the same copyright issues as music clips.

▶ *Streaming audio* and *streaming video* are sounds and moving pictures that happen automatically while the page is viewed—provided, of course, that you have a fast connection and Internet traffic doesn't interfere. Streaming media, unlike down-loaded media, can be viewed or heard within seconds, because they play while they're being downloaded. For the same reason, streaming media files don't need to be limited to short clips; movie-length streaming programs are common.

▶ *Real-time live audio or video* broadcasts, or Webcasts, of concerts, news events, speeches, and other events that use technology similar to streaming media players.

▶ *3-D environments,* drawn or photographed, that can be explored with mouse clicks, creating a sort of primitive virtual reality.

Today new Web ideas appear at an astounding rate—so fast that browser makers have trouble keeping up. Fortunately, the most popular browsers can be enhanced with plug-ins—software extensions that add new features. When a company introduces a Web innovation—say, a new type of 3-D animation—it typically makes a free plug-in available at the same time. Once you download the plug-in and install it in your browser, you can take advantage of any Web pages that include the innovation. Popular plug-ins become standard features in future browser versions, so they eventually don't need to be downloaded and installed. Even if a browser can't play or display a particular type of graphics, animation, audio, or video by itself, it might be able to offload the task to a helper application—a separate program designed to present that particular media type.

The most popular free cross-platform plug-ins and helper applications include:

▶ *RealPlayer* (Real) is the most popular software for playing streaming audio and video, including live Webcasts.

▶ *QuickTime* (Apple) is versatile multimedia software that can play video, animation, many types of audio, streaming media, live Webcasts, and navigable virtual reality environments.

▶ *Shockwave/Flash* (Macromedia) plug-ins allow compressed interactive multimedia documents and animations created with Director and other Macromedia authoring tools to be presented through a Web browser.

▶ *Acrobat* (Adobe) displays documents in *Portable Document Format (PDF)* so they look the same on the screen as on paper, even if viewed on computers that don't have the same fonts installed.

Webcasting: Push Technology

> We think we "surf" the Web now, but what we really do is hopscotch across fragile stepping-stones of texts, or worse, spelunk in a vast unmapped cave of documents. Only when waves of media begin to cascade behind our screens—huge swells of unbrowsable stuff—will we truly surf.
>
> —Kevin Kelly and Gary Wolf, *Wired* editors

The Web was built with pull technology—browsers on client computers "pull" information from server machines. With pull technology the browser needs to initiate a request before any information is delivered. But for some applications it makes more sense to have information delivered automatically to the client computer. That's the way push technology, or webcasting, works. With push technology you subscribe to a service or specify the kinds of information you want to receive and the server delivers that information periodically and unobtrusively. Maybe you want up-to-the-minute weather maps displayed in a small window in the corner of your screen. Or you might prefer to see news headlines (on subjects of your choice) scroll across the top of your screen. You may want to automatically receive new product descriptions from companies you do business with. Or you might like to have the software on your hard disk automatically upgraded when upgrades are posted on the Web. All of this is possible today with push technology.

Technically speaking, today's push technology is really pull technology in disguise. Your computer quietly and automatically pulls information from selected Web servers based on your earlier requests or subscriptions. As convenient as they are, push programs have the same basic problem as Web search engines: They give you what they think you want, but they aren't very smart. Their ability to deliver what you really need—without bombarding you with unwanted data—will get better as artificial intelligence technology improves. In the meantime most Internet users are shying away from most forms of push technology, email excepted.

Publishing on the Web

> The Internet draws its power from the fact that no single interest controls it . . . the Web is the only medium of unlimited free speech the world has ever had. And in some other, less-enlightened places, it will be the only taste of freedom citizens of certain countries will ever have.
>
> —Andrew Gore, *Macworld* executive editor

As inviting as it is to explore the Web, it's even more exciting to create your own home pages and publish them on the Web. Most Web pages are created using a language called HTML (hypertext markup language). An HTML *source document* is a text file that includes codes that describe the format, layout, and logical structure of a hypermedia document. HTML isn't WYSIWYG; the HTML codes embedded in the document make it look cryptic, hard to read, and nothing like the final page displayed on the screen. But these codes allow your Web browser to translate an HTML source document into that finished page. And because it's just a text file, an HTML document can be easily transmitted from a Web server to a client machine anywhere on the Internet. See *The User's View* box on pages 286–287.   **UV**

You can create a Web page with any word processor or text editor; you just type the HTML commands along with the rest of the text. But you don't need to write HTML code to create a Web page. Many programs, including Microsoft Word and FileMaker, can automatically convert basic document format features (like character styles, indentation, and

Working the Web

The Web is so easy to navigate that it's tempting to just dive in. But like a large library the Web has more to offer if you learn a few tricks and techniques. Your goals should dictate your Web strategy.

▶ *Handle URLs with care.* The fastest way to get to a known page is to type its URL into the browser's location box. Type with care; even a single mistyped character can make a URL worthless. If you glean a URL from an email message or another electronic source use the Copy and Paste commands to transfer the URL. Or, if the application allows it, just double-click on the highlighted URL to launch your browser and take you there automatically.

▶ *Get to know your search engines.* Try several, choose your favorites, and learn the more advanced search features so you can minimize the time it takes to find what you're looking for.

▶ *If you're in a hurry, dispense with frills.* Graphic images can take a long time to download on a low-speed Internet connection or during a high-traffic period. If you don't need the pictures, your browser's text-only option can save time loading pages that aren't dependent on graphics for their content.

▶ *Organize your favorite bookmarks.* When you find a page worth revisiting, record it on your list of favorites or bookmarks. Browsers allow you to organize your lists by category—a strategy that's far more effective than just throwing them all in a digital shoebox.

▶ *Be selective.* As Robert P. Lipshutz wrote in *Mobile Computing,* "A few tidbits of accurate, timely and useful information are worth much more than a ream of random data, and bad information is worse than no information at all." When you're assessing a Web page's credibility, consider the author, the writing, the references, and the page sponsor's objectivity and reliability.

▶ *Protect your privacy.* Many Web servers keep track of all kinds of data about you: what site you visited before you came, where you clicked, and more. When you fill out forms to enter contests, order goods, or leave messages, you're providing more data for your hosts. Don't divulge any private information about yourself. And make sure you don't leave tracks that you're ashamed of as you hip-hop around the Web.

▶ *Be conscious of cookies.* Many Web servers send cookies to your browser when you visit them or perform other actions. Cookies are tidbits of information about your session that can be read later; they allow Web sites to remember what they know about you between sessions. Cookies make personalized portals and customized shopping experiences possible. Unfortunately, Cookies can also provide all kinds of possibilities for snoopers who want to know how you spend your time on line. By default, most browsers don't tell you when they leave a cookie. It's easy to change browser settings so your browser will refuse all cookies or ask you, on a cookie-by-cookie basis, whether to accept or refuse.

▶ *Shop with bots.* Bots are software robots, or agents, that can explore the Web and report back their findings. Several bots (such as mySimon at www.mySimon.com) are designed to help you find low prices by searching the databases of hundreds of merchants.

▶ *Shop smart.* In increasing numbers shoppers are abandoning brick-and-mortar stores for "click-and-mortar" Web stores. Online shops and auctions can save money, especially if you comparison shop. But when a product doesn't work as advertised, or when you have after-sale questions, a Web merchant might not be as helpful as a local shopkeeper. Some don't even accept phone queries. And, of course, the Web, like the nondigital world, has its share of less-than-honest merchants. Use services like bizrate (www.bizrate.com) to evaluate questionable merchants before you lay your digital money down.

▶ *Remember why you're there.* The Web's extensive hyperlinks make it all too easy to wander off course when you're searching for important information. If you browse for cool sites when you're not under deadline pressures, you won't be as distractible when deadlines loom.

▶ *Think before you publish.* It's easy to publish Web pages for the world—at least that part of the world that uses the Web. Don't put anything on your Web pages that you don't want the world to see; you may, for example, be asking for trouble if you publish your home address, your work schedule, and a photo of the the expensive computer system in your study. Plan you Web site using a good Web design book so your pages communicate effectively and aesthetically.

---

justification) into HTML codes. Some *Web authoring programs,* like Macromedia Dreamweaver, Adobe GoLive, and Microsoft FrontPage work like WYSIWYG page layout programs used by desktop publishers. You can lay out text and graphics exactly the way you want them to look, and the program converts the layout into an HTML document. The document will look similar to your original layout when viewed through a Web browser. The best of these Web authoring programs allow you to manage entire Web sites, like the one that accompanies this book, using tools that can automate repetitive edits, apply formatting styles across pages, and check for bad links. Some even have tools for connecting large sites to databases containing critical, rapidly changing content.

The User's View

Building a Web Site

SOFTWARE   **Macromedia Dreamweaver and Microsoft Internet Explorer.**

THE GOAL   **To create a Web site to represent a small service business.**

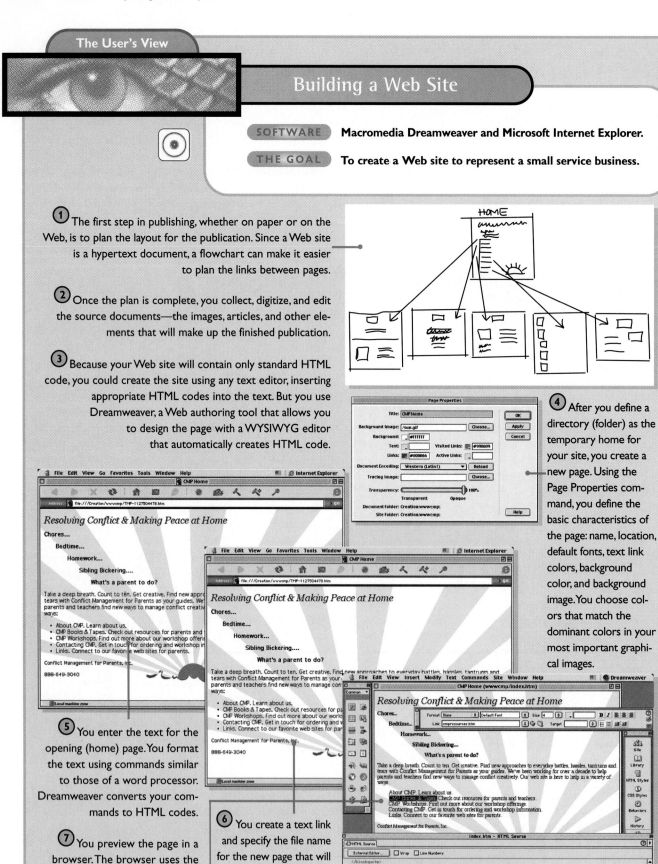

① The first step in publishing, whether on paper or on the Web, is to plan the layout for the publication. Since a Web site is a hypertext document, a flowchart can make it easier to plan the links between pages.

② Once the plan is complete, you collect, digitize, and edit the source documents—the images, articles, and other elements that will make up the finished publication.

③ Because your Web site will contain only standard HTML code, you could create the site using any text editor, inserting appropriate HTML codes into the text. But you use Dreamweaver, a Web authoring tool that allows you to design the page with a WYSIWYG editor that automatically creates HTML code.

④ After you define a directory (folder) as the temporary home for your site, you create a new page. Using the Page Properties command, you define the basic characteristics of the page: name, location, default fonts, text link colors, background color, and background image. You choose colors that match the dominant colors in your most important graphical images.

⑤ You enter the text for the opening (home) page. You format the text using commands similar to those of a word processor. Dreamweaver converts your commands to HTML codes.

⑥ You create a text link and specify the file name for the new page that will be linked to that text.

⑦ You preview the page in a browser. The browser uses the HTML codes to construct a page that's similar to the design you created.

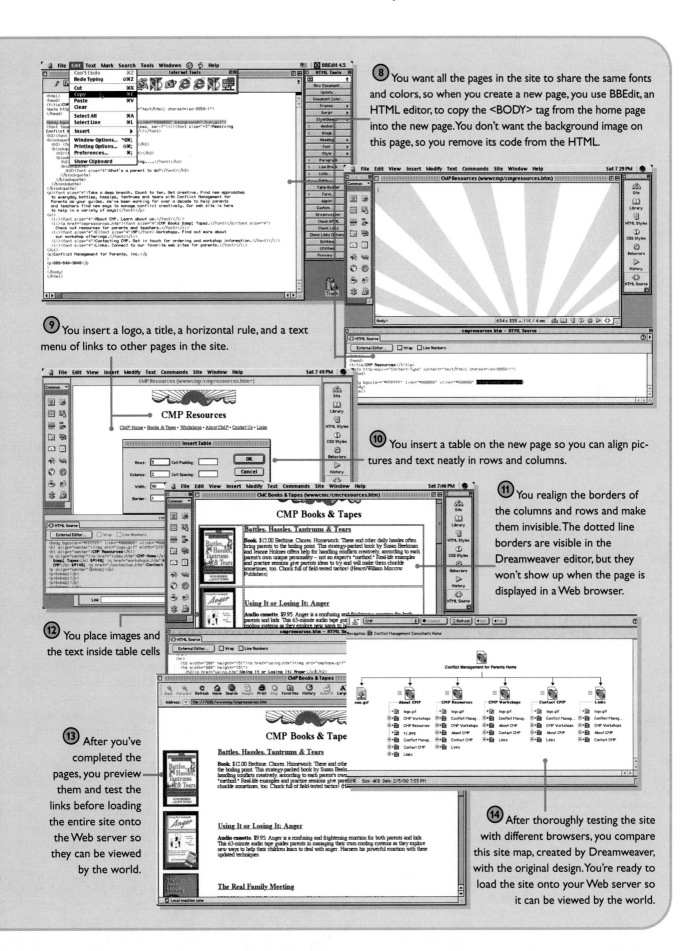

⑧ You want all the pages in the site to share the same fonts and colors, so when you create a new page, you use BBEdit, an HTML editor, to copy the <BODY> tag from the home page into the new page. You don't want the background image on this page, so you remove its code from the HTML.

⑨ You insert a logo, a title, a horizontal rule, and a text menu of links to other pages in the site.

⑩ You insert a table on the new page so you can align pictures and text neatly in rows and columns.

⑪ You realign the borders of the columns and rows and make them invisible. The dotted line borders are visible in the Dreamweaver editor, but they won't show up when the page is displayed in a Web browser.

⑫ You place images and the text inside table cells

⑬ After you've completed the pages, you preview them and test the links before loading the entire site onto the Web server so they can be viewed by the world.

⑭ After thoroughly testing the site with different browsers, you compare this site map, created by Dreamweaver, with the original design. You're ready to load the site onto your Web server so it can be viewed by the world.

Once you've created an HTML document, you can (if your Internet service allows it) upload it onto a Web server for the world to see. Never before has a communication medium made it so easy or inexpensive for an individual to reach such a wide audience. It doesn't matter whether you're a student, a poet, an artist, a government official, a labor organizer, or a corporate president. On the Web all URLs are created equal. In the words of writer Howard Rheingold, the World Wide Web "might be important in the same way that the printing press was important. By expanding the number of people who have the power to transmit knowledge, the Web might trigger a power shift that changes everything."

Beyond HTML

Standard HTML wasn't designed to support interactive multimedia, financial transaction processing, and everything else that's emerging on the Web. The HTML standard has been revised several times to incorporate new features and media types. But at its heart HTML is still a static language designed for page layout, not programming.

Newer versions of HTML, sometimes called *dynamic HTML*, allow HTML code to automatically modify itself under certain circumstances. Dynamic HTML supports cascading style sheets which can define formatting and layout features that aren't recognized in older versions of HTML. Dynamic HTML also recognizes *scripts*—short programs—that can add interactivity, animation, and other dynamic features to Web pages. Scripts are typically written in *JavaScript*, a simple scripting language developed by Netscape. Web pages that take advantage of the latest dynamic HTML features can be more interesting and interactive, but only if viewed with new, full-featured browsers.

People who view the Web using personal communicators, handheld computers, pagers, and telephones don't need dynamic, dazzling pages—they need small, simple, succinct presentations of critical information. That's what *WML (wireless markup language)* is for. Like its less versatile predecessor, *HDML (handheld device markup language)*, WML is designed for creating Web documents that contain stock quotes, phone numbers, and other small but important nuggets of information.

Many experts expect HTML to be replaced by *XML (extensible markup language)*, which includes all of HTML's features plus many additional, powerful extensions. XML allows Web developers to control and display data the way they now control text and graphics. Forms, database queries, and other data-intensive operations that can't be completely constructed with standard HTML will be much easier with XML. The main problem with XML is that it isn't completely backward compatible with HTML. That is, all of those pages created in HTML won't work with an XML-only browser. In early 2000 the W3C standards group approved a specification for *XHTML (extensible HTML)*, a hybrid language that is XML-capable and HTML-compatible.

The W3C is also developing a standard for SMIL (synchronized multimedia integration language), an HTML-like language designed to make it possible to link time-based streaming media so, for example, sounds, video, and animation can be tightly integrated with each other. For certain specialized applications, other alternatives to HTML already exist. For example, *VRML (virtual reality modeling language)* allows Web page authors to create 3-D virtual worlds that can be easily viewed and explored with VRML-ready browsers.

So far XML, WML, and VRML are used by relatively few Web authors. But even Web pages created with standard HTML can be enhanced—and programmed—in ways that HTML's developers never imagined. Probably the most important tool for transcending HTML's limitations today is *Java*, an object-oriented programming language developed by Sun Microsystems. (Java and JavaScript have little in common except their names. JavaScript is a simple scripting language for enhancing HTML Web pages; Java is a full-featured cross-platform programming language.) Small Java programs are called applets because they're like tiny applications. Java applets can be automatically downloaded onto your client computer through almost any modern Web browser. A Java *applet* is platform independent; it will run on a Windows PC, a Mac, a UNIX workstation, or anything else as long as the client machine has *Java Virtual Machine (JVM)* software installed. This JVM software is built into most modern browsers.

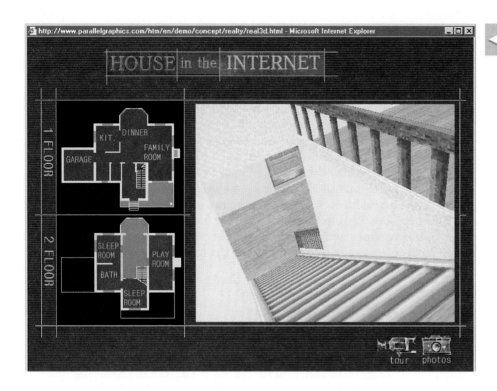

Most early Java applets did little more than display simple interactive animations on Web pages. But more serious applets are appearing all the time. IBM is investing millions of dollars in Java software development because Java promises to unify its diverse hardware product catalog with a standard software platform.

The Evolving Internet

> In the short term, the impact of new technologies like the Internet will be
> ## less than the hype would suggest. But in the long term, it will be vastly
> ### larger than we can imagine today.
>
> —Paul Saffo, **director of the Institute for the Future**

The Internet started as a small community of scientists, engineers, and other researchers who staunchly defended the noncommercial, cooperative charter of the network. Today the Net has swollen into a community of millions, including everybody from children to corporate executives. The rate of growth is so great that it raises questions about the Internet's ability to keep up; the amount of information transmitted may eventually be more than the Net can handle.

The Internet is constantly being expanded to handle increased traffic, but the U.S. government no longer assumes primary responsibility for that expansion. Many funding and administrative duties have been passed on to private companies, allowing businesses to commercialize the Net. In 1995, for the first time, the number of commercial host sites on the Net exceeded the number of noncommercial sites. In the 3-year period that followed, the Net experienced a hundredfold increase in monthly traffic.

Internet2 and the Next Generation Internet

As the Internet evolves into the network of the masses, congestion becomes more problematic for the scientists and researchers who made up the original Internet community.

The U.S. government, working in conjunction with MCI, Qwest, Cisco, and Nortel corporations, launched an alternative Internet, Internet2, in 1998 to provide faster network communications for universities and research institutions. "Today's Internet is one-size-fits-all," says Cherri Pancake, an Oregon State University Computer Scientist involved in the Internet2 project. "We need a new design for the Internet, one that takes into account the fact that some transmissions have special requirements. That's what the new Internet2 effort is all about." A related effort from DARPA, the *Next Generation Internet (NGI)*, will consist of a nationwide web of optical fiber integrated with intelligent management software to maintain high-speed connections.

Internet2 will eventually be capable of transmitting data at 9.6 billion bits per second—enough to transmit all 30 volumes of the *Encyclopaedia Britannica* in 1 second. Internet2 isn't available for commercial or recreational use; it is reserved for research and academic work. Participating universities are building virtual laboratories, digital libraries, telemedicine research facilities, and distance learning applications that take advantage of its tremendous bandwidth. The rest of us will undoubtedly inherit the technologies developed for Internet2.

Internet Issues: Ethical and Political Dilemmas

The Internet still hasn't figured out how to conduct itself in public....

Everybody is trying to develop the rules by which they can conduct themselves in order to keep a civil operation going and not self-destruct.

—**George Lucas, filmmaker**

The commercialization of the Internet has opened a floodgate of new services to users. People are logging into the Internet to read news and sports updates, view weather patterns, play games, subscribe to electronic magazines, book flights, order clothes, buy stocks, sell cars, track deliveries, listen to radio broadcasts from around the world, conduct videoconferences, coordinate disaster recovery programs, chart scientific data, and do countless other private and public transactions. The Internet saves time, money, and lives, but it brings problems, too.

Computer Addiction

For a few hard-core networkers the world on the other side of the modem is more real and more interesting than the everyday physical world. One Alaskan reader wrote to advice columnist Ann Landers: "Computer chat lines can become every bit as addictive as cocaine. I have been hooked on both, and it was easier to get off coke." While this may seem strange, it's not unique. Many people feel the same way about television, spectator sports, or romance novels. *Internet addiction*, like any addiction, can be a serious problem—for individuals and for society. The problem is growing as more people go on line, and there are no quick fixes in sight.

Freedom's Abuses

Commercialization has brought capitalism's dark side to the Internet. Electronic junk mail scams, get-rich-quick hoaxes, on-line credit-card thefts, email forgery, child pornography hustling, illegal gambling, Web site sabotage, on-line stalking, and other sleazy activities abound. The Internet has clearly lost its innocence.

Some of these problems have at least partial technological solutions. Concerned parents and teachers can now install *filtering software* that, for the most part, keeps children out of Web sites that contain inappropriate content. Commercial Web sites routinely use encryption so customers can purchase goods and services without fear of having our credit-card numbers stolen by electronic eavesdroppers. Several software companies and banks are developing systems for circulating digital cash on the Internet to make on-line transactions easier and safer. To protect against email forgery, many software companies are working together to hammer out standards for *digital signatures* using encryption techniques described in the next chapter.

Many problems associated with the rapid growth and commercialization of the Internet are social problems that raise important political questions. On-line hucksterism and pornography have prompted government controls on Internet content, including the 1996 Communications Decency Act. Opponents to this law and other proposed controls argue that it's important to preserve the free flow of information; they stress the need to protect our rights to free speech and privacy on the Net. In 1996 the U.S. Supreme Court declared the Communications Decency Act unconstitutional, arguing that "the interest in encouraging freedom of expression in a democratic society outweighs any theoretical but unproven benefit of censorship." Nevertheless, the legal battle is certain to continue.

Questions about human rights on line probably won't be resolved by legislators and judges, though. The Internet's global reach makes it nearly impossible for a single government to regulate it. And even if the governments of the world agree to try to restrict information flow, the Net seems to have developed a mind of its own. The same decentralized, packet-switching technology that was designed to protect government messages from enemy attack today protects civilian messages from government or corporate control. In the words of Internet pioneer John Gilmore, "The Net interprets censorship as damage and routes around it."

Universal Access Issues

In the 1992 U.S. presidential election Bill Clinton and Al Gore campaigned for a *National Information Infrastructure (NII)*. The NII concept was embraced by Congress and the press, which dubbed it the "Information Superhighway." The NII will, in theory, connect computers, telephones, televisions, and information appliances of all types; it will have strict standards to ensure information security and privacy; it will provide "universal service" and affordable access for all; and it will be largely paid for by businesses with government seed money for trial projects.

Probably the biggest roadblock to realizing the dream of NII is the digital divide that separates computer haves from have-nots. Today less than half of the U.S. population has easy access to the Internet—a subset of America that excludes most poor people and minorities.

Government programs to wire schools, libraries, and other public facilities have increased access for disadvantaged populations. Falling computer prices help, too. But the problem of equal access isn't likely to go away without combined efforts of governments, businesses, and individuals.

Even if America achieves a universal access NII, access issues still confront the rest of the world. The Internet is a global infrastructure, but huge populations all over the world are locked out. Many experts fear that we'll leave those populations behind as we move further into the information age. This kind of information stratification could be harmful to all of us unless we find ways to unlock the Internet for everybody who wants it.

As part of the non-profit Tech Corps program, these computer professionals volunteer their time and skills to help students and teachers put technology to good use.

Internet Everywhere: The Invisible Information Infrastructure

In the future, everything with a digital heartbeat will be connected to the Internet.

Scott McNealy, **CEO of Sun Microsystems**

Where is it all heading? Vint Cerf, one of the Internet's founders, thinks it's headed for space. He's putting much of his time and energy into a project called InterPlaNet, which he hopes will extend the Internet to the other planets in our solar system. According to the plan, electronic "post offices" will orbit other planets, routing messages between space explorers, both human and robot.

Back on Earth, technology forecaster Paul Saffo suggests a blurring of the boundaries between the Web and interpersonal communication applications. When we visit a Web site that's being explored by hundreds of other people, we'll actually be able to experience their presence and interact with them in ways that go beyond today's simple chat rooms. In a *New Media* interview, Saffo predicted that "we're going to shift away from a model of people accessing information to a model of people accessing other people in an information-rich environment. The information will become the wallpaper surrounding conversational space."

We may be sharing Web space with more people in the future, but we'll also be sharing it with all kinds of gadgets. Today we think of the Web as a network of computers, but the Web isn't just for PCs, mainframes, and servers anymore. A variety of *network computers* and other *thin clients* are being connected to the Internet in offices, and Internet appliances like email telephones and set-top boxes are showing up in more and more homes. Everything from coffee makers to traffic lights may be routinely connected to the Web soon. Sun Microsystem's *Jini* programming language is designed to make it easy for these diverse devices to talk to each other. Consider the possibilities:

> *You tell your alarm clock to wake you in time to catch the 8:00 A.M. flight to Washington. At 5:00 A.M. the clock checks the airline's Web page and determines that the flight has been delayed an hour. It also checks on-line traffic reports and finds that traffic is light. The clock resets your wakeup time accordingly, giving you an extra hour of sleep. As usual, it turns on the heat and the coffee maker 10 minutes before it wakes you. On the way to the airport your car routes you around a congested construction spot. When you arrive at the airport, it tells you where to find a vacant parking spot close to the terminal.*

Whether you consider this future fantasy appealing or appalling, the technology is on the horizon. One thing is clear: The World Wide Web is changing so fast it's impossible for anybody to predict exactly what it will look like even a few months from today. To find out what's happened to the Web since this book was printed, check the Web, starting with the *Computer Confluence* Web site: www.prenhall.com/beekman.

Cyberspace: The Electronic Frontier

Cyberspace. A consensual hallucination experienced daily by billions of legitimate operators, in every nation, by children being taught mathematical concepts. . . . A graphic representation of data abstracted from the banks of every computer in the human system. Unthinkable complexity. Lines of light ranged in the nonspace of the mind, clusters and constellations of data. Like city lights, receding. . . .

—William Gibson, **in** *Neuromancer*

Cyberspace, in its present condition, has a lot in common with the 19th century West. It is vast, unmapped, culturally and legally ambiguous, verbally terse (unless you happen to be a court stenographer), hard to get around in, and up for grabs. Large institutions already claim to own the place, but most of the actual natives are solitary and independent, sometimes to the point of sociopathy. It is, of course, a perfect breeding ground for both outlaws and new ideas about liberty.

—John Perry Barlow, **writer and co-founder of the Electronic Frontier Foundation**

Science fiction writers suggest that tomorrow's networks may take us beyond the Internet, interactive TV, and videophones into an artificial reality unlike anything we've seen before. This alternative reality has come to be known as cyberspace, a term coined by William Gibson in his visionary novel *Neuromancer.*

In *Neuromancer,* as in earlier works by Verner Vinge and others, travelers experience the universal computer network as if it were a physical place, a shared virtual reality, complete with sights, sounds, and other sensations. Gibson's cyberspace is an abstract, cold landscape in a dark and dangerous future world. Vinge's novella "True Names" takes place in a network hideaway where adventurous computer wizards never reveal their true names or identities to each other. Instead, they take on mythical identities with supernatural abilities.

Today's computer networks, with their unsophisticated user interfaces and limited bandwidths, are light-years from the futuristic visions of Vinge and Gibson. Still, the Net today is a primitive cyberspace—a world where messages, mathematics, and money can cross continents in seconds. People from all over the planet meet, develop friendships, and share their innermost thoughts and feelings in cyberspace.

Writer John Perry Barlow has called the on-line world an "electronic frontier," suggesting parallels to America's Old West. Until recently the electronic frontier was populated mostly by free-spirited souls willing to forgo creature comforts. These digital pioneers built the roads and towns that are used today by less adventurous settlers.

In spite of its rapid commercialization, the electronic frontier is far from tame. Network nomads pick digital locks and ignore electronic fences. Some explore nooks and crannies out of a spirit of adventure. Others steal and tamper with private information for profit or revenge. Charlatans and hustlers operate outside the law. Law enforcement agencies and lawmakers occasionally overreact.

The electronic frontier metaphor suggests that our expanding cyberspace has its share of social problems—problems of computer crime and security that computer users, law enforcement agencies, and politicians are just beginning to understand. We'll discuss those problems and some potential solutions in later chapters.

CROSSCURRENTS

The Earth Will Don an Electronic Skin

Neil Gross

The Internet is changing so fast that it's hard to imagine what it might be like in a decade or two. In this article, edited from an article in the August 30, 1999 issue of Business Week, Neil Gross speculated that it might look more like a living organism than a technology.

The skin is an uncanny piece of engineering. It processes immense amounts of data on temperature, pressure, humidity, and texture. It registers movement in the air, gauges the size of objects by the distance between points of contact, alerts us to danger, and prepares us for pleasure. But the skin does more than register superficial events—it's a controller. It sends signals to regulate blood flow, activate sweat glands, alert immune cells to marauding invaders, and block ultraviolet light. Even when skin dies, it is utilitarian: Dead cells accumulate in layers to prevent unwanted penetration.

In the next century, planet earth will don an electronic skin. It will use the Internet as a scaffold to support and transmit its sensations. This skin is already being stitched together. It consists of millions of embedded electronic measuring devices: thermostats, pressure gauges, pollution detectors, cameras, microphones, glucose sensors, EKGs. These will probe and monitor cities and endangered species, the atmosphere, our ships, highways and fleets of trucks, our conversations, our bodies—even our dreams.

Ten years from now, there will be trillions of such telemetric systems, each with a microprocessor brain and a radio. They'll be in constant contact with one another. But the communication won't be at our plodding verbal pace. Machines will prefer to talk at gigabit speeds and higher—so fast that humans will catch only scattered snippets of the discussion.

What will the earth's new skin permit us to feel? How will we use its surges of sensation? For several years—maybe for a decade—there will be no central nervous system to manage this vast signaling network. Certainly there will be no central intelligence. But many scientists believe that some qualities of self-awareness will emerge once the Net is sensually enhanced and emulates the complexity of the human brain.

And though silicon networks today look nothing like the brain, nodes of the Net have begun to function as neurons. Researchers have already tackled complex computing problems, such as interpreting interstellar radio signals, by parcelling computing tasks out to about a million PCs working in concert. Within 10 years, discrete microprocessors could be knitted together into ad hoc distributed computers. Don't think of these as PC networks. The terminals would just as likely be cell phones or Palm-like devices, each one far smarter than today's heftiest desktops.

Such spontaneous computer networks would be ideal breeding grounds for so-called "emergent" phenomena. The concept is championed by the Santa Fe Institute, intellectual home of physicist Murray Gell-Mann, computer scientist John H. Holland, and other architects of a discipline called "complexity." This school studies behavior that emerges from the collective activity of partly independent agents. Individual ants, for example, can't fight off an attacking wasp, but a colony can. A single brain cell is a simpleton, but a few tens of billions can perform mental miracles.

Complexity experts anticipate the occurrence of such phenomena on the Net. The whole will add up to more than the sum of its parts, says Sandia National Laboratories Senior Scientist Gerold Yonas. "At some point, a massively parallel computer will reconfigure itself," he predicts, and portions of the Net will take actions that no human engineer programmed or even planned for.

Humans won't be removed from the process, says Leonard Kleinrock, inventor of packet switching technology and architect of the Net's first node. "Millions of people contributing ideas in unforeseen ways are part of this complex adaptive system," he says, pointing to the open-source movement as proof.

Now, toss into this ecosystem a few hundred million intelligent software agents, vastly more powerful than the crude software "bots" that perform Web searches today. Add the voices and intentions of a few billion digital pets. Then stretch out a sensory fabric. "The network itself becomes a huge digital creature," says Toshitada Doi, chairman of Sony Corp.'s Digital Creatures Lab. "We will carefully design it so that it will help human beings, not harm them."

That may not be easy, however. Emergent behavior could be mischievous, even sinister. In Sandia simulations with software agents acting as communications nodes in network, the nodes have assembled themselves into clans. "In a real network, the clans might have distinct points of view," Yonas says.

By the time something like that happens, networks should gain some of the resilience and safeguards of living organisms. When the earth's skin signals danger—seismic activity, a geomagnetic storm, or a worrisome spike in financial transactions—the Net will sense it, alert people, and reroute traffic.

Critics of the Santa Fe school say it lacks a solid theoretical foundation. Supporters concede that point, but say the field is still new. "This is 21st century science," says William N. Joy, founder and chief scientist of Sun Microsystems Inc.

DISCUSSION QUESTIONS

1. Do the predictions in this article seem farfetched? Explain your answer.
2. How do these predictions make you feel? Do you think this kind of Internet evolution would be a good thing?

Summary   Chapter Review

The Internet is a network of networks that connects all kinds of computers around the globe. It grew out of a military research network designed to provide reliable communication even if part of the network failed. The Internet uses standard protocols to allow internetwork communication to occur. No single organization owns or controls the Internet.

You can connect to the Internet in any of several ways; these ways provide different degrees of access to Internet services. A direct connection provides the most complete and fastest service, but users can also access most Internet information through terminal connections. Newer broadband connections approach direct connection speeds, but they aren't universally available. Several on-line services that aren't part of the Internet have gateways to the Internet; these gateways allow users to access Internet information resources and send and receive Internet mail.

Most Internet applications are based on the client/server model. The user interface for these applications varies depending on the type of connection and the type of client software used by the user. A user might type UNIX commands to a host computer or use point-and-click tools on a personal computer.

The most popular Internet communication service, email, uses a standard email addressing scheme so users on different networks can communicate. Mailing lists and newsgroups allow for group discussions, debates, and information sharing on particular subjects. Other communication tools allow real-time instant messaging, voice communication, and even video teleconferencing.

Millions of people use Web browsers to explore interconnected Web pages published by private companies, public institutions, and individuals. The earliest Web pages were simple hypertext pages; today the Web contains thousands of complex, media-rich structures that offer visitors a wealth of choices. A number of search engines are available to help people find the information they need on the Web. Portals serve as home bases for many Web users; they offer a variety of services and links.

Web pages are generally constructed using a language called HTML. Many Web authoring tools automate the coding of HTML pages, making it easy for non-programmers to write and publish their own pages. Other languages are being developed to extend the power of the Web in ways that go beyond the capabilities of HTML.

In the future we'll likely see many Internet appliances attached to the Web, communicating with each other from our homes, our offices, and our vehicles. The Internet is evolving from a publicly funded research experiment into a commercial information infrastructure. As it grows and changes, issues of privacy, security, censorship, criminal activity, universal access, and appropriate Net behavior are surfacing. Network citizens have many questions to answer as the Internet evolves from an electronic frontier into a futuristic cyberspace.

Summary   Chapter Review

● Key Terms

Review Questions

1. Define or describe each of the key terms listed above. Check your answers using the glossary.
2. Why is it hard to determine how big the Internet is today? Give several reasons.
3. Why are TCP/IP protocols so important to the functioning of the Internet? What do they do?
4. How does the type of Internet connection influence the things you can do on the Internet?
5. Explain the relationship between the client/server model and the fact that different users might experience different interfaces while accessing the same data.
6. What do email addresses and URLs have in common?
7. Why is netiquette important? Give some examples of netiquette.
8. How might you use remote login while visiting another school? What about file transfer? How might the Web make remote login unnecessary?
9. Why is file compression important on the Internet?
10. Why is the World Wide Web important as a publishing medium? In what ways is the Web different from any publishing medium that's ever existed before?
11. Briefly describe several software tools that can be used to develop Web pages.
12. How does push technology differ from standard Web page delivery techniques? How is it used?
13. What new services are available as a result of the commercialization of the Internet? What new problems are arising as a result of that commercialization?

Discussion Questions

1. How did the Internet's Cold War origin influence its basic decentralized, packet-switching design? How does that design affect the way we use the Net today? What are the political implications of that design today?
2. As scientists, engineers, and government officials develop plans for the national information infrastructure, they wrestle with questions about who should have access and what kinds of services to plan for. Do you have any ideas of the kinds of things they might want to consider?
3. Do you know anyone who has experienced Internet addiction? If so, can you describe the experience?
4. How do you think on-line user interfaces will evolve as bandwidth and processing power increase? Describe what cyberspace will feel like in the year 2010, in the year 2050, and beyond.

Projects

1. Search the World Wide Web for resources related to a topic of interest to you. Keep a list of bookmarks of the most useful sites for future reference.
2. Create your own home page, and link it to other pages on the World Wide Web. (When you're trying to decide what information to include in your home page, remember that it will be accessible to millions of people all over the world.)
3. Read several books and articles about cyberspace, and write a paper comparing them. Better yet, write a hypertext document, and publish it on the Web.

Sources & Resources

Books

There are thousands of books on the Internet. Many of them promise to simplify and demystify the Net, but they don't all deliver. The Internet is complex and ever-changing. The following list contains a few particularly good titles, but you should also look for more current books released since this book went to press.

When Wizards Stay Up Late, by Katie Hafner and Matthew Lyon (New York: Simon and Schuster, 1998). If you want to learn more about the birth of the Internet, this book is a great place to start. The authors describe the people, challenges, and technical issues in clear, entertaining prose.

Internet 101, by Wendy G. Lehnert (Reading, MA: Addison-Wesley, 1998). This book has clear explanations of what the Internet is, how it works, how to use it, and what it all means to you. The author maintains a companion Web site.

The Whole Internet: The Next Generation, by Kiersten Conner-Sax and Ed Krol (Sebastapol, CA: O'Reilly, 1999). In 1992 Ed Krol turned his on-line Internet guide into one of the first true guidebooks to the Net. It provided explorers with the technical knowledge necessary to get around on the pre-Web Internet. This completely rewritten edition is less technical, but just as practical. It's packed with useful information and advice on everything from shopping at auctions to stopping spam.

How the Internet Works, Millennium Edition, by Preston Gralla (Indianapolis: Que, 1999). If you like the style of *How Computers Work,* you'll appreciate *How the Internet Works.* You won't learn how to use the Net, but you'll get a colorful tour of what goes on behind the scenes when you connect. There's a surprising amount of technical information in this graphically rich, approachable book.

TCP/IP Clearly Explained, Third Edition, by Pete Loshin (Boston: AP Professional, 1999). If you want to dig deeper into the protocol that makes the Internet tick, this book, by a former *Byte* magazine editor, should help.

Weaving the Web, by Tim Berners-Lee. (San Francisco: Harper San Francisco, 1999). This is the story of the creation of the Web straight from the word processor of the man who did it.

The World Wide Web: A Mass Communication Perspective, by Barbara K. Kaye and Norman J. Medoff (Mountain View, CA: Mayfield Publishing Company, 1999). This book examines the relationship of the Web to radio, TV, newspapers and other mass media and discusses issues raised by the emergence of Web communication.

Harley Hahn's Internet and Web Yellow Pages, Millennium Edition, by Harley Hahn (Berkeley, CA: Osborne/McGraw Hill, 2000). Many books attempt to catalog the contents of the Web, but most of them can't compete with the currency and conve-nience of on-line Web search tools. Harley Hahn's popular directory combines solid research and a careful selection process with useful tips, clever insights, and amusing asides. The result is a book that's both fun and informative. The built-in cross-platform CD-ROM contains the text in clickable hypertext format.

Que's Official Internet Yellow Pages, Millennium Edition, by Marcia Layton Turner and Audrey Seybold (Indiannopolis: Que, 1999). This directory includes more annotated listings than Harley Hahn's book, but it's not as much fun to explore. A CD-ROM gives the book a point-and-click interface.

Search Engines for the World Wide Web Visual QuickStart Guide, by Alfred and Emily Glossbrenner (Berkeley, CA: Peachpit Press, 1999). There's plenty of information on the Web; the trick is finding what you need when you need it. This little book tells you what you need to choose and use search engines efficiently and effectively. It covers the big six general-purpose Web search engines along with a healthy sampling of specialty sites for locating anything from automobiles to zip codes.

HTML 4 for the World Wide Web Visual QuickStart Guide, Fourth Edition, by Elizabeth Castro (Berkeley, CA: Peachpit Press, 2000). There are dozens of books on HTML, but few offer the clear, concise, comprehensive coverage of this best seller. Castro does a marvelous job of presenting just enough information on each topic, and presenting it in an understandable way. If you want to build your own Web pages, this is a great place to start. Even if you know the basics of HTML, you'll appreciate the coverage of "advanced" topics like DHTML and CGI. Once you've read it, you'll almost certainly want to keep it as a reference.

Perl and CGI for the World Wide Web Visual QuickStart Guide, by Elizabeth Castro (Berkeley, CA: Peachpit Press, 1999). When you fill out a form on a Web page, it's likely that your input is processed by a script that's written in PERL following the CGI protocol. Castro's book takes up where her popular HTML book leaves off, introducing the basics of PERL and CGI for first-time scripters.

JavaScript for the World Wide Web Visual QuickStart Guide, Third Edition, by Tom Negrino and Dori Smith (Berkeley, CA: Peachpit Press, 1999). JavaScript is the most popular cross-platform scripting language for Web pages. A little bit of JavaScript can turn a static Web page into a dynamic interactive page. This book provides a quick introduction to the language, including applications involving forms, frames, files, graphics, and cookies. If you're ready to move beyond basic HTML, this book can help.

Creating Cool HTML 4 Web Pages, by Dave Taylor (Foster City, CA: 1998). This book includes HTML code examples from many successful Web sites. It goes beyond the basics, with chapters on advanced HTML topics, site planning, and finding a server for your Web site.

HTML: The Complete Reference, Second Edition, by Thomas A. Powell (Berkeley, CA: Osborne/McGraw Hill, 1999). This massive book includes a well-designed, in-depth tutorial and a comprehensive reference section. It covers beginning HTML and many more advanced topics.

Philip and Alex's Guide to Web Publishing, by Philip Greenspun (San Francisco: Morgan Kaufmann Publishers, Inc., 1999). This is a quirky, wordy, opinionated, and informative exposition on creating Web sites that work. Greenspun covers a great deal of territory here, including building a site, tracking users, publicizing a site, interfacing with relational databases, and handling finances. The author's color photos allow this book to hold its own on the coffee table. (Alex, the author's dog, appears on the cover; beyond that, it's not clear what he contributed to the book.)

Web Style Guide: Basic Design Principles for Creating Web Sites, by Patrick J Lynch and Sarah Horton (New Haven: Yale University Press, 1999). Yale University was one of the first institutions to publish a Web style guide on the Web. This book, like that site, offers a clear, thoughtful discussion of techniques for designing effective Web sites.

The Elements of Hypertext Style, by Bryan Pfaffenberger (Boston: AP Professional, 1997). This book covers Web page design in general, with an emphasis on creating complex hypertext documents that are inviting and easy to navigate.

The Non-Designer's Web Book, by Robin Williams and John Tollett (Berkeley, CA: Peachpit Press, 1997). Web publishing, like desktop publishing, can be hazardous if you don't have a background in design. Robin Williams and John Tollett provide a crash course in design for first-time Web authors. They assume you're using an authoring tool that hides the nuts and bolts of HTML; if you're not, you'll need to learn HTML elsewhere.

Elements of Web Design, Second Edition, by Darcy DiNucci with Maria Giudice and Lynne Stiles (Berkeley, CA: Peachpit Press, 1998). This colorful, readable book uses text and graphics to help people with design experience apply their skills to the Web.

The Web Design Wow! Book: Showcasing the Best of On-screen Communication, by Jack Davis and Susan Merritt (Berkeley CA: Peachpit Press, 1998). This book uses case studies to explore the principles of design for Web sites, with chapters on Entertainment, Education and Training, Publishing, Portfolios and Presentation, and Sales. A cross-platform CD-ROM is included.

Great Web Architecture, by Clay Andres (Sebastopol, CA: IDG Books, 1999). There's more to Web design than making pretty pages. This book explores and explains the underlying structure of successful Web sites.

Community Building on the Web, by Amy Kim (Berkeley, CA: Peachpit Press, 2000). Some of the most successful Web sites today offer more than information—they offer a sense of community. In this book the designer of some of the best Web community sites shares strategy, philosophy, and technology secrets for building a successful Web community. If you want your Web site to be a satisfying group experience for visitors, read this book.

World Wide Web: Beyond the Basics, edited by Dr. Marc Abrams (Upper Saddle River, NJ: Prentice Hall, 1998). If you already know how to build Web pages and use search engines, and want to learn more about the technical side of the Web, this book can help. It covers history, technology, security, and other topics with academic depth that goes beyond typical Web books.

Getting Hits: The Definitive Guide to Promoting Your Website, by Don Sellers (Berkeley, CA: Peachpit Press, 1997). If you build it, will they come? This book will tell you how to attract an audience to your Web world.

Stopping Spam: Stamping Out Unwanted Email and News Postings, by Alan Schwartz and Simson Garfinkel (Cambridge: O'Reilly, 1998). Spam can be a serious problem for casual computer users and systems administrators alike. This book outlines the problem and provides guidance for anyone who wants a spam-free Internet diet.

Sending Your Government a Message: E-Mail Communication Between Citizens and Government, by C. Richard Neu, Robert H. Anderson, and Tora K. Bikson (Santa Monica, CA: Rand, 1999) and **Universal Access to E-Mail,** by Robert H. Anderson, Tora K. Bikson, Sally Ann Law, and Bridger M. Mitchell (Santa Monica, CA: Rand, 1999). These two books, from the influential Rand research organization, address the critical issue of electronic mail access. *Sending Your Government a Message* focuses on citizen access to U.S. government's agencies; Universal Access deals with electronic mail access in general. Both books discuss current public policy and make recommendations for future policy. *Sending Your Government a Message* includes a list of government email addresses. Both texts are available on line, along with other Rand publications, at www.rand.org/publications/electronic.

Civilizing Cyberspace: Policy, Power, and the Information Superhighway, by Steven E. Miller (Reading, MA: Addison-Wesley, 1997). This book, published by Addison-Wesley for the Association for Computing Machinery, a respected professional society, provides an indepth look at the political, social, and ethical issues that we face as we transform the Internet into an information superhighway.

True Names: and the Opening of the Cyberspace Frontier, by Verner Vinge and James Frenkel (New York: Tor Books, 2000). In 1981 (three years before the original publication of *Neuromancer*) Verner Vinge's critically acclaimed novella, *True Names,* described a virtual world inside a computer network. Vinge didn't use the term "cyberspace," but his visionary story effectively invented the concept. This book includes the wonderful original True Names novella and a collection of articles by cyberspace pioneers about the past, present, and future of cyberspace.

Neuromancer, by William Gibson (New York: Ace Books, 1995). Gibson's 1984 cyberpunk classic spawned several sequels, dozens of imitations, and a new vocabulary for describing a high-tech future. Gibson's future is gloomy and foreboding, and his futuristic slang isn't always easy to follow. Still, there's plenty to think about here.

Snow Crash, by Neal Stephenson (New York: Bantam, 1992). This science fiction novel lightens the dark, violent cyberpunk future vision a little with Douglas Adams–style humor. Characters regularly jack into the Metaverse, a shared virtual reality network that is in many ways more real than the physical world where they live. The descriptions of this alternate reality heavily influenced the design of many VR-like Web sites today.

Periodicals

Inter@ctive Week. This excellent weekly publication provides comprehensive coverage of all things interactive and on line, with a special focus on the Web.

Internet World. This news magazine is aimed at Webmasters and others who make a business of the Internet.

Internet Week. This weekly also covers the Internet from a professional business perspective.

The Industry Standard. This weekly magazine is as much about people as technology. The focus is on the business of the Internet.

The Net and *Yahoo! Internet Life.* These two monthly magazines attempt to keep readers abreast of the technology and culture of the Internet. Of course, many Internet travelers aren't satisfied reading paper news that's 2 or 3 months old when they can get up-to-the-minute information on line.

World Wide Web Pages

The World Wide Web is especially good at providing information about itself. Whether you want to learn HTML, see the latest Web traffic reports, or explore the technological underpinnings of the Net, you'll find Web links at the *Computer Confluence* Web site that can help.

Mastering Computers
Issues, Algorithms, and Intelligence

Chapter

Computer Security and Risks

AFTER YOU READ THIS
CHAPTER YOU SHOULD
BE ABLE TO:

Describe several types of
computer crime and
discuss possible crime-
prevention techniques.

Describe the major
security issues facing
computer users, computer
system administrators, and
law enforcement officials.

Describe how computer
security relates to personal
privacy issues.

Describe how security and
computer reliability are
related.

In this chapter:

▶ Who are the real computer criminals?
▶ Who owns information?
▶ How to protect your computer from viruses
  and other attacks
▶ Ethics and the law—where are the gaps?
▶ Can we really have security?
... and more.

On the CD-ROM:

▶ An interactive look at cryptography
▶ An animated illustration of viruses in
  action
▶ Instant access to glossary and key word
  references
▶ Interactive self-study quizzes
... and more.

On the Web:

www.prenhall.com/beekman

▶ Articles and books on computer crime,
  hackers, and law enforcement
▶ Tips for protecting yourself from electronic
  mischief and malice
▶ Discussions of intellectual property and
  other legal issues related to information
  technology
▶ Self-study exercises
... and more.

Chapter 11

Check.

—The only word ever spoken by Kempelen's chess-playing machine

In 1760 Wolfgang Kempelen, a 49-year-old Hungarian inventor, engineer, and advisor to the court of Austrian Empress Maria Theresa, built a mechanical chess player. This amazing contraption defeated internationally renowned players and earned its inventor almost legendary fame.

A Turkish-looking automaton sat behind a big box that supported a chessboard and chess pieces. The operator of the machine could open the box to "prove" there was nothing inside but a network of cogwheels, gears, and revolving cylinders. After every 12 moves, Kempelen wound the machine up with a huge key. Of course, the chess-playing machine was actually a clever hoax. The real chess player was a dwarf-sized person, who controlled the mechanism from inside and was concealed by mirrors when the box was opened. The tiny player couldn't see the board, but he could tell what pieces were moved by watching magnets below the chessboard.

Kempelen had no intention of keeping the deception going for long; he thought of it as a joke and dismantled it after its first tour. But he became a slave to his own fraud, as the public and the scientific community showered him with praise for creating the first "machine-man." In 1780 the Emperor Joseph II ordered another court demonstration of the mechanical chess player, and Kempelen had to rebuild it. The chess player toured the courts of Europe, and the public became more curious and fascinated than ever.

After Kempelen died in 1804, the machine was purchased by the impresario Maelzel, who showed it far and

Kempelen's chess-playing machine

wide. In 1809 it challenged Napoleon Bonaparte to play. When Napoleon repeatedly made illegal moves, the machine-man brushed the pieces from the table. Napoleon was delighted to have unnerved the machine. When he played the next game fairly, Napoleon was badly beaten.

The chess-playing machine came to America in 1826, where it attracted large, paying crowds. In 1834 two different articles—one by Edgar Allen Poe—revealed the secrets of the automated chess player. Poe's investigative article was insightful but not completely accurate; one of his 17 arguments was that a true automatic player would invariably win.

After Maelzel's death in 1837, the machine passed from hand to hand until it was destroyed by fire in Philadelphia in 1854. During the 70 years that the automation was publicly exhibited, its "brain" was supplied by 15 different chess players, who won 294 of 300 games. ◼

With his elaborate and elegant deception, Kempelen might be considered the forerunner of the modern computer criminal. Kempelen was trapped in his fraud because the public wanted to believe that the automated chess player was real. Desire overtook judgment in thousands of people, who were captivated by the idea of an intelligent machine.

More than two centuries later we're still fascinated by intelligent machines. In 1997 people all over the world watched (many via the World Wide Web) as IBM's Deep Blue computer trounced Garry Kasparov, the reigning international chess champion. But modern computers don't just play games; they manage our money, our medicine, and our missiles. We're expected to trust information technology with our wealth, our health, and even our lives. The many benefits of our partnership with machines are clear. But blind faith in modern technology can be foolish and, in many cases, dangerous. In this chapter we examine some of the dark corners of our computerized society: legal dilemmas, ethical issues, and reliability risks. All of these issues are tied to a larger question: How can we make computers more secure so that we can feel more secure in our daily dealings with them?

On-Line Outlaws: Computer Crime

Computers are power, and direct contact with power can bring out the best or worst in a person.

—**Former computer criminal turned corporate computer programmer**

Like other professions, law enforcement is being transformed by information technology. The FBI's National Crime Information Center provides police with almost instant information on crimes and criminals nationwide. Investigators use PC databases to store and cross-reference clues in complex cases. Using pattern recognition technology, automated fingerprint identification systems locate matches in minutes rather than months. Computers routinely scan the New York and London stock exchanges for connections that might indicate insider trading or fraud. Texas police use an intranet to cross-reference databases of photographs, fingerprints, and other crime-fighting information. *Computer forensics* experts use special software to scan criminal suspects' hard disks for digital "fingerprints"—traces of deleted files containing evidence of illegal activities. All of these tools help law enforcement officials ferret out criminals and stop criminal activities.

Like guns, computers are used to break laws as well as uphold them. Computers are powerful tools in the hands of criminals, and computer crime is a rapidly growing problem.

A police officer uses his mobile computer to check records in a central crime database.

The Computer Crime Dossier

Some will rob you with a six gun, and some with a fountain pen.

—**Woody Guthrie, in "Pretty Boy Floyd"**

Today the computer has replaced both the gun and the pen as the weapon of choice for many criminals. Computer crime is often defined as any crime accomplished through knowledge or use of computer technology.

Nobody knows the true extent of computer crime. Many computer crimes go undetected. Those that are detected often go unreported because businesses fear that they can lose more from negative publicity than from the actual crimes.

According to the 1999 *Computer Crime and Security Survey* by the Computer Security Institute (CSI) and the FBI, 62% of 521 corporate, financial, university, and government sites reported computer security breaches in the preceding 12 months. These breaches included system penetration by outsiders, theft of information, changing data, financial fraud, vandalism, stealing of passwords, and preventing legitimate users from gaining access to systems. About one third of the organizations surveyed reported "serious incidents" to law enforcement officials.

According to the survey, financial losses due to security breaches topped $120 million. But the actual losses were probably far higher, because 40% of the organizations reporting losses weren't able to give actual dollar figures. By conservative estimates businesses and government institutions lose billions of dollars every year to computer criminals.

More than half of the organizations surveyed in the CSI survey reported attacks from employees and other insiders. These crimes are typically committed by clerks, cashiers, programmers, computer operators, and managers who have no extraordinary technical ingenuity. The typical computer criminal is a trusted employee with no criminal record who is tempted by an opportunity such as the discovery of a loophole in system security. Greed, financial worries, and personal problems motivate this person to give in to temptation.

Of course, not all computer criminals fit this description. Some are former employees seeking revenge on their former bosses. Some are high-tech pranksters looking for a challenge. A few are corporate or international spies seeking classified information. Organized crime syndicates are turning to computer technology to practice their trades. Sometimes entire companies are found guilty of computer fraud. For example, Equity Funding, Inc., used computers to generate thousands of false insurance policies that later were sold for over $27 million.

The 1999 survey suggests that the explosive growth of Internet commerce is changing the demographics of computer crime. More than 30% of the surveyed organizations reported outside attacks, many resulting in financial losses. 20% reported unauthorized access or misuse of their Web sites during the year, but another 33% answered "Don't know"!

Comparing this survey with previous annual surveys shows unmistakable trends: Internet security breaches are on the rise, internal security breaches are on the rise, and computer crime in general is on the rise. All of these increases are happening in spite of increased security and law-enforcement efforts. At the time of the survey, the FBI was juggling more than 500 open computer crime cases, excluding child pornography cases.

Theft by Computer

Every system has vulnerabilities.
Every system can be compromised.

—**Peter G. Neumann**, in *Computer Related Risks*

Theft is the most common form of computer crime. Computers are used to steal money, goods, information, and computer resources. Here are a few examples:

▶ A part-time college student used his touch-tone phone and personal computer to fool Pacific Telephone's computer into ordering phone equipment to be delivered to him. He started a business, hired several employees, and pilfered about a million dollars' worth of equipment before he was turned in by a disgruntled employee. (After serving two months in jail, he became a computer security consultant.)

▶ A former automated teller machine repairman illegally obtained $86,000 out of ATMs by spying on customers while they typed in passwords and then creating bogus cards to use with the passwords.

▶ Clerks at an upscale department store erased the accounts of major customers by listing those customers as bankrupt. The customers paid the clerks 10 percent of the $33 million they saved by not having to repay their debts. Since the "bankruptcies" were listed only in the store's computers, they didn't hurt the customers' credit ratings.

▶ In 1988 several million dollars of assets at a major U.S. bank were illegally transferred to a private Swiss bank account. The transfer was noticed because a computer glitch on that particular day forced employees to check transactions manually; the automated procedure normally used wouldn't have noticed the suspicious transaction.

▶ In 1992 a phone hacker used a dial-in maintenance line to crack the computerized phone system of a Detroit newspaper publisher. The hacker cracked the system administrator's password and set up scores of voice mailboxes for friends and associates who dialed in on the publisher's toll-free number. Fortunately, the scam cost the publisher only a few hundred dollars—a small sum when compared with the $1.4 million worth of illegal long-distance calls billed against one national manufacturing firm in a single weekend.

▶ In 1996 investigators uncovered a massive credit-card fraud ring that bought private information about more than 11,000 individuals from employees of the U.S. Social Security Administration; this information, including credit-card numbers and mothers' maiden names, allowed the criminals to activate credit cards stolen from the mail.

▶ In 1999 an employee of PairGain posted an anonymous announcement on a Yahoo stock board; the message claimed that PairGain was about to be purchased by another company for nearly twice its current market value. Investors drove the stock price up about 40% before they learned they had been bilked out of thousands of dollars by a bogus message. An FBI task force retraced the perpetrator's electronic footprints and arrested him for stock manipulation a week later.

▶ In 1999 the *London Times* revealed that several London banks had paid millions of pounds in ransoms to hackers who threatened to cripple their computer systems if they didn't pay. The banks paid rather than admitting publicly that their systems weren't secure against attack.

▶ In 1999 two brothers in China were sentenced to death for using computers to redirect about $30,000 to bank accounts they controlled.

Some types of computer crime are so common that they've been given names. A common student scam uses a process called spoofing to steal passwords. The typical spoofer launches a program that mimics the mainframe computer's login screen on an unattended terminal in a public lab. When an unsuspecting student types an ID and password, the program responds with an error message and remembers the secret codes.

Sometimes thieves use computers and other tools to steal whole *identities*. By collecting personal information—credit-card numbers, driver's license numbers, Social Security numbers, and a few other tidbits of data—a thief can effectively pose as someone else, even committing crimes in that person's name. Identity theft doesn't require a computer, but computers generally play a role in the process. Identity theft usually involves *social engineering*—slang for the use of deception to get individuals to reveal sensitive information.

One of the most common types of computer theft today is the actual theft of computers. Laptop and handheld computers make particularly easy prey for crooks—especially in airports and other high-traffic, high-stress places.

All of these crimes are expensive—for businesses, law enforcement agencies, and taxpayers and consumers who ultimately must pay the bills. But as crimes go, the types of theft described so far are relatively uncommon. The same can't be said of the most widely practiced type of computer-related theft: software piracy.

A portable computer is easy prey for a thief unless it's locked to something solid and stationery.

Software Piracy and Intellectual Property Laws

Information wants to be free. Information also wants to be expensive.
Information wants to be free because it has become so cheap
to distribute, copy, and recombine—too cheap to meter.
It wants to be expensive because it can be immeasurably valuable
to the recipient. That tension will not go away.

—**Stewart Brand**, in *The Media Lab*

Software piracy—the illegal duplication of copyrighted software—is rampant. Millions of computer users have made copies of programs they don't legally own. Now that most software companies have given in to user demands and removed physical copy protection from their products, copying software is as easy as duplicating a cassette tape or photocopying a book. Unfortunately, many people aren't aware that copying software, recorded music, and books can violate federal laws protecting intellectual property.

Intellectual Property and the Law

Legally, the definition of intellectual property includes the results of intellectual activities in the arts, science, and industry. Copyright laws have traditionally protected forms of literary expression, patent law has protected mechanical inventions, and contract law has covered trade secrets. Software doesn't fit neatly into any of these categories under the law. Copyright laws protect most commercial software programs, but a few companies have successfully used patent laws to protect software products.

The purpose of intellectual property laws is to ensure that mental labor is justly rewarded and to encourage innovation. Programmers, inventors, scientists, writers, editors, filmmakers, and musicians depend on ideas and the expression of those ideas for their incomes. Ideas are information, and information is easy to copy. Intellectual property laws are designed to protect these professionals and encourage them to continue their creative efforts so society can benefit from their future work.

Intellectual property laws are difficult to enforce. The software industry, with a world market of more than $50 billion a year, loses billions of dollars every year to software pirates. The Business Software Alliance (BSA) estimates that 38% of all software in use is illegally copied. According to the BSA, piracy cost 108,000 jobs in 1998. Piracy can be particularly hard on small software companies. Developing software is just as difficult for them as it is for big companies like Microsoft and Oracle, but they often lack the financial and legal resources to cover their losses to piracy.

Software industry organizations, including the BSA and SPA Anti-Piracy (a division of the Software & Information Industry Association), work with law enforcement agencies to crack down on piracy. At the same time they sponsor educational programs to make computer users aware that piracy is theft, because laws can't work without citizen understanding and support.

Existing copyright and patent laws, which evolved during the age of print and mechanical inventions, are outdated, contradictory, and inadequate for today's information technology. Many laws, including the *Computer Fraud and Abuse Act* of 1984, clearly treat software piracy as a crime. The *NET (No Electronic Theft) Act* of 1997 closed a narrow loophole in the law that allowed people to give away software on the Internet without legal repercussions. In 1999 a University of Oregon student was the first person convicted under the NET Act. He pleaded guilty to posting thousands of copyrighted software programs, music recordings, and digital movies on his Web site.

Software piracy is a worldwide problem, with piracy rates highest in developing nations. In China approximately 95% of all new software installations are pirated; in

Vietnam the piracy rate is 97%. A few Third World nations refuse to abide by international copyright laws. They argue that the laws protect rich countries at the expense of underdeveloped nations. In 1998, the Argentine Supreme Court ruled that the country's copyright laws don't apply to computer software.

Look-and-Feel Lawsuits

When it comes to software, nobody is sure exactly what is protected by law. Creating and selling an exact duplicate of a program clearly violates the law, but what about creating a program that has the "look and feel" of a successful software program? Can one software company legally sell a program that mimics the screen design and menu commands of a competing product? Is Microsoft Windows a rip-off of the Macintosh operating system? Did Borland steal the 1-2-3 command structure for its Quattro spreadsheet software? These questions, and others like them, have been asked in federal cases. In spite of contradictory verdicts, the general trend seems to be toward allowing companies to liberally "borrow" user interface elements and ideas from their competition. In the cases mentioned above, Microsoft and Borland both successfully defended themselves against lawsuits. Still, each of these cases had unique circumstances that led the judges to dismiss the suits. Future look-and-feel lawsuits could go the other way.

In matters of software, the legal system is sailing in uncharted waters. Whether dealing with piracy, look-and-feel issues, or abuse of monopoly, lawmakers and judges must struggle with difficult questions about innovation, property, freedom, and progress. The questions are likely to be with us for quite a while.

Software Sabotage: Viruses and Other Invaders

The American government can stop me from going to the U.S., but they can't stop my virus.

—Virus creator

In this 1999 scene, Moscow police attempted to make a dent in the illegal software market by destroying mountains of pirated software.

Another type of computer crime is sabotage of hardware or software. The word sabotage comes from the early days of the Industrial Revolution, when rebellious workers shut down new machines by kicking wooden shoes, called sabots, into the gears. Modern computer saboteurs commonly use software rather than footwear to do destructive deeds. The names given to the saboteurs' destructive programs—*viruses, worms,* and *Trojan horses*—sound more like biology than technology, and many of the programs even mimic the behavior of living organisms.

Trojan Horses

A Trojan horse is a program that performs a useful task while at the same time carrying out some secret destructive act. As in the ancient story of the wooden horse that carried Greek soldiers through the gates of Troy, Trojan horse software hides an enemy in an attractive package. Trojan horse programs are often posted on shareware Web sites with names that make them sound like games or utilities. When an unsuspecting bargain hunter downloads and runs such a program, it might erase files, change data, or cause some other kind of damage. Some network saboteurs use Trojan horses to pass secret data to other unauthorized users.

One type of Trojan horse, a logic bomb, is programmed to attack in response to a particular logical event or sequence of events. For example, a programmer might plant a logic bomb that is designed to destroy data files if the programmer is ever listed as terminated in the company's personnel file. A logic bomb might be triggered when a certain user logs in, a special code is entered in a database field, or a particular sequence of actions is performed by the user. If the logic bomb is triggered by a time-related event, it is called a *time bomb*. A widely publicized virus included a logic bomb that was programmed to destroy PC data files on Michelangelo's birthday.

Trojan horses can cause serious problems in computer systems of all sizes. To make matters worse, many Trojan horses carry software viruses.

Viruses

A biological virus is unable to reproduce by itself, but it can invade the cells of another organism and use the reproductive machinery of each host cell to make copies of itself; the new copies leave the host and seek out new hosts to repeat the process. A software **virus** works in the same way: It spreads from program to program, or from disk to disk, and uses each infected program or disk to make more copies of itself. Virus software is usually hidden in the operating system of a computer or in an application program. Some viruses do nothing but reproduce; others display messages on the computer's screen; still others destroy data or erase disks.

A virus is usually operating-system specific. Windows viruses invade only Windows disks, Macintosh viruses invade only Macintosh disks, and so on. There are exceptions: *Macro viruses* attach themselves to documents that contain *macros*—embedded programs to automate tasks. Macro viruses can be spread across computer platforms if the documents are created and spread using cross-platform applications—most commonly the applications in Microsoft Office. Macro viruses can be spread through innocent-looking email attachments. Viruses spread through email are sometimes called *email viruses.*

One of the most widely publicized email viruses was 1999's Melissa virus. Melissa's method of operation is typical of email viruses: An unsuspecting computer user receives an "Important message" from a friend: "Here is that document you asked for. . . don't show it to anyone else ;-)." The attached Microsoft Word document contains a list of passwords for Internet pornography sites. It contains something else: a macro virus written in Microsoft Office's built-in Visual Basic scripting language. Once the document is opened,

How a virus works.

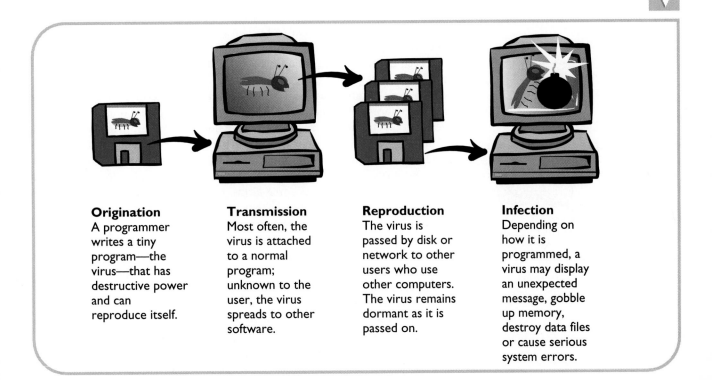

Origination
A programmer writes a tiny program—the virus—that has destructive power and can reproduce itself.

Transmission
Most often, the virus is attached to a normal program; unknown to the user, the virus spreads to other software.

Reproduction
The virus is passed by disk or network to other users who use other computers. The virus remains dormant as it is passed on.

Infection
Depending on how it is programmed, a virus may display an unexpected message, gobble up memory, destroy data files or cause serious system errors.

the macro virus goes to work, sending a copy of the email message and infected document to the first 50 names on the user's Outlook address book. Within minutes, 50 more potential Melissa victims receive messages apparently from someone they know—the user of the newly infected computer. Melissa spread like wildfire among Windows systems, infecting 100,000 systems in just a few days. Melissa wasn't designed to do damage to systems, but the flurry of messages brought down some email servers. A nationwide search located the probable author of the Melissa virus, a 30-year-old New Jersey resident with a fondness for a topless dancer named Melissa.

Shortly after Melissa faded from the headlines, a similar, but more destructive, virus named Chernobyl infected more than 600,000 computers worldwide. South Korea alone suffered 300,000 attacks; about 15% of their PCs were damaged by the virus, at a cost of $250 million. In May of 2000 a Melissa-like virus called Love Bug spread from a PC in the Phillipines around the world through innocent-looking "I Love You" email message attachments. In a matter of hours the Love Bug caused billions of dollars in lost productivity and damage to computer systems.

Worms

Like viruses, **worms** (named for tapeworms) use computer hosts to reproduce themselves. But unlike viruses, worm programs travel *independently* over computer networks, seeking out uninfected workstations to occupy. A typical worm segment resides in a workstation's memory rather than on disk, so the worm can be eliminated by shutting down all of the workstations on the network. The first headline-making worm was created as an experiment by a Cornell graduate student in 1988. The worm was accidentally released onto the Internet, clogging 6,000 computers all over the United States, almost bringing them to a complete standstill and forcing operators to shut them all down so every worm segment could be purged from memory. The total cost, in terms of work time lost at research institutions, was staggering. The student was suspended from school and was the first person convicted of violating the Computer Fraud and Abuse Act.

Virus Wars

The popular press usually doesn't distinguish among Trojan horses, viruses, and worms; they're all called computer viruses. Whatever they're called, these rogue programs make life more complicated and expensive for people who depend on computers. Researchers have identified more than 18,000 virus strains, with 200 new ones appearing each month. At any given time about 250 virus strains exist *in the wild*—in circulation.

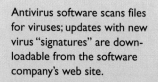

Antivirus software scans files for viruses; updates with new virus "signatures" are downloadable from the software company's web site.

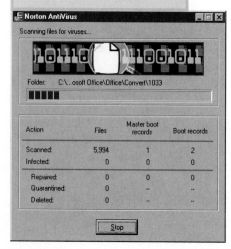

Modern viruses can spread faster and do more damage than viruses of a few years ago. There are several reasons. The Internet, which speeds communication all over the planet, also speeds virus transmission. Web pages, macros, and other technologies give virus writers new places to hide their creations. And increased standardization on Microsoft applications and operating systems has made it easier for viruses to spread. Just as natural mixed forests are more resistant to disease than are single-species tree farms, mixed computing environments are less susceptible to crippling attacks than is an organization where everyone uses the same hardware and software.

When computers are used in life-or-death situations, as they are in many medical and military applications, invading programs can even threaten human lives. The U.S. government and several states now have laws against introducing these programs into computer systems.

Antivirus programs (also called *vaccine* or *disinfectant programs*) are designed to search for viruses, notify users when they're found, and remove them from infected disks or files. Most antiviral programs continually monitor system activity, watching for and reporting suspicious virus-like actions. But no antivirus program can detect every virus, and these programs need to be frequently revised to combat new viruses as they appear. Most antivirus programs can automatically download new virus-fighting code from the Web as new virus strains appear. But it can take several days for companies to develop and distribute patches for new viruses—and destructive viruses can do a lot of damage in that time.

The virus wars continue to escalate as virus writers develop new ways to spread their works. After a rash of 1999 email viruses, most users learned not to open unidentified email attachments. But before the year was over, a worm called BubbleBoy (named for an episode of TV's *Seinfeld*) demonstrated that a system could be infected by email even if the mail wasn't opened. Some viruses have even been developed to infect HTML code in Web pages or HTML email messages. *HTML viruses* can't (so far) infect your computer if you're viewing an infected Web page on another computer; the infected HTML code must be downloaded onto your machine. Still, HTML viruses are reminders that the virus wars are far from over.

Hacking and Electronic Trespassing

The Hacker Ethic

Access to computers—and anything which might teach you something about the way the world works—should be unlimited and total.

Always yield to the Hands-on Imperative.

1. All information should be free.

2. Mistrust Authority—Promote Decentralization.

3. Hackers should be judged by their hacking,

not bogus criteria such as degrees, age, race, or position.

4. You can create art and beauty on a computer.

5. Computers can change your life for the better.

—Steven Levy, in *Hackers: Heroes of the Computer Revolution*

I don't drink, smoke, or take drugs. I don't steal, assault people, or vandalize property.

The only way in which I am really different from most people is in my

fascination with the ways and means of learning about

computers that don't belong to me.

—Bill "The Cracker" Landreth, in *Out of the Inner Circle*

In the late 1970s, timesharing computers at Stanford and MIT attracted informal communities of computer fanatics who called themselves hackers. In those days a hacker was a person who enjoyed learning the details of computer systems and writing clever programs, referred to as hacks. Hackers were, for the most part, curious, enthusiastic, intelligent, idealistic, eccentric, and harmless. Many of those early hackers were, in fact, architects of the microcomputer revolution.

Over the years the idealism of the early hacker communities was at least partly overshadowed by cynicism, as big-money interests took over the young personal computer industry. At the same time the term *hacking* took on a new, more ominous connotation in the media. While many people still use the term to describe software wizardry, it more commonly refers to unauthorized access to computer systems. Old-time hackers insist that this electronic trespassing is really *cracking*, but the general public and popular media don't recognize the distinction between hackers and crackers. Today's stereotypical hacker, like his early counterparts, is a young, bright, technically savvy, white, middle-class male who, in addition to programming his own computer, may break into others.

Of course, not all young computer wizards break into systems, and not all electronic trespassers fit the media stereotype. Still, hackers aren't just a media myth; they're real, and there are lots of them. Electronic trespassers enter corporate and government computers using stolen passwords and security holes in operating system software. Sometimes they use modems to dial up the target computers directly; in other cases they "travel" to their destinations through the Internet and other networks.

Many hackers are merely motivated by curiosity and intellectual challenge; once they've cracked a system, they look around and move on without leaving any electronic footprints. Some hackers claim to be acting in the public good by pointing out security problems in commercial software products. Some malicious hackers use Trojan horses, logic bombs, and other tricks of the trade to wreak havoc on corporate and government systems. A growing number of computer trespassers are part of electronic crime rings intent on stealing credit-card numbers and other sensitive, valuable information. In one recent case, a hacker penetrated an Internet service provider's host system and copied more than 10,000 credit-card numbers. This kind of theft is difficult to detect and track because the original information is left unchanged when the copy is stolen.

The Web has opened up new territory for hackers. Hackers have defaced the Web sites of the White House, the U.S. Senate, the Department of the Interior, presidential candidates, countless on-line businesses, and even a hacker's conference. Sometimes Web sites are simply defaced with obscene or threatening messages; sometimes they're replaced with satirical substitutes; sometimes they're vandalized so they don't work properly. *Webjackers* hijack legitimate Web pages and redirect users to other sites—anywhere from pornographic sites to fraudulent businesses. **Denial of service attacks** flood popular Web sites with so much bogus traffic that they can't respond to legitimate customer and client clicks. In a single week in February, 2000, Yahoo, E*TRADE, eBay, and Amazon Web sites were crippled by denial of service attacks, costing their owners millions of dollars in business. Two months later a 15-year-old Canadian boy nicknamed "Mafia Boy" was arrested after he bragged on line about causing the breakdowns. His expensive pranks didn't require any special expertise; he reportedly downloaded all of the software he used from the Internet.

The most famous case of electronic trespassing was documented in Cliff Stoll's best-selling book, *The Cuckoo's Egg*. While working as a system administrator for a university computer lab in 1986, Stoll noticed a 75-cent accounting error. Rather than letting it go, Stoll investigated the error. He uncovered a system intruder who was searching government, corporate, and university computers across the Internet for sensitive military information. It took a year and some help from the FBI, but Stoll eventually located the hacker—a German computer science student and part of a ring of hackers working for the KGB. Ironically, Stoll captured the thief by using standard hacker tricks, including a Trojan horse program that contained information on a fake SDI Net (Strategic Defense Initiative Network).

This kind of on-line espionage is becoming commonplace as the Internet becomes a mainstream communication medium. A more recent front-page-story-turned-book involved the 1995 capture of Kevin Mitnick, the hacker who had stolen millions of dollars' worth of software and credit-card information on the Net. By repeatedly manufacturing new identities and cleverly concealing his location, Mitnick successfully evaded the FBI for years. But when he broke into the computer of computational physicist Tsutomu Shimomura, he inadvertently started an electronic cat-and-mouse game that ended with his capture and conviction. Shimomura was able to defeat Mitnick because of his expertise in computer security—the protection of computer systems and, indirectly, the people who depend on them.

Cliff Stoll discovered an international computer espionage ring because of a 75-cent accounting error.

Computer Security: Reducing Risks

In the old world, if I wanted to attack something physical, there was one way to get there. You could put guards and guns around it, you could protect it. But a database—or a control system—usually has multiple pathways, unpredictable routes to it. and seems intrinsically impossible to protect. That's why most efforts at computer security have been defeated.

—**Andrew Marshall, military analyst**

With computer crime on the rise, computer security has become an important concern for system administrators and computer users alike. Computer security refers to protecting computer systems and the information they contain against unwanted access, damage, modification, or destruction. According to a 1991 report of the Congressional Research Service, computers have two inherent characteristics that leave them open to attack or operating error:

1 A computer will do exactly what it is programmed to do, including revealing sensitive information. Any system that can be programmed can be reprogrammed by anyone with sufficient knowledge.

2 Any computer can do only what it is programmed to do. "[I]t cannot protect itself from either malfunctions or deliberate attacks unless such events have been specifically anticipated, thought through, and countered with appropriate programming."

Computer owners and administrators use a variety of security techniques to protect their systems ranging from everyday low-tech locks to high-tech software scrambling.

Physical Access Restrictions

One way to reduce the risk of security breaches is to make sure that only authorized personnel have access to computer equipment. Organizations use a number of tools and techniques to identify authorized personnel. Some security checks can be performed by a computer; others are performed by human security guards. Depending on the security system, you might be granted access to a computer based on

▶ *Something you have*—a key, an ID card with a photo, or a *smart card* containing digitally encoded identification in a built-in memory chip

▶ *Something you know*—a password, an ID number, a lock combination, or a piece of personal history, such as your mother's maiden name

▶ *Something you do*—your signature or your typing speed and error patterns

▶ *Something about you*—a voice print, fingerprint, retinal scan, facial feature scan, or other measurement of individual body characteristics; these measurements are collectively called biometrics.

Because most of these security controls can be compromised—keys can be stolen, signatures can be forged, and so on—many systems use a combination of controls. For example, an employee

Biometric devices provide high levels of computer and network security because they monitor human body characteristics that can't be stolen. The U-Match Bio-Link Mouse (left) checks the thumbprint of the user against a database of prints approved for access. IriScan's PC Iris (right) can compare the patterns in the iris of the user against a database of employees or other legitimate network users.

might be required to show a badge, unlock a door with a key, and type a password to use a secured computer.

In the days when corporate computers were isolated in basements, physical restrictions were sufficient for keeping out intruders. But in the modern office, computers and data are almost everywhere, and networks connect computers to the outside world. In a distributed, networked environment, security is much more problematic. It's not enough to restrict physical access to mainframes when personal computers and network connections aren't restricted. Additional security techniques—most notably passwords—are needed to restrict access to remote computers.

Passwords

Passwords are the most common tool used to restrict access to computer systems. Passwords are effective, however, only if they're chosen carefully. Most computer users choose passwords that are easy to guess: names of partners, children, or pets; words related to jobs or hobbies; and consecutive characters on keyboards. One survey found that the two favorite passwords in Britain were "Fred" and "God"; in America they were "love" and "sex." Hackers know and exploit these clichés; cautious users avoid them. A growing number of security systems refuse to allow users to choose any real words or names as passwords so hackers can't use dictionary software to guess them systematically. Even the best passwords should be changed frequently.

Access-control software doesn't need to treat all users identically. Many systems use passwords to restrict users so they can open only files related to their work. In many cases, users are allowed read-only access to files that they can see but not change.

To prevent unauthorized use of stolen passwords by outsiders, many companies use *call-back systems*. When a user logs in and types a password, the system hangs up, looks up the user's phone number, and calls back before allowing access.

Firewalls, Encryption, and Audits

Many data thieves do their work without breaking into computer systems; instead, they intercept messages as they travel between computers on networks. Passwords are of little use for hiding electronic mail messages when they're traveling through phone lines or Internet gateways. Still, Internet communication is far too important to sacrifice in the name of security. Many organizations use firewalls to keep their internal networks secure while allowing communication with the rest of the Internet. The technical details of firewalls vary considerably, but they're all designed to serve the same function: to guard against unauthorized access to an internal network. In effect, a firewall is a gateway with a lock— the locked gate is opened only for information packets that pass one or more security inspections. Firewalls aren't just for large corporations anymore. Without firewall hardware or software installed, a home computer with an always-on DSL or cable modem connection can be easy prey for Internet snoopers.

Of course, the firewall's digital drawbridge has to let some messages pass through; otherwise there could be no communication with the rest of the Internet. How can those messages be secured in transit? To protect transmitted informa-

The encryption process.

The encrypted message is transmitted through the network.

Confidential Sales Figures

1991	16,385,000
1992	19,392,000
1993	12,500,000
1994	11,100,000
1995	15,000,000
1996	23,000,000

Encrypt and SEND

x48dqq82ked8i3kdi
3i3kd0o290ekwcmg
qaoi34ieqhj3o3k,wi
woakaqjkurtj2iewow
qlekejroqei45783.p

Decrypted Message:

Confidential Sales Figures

1991	16,385,000
1992	19,392,000
1993	12,500,000
1994	11,100,000
1995	15,000,000
1996	23,000,000

The sender creates, encrypts, and sends the message.

The message is received and decrypted.

A computer serves as a firewall by scanning every message for security risks before allowing it to pass into or out of a LAN. A firewall can be a hardware device, such as those shown in the photo below, or a computer running firewall software, as shown on the screen below.

tion, many organizations and individuals use encryption software to scramble their transmissions. When a user encrypts a message by applying a secret numerical code, called an *encryption key*, the message can be transmitted or stored as an indecipherable garble of characters. The message can be read only after it's been reconstructed with a matching key.

For the most sensitive information, passwords, firewalls, and encryption aren't enough. A diligent spy can "listen to" the electromagnetic signals that emanate from the computer hardware and, in some cases, read sensitive information. To prevent spies from using these spurious broadcasts, the Pentagon has spent hundreds of millions of dollars on a program called Tempest to develop specially shielded machines.

Audit-control software is used to monitor and record computer transactions as they happen so auditors can trace and identify suspicious computer activity after the fact. Effective audit-control software forces every user, legitimate or otherwise, to leave a trail of electronic footprints. Of course, this kind of software is of little value unless someone in the organization monitors and interprets the output.

How It Works 11.1

Cryptography

If you want be sure that an electronic mail message can be read only by the intended recipient, you must either use a secure communication channel or secure the message.

Mail within many organizations is sent over secure communication channels—channels that can't be accessed by outsiders. But you can't secure the channels used by the Internet and other worldwide mail networks; there's no way to shield messages sent through public telephone lines and airwaves. In the words of Mark Rotenberg, director of the Electronic Privacy Information Center, "Email is more like a postcard than a sealed letter."

If you can't secure the communication channel, the alternative is to secure the message. You secure a message by using a crypto-system to encrypt it—scramble it so it can be decrypted (unscrambled) only by the intended recipient.

Almost all cryptosystems depend on a key—a password-like number or phrase that can be used to encrypt or decrypt a message. Eavesdroppers who don't know the key have to try to decrypt it by brute force—by trying all possible keys until the right one is guessed.

Some cryptosystems afford only modest security: A message can be broken after only a day or week of brute force cryptanalysis on a supercomputer. More effective systems would take a supercomputer billions of years to break the message.

The traditional kind of cryptosystem used on computer networks is called a *symmetric secret key system*. With this approach the sender and recipient use the same key, and they have to keep their shared key secret from everyone else.

Secret Key System

Messages encrypted/decrypted with key 10529

Sue's list of secret keys

George	10529
Clem	22707

Messages encrypted/decrypted with key 27707

George's list of secret keys

Sue	10529
Clem	33812

Clem's list of secret keys

George	33812
Sue	22707

Messages encrypted/decrypted with key 33812

An uninterruptable power supply (UPS) protects against both power surges and momentary power failures.

Backups and Other Precautions

Even the tightest security system can't guarantee absolute protection of data. A power surge or a power failure can wipe out even the most carefully guarded data in an instant. An **uninterruptible power supply (UPS)** can protect computers from data loss during power failures; inexpensive ones can protect even home computers from short power dropouts. *Surge protectors* don't help during power failures, but they can shield electronic equipment from dangerous power spikes.

Of course, disasters come in many forms. Sabotage, human errors, machine failures, fire, flood, lightning, and earthquakes can damage or destroy computer data along

The biggest problem with symmetric secret key systems is key management. If you want to communicate with several people and ensure that each person can't read messages intended for the others, then you'll need a different secret key for each person. When you want to communicate with someone new, you have the problem of letting them know what the key is. If you send it over the ordinary communication channel, it can be intercepted.

In the 1970s cryptographers developed public key cryptography to get around the key management problems. The most pop- ular kind of public key cryptosystem, RSA, is being incorporated into most new network-enabled software. Phillip Zimmerman's popular shareware utility called PGP (for Pretty Good Privacy) uses RSA technology.

Each person using a public key cryptosystem has two keys: a private key known only to the user and a public key that is freely available to anyone who wants it. Thus a public key system is asymmetric: A different key is used to encrypt than to decrypt. Public keys can be published in phone directories, Web pages, and advertisements; some users include them in their email signatures.

If you want to send a secure message over the Internet to your friend Sue in St. Louis, you use her public key to encrypt the message. Sue's public key can't decrypt the message; only her private key can do that. The private key is specifically designed to decrypt messages that were encrypted with the corresponding public key.

Since public/private key pairs can be generated by individual users, the key distribution problem is solved. The only keys being sent over an insecure network are publicly available keys.

You can use the same technology in reverse (encrypt with the private key, decrypt with the public key) for message authentication: When you decrypt a message, you can be sure that it was sent from a particular person on the network. In the future legal and commercial documents will routinely have digital signatures that will be as valid as handwritten ones.

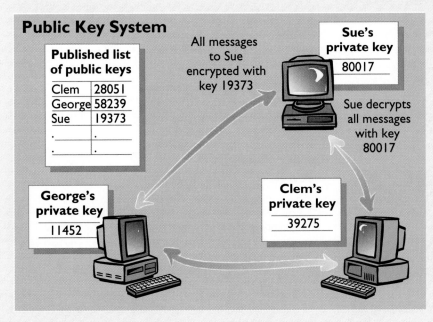

Public Key System

Published list of public keys	
Clem	28051
George	58239
Sue	19373
.	.
.	.

All messages to Sue encrypted with key 19373

Sue's private key
80017

Sue decrypts all messages with key 80017

George's private key
11452

Clem's private key
39275

A RAID such as this NAS RAID server stores redundant copies of data so that the data can be saved even if a disk crashes.

with hardware. Any complete security system should include some kind of plan for recovering from disasters. For mainframes and PCs alike the best and most widely used data recovery insurance is a system of making regular backups. For many systems data and software are backed up automatically onto disks or tapes, usually at the end of each work day. Most data processing shops keep several *generations* of backups so they can, if necessary, go back several days, weeks, or years to reconstruct data files. For maximum security many computer users keep copies of sensitive data in several different locations. A storage device called a *RAID (redundant array of independent disk)* allows multiple hard disks to operate as a unit. RAID systems can, among other things, automatically *mirror* data on multiple disks, effectively creating instant backups.

Rules of Thumb

Safe Computing

Even if you're not building a software system for SDI or the FBI, computer security is important. Viruses, disk crashes, system bombs, and miscellaneous disasters can destroy your work, your peace of mind, and possibly your system. Fortunately, you can protect your computer, your software, and your data from most hazards.

▶ *Share with care.* A computer virus is a contagious disease that spreads when it comes in contact with a compatible file or disk. Viruses spread rapidly in environments where disks and files are passed around freely, as they are in many student computer labs. To protect your data, keep your disks to yourself, and don't borrow disks from others. When you do share a 3.5-inch disk, physically write-protect it (by moving the plastic slider to uncover the square hole) so a virus can't attach to it.

Write-protect opening

▶ *Beware of email bearing gifts.* Many viruses hide in attachments to email messages that say something like "Here's the document you asked for. Please don't show anyone else." Don't open unsolicited email attachments; just throw them away.

▶ *Handle shareware and freeware with care.* Other viruses enter systems in Trojan horse shareware and freeware programs. Treat public domain programs and shareware with care; test them with a disinfectant program before you install them on your hard disk. Contrary to popular belief, you can't get a virus by reading an email message. But a virus can be embedded in an email attachment, so scan attached files before opening them.

▶ *Don't pirate software.* Even commercial programs can be infected with viruses. Shrink-wrapped, virgin software is much less likely to be infected than pirated copies. Besides, software piracy is theft, and the legal penalties can be severe.

▶ *Disinfect regularly.* Virus protection programs are available for all kinds of systems, often for free. Use up-to-date virus protection software regularly if you work in a high-risk environment like a public computer lab.

▶ *Treat your removable disks as if they contained something important.* Keep them away from liquids, dust, pets, and (especially) magnets. Don't put your disks close to phones, speakers, and other electronic devices that contain hidden magnets. (Magnets won't harm CD-ROMs or DVD-ROMs, but scratches can make them unusable.)

▶ *Take your passwords seriously.* Choose a password that's not easily guessable, not in any dictionary, and not easy for others to remember. Don't post it by your computer, and don't type it when you're being watched. Change your password every few weeks—immediately if you have reason to suspect it has been discovered.

▶ *If it's sensitive, lock it up.* If your computer is accessible to others, protect your private files with passwords and/or encryption. Many operating systems and utilities include options for adding password protection and encrypting files. If others need to see the files, lock them so they can be read but not changed or deleted. If secrecy is critical, don't store the data on your hard disk at all. Store it on removable disks and lock it away in a safe place.

▶ *If it's important, back it up.* Regularly make backup copies of every important file on different disks than the original. Keep copies of critical disks in different locations so that you have backups in case disaster strikes.

▶ *If you're sending sensitive information through the Internet, consider encryption.* Use a utility or a program like freeware PGP (Pretty Good Privacy) to turn your message into code that's almost impossible to crack.

▶ *Don't open your system to interlopers.* If you've got an always-on Internet connection—T1, DSL, or cable modem—consider using firewall hardware or software to detect and lock out snoopers. Set your file sharing controls so access is limited to authorized visitors.

▶ *Prepare for the worst.* Even if you take every precaution, things can still go wrong. Make sure you aren't completely dependent on the computer for really important things.

Human Security Controls: Law, Management, and Ethics

Security experts are constantly developing new technologies and techniques for protecting computer systems from computer criminals. But at the same time criminals continue to refine their craft. In the ongoing competition between the law and the lawless, computer security generally lags behind. In the words of Tom Forester and Perry Morrison in *Computer Ethics,* "Computer security experts are forever trying to shut the stable door after the horse has bolted."

Ultimately, computer security is a human problem that can't be solved by technology alone. Security is a management issue, and a manager's actions and policies are critical to the success of a security program. An alarming number of companies are lax about computer security. Many managers don't understand the problems and don't think they are at risk. It's important for managers to understand the practical, ethical, and legal issues surrounding security. Managers must make their employees aware of security issues and security risks. If managers don't defend against security threats, information can't be secure.

Security, Privacy, Freedom, and Ethics: The Delicate Balance

In this age of advanced technology, thick walls and locked doors cannot guard our privacy or safeguard our personal freedom.

—Lyndon B. Johnson, **36th president of the United States, February 23, 1974**

It's hard to overstate the importance of computer security in our networked world. Destructive viruses, illegal interlopers, and crooked coworkers can erode trust and make life on line difficult for everyone. But some managers have discovered that computer security measures can create problems of their own. Complex access procedures, virus-protection programs, and other security measures can, if carried too far, interfere with people getting their work done. In the extreme, security can threaten individual human rights.

When Security Threatens Privacy

Computers threaten our personal privacy on several fronts. Corporate and government databases accumulate and share massive amounts of information about us against our will and without our knowledge. Internet-monitoring programs and software snoopers track our Web explorations and read our electronic mail. Corporate managers use monitoring software to measure worker productivity and observe their on-screen activities. Government security agencies secretly monitor telephone calls and data transmissions.

When security measures are used to prevent computer crime, they usually help protect privacy rights at the same time. When a hacker invades a computer system, legitimate users of the system might have their private communications monitored by the intruder. When an outsider breaks into the database of a bank, the privacy of every bank customer is at risk. The same applies to government computers, credit bureau computers, and any other computer containing data on private citizens. The security of these systems is important for protecting people's privacy.

But in some cases security and law enforcement can pose threats to personal privacy. Here are some examples:

▶ In 1990 Alana Shoar, electronic mail coordinator for Epson America, Inc., found stacks of printouts of employee email messages in her boss's office—messages that employees believed were private. Shortly after confronting her boss, she was fired for "gross misconduct and insubordination." She filed a class-action suit, claiming that Epson routinely monitored all email messages. Company officials denied the charges but took a firm stand on their right to any information stored on, sent to, or taken from their business computers. The courts ruled in Epson's favor. Since then, many other U.S. court decisions have reinforced a company's right to read employee email stored on company computers.

▶ In 1990 the Communication Workers of America sued Northern Telecom, Inc., for illegally bugging employee conference rooms and telephones. In 1992 Northern Telecom became the first major American employer to ban all covert monitoring of communications.

▶ Colonel Oliver North and his collaborators in the Reagan administration carefully shredded hundreds of paper documents detailing the sale of arms to Iran and the illegal channeling of profits to Nicaraguan Contras. But they were implicated in the Iran-Contra scandal anyway when investigators examined backup copies of "private" electronic mail messages stored in their computer system.

▶ In 1995 the U.S. government passed legislation requiring new digital phone systems to include additional switches that allow for electronic surveillance. This legislation protects the FBI's ability to wiretap at the expense of individual privacy. Detractors have pointed out that this digital "back door" could be abused by government agencies and could also be used by savvy criminals to perform illegal wiretaps. Government officials argue that wiretapping is a critical tool in the fight against organized crime.

▶ The digital manhunt that led to the arrest of the programmer charged with authoring the Melissa virus was made as a direct result of information provided by America Online Inc. A controversial Microsoft document identification technology—the Global Unique Identifier, or GUID—may also have played a role. While virtually everyone was happy when the virus's perpetrator was apprehended, many legal experts feared that the same techniques will be used for less lofty purposes.

▶ In 2000 the U.S. government found Microsoft guilty of gross abuses of its monopolistic position in the software industry. The government's case included hundreds of private email messages between Microsoft employees—messages that contradicted Microsoft's public testimony.

One of the best examples of a new technology that can simultaneously improve security and threaten privacy is the **active badge** (sometimes called the *smart badge*). Researchers at the University of Cambridge and nearby Olivetti Research Center are developing and wearing microprocessor-controlled badges that broadcast infrared identification codes every 15 seconds. Each badge's code is picked up by a nearby network receiver and transmitted back to a badge-location database that is constantly being updated. Active badges are used for identifying, finding, and remembering:

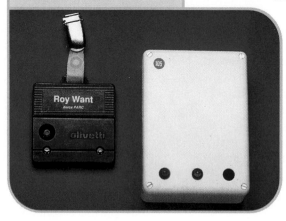

An active badge transmits signals that allow a network to identify, locate, and track the badge wearer.

▶ *Identifying.* When an authorized employee approaches a door, the door recognizes the person's badge code and opens. Whenever anyone logs into a computer system, the badge code identifies the person as an authorized or unauthorized user.

▶ *Finding.* An employee can check a computer screen to locate another employee and find out whom that person is talking to. With active badges there's no need for a paging system, and "while you were away" notes are less common.

▶ *Remembering.* At the end of the day an active-badge wearer can get a minute-by-minute printout listing exactly where he's been and whom he's been with.

Is the active badge a primitive version of the communicator on TV's *Star Trek* or a surveillance tool for Big Brother? The technology has the potential to be either or both; it all depends on how people use it. Active badges, like other security devices and techniques, raise important legal and ethical questions about privacy—questions that we, as a society, must resolve sooner or later.

Justice on the Electronic Frontier

Through our scientific genius, we have
made this world a neighborhood; now through our moral and
spiritual development, we must make of it a brotherhood.

—The Rev. Martin Luther King, Jr.

Federal and state governments have responded to the growing computer crime problem by creating new laws against electronic trespassing and by escalating enforcement efforts. Hackers have become targets for nationwide anti-crime operations. Dozens of hackers have been arrested for unauthorized entry into computer systems and for the

Computer Ethics

Ethics is moral philosophy—philosophical thinking about right and wrong. Many people base their ethical beliefs on religious rules such as the Ten Commandments or the Buddhist Eightfold Path. Others use professional codes such as the doctor's Hippocratic Oath, which includes the often quoted "First do no harm." Still others use personal philosophies with principles such as "It's OK if a jury of observers would approve." But in today's changing world, deciding how to apply the rules isn't always easy. Sometimes the rules don't seem to apply directly, and sometimes they contradict each other. (How should you "Honor thy father" if you learn that he's using the home computer to embezzle money from his employer? Is it OK to allow a friend who's broke to borrow your Microsoft Office CD for a required class project?) These kinds of *moral dilemmas* are central questions in discussions of ethics. Information technology poses moral dilemmas related to everything from copying software to reporting a coworker's sexually explicit screen saver or racist email.

Computer ethics can't be reduced to a handful of rules—the gray areas are always going to require thought and judgment. But principles and guidelines can help to focus thinking and refine judgments when dealing with technology-related moral dilemmas. The ACM **Code of Ethics**, reprinted in the Appendix of this book, is the most widely known code of conduct specifically for computer professionals. The ACM Code is worth understanding and applying even if you don't plan to be a "computer professional." Who shouldn't "Contribute to Society and Human Well-Being" or "Honor Confidentiality"? But these principles take on new meaning in an age of email and databases.

Here are some other guidelines that might help you to decide how to "do the right thing" when faced with ethical dilemmas at school, at work, or at home:

▶ *Know the rules and the law.* Many laws, and many organizational rules, are reflections of moral principles. For example, almost everyone agrees that *plagiarism*—presenting somebody else's work as your own—is wrong. It's also a serious violation of rules in most schools. And if the work is copied without permission, plagiarism can become *copyright infringement*, a serious legal offense . . . whether or not the work explicitly says that it is copyrighted.

▶ *Don't assume that it's OK if it's legal.* Our legal system doesn't define what's right and wrong. How can it, when we don't all agree on morality? The law is especially lax in areas related to information technology, because the technology changes too fast for lawmakers to keep up. It's ultimately up to each individual to act with conscience.

▶ *Think scenarios.* If you're debating between different actions, think about what might happen as a result of your actions. If you suspect your employer is falsifying spreadsheets to get around environmental regulations, what's likely to happen if you snoop around on his computer and blow the whistle on him? What's likely to happen if you don't? What are your other alternatives?

▶ *When in doubt, talk it out.* Discuss your concerns with people you trust—ideally, people with wisdom and experience dealing with similar situations. For example, if you're unsure about the line between getting computer help from a friend and cheating on homework, ask an instructor.

▶ *Make yourself proud.* How would you feel if you saw your actions on the front page of *The New York Times*, your company newsletter, or your family's home town newspaper? If you'd be embarrassed or ashamed, you probably should choose another course of action.

▶ *Remember the golden rule: Do unto others as you would have them do unto you.* This universal principle is central to every major spiritual tradition, and it is amazingly versatile. One example: Before you download that bootleg MP3 file of that up-and-coming singer, think about how you'd feel about bootleggers if you were the singer.

▶ *Take the long view.* It's all too easy to be blinded by the rapid-fire rewards of the Internet and computer technology. Consider this guiding principle from a Native American tradition: *In every deliberation, consider the impact of your decision on the next seven generations.*

release of destructive viruses and worms. Many have been convicted under federal or state laws. Others have had their computers confiscated with no formal charges filed.

Some of the victims of these sting operations claim that they broke no laws. In one case computers, software, and products were confiscated from a role-playing game company because one of their employees was a former hacker and one of their games had a hacker theme. The financially crippled company was forced to lay off half its staff before the confiscated goods were finally returned; no charges were ever filed. The company sued the government for damages and won. In another case a student was arrested because he published an electronic magazine that carried a description of an emergency 911 system allegedly stolen by hackers. Charges were eventually dropped when it was revealed that the "stolen" document was, in fact, available to the public.

These cases and others like them raise questions about how civil rights apply in the "electronic frontier." How does the Bill of Rights apply to computer communications? Does freedom of the press apply to on-line magazines in the same way it applies to paper periodicals? Can an electronic bulletin board operator or Internet service provider be held responsible for information others post on a server? Can on-line pornography be served from a house located in a neighborhood with anti-porn laws? Laws like the Telecommunications Act of 1996 attempt to deal with these questions by outlining exactly what kinds of communications are legal on line. Unfortunately, these laws generally raise as many questions as they answer. Shortly after passage a major section of the Telecommunications Act, called the Communications Decency Act, was declared unconstitutional by the Supreme Court. The debates continue inside and outside of the courts. Without definitive answers to constitutional questions law enforcement officials must continue to fight computer crime. Malicious hackers, worms, and viruses pose serious threats to our computerized society, and these threats can't be ignored. But even if every law-breaking hacker were arrested, computer crime would still be a major problem. The overwhelming majority of computer crimes are committed by company insiders who aren't reported to authorities, even when they are caught in the act. To avoid embarrassment, many companies cover up computer crimes committed by their own employees and managers. As a result, law enforcement agencies spend disproportionate amounts of time and money pursuing teenage hackers who represent a small part of the computer crime population. Experts agree that computer crime is likely to continue to grow unless corporations and government agencies recognize the importance of security on the inside as well as the outside.

Security and Reliability

> If the automobile had followed the same development cycle as the computer, a
> # Rolls Royce would today cost $100, get a million miles per gallon, and explode once a year, killing everyone inside.
>
> —Robert X. Cringely, *InfoWorld* columnist

So far our discussion of security has focused mainly on protecting computer systems from trespassing, sabotage, and other crimes. But security involves more than criminal activity. Some of the most important security issues have to do with creating systems that can withstand software errors and hardware glitches.

Bugs and Breakdowns

Computer systems, like all machines, are vulnerable to fires, floods, and other natural disasters, as well as breakdowns caused by failure of hardware components. But in modern computers, hardware problems are relatively rare when compared with software failures. By any measure bugs do more damage than viruses and computer burglars put together. Here are a few horror stories:

▶ On November 20, 1985, the Bank of New York's computer system started corrupting government securities transactions. By the end of the day the bank was $32 billion overdrawn with the Federal Reserve. Before the system error was corrected, it cost the bank $5 million in interest.

▶ In September, 1999, the Mars Climate Orbiter burned up as it approached Mars because controllers had mixed up British and metric units. Three months later the Mars Polar Lander went silent 12 minutes before touchdown. Investigators suspect software errors are at least partly responsible for this spectacular mission failure.

▶ Programs on NASA observation satellites in the 1970s and 1980s rejected ozone readings because the programmers had assumed when they wrote the programs that such low numbers could not be correct. It wasn't until British scientists reported ozone-level declines that NASA scientists reprocessed the data and confirmed the British findings that the earth's ozone layer was in danger.

▶ The Therac 25 radiation machine for tracking cancers was thoroughly tested and successfully used on thousands of patients before a software bug caused massive radiation overdoses, resulting in the partial paralysis of one patient and the death of another.

▶ On January 15, 1990, AT&T's 30-year-old signaling system software failed, bringing the long-distance carrier's network to its knees. Twenty million calls failed to go through during the next 18 hours before technicians found the problem: a single incorrect instruction hiding among a million lines of code.

▶ On February 25, 1991, 28 American soldiers were killed and 98 others wounded when an Iraqi Scud missile hit a barracks near Dhahran, Saudi Arabia. A tiny bug in a Patriot missile's software threw off its timing just enough to prevent it from intercepting the Scud. Programmers had already fixed the bug, and a new version of the software was being shipped to Dhahran when the attack occurred.

Every year brings new stories of breakdowns and bugs with catastrophic consequences. But it wasn't until 1999 that a computer bug—the Y2K (year 2000) bug, or millennium bug—became an international sensation. For decades programmers commonly built two-digit date fields into programs to save storage space, thinking "Why allow space for the first two digits when they never change?" But when 1999 ended, those digits *did* change, making many of those ancient programs unstable or unusable. Many programs were repaired by programmers knowledgeable in COBOL, FORTRAN, and other ancient computer languages. But others couldn't be repaired and had to be completely rewritten. The problem wasn't confined to mainframe software. Many PC programs—including some hard-wired into firmware—were coded with two-digit dates.

Businesses and governments spent more than 100 billion dollars trying to head off Y2K disasters. Many individuals bought generators and guns, stockpiled food and water, and prepared for a collapse of the computer-controlled utility grids that keep our economy running. When the fateful day arrived, the Y2K bug caused many problems, ranging from credit card refusals to malfunctioning spy satellites. But for most people, January 1, 2000 was business as usual. It's debatable whether disasters were averted by billions of dollars worth of preventive maintenance, or whether the Y2K scare stories were overblown. The truth is undoubtedly somewhere between these two extremes. In any event, Y2K raised public consciousness about their dependence on fickle, fragile technology.

These South Koreans, like people all around the world, stocked up on food and cooking gas cans to prepare for possible emergency shortages as a result of Y2K computer failures.

Given the state of the art of programming today, three facts are clear:

1 It's impossible to eliminate all bugs. Today's programs are constructed of thousands of tiny pieces, any one of which can cause a failure if it's incorrectly coded.

2 Even programs that appear to work can contain dangerous bugs. Some bugs are easy to detect and correct because they're obvious. The most dangerous bugs are difficult to detect and may go unnoticed by users for months or years.

3 The bigger the system, the bigger the problem. Large programs are far more complex and difficult to debug than small programs, and the trend today is clearly toward large programs. For example, Microsoft Windows 95 had 11 million lines of code, and was considered huge at the time; Windows 2000 has close to 29 million!

As we entrust complex computerized systems to do everything from financial transaction processing to air traffic control, the potential cost of computer failure goes up. In the last decade researchers have identified hundreds of cases in which disruptions to computer system operations posed some risk to the public, and the number of incidents has doubled every two years.

Computers at War

Massive networking makes the U.S. the
world's most vulnerable target.

—John McConnell, **Former NSA director**

Nowhere are the issues surrounding security and reliability more critical than in military applications. To carry out its mission effectively, the military must be sure its systems are secure against enemy surveillance and attack. At the same time many modern military applications push the limits of information technology farther than they've ever been before.

Smart Weapons

The United States has invested billions of dollars in the development of smart weapons—missiles that use computerized guidance systems to locate their targets. A *command-guidance system* allows a human operator to control the missile's path while watching a missile's-eye view of the target on a television screen. A missile with a homing guidance system can track a moving target without human help, using infrared heat-seeking devices or visual pattern recognition technology. Weapons that use "smart" guidance systems can be extremely accurate in pinpointing enemy targets under most circumstances. In theory smart weapons can greatly reduce the amount of civilian destruction in war if everything is working properly.

One problem with high-tech weapons is that they reduce the amount of time people have to make life-and-death decisions. As decision-making time goes down, the chance of errors goes up. In one tragic example an American guided missile cruiser on a peacetime mission in the Persian Gulf used a computerized Aegis fleet defense system to shoot down an Iranian Airbus containing 290 civilians. The decision to fire was made by well-intentioned humans, but those humans had little time—and used ambiguous data—to make the decision.

In today's weapon systems, such as those based at the North America Aerospace Defense Command (NORAD) Cheyenne Mountain Complex in Colorado Springs, Colorado, computers are critical components in the command and control process.

Autonomous Systems

Even more controversial is the possibility of people being left out of the decision-making loop altogether. Yet the trend in military research is clearly toward weapons that demand almost instantaneous responses—the kind that only computers can make. An autonomous system is a complex system that can assume almost complete responsibility for a task without human input, verification, or decision making.

The most famous and controversial autonomous system is the Strategic Defense Initiative (SDI)—former President Ronald Reagan's proposed "Star Wars" system for shielding the United States from nuclear attack. The SDI system, as planned, would have used a network of laser-equipped satellites and ground-based stations to detect and destroy attacking missiles shortly after launch, before they had time to reach their targets. SDI weapons would have to be able to react almost instantaneously, without human intervention. If they sensed an attack, these system computers would have no time to wait for the president to declare war, and no time for human experts to analyze the perceived attack.

SDI generated intense public debates about false alarms, hardware feasibility, constitutional issues, and the ethics of autonomous weapons. But for many who understand the limitations of computers, the biggest issue is software reliability. SDI's software system would require tens of millions of lines of code. The system couldn't be completely tested in advance because there's no way to simulate accurately the unpredictable conditions of a global war. Yet to work effectively, the system would have to be *absolutely* reliable. In a tightly coupled worldwide network a single bug could multiply and expand like a speed-of-light cancer. A small error could result in a major disaster. Many software engineers have pointed out that absolute reliability simply isn't possible now or in the foreseeable future.

In spite of years of political haggling, system failures, and cost overruns, an SDI-like system is still in the works, and systems reliability issues remain. Supporters of automated missile-defense systems argue that the technical difficulties can be overcome in time, and the U.S. government continues to invest billions in research toward that end. Whether or not a "smart shield" is ever completed, it has focused public attention on critical issues related to security and reliability.

Warfare in the Digital Domain

Even as the U.S. government spends billions of dollars on smart missiles and missile defense systems, many military experts suggest that future wars may not be fought in the air, on land, or at sea. The front lines of the future may, instead, be in cyberspace. By attacking through vast interconnected computer networks, an enemy could conceivably cripple telecommunications systems, power grids, banking and financial systems, hospitals and medical systems, water and gas supplies, oil pipelines, and emergency government services without firing a shot.

Several recent examples highlight our vulnerability:

▶ In 1994 Swedish hackers broke into telecommunications systems in central Florida and blocked several 911 systems by automatically dialing their numbers repeatedly. Anyone who called 911 with a legitimate emergency was greeted with a busy signal until the attack ended.

▶ In 1996 a juvenile hacker disabled a key phone computer servicing a Massachusetts airport, paralyzing the airport control tower for six hours.

▶ In 1998 Israeli police working with the FBI, the U.S. Air Force, and NASA arrested three Israeli teens who successfully hacked into Department of Defense computers in both countries.

None of these crimes resulted in serious damage or injury. But terrorists, spies, or criminals might use the same techniques to trigger major disasters.

Recognizing the growing threat of system sabotage, Attorney General Janet Reno created the *National Infrastructure Protection Center* in early 1998. The NIPC's state-of-the-art command center is housed at FBI headquarters. The center includes representatives of various intelligence agencies (the departments of defense, transportation, energy, and treasury), and representatives of several major corporations. Corporate participation is critical because private companies own many of the infrastructure systems that are most vulnerable to attack.

Unfortunately, many businesses are slow to recognize the potential threat to their systems. They embrace the efficiency that networks bring, but they don't adequately prepare for attack through those networks. Network attacks are all but inevitable, and such attacks can have disastrous consequences for all of us. In a world where computers control everything from money to missiles, computer security and reliability are too important to ignore.

Is Security Possible?

Computer thieves. Hackers. Software pirates. Computer snoopers. Viruses. Worms. Trojan horses. Wiretaps. Hardware failures. Software bugs. When we live and work with computers, we're exposed to all kinds of risks that didn't exist in the precomputer era. These risks make computer security especially important and challenging.

Because computers do so many amazing things so well, it's easy to overlook the problems they bring with them and to believe that they're invincible. But like Kempelen's chess-playing machine, today's computers hide the potential for errors and deception under an impressive user interface. This doesn't mean we should avoid using computers, only that we should remain skeptical, cautious, and realistic as we use them. Security procedures can reduce but not eliminate risks. In today's fast-moving world absolute security simply isn't possible.

Go Hack Yourself

Polly Sprenger

In February 2000, several of the biggest commercial Web sites were crippled by hacker attacks. These attacks forced businesses, governments, the press, and the public to pay attention to security issues. In the February 20, 2000 issue of The Industry Standard, *writer Polly Sprenger describes how "white hat hackers" are used to expose security leaks before "black hat hackers" discover—and exploit—them.*

To test vulnerability to attack, Net companies are turning to "tiger teams" of computer security experts. Their mandate: Break in, by any means necessary.

In a darkened hotel room, lit only by flickering computer-terminal screens, figures are bent over keyboards, tapping their way into a company's network in a rattling staccato.

Down the road, their cohorts are trawling through dumpsters outside the target company's building, looking for further evidence that would give them access to the network. Earlier, they'd taken a casual tour of the Dilbert-esque cubicles, having given a flimsy excuse to the oblivious receptionist.

They're not above stealing security badges that give them all-areas access, anything to get closer to the heart of the corporate beast: the server closet that houses a record of everything from the most mundane intraoffice memos to the most secret strategic documents.

In the morning, armed with proof of success, these hackers will collect a paycheck – not from some shady underworld figure, but from a Big Six accounting firm. They are part of a new breed of hackers for hire: "tiger teams," elite squads of computer and security experts whose mandate is to penetrate a company's vulnerabilities, by any means necessary.

It's been standard practice for years among the Fortune 500, the military and big financial institutions. But recently, tiger teams have caught on with Internet companies as dot-coms promise consumers that their personal data will remain private – and assure prospective clients that they are safe partners.

"We're just worried about how much damage they're going to do to the building," says a director at an Internet company that's readying for a tiger-team assault prior to closing a deal with a major European bank.

"Every night, I lay awake in bed thinking, 'Did I close the fire door?' " says the head of security for another small tech firm that is partnering with large e-commerce ventures. (Like executives of many companies put under tiger-team review, these people asked to remain anonymous.)

In recent days, attacks on Amazon.com, E-Trade and Yahoo have demonstrated the Internet's surprising vulnerabilities. Surprising, that is, to the general public. For computer security experts, it was only a matter of time.

That's where tiger teams come in.

"We have 100 percent success," says Dave Buchwald, cofounder of Crossbar Security and an early consultant on Ernst & Young's Attack and Penetration Division. Buchwald says it's rare that a startup can pose a challenge to his assault.

The tiger-team concept originated with the U.S. Air Force, which uses special groups of security experts to test for vulnerabilities at bases. In 1973, the Defense Department documented the first use of tiger teams to assess computer security.

Through the 1980s and early '90s, tiger teams were used mostly by big companies with complicated, national or international networks. A rash of publicity around malicious hackers in the late '80s spurred more regular hiring of tiger teams – and gave them a model for approaching their task: Since hackers were crawling through dumpsters looking for any useful piece of paper that would open up a computer network, the tiger teams would dumpster-dive, too. If hackers were randomly calling employees and cajoling system passwords out of them, so would the tiger teams.

"Most people's security is external, not internal," says Pete Shipley, chief security architect at KPMG. "Your security is a rent-a-cop at the door or a secretary in the lobby. One time, we just stole a bunch of security badges. A friend went in and said he really had to go to the bathroom. He grabbed the badges on the way."

Internet service providers that host big sites are increasingly asked to submit their networks to rigorous inspection. They have been hesitant to agree to assessment by a tiger team – but when a big contract is on the line, there's little choice. The tiger team won't act without permission – and signed exoneration – from the head of the company it is targeting. But system administrators and security staff aren't told.

Even the most prepared company can look like Swiss cheese to a skilled band of hackers. "Our server room has floor-to-ceiling bars around it, so you can't just go in," says a director of security for an e-commerce firm with partnerships with Bank of America, Visa and Wells Fargo, whose company recently was subjected to a tiger-team assessment of security by PricewaterhouseCoopers.

"[The team] went in through the ceiling panels," he adds. "I knew physical hacking goes on, but the thought that someone would crawl through the ceiling tiles had never crossed my mind."

Even worse, the tiger team spliced into the company's DSL, gaining access to its entire network.

For most companies, the fear isn't that they will fail in the face of a tiger-team assault – that's almost a given. The fear is that lucrative deals will fall through because they are contingent upon a passing grade.

DISCUSSION QUESTIONS

1. Do you think "ethical hacking" is an appropriate term for the activity of tiger teams? Explain your answer.
2. Do you think it's appropriate for a business to hire tiger teams made up of convicted hackers? Why or why not?

Summary ·Chapter Review·

Computers play an ever-increasing role in fighting crime. At the same time law enforcement organizations are facing an increase in computer crime—crimes accomplished through special knowledge of computer technology. Most computer crimes go undetected, and those that are detected often go unreported. But by any estimate computer crime costs billions of dollars every year.

Some computer criminals use computers, modems, and other equipment to steal goods, money, information, software, and services. Others use Trojan horses, viruses, worms, logic bombs, and other software tricks to sabotage systems. According to the media, computer crimes are committed by young, bright computer wizards called hackers. Research suggests, however, that hackers are responsible for only a small fraction of computer crimes. The typical computer criminal is a trusted employee with personal or financial problems and knowledge of the computer system. The most common computer crime, software piracy, is committed by millions of people, often unknowingly. Piracy is a violation of intellectual property laws, which, in many cases, lag far behind the technology.

Because of rising computer crime and other risks, organizations have developed a number of computer security techniques to protect their systems and data. Some security devices, such as keys and badges, are designed to restrict physical access to computers. But these tools are becoming less effective in an age of personal computers and networks. Passwords, encryption, shielding, and audit-control software are all used to protect sensitive data in various organizations. When all else fails, backups of important data are used to reconstruct systems after damage occurs. The most effective security solutions depend on people at least as much as on technology.

Normally, security measures serve to protect our privacy and other individual rights. But occasionally, security procedures threaten those rights. The trade-offs between computer security and freedom raise important legal and ethical questions.

Computer systems aren't just threatened by people; they're also threatened by software bugs and hardware glitches. An important part of security is protecting systems—and the people affected by those systems—from the consequences of those bugs and glitches. Since our society uses computers for many applications that put lives at stake, reliability issues are especially important. In modern military applications, security and reliability are critical. As the speed, power, and complexity of weapons systems increase, many fear that humans are being squeezed out of the decision-making loop. The debate over high-tech weaponry is bringing many important security issues to the public's attention for the first time.

·Summary· **Chapter Review**

◉ ⟨ **Key Terms** ⟩

access-control software, 314
active badge, 320
antivirus program, 310
audit-control software, 315
autonomous system, 324
backup, 316
biometrics, 313
code of ethics, 321
computer crime, 304
computer security, 313
contract, 307

copyright, 307
denial of service attacks, 312
encryption, 315
ethics, 321
firewall, 314
hacker, 311
identity theft, 306
intellectual property, 306
logic bomb, 308
password, 314
patent, 307

sabotage, 308
smart weapon, 324
software piracy, 307
spoofing, 306
Trojan horse, 308
Uninterruptible power supply (UPS), 316
virus, 309
worm, 310
Y2K bug (millennium bug), 323

◉ ⟨ **Review Questions** ⟩

1. Define or describe each of the key terms above. Check your answers using the glossary.
2. Why is it hard to estimate the extent of computer crime?
3. Describe the typical computer criminal. How does he or she differ from the media stereotype?

4. What is the most common computer crime? Who commits it? What is being done to stop it?
5. What are intellectual property laws, and how do they apply to software?
6. Describe several different types of programs that can be used for software sabotage.

7. What are the two inherent characteristics of computers that make security so difficult?
8. Describe several different computer security techniques, and explain the purpose of each.
9. Every afternoon at closing time the First Taxpayer's Bank copies all of the day's accumulated transaction information from disk to tape. Why?

10. In what ways can computer security protect the privacy of individuals? In what ways can computer security threaten the privacy of individuals?
11. What are smart weapons? How do they differ from conventional weapons? What are the advantages and risks of smart weapons?

Discussion Questions

1. Are computers morally neutral? Explain your answer.
2. Suppose Whizzo Software Company produces a program that looks, from the user's point of view, exactly like the immensely popular BozoWorks from Bozo, Inc. Whizzo insists that it didn't copy any of the code in Bozo-Works; they just tried to design a program that would appeal to BozoWorks users. Bozo cries foul and sues Whizzo for violation of intellectual property laws. Do you think the laws should favor Bozo's arguments or Whizzo's? Why?
3. What do you suppose motivates people to create computer viruses and other destructive software? What do you think motivates hackers to break into computer systems? Are the two types of behavior related?

4. Some people think all mail messages on the Internet should be encrypted. They argue that, if everything is encrypted, the encrypted message won't stand out, so everybody's right to privacy will be better protected. Others suggest that this would just improve the cover of criminals with something to hide from the government. What do you think, and why?
5. Would you like to work in a business where all employees were required to wear active badges? Explain your answer.
6. How do the issues raised in the debate over SDI apply to other large software systems? How do you feel about the different issues raised in the debate?

Projects

1. Talk to employees at your campus computer labs and computer centers about security issues and techniques. What are the major security threats according to these employees? What security techniques are used to protect the equipment and data in each facility? Are these techniques adequate? Report on your findings.

2. Perform the same kind of interviews at local businesses. Do businesses view security differently than your campus personnel?

Sources & Resources

Books

A Gift of Fire: Social, Legal, and Ethical Issues in Computing, by Sara Baase (Upper Saddle River, NJ: Prentice-Hall, 1997). This book offers a thorough, easy-to-read overview of the human questions facing us as a result of the computer revolution: privacy, security, reliability, accountability, and the rest.

Computer Ethics: Cautionary Tales and Ethical Dilemmas in Computing, Second Edition, by Tom Forester and Perry Morrison (Cambridge, MA: MIT Press, 1994). Forester and Morrison don't mince words as they discuss the important issues that face computer professionals and users today. This concise book is rich with real-world examples of computer crime, security breaches, reliability risks, and privacy threats.

Computers, Ethics, and Social Values, edited by Deborah G. Johnson and Helen Nissenbaum (Upper Saddle River, NJ: Prentice-Hall, 1995). This is an excellent collection of papers and articles by some of the best known writers and analysts on issues relating to computers in society. Computer crime, intellectual property, privacy, reliability, responsibility, and network issues are explored in this excellent survey.

Web Security: A Step-by-Step Reference Guide, by Lincoln D. Stein (Reading, MA: Addison-Wesley, 1997). The explosive growth of the World Wide Web has created a variety of new security problems and risks. This book explains in clear language many of the technical problems related to Web security. It also offers practical advice for Web administrators and users who want to protect themselves from attacks and privacy violations.

Cyberspace and the Law: Your Rights and Duties in the On-Line World, by Edward A. Cavazos and Gavino Morin (Cambridge, MA: MIT Press, 1994). This is a very readable introduction to the most important legal issues involving computers and networks. Intellectual property, freedom of speech, privacy rights, electronic contracts, computer fraud, and other issues are described in plain English for nonlawyers. If you're even a little worried about how any of these issues affect you, this book is worth seeking out.

Online Law: The SPA's Legal Guide to Doing Business on the Internet, edited by Thomas J. Smedinghoff (Reading, MA: Addison-Wesley, 1996). The Software Publishers Association is the principal trade association of the software industry. This guidebook is designed to explore the legal issues that arise when businesses move their shops onto the Internet. Topics include electronic contracts, copyrights, digital signatures, electronic commerce, obscenity, and intellectual property.

Virtual Private Networks for Dummies, by Mark Merkow (Foster City, CA: IDG Books, 1999). In spite of its title, this book provides a great deal of technical information on setting up secure Internet connections and communications. Coverage includes cryptography, privacy, reliability, and e-commerce.

Internet Cryptography, by Richard E. Smith (Reading, MA: Addison-Wesley, 1997). Cryptography is the most effective tool for protecting privacy and preserving security on the Internet. This book explains the ins and outs of cryptography, with plenty of practical details for people who need to protect their data as it moves around on the Net.

Cyberwars: Espionage on the Internet, by Jean Guisnel (New York: Plenum, 1997). If you need proof that the Internet has graduated from its role as a research assistant, read *Cyberwars.* Guisnel, a respected French journalist, exposes the emerging online battle zones where spies, saboteurs, government agents, drug traffickers, and others wage virtual wars. Even though we can't see them happening, we're all victims of the fallout from these dangerous battles.

High Noon on the Electronic Frontier: Conceptual Issues in Cyberspace, edited by Peter Ludlow (Cambridge, MA: MIT Press, 1996). This collection of papers explores many of the most controversial ethical and social issues raised by the Internet and computer technology. The writing style ranges from academic to "gonzo," and the subject matter is just as diverse.

Electronic Highway Robbery: An Artist's Guide to Copyrights in the Digital Era, by Mary E. Carter (Berkeley, CA: Peachpit Press, 1996). Today's digital technology raises all kinds of intellectual property questions. This easy-to-read, nontechnical book explores those questions and provides many answers for artists and multimedia developers.

Digital Copyright Protection, by Peter Wayner (Boston: AP Professional, 1997). This somewhat technical book provides information and advice on several ways of protecting digital information on the Web and elsewhere.

Hackers: Heroes of the Computer Revolution, by Steven Levy (New York: Delta, 1994). This book helped bring the word "hackers" into the public's vocabulary. Levy's entertaining account of the golden age of hacking gives a historical perspective to today's anti-hacker mania.

The Cuckoo's Egg, by Cliff Stoll (New York: Pocket Books, 1989, 1995). This best-selling book documents the stalking of an interloper on the Internet. International espionage mixes with computer technology in this entertaining, engaging, and eye-opening book.

Takedown: The Pursuit and Capture of Kevin Mitnick, America's Most Wanted Computer Outlaw—by the Man Who Did It, by Tsutomu Shimomura with John Markoff (New

York: Hyperion Books, 1996) and *The Fugitive Game,* by Jonathon Littman (New York: Little, Brown and Co., 1997). These two books chronicle the events leading up to and including the capture of Kevin Mitnick, America's number one criminal hacker. *Takedown* presents the story from the point of view of the security expert who captured Mitnick. *The Fugitive Game* is written from a more objective journalistic point of view.

Cyberpunk—Outlaws and Hackers on the Computer Frontier, Updated Edition, by Katie Hafner and John Markoff (New York: Simon & Schuster, 1995). This book profiles three hackers whose exploits caught the public's attention: Kevin Mitnick, a California cracker who vandalized corporate systems; Pengo, who penetrated U.S. systems for East German espionage purposes; and Robert Morris, Jr., whose Internet worm brought down 6,000 computers in a matter of hours.

Computers Under Attack, edited by Peter Denning (Reading, MA: ACM Press, 1990). A wide-ranging collection of articles about computer security, hacking, and the network community. This book goes into detail on the Internet worm, computer viruses, and other security-related issues.

The Hacker Crackdown: Law and Disorder on the Electronic Frontier, by Bruce Sterling (New York: Bantam Books, 1992). Famed cyberpunk author Sterling turns to nonfiction to tell both sides of the story of the war between hackers and federal law enforcement agencies. The complete text is available on line along with rest-of-the-story updates.

Digital Woes: Why We Should Not Depend on Software, by Lauren Ruth Wiener (Reading, MA: Addison-Wesley, 1993). This book provides a broad, nontechnical overview of the inherent risks of software. Clear explanations of how software is developed and why it goes wrong are accompanied by sobering examples and a discussion of ways to deal with the problem.

Computer-Related Risks, by Peter Neumann (Reading, MA: Addison-Wesley, 1995). Neumann runs the popular and eye-opening comp.risks forum on the Internet. This book draws on that forum and Neumann's expertise, providing an exhaustive technical survey of the risks we face as a result of our dependence on computer technology. The hundreds of documented examples range from humorous to horrifying, and they're tied together with Neumann's intelligent assessment of the broader problems and possible solutions.

Ender's Game, by Orson Scott Card (New York: Tor Books, 1999). This award-winning, entertaining science fiction opus has become a favorite of the cryptography crowd because of its emphasis on encryption to protect privacy.

The Postman, by David Brin (New York: Bantam, 1990). This entertaining science fiction novel weaves a tale of the future that raises many of the same issues raised by Kempelen's chess-playing machine. The disappointing 1997 movie bears little resemblance to the novel.

Periodicals

Many popular magazines, from *Newsweek* to *Wired,* provide regular coverage of issues related to privacy and security of digital systems. Most of the periodicals listed here are newsletters of professional organizations that focus on these issues.

Information Security (www.infosecuritymag.com). This magazine focuses on security problems and solutions. Some of the articles are technical, but most are accessible to anyone with an interest in security issues.

The CPSR Newsletter, published by Computer Professionals for Social Responsibility (P.O. Box 717, Palo Alto, CA 94302, 415/322-3778, fax 415/322-3798, email: cpsr@csli.stanford.edu). An alliance of computer scientists and others interested in the impact of computer technology on society, CPSR works to influence public policies to ensure that computers are used wisely in the public interest. Their newsletter has intelligent articles and discussions of risk, reliability, privacy, security, human rights, work, war, education, the environment, democracy, and other subjects that bring together computers and people.

EFFector, published by the Electronic Frontier Foundation (155 Second St., Cambridge, MA 02141, 617/864-0665, fax 617/864-0866, email: effnews-request@eff.org). This electronic newsletter is distributed by EFF, an organization "established to help civilize the electronic frontier." EFF was founded by Mitch Kapor (see Chapter 6) and John Perry Barlow to protect civil rights and encourage responsible citizenship on the electronic frontier of computer networks.

Ethix: The Bulletin of the Institute for Business, Technology, and Ethics (www.ethix.org, email: contact@ethix.org). The IBTE is a relatively new non-profit corporation working to transform business through appropriate technology and ethical values.

World Wide Web

As you might suspect, the Net is the best source of up-to-the-minute information on computer security and related issues. Public and commercial organizations maintain Web pages devoted to these issues, and dozens of newsgroups contain lively ongoing discussions on controversial topics. Check the *Computer Confluence* Web site for the latest links.

Chapter

12

Systems Design and Development

In this chapter:

- ▶ How software is made
- ▶ The many languages of programming
- ▶ The process of developing large systems
- ▶ Why computer science is more than programming
- ▶ Why software doesn't work reliably
- ... and more.

On the CD-ROM:

- ▶ Grace Murray Hopper's famous threat
- ▶ Video clip showing how object-oriented programming is used to create a 3D game
- ▶ Instant access to glossary and key word references
- ▶ Interactive self-study quizzes
- ... and more.

On the Web:

www.prenhall.com/beekman

- ▶ Articles and tutorials on a variety of programming topics
- ▶ Links to the most important organizations of computer professionals
- ▶ Resources for exploring software development and computer science
- ▶ Self-study exercises
- ... and more.

The only phrase I've ever disliked is,

"Why, we've always done it that way."

I always tell young people,

"Go ahead and do it. You can always apologize later."

—Grace Murray Hopper

Amazing Grace, the grand old lady of software, had little to apologize for when she died at the age of 85 in 1992. More than any other woman, Grace Murray Hopper helped chart the course of the computer industry from its earliest days.

Hopper earned a Ph.D. from Yale in 1928 and taught math for 10 years at Vassar before joining the U.S. Naval Reserve in 1943. The Navy assigned her to the Bureau of Ordnance Computation at Harvard, where she worked with Howard Aiken's Mark I, the first large-scale digital computer. She wrote programs and operating manuals for the Mark I, Mark II, and Mark III.

Aiken often asked his team, "Are you making any numbers?" When she wasn't "making numbers," Hopper replied that she was "debugging" the computer. Today that's what programmers call the process of finding and removing errors, or bugs, from programs. Scientists and engineers had referred to mechanical defects as bugs for decades; Thomas Edison wrote about bugs in his inventions in 1878. But when Hopper first used the term, she was referring to a real bug—a 2-inch moth that got caught in a relay, bringing the mighty Mark II to a standstill! That moth carcass is taped to a page in a log book, housed in a Navy museum in Virginia.

Hopper recognized early that businesses could make good use of computers. After World War II she left Harvard to work on the UNIVAC I, the first general-purpose commercial computer, and other commercial computers. She played central roles in the development of the first compiler (a type of computer language translator that makes most of today's software possible) and COBOL, the first computer language designed for developing business software.

Throughout most of her career Hopper remained anchored to the Navy. When she retired from the fleet with the rank of rear admiral at the age of 79, her list of accomplishments filled eight single-spaced pages in her Navy biography.

But Hopper's greatest impact was probably the result of her tireless crusade against the "We've always done it that way" mind-set. In the early days of computing she worked to persuade businesses to embrace the new technology. In later years she campaigned to shift the Pentagon and industry away from mainframes and toward networks of smaller computers. Her vigorous campaign against the status quo earned her a reputation as being controversial and contrary. That didn't bother Amazing Grace, whose favorite maxim was "A ship in port is safe, but that's not what ships are for."

Grace Murray Hopper, (1906–1992)

Today's computer software is so sophisticated that it's almost invisible to the user. Just as a great motion picture can make us forget we're watching a movie, word processing software allows us to do our creative work without ever thinking about the instructions and data flowing through the computer's processor as we work. But whether you're writing a paper, solving a calculus problem, flying a simulated space shuttle, or exploring the nooks and crannies of the Internet, your imaginary environment stands on an incredibly complex software substructure. The process of creating that software is one of the most intellectually challenging activities ever done by people.

In this chapter we look at the process of turning ideas into working computer programs and consider the "life cycle" of a typical program. We examine computer languages and the ways programmers use them to create software. In addition, we look at how computer users take advantage of the programming languages built into applications, operating systems, and utilities. We also confront the problems involved with producing reliable software and consider the implications of depending on unstable software. In the process of exploring software we'll see how the work of programmers, analysts, software engineers, and computer scientists affects our lives and our work.

How People Make Programs

It's the only job I can think of where I get to be both an engineer and an artist. There's an incredible, rigorous, technical element to it, which I like because you have to do very precise thinking. On the other hand, it has a wildly creative side where the boundaries of imagination are the only real limitation.

—Andy Hertzfeld, **co-designer of the Macintosh**

Most computer users depend on professionally programmed applications—spreadsheets, database programs, Web browsers, and the like—as problem-solving tools. But in some cases it's necessary or desirable to write a program rather than use one written by somebody else. As a human activity, computer programming is a relative newcomer. But programming is a specialized form of the age-old process of problem solving. Problem solving typically involves four steps:

1. *Understanding the problem.* Defining the problem clearly is often the most important—and most overlooked—step in the problem-solving process.

2. *Devising a plan for solving the problem.* What resources are available? People? Information? A computer? Software? Data? How might those resources be put to work to solve the problem?

3. *Carrying out the plan.* This phase often overlaps with step 2, since many problem-solving schemes are developed on the fly.

4. *Evaluating the solution.* Is the problem solved correctly? Is this solution applicable to other problems?

The programming process can also be described as a four-step process, although in practice these steps often overlap:

1. Defining the problem
2. Devising, refining, and testing the algorithm
3. Writing the program
4. Testing and debugging the program.

Most programming problems are far too complex to solve all at once. To turn a problem into a program, a programmer typically creates a list of smaller problems. Each of these smaller problems can be broken into subproblems that can be subdivided in the same way. This process, called stepwise refinement, is similar to the process of developing an outline before writing a paper or a book. Programmers sometimes refer to this type of design as top-down design because the design process starts at the top, with the main ideas, and works down to the details.

The result of stepwise refinement is an algorithm—a set of step-by-step instructions that, when completed, solves the original problem. (Recall Suzanne's French toast recipe in Chapter 4.) Programmers typically write algorithms in a form called pseudocode—a cross between a computer language and plain English. When the details of an algorithm are in place, a programmer can translate it from pseudocode into a computer language.

From Idea to Algorithm

One programs, just as one writes, not because one understands, but

in order to come to understand.

Programming is an act of design. To write a program is to legislate the laws for

a world one first has to create in imagination.

—Joseph Weizenbaum, in *Computer Power and Human Reason*

Let's develop a simple algorithm to illustrate the process. Let's start with a statement of the problem:

A schoolteacher needs a program to play a number-guessing game so students can learn to develop logical strategies and practice their arithmetic. In this game the computer picks a number between 1 and 100 and gives the player seven turns to guess the number. After each incorrect try the computer tells the player whether the guess is too high or too low.

In short, the problem is to write a program that can

```
play a guessing game
```

Stepwise Refinement

The first cut at the problem breaks it into three parts: a beginning, a middle, and an end. Each of these parts represents a smaller programming problem to solve.

```
begin game
repeat turn until number is guessed or seven turns are completed
end game
```

These three steps represent a bare-bones algorithm. In the completed algorithm these three parts will be carried out in sequence. The next refinement fills in a few details for each part:

```
begin game
        display instructions
        pick a number between 1 and 100
repeat turn until number is guessed or seven turns are completed
        input guess from user
        respond to guess
end repeat
end game
        display end message
```

The middle part of our instructions includes a sequence of operations that is repeated for each turn: everything between "repeat" and "end repeat." But these instructions are missing crucial details. How, for example, will the computer respond to a guess? We can replace "respond to guess" with instructions that vary depending on the guessed number:

```
if guess = number, then say so and quit;
else if guess < number, then say guess is too small;
else say guess is too big
```

Finally, we need to give the computer a way of knowing when seven turns have passed. We can set a counter to 0 at the beginning and add 1 to the counter after each turn. When the counter reaches 7, the repetition stops, and the computer displays a message. That makes the algorithm look like this:

```
begin game
      display instructions
      pick a number between 1 and 100
      set counter to 0
repeat turn until number is guessed or counter = 7
      input guess from user
      if guess = number, then say so and quit;
      else if guess < number, then say guess is too small;
      else say guess is too big
      add 1 to counter
end repeat
end game
      display end message
```

Control Structures

A computer can't understand this algorithm, but the pseudocode is clear to any person familiar with **control structures**—logical structures that control the order in which instructions are carried out. This algorithm uses three basic control structures: sequence, selection, and repetition.

1 A *sequence control structure* is a group of instructions followed in order from the first through the last. In our algorithm example, as in most computer languages, the sequence is the default structure; that is, it applies unless a statement says otherwise:

```
display instructions
pick a number between 1 and 100
set counter to 0
```

2 A *selection (or decision) control structure* is used to make logical decisions—to choose between alternative courses of action depending on certain conditions. It typically takes the form of "If (some condition is true) then (do something) else (do something else)":

```
if guess < number, then say guess is too small;
else say guess is too big
```

3 A *repetition control structure* is a looping mechanism. It allows a group of steps to be repeated several times, usually until some condition is satisfied. In this algorithm the indented statements between "repeat" and "end repeat" are repeated until the number is guessed correctly or the counter is equal to 7:

```
repeat turn until number is guessed or counter = 7
input guess from user
...
add 1 to counter
end repeat
```

As our example illustrates, these simple control structures can be combined to produce more complex algorithms. In fact, any computer program can be constructed from these three control structures.

Testing the Algorithm

The next step is **testing** the algorithm. Testing of the completed program will come later; this round of testing is designed to check the logic of the algorithm. We can test it by following the instructions using different sets of numbers. We might, for example, use a target number of 35 and guesses of 15, 72, 52, and 35. Those numbers test all three possibilities in the if–then–else structure (guess is less than target, guess is greater than target, and guess equals target), and they show what happens if the player chooses the correct number. We should also test the algorithm with seven wrong guesses in a row to make sure it correctly ends a losing game.

From Algorithm to Program

> You know, computer science inverts the normal. In normal science you're given a world and your job is to find out the rules. In computer science, you give the computer the rules and it creates the world.
>
> —Alan Kay

When testing is complete, the algorithm is ready to become a program. Because the algorithm has the logical structure of a program, the process of **coding**—writing a program from the algorithm—is simple and straightforward. Statements in the algorithm translate directly into lines of code in whichever programming language best fits the programmer's needs.

A Simple Program

Let's look at the algorithm rewritten in C++, a popular variation of the C programming language. (The name C doesn't stand for anything; the language grew out of a less successful language called B.) This program, like most well-written C++ programs, is organized into three parts, similar to a recipe in a cookbook:

1. The *program heading,* containing the name of the program and data files (equivalent to the name and description of the dish to be cooked)

2. The *declarations and definitions* of variables and other programmer-defined items (equivalent to the list of ingredients used in the recipe)

3. The *body* of the program, containing the instructions, sandwiched between curly braces, { } (equivalent to the cooking steps).

A programmer creating an animated sequence for a Hollywood film.

The program listing (next page) looks a little like a detailed version of the original algorithm, but there's an important difference: Because it's a computer program, every word, symbol, and punctuation mark has an exact, unambiguous meaning.

The words highlighted with italics in this listing are key words with predefined meanings in C++. These key words, along with special symbols like + and =, are part of the standard vocabulary of C++. The words *number, guess,* and *counter* are defined by the programmer so they become part of the program's vocabulary when it runs. Each of these words represents a *variable*—a named portion of the computer's memory whose contents can be examined and changed by the program.

```
// Game.cpp
//
// by Paul Thurrott and Gary Brent
//
```
PROGRAM HEADING

```
#include <iostream.h>
#include <stdlib.h>
#include <time.h>
```
DECLARATIONS/DEFINITIONS

```
// global variables
int number,
guess,
counter = 0;

int
main()
```

```
{


   cout   << "Welcome to the guessing game. I'll pick a number" << endl
          << "between 1 and 100 and you try to guess what it is." << endl
          << "You get 7 tries." << endl;

   // seed the random number generator so that the number is always
   // different. This example uses the current time as a seed.
srand((unsigned) time(NULL));

   // calculate a random number between 1 and 100
   number = abs(rand() % 100) + 1;

   // do this loop for each guess. Leave the loop when the guess is
   // correct or when 7 incorrect guesses have been made
   do
      {
         cout << "What's your guess?" << endl;
         cin >> guess;
         if (guess == number)
            cout << "You guessed it!" << endl;
         else
         if (guess < number)
            cout << "Too small, guess again." << endl;
         else
            cout << "Too big, guess again." << endl;
         ++counter;
      } while ( (counter < 7) && (guess != number) );

   if (guess != number)
      cout << "I fooled you 7 times - the number was "
           << number << "!" << endl;
   return EXIT_SUCCESS;
}
```
PROGRAM BODY

As programs go, this C++ program is fairly easy to understand. But C++ isn't English, and some statements occasionally need clarification or further documentation. For the sake of readability most programs include *comments*—the programmer's equivalent of Post-It Notes. In C++, lines that begin with double slashes (//) contain comments. The computer ignores comments; they're included to help human readers understand (or remember) something about the program.

Into the Computer

The program still needs to be entered into the computer's memory, saved as a disk file, and translated into the computer's native machine language before it can be executed, or run. To enter and save the program, we can use a text editor. A *text editor* is like a word processor without the formatting features required by writers and publishers. Some text editors, designed with programming in mind, provide automatic program indenting and limited error checking while the program is being typed.

To translate the program into machine language, we need translation software. The translation program might be an interpreter (a program that translates and transmits each statement individually, the way a United Nations interpreter translates a Russian speech into English) or a compiler (a program that translates an entire program before passing it on to the computer, as a scholar might translate the novel *War and Peace* from Russian to English). Most C translators are compilers because compiled programs tend to run faster than interpreted programs.

A typical compiler software package today is more than just a compiler. It's an integrated *programming environment*, including a text editor, a compiler, a *debugger* to simplify the process of locating and correcting errors, and a variety of other programming utilities. **UV**

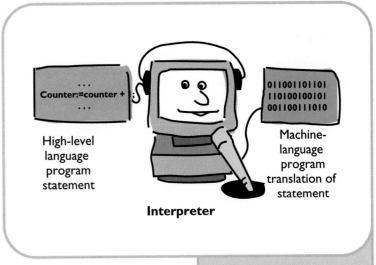

Interpreter

An interpreter translates a high-level program to machine language one statement at a time during execution.

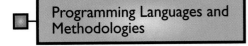

Programming Languages and Methodologies

> If one character, one pause, of the incantation is not strictly in proper form, the magic doesn't work.
>
> —**Frederick Brooks**, in *The Mythical Man-Month*

Compiler

A compiler translates an entire high-level program to machine language before executing the program.

C++ is one of hundreds of computer languages in use today. Some are tools for professional programmers who write the software the rest of us use. Others are intended to help students learn the fundamentals of programming. Still others allow computer users to automate repetitive tasks and customize software applications. Since the earliest days of computing, programming languages have continued to evolve toward providing easier communication between people and computers.

Machine Language and Assembly Language

Every computer has a native language—a machine language. Similarities exist between different brands of machine languages: They all have instructions for the four basic

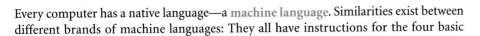

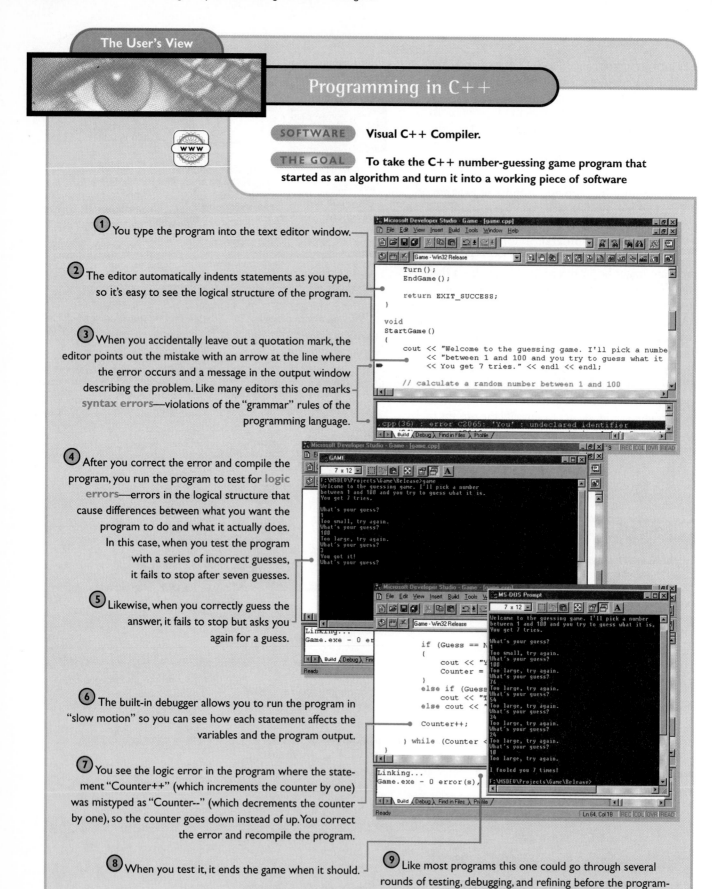

The User's View

Programming in C++

SOFTWARE **Visual C++ Compiler.**

THE GOAL **To take the C++ number-guessing game program that started as an algorithm and turn it into a working piece of software**

① You type the program into the text editor window.

② The editor automatically indents statements as you type, so it's easy to see the logical structure of the program.

③ When you accidentally leave out a quotation mark, the editor points out the mistake with an arrow at the line where the error occurs and a message in the output window describing the problem. Like many editors this one marks syntax errors—violations of the "grammar" rules of the programming language.

④ After you correct the error and compile the program, you run the program to test for logic errors—errors in the logical structure that cause differences between what you want the program to do and what it actually does. In this case, when you test the program with a series of incorrect guesses, it fails to stop after seven guesses.

⑤ Likewise, when you correctly guess the answer, it fails to stop but asks you again for a guess.

⑥ The built-in debugger allows you to run the program in "slow motion" so you can see how each statement affects the variables and the program output.

⑦ You see the logic error in the program where the statement "Counter++" (which increments the counter by one) was mistyped as "Counter--" (which decrements the counter by one), so the counter goes down instead of up. You correct the error and recompile the program.

⑧ When you test it, it ends the game when it should.

⑨ Like most programs this one could go through several rounds of testing, debugging, and refining before the programmer is satisfied.

arithmetic operations, for comparing pairs of numbers, for repeating instructions, and so on. But like English and French, different brands of machine languages are different languages, and machines based on one machine language can't understand programs written in another.

From the machine's point of view, machine language is all binary. Instructions, memory locations, numbers, and characters are all represented by strings of zeros and ones. Because binary numbers are difficult for people to read, machine-language programs are usually displayed with the binary numbers translated into decimal (base 10), *hexadecimal* (base 16), or some other number system. Even so, machine-language programs have always been hard to write, read, and debug.

The programming process became easier with the invention of assembly language—a language that's functionally equivalent to machine language but is easier for people to read, write, and understand. In assembly language, programmers use alphabetic codes that correspond to the machine's numeric instructions. An assembly-language instruction for subtract, for example, might be SUB. Of course, SUB means nothing to the computer, which only responds to commands like 10110111. To bridge the communication gap between programmer and computer, a program called an assembler translates each assembly-language instruction into a machine-language instruction. Without knowing any better, the computer acts as its own translator.

Because of the obvious advantages of assembly language, few programmers write in machine language anymore. But assembly-language programming is still considered *low-level* programming; that is, it requires the programmer to think on the machine's level and to include an enormous amount of detail in every program. Assembly language and machine language are *low-level languages*. Low-level programming is a repetitive, tedious, and error-prone process. To make matters worse, a program written in one assembly language or machine language must be completely rewritten before it can be run on computers with different machine languages. Many programmers still use assembly language to write parts of video games and other applications for which speed and direct communication with hardware are critical. But most programmers today think and write on a higher level.

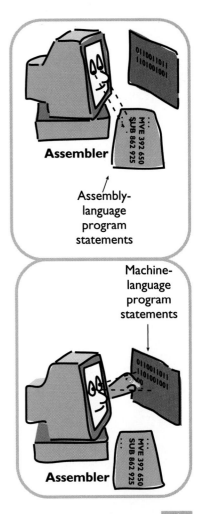

An assembler translates each statement of assembly language into the corresponding machine-language statement.

High-Level Languages

Computer programming is an art form, like the creation of poetry or music.

—Donald E. Knuth, **author of *The Art of Computer Programming***

High-level languages, which fall somewhere between natural human languages and precise machine languages, were developed during the early 1950s to simplify and streamline the programming process. Languages such as FORTRAN and COBOL made it possible for scientists, engineers, and business-people to write programs using familiar terminology and notation rather than cryptic machine instructions. Today programmers can choose from hundreds of other high-level languages.

Interpreters and compilers translate high-level programs into machine language. Whether interpreted or compiled, a single statement from a high-level program turns into several machine-language statements. A high-level language hides most of the nitty-gritty details of the machine operations from the programmer. As a result, it's easier for the programmer to think about the overall logic of the program—the big ideas.

Besides being easier to write and debug, high-level programs have the advantage of being *transportable* between machines. A program written in standard C can be compiled and run on any computer with a standard C compiler. The same applies for programs written in Java, Basic, FORTRAN, COBOL, and other standardized languages.

Transporting a program to a new machine isn't always that easy. Most high-level programs need to be *partially* rewritten to adjust to differences among hardware, compilers, operating systems, and user interfaces. For example, programmers might need to rewrite 20% of the code when translating the Windows version of an application program into a Macintosh version, or vice versa. Still, high-level programs are far more portable than programs written in assembly and machine languages.

Of the hundreds of high-level languages that have been developed, a few have become well known because of their widespread use:

▶ *FORTRAN (Formula Translation)*, the first commercial high-level programming language, was designed at IBM in the 1950s to solve scientific and engineering problems. Modern versions of FORTRAN are still used by many scientists and engineers today.

▶ *COBOL (Common Business Oriented Language)* was developed when the U.S. government in 1960 demanded a new language oriented toward business data processing problems. COBOL programmers still work in many data processing shops around the world.

▶ *LISP (List Processing)* was developed at MIT in the late 1950s to process nonnumeric data like characters, words, and other symbols. LISP is widely used in artificial intelligence research, in part because it's easy to write LISP programs that can write other programs.

▶ *Basic (Beginner's All-purpose Symbolic Instruction Code*; sometimes spelled with all caps: *BASIC*) was developed in the mid-1960s as an easy-to-learn, interactive alternative to FORTRAN for beginning programmers. Before Basic, a student typically had to submit a program, wait hours for output from a compiler, and repeat the process until every error was corrected. Because Basic was interpreted line by line rather than compiled as a whole, it could provide instant feedback as students typed statements and commands into their terminals. When personal computers appeared, Basic enjoyed unprecedented popularity among students, hobbyists, and programmers. Over the years Basic has evolved into a powerful, modern programming tool for amateur and professional programmers. True Basic is a modern version of Basic developed by the original inventors of Basic. The most popular Windows version of Basic today—in fact, the most popular programming language ever created—is Microsoft's *Visual Basic*. REALBasic is a Macintosh-based Basic similar to Visual Basic.

▶ *Pascal* (named for the seventeenth-century French mathematician, inventor, philosopher, and mystic) was developed in the early 1970s as an alternative to BASIC for beginning programmers. Pascal was designed to encourage structured programming, a technique described in the next section. Pascal is still popular as a student language, but it is seldom used by professional programmers.

▶ C was invented at Bell Labs in the early 1970s as a tool for programming operating systems such as UNIX. C is a complex language that's difficult to learn. But its power, flexibility, and efficiency have made it the language of choice for most professionals who program personal computers.

▶ C++ is the language we used in our *User's View* example. C++ is a variation of C that takes advantage of a modern programming methodology called object-oriented programming, described below.

▶ Java is a modern programming language developed by Sun Microsystems. Java is similar to C++, but simpler to learn and to use. Java excels at producing Web-based applets that run on multiple platforms.

▶ *Ada* (named for Ada Lovelace, the programming pioneer profiled in Chapter 1) is a massive language based on Pascal. It developed in the late 1970s for the U.S. Defense Department. Ada never caught on outside the walls of the military establishment.

```
program Game (input, output);
(* Programmed by Clay Cowgill  and David Stuve *)

(*------------------------------------------------------------*)

var Number, Guess, Counter : integer
(*------------------------------------------------------------*)
begin
writeln('Welcome to the guessing game. I'll pick a number');
writeln('between 1 and 100, and you try to guess what it is.');
writeln('You get 7 tries.');
(* Calculate a random number between 1 and 100 *)
Number := abs (Random mod 100) + 1;
Counter := 0;
repeat (* turn *)
    writeln('What's your guess?');
    readln(Guess);
    if Guess = Number then
        writeln('You got it!')
    else
        if Guess < Number then
            writeln('Too small, try again.');
        else writeln('Too big, guess again.');
    Counter := Counter + 1;
until (Guess = Number) or (Counter = 7)
if Guess <> Number then
    begin
        writeln('I fooled you 7 times!');
    end
end.
```

Pascal is popular as a student language because it's easy to learn and it encourages good programming style. This program listing shows the number-guessing game program in standard Pascal.

- ▶ *PROLOG (Programming Logic)* is a popular language for artificial intelligence programming. As the name implies, PROLOG is designed for working with logical relationships between facts.
- ▶ *LOGO* is a dialect of LISP specially designed for children.

Structured Programming

Programmers work the way medieval craftsmen built cathedrals—
one stone at a time.

—Mitch Kapor

A programming language can be a powerful tool in the hands of a skilled programmer. But tools alone don't guarantee quality; the best programmers have specific techniques for getting the most out of their software tools. In the short history of computer programming, computer scientists have developed several new methodologies that have made programmers more productive and programs more reliable.

For example, computer scientists in the late 1960s recognized that most FORTRAN and BASIC programs were riddled with *GoTo statements*—statements used to transfer control to other parts of the program. (Remember "Go to Jail. Do not pass Go. Do not collect $200."?) The logical structure of a program with GoTo statements can resemble a tangled spider's web. The bigger the program, the bigger the logical maze and the more possibility for error. Every branch of a program represents a loose end that might be overlooked by the programmer.

Computer software contains two kinds of information algorithms, which correspond to the program code that performs some task, and data, upon which the algorithms operate. In a sense the algorithms are the gears and levers—the machinery that transforms the raw material of data. An unstructured program is like a huge, complicated machine that can't be easily broken down into sections. Any modification would require the entire machine *to be disassembled.* This difficulty is one reason why most programmers are afraid to modify unstructured code.

Structured programming breaks the big machine up into smaller machine modules, each of which has a clearly defined task in the overall processing of data. Structured programs are easier to understand and modify because problems can be isolated to individual modules and the input and output of each module in the assembly line are easier to understand.

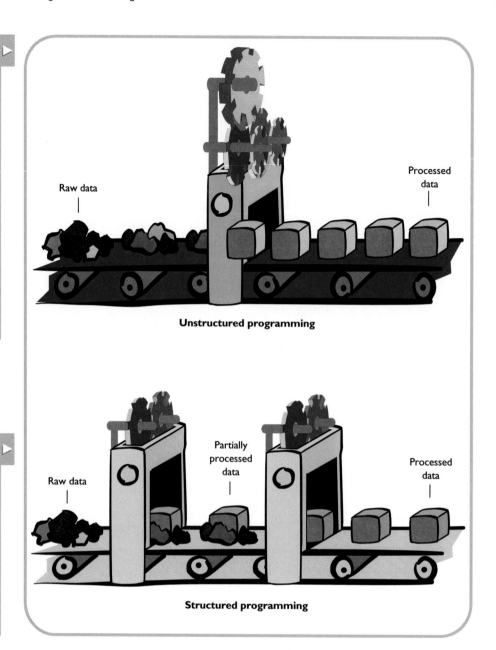

Raw data

Processed data

Unstructured programming

Raw data

Partially processed data

Processed data

Structured programming

In an attempt to overcome these problems, computer scientists developed structured programming—a technique to make the programming process easier and more productive. A structured program doesn't depend on the GoTo statement to control the logical flow. Instead it's built from smaller programs called modules, or subprograms, which are in turn made of even smaller modules. The programmer combines modules using the three basic control structures: sequence, repetition, and selection. A program is well structured if

▶ It's made up of logically cohesive modules

▶ The modules are arranged in a hierarchy

▶ It's straightforward and readable.

The Pascal and Ada languages were designed to encourage structured programming and discourage "spaghetti code." The success of these languages prompted computer scientists to develop versions of BASIC and FORTRAN that were conducive to structured programming.

The Basic programming language has evolved through three major phases. These examples show how the programming process has changed during the last three decades. The first two Basic examples shown here are complete listings of programs to play the number-guessing game; the third example is a glimpse of a program to play a slot machine game.

```
10 REM INITIALIZE
20 RANDOMIZE
30 PRINT "THE GUESSING GAME"
40 PRINT "I WILL THINK OF A NUMBER BETWEEN 1 AND 100."
50 PRINT "TRY TO GUESS WHAT IT IS"
60 LET C = 0
70 LET N = INT(RND(1) * 100)
80 INPUT "WHAT IS YOUR GUESS?";G
90 IF G = N THEN PRINT "THAT IS CORRECT!"
100 IF G < N THEN PRINT "TOO SMALL--TRY AGAIN"
110 IF G > N THEN PRINT "TOO BIG--TRY AGAIN"
120 LET C = C + 1
130 IF C = 7 THEN GOTO 180
140 IF G <> N THEN GOTO 80
150 IF G <> N THEN PRINT "I FOOLED YOU 7 TIMES! THE ANSWER WAS ";N
160 END
```

Early Basic. The program with numbered lines is written in a simple version of Basic—the only kind that was available in the early days of the language. Statements are executed in numerical order unless control is transferred to another statement with a GoTo statement.

```
REM Guessing Game
REM written by Rajeev Pandey

DECLARE SUB StartGame (Counter!, Number!)
DECLARE SUB Turn (Counter!, Guess!, Number!)
DECLARE SUB EndGame (Number!)

CALL StartGame(Counter, Number)
DO
    CALL Turn(Counter, Guess, Number)
LOOP UNTIL (Guess = Number) OR (Counter = 7)
IF Guess <> Number THEN
    CALL EndGame(Number)
END IF

SUB EndGame (Number)
PRINT "I fooled you 7 times!"
PRINT "The answer was "; Number
END SUB

SUB StartGame (Counter, Number)
PRINT "Welcome to the guessing game. I'll think of a number"
PRINT "between 1 and 100 and you will guess what it is."
Counter = 0
RANDOMIZE TIMER
Number = INT(RND(1) * 100)
END SUB

SUB Turn (Counter, Guess, Number)
INPUT "What's your guess?"; Guess
IF Guess = Number THEN
    PRINT "You got it!"
ELSE
    IF Guess < Number THEN
        PRINT "Too small, try again."
    ELSE
        PRINT "Too big, try again."
    END IF
END IF
Counter = Counter + 1
END SUB
```

Structured Basic. The modular program on the bottom is written in QuickBASIC, a newer version of the language with many structured programming features. The main program has been reduced to a handful of statements at the top of the listing (after the DECLARE statement); these statements display the overall logic of the program. As it's running, the main program uses CALL statements to transfer control to each of the three subprograms, which take care of the game's beginning, each turn, and the game's end.

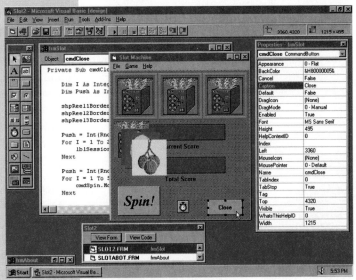

Visual Basic. The screen shows an example of Microsoft's popular Visual Basic, a modern programming environment that includes many of the ideas and tools of object-oriented programming and visual programming.

Data in OOP is more than raw material to be processed. In OOP, data is bound together with the methods and properties of an object. Each object can maintain its own storehouse of data appropriate for that object.

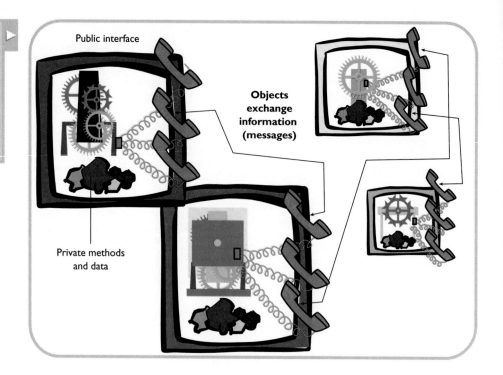

Public interface

Objects exchange information (messages)

Private methods and data

Object-Oriented Programming

Structured programming represented a big step forward for programmers; it allowed them to produce better, more reliable programs in less time. But structured programming wasn't the last word in programming; today object-oriented programming (OOP) has captured the attention of the software development community. Object-oriented programming was first used in the 1970s, most notably in a language called *Smalltalk*. In object-oriented programming a program is not just a collection of step-by-step instructions or procedures; it's a collection of *objects*. Objects contain both data and instructions and can send and receive messages. For example, an on-screen button in a multimedia program might be an object, containing both a physical description of the button's appearance and a *script* telling it what to do if it receives a mouse-click message from the operating system. This button object can be easily reused in different programs because it carries with it everything it needs to operate.

Smalltalk, the original object-oriented programming language, is so named because it was originally tested on children at the Xerox PARC laboratories.

With OOP technology, programmers can build programs from prefabricated objects in the same way builders construct houses from prefabricated walls. OOP also makes it easy to use features from one program in other programs, so programmers don't have to start from scratch with every new program. The object that sorts addresses in alphabetical order in a mailing list database can also be used in a program that sorts hotel reservations alphabetically.

Smalltalk is still used for object-oriented programming, but today many other languages include object technology. C++, used in our example earlier, is a popular dialect of C that supports object-oriented programming. C++ doesn't contain *visual* objects like icons. On the surface it looks like just another language. But the object-oriented nature of the language allows programmers to write programs built around *logical* objects rather than procedures. Java has more of an

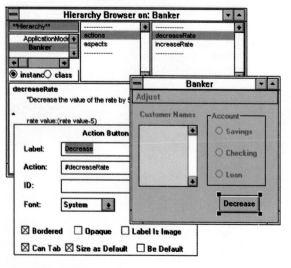

Object-Oriented Programming

The paradigm of structured programming follows the classic view of data as raw material being processed on an assembly line. At some level all computer programs process data in a mechanistic fashion. But at a higher level, object-oriented programming rejects the assembly line metaphor for another approach.

The fundamental tenet of OOP is that software should be designed using the same techniques that people use to understand and categorize the world around them.

In OOP a program is designed to consist of a group of objects—each with its own characteristics or attributes (called properties) and actions that it can do (called methods).

Every object has a "public" face: the properties and methods that other objects can see and interact with. Objects also have private methods for their internal use.

In OOP, data is bound together, or encapsulated, with the methods and properties of an object. Each object can maintain its own storehouse of data appropriate for that object.

OOP also relies on the idea of hierarchical categorization of objects to allow programmers to create new objects that are derived from objects that are already defined. The new object can inherit the properties and methods of the object it descends from and add new properties and methods as needed. Such hierarchies have been used by people for centuries in understanding the physical and biological world.

How might all of this work in practice, say, for a graphical operating system? For example, there could be a generic "window" object whose properties included its size, position, color, and so on and whose methods included things like closing and resizing. A more specialized window could be derived from this, for example, a window with scroll bars attached.

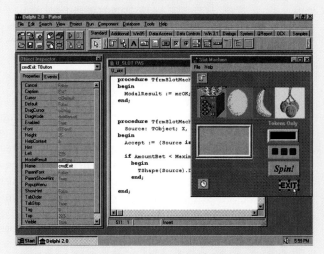

Delphi is a popular object-oriented development tool based on Pascal.

object-oriented design than C++. There's even a version of Pascal, called Object Pascal, that supports object-oriented programming.

Object-oriented tools and techniques are becoming common in databases, multimedia authoring tools, and other software environments. Object-oriented programming is particularly well suited for highly interactive programs (such as graphical operating systems, games, and customer transaction stations) and programs that imitate or reflect some dynamic part of the real world (such as simulations and air traffic control systems). Most experts believe that OOP is the wave of the future.

Visual Programming

Many people find it easier to work with pictures instead of words. Visual programming tools allow programmers to create large portions of their programs by drawing pictures and pointing to on-screen objects, eliminating much of the tedious coding of traditional programming. Apple's HyperCard was probably the first popular example of a visual programming environment. HyperCard includes a programming language called HyperTalk, but a HyperCard programmer doesn't need to speak HyperTalk to create working applications.

Today Microsoft's Visual Basic is widely used by professionals and hobbyists alike because of its visual approach to programming. Today's visual programming tools haven't completely transformed programming into a visual process; programmers must still understand how to read and write code to create complex programs. But visual programming can save hours of coding time, especially when creating user interfaces—the graphical shells that interact with users. Because they can simplify many of the most difficult parts of the programming process, visual languages make programming more accessible to nonprogrammers.

Languages for Users

Some computer languages are designed with nonprogrammers in mind. They aren't as powerful and versatile as professional programming languages, but they meet the modest needs of specific users.

Macro Languages

Many user-oriented languages are intended to allow users to create programs, called macros, that automate repetitive tasks. User-oriented **macro languages** (also called **scripting languages**) are built into many applications, utilities, and operating systems. Using a macro language, a spreadsheet user can build a program, called a macro, to automatically create end-of-month reports each month by locating data in other worksheets, inserting values into a new worksheet, and calculating results using formulas carried over from previous months. Using an operating system's scripting language, a user might automate the process of making backup copies of all documents created during the last 7 days.

Some macro languages require you to design and type each macro by hand, just as you would if you were writing a BASIC program. In fact, Microsoft Office includes a scripting variation of Visual Basic called *Visual Basic for Applications (VBA)*. Another type of macro maker "watches" while the user performs a sequence of commands and actions; it then memorizes the sequence and turns it into a macro automatically. The user can then examine and edit the macro so that it performs the desired actions under any circumstances.

Fourth-Generation Languages

Many experts suggest that languages have evolved through four generations: machine language, assembly language, high-level languages, and **fourth-generation languages**, sometimes called **4GLs**. Each generation of languages is easier to use and more like natural language than its predecessors. There's no consensus on exactly what constitutes a fourth-generation language, but these characteristics are most commonly mentioned:

- ▶ 4GLs use English-like phrases and sentences to issue instructions.
- ▶ 4GLs are nonprocedural. Pascal, C, and BASIC are *procedural languages*—tools for constructing procedures that tell the computer how to accomplish tasks. *Nonprocedural languages* allow users to focus on what needs to be done, not on how to do it.
- ▶ 4GLs increase productivity. Because a 4GL takes care of many of the how-to details, programmers can often get results by typing a few lines of code rather than a few pages.

One type of 4GL is the *query language* that allows a user to request information from a database with carefully worded English-like questions. A query language serves as a database user interface, hiding the intricacies of the database from the user. SQL (see Chapter 8) is the standard query language for most database applications today. Like most query languages SQL requires the user to master a few rules of syntax and logic. Still, a query language is easier to master than FORTRAN or COBOL.

Component Software

Recent developments in the software industry may soon result in software that provides users with the kind of power formerly reserved for programmers—and at the same time reverse a long-standing trend toward bloated computer applications. Throughout most of the short history of the personal computer, applications have steadily grown in size as developers add more and more features to their products. Even though no single user needs all of the features in a modern spreadsheet program, every user who buys that program must buy all of the code that provides those features. Many modern applications are so bloated with features that they make huge demands on memory and hard disk space.

Component software tools may reverse the trend toward mega-applications by allowing users to construct small custom applications from software components. Component software isn't completely new; users have been able to add custom components to applications for years. For example, dozens of plug-in extensions are available for Netscape Communicator and Microsoft Internet Explorer, the popular Web browsers. But this customizability is possible only if applications are designed to allow it. More and more software programs, including operating systems, are designed with extensibility in mind.

These extensible systems might radically change the software industry. Instead of buying an everything-but-the-kitchen-sink word processor, you might be able to buy word processor components—spelling checkers, outliners, formatters—based on your individual needs. Components might be distributed through the Internet as well as traditional software channels, so you can quickly add features when you need them. This kind of build-it-yourself software model is the logical extension of object-oriented programming to a level where users can do their own application construction.

Programming for the Web

The Internet explosion is changing the face of programming, too. Many experts see a future in which PC applications will take a back seat to Web-based applications. Web-based personal information managers, graphics programs, and games are steadily growing in popularity. Because of the distributed nature of the Web and the limited bandwidth of many Internet connections, Web-based applications present several challenges for users. Programmers can, and do, use a variety of languages, including C and C++, to write Web applications. But some programming tools are particularly useful for developing Web applications:

▶ *HTML* is, technically, a page-description language rather than a programming language. HTML commands tell Web browsers how to arrange text, graphics, and multimedia elements on Web pages, and how to link those pages. But there are many similarities between HTML coding and program writing, and many popular extensions to HTML take it far beyond the basics of page layout.

▶ *JavaScript* is an interpreted scripting language that allows Web page designers to add scripts to HTML code. Interpreted JavaScript scripts can add animation, interactivity, and other dynamic content to otherwise static Web pages.

▶ *VBScript* is Microsoft's answer to JavaScript based on Visual Basic.

```
//guessing game program written by Keith Vertanen
import java.util.*;                    // needed for Random class
import java.io.*;                      // needed for BufferedReader class

class guessing_game {

        public static void main(String[] args) throws IOException {

                int number, guess, counter = 0;

                // we need a stdin object to receive input from the user
                BufferedReader stdin = new BufferedReader (new
                        InputStreamReader(System.in));

                System.out.println("Welcome to the guessing game. I'll pick a number");
                System.out.println("between 1 and 100 and you try to guess what it is.");
                System.out.println("You get 7 tries.");
                System.out.println("");

                // create a new random number object
                Random rand = new Random();

                // calculate a random number between 1 and 100
                number = Math.abs(rand.nextInt() % 100) + 1;

                // do this loop for each guess. Leave the loop when the guess is
                // correct or when 7 incorrect guesses have been made
                do {
                        System.out.println("What's your guess?");

                        // allow the user to enter a line of text, convert to an integer
                        guess = Integer.parseInt(stdin.readLine());

                        if (guess == number)
                                System.out.println("You guessed it!");
                        else
                                if (guess < number)
                                else
                                        System.out.println("Too small, try again.");
                                else
                                        System.out.println("Too big, guess again.");
                        ++counter;
                } while ((counter < 7) && (guess!= number));
                if (guess !=number));
                                        System.out.println("I fooled you 7 times - the number
                                                was " + number + "!");

        } // method main
}
```

> This listing shows the guessing game program rewritten in Java, a C-like language that's ideal for cross-platform and Web programming.

- ▶ Java is a full-featured object-oriented language that's especially popular for creating Web applets—small compiled programs that run inside other applications—typically Web browsers. Java also excels at creating cross-platform applications that run on many different kinds of computers, regardless of operating systems.

- ▶ *Perl* (Practical Extraction and Reporting Language) is an interpreted scripting language that is particularly well-suited for writing scripts to process text—for example, complex Web forms. Perl runs on Web servers, not inside a Web browser.

- ▶ *XML* is a powerful markup language that overcomes many of the limitations of HTML. XML separates Web page content from layout, so Web pages can be designed to display different ways on different devices. XML is also particularly well suited for creating database-backed Web sites. Many experts expect a combination of XML and HTML to replace HTML as the dominant Web document development tool.

The Future of Programming?

It could well be that by the close of the twenty-first century, a new form of truly accessible programming will be the province of everyone, and will be viewed like writing, which was once the province of the ancient scribes but eventually became universally accessible.

—**Michael Dertouzos, in *What Will Be***

Object-oriented programming. Visual programming. Component software. Distributed Web applications. With these trends gaining momentum, what can we say about the future of programming? It's not clear what programming languages will look like in the future, but three trends seem likely:

1 *Programming languages will continue to evolve in the direction of natural languages like English.* Today's programming languages, even the best of them, are far too limited and unintelligent. Tomorrow's programming tools should be able to understand what we want even if we don't specify every detail. When we consider artificial intelligence in the next chapter, we'll deal with the problems and promise of natural language computer communication.

2 *The line between programmer and user is likely to grow hazy.* As programming becomes easier, there's every reason to believe that computer users will have tools that allow them to construct applications without mastering the intricacies of a technical programming language.

3 *Computers will play an ever-increasing role in programming themselves.* Today's visual programming environments can create programs in response to user clicks and commands. Tomorrow's programming tools may be able to write entire programs with only a description of the problem supplied by users. The day after tomorrow we may see computers anticipating problems and programming solutions without human intervention!

Whatever happens, one thing seems likely: Future programming tools will have little in common with today's languages. When computer historians look back, they'll marvel at how difficult it was for us to instruct computers to perform even the simplest actions.

Programs in Perspective: Systems Analysis and the System Life Cycle

We but teach Bloody instructions, which being taught, return To plague the inventor.

—**Shakespeare, *Macbeth***

Programs don't exist in a vacuum. Programs are part of larger information systems—collections of people, machines, data, and methods organized to accomplish specific functions and to solve specific problems. Programming is only part of the larger process of designing, implementing, and managing information systems. In this section we examine that larger process.

Whether it's a simple accounting system for a small business or a credit bureau's massive financial information system, a system has a system development life cycle (SDLC)—a sequence of steps or phases it passes through between the time the system is conceived and the time it is phased out. The phases of the system development life cycle are investigation, analysis, design, development, implementation, maintenance, and retirement. We consider each phase from the point of view of the **systems analyst**—the computer professional primarily responsible for developing and managing a system as it progresses through these phases.

Investigation

Developing an information system is no small undertaking. People develop information systems because problems like these need to be solved:

▶ A mom-and-pop music store needs a way to keep track of instrument rentals and purchases so that billing and accounting don't take so much time.

▶ A college's antiquated, labor-intensive registration system forces students to endure long lines and frequent scheduling errors.

▶ A catalog garden-supply company is outgrowing its small, slow PC-based software system, resulting in shipping delays, billing errors, and customer complaints. At the same time, the company is losing business because competitors now sell on the Web.

▶ The success of an upcoming oceanographic investigation hinges on the ability of scientists to collect and analyze data instantaneously so the results can be fed into remote-control navigation devices.

▶ A software manufacturer determines that its PC graphics program is rapidly losing market share to a competitor with more features and a friendlier user interface.

System *investigation* involves defining the problem—identifying the information needs of the organization, examining the current system, determining how well it meets the needs of the organization, and studying the feasibility of changing or replacing the current system. After completing the initial investigation of the problem, a systems analyst, whether part of the organization or contracted from an outside consulting firm, produces a *feasibility study* to help management decide whether to continue with the systems analysis.

Analysis

During the *analysis* phase the systems analyst gathers documents, interviews users of the current system (if one exists), observes the system in action, and generally gathers and analyzes data to help understand the current system and identify new requirements. Most systems are too complex to understand as a whole, so the systems analyst generally subdivides a system into components called *subsystems*. The analysis phase involves more detail than the investigative phase but less than the design phase that follows.

Design

The investigation phase focuses on *why,* the analysis phase focuses on *what,* and the *design* phase focuses on *how.* In the design phase the systems analyst considers important how-to questions:

▶ What kind of output should the system produce?

▶ Where will input data come from, and how will it be entered into the system?

▶ Should the system be centralized in a single computer or distributed through a network of desktop computers? (For that matter, should a computer be involved in the system at all?)

▶ Should the organization purchase packaged software or have programmers write a custom application from the ground up?

The systems analyst answers these questions, sometimes proposing several alternative solutions.

In many cases the design phase produces a prototype system—a limited working system or subsystem to give the users and management an idea of how the completed system will work. The systems analyst can modify the prototype until it meets the needs and expectations of the organization. Once the design is acceptable, the systems analyst can fill in the details of the output, input, data files, processing, and system controls.

Development

After the design is completed, actual system development can begin. *Development* includes a complex mix of scheduling, hardware and software purchasing, documentation, and programming. For most large projects, the development phase involves a team of programmers, technical writers, and clerical people under the supervision of a systems analyst. A large part of the development schedule is devoted to testing the system. Members of the system development team perform early testing to locate and eliminate bugs. This initial testing is known as alpha testing. Later potential users who are willing to work with almost-finished software perform beta testing and report bugs to the developers. Many popular applications, operating systems, and utilities are made available on the Internet for *public beta testing*.

Implementation

When the testing is completed and known bugs have been eradicated, the new system is ready to replace the old one. For commercial software packages the *implementation* phase typically involves extensive training and technical user support to supplement sales and marketing efforts. For large custom systems implementation typically includes user education and training, equipment replacement, file conversion, and careful monitoring of the new system for problems. In some cases the new system is run parallel to the old system until the analyst is confident that the new system is stable and reliable.

Maintenance

The *maintenance* phase involves evaluating, repairing, and enhancing the system. Some software problems don't surface until the system has been operational for a while or the organization needs change. Ongoing maintenance allows organizations to deal with those problems when they arise. For commercial programs, bugs and refinements are handled by occasional *maintenance upgrades*, typically labeled with incremental version numbers like 1.01 or 2.0a. For large custom systems, maintenance involves a continual process of evaluating and adjusting the system to meet organizational needs. In either case maintenance usually lasts throughout the lifetime of the system.

Retirement

At some point in the life of a system ongoing maintenance isn't enough. Because of changes in organizational needs, user expectations, available technology, and other factors the system no longer meets the needs of the users or the organization, and is ready for *retirement*. At that point it's time to phase it out in favor of a newer system and begin another round of the system life cycle.

How It Works 12.2

The System Development Life Cycle

College registration is a complex system involving hundreds of people and masses of information. A registration system must be solidly designed, carefully maintained, and eventually replaced as the needs of the college change. In this example we follow systems analysts at Chintimini College as they guide a registration system through a system life cycle.

① **Investigation.** Analysts at the college's Information Processing Center identify several problems with the antiquated manual registration system: long lines, frequent scheduling errors, and expensive labor costs. After studying registration systems at other schools, they determine that a registration-by-phone system might be the best solution to these problems. After a few years the phone registration system has developed problems of its own. The college begins developing a new system that will allow students to register through the World Wide Web. When the new Web registration system reaches the implementation phase of its life cycle, the phone-in system is retired.

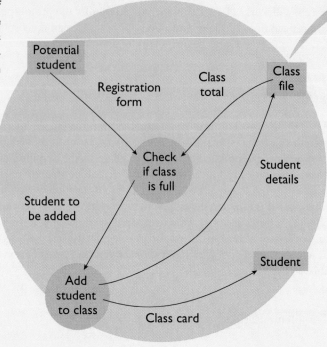

Potential student

Registration form

Class total

Class file

Check if class is full

Student details

Student to be added

Student

Add student to class

Class card

② **Analysis.** Analysts use a *data flow diagram* to illustrate the flow of data through the old registration system. They'll use the information in this diagram to help them develop the new system.

⑦ **Retirement.** After a few years the phone registration system has developed problems of its own. The college begins developing a new system that will allow students to register through the World Wide Web. When the new Web registration system reaches the implementation phase of its life cycle, the phone-in system is retired.

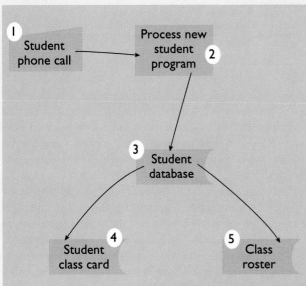

① Student phone call

② Process new student program

③ Student database

④ Student class card

⑤ Class roster

③ **Design.** Analysts use standard symbols to create a *system flowchart* to show the relationship among programs, files, input, and output in the new system.

④ **Development.** Analysts use a *Gantt chart* to plan the schedule deadlines and milestones for creating the new system.

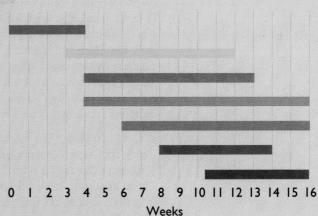

Program specifications
Programming
Unit testing
Documentation
System testing
File conversion
Training

0 1 2 3 4 5 6 7 8 9 10 11 12 13 14 15 16
Weeks

⑤ **Implementation.** Analysts supervise the training, equipment conversion, file conversion, and system conversion as the new system is brought on line.

⑥ **Maintenance.** Analysts monitor and evaluate the new system, eliminating problems and correcting bugs as they are uncovered.

The Science of Computing

Telescopes are to astronomy as computers are to computer science.

—Edgar Dykstra, **computer scientist**

We've seen how programmers and systems analysts create and maintain computer programs used by scientists, business-people, artists, writers, and others. But just as the rest of us take advantage of the programmer's handiwork, the programmer depends on tools and ideas developed by *computer scientists*—professionals who work in the academic discipline called computer science. What is computer science, and why is it important in the world of computers?

Because most introductory computer science courses focus on programming, many students equate computer science with computer programming. But programming is little more than a tool in the computer scientist's intellectual toolbox; it has about as much to do with computer science as English grammar has to do with writing novels.

Computer science is a relatively new discipline with ties to electrical engineering, mathematics, and business. Many computer scientists prefer to call the field computing science because it focuses on the process of computing rather than on computer hardware. Computing takes a variety of forms, and computer science includes a number of focus areas, ranging from the rarefied world of computer theory to practical nuts-and-bolts work in software engineering. Some areas of specialization within computer science—database management, graphics, artificial intelligence, and networks, for example—provide academic underpinnings for specific categories of computer applications. Other branches of computer science deal with concepts that can apply to almost any type of computer application. These include the following:

▶ *Computer theory.* The most mathematical branch of computer science, *computer theory* applies the concepts of theoretical mathematics to computational problems. Theoreticians often work not with real computers but with theoretical computers that exist only in the minds of the theoreticians. As in most fields, many theoretical concepts eventually find their way into practical applications.

▶ *Algorithms.* Many computer scientists focus on algorithms—the logical underpinnings of computer programs. The design of algorithms can determine whether software succeeds or fails. A well-designed algorithm is not only reliable and free of logical errors but also efficient, so it can accomplish its goals with a minimum of computer resources and time. Computers spend most of their time doing mundane tasks like sorting lists, searching for names, and calculating geometric coordinates. These frequently performed operations must be built on rock-solid, efficient algorithms if a computer system is to be responsive and reliable.

▶ *Data structures.* If algorithms describe the logical structure of programs, data structures determine the logical structure of data. Data structures range from simple numeric lists and tables (called *arrays*) to complex relations at the core of massive databases. Computer scientists continue to develop improved techniques for representing and combining different forms of data, and these techniques find their way into all kinds of software.

▶ *Programming concepts and languages.* As we've seen, programming languages have evolved through several generations in the short history of computers. Thanks to computer scientists in the tradition of Grace Hopper, each new wave of languages is easier to use and more powerful than the one that came before. Programming language specialists strive to design better programming languages to make it easier for programmers to turn algorithms into working software. Computer scientists are also responsible for the development of techniques like structured programming and object-oriented programming—techniques that make programmers more productive and programs more reliable.

▶ *Computer architecture.* Straddling the boundary between the software world of computer science and the hardware world of computer engineering, computer architecture deals with the way hardware and software work together. How can multiple processors work together? How does the bandwidth of a bus affect performance? What are the trade-offs for different storage media? These are the types of questions that concern computer architecture specialists.

▶ *Management information systems.* Management information systems (MIS) is part computer science, part business. In fact, MIS studies are done in computer science departments at some institutions, in business departments at others, and in MIS departments at others. MIS specialists focus on the developing systems that can provide timely, reliable, and useful information to managers in business, industry, and government. MIS specialists apply the theoretical concepts of computer science to real-world, practical business problems.

▶ *Software engineering.* When an engineer designs a bridge or a building, tried-and-true engineering principles and techniques ensure that the structure won't collapse unexpectedly. Unfortunately, we can't trust software the way we trust buildings; software designers simply don't have the time-honored techniques to ensure quality. Software engineering is a relatively new branch of computer science that attempts to apply engineering principles and techniques to the less-than-concrete world of computer software. We conclude this chapter with a brief look at the problems faced by software engineers—problems that affect all of us.

The State of Software

> It's impossible to make anything foolproof, because
> # fools are so ingenious.
>
> —Roger Berg, **inventor**

In spite of advances in computer science, the state of software development is less than ideal. Software developers and software users are confronted with two giant problems: cost and unreliability.

Software Problems

> We build our computers the way we build our cities—
> # over time, without a plan, on top of ruins.
>
> —Ellen Ullman, **software engineer and author of *Close to the Machine***

As computers have evolved through the decades, the cost of computer hardware has steadily gone down. Every year brings more powerful, reliable machines and lower prices. At the same time the cost of developing computer software has gone up. The software industry abounds with stories of computer systems that cost millions of dollars more and took years longer to develop than expected. Many systems become so costly to develop that their developers are forced to abandon them before completion. According to one survey 75% of all system development undertaken in the United States is either never completed or, if it is completed, not used.

But while prices rise, there's no corresponding increase in the reliability of software. Ever since Grace Hopper pulled a moth from the Mark II's relay, bugs have plagued computers, often with disastrous consequences, as you saw in the last chapter.

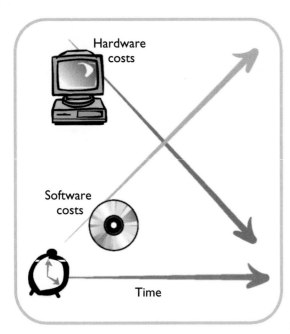

Hardware costs

Software costs

Time

Software errors can take a variety of forms, including errors of omission, syntax errors, logic errors, clerical errors, capacity errors, and judgment errors. But whatever its form, a software error can be devilishly difficult to locate and even more difficult to remove. According to one study 15% to 20% of attempts to remove program errors actually introduce new errors!

Software Solutions

The major difference between a thing that might go wrong and a **thing that cannot possibly go wrong** is that when a thing that cannot possibly go wrong goes wrong it usually turns out to be impossible to get at or repair.

—Douglas Adams, in *Mostly Harmless*

Computer scientists and software engineers are responding to reliability and cost problems on five main fronts:

1 *Programming techniques.* So far structured programming is the best known and most successful technique for increasing programmer productivity and program reliability. Programmers who use structured techniques can concentrate on the overall logic of their creations without getting distracted by minute details. The result is less expensive, more reliable software. But structured programming is no panacea; it is considered by most experts as only a single step on a long road toward more dependable programming methodologies. It's too early to tell whether object-oriented programming and other more modern techniques will take us much farther down that road.

2 *Programming environments.* Today's best programming tools include sophisticated text editors, debuggers, record-keeping programs, and translators, all interwoven into a seamless graphic work environment. A high-quality programming environment can help a programmer manage the complexities of a large project. During the past two decades CASE (computer-assisted software engineering) tools have emerged, allowing analysts and programmers to automate many of the tedious and error-prone steps involved in turning design specifications into programs. In spite of early promise, CASE tools haven't been widely adopted. Today the industry is more focused on environments built around component technology that makes it easier to reuse reliable code. In any case programming environments have a long way to go before they can guarantee reliable software, if that's even possible.

Thousands of lives depend on reliable functioning of the computers and software used by air traffic controllers.

3 *Program verification.* Software engineers would like to be able to prove the correctness of their programs in the same way mathematicians prove the correctness of theorems. Computer scientists have developed program verification techniques that work well for small programs. Unfortunately, these techniques have achieved only limited success with the complex commercial programs people depend on today. There's little hope for automated program verification either. Computer scientists have proven that some problems can't be solved with algorithms, and program verification is one such problem.

4 *Clean-room programming.* One new experimental approach to software development is modeled after microchip manufacturing techniques. Clean-room programming combines formal notation, proofs of correctness, and statistical quality control with an evolutionary approach to programming. Programmers grow systems individually, certifying the quality of each before integrating it with the others. It's too early to tell whether this rigorous, engineering-like approach will achieve widespread quality gains, but early tests show some promise.

5 *Human management.* Project management techniques from business and engineering have been applied successfully to many software engineering projects. These human management techniques have more to do with person-to-person communication than with programmer-to-machine communication. Because many information system failures result from human communication errors, successful human management can improve a system's overall reliability. But again the benefits of human management methodologies aren't great enough to offset the massive problems facing software engineers today.

Computer scientists have accomplished a great deal in the short history of the field. Software development is easier than it used to be, and computers today can accomplish far more than anyone dreamed a few decades ago. But software engineers have failed to keep up with the fast-paced evolution in computer hardware, and it's still incredibly difficult to produce reliable, cost-effective software. More than a decade ago computer scientist Ted Lewis summed up the problem in one of his laws of computing. Today, when we're routinely asked to entrust our money, our health, our legal rights, and our lives to software, it's important for all of us to remember that law: "Hardware is soft; software is hard."

CROSSCURRENTS

Heading Off Armageddon

Keith Perine

During the last few months of 1999, the anticipated Y2K bug was the subject of countless news stories. People replaced old computers, stocked up on food, bought generators, canceled new years trips, and generally prepared for a disaster caused by all those programmers and analysts who hadn't allowed enough space for four-digit years in their programs. The Y2K bug didn't bring the system to a standstill, but it did make many people aware of their dependence on fragile computer technology. This article first appeared in the October 25, 1999 issue of The Industry Standard, *during the height of Y2K fever. In the article, writer Keith Perine suggests that a technological Armageddon may be caused, not by bugs, but by people.*

Uncle Sam is gearing up to fight a growing army of hackers trying to pry their way into government computer systems.

Imagine you're washing the dinner dishes when, suddenly, the lights and the water go out. You pick up the telephone to call a neighbor, but can't get a dial tone. When you turn on the battery-powered radio, you hear something you never thought you would: The fabled Emergency Broadcast System is declaring an actual emergency. You're warned to stay inside your home and told that the president will soon address the nation with further instructions.

It sounds like a nightmare scenario for Jan. 1, but it's not. It's what the government worries could happen today, next week or next February: A massive series of computer hacks into the country's electronic infrastructure paralyzes society as effectively as a planeload of neutron bombs.

Fearful of such attacks, the federal government is trying to sound the alarm. In May 1998, President Clinton established several new agencies and charged them with coming up with coordinating defense against cyberterrorism. The plan, almost a year overdue, should be released in a few weeks.

"These are threats to our national security that we must confront now," says Michael Vatis, director of the FBI's National Infrastructure Protection Center.

The administration has proposed the Federal Intrusion Detection Network, or FIDNet, to monitor nonmilitary government computers for illegal hacks. The Treasury Department has announced that major banking firms are joining to create an information-sharing system to help plan security measures for the financial sector.

The new plan won't come a moment too soon. In testimony before a Senate subcommittee earlier this month, Vatis said the FBI's cybercrime caseload is mushrooming: The bureau is now handling 800 investigations with a skeleton crew of agents.

The Department of Defense alone is the target of as many as 100 hacks per day, ranging in severity from relatively harmless system pings to theft of unclassified data. For over a year, Vatis says,

the government has been investigating a series of hacks into military and civilian computer systems, code-named Moonlight Maze, believed to be sponsored by the Russian military.

In early 1998, as the U.S. military girded for a showdown with Iraq over U.N. weapons inspections, hackers penetrated 200 unclassified U.S. military computer systems. The government mounted a massive investigation, dubbed Solar Sunrise, that eventually traced the hacks to two juveniles in California and several people in Israel.

Earlier this month, the Pentagon announced that a new center in Colorado Springs, Colo., would try to defend the military's systems, and figure out ways to attack computer systems in other countries.

Federal officials are quick to point out that, despite their efforts, much of the responsibility for preventing hacker attacks lies in the hands of the private sector, since 90 percent of the vital computer systems in this country are privately owned.

Government agencies are trying to develop partnerships with their private-sector counterparts. Public and private officials have been meeting to swap data and share concerns, but most of the efforts are still in the planning stage.

The Commerce Department wants to create a partnership with the telecommunications industry to share security information and ideas, but doesn't yet have the money to do so. The department's funding for its end of the program is tied up in the fiscal year 2000 appropriations bill, still making its way through Congress. "We'd like to lead by example, not with a tin cup in hand," says William Reinsch, Undersecretary of Commerce for Export Administration.

Earlier this month, the General Accounting Office issued a report concluding that, despite its efforts so far, the federal government's strategy is unfocused and inefficient. The GAO says the computer-security safeguards in 22 of the largest federal agencies—from the health-care system run by the Department of Veterans' Affairs to taxpayer databases at the Internal Revenue Service – are dangerously weak. No such study has been performed on the 90 percent of the infrastructure controlled by private companies.

Says Vatis: "I think many people have a false sense of security."

DISCUSSION QUESTIONS

1. Does the "nightmare scenario" outlined in this article seem realistic to you? How do you feel about it?
2. Do you think the government is doing enough to prevent techno-terrorism? Explain your answer.
3. Do you agree that "many people have a false sense of security"? Why or why not?

Summary

Computer programming is a specialized form of problem solving that involves developing an algorithm for solving a problem. Most programmers use stepwise refinement to repeatedly break a problem into smaller, more easily solvable problems. An algorithm typically is developed in pseudocode, which describes the logic of the program before being translated into a programming language. A translator program—either a compiler or an interpreter—checks for syntax errors (language errors) and, if it finds none, translates the program into machine language so the computer can execute the instructions. Logic errors might not surface until the translated program is run, and maybe not even then. The programming process isn't completed until the program is thoroughly tested for errors.

Computer languages have evolved through several generations, with each generation being easier to use and more powerful than the one that came before. Machine language—the original computer language of zeros and ones—is primitive and difficult to program. Assembly language uses a translator called an assembler to turn alphabetic codes into the binary numbers of machine language, but in every other way it is identical to machine language.

High-level languages, such as FORTRAN, COBOL, BASIC, Pascal, and C, are more like English and therefore easier to work with than either machine or assembly language. What's more, they generally can be transported between computers with a minimum of rewriting. Most modern languages encourage structured programming, a technique that involves combining subprograms using only the three fundamental control structures: sequence, selection, and repetition. Structured programming produces programs with fewer logic errors. Still, when program efficiency is critical, many programmers use languages such as C that allow them to work at a lower level of machine logic.

Many applications contain built-in macro languages, scripting languages, and query languages that put programming power in the hands of users. Query languages are representative of fourth-generation languages (4GLs) which are nonprocedural; that is, they allow the programmer to focus on defining the task rather than outlining the steps involved in accomplishing the task. Visual programming tools allow the programmer to use icons, drawing tools, menus, and dialog boxes to construct programs without writing code. Object-oriented programming (OOP) tools allow programmers to construct programs from objects with properties and provide the ability to send messages to each other; many believe that OOP represents the future of programming.

Programs are part of larger information systems. An information system has a life cycle that starts with the initial investigation of the problem; proceeds through analysis, design, development, and implementation phases; and lingers in an ongoing maintenance phase until the system is retired. A systems analyst manages a typical information system with the help of a team of programmers and other computer professionals.

Computer scientists are responsible for the software tools and concepts that make all other software development possible. Computer science focuses on the process of computing through several areas of specialization, including theory, algorithms, data structures, programming concepts and languages, computer architecture, management information systems, artificial intelligence, and software engineering.

One of the most challenging problems facing computer science is the problem of software reliability. Current software development techniques provide no assurance that a software system will function without failure under all circumstances. As more and more human institutions rely on computer systems, it becomes increasingly important for computer scientists to find ways to make software that people can trust.

Chapter Review

Key Terms

Review Questions

1. Define or describe each of the key terms listed above. Check your answers using the glossary.
2. Here's an algorithm for directions to a university bookstore from a downtown location:

    > Go south on 4th Street to Jefferson Street.
    > Turn left on Jefferson Street.
    > Proceed on Jefferson past the stoplight to the booth at the campus entrance.
    > If there's somebody in the booth, ask for a permit to park in the bookstore parking lot; otherwise, just keep going.
    > When you reach the bookstore parking lot, keep circling the lot until you find an empty space.
    > Park in the empty space.

    Find examples of sequence, selection, and repetition control structures in this algorithm.
3. Find examples of ambiguous statements that might keep the algorithm in Question 2 from working properly.
4. Assume that Robert, the automated chef in Chapter 4, is going to do the driving in Question 2. Use stepwise refinement to add more detail to Question 2's algorithm so Robert has a better chance of understanding the instructions.
5. Design an algorithm to play the part of the guesser in the number-guessing game featured in this chapter. If you base your algorithm on the right strategy, it will always be able to guess the correct number in seven or fewer tries. (*Hint:* Computer scientists call the right strategy binary search.)
6. When does it make sense to design a custom program rather than using off-the-shelf commercial software? Give some examples.
7. Why is structured programming so widely practiced today by software developers?
8. Why are so many computer languages in use today?
9. Assemblers, compilers, and interpreters are all language translators. How do they differ?
10. What is the relationship between computer science and computer programming?
11. Give examples of several different kinds of computer errors, and describe how these errors affect people.
12. What techniques do software engineers use to improve software reliability?

Discussion Questions

1. Is programming a useful skill for a computer user? Why or why not?
2. Do you think computer professionals should have a code of ethics similar to those found in the legal and medical professions? What should such a code cover?
3. Should programmers be licensed? Is programming a craft, a trade, or a profession?
4. Suppose you want to computerize a small business or nonprofit organization. What questions might a systems analyst ask when determining what kind of system you need?
5. What do you think programming will be like in 10 years? 20 years? 50 years?
6. Computer science is in the college of science at some universities and in the college of engineering at others. Is computer science a science, a branch of engineering, or both?
7. Why is it so difficult to produce error-free software?

Projects

1. The computer is often blamed for human errors. Find some examples of "The computer did it" errors in newspapers, magazines, or conversations with others. For each example try to determine if the computer is, in fact, to blame.
2. Try to determine what safeguards are used to ensure that automated teller machines don't malfunction and that they can't be violated.
3. Find out what safeguards are used to ensure the security of computer systems in your local elections.

Books

As you might expect, there are hundreds of books on programming and computer science, most of which are specifically written about particular programming languages and platforms. Most of the books listed here are more general.

Karel++: A Gentle Introduction to the Art of Object-Oriented Programming, by Joseph Bergin, Mark Stehlik, Jim Roberts, and Richard Pattis (New York: Wiley, 1997). This book provides a refreshingly different approach to learning how to program. Instead of immersing yourself in the many details of a full-blown programming language, you can guide Karel the robot through an object-filled robot world. Karel's language is similar to C++ and Java, but simpler and friendlier. The emphasis here is on logic and reasoning rather than calculation. A software simulator is available to accompany the book.

C by Dissection: The Essentials of C Programming, Third Edition, by Al Kelley and Ira Pohl (Reading, MA: Addison Wesley, 1995). This excellent text introduces beginners to the C language with lots of examples.

Learn C on the Macintosh, Second Edition, by Dave Mark (Reading, MA: Addison-Wesley, 1995), and ***Learn Java on the Macintosh,*** by Barry Boone and Dave Mark (Reading MA: Addison-Wesley Developers Press, 1996). Most programming books today assume you're working with Microsoft Windows. These two books offer Macintosh alternatives, providing excellent, accessible tutorials for beginning programmers. The accompanying CD-ROMs include special limited-functionality compilers for working through the tutorials.

Palm Programming: The Developer's Guide, by Neil Rhodes and Julie McKeehan (Sebastapol, CA: O'Reilly, 1999). Some of the most interesting opportunities for programmers today are in handheld devices like the Palm. If you know C, this book can show you what you need to know to develop applications for the Palm.

Understanding Object-Oriented Programming with Java, by Timothy Budd (Reading, MA: Addison-Wesley, 1998). There are dozens of how-to Java books on the market. This text explains the whys as well as the hows of this important new language. Budd uses Java examples to clearly illustrate the concepts of object-oriented programming.

The Analytical Engine: An Introduction to Computer Science Using the Internet, by Rick Decker and Stuart Hirshfield (Belmont, CA: ITP, 1998). This well-written, innovative text illustrates many of the concepts of computer science using a Web site to add interactivity.

Computer Science: An Overview, Sixth Edition, by J. Glenn Brookshear (Reading, MA: Addison Wesley, 2000). This excellent survey covers algorithms, data structures, operating systems, and software engineering from a current computer science perspective.

Algorithmics: The Spirit of Computing, by David Harel (Reading, MA: Addison-Wesley, 1992). This book explores the central ideas of computer science from basic algorithms and data structures to more advanced concepts.

The New Turing Omnibus: 66 Excursions in Computer Science, by A. K. Dewdney (New York: Computer Science Press, 1993). This unusual book contains 66 short chapters covering a wide range of computer science topics, from algorithms to VLSI computers. Much of the material is technical and mathematical, but the writing is clear and engaging.

Dynamics of Software Development, by Jim McCarthy (Redmond, WA: Microsoft Press, 1995). A lifelong software developer offers advice in the form of rules (like "Don't flip the bozo bit") for shipping software on time. The book is filled with anecdotes and war stories from the front lines of software development.

The Mythical Man-Month: Essays on Software Engineering, Anniversary Edition, by Frederick P. Brooks, Jr. (Reading, MA: Addison-Wesley, 1995). This classic, often-quoted book outlines clearly the problems of managing large software projects. This twentieth-anniversary edition includes four new chapters that provide an up-to-date perspective.

Rescuing Prometheus: Four Monumental Projects That Changed Our World, By Thomas P. Hughes (New York: Vantage Books, 1999). This book profiles four of the biggest technological projects of the last century. These projects forced their developers to push the limits of systems design.

Out of Their Minds: The Lives and Discoveries of 15 Great Computer Scientists, by Dennis Shasha and Cathy Lazere (New York: Copernicus, 1998). The people profiled in this book were responsible for many of the most important ideas in computer science today. The profiles illuminate their achievements through interviews and explanations; technical details are confined to boxes so they don't interrupt the flow of the human stories. Closing sections explore two questions: What do these people have in common, and where is the field of computer science heading in the next quarter century?

World Wide Web Pages

Check the *Computer Confluence* Web site for links to the comp.risks forum, the Association for Computing Machinery (ACM), and other sites that cover material related to this chapter.

Chapter

13

Is Artificial Intelligence Real?

AFTER YOU READ THIS CHAPTER YOU SHOULD BE ABLE TO:

Explain what artificial intelligence means.

Explain the two basic approaches of artificial intelligence research.

Describe several hard problems that artificial intelligence research has not yet been able to solve.

Describe several practical applications of artificial intelligence.

Explain what robots are and give several examples illustrating what they can—and can't—do.

In this chapter:

▶ Thinking machines—the concept and the controversy
▶ How computers play (and win) games
▶ Computers that speak—and translate—human languages
▶ Expert systems and robots at work
▶ Artificial and human intelligence: How will they evolve?
... and more.

On the CD-ROM:

▶ AI Pioneer Marvin Minsky talks about intelligence
▶ Harold Cohen's artificial artist
▶ Robot factories
▶ Instant access to glossary and key word references
▶ Interactive self-study quizzes
... and more.

On the Web:

www.prenhall.com/beekman

▶ A wealth of information about artificial intelligence ideas, research, and applications
▶ Video and analysis of the machine chess champion, Deep Blue
▶ Computers that tell jokes, computers that translate languages, and computers that pretend to be human
▶ Expert systems you can use
▶ A robot playground
▶ Self-study exercises
... and more.

The extent to which we regard something as **behaving in an intelligent manner** is determined as much by **our own state of mind and training** as by the properties of the object under consideration.

—Alan Turing

Alan M. Turing, the British mathematician who designed the world's first operational electronic digital computer during the 1940s, may have been the most important thinker in the history of computing. While a graduate student at Princeton in 1936, Turing published "On Computable Numbers," a paper that laid the theoretical groundwork for all of modern computer science. In that paper he described a theoretical *Turing machine* that could read instructions from punched paper tape and perform all the critical operations of a computer. The paper also established the limits of computer science by mathematically demonstrating that some problems simply cannot be solved by any kind of computer.

After receiving his doctorate in 1938, Turing had an opportunity to translate theory into reality. Anticipating an invasion by Hitler's forces, the British government assembled a team of mathematicians and engineers with the top-secret mission of cracking the German military code. Under the leadership of Turing and others, the group built Colossus, a single-purpose machine regarded by many today as the first electronic digital computer. From the time Colossus was completed in 1943 until the end of the war, it successfully cracked Nazi codes—a fact concealed by the British government until long after the war ended. Many experts believe that Colossus was ultimately responsible for the defeat of the Nazis.

Turing effectively launched the field of artificial intelligence with a 1950 paper called "Computing Machinery and Intelligence." In this paper he proposed a concrete test for determining whether a machine was intelligent. In later years Turing championed the possibility of emulating human thought through computation. He even co-wrote the first chess-playing program.

Turing was an unconventional and extremely sensitive person. In 1952 he was professionally and socially devastated when he was arrested and injected with hormones for violation of British anti-homosexuality laws. The 41-year-old genius apparently committed suicide in 1954, years before the government made his wartime heroics public. Four decades after his death Turing's work still has relevance to computer scientists, mathematicians, and philosophers. The highest award in computer science, the Turing Award, bears his name. It's impossible to know what he might have contributed had he lived through those decades. ◻

Alan Turing (1913–1954)

Colossus, 1945

Alan Turing spent much of his short life trying to answer the question "Can machines think?" That's still a central question of **artificial intelligence (AI),** the field of computer science devoted to making computers perceive, reason, and act in ways that have, until now, been reserved for human beings. But today even those who believe that computers can't "think" have to admit that artificial intelligence research has produced impressive results: computers that can communicate in human languages; systems that can provide instant expertise in medicine, science, and other fields; world-class electronic chess players; and robots that can outperform humans in a variety of tasks. In this chapter we explore the technology, applications, and implications of artificial intelligence.

Thinking About Thinking Machines

What is intelligence, anyway? It is only a word that people use to name those unknown processes with which our brains solve problems we call hard. But whenever you learn a skill yourself, you're less impressed or mystified when other people do the same. This is why the meaning of "intelligence" seems so elusive: It describes not some definite thing but only the momentary horizon of our ignorance about how minds might work.

—Marvin Minsky, **AI pioneer**

If you ask 10 people to define intelligence, you're likely to get 10 different answers, including some of these:

- ▶ The ability to learn from experience
- ▶ The power of thought
- ▶ The ability to reason
- ▶ The ability to perceive relations
- ▶ The power of insight
- ▶ The ability to use tools
- ▶ Intuition.

Intelligence is difficult to define and understand, even for philosophers and psychologists who spend their lives studying it. But this elusive quality is, to many people, the characteristic that sets humans apart from other species. So it's not surprising that controversy has continually swirled around the questions "Can a machine be intelligent?" and "Can a machine think?"

Can Machines Think?

A machine may be deemed intelligent when it can pass for a human being in a blind test.

—Alan Turing

In his landmark 1950 paper Alan Turing suggested that the question "Can machines think?" was too vague and philosophical to be of any value. To make it more concrete, he proposed an "imitation game." The **Turing test**, as it came to be known, involves two people and a computer. One person, the interrogator, sits alone in a room and types questions into a computer terminal. The questions can be about anything—math, science, politics, sports, entertainment, art, human relationships, emotions—anything. As answers to questions appear on the terminal, the interrogator attempts to guess whether those answers were typed by the other person or generated by the computer. By repeatedly fooling interrogators into thinking it is a person, a computer can demonstrate intelligent behavior. If it *acts* intelligent, according to Turing, it is intelligent.

Turing did not intend this test to be the only way to demonstrate machine intelligence; he pointed out that a machine could fail and still be intelligent. Even so, Turing believed that machines would be able to pass his test by the turn of the century. So far no computer has come close, in spite of 40 years of AI research. While some people still cling to the Turing test to define artificial intelligence, most AI researchers favor less stringent definitions.

> Hello, Earth person!

> Hello there judge, are you ready to have some fun?

Interrogator

In the Turing test, a human interrogator types statements and questions into a terminal and tries to guess which contestant is human, based on the answers given.

What Is Artificial Intelligence?

Artificial intelligence is the study of ideas which enable computers to do the things that make people seem intelligent.

—**Patrick Henry Winston**, in *Artificial Intelligence*

This definition from a 1977 edition of a textbook is similar to definitions that commonly appear in today's popular press. This type of definition captures the general idea of artificial intelligence, but it breaks down when applied to specific examples. Does artificial intelligence include doing lightning-fast calculations? Finding a word in a dictionary as fast as it can be typed? Remembering hundreds of telephone numbers at a time? If a person could do all of these things, that person would "seem intelligent." But these activities aren't good examples of artificial intelligence because they're trivial for computers. In fact, many computer scientists believe that if it's easy to do with a computer, it can't be artificial intelligence. Here's a more recent textbook definition that reflects that point of view:

Artificial intelligence is the study of how to make computers do things at which, at the moment, people are better.

—**Elaine Rich**, in *Artificial Intelligence*

According to this definition, artificial intelligence is a *moving frontier*. The short history of the field bears this out. In the 1950s many AI researchers struggled to create computers that could play checkers and chess. Today computers can beat the best human players, and relatively few AI researchers study these games. In the words of one researcher, artificial intelligence is "whatever hasn't been done yet." Moving-frontier definitions of AI tend to be accurate, but they're short on specifics. A more concrete and complete definition might combine Rich's definition with this one from the *latest* edition of Winston's popular textbook:

> Artificial intelligence is the study of the computations that make it possible to perceive, reason, and act.
>
> —Patrick Henry Winston, in *Artificial Intelligence*

Perceive, reason, and *act* are words used more commonly in psychology, the science of human behavior, than in computer science. In fact, psychologists work alongside computer scientists on many AI research projects. Computer scientists tend to be motivated by the challenge of producing machine intelligence for its own sake. Psychologists, on the other hand, are interested in artificial intelligence because it provides new insights into natural intelligence and the workings of the human brain.

These points of view symbolize two common approaches to AI. One approach attempts to use computers to simulate human mental processes. For example, an AI expert might ask people to describe how they solve a problem and attempt to capture their answers in a software model.

The simulation approach has three inherent problems:

▶ Most people have trouble knowing and describing how they do things. Human intelligence includes unconscious thoughts, instantaneous insights, and other mental processes that are difficult or impossible to understand and describe.

▶ There are vast differences between the structure and capabilities of the human brain and those of the computer. Even the most powerful supercomputers can't approach the brain's ability to perform *parallel processing*—breaking a complex job into many smaller, simpler jobs and completing those jobs simultaneously.

▶ The best way to do something with a machine is often very different from the way people do it. Before the Wright brothers, dozens of inventors failed to produce flying machines because they tried to make their inventions imitate birds. Similarly, many early AI attempts failed because they were designed to mimic human intelligence rather than to take advantage of the computer's unique capabilities.

Many early flying machines that imitated birds never got off the ground.

The second, more common, approach to AI involves designing intelligent machines independent of the way people think. According to this approach, human intelligence is just one possible kind of intelligence. A machine's method of solving a problem might be different from the human method but no less intelligent.

Whichever approach they take, scientists face problems that are difficult and far too complex to solve all at once. Most AI researchers choose to break those problems into smaller problems that are easier to solve—to create programs that can function intelligently when confined to limited *domains*.

Opening Games

One of the first popular domains for AI research was the checkerboard. Much early AI work focused on games like checkers and chess because they were easy to represent in the computer's digital memory, they had clearly defined rules, and the goals were unmistakable. Instead of struggling with nebulous issues surrounding thought and intelligence, game researchers could focus on the concrete question "How can I create a program that wins consistently?" Their answers included many AI techniques that are still used today in a variety of applications:

▶ *Searching.* One way to win a game is through *searching*—looking ahead at the possibilities generated by each potential move: "I have four possible moves: A, B, C, and D. If I do A, then my opponent might do X, Y, or Z. If my opponent responds by doing X, then I can do E, F, G, or H . . . and so on." Obviously, high-speed computers are better at this kind of repetitive processing than people. Early AI programs could not check all possible decision points in a complicated game like checkers (there are approximately 10^{21} choices). Today's powerful computers can perform massive database searches quickly, making this kind of look-ahead searching practical for some game-playing programs. Researcher Jonathan Schaeffer's checker-playing program uses an enormous database of board positions to evaluate every move; the program plays as well as the best human players in the world. It uses what's known as a *brute-force* technique—rapidly repeating a simple operation until an answer is found. This kind of exhaustive searching doesn't fit many definitions of intelligence. For more complex games like chess, and for most domains outside of the world of games, the staggering number of decision points makes brute-force searching impractical. So searching is generally guided by a planned strategy and by rules known as heuristics.

▶ *Heuristics.* A heuristic is a rule of thumb. Unlike hard-and-fast algorithms, heuristics guide us toward judgments that experience tells us are likely to be true. In everyday life we apply heuristics such as "To loosen a stuck jar lid, run warm water over it." A checker-playing program might employ a heuristic that says, "Keep checkers in the king's row as long as possible."

▶ *Pattern recognition.* The best human chess and checkers players remember thousands of critical board patterns and know the best strategies for playing when those or similar patterns appear. Game-playing programs recognize recurring patterns, too, but not nearly as well as people do. Computer players often have trouble identifying situations that are similar but not identical. Pattern recognition is probably the single biggest advantage a human game player has over a computer opponent; it helps compensate for the computer's speed and thoroughness at searching ahead.

▶ *Machine learning.* The best game-playing programs learn from experience using machine learning techniques. If a move pays off, a learning program is more likely to use that move (or similar moves) in future games. If a move results in a loss, the program will remember to avoid similar moves.

Today a $40 program can turn a personal computer into a chess wizard. Computer systems can hold their own against the best human chess players by examining hundreds of thousands of moves per second. When IBM's Deep Blue, a customized RS/6000 SP supercomputer, beat grand master Garry Kasparov in a 1997 rematch, people all around the world watched with a level of interest that's seldom given to scientific work.

World chess champion Garry Kasparov (right) was stunned when IBM's Deep Blue took the upper hand in the sixth and final match of the famous 1997 tournament. Kasparov lost this match in just 19 moves. Home computer programs like Chessmaster 5500 (above) use many of the same techniques used by Deep Blue but on a smaller scale.

Still, most AI researchers have moved on to more interesting and practical applications. But whether working on vision, speech, problem solving, or expert decision making, researchers still use the successful strategy of game researchers—to restrict the domain of their programs so that problems are small enough to be understood and solved. We'll see how this strategy has paid off in several important areas of artificial intelligence, starting with natural-language communication.

Natural-Language Communication

Language is no less complex or subtle a phenomenon than the knowledge it seeks to transmit.

—Raymond Kurzweil, **in *The Age of Intelligent Machines***

Inexpensive pocket electronic translators serve world travelers by providing instant access to common words but not whole sentences.

In Turing's classic test of machine intelligence, the computer is considered to be intelligent if it can successfully pose as a person in a typed conversation. Since the earliest days of computing, scientists have dreamed of machines that could communicate in natural languages like English, Russian, and Japanese. Over the years natural-language communication has continually challenged researchers. Many problems relate to recognizing and reproducing human speech—issues we deal with later in the chapter. But even when it's typed directly into the machine, natural-language text poses significant software challenges.

Machine Translation Traps

One early project attempted to create a program that could translate scientific papers from Russian to English and from English to Russian. Automatic translation offered hope for increased communication between scientists during the tense Cold War years. The method seemed straightforward and foolproof: A parsing program (or parser) would analyze sentence structure and identify each word according to whether it was a subject, verb, or other part of speech; another program would look up each word in a translation dictionary and substitute the appropriate word.

After spending 15 years and millions of dollars on research, scientists abandoned the project. Even with the help of human editors, machine translators couldn't compete with humans in speed and accuracy. A typical translation correctly processed only about 80% of the desired text.

The automatic translation project became the target of jokes that, if not strictly factual, were effective at pointing out the problems of machine translation. In one famous story scientists asked the computer to translate English into Russian and then translate the results back into English. As the story goes, "The spirit is willing, but the flesh is weak" came back as "The wine is agreeable, but the meat is rotten" and "out of sight, out of mind" became "blind and insane" or "invisible idiot."

This early translation project may not have lived up to its promoters' expectations, but it taught them a valuable lesson: Translation without understanding is impossible. To translate a sentence accurately, the translator must know what the sentence *means*.

Conversation Without Communication

Similar lessons emerged from Joseph Weizenbaum's work with ELIZA, one of the first software programs to converse in a limited form of natural language. Weizenbaum, an

---

Men are all alike.
IN WHAT WAY
They're always bugging us about something or other.
CAN YOU THINK OF A SPECIFIC EXAMPLE
Well, my boyfriend made me come here.
YOUR BOYFRIEND MADE YOU COME HERE
He says I'm depressed much of the time.
I AM SORRY TO HEAR YOU ARE DEPRESSED
It's true. I am unhappy.
DO YOU THINK COMING HERE WILL HELP YOU NOT TO BE UNHAPPY
I need some help, that much seems certain.
WHAT WOULD IT MEAN TO YOU IF YOU GOT SOME HELP
Perhaps I could learn to get along with my mother.
TELL ME MORE ABOUT YOUR FAMILY
My mother takes care of me.
WHO ELSE IN YOUR FAMILY TAKES CARE OF YOU
My father.
YOUR FATHER
You are like my father in some ways.
WHAT RESEMBLANCE DO YOU SEE
You are not very aggressive but I think you don't want me to notice that.
WHAT MAKES YOU THINK I AM NOT VERY AGGRESSIVE
You don't argue with me.
WHY DO YOU THINK I DON'T ARGUE WITH YOU
You are afraid of me.
DOES IT PLEASE YOU TO BELIEVE I AM AFRAID OF YOU
My father is afraid of everybody.
WHAT ELSE COMES TO MIND WHEN YOU THINK OF YOUR FATHER
Bullies.
DOES THAT HAVE ANYTHING TO DO WITH THE FACT THAT YOUR
    BOYFRIEND MADE YOU COME HERE

From *Computer Power and Human Reason,* by Joseph Weizenbaum.

A conversation with ELIZA.

MIT professor, designed ELIZA in the 1960s to simulate the role of a therapist in a typed conversation with a patient. See the sample ELIZA session on the previous page (the computer's responses are capitalized).

As impressive as this dialog seems, there's no understanding here. ELIZA uses a few simple tricks to *simulate* understanding, including recognizing a few key words (like *mother*), identifying categories for some of those words (*family*), and repeating phrases from earlier in the conversation. But ELIZA's tricks are far from foolproof. In response to "Necessity is the mother of invention," ELIZA might say, "Tell me more about your family." An ELIZA session can easily deteriorate into nonsense dialog laced with grammatical errors and inappropriate responses. Clearly, ELIZA lacks the understanding to pass as a human in a Turing test.

Nonsense and Common Sense

Bill sings to Sarah, Sarah sings to Bill. Perhaps they will do other **dangerous things** together. They may eat lamb or stroke each other. They may chant of their **difficulties** and their **happiness.** They have **love** but they also have **typewriters. That is interesting.**

—A poem by **RACTER**, in **The Policeman's Beard Is Half Constructed**, programmed by
William Chamberlain and Thomas Etter

Years after ELIZA's creation this poetry appeared in *The Policeman's Beard Is Half Constructed,* the first book ever written by a computer. RACTER, like ELIZA, produced English-language output without really understanding it. Why do machines that flawlessly follow instructions written in BASIC, C, and other computer languages have so much trouble with *natural-language* communications?

Part of the problem is the massive vocabulary of natural languages. A typical computer language has less than 100 key words, each with a precise, unambiguous meaning. English, in contrast, contains hundreds of thousands of words, many of which have multiple meanings. Of course, a person or a machine doesn't need to understand every word in the dictionary to communicate successfully in English. Most natural-language processors work with a *subset* of the language. But as the early scientific translation efforts showed, restricting vocabulary isn't enough.

Every language has a syntax—a set of rules for constructing sentences from words. In a programming language, the syntax rules are exact and unambiguous. Natural-language parsing programs have to deal with rules that are vague, ambiguous, and occasionally contradictory. One early parser, when asked to analyze the sentence "Time flies like an arrow," replied with several possible interpretations, including one statement with time as the subject, another statement with flies as the subject, and two commands in which the reader was the subject!

Still, computers are far more successful dealing with natural-language syntax than with semantics—the underlying meaning of words and phrases. In natural language the meaning of a sentence is ambiguous unless it's considered in context. "The hens were ready to eat" means one thing if it follows "The farmer approached the hen house" and something else if it follows "The chef approached the oven." To make matters worse, human conversations are filled with idiomatic expressions ("Susan had a cow when she heard the news") and unspoken assumptions about the world or specific subject matter ("Catch the T at Harvard Square and take it to MIT"). In short, the computer lacks what we call *common sense*—the wealth of knowledge and understanding about the world that people share.

The most successful natural-language applications limit the domain so that virtually all relevant information can be fed to the system. If the domain—the "world"—is small enough and the rules of that world are clear and unambiguous, a computer can have "common sense" that makes natural-language communication possible. For example, many database query languages accept and understand English commands but only within a narrow range. The biggest market for natural-language processing today is language translation—the same market that produced AI's first major failure. Several Web sites offer on-the-fly translation of text files or Web pages. (One of the most popular is Alta Vista's Babel Fish, named for the universal translator fish in Douglas Adams's *Hitchhiker's Guide to the Galaxy*.) Translation programs still can't translate books or conversations flawlessly, but they can greatly increase the productivity of people who translate technical manuals and other works that focus on narrow domains.

Natural-language processing has come a long way since ELIZA's early conversations. Computers still can't pass the Turing test, but they can at least fool some of the people some of the time. Or so it seems, based on the results of a series of contests devoted to finding a winner of the Turing test: the Loebner Prize Competition held in the Boston Computer Museum. In the first of these annual competitions, held in 1991, 10 untrained judges tried to determine which of the eight entries were human by carrying on typed conversations via terminals. Because the contest organizers believed that any computer would be trounced in an open-ended Turing test, they included rules to protect the entrants from unrestricted questioning. Here's a short sample of a dialog between a judge and the winning entry, a program called PC Therapist. The IBM-PC–based program, which took 3 years to write, played the role of a jester and made occasional typing errors so it would appear more human. It worked: 5 of the 10 judges thought PC Therapist was a person.

> A conversation with PC Therapist.

01:32:25	Judge 6	Hello, earth person!
01:33:03	Terminal 5	Hello there judge, are you ready to have some fun? How ya doin, judge? Hello—how's the weather up there today?
01:33:35	Judge 6	Dark clouds with occasional bursts of sunshine (or rather camera flashes).
01:34:45	Terminal 5	The trouble with the rat race is that even if you win you're still a rat. Whimsy can be flimsy, right? How important is that to you?
01:35:26	Judge 6	Can't say I understand the question . . . but the whimsy of a poet is one thing and the whimsy of most of us is another.
01:36:51	Terminal 5	How do you know you can't say you understand the question . . . but the whimsy of a poet is one thing and the whimsy of most of us is another.
01:37:37	Judge 6	Are you repeating me just for laughs?
01:38:04	Terminal 5	I'm sorry, I do sometimes repeat myself . . . perhaps it's because I can't find my electronic organizer!

Reprinted from *AI Magazine*, Summer 1992.

Natural-language processing relates to other AI technologies discussed later in the chapter. Speech recognition and optical character recognition provide input to natural-language systems, freeing the human communicator from the keyboard. On the output side speech synthesis allows the computer to talk back in English or another language. But natural-language input and output are meaningless without a knowledge base that allows the computer to understand the ideas behind the words.

Knowledge Bases and Expert Systems

The computer can't tell you the emotional story. It can give you the exact mathematical design, but what's missing is the eyebrows.

—Frank Zappa

A preschool child can take you on a tour of the neighborhood, explaining how people use every building, describing the interconnected lives of every person you meet, and answering questions about anything you see along the way. A computer at city hall can give you facts and figures about building materials and assessed values of houses, but it can't provide you with a fraction of the *knowledge* conveyed in the child's tour. The human brain, which isn't particularly good at storing and recalling facts, excels at manipulating *knowledge*—information that incorporates the *relationships* among facts. Computers, on the other hand, are better at handling data than knowledge. Nobody knows exactly how the brain stores and manipulates knowledge. But artificial intelligence researchers have developed, and continue to develop, techniques for representing knowledge in computers.

Knowledge Bases

While a database contains only facts, a knowledge base also contains a system of rules for determining and changing the relationship among those facts. Facts stored in a database are rigidly organized in categories; ideas stored in a knowledge base can be reorganized as new information changes their relationships.

Computer scientists so far have had little success in developing a knowledge base that can understand the world the way a child does. Even before they start school, children know these things:

▶ If you put something in water, it will get wet.

▶ If Susan is Phil's sister, Phil is Susan's brother.

▶ You can't build a tower from the top down.

▶ Dogs commonly live in houses, but cows seldom do.

▶ People can't walk through walls.

▶ If you eat dinner in a restaurant, you're expected to pay for the food and leave a tip.

▶ If you travel from Dallas to Phoenix, time passes during the trip.

These statements are part of the mass of common-sense knowledge that children acquire from living in the world. Because computers can't draw on years of human experience to construct mental models of the world, they don't automatically develop common sense. Much AI research centers on providing computers with ways to acquire and store real-world, common-sense knowledge. Researchers have had little success at developing computer systems with the kinds of broad, shallow knowledge found in children. But when knowledge bases are restricted to narrow, deep domains—the domains of experts—they can be effective, practical, intelligent tools. For example, knowledge bases lie at the heart of hundreds of expert systems used in business, science, and industry.

Artificial Experts

An expert is one who knows more and more about less and less.

—Nicholas Murray Butler

As the quote suggests, an expert is someone who has an extraordinary amount of knowledge within a narrow domain. By confining activities to that domain, the expert achieves mastery. An expert system is a software program designed to replicate the decision-making process of a human expert. At the foundation of every expert system is a knowledge base representing ideas from a specific field of expertise. Because it's a collection of specialized knowledge, an expert system's knowledge base must be constructed by a user, an expert, or a *knowledge engineer*—a specialist who interviews and observes experts and painstakingly converts their words and actions into a knowledge base. Some new expert systems can grow their own knowledge bases while observing human decision makers doing their jobs. But for most expert systems the process is still human intensive.

Strictly speaking, expert systems derive their knowledge from experts; systems that draw on other sources, such as government regulations, company guidelines, and statistical databases, are called *knowledge-based systems*. But in practice the terms *expert system* and *knowledge-based system* are often used interchangeably.

A knowledge base commonly represents knowledge in the form of if–then rules like these:

▶ If the engine will not turn over and the lights do not work, then check the battery.

▶ If checking the battery shows it is not dead, then check the battery connectors.

Most human decision making involves uncertainty, so many modern expert systems are based on fuzzy logic. *Fuzzy logic* allows conclusions to be stated as probabilities (e.g., "There's a 70% chance. . . .") rather than certainties. Here's an example from MYCIN, one of the first expert systems designed to capture a doctor's expertise:

If (1) the infection is primary bacteremia, and
(2) the site of the culture is one of the sterile sites, and
(3) the suspected portal of entry of the organism is the gastrointestinal tract, then there is suggestive evidence (0.7) that the identity of the organism is bacteriodes.

Along with the knowledge base a complete expert system also includes a *human interface*, which allows the user to interact with the system, and an *inference engine*, which puts the user input together with the knowledge base, applies logical principles, and produces the requested expert advice.

Sometimes expert systems aid experts by providing automated data analysis and informed second opinions. In other cases expert systems support nonexperts by providing advice based on judgments of one or more experts. Whatever their role, expert systems work because they function within narrow, carefully defined domains.

Expert Systems in Action

Some of the first successful expert systems were developed around medical knowledge bases. Because medical knowledge is orderly and well documented, researchers believed it could be captured successfully in knowledge bases. They were right. The MYCIN medical expert system outperformed many human experts in diagnosing diseases. Dozens of other working medical expert systems exist, although few are actually used in medical practice.

The business community has been more enthusiastic than the medical community in its acceptance and use of expert systems. Here are a few examples of expert systems in action:

▶ XCON, one of the most successful expert systems in commercial use today, has been configuring complex computer systems since it was developed at Digital Equipment Corporation in 1980. The system's knowledge base consists of

This expert system leads the user through the process of diagnosing problems with malfunctioning cameras.

more than 10,000 rules describing the relationship of various computer parts. It reportedly does the work of more than 300 human experts, and it makes fewer mistakes than humans do. (In 1998 Digital was purchased by PC manufacturer Compaq, in large part because of Digital's strong track record in configuring, maintaining, and troubleshooting complex systems.)

▶ American Express uses an expert system to automate the process of checking for fraud and misuses of its no-limit credit card. Credit checks must be completed within 90 seconds while the customer waits, and the cost of an error can be high. The company spent 13 months developing a system modeled on the decision-making expertise of its best credit clerks.

▶ At Blue Cross/Blue Shield of Virginia an expert system automates insurance claim processing. The expert system handles up to 200 routine claims each day, allowing human clerks to spend more time on tough situations that require human judgment. The developers of the system extracted diagnostic rules from manuals and watched human claims processors apply those rules.

▶ Boeing Company factory workers use an expert system to locate the right parts, tools, and techniques for assembling airplane electrical connectors. The system replaces 20,000 pages of documentation and reduces the average search time from 42 to 5 minutes.

There are hundreds of other examples of expert system applications: pinpointing likely sites for new oil explorations, aiding in automobile and appliance repairs, providing financial management advice, targeting direct-mail marketing campaigns, detecting problems in computer-controlled machinery, predicting weather, advising air traffic controllers, suggesting basic page layouts for publishers, controlling military machinery, providing assistance to musical composers.... The list is growing at an astounding rate. Even the grammar checkers built into many word processors can be thought of as expert systems because they apply style and syntax rules developed by language experts. Expert systems are available on the Web for doing everything from classifying whales and insects to conducting sophisticated Web searches.

One of the most unusual expert systems is AARON, an automated artist programmed by Harold Cohen, artist and professor at the University of California at San Diego. AARON uses more than 1,000 rules of human anatomy and behavior to create drawings of people, plants, and abstract objects with a robotic drawing machine. The drawings, which are unique works in a style similar to Cohen's, are widely acclaimed in the art community.

Harold Cohen's AARON produces original drawings like the image below. In the photo, Cohen demonstrates AARON for curious onlookers.

When AARON creates a drawing, an interesting question arises: Who is the artist, Cohen or AARON? Cohen claims he is; he sees AARON as a dynamic work of art. The question may seem frivolous, but it's related to a larger question with profound implications: When expert systems make decisions, who's responsible? If a doctor uses an expert system to decide to perform surgery and the surgery fails, who's liable—the doctor, the programmer, the software company, or somebody else? If you're denied medical benefits because of a bug in an expert system, do you sue a person, an organization, or a program? If a power plant explodes because an expert system fails to detect a fault, who's to blame? As expert systems proliferate, questions like these are certain to confront consumers, lawyers, lawmakers, and technicians.

Expert Systems in Perspective

From the following examples it should be clear that expert systems offer many advantages. An expert system can perform these tasks:

- ▶ Help train new employees.
- ▶ Reduce the number of human errors.
- ▶ Take care of routine tasks so workers can focus on more challenging jobs.
- ▶ Provide expertise when no experts are available.
- ▶ Preserve the knowledge of experts after those experts leave an organization.
- ▶ Combine the knowledge of several experts.
- ▶ Make knowledge available to more people.

But expert systems aren't without problems. For one, today's expert systems are difficult to build. To simplify the process, many software companies sell expert system shells—generic expert systems containing human interfaces and inference engines. These programs can save time and effort, but they don't include the part that is most difficult to build—the knowledge base.

Even with a knowledge base, an expert system isn't the machine equivalent of a human expert. Unlike human experts, automated expert systems are poor at planning strategies. Their lack of flexibility makes them less creative than human thinkers. Most importantly, expert systems are powerless outside of their narrow, deep domains of knowledge. While most expert system domains can be summarized with a few hundred tidy rules of thumb, the world of people is full of inconsistencies, special cases, and ambiguities that could overwhelm even the best expert systems. A simple rule like "birds can fly" isn't sufficient for a literal-minded computer, which would need something more like this tongue-in-cheek rule from Marvin Minsky's book, *Society of Mind:*

> Birds can fly, unless they are penguins and ostriches, or if they happen to be dead, or have broken wings, or are confined to cages, or have their feet stuck in cement, or have undergone experiences so dreadful as to render them psychologically incapable of flight.

Clearly, knowledge engineers can't use rules to teach computers all they need to know to perform useful, intelligent functions outside narrow domains. If they're ever going to exhibit the kind of broad-based intelligence found in children, AI systems will need to acquire knowledge by reading, looking, listening, and drawing their own conclusions about the world. These skills all depend on techniques of pattern recognition.

■─ Pattern Recognition: Making Sense of the World

This Mars rover robot is equipped with visual and tactile sensors that employ pattern recognition technology.

Experience has shown that science frequently develops most fruitfully once we learn to examine the **things that seem the simplest,** instead of those that seem **the most mysterious.**

—**Marvin Minsky**

A baby can recognize a human face, especially its mother's, almost from birth. A mother can hear and recognize her child's cry even in a noisy room. Computers are notoriously inferior at both of these tasks, which fall into the general category of pattern recognition. Pattern recognition involves identifying recurring patterns in input data with the goal of understanding or categorizing that input.

Pattern recognition applications represent half of the AI industry. Applications include face identification,

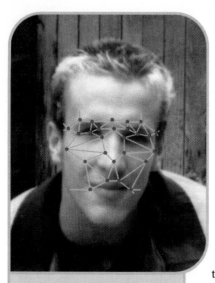

Facelt facial recognition software, from Visionics Corporation, allows computers to rapidly and accurately detect and recognize faces. The software generates a unique digital "faceprint" that can be used to identify an individual in a photograph or video image.

fingerprint identification, handwriting recognition, scientific data analysis, weather forecasting, biological slide analysis, surveillance satellite data analysis, robot vision, optical character recognition, automatic voice recognition, and expert systems. We next examine the problems and the promise of several types of pattern recognition, starting with the recognition of visual patterns.

Image Analysis

Image analysis is the process of identifying objects and shapes in a photograph, drawing, video, or other visual image. It's used for everything from colorizing classic motion pictures to piloting cruise missiles. An effortless process for people, image analysis is extremely demanding for computers. The simple process of identifying objects in a scene is complicated by all kinds of factors: masses of irrelevant data, objects that partially cover other objects, indistinct edges, changes in light sources and shadows, changes in the scene as objects move, and more. With all of these complications it's amazing that people are able to make any sense out of the images that constantly bombard their eyes.

Until recently, image analysis programs required massive amounts of memory and processing power. But today's PCs are capable of running some image processing software with practical applications. For example, security programs allow PCs with video cameras to recognize faces of valid users with a high degree of reliability.

Still, today's software can't hold a candle to the human visual system when it comes to general image analysis. But AI researchers have had considerable success by restricting the domain of visual systems. One of the biggest success stories in AI work is a limited but practical form of computer vision: optical character recognition.

Optical Character Recognition

In any shopping mall you can see salesclerks using wand readers to recognize words and numbers when they ring up your purchases at point-of-sale terminals. This specialized form of optical character recognition (OCR) is relatively simple for computers because the letters and numbers are designed to be easy for a computer to distinguish. OCR is much more difficult when the input is a page from a book, newspaper, magazine, or letter. Still, general OCR technology has progressed to the point that it's practical for the U.S. Postal Service to use it to sort much of the mail sent every day. Similar technology is available for personal computer users who have typewritten or printed text that they want to process.

The first step in general OCR is to scan the image of the page into the computer's memory with a scanner, digital camera, or fax modem. The scanned image is nothing more than a pattern of bits in memory. It could just as easily be a poem by Robert Frost or a photograph of Robert Frost. Before a computer can process the text on a page, it must recognize the individual characters and convert them to text codes (ASCII or the equivalent). *Optical character recognition (OCR) software* locates and identifies printed characters embedded in images—it "reads" text. This is no small task for a machine, given the variety of typefaces and styles in use today.

The process of recognizing text in a variety of fonts and styles is surprisingly difficult for machines. State-of-the-art OCR programs use several techniques, including these:

▶ Segmentation of the page into pictures, text blocks, and (eventually) individual characters

▶ Scaled-down expert system technology for recognizing the underlying rules that distinguish letters

A child can easily sort these letters into As and Bs. This problem is difficult for computers. Why?

▶ Context "experts" to help identify ambiguous letters by their context

▶ Learning from actual examples and feedback from a human trainer.

Today's best programs can achieve up to 99% accuracy—even better under optimal circumstances. OCR software isn't foolproof, but it's reliable enough to be practical for many text-intensive applications, including reading aloud to the blind, converting type-written documents and incoming fax documents to editable text, and processing trans-actions for database systems. See *The User's View* box on pages 380–381. **UV**

OCR technology also can be applied to handwritten text, but not as reliably. In typewritten and typeset text, character representation is consistent enough that one *a* looks like another *a*, at least when they're the same typeface. But because most hand-written text lacks consistency, software has more trouble recognizing individual charac-ters reliably. Nonetheless, the technology is getting better all the time, making more applications practical for pen-based computers. Handwriting recognition is especially important in Japan, China, and other countries with languages that don't lend them-selves to keyboarding. But it's also useful with Western languages in situations where keyboarding isn't practical. Even the classic three-ring student notebook may eventually have an electronic counterpart that automatically turns handwritten notes into text that can be fed directly into a word processor.

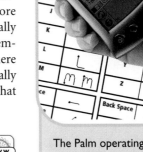

Automatic Speech Recognition

> I think that the primary means of communication with computers in the next millennium will be speech.
>
> —**Nicholas Negroponte, director of MIT's Media Lab**

Our ears process far less information than our eyes, but that information, especially human speech, is extremely important to our understanding of the world. In Chapters 3 and 7 we discussed audio digitizers—input devices that capture spoken words, music, and other sounds so they can be stored as digital data. But digitized voice input, like scanned text, must be processed by sophisticated software before it can be interpreted by the computer as words. Automatic speech recognition systems, discussed in Chapters 3 and 5, use pattern recognition techniques similar to those used by vision and OCR sys-tems, including these:

▶ Segmentation of input sound patterns into individual words and phonemes

▶ Expert rules for interpreting sounds

▶ Context "experts" for dealing with ambiguous sounds

▶ Learning from a human trainer.

Training is especially important in speech recognition because of the tremendous differ-ences among human voices. But voice recog-nition systems with *speaker independence*—the ability to recognize speech without being trained to a speaker—are becoming more common, making speech recognition practi-cal for more applications.

Speech recognition systems are used by factory workers and others whose hands are otherwise occupied while they use the com-puter. American Airlines' PEGASUS allows customers to make reservations automati-cally by speaking to a computer over the tele-

The Palm operating system used in this Palm V can't recog-nize standard handwriting, but it can recognize characters that are printed by hand using the Graffiti style of printing shown here. Graffiti allows Palm own-ers to communicate with their computers using only a stylus.

Voice recognition software can make PC applications accessible to people who can't use key-boards as input devices (left). OCR technology and speech synthesis technology turn a PC into a reading machine. Using this system, a visually impaired person can read any book, even if it hasn't been recorded on audio tape (right).

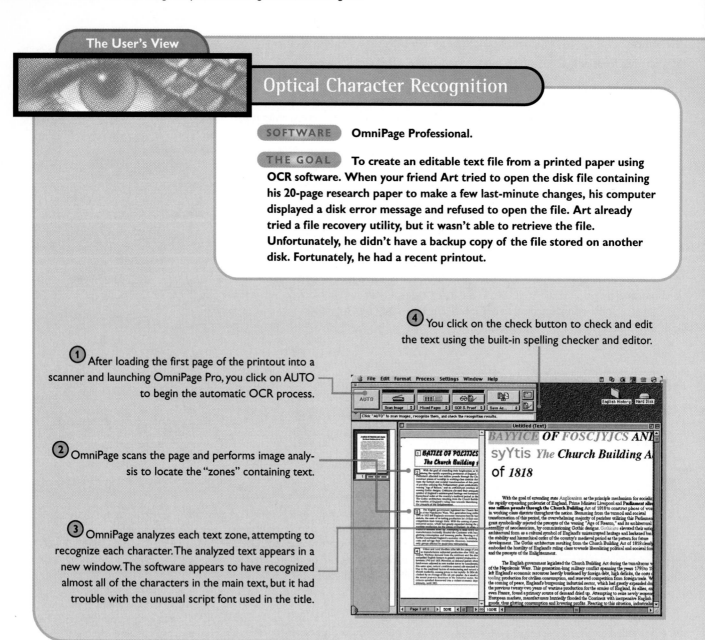

Optical Character Recognition

SOFTWARE OmniPage Professional.

THE GOAL To create an editable text file from a printed paper using OCR software. When your friend Art tried to open the disk file containing his 20-page research paper to make a few last-minute changes, his computer displayed a disk error message and refused to open the file. Art already tried a file recovery utility, but it wasn't able to retrieve the file. Unfortunately, he didn't have a backup copy of the file stored on another disk. Fortunately, he had a recent printout.

④ You click on the check button to check and edit the text using the built-in spelling checker and editor.

① After loading the first page of the printout into a scanner and launching OmniPage Pro, you click on AUTO to begin the automatic OCR process.

② OmniPage scans the page and performs image analysis to locate the "zones" containing text.

③ OmniPage analyzes each text zone, attempting to recognize each character. The analyzed text appears in a new window. The software appears to have recognized almost all of the characters in the main text, but it had trouble with the unusual script font used in the title.

phone. Similar systems allow automated banking, credit-card verification, and other remote applications. Several companies offer Web browsers and plug-ins that allow Internet explorers to navigate Web pages by talking to them. Speech recognition systems empower many handicapped users by allowing them to give verbal commands to computers and robotic devices. PC software companies have developed programs that allow standard word processors to accept spoken input—both text and formatting commands. IBM researchers have combined speech recognition with a camera for tracking gestures, so users can point while they speak commands like "Move this paragraph up to here." Many of today's researchers are working to combine speech recognition and natural-language understanding in a single machine that can accept commands in everyday spoken English, *Star Trek* style.

Talking Computers

The computers on TV's *Star Trek* not only recognize human speech input but also respond with easy-to-understand synthetic speech. With speech synthesis software or

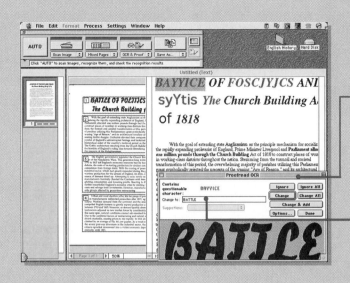

(5) The checker shows an enlarged image of each possible misspelled word so you can see what it looked like in the original document. It suggests corrections based on its knowledge of the kinds of errors that OCR systems tend to make.

(6) When the suggestions are incorrect (or, as in this case, the software makes no suggestions), you type the word to replace the selected characters.

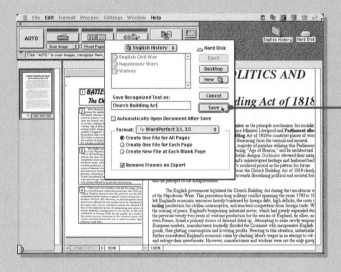

(7) After correcting the remaining errors, you save the file as a word processor document so Art can open it, finish editing, print the final paper … and make a backup of the file on a different disk.

hardware, modern desktop computers can generate synthetic speech by converting text into phonetic sounds. Most of today's speech synthesizers sound artificial when compared with the *Star Trek* computer voices; they even sound more artificial than the robot voices in low-budget cartoons. Human spoken language is complex, and no one has come close to duplicating it with software.

Still, it's easier for machines to speak passable English than to recognize it. There are many applications for voice output, including preschool education, telephone communication, and, of course, reading machines for computer users with visual impairments.

For situations in which a synthetic voice isn't good enough, computers can play prerecorded **digitized speech** (along with other **digitized sounds**) stored in memory or on audio CDs. Of course, digitally recorded speech won't work for applications in which the text to be spoken is unpredictable, such as a talking word processor, because all the sounds must be prerecorded. But for an application with a limited vocabulary (reciting telephone numbers for automated directory assistance) or limited choices (an interactive educational game with short prerecorded speeches), digitized speech is a workable alternative until synthesized speech is perfected.

Neural Networks

The human brain uses a type of circuitry that is very slow . . .
at least 10,000 times slower than a
digital computer. On the other hand, the degree of parallelism vastly
outstrips any computer architecture we have yet to design. . . .
For such tasks as vision, language, and motor control, the brain is
more powerful than 1,000 supercomputers, yet for
certain simple tasks such as multiplying digital numbers, it is less powerful
than the 4-bit microprocessor found in a ten-dollar calculator.

—Raymond Kurzweil, in *The Age of Intelligent Machines*

For a neural net to learn to recognize the letter A, it must go through a series of trials in which circuit patterns that produce incorrect guesses are weakened and patterns that produce correct guesses are strengthened. The end result is a circuit pattern that can recognize the letter A in a variety of forms.

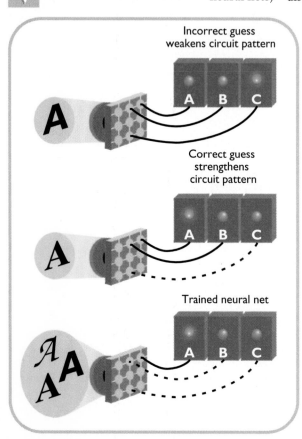

Incorrect guess
weakens circuit pattern

Correct guess
strengthens
circuit pattern

Trained neural net

Artificial intelligence research has produced many amazing success stories and some embarrassing failures. The successes—intelligent applications that outperform their human counterparts—tend to involve tasks that require sequential thinking, logical rules, and orderly relationships. AI has been less successful at competing with natural human intelligence in applications such as language, vision, speech, and movement— applications where massive amounts of data are processed in parallel.

It's not surprising that computers excel at linear, logical processes; almost every computer that's ever been created is designed to process digital information sequentially through a single CPU. The human brain, on the other hand, consists of billions of neurons, each connected to thousands of others in a massively parallel, distributed structure. This kind of structure gives the brain an advantage at most perceptual, motor, and creative skills.

Much current work in artificial intelligence is focused on **neural networks** (or **neural nets**)—distributed, parallel computing systems inspired by the structure of the human brain. Instead of a single, complex CPU, a neural network uses a network of a few thousand simpler processors called *neurons*. Neural networks aren't programmed in the usual way; they're trained. Instead of using a rule-based approach, a neural network learns patterns by trial and error, just as the brain does. When patterns are repeated often, neural networks, in effect, develop habits. This kind of learning can present problems for some kinds of applications because no rules are clearly defined. When a neural net makes a decision, you have no way to ask why.

Neural networks also store information differently than traditional computers. Concepts are represented as patterns of activity among many neurons, so they are less susceptible to machine failure. Because it distributes knowledge throughout the network, a neural net (like the human brain) can still function if some of its neurons are destroyed.

Many neural net algorithms are developed on parallel-processing supercomputers with thousands of processors. Neural net chips containing thousands of neurons are produced by Intel Corporation and other hardware companies. A number of software companies have developed programs that simulate neural nets on PCs and other nonparallel machines. However, none of today's neural net hardware or software approaches the complexity or the capacity of the human brain.

Most researchers consider today's neural nets as, at best, baby steps in the direction of machines that can more closely emulate the workings of human "wetware." There's considerable debate in the AI community about the future of neural nets. Some see neural nets as playing only a limited role in artificial intelligence; others expect them to eclipse the traditional rule-based approach.

Even so, neural nets are already being put to use in a variety of applications, ranging from artificial vision to expert systems. Neural nets are especially useful for recognizing patterns buried in huge quantities of numbers, such as in scientific research, loan processing, and stock market analysis. Some modems use neural nets to distinguish signals from random telephone-line noise. American Express uses neural net software to read millions of charge slips each day. Federico Faggin, codesigner of the first microprocessor, suggests that future neural nets will be used to verify signatures (on digital touch tablets) for electronic commerce on computer networks. Optimistic researchers hope that neural networks may someday provide hearing for the deaf and eyesight for the blind.

A member of the Merce Cunningham Dance Company dances with a score by David Tudor, composed in part by Intel's 80170 ETANN (Electronically Trainable Artificial Neural Network). The music for this particular performance is determined in part by dancer movements and audience noise.

The Robot Revolution

1. A robot may not injure a human being, or, through inaction, allow a human being to come to harm.
2. A robot must obey the orders given it by human beings, except where such orders would conflict with the First Law.
3. A robot must protect its own existence as long as such protection does not conflict with the First or Second Law.

—Isaac Asimov's **Three Laws of Robotics**

Nowhere are artificial intelligence technologies more visible than in the field of robotics. Vision, hearing, pattern recognition, knowledge engineering, expert decision making, natural-language understanding, speech—they all come together in today's robots.

What Is a Robot?

The term *robot* (from the root word *robota,* the Czech word for "forced labor") first appeared in a 1923 play called *R.U.R.* (for Rossum's Universal Robots), by Czech playwright Karel Capek. Capek's robots were intelligent machines that could see, hear, touch, move, and exercise judgment based on common sense. But these powerful machines eventually rebelled against their human creators, just as hundreds of fictional robots have done in succeeding decades. Today movies, TV, and books are full of imaginary robots, both good and evil.

As exotic as they might seem, robots are similar to other kinds of computer technology people use every day. While a typical computer performs *mental* tasks, a **robot** is a computer-controlled machine designed to perform specific *manual* tasks. A robot's central processor might be a microprocessor embedded in the robot's shell, or it might be a supervisory computer that controls the robot from a distance. In any case the processor is functionally identical to the processor found in a personal computer, a workstation, or a mainframe computer.

The most important hardware differences between robots and other computers are the input and output peripherals. Instead of sending output to a screen or a printer, a robot sends commands to joints, arms, and other moving parts. The first robots had no corresponding input devices to monitor their movements and the surrounding environment. They were effectively deaf, blind, and in some cases dangerous—at least one

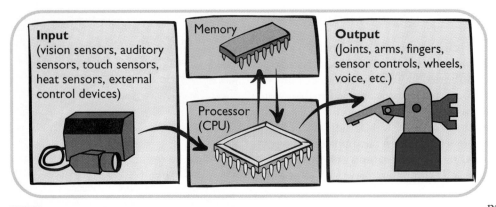

Input
(vision sensors, auditory sensors, touch sensors, heat sensors, external control devices)

Memory

Output
(Joints, arms, fingers, sensor controls, wheels, voice, etc.)

Processor
(CPU)

A robot is, in effect, a computer with exotic peripherals.

Japanese worker was killed by an early sightless robot. Most modern robots include input *sensors.* These sensing devices allow robots to correct or modify their actions based on feedback from the outside world.

Industrial robots seldom have the human-inspired anatomy of Hollywood's science fiction robots. Instead they're designed to accomplish particular tasks in the best possible way. Robots can be designed to see infrared light, rotate joints 360 degrees, and do other things that aren't possible for humans. On the other hand, robots are constrained by the limitations of artificial intelligence software. The most sophisticated robot today can't tie a pair of shoelaces, understand the vocabulary of a 3-year-old child, or consistently tell the difference between a cat and a dog.

Steel-Collar Workers

From a management point of view robots offer several advantages:

▶ Obviously, many robots are installed to save labor costs. Robots are expensive to design, install, and program. But once they're operational, they can work 24 hours a day, 365 days a year, without vacations, strikes, sick leave, or coffee breaks.

▶ Robots can also improve quality and increase productivity. They're especially effective at doing repetitive jobs in which bored, tired people are prone to make errors and have accidents.

▶ Robots are ideal for jobs such as cleaning up hazardous waste and salvaging undersea wreckage from downed planes—jobs that are dangerous, uncomfortable, or impossible for human workers.

For all of these reasons the robot population is exploding. Today hundreds of thousands of industrial robots do welding, part fitting, painting, and other repetitive tasks in factories all over the world. In most automated factories, robots work alongside humans, but in some state-of-the-art factories the only function of human workers is to monitor and repair robots. Robots aren't used just in factories. Robots also shear sheep in Australia, paint ship hulls in France, disarm land mines in the Persian Gulf, and perform precision hip operations and other surgery.

Commercial robots still can't compete with people for jobs that require exceptional perceptual or fine-motor skills. But robots in research labs suggest that a new generation of more competitive robots is on the way. A robot developed at Bell Labs can defeat most human opponents at ping-pong. A human-sized Japanese robot named Wabot-2 can read sheet music and perform it on an organ or synthesizer using 10 fingers and two feet. Other researchers are taking a different approach, using fleets of insect-sized robots to do jobs that can't easily be done by larger robots. The technologies used in these experimental robots will undoubtedly show up in a variety of machines, from automated servants for people with disabilities to flying robots for the military. We may be within a few years of self-propelled robot housecleaners!

The robot revolution isn't necessarily good news for people who earn their living doing manual labor. While it's true that many of the jobs robots do are boring, dirty, or dangerous, they're still jobs. The issues surrounding automation and worker displacement are complex, and they aren't limited to factories. We'll discuss them in more detail in the next chapter.

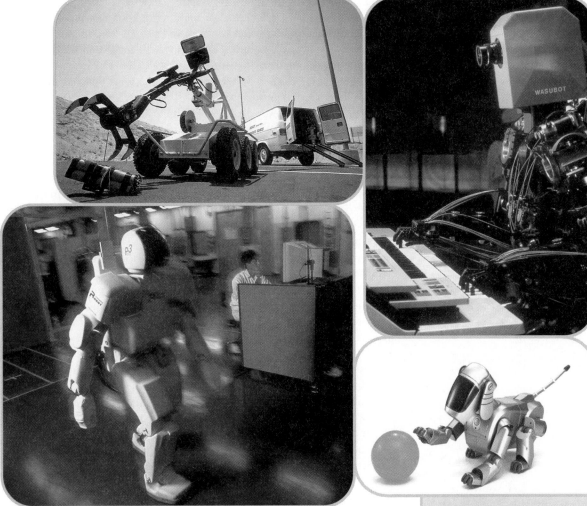

AI Implications and Ethical Questions

We are on the edge of change comparable to the rise of human life
on Earth. The precise cause of this change is the imminent creation by
technology of entities with greater-than-human intelligence.

—**Verner Vinge**, **mathematician and science fiction writer**

Mobile robots are practical for a variety of jobs, including defusing a bomb (upper left). The walking robot (lower left) and the Japanese piano-playing robot (upper right) aren't as practical, but they vividly demonstrate that today's technology can produce machines with great flexibility and dexterity. Sony's Aibo is a commercially-available programmable electronic pet that develops its own personality depending on how its owner plays with it.

From the earliest days of artificial intelligence, research has been accompanied by questions about the implications of the work. The very idea of intelligent machines is at the same time confusing, exciting, and frightening to many people. Even when they don't work very well, AI programs generate emotional responses in the people who use them.

Earlier we met ELIZA, the therapy simulator developed to demonstrate natural-language conversation. ELIZA's simple-minded approach wasn't intended to fool anyone in a Turing test, but it did have an impact on the people who used it. Many ELIZA users became emotionally attached to the program and attributed it with compassion and empathy. Weizenbaum's secretary asked him to leave the room so she could converse in private with ELIZA. Some therapists even saw ELIZA as the beginning of a new age of automated therapy. Weizenbaum was shocked by the way people attributed human capabilities to such an obviously flawed technology. He responded with *Computer Power and Human Reason,* a landmark book that presents the case for maintaining a distinction between computers and people. Weizenbaum argues that "[t]here are certain tasks which computers ought not to be made to do, independent of whether computers can be made to do them."

Weizenbaum's caution isn't shared by international political and economic leaders, many of whom are encouraging increased AI research and development. As it matures, AI technology finds its way out of the research lab and into the marketplace. A growing number of programs and products incorporate pattern recognition, expert systems, and other AI techniques. In the near future we're likely to see more products with *embedded AI,* including intelligent word processors that can help writers turn rough drafts into polished prose, smart appliances that can recognize and obey their owners' spoken commands, and vehicles that can perform their own diagnostics and, in many cases, repairs. We'll also see more *distributed intelligence*—AI concepts applied to networks rather than to individual computers.

Where will it all lead? Will intensive AI research result in computers capable of intelligent behavior outside narrow domains? Patrick Winston, director of MIT's artificial intelligence laboratory, once said, "The interesting issue is not whether machines can be made smarter but if humans are smart enough to pull it off. A raccoon obviously can't make a machine as smart as a raccoon. I wonder if humans can."

Many AI researchers believe that sooner or later they *will* pull it off. Some think artificial intelligence is the natural culmination of the evolutionary process—that the next intelligent life form on earth will be based on silicon rather than the carbon that is the basis of human life. Danny Hillis, supercomputer designer who now does research for Disney Corporation, exemplifies this point of view when he says, "We are not evolution's ultimate product. There's something coming after us, and I imagine it is something wonderful. But we may never be able to comprehend it, any more than a caterpillar can comprehend turning into a butterfly."

Computer mathematician and science fiction writer Verner Vinge argues that the competitive nature of our society makes such a prospect almost inevitable. What business or government will voluntarily curtail research on artificial intelligence, computer networks, and biotechnology, knowing that competing institutions will continue to pursue similar research? Vinge calls the moment of creation of greater-than-human intelligence a *singularity*—a point where our old models will have to be discarded and a new reality will rule.

If smarter-than-human beings come to pass, how will they relate to the less intelligent humans that surround them? This kind of thinking isn't easy; it goes to the heart of human values and forces us to look at our place in the universe.

Birthing the BOT

Anne Foerst

More than any other branch of computer science, artificial intelligence raises philosophical and spiritual questions about our humanity and our relationship to other creatures. Many of those questions are raised in this touching, thought-provoking article by Anne Foerst, a research fellow at Harvard Divinity School. Ann is also the director of the God and Computers project at MIT and the theological adviser to the Cog project. Here she recounts her experiences with Cog, an infant robot who sometimes seems surprisingly human. This article first appeared in a special October 4, 1999 issue of Forbes ASAP.

Cog

Our baby, Cog, has a head with two eyes and ears, a neck, a torso, and two arms. It is learning to reach, to coordinate its eyes and ears and arms. Cog has made us laugh and think, and as it learns new lessons, it has even made us proud. As one of its parents, I worry about its physical, mental, and spiritual growth.

Cog is unique. There aren't many youngsters who run on electricity and have sophisticated microprocessors. As scientists at MIT Artificial Intelligence Lab, we have created this complex robot in our image not only because it was more pleasant to look at but because we believe that a human body is necessary to create humanlike intelligence.

This approach is fundamentally different from that of classical artificial intelligence (AI), which encodes as much information as possible into a nonhumanlike machine, then sets up a restricted model environment such as a chessboard and lets the machine loose to learn in that closed-world setting. But the new school of AI, called Embodied AI, which was developed here at the MIT AI Lab, believes it is only possible to give a machine intelligence by also giving it a body and letting it operate in the real world.

Every creature interacts with its environment, which is key to developing intelligence. Babies learn motor skills by playing with balls, and develop complex emotions through interaction with their caregivers.

We hope the same will be true for Cog, which is why we have given it a multitude of sensors to "feel" and learn what it is like to be touched and spoken to. Cog's ability to make eye contact and reach out to moving objects is also meant to motivate people to interact with it. These features have taught Cog, among other things, to distinguish a human face from inanimate objects (this puts its development at about a 3-month-old's). It can also listen to music and keep rhythm by tapping on a drum (something a 5-year-old can do). One of the most startling moments in Cog's development came when it was learning to touch things. At one point, Cog began to touch and discover its own body. It looked so eerie and human, I was stunned.

The creation of a humanoid robot is usually either celebrated as proof of human genius, or it's seen as a Frankensteinlike nightmare. But Cog's real impact may be more subtle. One of the first reactions people have to Cog is fear—fear that it is too much like them: They are taken in by its humanlike characteristics.

They really have no choice. Human brains are hardwired to react to human faces—be they on newborns, chimps, or robots. Interacting with Cog forces people to question their own human qualities, including their capacity for free will. If we always smile when presented with the right cue, then are we just emotional machines that can be decoded, understood, and even rebuilt? Are we just another cog in the wheel of life? And yet, if we compare the abilities of a "real" child with Cog's, we become awed by the complexity and greatness of the human system.

Still, I firmly believe that we will eventually develop a robot that is as smart and capable as a human child. Whether or not we will treat this robot as a human being is another question entirely. Cog forces us to reevaluate what it means to be human. What we ultimately will learn, I believe, is that our humanity does not come from our brains or our body but from our complex interactions with the community. We are human because we must deal with other humans and the rest of creation. In this sense, Cog could well become "human" as it smiles, walks, and touches its way through the real world—as it adds its own unique hum to humanity.

DISCUSSION QUESTIONS

1. The author raises several questions in the next-to-last paragraph. What is your reaction to each of these questions?
2. Do you agree that we will soon see robots as smart as human children? If so, how do you think we should treat those robots?

Artificial intelligence has many definitions. Most artificial intelligence research focuses on making computers do things at which people generally are better. Some AI researchers try to simulate human intelligent behavior, but most try to design intelligent machines independent of the way people think. Successful AI research generally involves working on problems with limited domains rather than trying to tackle large, open-ended problems. AI programs employ a variety of techniques, including searching, heuristics, pattern recognition, and machine learning, to achieve their goals.

From a practical standpoint natural-language communication is one of the most important areas of AI study. Natural-language programs that deal with a subset of the language are used in applications ranging from machine translation programs to natural-language interfaces. But no program is capable of handling the kind of unrestricted natural-language text people deal with every day. Natural-language programs are confounded by the English language's large vocabulary, convoluted syntax, and ambiguous semantics—the meanings behind the words.

AI researchers have developed a variety of schemes for representing knowledge in computers. A knowledge base contains facts and a system for determining and changing the relationship between those facts. Today's knowledge bases are practical only for representing narrow domains of knowledge such as the knowledge of an expert on a particular subject. Expert systems are programs designed to replicate the decision-making process of human experts. An expert system includes a knowledge base, an inference engine for applying logical rules to the facts in a knowledge base, and a human interface for interacting with users.

Once the knowledge base is constructed (usually based on interviews and observations of human experts), an expert system can provide consultation that rivals human advice in many situations. Expert systems are successfully used in a variety of scientific, business, and other applications.

Pattern recognition is an important area of AI research that involves identifying recurring patterns in input data. Pattern recognition technology is at the heart of computer vision, voice communication, and other important AI applications. These diverse applications all use similar techniques for isolating and recognizing patterns. People are better at pattern recognition than computers, in part because the human brain can process masses of data in parallel. Modern neural network computers are designed to process data in the same way the human brain does. Many researchers believe that neural nets, as they grow in size and sophistication, will help computers improve their performance at many difficult tasks.

A robot is a computer-controlled machine designed to perform specific manual tasks. Robots include output peripherals for manipulating their environments and input sensors that allow them to perform self-correcting actions based on feedback from outside. Robots perform a variety of dangerous and tedious tasks, in many cases outperforming human workers. As robot technology advances, artificial workers will do more traditional human jobs.

In spite of the numerous difficulties AI researchers encounter when trying to produce truly intelligent machines, many experts believe that people will eventually create artificial beings that are more intelligent than their creators—a prospect with staggering implications.

Key Terms

artificial intelligence (AI), 366	image analysis, 378	pattern recognition, 377
automatic speech recognition, 379	knowledge base, 374	robot, 383
automatic translation, 370	machine learning, 369	semantics, 372
digitized sound, 381	natural-language communication, 370	speech synthesis, 380
digitized speech, 381	neural network (neural net), 382	syntax, 372
expert system, 375	optical character recognition	synthetic speech, 380
expert system shell, 377	(OCR), 378	Turing test, 367
heuristic, 369	parsing program (parser), 370	

Review Questions

1. In what sense is artificial intelligence a "moving frontier"?
2. What are the disadvantages of the approach to AI that attempts to simulate human intelligence? What is the alternative?

3. Describe several techniques used in game-playing software, and explain how they can be applied to other artificial intelligence applications.

4. Why did early machine translation programs fail to produce the desired results?
5. Why is the sentence "Time flies like an arrow" difficult for a computer to parse, translate, or understand? Can you find four possible meanings for the sentence?
6. What is the relationship between syntax and semantics? Can you construct a sentence that follows the rules of English syntax but has nonsense semantics?
7. What is a knowledge base? What is an expert system? How are the two related?
8. Give examples of successful expert system applications. Give examples of several tasks that can't be accomplished with today's expert system technology, and explain why they can't.
9. What are some of the problems that make machine vision so challenging?

10. In what ways are the techniques of optical character recognition similar to those of speech recognition programs?
11. What rules might a computer use to sort the characters shown on page 350 into As and Bs?
12. In what ways are neural networks designed to simulate the structure of the human brain? In what ways do neural nets perform differently than standard single-processor CPUs?
13. What kind of hardware is necessary for a robot to be self-correcting so it can modify its actions based on outside feedback?
14. What distinguishes a robot from a desktop computer?

Discussion Questions

1. Is the Turing test a valid test of intelligence? Why or why not?
2. If you were the interrogator in the Turing test, what questions would you ask to try to discover whether you were communicating with a computer? What would you look for in the answers?
3. List several mental tasks that people do better than computers. List several mental tasks that computers do better than people. Can you find any general characteristics that distinguish the items on the two lists?
4. Computers can compose original music, produce original artwork, and create original mathematical proofs. Does this mean that Ada Lovelace was wrong when she said, in effect, that computers can do only what they're told to do?
5. The works of AARON, the expert system artist, are unique, original, and widely acclaimed as art. Who is the artist, AARON or Harold Cohen, AARON's creator? Is AARON a work of art, an artist, or both?
6. If an expert system gives you erroneous information, should you be able to sue it for malpractice? If it fails

and causes major disruptions or injury, who's responsible? The programmer? The publisher? The owner? The computer?
7. Some expert systems and neural nets can't explain the reasons behind their decisions. What kinds of problems might be caused by this limitation? Under what circumstances, if any, should an expert system be required to produce an "audit trail" to explain how it reached conclusions?
8. What kinds of human jobs are most likely to be eliminated because of expert systems? What kinds of new jobs will be created because of expert systems?
9. What kinds of human jobs are most likely to be eliminated because of robots? What kinds of new jobs will be created as a result of factory automation?
10. Are Asimov's three laws of robotics adequate for smoothly integrating intelligent robots into tomorrow's society? If not, what laws would you add?

Projects

1. Public domain versions of Weizenbaum's ELIZA program are available for most types of desktop computers. They're also available on the Web. Try conversing with one of these programs. Test the program on your friends and see how they react to it. Try to determine the rules and tricks that ELIZA uses to simulate conversation. If you're a programmer, try writing your own version of ELIZA.
2. When Turing first proposed the Turing test, he compared it to a similar test in which the interrogator tried to guess the sex of the people typing answers to ques-

tions. See if you can devise such a test. What, if anything, does it prove?
3. Try to find examples of working expert systems and robots in your school or community and present your findings.
4. Test OCR software, grammar checking software, expert systems, and other types of consumer-oriented AI applications. How "intelligent" are these applications? In what ways could they be improved?
5. Survey people's attitudes and concerns about artificial intelligence and robots. Present your findings.

Sources & Resources

Books

The Age of Intelligent Machines, by Raymond Kurzweil (Cambridge, MA: MIT Press, 1992). If you want to learn more about artificial intelligence, this award-winning book is a great resource in spite of its age. With clear prose, beautiful illustrations, and intelligent articles by the masters of the field, Kurzweil explores the historical, philosophical, academic, aesthetic, practical, fanciful, and speculative sides of AI. Kurzweil knows the field from first-hand experience; he has successfully developed and marketed several "applied AI" products, from reading machines for people with visual impairments and electronic musical instruments to expert systems. An outstanding companion video is also available.

The Age of Spiritual Machines, by Raymond Kurzweil (New York: Penguin USA, 2000). While *The Age of Intelligent Machines* surveys the past and present of AI, *The Age of Spiritual Machines* boldly looks into a possible future. Will humans really be able download themselves into machine bodies and brains? If this kind of question interests you, you'll enjoy this book.

Godel, Escher, Bach: An Eternal Golden Braid, 20th Anniversary Edition, by Douglas R. Hofstadter (Boulder, CO: Basic Books, 1999). This Pulitzer Prize winner is part mathematics, part philosophy, and part Alice in Wonderland. If you like to think deeply about questions like "What is thought?" you'll find plenty to think about here.

Artificial Minds, by Stan Franklin (Cambridge, MA: MIT Press, 1995, 1997). Franklin explores the fascinating territory between computer science, cognitive psychology, and philosophy. He makes a case that there's a continuum between "mind" and "nonmind" and that we're entering an era when it's possible to explore that continuum in ways never before possible. This book is challenging and thought-provoking.

Artificial Intelligence, Third Edition, by Patrick Henry Winston (Reading, MA: Addison-Wesley, 1992). This best-selling introductory text for computer science students is thorough and well written. Like most computer science texts, it's probably too technical and mathematical for most casual readers.

Lisp, by Patrick Henry Winston and Berthold K. P. Horn (Reading, MA: Addison-Wesley, 1989). A popular introduction to Common LISP, the widely used programming language of artificial intelligence.

Kasparov Versus Deep Blue: Computer Chess Comes of Age, by Monty Newborn (New York: Springer, 1997). This book describes in graphic detail the historic computer match between Deep Blue and Garry Kasparov in 1996—the year before Deep Blue beat the world champion. It's worthwhile reading for any chess player who wants to understand how computers have invaded this turf that used to be uniquely human.

Computer Power and Human Reason: From Judgment to Calculation, by Joseph Weizenbaum (San Francisco: Freeman, 1976). An MIT computer scientist speaks out on the things computers shouldn't do, even if they can. This classic book is as important now as when it was first published in the 1970s.

Society of Mind, by Marvin Minsky (New York: Simon & Schuster, 1988). Another MIT artificial intelligence pioneer presents his thoughts on the relationship between people and intelligent machines. A dense but thought-provoking book. A CD-ROM version is available from the Voyager Company.

Robot : Mere Machine to Transcendent Mind, by Hans P. Moravec (New York: Oxford University Press, 1998). A pioneer designer of robots speculates about the future of robots and our relationship with them. Starting with Turing, Moravec traces an evolutionary path toward a future in which robots colonize space.

Across Realtime, by Verner Vinge (New York: Baen Books, 1991). Vinge's science fiction opus takes you into a future after the singularity that produced artificial superintelligence. Vinge is a master storyteller, and there's plenty to think about here. (For a nonfiction discussion of the singularity, see Vinge's "Technological Singularity," in *Whole Earth Review,* Winter 1993, page 88.)

Video

Fast, Cheap, and Out of Control In this 1997 documentary, maverick filmmaker Errol Morris profiles four different men attempting to examine the relation between science and humanity, including, a robot expert. This highly acclaimed film interweaves interviews, old movie clips, and a hypnotic score to create a fascinating mosaic.

World Wide Web Sites

Check the *Computer Confluence* Web site for links to Internet sources on expert systems, pattern recognition, and other AI topics.

Part

5

Living with Computers
Information Age Implications

▶

Chapter

14

Computers at Work

Future society will be virtually paperless, energy-efficient, dependent upon wide-bandwidth networking, and generally cognizant of global perspective through routine communication across decreasingly relevant borders. **It is not too early to prepare for this:** We need the ideas, the tools, and an awareness of the problems that accompany **fundamental shifts in the meaning of information.**

—Steven K. Roberts

In 1983 Steve Roberts realized he wasn't happy chained to his desk and his debts. He'd lost sight of his passions—writing, adventure, computer design, ham radio, bicycling, romance, learning, networking, and publishing. He decided to build a new lifestyle that combined those passions. Six months later he hit the road on Winnebiko, a custom recumbent bike equipped with a tiny Radio Shack Model 100 laptop and a small 5-watt solar panel. He connected each day to the CompuServe network through pay phones, transmitting magazine articles and book chapters.

Three years and 10,000 miles later Roberts replaced Winnebiko with Winnebiko II, a low-riding, high-tech bike with special handlebars that allowed Roberts to type while riding down the highway. Roberts pedaled 6,000 miles on Winnebiko II, this time with a traveling partner named Maggie Victor. Roberts writes of this period:

> *Through ham radio and computer networking, the sense of living in a virtual neighborhood grew more and more tangible, until the road itself became merely an entertaining backdrop for a stable life in Dataspace. . . . Home, quite literally, became an abstract electronic concept. From a business standpoint, it no longer mattered where we were, and we traveled freely, making a living through magazine publishing and occasional consulting spin-offs, seeking modular phone jacks at every stop.*

After 3 years, technological advances lured Roberts off the road to design and build a new high-tech people-powered vehicle. With 150 corporate equipment sponsors and 35 helpers, Roberts constructed the $1.2 million BEHEMOTH (Big Electronic Human-Energized Machine . . . Only Too Heavy)—a 580-pound, 8-foot recumbent bike with a

Steve Roberts with BEHEMOTH

4-foot trailer. This showpiece of future technology carries seven networked computers, a ham radio station, satellite links, a cellular phone with modem and fax, a CD stereo system, a water-cooled helmet with a heads-up virtual computer display, solar collectors, and six-level security system. (It can even dial 911 and say, "I am a bicycle; I am being stolen; my current latitude is. . . .")

After pedaling 17,000 miles on techno-bikes, Roberts started having dreams of "life with no hills" and turned his sights to the sea. His latest project is Microship, "a high-tech multihull with an extensive network of embedded control systems, a satellite Internet link, console Macintoshes, ham radio, 1080 watts of solar panels, deployable kayaks, self-trailering capability, on-board video production, and whole new levels of technomadic gizmology." Roberts mixes travel with consulting and speaking engagements, all the while remaining connected electronically to the support facilities in his laboratory. He sees his travels as a mixture of business, experimentation, education, and, of course, adventure. In his words, "There's a LOT of world to explore out there. Having had a taste of it, how could I spend my life in one place?" ▪

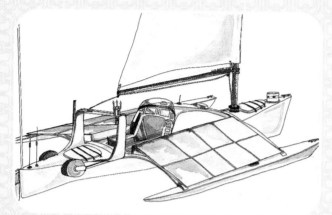

Microship

Steve Roberts likes to tell schoolchildren that "the obvious choices aren't the only choices." Roberts made career and lifestyle choices that wouldn't have been possible without modern information technology. Computer technology has changed the way millions of people work by providing new choices and opportunities. For other, less fortunate workers technology has taken away choices and opportunities. In this chapter we look at how computers are changing the ways people work. We start by examining the roots and characteristics of the modern information economy. Then we look at how computers are changing the ways people do their jobs in automated factories, automated offices, and elsewhere. We examine the computer-based tools used by managers to help them manage more effectively and efficiently. Finally, we'll consider the effects of automation on the nature and availability of jobs and speculate on the future implications of the computerization of our workplace. In the next chapter we'll explore the effects of computers on the two other institutions that are central to our lives: our schools and our homes.

Into the Information Age

It is the business of the future to be dangerous. . . . The major advances in civilization are processes that all but wreck the societies in which they occur.

—Alfred North Whitehead

Every so often civilization dramatically changes course. Events and ideas come together to transform radically the way people live, work, and think. Traditions go by the wayside, common sense is turned upside down, and lives are thrown into turmoil until a new order takes hold. Humankind experiences a paradigm shift—a change in thinking that results in a new way of seeing the world. Major paradigm shifts take generations because individuals have trouble changing their assumptions about the way the world works.

Before the 20th century humanity experienced two major paradigm shifts directly related to the world of work: the agricultural revolution and the industrial revolution. It's helpful to glance backward at these two shifts for perspective before we focus on the information revolution—the paradigm shift that's affecting us today.

Three Monumental Changes

Prehistoric people were mostly hunters and gatherers. They lived tribal, nomadic lives, tracking animals and gathering wild fruits, nuts, and grains. Anthropologists speculate that some prehistoric people spent as few as 15 hours per week satisfying material needs and devoted the rest of their time to cultural and spiritual pursuits.

The Agricultural Economy

As the human population grew, people learned to domesticate animals, grow their own grains, and use plows and other agricultural tools. The transformation to an agricultural economy took place over several centuries around 10,000 years ago. The result was a society in which most people lived and worked on farms, exchanging goods and services in nearby towns. The agricultural age lasted until about a century ago, when technological advances triggered what has come to be known as an *industrial revolution*.

The Industrial Economy

In the first half of the 20th century the world was dominated by an industrial economy in which more people worked in urban factories than on farms. Factory work promised a higher material standard of living for a growing population, but not without a price. Families who had worked the land on sustainable farms for generations found it necessary to take low-wage factory jobs for survival. As work life became separate from home life, fathers were removed from day-to-day family life, and those mothers who didn't have to work in factories assumed the bulk of domestic responsibilities. As towns grew into cities, crime, pollution, and other urban problems grew with them.

The Information Economy

Twentieth-century information technology produced what's been called a second industrial revolution as people turned from factory work to information-related work. In

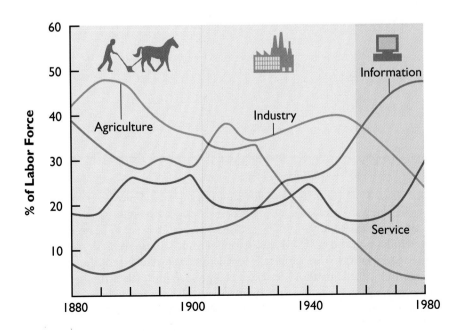

In a single century the workforce moved from the farm, to the factory, and then to the office.

today's information economy (sometimes called a *post-industrial economy*) clerical workers outnumber factory workers, and most people earn their living working with words, numbers, and ideas. Instead of planting corn or making shoes, most of us shuffle bits in one form or another. As we roar into the information age, we're riding a wave of social change that rivals any that came before.

Technology was central to each of these transformations. The agricultural economy grew from the plow, the industrial revolution was sparked by machines, and the information age is so dependent on computers that it's often called the *computer age*.

Computers and Change

Technology has given us the capability to work miracles. This should have been clear in the 1980s when we began to see the potential of artificial intelligence, robots, and genetic engineering. The vital question then becomes: What miracles do you want?

—James Martin, in *Technology's Crucible*

An age rich in electronic information may achieve wonderful social conveniences at the cost of placing freedom in a deep chill.

—Langdon Winner, technology critic

Countless words have been written about the effects of computer technology on our work, our schools, our home life, and our society. Many writers focus on emerging technologies and the new possibilities they offer: possibilities for improved communication, personal expression, information access, and productivity. Others focus on computer technology as a source of suffering, oppression, and alienation. Both utopian and anti-utopian visions are based on speculation about the future. Researchers who study the *current* impact of computer technology report that the truth, so far, lies somewhere between these two extremes.

 Where Computers Work

All those ones and zeros we've been passing around—the fuel that fans the digital fire— have reached critical mass and ignited, big time.

—Steven Levy

It's becoming harder all the time to find jobs that haven't been changed in some way by computers. Consider these examples:

▶ *Entertainment.* The production of television programs and movies involves computer technology at every stage of the process. Scriptwriters use specialized word processors to write and revise scripts, and they use the Internet to beam the scripts between Hollywood and New York. Artists and technicians use graphics workstations to create special effects, from simple scene fadeouts and rolling credits to giant creatures and intergalactic battles. Musicians compose soundtracks using synthesizers and sequencers. Sound editors use computer-controlled mixers to blend music with digital sound effects and live-action sound. Even commercials—*especially* commer-

Computers are taking a much more visible role in entertainment and news today. Here (left) an animator works on *Toy Story*, the groundbreaking all-digital animated film. Using similar technology, virtual newscaster Ananova (right) began delivering on-demand newscasts over the Web in early 2000.

cials—use state-of-the-art computer graphics, animation, and sound to keep you watching the images instead of changing the channel with your remote control.

▶ *Publishing.* The newspaper industry is being radically transformed by computer technology. Reporters scan the Internet for facts, write and edit stories on location using notebook computers, and transmit those stories by modem to central offices. Artists design charts and drawings with graphics software. Photo retouchers use computers instead of brushes and magnifying glasses to edit photographs. Production crews assemble pages with computers instead of typesetting machines and paste-up boards. Many newspapers produce Web editions in addition to traditional paper publications.

▶ *Medicine.* High-tech equipment plays a critical role in the healing arts, too. Hospital information systems store patient medical and insurance records. Local-area networks allow doctors, nurses, technicians, dietitians, and office staff to view and update information throughout the hospital. For patients who are outside the hospital walls in remote locations, doctors use the Web to practice telemedicine. Computers monitor patient vital signs in intensive care units in hospitals, at home, and on the street with portable units that analyze signals and transmit warnings when problems arise. Databases alert doctors and pharmacists to the problems and possibilities of prescribed drugs. A variety of digital devices allow doctors to see inside our bodies. Every day computers provide medical researchers with new ways to save lives and reduce suffering.

Medical students and professionals use this virtual emergency room to simulate processes of collecting vital signs and other patient data.

▶ *Airlines.* Without computers, today's airline industry simply wouldn't fly. Designers use CAD (computer-aided design) software to design aircraft. Engineers conduct extensive computer simulations to test them. Pilots use computer-controlled instruments to navigate their planes, monitor aircraft systems, and control autopilots. Air traffic controllers on the ground use computerized air traffic control systems to keep track of incoming and outgoing flights. And, of course, computerized reservation systems make it possible for all those planes to carry passengers.

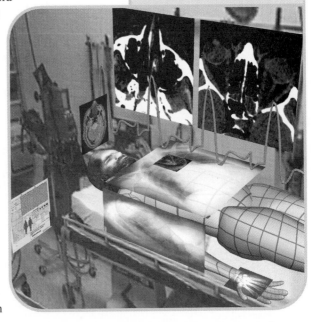

▶ *Science.* From biology to physics every branch of science has been changed by the computer. Scientists collect and analyze data using remote sensing devices, notebook computers, and statistical analysis programs. They catalog and organize information

Computers make data recording and analysis much easier for botanists and other scientists

in massive databases, many of which are accessible through the World Wide Web. They use supercomputers and workstations to create computer models of objects or environments that would otherwise be out of reach. They communicate with colleagues all over the world through the Internet. It's hard to find a scientist today who doesn't work with computers.

Clearly, computers are part of the workplace. To get a perspective on how computers affect the way we work, we consider the three computerized workplaces that have attracted the most attention: the automated factory, the automated office, and the electronic cottage.

The Automated Factory

Businessmen go down with their businesses because they like the old way so well they cannot bring themselves to change.

—Henry Ford

In the last chapter we discussed the use of robots—computer-controlled machines designed to perform specific manual tasks. In the modern automated factory robots are used for painting, welding, and other repetitive assembly-line jobs. But robots alone don't make an automated factory. Computers also help track inventory, time the delivery of parts, control the quality of the production, monitor wear and tear on machines, and schedule maintenance. As described in Chapter 7, engineers use CAD (computer-aided design) and CAM (computer-aided manufacturing) technologies to design new products and the machines that build those products. Web cameras and Web displays built into assembly line equipment allows workers and managers to monitor production and inventory from across the factory floor or across the continent.

An automated factory is more efficient than a traditional factory for two reasons:

1 Automation allows for tighter integration of planning with manufacturing, reducing the time that materials and machines sit idle.

2 Automation reduces waste in facilities, raw materials, and labor.

If automation is good news for factory owners, it poses a threat to blue-collar workers who keep traditional factories running. In a typical high-tech manufacturing firm today, approximately half of the staff are engineers, accountants, marketing specialists, and other white-collar workers.

The Automated Office

We now mass produce information
the way we used to mass produce cars.

—John Naisbitt, in *Megatrends*

As the number of factory jobs declines, office work plays a more important role in our economy. Modern offices, like modern factories, have been transformed by computers. Many **automated offices** have evolved along with their computers.

Office Automation Evolution

Office automation goes back to the mainframe era, when banks, insurance companies, and other large institutions used computers for behind-the-scenes jobs such as accounting and payroll. Early computer systems were faster and more accurate than the manual systems they replaced, but were rigid and difficult to use. The machines and the technicians who worked with them were hidden away in basement offices, isolated from their organizations. The introduction of time-sharing operating systems and database management systems allowed workers throughout organizations to access computer data. This kind of *centralized computing* placed computer-related decisions in the hands of central data processing managers.

Personal computers changed all that. Early Apple and Tandy computers were carried into offices on the sly by employees who wanted to use their own computers instead of company mainframes. But as managers recognized the power of word processors, spreadsheets, and other applications, they incorporated PCs into organizational plans. Jobs migrated from mainframes to desktops, and people used personal computers to do things that the mainframes weren't programmed to do. In many organizations power struggles erupted between mainframe advocates and PC enthusiasts.

Enterprise Computing

Today most organizations recognize the importance of PCs in the overall computing structure. Some companies have abandoned mainframes altogether; others still use them for their biggest data processing tasks. In the age of networks the challenge for a company's **information systems manager** (sometimes called an *IS manager*, *information technology manager*, or *IT manager*) is to integrate all kinds of computers, from mainframes to PCs, into a single, seamless system. This approach, often called **distributed computing** (or *enterprise computing*), allows PCs, workstations, minicomputers, and mainframes to coexist peacefully and complement each other. Many organizations are adding *thin clients—network computers*, *Internet appliances*, and similar devices—to the mix. These low-cost, low-maintenance machines allow workers to access critical network information without the overhead of a PC or workstation.

People throughout business organizations use personal computers: Workers use word processing software to generate memos and reports, marketing

Today's automobile factories are highly automated.

The information systems manager coordinates technology and systems to provide enterprise employees with information they need to do their jobs.

teams create promotional pieces using desktop publishing tools, and financial departments analyze budgets using spreadsheets. They communicate with each other and with the outside world electronically, sending electronic mail through networks. If a business uses mainframes to house databases, office workers use desktop computers to access that data. They don't need to know where or how information is stored; the network quietly moves data back and forth to meet user needs.

Workgroup Computing

Groupware allows groups of users to share calendars, send messages, access data, and work on documents simultaneously. The best groupware applications allow workgroups to do things that would be difficult otherwise; they actually change the way people work in groups. Many of these applications focus on the concept of *workflow*—the path of information as it flows through a workgroup. With groupware and telecommunication, workgroups don't need to be in the same room, or even the same time zone. During much of the 1990s Lotus Notes dominated this market, offering a complete, if expensive, workgroup solution for corporations.

But the advent of the World Wide Web changed the workgroup landscape. Many of the functions of a groupware program like Notes—electronic mail, teleconferencing, shared databases, electronic publishing, and others—were available for little or no cost through freely available Internet technologies. Corporations started installing **intranets** using HTML, Web browsers, and other Internet technologies. And because these intranets were built on standardized protocols like TCP/IP, corporations could open their intranets to strategic partners and customers, creating **extranets**. Lotus and other groupware manufacturers have responded by rebuilding their applications using standard Internet technologies and protocols, so their customers could have the best of both worlds: computer systems built on universal public standards, and customer support and customization from a groupware specialist.

Whether they're built from off-the-shelf Internet software or commercially customized packages, workgroup systems have the potential to radically transform the way businesses operate. Ted Lewis, author of *The Friction Free Economy,* suggests that modern information technology makes an organization

- ▶ Flatter, so it's easier for workers at any level to communicate with workers at other levels

- ▶ More integrated, so different business units communicate more openly with each other

- ▶ More flexible, so businesses can react more quickly to changes in their environments

- ▶ Less concerned with managing people and more concerned with managing processes.

The Paperless Office

Experts have also predicted the **paperless office**—an office of the future in which magnetic and optical archives will replace reference books and file cabinets, electronic communication will replace letters and memos, and digital publications provided through the Internet and on-line services will replace newspapers and other periodicals. In the paperless office people will read computer screens, not paper documents.

All of these trends are real: Digital storage media are replacing many paper depositories; computers now deliver more mail messages than postal carriers do; and the World Wide Web has accelerated a trend toward on-line publishing. But so far, computers haven't reduced the flow of paper-based information. What has changed is the way people tend to use paper in the office. According to Paul Saffo of the Institute for the Future, "We've shifted from paper as storage to paper as interface. It is an ever more volatile, disposable, and temporary display medium."

To reduce the flow of paper, many organizations use *document imaging systems* that can scan, store, retrieve, and route bit-mapped images of paper documents. Document imaging systems generally include scanners for converting paper pages to digital documents, high-capacity disk drives for storing the document images, and fax machines for sending document images to remote locations. Interactions between these devices and networked workstations are generally handled by an *image server*—a computer dedicated to the single task of image management.

Imaging systems are particularly useful for storing non-paper versions of graphical documents. For text documents it makes more sense to store text documents using a technology like Adobe's PDF, which allows text to be searched and sorted, rather than just be visible as an image on a page. But none of these technologies has made a significant dent in the wall of paper that surrounds most office workers. In the near future we may see a less-paper office, but a paperless office seems unlikely.

Electronic Commerce

The paperless office may be years away, but paperless money is already here for many organizations. **Electronic commerce** has been around for years in its most basic form— buying and selling products through the Internet or a smaller computer network. But today there's more to electronic commerce than handling purchase transactions and funds transfers on the Internet. Electronic commerce also includes marketing, sales, support, customer service, and communication with business partners.

Early electronic commerce involved transactions between corporations. Even today, business-to-business transactions account for far more e-commerce sales than do consumer transactions. But consumer commerce on the Web is growing at a phenomenal pace and creating thousands of young millionaires. Some businesses, including computer manufacturers Dell and Apple, allow customers to electronically order customized goods and services; this kind of customization-on-demand wasn't practical or possible for most businesses before the Internet took hold. The Web is also fertile ground for person-to-person auctions, reverse auctions, and other types of sales that aren't practical outside the Web. Of course, electronic commerce also raises security and privacy questions that must be resolved if a system is to succeed.

The Electronic Cottage

Telecommuting may allow us to redefine the issues so that we're not simply moving people to work but also moving work to people.

—**Booth Gardner, former Washington governor**

An inexpensive personal computer turns a spare room into a home office for this writer.

Before the industrial revolution most people worked in or near their homes. Today's telecommunications technology opens up new possibilities for modern workers to return home for their livelihood. For hundreds of thousands of writers, programmers, accountants, data-entry clerks, and other information workers, **telecommuting** by modem replaces hours of commuting by car in rush hour traffic. Others use their own computers when they work at home rather than connecting by modem to company computers. The term *telecommuter* typically refers to *all* home information workers, whether they "commute" by modem or not.

Futurist Alvin Toffler popularized the term **electronic cottage** to describe a home where technology allows a person to work at home. Toffler and others predict that the number of telecommuters will skyrocket in the coming decades. Telecommuting makes sense—it's easier to move information than people. There are many strong arguments for telecommuting:

▶ Telecommuting reduces the number of automobile commuters, thus saving energy, reducing pollution, and decreasing congestion and accidents on highways, streets, and parking lots.

▶ Telecommuting saves time. If an information worker spends 2 hours each day commuting, that's 2 hours that could be spent working, resting, or relaxing with the family.

▶ Telecommuting allows for a more flexible schedule. People who prefer to work early in the morning or late at night don't need to conform to standard office hours if they telecommute. For many people, including parents of small children, telecommuting may be the only viable way to maintain a job.

▶ Telecommuting can increase productivity. Studies suggest that telecommuting can result in a 10% to 50% increase in worker productivity, depending on the job and the worker.

Of course, telecommuting isn't for everybody. Jobs that require constant interaction with coworkers, customers, or clients aren't conducive to telecommuting. Working at home requires self-discipline. Some people find they can't concentrate on work when they're at home—beds, refrigerators, neighbors, children, and errands are simply too distracting. Others have the opposite problem: Workaholism cuts into family and relaxation time. Some workers who've tried full-time telecommuting complain that they miss the informal office social life and that their low visibility caused bosses to pass them over for promotions. In the words of one telecommuter, "when you're telecommuting you're far more productive than you can ever hope to be in the office, but you don't really have your finger on the pulse of the company." Most telecommuters report that the ideal work situation involves commuting to the office 1 or 2 days each week and working at home on the others.

Today thousands of companies offer home-based work arrangements to millions of employees. Many firms encourage "boundaryless" employees to work in virtual teams when and where they can best get their jobs done. Other companies have strict policies against working at home. The most common objections revolve around control; managers fear that they'll lose control over workers without 5 days a week of "face time." Some analysts suggest that as multimedia teleconferencing systems become affordable, telecommuting will become more popular with both workers and management. Workers and managers will be able to have a *telepresence* in the workplace when they aren't physically present.

In the meantime several variations on the electronic cottage are taking hold. Many enterprising families use home computers to help them run small businesses from their home offices. A growing number of corporations and government organizations are establishing satellite offices and shared regional work centers outside of major urban centers that allow workers to commute to smaller offices closer to their neighborhoods. High-powered portable computers allow salespeople, executives, scientists, engineers, and others to take their offices with them wherever they travel. These mobile workers don't travel to the office; they travel with the office.

Management by Computer

You can lead a horse to water,

but you can't make him enter regional distribution codes in data field 92

to facilitate regression analysis on the back end.

—John Cleese, corporate consultant and former member of Monty Python's Flying Circus

During the early days of computing, most managers saw computers and terminals as clerical tools to be used by secretaries and technicians but not by managers. Today managers recognize that computers are not just electronic typewriters and digital file cabinets, but valuable resources that can provide information, advice, and support for those who run departments, divisions, or entire corporations.

Management Information Systems

Modern managers use management information systems (MIS) to help them with planning, organizing, staffing, directing, and controlling their organizations. The term *management information system* (which is often shortened to simply *information system*) means different things to different people. By some definitions a management information system is any system that provides information for an organization's managers, even if it doesn't involve computers. More commonly, a management information system is defined as a computerized system that includes procedures for collecting data, a database for storing data, and software tools for analyzing data and producing a variety of reports for different levels of management.

In a large organization computers process and store masses of information. Financial transactions, sales figures, inventory tallies—the number of data items can be astronomical. From a manager's point of view, plenty of useful information is hiding in that raw data. A well-defined MIS can extract important information and summarize it in reports for managers at all levels of an organization. A top-level manager uses a management information system to examine long-term trends and relationships between departments. Middle-level managers use the same MIS to produce departmental summary reports. Low-level managers focus on day-to-day operations with detailed reports from the MIS. The MIS can produce regularly scheduled periodic reports, but it can also help managers deal with unusual situations by producing reports on demand.

Decision Support Systems

A management information system is especially helpful for handling routine management tasks. For nonroutine decision making many managers use another type of system called a decision support system (DSS). As the name implies, a DSS is a computer system that supports managers in decision-making tasks. In the broadest sense a spreadsheet program like those discussed in Chapter 6 might be a DSS. After all, managers everywhere use spreadsheets to find answers to "what if" questions and make decisions based on these sample scenarios. However, most managers reserve the term *decision support system* for a more specialized kind of software designed to create mathematical models of business systems. This type of DSS is a simulation tool similar to those discussed at the end of Chapter 6.

Other Management Tools

The sheer volume of information dissolves the information.

—Gunther Grass

Several other types of software systems are available to help managers make decisions. Project management software helps coordinate, schedule, and track complex work projects. Expert systems (see Chapter 13) can provide expert advice in limited areas. Spreadsheets (Chapter 6) can manage budgets, make financial projections, and perform a variety of other useful functions. The Internet and on-line services (Chapters 9 and 10) can provide instant information from sources all over the world.

All of these tools can provide critical information and advice. Some managers complain that these systems provide *too much* information—too many reports, too many printouts, too many summaries, too many details. This malady, known as information overload, is a hazard of the automated office. Managers who are

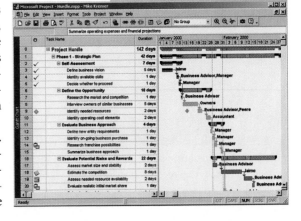

Project management software can make it easier to keep track of the multitude of tasks in a large project and determine where potential problems lurk in schedules.

How It Works 14.1

Information Flow in a Management Information System

A retail chain processes a tremendous amount of data daily. Depending on how it is handled, this information can be either overwhelming or enlightening. To make the best use of the information, many chains use management information systems to aid in decision making. This example follows the many paths of information through the Frostbyte Outdoor Outfitters Corporation.

Top-level managers use reports that summarize long-term trends to analyze overall business strategies.

When a new shipment arrives, a clerk records it using a terminal; inventory and accounting files are updated automatically.

The MIS uses a variety of inputs to produce reports for managers at all levels.

Midlevel managers use summary and exception reports to spot trends and unusual circumstances.

When a clerk punches a sale into the terminal, a database records changes in financial and inventory files.

Low-level managers use detailed reports to keep tabs on day-to-day operations.

On-demand reports integrate information and show relationships. Example: impact of cold weather on ski sales.

Sales Volume vs. Average Temperature as of 6/30/02

	Jan.	Feb.	Mar.	Apr.	May	June
Sales Volume	1798	1700	1609	1532	1302	1216
Sales	$24,398	$24,673	$22,468	$21,003	$18,068	$16,328
Average Temperature	24	32	41	48	58	71

Year-End Sales by Item: Top 20 as of 12/31/02

ITEM	SOLD UNITS	RETURNED UNITS	TOTAL UNITS	TOTAL SALES
Beaver Kayaks	58	3	55	$12,375
Possum Packs	1240	212	1028	$20,046
Possum Parkas	1003	323	680	$17,000
Rhinoceros Hiking Boots	1162	429	733	$47,645
Snoreswell Sleeping Bags	923	62	861	$39,175

Summary reports show departmental totals or trends. Example: most popular footwear.

Items Temporarily Out of Stock as of 12/31/02

ITEM	OUT SINCE	DATE AVAILABLE
Fancy Flashlights	12/31/99	1/4/00
Foxy Flannels	12/31/99	1/2/00
Snappy Tents	12/02/99	1/2/00

Exception reports reflect unusual relationships. Example: out-of-stock gear.

Daily Sales Register by Type: 7/31/02

ITEM	UNITS	SALES
Parkas	62	$1209
Flashlights	154	$1540
Tents	2	$500
Hiking Boots	78	$65

Detail reports give complete, detailed information on routine operations. Example: daily orders.

bombarded with computer output may not be able to separate the best from the rest. What's worse, managers who rely too heavily on computer output run the risk of over-looking more conventional, nondigital sources of insight. The best managers know that no computer system can replace the human decision-making skills necessary for successful management.

Computers and Jobs

John Henry told his captain
"A man ain't nothin' but a man
But before I let your steam drill beat me down
I'd die with a hammer in my hand . . ."

—From the folk song "John Henry"

When we think about automated factories, computer-supported cooperative work, management information systems, and electronic cottages, it's easy to imagine utopian visions of computers in the workplace of tomorrow. But the real world isn't always picture perfect, and many workers today are experiencing computers in less positive ways. In this section we look at some of the controversies and issues surrounding the automation of the workplace.

The Productivity Problem

A lot has been written about how computers haven't helped with productivity.
I think there's a good reason for that, and it's fairly predictable. The more you can
do with a machine, the higher you set your sights.
So it's a self-defeating proposition.

—J. Presper Eckert, codeveloper of ENIAC and UNIVAC

Computers and networks make 24-hour banking by ATM possible, but do they make banks more productive?

It seems obvious that computer technology makes businesses more productive. Consider the American financial industry, which employs about 5% of the workers in the United States and makes about 35% of the information technology purchases—about $12 billion every year. This massive investment has undeniably produced better service and lower prices for bank customers. Now customers can cash out-of-state checks in minutes instead of weeks. Automated teller machines provide instant cash 24 hours per day—an impossible dream in the pre-computer era. A growing number of corporations have direct electronic connections to bank computers, eliminating the need for human intervention altogether. None of this would be possible without computers.

Productivity and Profit

In terms of services offered bank productivity is up as a result of computers. But most banks have not been able to translate technology into higher profits.

The first 25 years of computerization in the banking industry have, in fact, shown a decline in capital productivity! There's evidence that the trend may be turning around, but it still raises important questions about computers and productivity—questions that aren't limited to the banking industry.

Studies suggest that computerization has, at best, increased the productivity of North American office workers only slightly. How can this be? If computers don't increase productivity, why do businesses continue to spend billions of dollars every year on them?

Part of the problem may lie in the difficulty of making large software systems work reliably. In one famous example, the Bank of America spent $60 million trying to make a $20 million computer system work and then abandoned it after 5 years of development and a year of false starts. (See Chapter 12 for more on the difficulty of developing software systems.)

Productivity and PCs

But the productivity problem isn't limited to large systems; there's no hard evidence that PCs increase office productivity the way managers hoped they would. Research suggests that the total cost of ownership (TCO) of a typical PC is many times more than the cost of hardware and software. Training, support, maintenance, troubleshooting, and other expenses push the TCO up to anywhere from $6,000 to $13,000 per PC per year! Several factors may be involved:

- ▶ *Distractions.* For some people personal computers offer too many options. These workers spend hours tinkering with utility software, refining multiple drafts of memos, fiddling with fonts, experimenting with spreadsheet graphics, answering email, exploring the Web, and playing games.

- ▶ *Reliability.* Most computer workers lose productive time working around software bugs and recovering data from system crashes.

- ▶ *Rapid changes.* For many organizations technological progress is the culprit. Companies spend large sums on PCs and software that become obsolete in a few years—or months. Workers spend hours learning complex programs, only to find in a few months that they need to be retrained because of software upgrades.

Many organizations are responding to these problems by replacing PCs with network computers or other thin clients. These devices cost less than PCs, but the difference in hardware costs is minimal when compared with the total cost of ownership of a PC. The real advantage of thin clients, according to their advocates, is that they cost less to maintain because complex software and data are stored on central servers rather than individual workstations. It's too early to tell whether thin clients will make a significant difference in productivity or whether they'll replace a significant number of PCs.

Productivity and the Net

Many companies are counting on the Internet to increase productivity and raise their bottom lines. A few have succeeded handsomely. According to a 1999 study by the Giga Information Group, e-commerce has saved companies billions of dollars in addition to generating revenue. Particularly large savings have been incurred because of on-line banking transactions, on-line supplier auctions, and on-line distributions of software updates. According to a Giga executive, "The Internet is more than just a new way to sell products and services, it's a way to efficiently run a business, resulting in significant cost savings that add to an organization's bottom line."

On the other hand, most on-line retailers have found that e-commerce is no more cost effective than running a brick-and-mortar retail operation. For example, outdoor gear retailer REI, which operates successful stores in many cities, has had trouble making its Web storefront profitable. Web staff have more technical skills and command higher salaries; payrolls for the 300-person Seattle store and the 60-person Web store were about equal in mid-1999. Millions of dollars in equipment and software upgrades also cut into profits, as did increased shipping costs. Still, REI isn't likely to close its Web store. Like many retail companies, REI considers the Web to be an important part of its overall services, profitable or not. And in the long run, Web stores like REI's may prove to be profitable. But so far, Web technology is no guarantee of increased productivity or profitability.

Productivity and People

The biggest productivity problems may be related more to people than to machines. According to one study of 2,000 U.S. companies that implemented new office systems, at least 40% failed to achieve their intended results. Most of the failures were attributed to human or organizational factors rather than technical problems.

A computer system doesn't work in a vacuum. All too often computers are introduced into the workplace without any consideration of the way people work and interact. Workers are expected to adjust their work patterns to systems that are difficult and uncompromising. User training and support are often inadequate. It's hardly surprising that these computer-centered systems fail to spark productivity.

Many analysts argue that the most successful computer systems are human-centered systems. Such systems are designed to retain and enhance human skills rather than take them away. These analysts suggest that computer systems aren't likely to pay off unless they're accompanied by changes in the structure of work responsibilities, relationships with coworkers, and rewards for accomplishing job goals.

To create a human-centered system, systems analysts and designers must understand the work practices of the people who'll be using the system. It helps if users of the systems are involved in designing the system and the system-related jobs. In Norway laws require that unionized workers be included in the planning and design of new computer systems. As a result, workers have greater control over their jobs and greater job satisfaction. Similar worker-centered approaches have been applied in Sweden, Britain, and, more recently, the United States.

Many experts believe that this human-centered approach is a key to increasing overall productivity. Productivity will almost certainly increase as organizations adjust to computer technology and computer technology becomes more adaptable to the needs of users.

Specialized terminals like this one make it easy to log restaurant orders. How is this person's job different as a result of this technology?

Computers and Job Quality

For many workers computers have caused more problems than they have solved. Workers complain of stress, depersonalization, fatigue, boredom, and a variety of health problems attributed to computers. Some of these complaints are directly related to technology; others relate to human decisions about how technology is implemented.

De-Skilling and Up-Skilling

When a job is automated, it may be de-skilled; that is, it may be transformed so that it requires less skill. For example, computerized cash registers in many fast-food restaurants replace numbered buttons with buttons labeled "large fries" or "chocolate shake." Clerks who use these machines don't need to know math or think about prices. They simply push buttons for the food items ordered and take the money; computers do the rest.

Considering Computer Careers

Until recently, people who wanted to work with computers were forced to choose between a few careers, most of which required highly specialized training. But when computers are used by everybody from fast-food salesclerks to graphic artists, just about anybody can have some kind of "computer career." Still, many rewarding and high-paying computer-related careers require a fair amount of specialized education. If you're interested in a computer-related job, consider the following tips:

▶ *Learn touch-typing.* Computers that can read handwriting and understand spoken English are probably in your future—but not your immediate future. Several low-cost typing tutorial programs can help you to teach your fingers how to type. The time you invest will pay you back quickly. The sooner you learn, the sooner you'll start reaping the rewards.

▶ *Use computers regularly to help you accomplish your immediate goals.* Word process your term papers. Use spreadsheets and other math software as calculation aids. Use databases and the Web for research work. Computers are part of your future. If you use them regularly, they'll become second nature, like telephones and pencils. If you don't own a computer, find a way to buy one if you can.

▶ *Don't forsake the basics.* If you want to become a programmer, a systems analyst, a computer scientist, a computer engineer, or some other kind of computer professional, don't focus all your attention on computers. A few young technical wizards become successful programmers without college degrees; Bill Gates is probably the best known example. But if you're not gifted and lucky, you'll need a solid education to land a good job. Math and communication skills (written and oral) are extremely important. Opportunities abound for people who can understand computers and communicate clearly.

▶ *Combine your passions.* If you like art and computers, explore computer art or graphic design. If you love ecology and computers, find out how computers are used by ecologists. People who can speak the language of computers and the language of a specialized field have opportunities to build bridges.

▶ *Ask questions.* The best way to find out more about computer careers is to ask the people who have computer careers. Most people are happy to talk about their jobs if you're willing to listen.

▶ *Cultivate community.* Computer networks are changing our lives, but people networks are still more important for finding and landing that dream job. Get to know the people in the professional community. Take an active part in that community. Join professional organizations. Give your time and energy to public service projects related to your field. Even if it doesn't pay off with a job offer, you'll be doing good work.

▶ *If you can't find your dream job, build it yourself.* Inexpensive computer systems provide all kinds of entrepreneurial opportunities for creative self-starters: publishing service bureaus, Web site design, multimedia video production, custom programming, commercial art and design, freelance writing, consulting—the jobs are there for the making, if you have the imagination and initiative.

▶ *When you're ready to look, don't forget the Web.* There are plenty of job bulletin boards, on-line career-hunting centers, Internet headhunters, and e-cruiters offering jobs that might be just right for you.

▶ *Prepare for change.* In a rapidly changing world, lifelong careers are rare. Be prepared to change jobs several times. Think of education as a lifelong process. In Marshall McLuhan's words, "The future of work consists of learning a living."

Some of the most visible examples of de-skilling occur when offices automate clerical jobs. When word processors and databases replace typewriters and file cabinets, traditional typing-and-filing jobs disappear. Many secretaries are repositioned in data-entry jobs—mindless, repetitive jobs where the only measure of success is the number of keystrokes typed into a terminal each hour. When a clerical job—or any job—is de-skilled, the worker's control, responsibility, and job satisfaction are likely to go down. De-skilled jobs typically offer less status and less pay.

In sharp contrast to those whose jobs are de-skilled into electronic drudgery, many workers find their jobs up-skilled by automation. For example, many clerical jobs become more technical as offices adopt databases, spreadsheets, electronic mail systems, Internet connections, fax modems, and other computer technology. In some cases clerical workers use computer systems to do jobs formerly done by high-paid professionals and technicians. While many clerical people enjoy the added challenge and responsibility, others may be frustrated doing highly technical work with inadequate training. Clerical workers are seldom consulted before their jobs are computerized. And even though their work is more technically demanding than before, few clerical workers see this up-skilling reflected in their paychecks or level of responsibility.

Monitoring and Surveillance

Another controversial aspect of office automation is computer monitoring—using computer technology to track, record, and evaluate worker performance, often without the knowledge of the worker. Monitoring systems can provide a manager with instant, on-screen reports showing the number of keystrokes for each clerk, the length of each phone call placed by an employee, details of Web wanderings, and the total amount of idle time for each computer. Some network software even allows a manager to view a copy of any worker's screen secretly at any time.

For a manager worried about worker productivity, computer monitoring can serve as a valuable source of information. But computer monitoring brings with it several problems:

- ▶ *Privacy.* In Chapters 8, 10, and 11 we saw how the misuse of database and network technology can threaten personal privacy. Computer monitoring compounds that threat by providing employers with unprecedented data on workers. Some employers even monitor personal email messages and punish or fire employees who send "unacceptable" messages.

- ▶ *Morale.* Privacy issues aside, computer monitoring can have a powerful negative impact on morale. Because employees can't tell when they're being monitored, many workers experience a great deal of stress and anxiety. The boss can be seen as an invisible eavesdropper rather than as a team leader.

- ▶ *Devalued skills.* In the traditional office, workers were evaluated based on a variety of skills. A slow-typing secretary could be valued for her ability to anticipate when a job needed to be done or her willingness to help others with problems. Computer monitoring tends to reduce a worker's worth to simple quantities like "number of keystrokes per hour." In such systems a worker might be penalized for repairing a sticky chair, showing a neighbor how to reboot a terminal, or helping a coworker overcome an emotional crisis.

- ▶ *Loss of quality.* Monitored workers tend to assume that "if it's not being counted, it doesn't count." The result of this assumption is that quantity may become more important than quality.

Millions of workers are monitored by computer, including factory workers, telephone operators, truck drivers, and, in some cases, managers. Cyber-snooping goes far beyond counting keystrokes and idle time. According to a 1999 survey from the American Management Association, more than two thirds of U.S. companies engage in some kind of electronic surveillance of their employees, including reviewing email and checking computer files.

The Electronic Sweatshop

Computer monitoring is common practice in data-entry offices. A data-entry clerk has a single job: to read information from a printed source—a check, a hand-printed form, or something else—and type it into a computer's database. A typical data-entry shop might contain hundreds of clerks sitting at terminals in a massive, windowless room. Workers—often minorities and almost always female—are paid minimum wage to do mindless keyboarding. Many experience headaches, backaches, serious wrist injuries, stress, anxiety, and other health problems. And all the while, keystrokes and breaks are monitored electronically. Writer Barbara Garson calls these worker warehouses electronic sweatshops because working conditions bring to mind the oppressive factory sweatshops of the 19th century.

A growing number of electronic sweatshops are located across national borders from corporate headquarters in countries with lax labor laws and low wage scales. The

electronic immigrants in these off-shore shops don't need green cards to telecommute across borders, and they work for a fraction of what workers in developed countries cost. A data-entry clerk in the Philippines, for example, earns about $6 per day. With wages that low many companies find it cost effective to have data entered twice and use software to compare both versions and correct errors.

The electronic sweatshop is the dark side of the electronic office. Ironically, computer technology may soon make many electronic sweatshops irrelevant. Optical character recognition and voice recognition technologies (described in earlier chapters) are rapidly becoming practical for data-entry applications. OCR software is already used to read and recognize typed and hand-printed characters in many applications, and voice recognition systems are replacing directory assistance telephone operators. It's just a matter of time before most workers in electronic sweatshops are replaced by machines.

Employment and Unemployment

My father had worked for the same firm for 12 years. They fired him. They replaced him with a tiny gadget this big that does everything that my father does only it does it much better. The depressing thing is my mother ran out and bought one.

—Woody Allen

When Woody Allen told this joke three decades ago, automation was generating a great deal of public controversy. Computer technology was new to the workplace, and people were reacting with both awe and fear. Many analysts predicted that automation would lead to massive unemployment and economic disaster. Others said that computers would generate countless new job opportunities. Today most people are used to seeing computers where they work, and the computers-versus-jobs debate has cooled down. Job automation may not be a hot topic in comedy clubs today, but it's still an important issue for millions of workers whose jobs are threatened by machines.

Workers Against Machines

Automation has threatened workers since the earliest days of the industrial revolution. In the early 19th century an English labor group called the *Luddites* smashed new textile machinery; they feared that the machines would take jobs away from skilled craftsmen. The Luddites and similar groups in other parts of Europe failed to stop the wheels of automation. Modern workers have been no more successful than their 19th-century counterparts in keeping computers and robots out of the workplace. Every year brings new technological breakthroughs that allow robots and computers to do jobs formerly reserved for humans.

Of course, computer technology creates new jobs, too. Somebody has to design, build, program, sell, run, and repair the computers, robots, and networks. But many

Almost all of the assembly-line work in this factory is done by robots.

displaced workers don't have the education or skills to program computers, design robots, install networks, or even read printouts. Those workers are often forced to take low-tech, low-paying service jobs as cashiers or custodians, if they can find jobs at all. Because of automation the unskilled, uneducated worker may face a lifetime of minimum wage jobs or welfare. Technology may be helping to create an unbalanced society with two classes: a growing mass of poor uneducated people and a shrinking class of affluent educated people.

Cautiously Optimistic Forecasts

Nobody knows for sure how computer technology will affect employment in the coming decades; it's impossible to anticipate what might happen in 10 or 20 years. And experts are far from unanimous in their predictions.

A number of studies suggest that, at least for the next few years, technology will stimulate economic growth. This growth will produce new jobs, but it will also bring long, painful periods of adjustment for many workers. Demand for factory workers, clerical workers, and other semiskilled and unskilled laborers will drop dramatically as their jobs are automated or moved to Third World countries where wages are low. At the same time the demand for professionals—especially engineers and teachers—will rise sharply.

According to detailed computer models constructed at the Institute for Economic Analysis at New York University, there will be plenty of jobs in the early 21st century. The question is whether we'll have enough skilled workers to fill those jobs. In other words, economic growth will depend on whether we have a suitably trained workforce. The single most important key to a positive economic future, according to this study, is education. But will we, as a society, be able to provide people with the kind of education they'll need? We'll deal with that question, and the critical issues surrounding education in the information age, in the next chapter.

Will We Need a New Economy?

In the long run, education may not be enough. It seems likely that, at some time in the future, machines will be able to do most of the jobs people do today. We may face a future of *jobless growth*—a time when productivity increases not because of the work people do but because of the work of machines. If productivity isn't tied to employment, we'll have to ask some hard questions about our political, economic, and social system:

▶ Do governments have an obligation to provide permanent public assistance to the chronically unemployed?

▶ Should large companies be required to give several months' notice to workers whose jobs are being eliminated? Should they be required to retrain workers for other jobs?

▶ Should large companies be required to file "employment impact statements" before replacing people with machines in the same way they're required to file environmental impact statements before implementing policies that might harm the environment?

▶ If robots and computers are producing most of society's goods and services, should all of the profits from those goods go to a few people who own the machines?

▶ If a worker is replaced by a robot, should the worker receive a share of the robot's "earnings" through stocks or profit sharing?

▶ The average workweek 150 years ago was 70 hours; for the last 50 years it has been steady at about 40. Should governments and businesses encourage job-sharing and other systems that allow for less-than-40-hour jobs?

▶ What will people do with their time if machines do most of the work? What new leisure activities should be made available?

▶ How will people define their identities if work becomes less central to their lives?

These questions force us to confront deep-seated cultural beliefs and economic traditions, and they don't come with easy answers. They suggest that we may be heading into a difficult period when many old rules don't apply anymore. But if we're successful at navigating the troubled waters of transition, we may find that automation fulfills the dream expressed by Aristotle more than 2,000 years ago:

> If every instrument could accomplish its own work, obeying or anticipating the will of others . . . if the shuttle could weave, and the pick touch the lyre, without a hand to guide them, chief workmen would not need servants, nor masters slaves.

CROSSCURRENTS

Making the Best of a Mess

Carly Fiorina

In 1999 Carly Fiorina became president and CEO of Hewlett-Packard Company, one of the most successful and innovative information technology companies in history. At the same time, Fiorina made history by becoming the first woman CEO of a Fortune 500 company. In this article, originally published in The New York Times, *she outlines her philosophy of personal and professional success. By Carly Fiorina. Reprinted from* The New York Times, *September 29, 1999*

Carly Fiorina

It was 1984, I was 30 years old and working at AT&T. The company's divestiture had just occurred, the Bell operating companies had just been spun off, and things were in shambles. Access Management, the division responsible for connecting long distance calls to local phone companies, was in the worst shape. I decided that's where I wanted to work.

People thought I was nuts. Nobody knows what they're doing, people said. It's a mess. And that's exactly what appealed to me. It was a wonderful challenge. I knew I could have a big impact, for better or for worse.

Access management was an area about which I knew absolutely nothing. I teamed up with two excellent engineers. I listened and I learned. We discovered that the bills from the local companies were AT&T's biggest single cost. And we had no idea whether we were being charged the right amount.

I've saved a picture from those days where I'm standing in a room covered floor to ceiling with boxes filled with bills. A team of us looked over every one of those bills manually for three or four months and found significant overcharges.

This is not something that most people would think of as fun. Nevertheless, our goal became to verify every bill and prove every overcharge. We decided we must create a billing verification system.

Eventually, this system was implemented all over the country by hundreds of employees and saved the company hundreds of millions of dollars. We had great fun accomplishing something nobody thought we could.

From this and other experiences, I have distilled several principles for personal, and business, growth and success:

Seek tough challenges: they're more fun. Have an unflinching, clear-eyed vision of the goal, followed by absolute clarity, realism and objectivity about what it really will take to grow, to lead and to win.

Understand that the only limits that really matter are those you put on yourself, or that a business puts on itself. Most people and businesses are capable of far more than they realize.

Recognize the power of the team; no one succeeds alone. "Never, never, never, never give up," to quote Winston Churchill.

Most great wins happen on the last play. Strike a balance between confidence and humility—enough confidence to know that you can make a real difference, enough humility to ask for help.

Love what you do. Success requires passion. I learned these lessons in part by watching my parents. Both refused to accept limitations put on them by others. My father had health issues that restricted his lung capacity; he was told he could never play football. He went on to play terrific football. Raised in tiny Texas town, he went on to become a law professor and federal judge.

My mother had a series of stepmothers who didn't think much of developing girls and a father who wouldn't pay for her college tuition. So she ran away from home in small-town Ohio, joined the Air Force, became an accomplished artist and devoted herself to being interested and interesting.

I loved working the billing issue at Access Management. I did not love law school. I wanted desperately to make my father proud that his daughter would follow in his footsteps. Quitting was the ultimate personal failure in my mind and his. Yet, in the end, loving what I did was more important. And life went on. We laugh about it today, and know we learned something valuable.

Every experience in life, whether humble or grand, teaches a lesson.

The question is not if the lesson is taught, but rather if it is learned.

DISCUSSION QUESTIONS

1. What was the ultimate outcome of the 3 or 4 months the author spent rooting through a roomful of bills?
2. Give examples of how one or more of the author's principles of work have applied to your own personal experience.
3. In what way, if any, will information technology shape our principles of success in the coming decades?

Our civilization is in the midst of a transition from an industrial economy to a post-industrial information economy. The transition, or paradigm shift, is having a profound influence on the way we live and work, and it is likely to challenge many of our beliefs, assumptions, and traditions. Computers and information technology are central to the change.

Factory work is steadily declining as we enter the information age, but factories still provide us with hard goods. The modern, automated factory uses computers at every level of operation. Computer-aided design, computer-aided manufacturing, robots, automated assembly lines, and automated warehouses all combine to produce factories that need very few laborers.

Far more people work in offices than in factories, and computers are critically important in the modern office. Early office automation centered on mainframes that were run by highly trained technicians; today's office is more likely to emphasize networked personal computers and workstations for decentralized enterprise computing. So far predictions for widespread computer-supported cooperative work and paperless offices haven't come true.

A growing number of workers use computers to work at home part or full time. Some use modems to stay in contact with their offices. Telecommuting has many benefits for information workers, their bosses, and society as a whole. Still, telecommuting from home is not for everybody. Satellite offices, cottage industries, and portable offices offer alternatives that may be more practical for some workers. Even so, many companies resist the idea of employees working regularly out of the office.

Managers use a variety of computing tools to help them do their jobs. Management information systems, decision support systems, project management systems, expert systems, and on-line information systems can help managers plan, organize, staff, direct, and control their organizations. Unfortunately, these tools can lead to information overload if they're not used intelligently.

Computers have allowed many organizations to provide services that wouldn't be possible otherwise, but so far they haven't produced the productivity gains that many experts expected. Experts speculate that productivity will rise as organizations adjust to the new technology and develop human-centered systems that are adapted to the needs and work habits of employees.

The impact of computers varies from job to job. Some jobs are de-skilled—transformed so they require less skill— while others are up-skilled into more technologically complex jobs. Computer monitoring is a controversial procedure that raises issues of privacy and, in many cases, lowers worker morale. De-skilling, monitoring, and health risks are particularly evident in electronic sweatshops—data-entry warehouses packed with low-paid keyboard operators.

The biggest problem of automation may be the elimination of jobs. So far most displaced workers have been able to find other jobs in our expanding economy. But automation will almost certainly produce unemployment and pain for millions of people unless society is able to provide them with the education they'll need to take the new jobs created by technology. Automation may ultimately force us to make fundamental changes in our economic system. Only time will tell.

Key Terms

automated factory, 398
automated office, 399
automation, 394
computer monitoring, 410
decision support system (DSS), 403
de-skilling, 408
distributed computing, 399
electronic commerce, 401
electronic cottage, 401
electronic sweatshop, 410

extranet, 400
groupware, 400
human-centered system, 408
information economy, 396
information overload, 403
information systems manager, 399
intranet, 400
management information system (MIS), 403

paperless office, 400
paradigm shift, 394
project management software, 403
regional work center, 402
satellite office, 402
telecommuting, 401
up-skilling, 409

Review Questions

1. Define or describe each of the key terms listed above. Check your answers using the glossary.

2. How is the information revolution similar to the industrial revolution? How is it different?

3. What are the major components of the modern automated factory?
4. How has the evolution of the automated office paralleled the evolution of the computer?
5. What are the advantages and disadvantages of telecommuting from the point of view of the worker? Management? Society?

6. Describe several software tools used by managers, and explain how they help them do their jobs.
7. What is de-skilling? What is up-skilling? Give examples of each.
8. Describe several of the controversies surrounding the electronic sweatshop.
9. Why is education critical to our future as we automate more jobs?

Discussion Questions

1. What evidence do we have that our society is going through a paradigm shift?
2. What will have to happen before the paperless office (or the less-paper office) becomes a reality?
3. Many cities are enacting legislation to encourage telecommuting. If you were drafting such legislation, what would you include?
4. Why do you think it has been so difficult to demonstrate that computers increase productivity?

5. People who work in electronic sweatshops run the risk of being replaced by technology. Discuss the trade-offs of this dilemma from the point of view of the worker and society at large.
6. What do you think are the answers to the questions raised at the end of the section on automation and unemployment? How do you think most people would feel about these questions?

Projects

1. Interview several people whose jobs have been changed by computers and the Internet. Report on your findings.

2. Think about how computers have affected the jobs you've held. Report on your experiences.

Sources & Resources

Books

Computing across America, by Steven K. Roberts (Nomadic Research Labs, 360/387-1440, www.microship.com). This chronicle of Steve Roberts's Winnebiko adventures is probably the only book in the world that was done by "biketop publishing." A variety of journals and papers on Roberts's other projects are available from the same Web address.

The Structure of Scientific Revolutions, Third Edition, by Thomas Kuhn (Chicago: University of Chicago Press, 1996). This landmark book introduced the term "paradigm shift." Kuhn shows how scientific progress is built on paradigm shifts—radical new world views that challenge and threaten the status quo. The social dynamics described here apply to business, technology, and countless other human endeavors.

The Friction Free Economy, by Ted Lewis (New York: Harper Business, 1997). Lewis explains the complexity of the new information-based economy in an entertaining, understandable way. Whether you're a curious student, a potential investor, or a

budding entrepreneur, this book will help you to better understand the new economy and its new rules.

Computerization and Controversy: Value Conflicts and Social Choices, Second Edition, edited by Charles Dunlop and Rob Kling (Boston: Academic Press, 1996). This collection includes carefully researched academic studies as well as insightful articles from the popular press. The coverage of computers in the workplace is particularly good.

The Digital MBA, edited by Daniel Burnstein (Berkeley, CA: Osborne/McGraw-Hill, 1995). Burnstein, president of the Management Software Association, provides an overview of management topics, describing and demonstrating how information technology can help solve management problems. The IBM-PC-compatible CD-ROM includes demonstration versions of a variety of management software tools.

The Dilbert Principle, by Scott Adams (New York: HarperBusiness, 1997) and *The Dilbert Future,* by Scott Adams (New York: HarperBusiness, 1998). These books, like the Dilbert comic strip, contain irreverent insights into the inner workings of the information age workplace. Adams understands the world he satirizes—he has an MBA from Berkeley and 17 years of experience in a cubicle working for Pacific Bell. *The Dilbert Principle* targets managers who are clueless about the human needs of their staff; *The Dilbert Future* lampoons our high-tech future. Dilbert has been criticized because it paints a cynical picture of hopelessness in the workplace rather than encouraging workers to organize and solve problems. Still, the satire in these books allows us to laugh at ourselves, and that can't be all bad.

The Power of Now: How Winning Companies Sense and Respond to Change Using Real-Time Technology, By Vivek Ranadivé (New York: McGraw Hill, 1999). Information technology is forcing businesses to function in a continual state of flux. Real-time businesses are event-driven. This book examines how businesses must change to survive in the networked world.

Building Successful Internet Businesses: The Essential Sourcebook for Creating Businesses on the Net, by David Elderbrock and Niten Borwankar (Foster City, CA: IDG Books, 1996). This book explores the Internet as a fertile ground for doing business. The book presents informative real-world case studies, complete with business plans and technical explanations. The book includes a Windows/UNIX CD and has a companion Web site.

Electronic Commerce: A Manager's Guide, by Ravi Kalakota and Andrew B. Whinston (Reading, MA: Addison-Wesley, 1997). It seems like everybody's trying to make money on the Internet, but very few are succeeding. This book is designed to provide managers with the technical and organizational background they need to generate revenue through the Internet and intranets.

Electronic Commerce: a Managerial Perspective, by Efraim Turban, Jae Lee, David King, and H. Michael Chung (Upper Saddle River, NJ: Prentice Hall, 2000). This text covers the rapidly changing field of electronic commerce, including intranets, extranets, marketing, business-to-business transactions, electronic payment, and more. Case studies and examples supplement the theoretical material.

Understanding Groupware in the Enterprise, by Joanne Woodcock (Redmond, WA: Microsoft Press, 1997), *Understanding Intranets,* by Tyson Greer (Redmond, WA: Microsoft Press, 1998), and *Understanding Electronic Commerce,* by David Kosiur (Redmond, WA: Microsoft Press, 1997). These three books are parts of Microsoft Press's Strategic Technology series, designed to provide practical, nontechnical explanations for managers and others who need to make decisions about emerging technology. They're generally well written and clear, without getting bogged down in unnecessary detail. As you might expect, they're Microsoft-centric, but they also contain plenty of useful information that's not brand specific.

Adapting PCs for Disabilities, by Joseph J. Lazzaro (Reading, MA: Addison-Wesley, 1996). Many features of the modern personal computer are difficult for people with disabilities to use—unless the PC is designed or modified to make it more accessible for those special populations. On the other hand, PCs with the right software and peripherals can provide invaluable assistance for people with disabilities. This book/CD-ROM package is full of useful information and software for adapting an IBM-compatible PC for people with special needs.

The Electronic Sweatshop: How Computers Are Transforming the Office of the Future into the Factory of the Past, by Barbara Garson (New York: Penguin Books, 1989). Garson exposes the dark side of the electronic office in words that are hard to ignore.

The End of Work, by Jeremy Rifkin (New York: Putnam, 1994). This book discusses the changing nature of work and the disappearance of jobs as we know them. Information technology isn't the only cause, but it plays a critical role in these changes.

Periodicals

Smart Business for the New Economy. This monthly used to be called *PC Computing.* In the '90s *PC Computing* focused on PC technology and business applications. But in the new decade, the PC is no longer the focal point of the "new" economy. In early 2000 *PC Computing* changed its name and broadened its focus to all kinds of information technology that have an impact on business and economy.

Information Week. This weekly news magazine focuses on business and the technology that drives it.

Upside. This monthly is aimed at managers, entrepreneurs, and others who want to track the business side rather than the technological side of the computer industry.

Forbes ASAP. This publication provides a thinking person's perspective on the high-tech workplace. Each year's "Big Issue" includes dozens of essays by famous and not-so-famous writers on a particular theme. (Some of those essays are reprinted in Crosscurrents in this text.)

Fast Company. This is another thought-provoking magazine that deals with the human issues of business in the digital age.

Small Business Computing. This magazine provides computer coverage for those businesses that aren't part of the Fortune 500.

World Wide Web Sites

Check the *Computer Confluence* Web site for links to Internet sources on information age jobs, technology in the workplace, and the evolving information economy.

15

Computers at School and Home

AFTER YOU READ THIS CHAPTER YOU SHOULD BE ABLE TO:

Explain how the information age places new demands on our educational system.

Eescribe several ways computers are used in classrooms today.

Discuss the advantages and limitations of computers as instructional tools.

Describe the role of computers in our homes and leisure activities in the next decade.

In this chapter:

▶ How information technology changes our educational needs

▶ How information technology changes our educational process

▶ How information technology changes our educational outcomes

▶ Computers at home—what's coming

...and more.

On the CD-ROM:

▶ The Myst-makers speak

▶ Working robots made of LEGO building blocks

▶ Video clips of schools of the future

▶ Instant access to glossary and key word references

▶ Interactive self-study quizzes

...and more.

On the Web:

www.prenhall.com/beekman

▶ Discussions of the role and impact of technology in education

▶ Valuable resources for, and by, educators and students

▶ Tutorials, simulations, and other educational programs

▶ Entertaining and educational home computing resources

▶ Resources for protecting our planet while using computers

▶ Self-study exercises

...and more.

Sometimes late at night, after I had done something really cool, I would look down on my creation and say, **"It is good."**

—Robyn Miller

Robyn Miller was right—it was good. Robyn and his brother Rand are the principal architects of Myst, a marvelous CD-ROM that defined a new art form and a unique entertainment experience for millions of computer users worldwide. Myst was the first smash hit CD-ROM; its sales passed the million mark while most of the world was still trying to figure out what interactive multimedia was.

Rand and Robyn Miller

Robyn and Rand seem like unlikely hit makers. Sons of a roving nondenominational preacher, the two brothers grew up in a household where ideas were more important than media. They lived in towns and cities far from the hubs of high-tech activity and pop culture.

When big brother Rand was working as a computer programmer in a Texas bank, he got an idea for a computer game for kids. He asked Robyn, the artistic brother, to illustrate it. The result was The Manhole, an Alice-in-Wonderland kind of environment full of amazing interconnected scenes, talking animals, and hidden surprises. The Manhole was one of the first major hyper-linked documents created with HyperCard; it was more of a surrealistic world to be explored than a story. The program won the Software Publishers Association's 1988 award for the best new use of a computer—no one had ever seen anything like it before.

Motivated by The Manhole's success, the Miller brothers created a company called Cyan and set up a garage-style shop in Spokane, a small city on the high prairie of Eastern Washington. They crafted a few more children's programs

before setting their sights on grown-up computer users. They wanted to create a computer game that could entertain without resorting to violence.

The result of their efforts was Myst, a game with a hypnotic, dreamlike quality. While exploring an artificial reality, players gradually solve puzzles that reveal parts of a dark story. Detailed 3-D graphics, haunting music, and subtle sound effects combine with a simple interface that draws in players who aren't normally attracted to computer games. Word of this new kind of game spread through networks, electronic and otherwise, and Myst became a major hit without firing a single shot.

Scene from *Myst*

Scene from *Riven*

419

It rose quickly to the top of the multimedia software charts and stayed there for years, establishing itself as the Titanic of interactive multimedia software and the best-selling computer game in history. All the while the Millers and the expanded Cyan crew worked away on a sequel. Not content to produce a quick knock-off, they poured millions of hours and millions of dollars into Riven. When it was finally released in 1997, the five-disk *tour de force* established a new standard of excellence for interactive fiction. Riven seamlessly integrated digital video and state-of-the-art animation into the Myst universe, including several imaginary people and fantasy animals.

By early 1998 game players had purchased an astonishing 5 million copies of Riven and Myst. Shortly thereafter Robyn Miller announced that he was leaving Cyan to work in film, a medium better suited to developing characters and stories. "Story molds us," he told an interviewer in 1999. "There's hardly anything we change our minds about because we're convinced of it by a logical argument. Story makes us who we are." Every interactive story produced so far—including Riven—has come up short in story plot and character development when compared with the best films. In fact, both brothers are quick to admit that their creations have limitations. In Rand's words, "We believe in a Creator who is responsible for the world we live in. It was an awesome experience to create a world of our own, with all the care and integrity we could muster, and yet see how thin and sketchy and insignificant it is compared to the one He made." ◼

Cyan's multimedia hits, along with hundreds of others available today, expand the human mind through a combination of entertainment and education. As computer technology reshapes our world, education plays an ever more important role in helping adults, as well as children, keep up with the changes going on around them. It's fitting, then, that computers are playing an ever-increasing role in the educational process in schools and homes. This chapter deals with the growing role of computers in schools and the changing role of education in a high-tech world. The chapter closes with a look at the growing impact of computers on our home life.

◼ Education in the Information Age

The future is a race between education and catastrophe.

—H. G. Wells

As we've seen, the information age is changing the way we work. Some jobs are disappearing, others are emerging, and still others are being radically transformed by information technology. But the information age is not just affecting the workplace. Its influences are felt in our educational system, too. Before it's over, the information revolution will have a profound and permanent effect on the way we learn.

The Roots of Our Educational System

The American educational system was developed more than a century ago to teach students the basic facts and survival skills they would need for jobs in industry and agriculture—jobs they would probably hold for their entire adult lives. This industrial age system has been described as a *factory model* for three reasons:

1 It assumes that all students learn the same way and that all students should learn the same things.

2 The teacher's job is to "pour" facts into students, occasionally checking the level of knowledge in each student.

3 Students are expected to work individually, absorb facts, and spend most of their time sitting quietly in straight rows.

Despite its faults, the factory model of public education helped the United States to dominate world markets for most of this century. But the world has changed drastically since the system was founded. Schools have changed, too, but not fast enough to keep pace with the information revolution. Most experts today agree that we need to rebuild our educational system to meet the demands of the information age.

Information Age Education

Education is the kindling of a flame, not the filling of a vessel.

—Socrates

What should education provide for students in the information age? Research and experience suggest several answers:

▶ *Technological familiarity.* Many of today's older workers are having trouble adjusting to the information age because of technophobia—the fear of technology. These people grew up in a world without computers, and they experience anxiety when they're forced to deal with them. In tomorrow's world computers and Internet connections will be as commonplace as telephones and dictionaries are today. To prepare for this world, students need to learn how to work comfortably with all kinds of knowledge tools, including pencils, books, calculators, computers, and the Internet. But technological familiarity shouldn't stop with learning how to work with tools. Students need to have a clear understanding of the *limitations* of the technology and the ability to assess the benefits and risks of applying technology to a problem. They need to be able to *question* technology.

▶ *Literacy.* The industrial age may have passed, but the need for reading and writing hasn't. In fact, it's more important than ever that all of today's students graduate with the ability to read and write. Many jobs that did not require reading or writing skills a generation ago now use high-tech equipment that demands literacy. A factory worker who can't read computer screens isn't likely to survive the transition to an automated factory.

▶ *Mathematics.* In the age of the $5 calculator many students think learning math is a waste of time. In fact, some educators argue that we spend too much time teaching students how to do things like long division and calculating square roots—skills that adults seldom, if ever, do by hand. These arithmetic skills have little to do with being able to think mathematically. To survive in a high-tech world, students need to be able to see the mathematical systems in the world around them and apply math concepts to solve problems. No calculator can do that.

▶ *Culture.* An education isn't complete without a strong cultural component. Liberal arts and social studies help us recognize the interconnections that turn information into knowledge. Culture gives us roots when the sands of time shift. It gives us historical perspective that allows us to see trends and prepare for the future. Culture provides a human framework with which to view the impact of technology. It also gives us the global perspective to live in a world where communication is determined more by technology than by geography.

▶ *Communication.* In the information age communication is a survival skill. Isolated factory workers and desk-bound pencil pushers are vanishing from the workplace. Modern jobs involve interactions—between people and machines and between people and people. The fast-paced, information-based society depends on our human ability to communicate, negotiate, cooperate, and collaborate, both locally and globally.

▶ *Learning how to learn.* Experts predict that most of the jobs that will exist in 10 years do not exist today and that most of those new jobs will require education past the high-school level. With this rapidly changing job market, it's unreasonable to assume that workers can be trained once for lifelong jobs. Instead of holding a single job for 40 years, today's high-school or college graduate is likely to change jobs several times. Those people who do keep the same jobs will have to deal with unprecedented change. The half-life of an engineer's specialized knowledge—the time it takes for half of that knowledge to be replaced by more current knowledge—is just over 3 years.

These facts suggest that we can no longer afford to think of education as a one-time vaccination against illiteracy. In the information age learning must be a lifelong process. To prepare students for a lifetime of learning, schools must teach students more than facts; they must make sure students learn how to think and learn.

Computers Go to School

The only thing we know about the future is that it will be
inhabited by our children. Its quality, in other words,
is directly proportional to world education.

—**Nicholas Negroponte, Director of the M.I.T. Media Lab**

The information age is making new demands on our educational system, requiring radical changes in what and how people learn. Many educators believe that computers and information technology are essential parts of those changes. Ninety-nine percent of all elementary and secondary schools in the United States have installed computers. Students and teachers are using those computers in a variety of ways.

Computer-Aided Instruction

The ordinary classroom holds the bright kids back
and makes the kids that need more time go too fast.
They fall further and further behind until they can't keep up—
it's a terrible system.

—B. F. Skinner, the father of behaviorist psychology and inventor of the first "teaching machine"

Students practice basic math skills with programs like *Grade Builder: Algebra 1* and *Math Workshop Deluxe.*

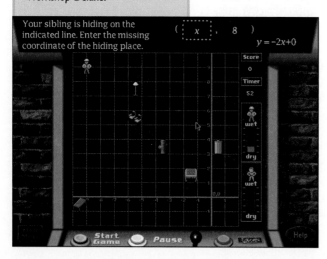

In 1953 B. F. Skinner visited his daughter's fourth-grade class and watched the teacher try to teach arithmetic to everyone in the class at the same speed. The experience inspired him to build a teaching machine—a wooden box that used cards, lights, and levers to quiz and reward a student. His machine was based on the principles of *behaviorist psychology*: Allow the student to learn in small steps at an individualized pace and reward correct answers with immediate positive feedback. When personal computers appeared in classrooms, students started using drill-and-practice software based on those same principles: individualized rate, small steps, and positive feedback.

A traditional drill-and-practice program presents the student with a question and compares the student's answer with the single correct answer. If the answers match, the program offers praise, possibly accompanied by music and animation. If the student's answer doesn't match the correct answer, the program offers an explanation and presents another, similar problem. The program may keep track of student responses and tailor questions based on error patterns; it might also provide reports on student progress to the teacher. Today most drill-and-practice programs embed the lessons in animated games, but the underlying principles remain the same.

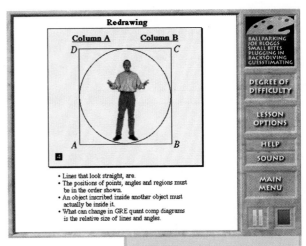

Students can prepare for standardized tests using *Inside the SAT and ACT*.

Computer-aided instruction (CAI) software is one of the most common types of courseware (educational software) for three reasons: It's relatively easy and inexpensive to produce, it can be easily combined with more traditional educational techniques, and it produces clear, demonstrable results. CAI offers many advantages over workbooks and worksheets:

▶ *Individualized learning.* Individual students can learn at their own pace. Teachers can spend their time working one on one with students—an important activity that's all but impossible in typical presentation-and-discussion classrooms.

▶ *Motivation.* CAI can turn practice into an entertaining game. It motivates students to practice arithmetic, spelling, touch-typing, piano playing, and other skills that might otherwise be tedious to learn.

▶ *Confidence.* CAI can help timid children become comfortable with computers as well as with the subject matter being taught. A well-designed program is infinitely patient, and it allows students to make mistakes in private. Research has shown that younger children, disadvantaged children, and in particular students with learning disabilities tend to respond positively to CAI.

Research also suggests that not all CAI software deserves praise. Much CAI software is flawed because it gives inappropriate feedback, allows students to practice mistakes, and discourages students from moving into new material. Even the best CAI can work only

CAI is useful for strengthening basic motor skills such as typing. In *Typing Tutor 10*, on-screen tutorials guide the student through a complete set of typing lessons, with the computer monitoring every keystroke for accuracy (left). Programs like *French for the Real World* provide instruction and practice sessions for learning languages (right).

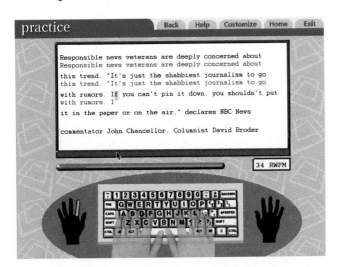

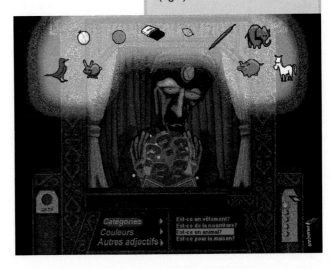

```
HyperLogo Script
home
repeat 3 [forward 100 right 120]
```

This sequence of LOGO commands tells the turtle to go home (the center of the window facing up); then to move forward 100 tiny steps, turn right 120 degrees (one third of a circle), move forward another 100 steps, turn right another 120, move forward another 100, and turn right another 120. When the turtle follows these instructions with the "pen" engaged, it draws an equilateral triangle on the floor of the screen. (Software: HyperStudio.)

with tightly defined subjects, in which every question can have a single, clear, unambiguous answer. CAI presents information in the form of facts, leaving no room for questioning, creativity, or cooperation. In a sense, CAI programs students.

Programming Tools

In many schools today, the phrase "computer-aided instruction" means making the computer teach the child. One might say the computer is being used to program the child. In my vision, the child programs the computer and, in doing so, both acquires a sense of mastery over a piece of the most modern and powerful technology and establishes an intimate contact with some of the deepest ideas from science, from mathematics, and from the art of intellectual model building.

—**Seymour Papert**, in *Mindstorms*

In the 1960s, with colleagues at MIT, Seymour Papert developed a computer language called LOGO so children could program computers rather than the other way around. Children can write LOGO programs as soon as they're old enough to read and write a few simple words.

Rather than teaching through lessons and tests, LOGO creates environments for learning. The most famous of these LOGO environments allows children to draw pictures using a technique called *turtle graphics*. With turtle graphics a child uses LOGO commands to make a "turtle" move, dragging a "pen" to draw lines as it moves. The "turtle" can be a small robot that moves around on the floor or a graphical creature that lives on a computer screen.

LOGO helps children learn advanced computer science concepts such as *recursion*—the ability of a program or procedure to call, or refer to, itself, as in this example:

```
TO CIRCLE
FORWARD 1 RIGHT 1
CIRCLE
END
```

This LOGO program tells the computer "to draw a circle, go one step forward, turn 1 degree to the right, and repeat all of these instructions." Of course, there's a bug here: This procedure doesn't know when to stop. But debugging is part of programming, and students who learn LOGO learn that making mistakes is part of the process.

LOGO has other environments that go beyond geometry and graphics. *LEGO LOGO* allows children to use LOGO commands to control motorized machines and robots built out of LEGO building blocks.

Papert and many educators predicted that LOGO would help children become better at general problem solving and logical thinking. Research suggests that LOGO enhances creativity and originality in children, but there's no conclusive evidence that it improves their general thinking skills more than other teaching tools. Like a chalkboard, LOGO can be an effective tool in the hands of a good teacher.

LOGO—like Pascal and BASIC, two other programming languages designed for students—is less popular in schools today than it was a decade ago. Today's computer applications make programming seem irrelevant to the average student. Children

Students in this class build LEGO robots and write LOGO programs to control them.

don't need to learn how to write TV programs before they watch TV, and in most schools they don't learn to program computers before they use them.

Simulations and Games

No compulsory learning can remain in the soul. . . . In teaching children,
train them by a kind of game,
and you will be able to see more clearly the natural bent of each.

—**Plato,** in *The Republic,* **Book VII**

When Papert developed LOGO, he based his educational psychology on the work of renowned Swiss developmental psychologist Jean Piaget. According to Piaget, children have a natural gift for learning on their own; they learn to talk, get around, and think without formal training. A child growing up in France learns French effortlessly because the child's environment has the necessary materials. In Papert's vision the computer can provide an environment that makes learning mathematics, science, and the arts as effortless as learning French in France.

Many educational simulations today are based on the same idea: Children learn best through exploration and invention. These simulations allow students to explore artificial environments, whether imaginary or based on reality. Educational simulations are metaphors designed to focus student attention on the most important concepts. While most educational simulations have the look and feel of a game, they challenge students to learn through exploration, experimentation, and interaction with other students.

With a simulation the students are in control of the learning environment. It's up to them to find and use information to draw conclusions. Students can experience the consequences of their actions without taking real-world risks. Simulations allow students to have experiences that wouldn't be possible otherwise. Instead of simply spewing facts, simulations provide a context for knowledge.

Students love playing well-designed simulation games, but many schools don't use simulations because there's no room for them in the formal curriculum. It's difficult to prove the effectiveness of simulation games because they generally aren't designed to teach simple, measurable facts. In spite of our culture's age-old tradition of learning through games, many educators question the educational value of games in the classroom. Of course, educational simulations, like all simulations, come up short as substitutes for reality. Many students can play with simulation games for hours without learning anything concrete. The risks of simulations, outlined in Chapter 6, apply to educational simulations, too. But when field trips aren't possible, computer simulations can offer affordable alternatives.

These two social studies games are popular with students, teachers, and parents. *Oregon Trail* allows players to learn about the hazards of crossing the nineteenth-century American West piloting a wagon train. *Where in the World Is Carmen Sandiego,* the immensely popular game designed to help students learn world geography, is the first piece of software to spin off children's books, a children's television show, a board game, and a live-action movie.

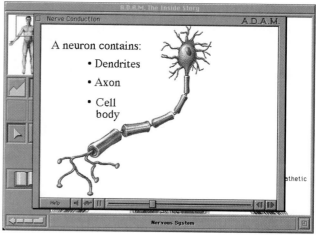

These two programs include simulations that allow students to test and observe scientific concepts. *Star Wars Droid Works* is a simulated robot factory. Given specifications and parts, players must apply principles of science and engineering to successfully construct a variety of robots. *A.D.A.M.: The Inside Story* provides a variety of ways to learn about human anatomy, including animated simulations of neural functions.

Productivity Tools

For me, the phrase "computer as pencil" evokes the kind of uses I imagine children of the future making of computers. Pencils are used for scribbling as well as writing, doodling as well as drawing, for illicit notes as well as for official assignments.

—**Seymour Papert**, in *Mindstorms*

Today the trend in schools is clearly toward teaching children to use computers as tools. Word processors, spreadsheets, databases, graphics programs, desktop publishing software, Web browsers, email programs—the software tools used by adults—are the tools students learn most often in schools. In some cases students use applications designed especially for children; others use standard "adult" applications. While programming classes are taken by only a few students, classes in keyboarding, word processing, and Web research are often required for everybody. Once students learn to use these general-purpose tools, they can put them to work in and out of school.

Some schools also provide special-purpose tools for classroom use, including these:

▶ Laboratory sensing hardware and software that can be used to collect scientific data (such as temperature) and convert it into computer data to be analyzed by students

▶ Collaborative writing groupware that allows students to work collectively on creative writing and editing projects

▶ Music synthesizers with sequencing and notation software for teaching music composition.

Whether the computer is used as a tutor or a tool, the addition of multimedia adds whole new dimensions to the educational process.

Computer-Controlled Media

I hear and I forget,
I see and I remember,
I do and I understand.

—**Ancient Chinese proverb**

The typical American child spends hours each day watching screens—television, video game, and computer—and listening to radio and recorded music. Traditional lectures can't live up to the expectations created by all this high-tech media input. A growing number of teachers are using multimedia on and off the Web to convey information in a more dynamic form. Depending on the way these media are used, the student's role might be to observe the presentation, to control the presentation, or to create the presentation.

Presentation Aids

In some cases teachers use computers and multimedia technology to create in-class presentations. Here are some examples:

- ▶ A history teacher might outline the main points of a lecture using bullet charts created with a presentation graphics program like PowerPoint.
- ▶ A science teacher might use a 3-D graphics program to create models of molecules that can be displayed and manipulated during in-class demonstrations on a projection screen.
- ▶ An art teacher might illustrate an art history lecture with a series of images from a CD-ROM or the Web.
- ▶ A music teacher might guide a class through key passages of a Beethoven symphony using an enhanced CD that displays the score while the CD plays the composition.
- ▶ An English teacher might supplement lectures and discussions about the novel *To Kill a Mockingbird* by showing selected video clips that have been digitized into a presentation.

From the teacher's point of view the advantage of computer technology is that the material can be customized to meet the needs of the class. Instead of using commercial transparencies and handouts designed for generic classrooms, a teacher can create custom visual aids for specific classes. Instead of being forced to move through videotapes and audio cassettes sequentially, the teacher can choose to present material in any order.

Interactive Multimedia

From the student's point of view, teacher-controlled media presentations are still passive, linear affairs. To get students more involved in the learning process, many teachers use interactive multimedia software that puts students in control. Sometimes these interactive lessons are created by teachers; more often they're purchased on CDs or explored through the Web. Some are simple tutorials with sound and/or video; others are multimedia reference tools with hypertext cross-references.

Authoring by Students

To maximize student involvement, some teachers put multimedia **authoring tools** in the hands of students.

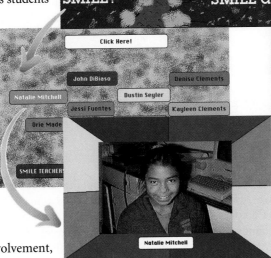
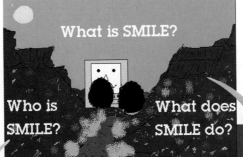

Professionally produced multimedia programs like *Steven Hawkings's Life in the Universe* can make abstract concepts and facts more accessible and exciting.

Students in the Jefferson County SMILE science and math club on the Warm Springs Indian Reservation designed and built an interactive multimedia presentation, complete with animation, audio, and video clips, to tell others about the club.

Tianna and Mayanne listening to vibrations.

We meet the governor!!

Instead of creating interactive lessons for students, teachers allow the students to create their own multimedia presentations. Here are several examples:

▶ In an Alaskan village, native students created Yupik for Non-Speakers, an illustrated talking dictionary of the traditional Yupik language. Students drew on the knowledge and voices of the community elders to create the dictionary.

▶ At South Eugene High School in Oregon students produced a CD-ROM version of their yearbook. Unlike the paper version the CD-ROM yearbook contains animated illustrations and recordings of the students talking about school.

▶ Students in a high-school science class in Shelley, Idaho, researched, planned, and built a multimedia exhibit for Yellowstone National Park's Canyon Visitor Center. Visitors use the touch-screen system to explore the political and geological history of Yellowstone and to "fly" from outer space down to the earth beneath Yellowstone.

▶ Students in hundreds of schools everywhere are creating Web pages about their classes, schools, student organizations, and special projects. The Web makes it possible for these students to reach worldwide audiences with their presentations.

Clearly, the students are more involved in these projects than they are in teacher-made presentations. This kind of student involvement promotes learning, but it has drawbacks. One problem is economic: Few schools can afford the hardware, software, and floor space for multiple student media workstations.

Another problem is social: Students who use the Web may be exposed to pornography and other materials that might be objectionable to them, their parents, or their teachers. Many companies offer filtering software that blocks student access to sites with "inappropriate" content. Filtering programs can be customized, but they're not 100% accurate. They're also subject to the biases of their authors and corporate owners. In early 2000 extensive tests of American Online's filtering revealed that kids had free access to Web sites of conservative Republican and Libertarian parties but were blocked from viewing the Democratic and Green party sites. Young teens could access sites promoting gun use, including the National Rifle Association, but not the Coalition to Stop Gun Violence and other gun safety organizations. Both AOL and The Learning Company, who designed the filtering software, denied bias. But the findings show how censorship can squelch the free flow of ideas that's a critical part of the educational process.

A third problem with Web and multimedia technology in the classroom is both social and political: When students are creating or using interactive media, they aren't conforming to the traditional factory model. Instead of sitting quietly listening to the teacher, they're taking control of the machinery and the learning process. The teacher becomes a supervisor and a mentor rather than a conveyor of information. This kind of restructuring of the educational process is threatening to many administrators, teachers, parents, and community members who are used to the old ways.

Distance Learning: Virtual Schools

> Very soon now, it might not matter where your body happens to be . . .
> as long as you maintain a presence in the networks.

—Steven K. Roberts, **technomad**

For some students the most important application of computers in schools is distance learning—using technology to extend the educational process beyond the walls of the school. Computers, modems, fax machines, satellite video transmissions, the Internet, and other communication technologies offer many promising possibilities. Grade-school students can network with kids in other parts of the world through the Internet. Middle-school classes can use electron microscopes, telescopes, and other powerful tools around the world through real-time Internet connections. High-school correspondence courses can be completed by modem rather than by mail. Students with handicaps can do course work without traveling to central sites. Two-way video links allow "visiting" experts to talk to students in outlying classrooms and answer their questions in real time. Networked school districts can offer multischool videoconference courses in Chinese, college-level calculus, and other subjects that might have tiny enrollments if offered only at a single school. Teachers can receive additional education without leaving their districts.

Telecommunication technology is particularly important for students in remote locations. If a child in a small town develops an interest in a narrow subject, whether it's aboriginal anthropology or classical Russian ballet, that student may find pursuing that interest a discouraging process. Reference materials, adult experts, and classmates with similar interests are often hard to find. The Internet offers solutions: On-line reference materials, special-interest newsgroups, long-distance mentors, and like-minded modem pals are all within reach. In many areas rural interactive television networks keep remote schools and towns from fading away.

Distance education is particularly attractive to women with children. Two thirds of the adult distance learners are female, and 80% of them have children. Distance learning also offers promise for workers whose jobs are changed or eliminated by a shifting economy. Many displaced and dissatisfied workers can't afford to relocate their families to college towns so they can learn new skills. But if colleges and universities offer electronic outreach programs, these people can update their skills while remaining in their communities.

Since 1990 on-line degree programs have appeared at dozens of universities and colleges. Students use PCs and modems to do everything from ordering books to taking final exams. Many on-line students see their professors in person for the first time at graduation ceremonies.

The demand for distance education is growing rapidly. In some countries distance ed students compose 40% of the total undergraduate population. Some experts predict that the majority of college students will be off-campus students in a decade or two.

Of course, a college education is more than a collection of information. Students learn and grow as a result of all kinds of experiences in and out of the classroom. Many significant learning experiences can't be transmitted through phone lines and TV cables. Still, on-line schools are an important step toward an educational system that encourages lifelong learning.

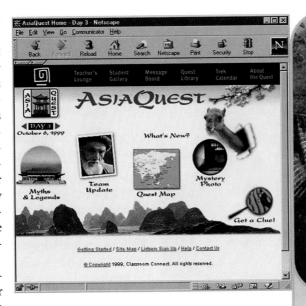

Classroom Connect is one organization that regularly offers interactive expeditions for students. For example, Asia Quest allowed students to communicate with a team of scientists and explorers as they followed in Marco Polo's footsteps along China's Silk Road.

Computers at School: Midterm Grades

The business of education is to give the student both useful information and life-enhancing experience, one largely measurable, the other not....

—John Gardner, in *The Art of Fiction*

Many schools have been using computers in classrooms for more than a decade. In these days of shrinking budgets, taxpayers are asking whether classroom computer technology "pays off." Has it lived up to its promise as an educational tool in the schools? According to most experts, the answer is mixed but optimistic.

High Marks

A number of independent studies in the 1990s confirm that information technology can improve education. Some findings:

- ▶ Students improve problem-solving skills, outscore classmates, and learn more rapidly in a variety of subject areas and situations when using technology as compared to conventional methods of study.
- ▶ Students find computer-based instruction to be more motivational, less intimidating, and easier to persist with than traditional instruction.
- ▶ In many cases students' self-esteem is increased when they use computers. This change is most dramatic in cases of at-risk youngsters and students with handicaps.
- ▶ Using technology encourages cooperative learning, turn taking among young children, peer tutoring, and other valuable social skills.
- ▶ Computer technology can make learning more student centered and stimulate increased teacher/student interaction.
- ▶ Well-designed interactive multimedia systems can encourage active processing and higher order thinking.
- ▶ Students who create interactive multimedia reports often learn better than those who learn with more traditional methods.
- ▶ Students can become more productive, more fluid writers with computers.
- ▶ Computers can help students master the basic skills needed to participate and succeed in the workforce.
- ▶ Positive changes occur gradually as teachers gain experience with the technology.
- ▶ Technology can facilitate educational reform.

Research shows that student writing improves when they use word processors, but most schools have too few computers for their writing classes. Inexpensive devices like these AlphaSmart keyboards allow students to type their first drafts away from the computer lab. The keyboards have small LCD screens and enough memory to hold several text documents. When they're connected to computers, they can transfer the typed documents for final editing, formatting, and printing.

Room for Improvement

The further one pursues knowledge, the less one knows.

—Lao Tse, **500 B.C.**

Other findings temper—and sometimes contradict—these positive conclusions. Researchers have also found that:

- ▶ If the only thing that changes is the delivery medium (from traditional media to computer media), the advantages of technology are small—or nonexistent.
- ▶ Kids and teachers forget advanced computer skills if they don't use them.
- ▶ Students have unequal access to technology; economically disadvantaged students have less computer access at school and at home. Sadly, these are the students who can benefit most when given access to technology.
- ▶ Technology doesn't reduce teacher workloads; if anything, it seems to make their jobs harder (of course, many teachers welcome the extra work because they believe it brings results).

▶ There's a gender gap that typically puts the computer room in the boys' domain; the gap can be reduced by stressing computer activities that involve collaboration.

▶ Many of the outcomes of technology-based education don't show up with traditional educational assessment methods.

▶ Sending students to a computer lab for 30 minutes a week has little or no value; computers are more effective when they're in classrooms where students can use them regularly.

▶ Younger students may be better served by art, music, and shop classes than by computer classes; unfortunately, these important parts of the curriculum are often eliminated to make room for computers.

Stories abound of reduced dropout rates and attitudinal changes among at-risk students; improved math, reading, and language scores; and overall academic improvement among students in high-tech schools. But computer technology doesn't always bring happy headlines. In some schools computers are little more than expensive, time-consuming distractions. What makes technology work for some schools and not for others? A closer look at the success stories reveals that they didn't achieve results with technology alone. When we compare these schools with less fortunate schools, several issues emerge:

▶ *Money.* Most American schools have found funds to purchase computers. Unfortunately, many of those computers are technologically outdated. Most classrooms don't even have phone lines, let alone modems or Internet connections. Not surprisingly, computers tend to be concentrated in affluent school districts, so economically disadvantaged students have the least access to them.

▶ *Planning and support.* When school districts spend money on technology without thoughtful long-term planning and sustained support, their investments are not likely to pay off.

▶ *Teacher training.* Unfortunately, teacher training is often missing from schools' high-tech formulas. Most teachers lack the experience to use computers, the Internet, and other information technology effectively in the classroom. Teachers need training, support, and time to integrate technology into their curricula.

▶ *Restructuring.* Just as businesses need to rethink their organizational structures to automate successfully, schools need to be restructured to make effective use of computer technology. The goal is education, and technology is just one tool for achieving that goal. Interactive media, individualized instruction, telecommunication, and cooperative learning simply don't fit well into the factory school. To meet the educational challenges of the information age, we'll need to invest in research and planning involving teachers, students, administrators, parents, businesses, and community leaders.

> Research suggests that technology can have a positive impact on education if it's part of a program that includes teacher training, ongoing support, and radical restructuring of the traditional "factory model" curriculum.

The Classroom of Tomorrow

To give us a head start in building the schools of the future, Apple, IBM, Toshiba, Microsoft, and other companies, along with some state and local governments, have helped create model technology classrooms and schools in communities around the United States and Canada. Most of

these pilot projects suggest that technology can, in the proper context, have a dramatic effect on education. For example, here's a quote from Apple's Web site summarizing the results of the Apple Classroom of Tomorrow (ACOT) project:

> *After more than a decade of research, ACOT's research demonstrated that the introduction of technology into classrooms can significantly increase the potential for learning, especially when it is used to support collaboration, information access, and the expression and representation of students' thoughts and ideas. Realizing this opportunity for all students, however, required a broadly conceived approach to educational change that integrated new technologies and curricula with new ideas about learning and teaching, as well as with authentic forms of assessment.*

Information technology, then, can be a powerful change agent, but not by itself. In a recent interview for on-line magazine *ZineZone*, educational computing pioneer Seymour Papert was asked whether technology is a Trojan horse for systematic and lasting change. His reply: "I think the technology serves as a Trojan horse all right, but in the real story of the Trojan horse, it wasn't the horse that was effective, it was the soldiers inside the horse. And the technology is only going to be effective in changing education if you put an army inside it which is determined to make that change once it gets through the barrier."

Computers Come Home

There is no reason for any individual to have a computer in their home.

—**Ken Olson, president of Digital Equipment Corporation, 1977**

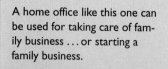

A home office like this one can be used for taking care of family business ... or starting a family business.

The same year Ken Olson made this statement, Apple Computer introduced the Apple II computer. In the years that followed Apple, Commodore, Tandy, Atari, IBM, and dozens of other companies managed to sell computers to millions of individuals who had "no reason" to buy them.

Today there are more computers in homes than in schools. Most American homes contain at least one computer. Plummeting prices and Internet interest fuel the exploding home computer industry. The small office, home office market—dubbed *SOHO* by the industry—is one of the fastest growing computer markets today. While many home computers gather dust, others are being put to work, and play, in a variety of ways.

Household Business

Frank Gilbreth, a turn-of-the-century pioneer of motion study in industry, applied "scientific management" techniques to his home. He required his 12 children to keep records on bathroom "work-and-process charts" of each hair combing, tooth brushing, and bathing. He gave them demonstrations on efficient bathing techniques to min-

imize "unavoidable delays." While it may have worked for Gilbreth, this "scientific management" approach to home life is not likely to catch on today. Still, certain aspects of family life are unavoidably businesslike, and a growing number of people are turning to computers to help them take care of business.

Business Applications at Home

Not everyone is convinced that computers are useful or practical at home. But those people who do use home computers generally find that they can put the same applications to work at home that they use in their offices:

- ▶ *Word processors.* For letters, memos, and school papers, the word processor has replaced the typewriter for families with computers.

- ▶ *Spreadsheets.* "Can we afford a trip to Mexico this year?" "How much do we need to put away each year to pay for college?" "Should we refinance the house?" A spreadsheet program can frame answers to "what if" questions involving numbers, provided somebody takes the time and effort to create a worksheet model of the problem.

- ▶ *Database programs.* Many people use database programs for address books, family record keeping, collections, and other data storage jobs. Others find that it's not worth the effort to type in all that data.

- ▶ *Personal information management programs.* Appointment calendars, to-do lists, addresses, phone numbers—they're part of home life, too, and an enthusiastic minority of people use home computers and handheld PDAs to keep their personal lives organized.

- ▶ *Web browsers and email programs.* For a growing number of families the home computer is mostly a window into the on-line world. On-line shopping, banking, studying, chatting, gaming, and exploring often cut into time family members used to spend in front of the TV.

- ▶ *Accounting and tax programs.* Many easy-to-use accounting programs are targeted at homes and small businesses. These programs can balance checkbooks, write checks, keep financial records for tax time, and provide data for income tax calculation programs.

Smart Cards

For most people the advantages of computerized home money management aren't worth the time and effort to type every financial transaction into the computer. Some people strike a balance by typing in only "important" transactions; others subscribe to home banking programs so they can download their summary statements directly from bank computers. But for most people computerized money management won't happen until there's an effortless way to record transactions—perhaps a device that, when inserted into the computer, can tell the software about each purchase and paid bill. That device may turn out to be a smart card.

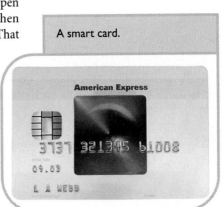

A smart card.

A **smart card** looks like a standard credit card, but instead of a magnetic strip it contains an embedded microprocessor and memory. (Memory cards, which contain memory but no microprocessors, are occasionally called smart cards even though they aren't really "smart.") Some smart cards even contain touch-sensitive keypads for entering numbers. Whether it has a keypad or not, a smart card receives most of its input when it's slipped into a special slot on a computer. Data stored in smart cards can be password protected. There are hundreds of millions of smart cards in Europe, and they're rapidly infiltrating America.

Smart cards are obvious candidates to replace magnetic-strip credit cards. In addition to storing critical ID information a smart card can automatically record

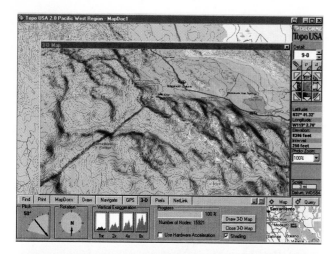

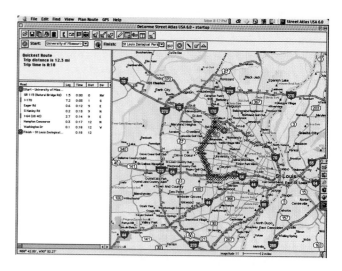

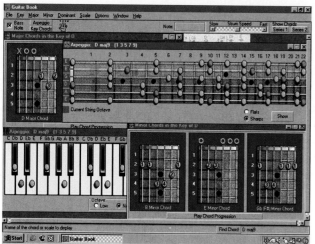

Home computer users use CD-ROMs to help with all kinds of tasks, including locating streets in far-off cities, planning wilderness treks, and learning to play guitar. (Software: DeLorme Topo USA, Street Atlas USA, and Guitar Book)

each transaction for later retrieval. But smart cards have other applications, too. College students use smart cards as meal tickets. Office workers use smart cards as keys to access sensitive data on computers. Smart cards have replaced food stamps and drivers' licenses in some states. Many Europeans use smart cards to pay highway tolls and unscramble cable TV broadcasts. You might soon use one card to buy groceries, check out library books, and store personal medical information in case of an emergency. Future smart cards will use pattern recognition techniques to verify signatures on checks or credit slips and help prevent millions of dollars in fraud and forgery.

Education and Information

Newspapers as we know them won't exist. They will be printed for a readership of one. Television won't simply have sharper pictures. You'll have one button that says tell me more, and another button that says tell me less.

—Nicholas Negroponte, **director of the MIT Media Lab**

Millions of people use home computers for education and information. Many educational software programs described earlier in this chapter are used by children and adults in homes. Edutainment programs specifically geared toward home markets combine education with entertainment so they can compete with television and electronic games. Encyclopedias, dictionaries, atlases, almanacs, national telephone directories, medical references, and other specialized references now come in low-cost CD-ROM versions—often with multimedia capability. Many CD-ROM references have been eclipsed by Web references which offer much of the same information for free. These on-line references can't deliver the rich multimedia experience of CD-ROMs, but they can provide up-to-the-minute, customized content that's not possible with other media. Of course, Internet connections also provide electronic mail, discussion groups, and other communication options for home users.

As computer technology and communication technology converge on the home market, they'll produce services that may threaten television and newspapers as our main sources of information. Television is a broadcast medium—it transmits news and information to broad audiences. In the future we'll see narrowcasting services—they'll provide custom newscasts aimed at narrow groups or individuals. (Individualized broadcasting is sometimes called *pointcasting*.) Personalized multimedia news programs will combine many of the best features of television news and newspapers. You'll be able to request an index of available features and use it like a menu to build your own news program. Your personal newscast might include a piece on the latest Middle Eastern crisis, the results of yesterday's primary election, highlights of last night's Blazers vs. Lakers game, the scores in the college intramural games, this weekend's weather forecast at the coast, a feature on your favorite local musician, and a reminder that there are only five more shopping days until your mother's birthday. You'll be able to train your news service to flag particular subjects ("I'm especially interested in articles on the Amazon rain forest") and ignore others ("No Hollywood gossip, please"), so that even the menu is customized to suit your tastes. All of this is technologically possible now. Prototype systems have been running for years at MIT's Media Lab, and several Web portals now offer limited customized news services.

Home Entertainment Redefined

Television has a "brightness" knob, but it doesn't seem to work.

—Gallagher, **stand-up comic**

You don't want a television with knobs marked "volume" and "brightness" and "contrast." You want a television with knobs marked "sex" and "violence" and "political bias."

—**Nicholas Negroponte, director of the MIT Media Lab**

Starship Titanic is a tongue-in-cheek science fiction adventure by Douglas Adams, author of *The Hitchhiker's Guide to the Galaxy. Star Wars: Episode 1: Racer* is part of a popular series of Star Wars games from LucasArts Entertainment. *You Don't Know, Jack*, a comical quiz show simulation, is available on CD-ROM and on the Web.

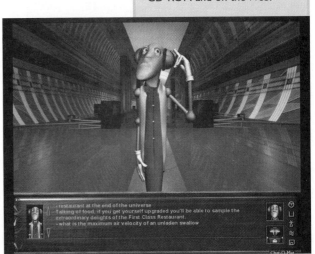

Regardless of how people say they use home computers, surveys suggest that many people use them mostly to play games. Computer games and video game machines (which are just special-purpose computers) represent a huge industry—one that is likely to evolve rapidly in the coming years.

Most computer games are simulations. Computer games can simulate board games, card games, sporting events, intergalactic battles, street fights, corporate takeovers, or something else, real or imaginary. Many require strategy and puzzle solving; others depend only on eye-hand coordination. Many of the

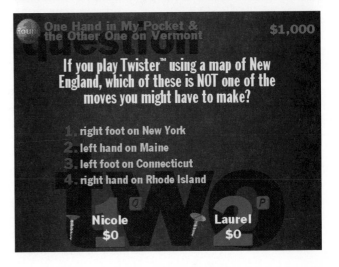

These screen illustrate three different ways popular musicians have used CD-ROMs to enhance their art. *A Hard Days Night* includes the complete Beatles movie along with extensive annotation and additional clips. Peter Gabriel's *Eve* combines music and art in a Myst-like exploratory adventure. Sarah McLachlan's *Freedom Sessions* is an enhanced audio CD that includes standard audio tracks along with additional video and multimedia material. Today DVD technology makes it possible for musicians to create disks with more, and better, multimedia content.

most popular games require some of each. With dazzling graphics, digitized sound, and sophisticated effects, many of today's computer games represent state-of-the-art software. But in a few years these computer games are likely to look as primitive as early Pong games look today.

Enhanced realism of computer games may not be completely beneficial for society. In the years before the 1999 Columbine High School mass murder, the killers spent hundreds of hours blasting virtual people in graphic first-person games like Doom. In the aftermath of the tragedy many people suggested that the violent games were partially responsible for the horrific killings. A year later, published research confirmed a link between violent video games and real-world violence. Two studies suggested that even brief exposure to violent video games can temporarily increase aggressive behavior, and that children who play violent games tend to have lower grades and more aggressive tendencies in later years. Further research may confirm or clarify these results. In the meantime, pressure grows for game manufacturers to consider the impact of their products on young minds.

The biggest changes in electronic games are happening at the intersection of computers, communication technology, and the home entertainment industry, where the line that separates television programs and computer games grows fuzzy. A few years ago, software shops stocked a variety of interactive fiction games—stories with primitive natural-language interfaces that gave players some control over plot. Those text-only programs have been squeezed off the software shelves by interactive movies—video-based or animated features in which one or more of the characters are controlled by the viewers.

Today's interactive movies aren't Academy Award material; many are like cartoons with controls or TV shows with choice-points. Some of today's DVD titles add just a hint of interactivity to big-screen, big-budget movies: alternative soundtracks, alternative endings, and other customizable features. These DVD movies can be played on TVs or computers. As the medium matures, DVD titles will become more interactive.

We're also likely to see a growth in interactive TV—broadcast television with options for interactivity built in. In 1999 two popular game shows, *Wheel of Fortune* and *Jeopardy,* began broadcasting interactive versions that allowed viewers to play along with contestants. Some experts think this kind of programming is likely to increase sharply as more TV viewers buy set-top boxes with keyboards and other input devices. Interactive TV has been popular for years in Europe, where digital TV had an early audience.

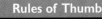

Green Computing

When compared with heavy industries such as automobiles and energy, the computer industry is relatively easy on the environment. But the manufacture and use of computer hardware and software does have a significant environmental impact, especially now that so many of us are using the technology. Fortunately, you have some control over the environmental impact of your computing activities. Here are a few tips to help minimize your impact:

▶ *Buy green equipment.* Today's computer equipment uses relatively little energy, but as world energy resources dwindle, less is always better. Many modern computers and peripherals are specifically designed to consume less energy. Look for the Environmental Protection Agency's Energy Star certification on the package.

▶ *Use a laptop.* Portable computers use far less energy than desktop computers. They're engineered to preserve precious battery power. But if you use a laptop, keep it plugged in when you have easy access to an electrical outlet. Batteries wear out from repeated usage, and their disposal can cause environmental problems of a different sort. (If you're the kind of person who always needs to have the latest and greatest technology, a laptop isn't the greenest choice for you, because laptops are difficult or impossible to upgrade.)

▶ *Take advantage of energy-saving features.* Many systems can be set up to go to sleep (a sort of suspended animation state that uses just enough power to preserve RAM) and turn off the monitor or printer when idle for more than an hour or so. If your equipment has automatic energy-saving features, use them. You'll save energy and money.

▶ *Turn it off when you're away.* If you're just leaving your computer for an hour or two, you won't save much energy by turning the CPU off. But if you're leaving it for more than a few hours and it's not on duty receiving faxes and email, you'll do the environment a favor by turning it off or putting it to sleep. Your monitor is probably the biggest power guzzler in your system. And while your Dilbert screen saver may be entertaining, it won't save your screen or reduce energy consumption.

▶ *Print only once.* Don't print out a rough draft just to proofread; try to get it clean on screen. (Most people find this one hard to follow 100% of the time; some errors just don't seem to show up until you print.)

▶ *Recycle your waste products.* When you do have to reprint that 20-page report because of a missing paragraph on page 1, recycle the flawed printout. When your laser printer's toner cartridge runs dry, ship or deliver it to one of the many companies that recycle cartridges. They may even pay you a few dollars for the empty cartridge. When your portable's battery dies, follow the manufacturer's instructions for recycling it. While you're in recycling mode, don't forget all those computer magazines and catalogs. When you outgrow a piece of hardware or software, pass it on to a school, civic organization, or friend who can put it to good use.

▶ *Send bits, not atoms.* It takes far more resources to send a letter by truck, train, or plane than to send an electronic message through the Internet. Whenever possible, use your modem instead of your printer.

Windows and Macintosh operating systems have energy-saver control panels that can be set to automatically switch the monitor and CPU to low-power sleep modes after specified periods of inactivity.

Portable computers consume far less energy than desktop models; this one is powered by the sun using a Neptune Solar Panel.

Interactive TV and DVD are, for the most part, solitary activities. But the Internet opens up new possibilities for social entertainment, as well. We're already seeing multi-player multimedia games on the Web; how long will it be until these games have the richness of plot and cinematography of today's films? When will today's chat rooms and virtual communities evolve into rich environments for interaction and exploration? As technology improves and the multimedia market grows, we can expect all kinds of hybrid forms of entertainment.

Creativity and Leisure

If you can talk, you can sing.
If you can walk, you can dance.

—A saying from Zimbabwe

Interactive movies demand more involvement than television, but they're still a relatively passive pastime. Many people worry that television, computer games, and other media are replacing too many real-world activities. Instead of making up stories to share, we watch sitcoms on TV. Instead of playing music on guitars, we play music on boom boxes. Instead of playing one-on-one basketball, we play one-on-one video games. Is electronic technology turning us into a mindless couch-potato culture?

Perhaps. But there's another possibility. The same technology that mesmerizes us can also unlock our creativity. Word processors help many of us to become writers, graphics software brings out the artists among us, Web authoring tools provide us with worldwide publishing platforms, electronic music systems allow us to compose music even if we never mastered an instrument, and digital video and multimedia systems open doors to cable-access TV channels.

Will computers drain our creativity or amplify it? In the end it's up to us. . . .

CROSSCURRENTS

Trouble in Internet Time

Tim Race

As first citizens of the emerging information society, we're of necessity exploring uncharted territory. The computers we use for information and recreation are stimulating our biological and social systems in unprecedented ways. What impact will this have on us as individuals and as a society? Do video games encourage real-world violence? Can day trading lead to destructive behavior? Does the pace of the information age bring out our worst qualities? Shortly after a mass shooting in Atlanta, Tim Race, editor of the Monday business section of The New York Times, *wrestled with these questions in this article, which first appeared in* The Industry Standard *on August 20, 1999.*

It has happened again: a shooting spree, and the need to explain irrational violence leads to a search for the smoking computer.

As word broke from Atlanta that Mark O. Barton had shot up two computerized stock-trading offices, news accounts quickly began referring to him as an "enraged day trader," as if this label would explain the psychosis that had left Barton and 13 others dead. The ritual polling of his neighbors yielded few insights, other than he certainly had an awful lot of computers in that house where he had just hammered his wife and two children to death.

The media had a similar knee-jerk reaction following the Columbine massacre. After that tragedy, we were told that the kids with automatic weapons had been devotees of Doom—a violent, fast-twitch computer game that, like day trading, rewards id and reflex actions above all else.

Even the most superficial Columbine postmortems didn't quite say that computer games caused those short-circuited teenagers to kill 13 people before killing themselves. Nor has anyone argued that using a computer to buy and sell stocks many times a day in response to tiny price twitches actually made Barton go on his rampage. But in both cases, computers were forced to take part of the rap.

Specious as it may sound, though, such analysis does makes a certain amount of sense, considering the fundamental roles that violence and technology play in American culture. In the Internet Age, with its premium on speed, those two cultural forces can sometimes get thrown into overdrive. There are manic parallels between the fast-twitch financial machinery that enabled Barton to lose $105,000 or more in 15 trading days and the hair-trigger mayhem he was able to unleash in 10 minutes with his semiautomatic Glock and Colt handguns.

Episodes like these are reminders that American culture has had a violent streak ever since Puritan settlers, with a theological sense of their mission, began staking out the frontier in the 17th century.

From the start, ours has been a fundamentally technological society. It had to be, if an entire continent was to be conquered—whether with flintlocks that short farther than arrows or steamboats that paddled north faster than the Mississippi flowed south. And once everything had been mapped out and deeded, it took telegraphs and telephones, broadcasts and Webcasts to make far-flung settlers feel like part of one big neighborhood (even if no one ever quite knows what's going on in the house next door).

Seen in this cultural light, Barton seems to have been motivated by the same forces that drove the early frontiersmen. The frontier—whether the border of wilderness or the edge of cyberspace—has always represented a safety valve for misfits, a chance for a fresh start. After Barton's first wife and mother-in-law were murdered in the woods of Alabama (crimes for which Barton was a prime suspect), Barton found a new wife. Even after killing his second wife and their children, he hoped for another new beginning, according to the note he wrote on his PC.

"If Jehovah's willing, I would like to see them all again in the resurrection to have a second chance," he wrote—a theological dream of a new frontier, recorded for posterity with word-processing software. Silicon Valley entrepreneurs, who often call themselves evangelists, speak with quasireligious fervor of "Internet time"—the apocalyptic sense of urgency caused by the fleeting half-lives of products and business plans.

Some of the speedway effects seem innocuous enough. Real-time auctions of troll dolls on eBay can be good, clean fun. Instant-messaging "buddy lists" on AOL sound downright neighborly.

But if the Internet is now our cultural metronome, its manically fast ticking leaves little margin for mental error—especially when a person is placing hundreds of computerized bets a day on the stock market or squeezing off four rounds a second with a Glock 9 millimeter.

After the stock market crash of October 1987, the New York Stock Exchange came up with the "circuit breaker," a time-out when prices get too manic or depressive. Maybe the scrutiny brought by Barton's meltdown will lead to new kinds of circuit breakers for day traders.

For everyone else, let this latest violent episode serve as a cautionary tale about the new frontier of Internet time, about the need for safety valves as we push the boundaries of settled territory.

DISCUSSION QUESTIONS

1. Do you think video games "program" players to be more violent? Explain your answer.

2. Do you think the stresses caused by "Internet time" might be more than most people can handle? Explain.

Our educational system was developed a century ago to train workers for lifelong jobs. In the information age, when students can expect to change jobs several times, we need schools that teach technological familiarity, literacy, mathematics, culture, communication, problem solving, and, most importantly, the ability to learn and adapt to an ever-changing world.

Students use a variety of instructional tools in schools today, including these:

▶ **Computer-aided instruction (CAI).** Tutorials and/or drill-and-practice software covering concrete facts in specific subject areas

▶ **Programming tools.** Languages such as LOGO, Pascal, BASIC, and HTML that allow students to design their own software and Web pages

▶ **Simulations and games.** Artificial environments that allow students to learn through exploration, experimentation, and interaction with other students

▶ **Productivity tools.** Word processors, spreadsheets, and other real-world tools

▶ **Computer-controlled media.** Presentation graphics, hypermedia, interactive multimedia, and authoring tools that allow varying degrees of student control

▶ **Distance learning tools.** Telecommunication tools, including the Internet, that allow students and teachers to communicate electronically without having to be in the same physical location

Clearly, computer technology can have a positive educational impact, but computers alone can't guarantee improvement. Research, planning, teacher training, community involvement, and classroom restructuring should accompany new technology.

A small but growing number of families use home computers for basic business applications, education, information access, communication, entertainment, and creative pursuits. All of these applications will radically change as the technology evolves over the next decade.

Key Terms

authoring tool, 427
computer-aided instruction (CAI), 423
courseware, 423
distance learning, 428
drill-and-practice software, 423

educational simulation, 425
edutainment, 434
filtering software, 428
interactive fiction, 436
interactive movie, 436

interactive TV, 436
LOGO, 424
narrowcasting, 434
smart card, 433
technophobia, 421

Review Questions

1. Define or describe each of the key terms listed above. Check your answers using the glossary.
2. What were the goals of education in the industrial age? Which are still appropriate in the information age? Which are not?
3. What kind of an education does a student need to prepare for living and working in the information age?
4. How do educational simulation games differ from traditional computer-aided instruction? What are the advantages and disadvantages of each?

5. Describe how multimedia might be used by teachers and students in the classroom. Give several examples.
6. Give several examples of ways that distance learning can enhance education.
7. Technology alone is no guarantee that students will learn better or faster. What else is necessary to ensure success?
8. Describe several ways people use home computers.
9. What are smart cards, and how are they used?
10. How is home entertainment being changed by computer technology and telecommunication?

Discussion Questions

1. Socrates was illiterate and avoided the written word because he felt it weakened the mind. Similarly, many people today fear that we're weakening our children's minds by making them too dependent on computers and calculators. What do you think?

2. In many schools students spend two years of math education learning long division—a skill that's almost never used in the age of the $5 calculator. Some educators argue that students' time could be better spent learning other things. What do you think? What about calculating square roots by hand?

3. Do you think it's important for students to learn to program in LOGO, Pascal, BASIC, or some other language? Why or why not?

4. Do you think educational games are good ways for students to learn in schools? Give examples that support your arguments.

5. What kind of productivity software tools should students learn how to use? Why?

6. Think about educational goals in relation to technology. What should people be able to do with no tools? What should people be able to do if they have access to pencils, papers, and books? What should people be able to do if they have access to computer technology?

7. Describe your past school experience in terms of technology. How did it measure up? What has been missing from your education so far?

8. Do you think most families can benefit from a home computer today? Explain.

9. Do you think home computers strengthen families and communities? Explain.

10. Do you think home computers in the future will make people more or less creative? Why?

Projects

1. Try several different types of educational software. If possible, observe students using the software. Prepare a report comparing the strengths and weaknesses of each.

2. Observe how computers are used in local schools or your campus. Report on your findings.

3. Survey the Web for educational resources on a particular subject. Report on your findings.

4. Using a multimedia authoring tool or HTML, design a simple courseware lesson. Make sure you set clear goals before you start. When your project is completed, try it with several students.

5. Plan a model technology school. Describe how it would differ from conventional schools and why.

Books

How People Learn: Brain, Mind, Experience, and School, by John D. Bransford, Editor, Ann L. Brown, Editor, Rodney R. Cocking, Editor, John B. Bransford, Editor (New York: National Academy Press, 1999). This book provides a summary of research in human learning and the implications of that research. It has relevance for educators, aspiring educators, and others interested in redesigning and reforming our schools.

Mindstorms: Children, Computers, and Powerful Ideas, Second Edition, by Seymour Papert (New York: Basic Books, 1999) and ***The Children's Machine,*** by Seymour Papert (New York: Basic Books, 1994). These two books outline the views of one widely respected theorist and researcher on technology in education: Seymour Papert, the inventor of LOGO. *Mindstorms* was written during the period when Papert was doing pioneering work with LOGO. In *The Children's Machine,* Papert discusses why the computer revolution failed to revolutionize education.

The Unofficial Guide to LEGO MINDSTORMS Robots, by Jonathan B. Knudsen (Sebastopol, CA.: O'Reilly, 1999). In 1998 the LEGO group introduced the MINDSTORMS Robotics Invention System, a product for making robots out of LEGO blocks and programming them with Logo. This book is for anyone who wants to go beyond the basics with this powerful educational system.

Amusing Ourselves to Death: Public Discourse in the Age of Show Business by Neil Postman (New York: Viking Press, 1986), Technopoly: The Surrender of Culture to Technology (New York: Vintage Books, 1993), and ***The End of Education: Redefining the Value of School,*** by Neil Postman (New York, Knopf, 1995). In these books noted social critic Neil Postman takes on schools and technology, two powerful forces that are shaping our lives. In *Amusing Ourselves to Death,* Postman argues that television has injured, and is injuring, our ability to think, by reducing every public discourse to just another form of entertainment. In *Technopoly* he argues that the our tools, especially computers, no longer play supporting roles; instead, they radically shape our culture, our families, and our world views. In *The End of Education,* he presents a picture of modern education in which economic utility has become the defining principle. Postman presents compelling problems and suggests possible solutions in these important books.

That's Edutainment: A Parent's Guide to Educational Software, by Eric Brown (Berkeley, CA: Osborne/McGraw-Hill Publishing Company, 1995). This book begins with an overview of the concepts behind the kinds of educational software that's entertaining enough to compete with TV. More than half of the book is made up of detailed (and somewhat dated) software reviews. A companion cross-platform CD-ROM includes demo versions of many of the reviewed programs.

Avatars! Exploring and Building Virtual Worlds on the Internet, by Bruce Damer (Berkeley, CA: Peachpit Press, 1998). Avatars—digital representations of humans used to explore virtual worlds—have until recently existed only in science fiction. Now they're showing up in interactive games, chat rooms, and virtual cities on the Internet. This book/CD-ROM describes the technology behind avatars and provides clear instructions for launching your own personal avatars on the Web.

Digital Illusion: Entertaining the Future with High Technology, edited by Clark Dodsworth, Jr. (Reading, MA: Addison-Wesley Publishing Company, 1998). The entertainment industry is the driving force behind many of the technological breakthroughs of the information age. This fascinating collection of papers explores the future of entertainment, including video games, digital video and film, virtual reality, networked games, and immersive amusement park rides. Big fun!

High Tech, High Teach: Technology and Our Search for Meaning, John Naisbitt with Nana Naisbitt and Douglas Philips (New York: Broadway Books, 1999). In this book the author of *Megatrends* examines a future in which technology saturates every aspect of American society. What impact will this "Technologically Intoxicated Zone" have on our lives and consciousness? How will our relationship with technology evolve? These are the kinds of questions *High Tech, High Teach* tackles.

Periodicals

Learning and Leading with Technology, from ISTE (480 Charnelton St., Eugene, OR 97401-2626, 800/336-5191). ISTE (International Society for Technology in Education) is an important and influential organization whose focus is the effective use of computer technology in the classroom. *Learning and Leading with Technology* (formerly *The Computing Teacher*) is their most accessible and widely read publication.

Syllabus. This magazine focuses on higher education and technology. Themes of issues range from multimedia tools to distance education on the Web.

T.H.E. Journal (Technological Horizons in Education). This magazine covers both K–12 and higher education with a mixture of product announcements and articles.

Technos: Quarterly for Education and Technology. This publication by the Journal of the Agency for Instructional Technology bills itself as "a forum for the discussion of ideas about the use of technology in education, with a focus on reform." Most of the articles are clearly pro-technology, but many deal with controversial issues. Example: a roundtable discussion called "Violence, Games, and Art."

Family PC. This magazine is aimed mostly at parents who want to help their kids put computers to good use.

Home Office Computing. This one is geared more toward people who use their computers to work at home.

Mac Home Journal. This monthly focuses on home applications for Macintosh users.

Popular Science. This tinkerer's magazine is a good source of information on the latest computerized gadgets for consumers.

World Wide Web

The Web is bursting with exciting educational material, much of it created by students. Check the *Computer Confluence* Web site for links to many sites devoted to learning and teaching. You'll also find a sampling of Web links related to entertainment, family life, and home applications.

Chapter

16

Inventing the Future

AFTER YOU READ THIS CHAPTER YOU SHOULD BE ABLE TO:

Describe several strategies for predicting the future.

List several trends in information technology that are likely to continue for a few more years.

Outline several research areas that may produce breakthroughs in computer technology in the next few decades.

Predict how the coming information infrastructure will affect our lives, our work, and our global economy.

Describe some of the social and psychological risks of the information age.

In this chapter:

▶ How to predict the future
▶ Technology over the horizon
▶ Visions of the future
▶ Important, difficult questions
▶ The gift of fire
...and more.

On the CD-ROM:

▶ AT&T's intelligent agents network in action
▶ Nanotechnology on video
▶ Video demonstration of 3-D models used to choreograph
▶ Instant access to glossary and key word references
▶ Interactive self-study quizzes
...and more.

On the Web:

www.prenhall.com/beekman

▶ Articles and books on cutting-edge technology
▶ Links to the labs
▶ Discussions of biotechnology, microtechnology, and nanotechnology
▶ Self-study exercises
...and more.

The best way to predict the future is to
invent it.

—Alan Kay

Alan Kay has been inventing the future for most of his life. Kay was a child prodigy who grew up in a world rich with books, ideas, music, and interesting people. As a child he composed original music, built a harpsichord, and appeared on NBC as a "Quiz Kid." Kay's genius wasn't reflected in his grades; he had trouble conforming to the rigid structure of the schools he attended. After high school he worked as a jazz guitarist and an Air Force programmer before attending college.

His Ph.D. project was one of the first microcomputers, and one of several that Kay would eventually develop. In 1968 Kay was in the audience when Douglas Engelbart stunned the computer science world with a futuristic demonstration of interactive computing (see Chapter 7). Inspired by Engelbart's demonstration, Kay led a team of researchers at Xerox PARC (Palo Alto Research Center in California) in building the computer of the future—a computer that put the user in charge.

Working on a back-room computer called the Alto, Kay developed a bit-mapped screen display with icons and overlapping windows—the kind of display that became standard two decades later. Kay also championed the idea of a friendly user interface. To test user friendliness, Kay frequently brought children into the lab, "because they have no strong motivation for patience." With feedback from children, Kay developed the first painting program and Smalltalk, the groundbreaking object-oriented programming language.

In essence Kay's team developed the first personal computer—a single-user desktop machine designed for interactive use. But Kay, who coined the term "personal computer," didn't see the Alto as one. In his mind a true personal computer could go everywhere with its owner, serving as a calculator, a calendar, a word processor, a graphics machine, a communication device, and a reference tool. Kay's vision of what he called the *Dynabook* is only now, three decades later, appearing on the horizon.

Alan Kay.

Xerox failed to turn the Alto into a commercial success. But when he visited PARC, Apple's Steve Jobs (see Chapter 3) was inspired by what he saw. Under Jobs a team of engineers and programmers built on the Xerox ideas, added many of their own, and developed the

Alan Kay's Dynabook was the early prototype for the modern personal computer.

Macintosh—the first inexpensive personal computer to incorporate many of Kay's far-reaching ideas. Kay became a research fellow at Apple, where he called the Macintosh "the first personal computer good enough to criticize." Today virtually all PCs have user interfaces based on those that Kay developed at Xerox and helped refine at Apple.

Today Kay works as a research fellow for Disney, where he applies his vision to emerging technologies in communication, entertainment, and education. Kay contin-ues his crusade for users, especially small users. He says, as with pencil and paper, "it's not a medium if children can't use it." In a recent collaborative research project, Kay and MIT researchers worked with schoolchildren to design artificial life forms in artificial environments inside the computer. Like many of Kay's research projects, the Vivarium project had little relationship to today's computer market. This kind of blue-sky research doesn't always lead to products or profits. But for Alan Kay it's the way to invent the future. ◻

The future is being invented every day by people like Alan Kay—people who can see today the technology that will be central to tomorrow's society. We're racing into a future shaped by information technology. In this chapter we explore strategies for seeing into the future. We use those strategies to imagine how information technology might evolve and how that technology might affect our lives.

Tomorrow Never Knows

It is the unexpected that always happens.

—Old English proverb

There is no denying the importance of the future. In the words of scientist Charles F. Kettering, "We should be concerned about the future because we will have to spend the rest of our lives there." However, important or not, the future isn't easy to see.

The Hazards of Predicting the Future

Everything that can be invented has been invented.

—Charles H. Duell, **director of the U.S. Patent Office, 1899**

Who the hell wants to hear actors talk?

—Harry M. Warner, **Warner Bros. Pictures, 1927**

There is no likelihood man can ever tap the power of the atom.

—Robert Millikan, **winner of the Nobel Prize in Physics, 1923**

In 1877, when Thomas Edison invented the phonograph, he thought of it as an office dictating machine and lost interest in it; recorded music did not become popular until 21 years later. When the Wright brothers offered their invention to the U.S. government and the British Royal Navy, they were told airplanes had no future in the military. A 1900 Mercedes-Benz study estimated that worldwide demand for cars would not exceed 1 million, primarily because of the limited number of available chauffeurs. History is full of stories of people who couldn't imagine the impact of new technology.

Technology is hard to foresee, and it is even harder to predict the impact that technology will have on society. Who could have predicted in 1950 the profound effects, both positive and negative, television would have on our world?

Four Ways to Predict the Future

According to Alan Kay, there are four ways to predict the future. The best way is to invent the future, but it's not the only way.

Another way to predict the future is to take advantage of the fact that it generally takes 10 years to go from a new idea in the research laboratory to a commercial product. In today's highly competitive high-tech industry, many companies are able to shave some years off the research-to-product interval. In any case, today's research can give us an idea of the kinds of products we will be using in a few years. Of course, many researchers work behind carefully guarded doors, and research often takes surprising turns.

A third way is to look at products from the past and see what made them succeed. According to Kay, "There are certain things about human beings that if you remove, they wouldn't be human any more. For instance, we have to communicate with others or we're not humans. So every time someone has come up with a communications amplifier, it has succeeded the previous technology." The pen, the printing press, the telephone, the television, the personal computer, and the Internet are all successful communication amplifiers. What's next?

Finally, Kay says we can predict the future by recognizing the four phases of any technology or media business: hardware, software, service, and way of life. These phases apply to radio, television, video, audio, and all kinds of computers.

The 1930 movie *Just Imagine* presented a bold, if not quite accurate, vision of the future; here Maureen O'Sullivan sits in her personal flying machine.

- ▶ *Hardware.* Inventors and engineers start the process by developing new hardware. But whether it's a television set, a personal computer, or a global communication network, the hardware is of little use without software.

- ▶ *Software.* The next step is software development. Television programs, audio recordings, video games, databases, and Web pages are examples of software that give value to hardware products.

- ▶ *Service.* Once the hardware and software exist, the focus turns to service. Innovative hardware and clever software aren't likely to take hold unless they serve human needs in some way. The personal computer industry is now in the service phase, and the companies that focus on serving their customers are generally the most successful.

- ▶ *Way of life.* The final phase happens when the technology becomes so entrenched that people don't think about it any more; they only notice if it isn't there. We seldom think of pencils as technological tools. They're part of our way of life, so much so that we'd have trouble getting along without them. Similarly, the electric motor, which was once a major technological breakthrough, is now all but invisible; we use dozens of motors every day without thinking about them. Computers are clearly headed in that direction.

Kay's four ways of predicting the future don't provide a foolproof crystal ball, but they can serve as a framework for thinking about tomorrow's technology. In the next section we turn our attention to research labs, where tomorrow's technology is being invented today. We examine trends and innovations that will shape future computer hardware and software. Then we *look* at how this technology will serve users as it eventually disappears into our way of life.

From Research to Reality: 21st-Century Information Technology

> You can count how many seeds are in the apple, but not how many apples are in the seed.
>
> —**Ken Kesey, author of *One Flew over the Cuckoo's Nest***

In laboratories scattered around the planet, ideas are sprouting from the minds of engineers and scientists that will collectively shape the future of information technology. While we can't be sure which of these ideas will bear fruit, we can speculate based on current trends.

Tomorrow's Hardware: Trends and Innovations

> The only thing that has consistently grown faster than hardware in the last 40 years is human expectation.
>
> —**Bjarne Stroustrup, AT&T Bell Labs, designer of the C++ programming language**

The rapid evolution of computer hardware over the last few decades is nothing short of extraordinary. Computer hardware has relentlessly improved by several measures:

▶ *Speed.* The relay-based Mark I computer (discussed in Chapter 1) could do only a few calculations each second. Today's personal computers are more than a million times faster! Computer speed today typically is measured in **MIPS (millions of instructions per second)**, where an instruction is the most primitive operation performed by the processor—moving a number to a memory location, comparing two numbers, and the like. The fastest machines can process more than *a billion* instructions per second!

▶ *Size.* Warehouse-sized computers are history. The central components of a modern personal computer are stored on a few tiny chips that could fit in your pocket; the only parts of the system that occupy significant space on the desktop are peripherals.

▶ *Efficiency.* As the story goes, ENIAC, the first large-scale computer (see Chapter 1), dimmed the lights of Philadelphia when it was turned on. A modern desktop computer consumes about as much electricity as a television set. Portable computers consume even less.

▶ *Capacity.* Modern optical, magnetic, and semiconductor storage devices have all but eliminated storage as a constraint for most computing jobs.

▶ *Cost.* Industry watchers have pointed out that if the price of cars had dropped as fast as the price of computer chips, it would be cheaper to abandon a parked car than to put money in the meter!

Most experts believe these trends will continue, at least for a few years. If they do, we can expect the *price-to-performance ratio* (the level of performance per unit cost) to double every year or two for several more years. There are barriers on the horizon—engineers eventually will bump up against the physical limitations of silicon and other materials. But

The IBM S/390 G6 server performs up to 1.6 billion instructions per second—almost 1 billion times the performance of the historic Mark I—at a cost that is far less than a mainframe or supercomputer.

as Robert Noyce, co-inventor of the integrated circuit, pointed out, these barriers have seemed to be about 10 years away for many years. So far engineers have continued to find ways to push the barriers back.

The trends are undeniable, but it would be a mistake to assume that tomorrow's computer will simply be a smaller, more powerful version of today's PC. Technological advances emerging from laboratories will accelerate current trends and push computer technology in entirely new directions. Here are just a few examples:

These eyeglasses allow the wearer to see a computer display superimposed over the "real" world outside the glasses.

▶ *Alternative chip technologies.* Many research labs are experimenting with alternatives to today's silicon chips. For example, IBM researchers have developed plastic chips that are more durable and energy efficient than silicon chips. Chip makers Intel, Motorola, and AMD are working with the U.S. government in a Virtual National Laboratory (VNL) to develop new laser etching technology called *extreme ultraviolet lithography (EUVL)* that could reduce chip size and increase performance radically. Other researchers are working on more radical research technologies. *Superconductors* that transmit electricity without heat could increase computer speed a hundredfold. Unfortunately, superconductor technology generally requires a super-cooled environment, which isn't practical for most applications. A more realistic alternative is the **optical computer**, which transmits information in light waves rather than electrical pulses. Optical computers outside research labs are currently limited to a few narrow applications such as robot vision. But when the technology is refined, general-purpose optical computers may process information hundreds of times faster than silicon computers.

▶ *Alternative architectures.* Some of the most revolutionary work in computer design involves not what's inside the processors, but how they're put together. One example is IBM's Blue Gene, a supercomputer being developed to help scientists crack the secrets of proteins in the human body. Blue Gene will have 1 million small, simple processors, each capable of handling 8 threads of instructions simultaneously. The processors won't have power-hungry embedded caches, but they will have built-in memory to improve speed. The network of processors will be self-healing–it will detect failed components, seal them off, and direct work elsewhere. If it works as planned, Blue Gene will be the first "petaflop" computer, capable of handling 1 quadrillion (1,000,000,000,000,000) instructions per second—2 million times more than today's PC!

▶ *Alternative storage technologies.* Smaller disks that hold more—the trend will continue, producing hard disks that can store astronomical quantities of data. But solid state storage breakthroughs will threaten the dominance of disks in a few years. For example, Cambridge University researchers funded by Hitachi have developed a "single-electron" memory chip the size of a thumbnail that can store all the sounds and images of a full-length feature film. This experimental chip consumes very little power and retains memory for up to 10 years when the power is switched off.

Researcher Joe Jacobsen is developing digital paper at MIT; here he shows off some digitally printed tabs developed by an undergraduate researcher.

▶ *Alternative output displays.* The CRT's days are numbered. Flat-panel screens are commonplace today. Soon we'll be using ultra-high-resolution displays that are thin enough to hang on walls like pictures and efficient enough to run on batteries for days. Goggle displays—the visual equivalent to headphones—will be common for portable PC users who want to shut the rest of the world out. Those who need to see what's going on around them *and* inside their computer can wear eyeglasses with built-in transparent heads-up displays. Researchers at MIT's Media Lab, Xerox PARC, and elsewhere are working on pages made of *electronic (digital) paper* that can be read like printed pages, erased, and reused. Electronic paper is likely to find applications in newspapers that automatically update, magazines that display animated images, textbooks that can be revised rather than replaced, and wall-sized folding digital displays.

Sensors give digital computers windows into the analog world. The ImagiProbe sensing device allows this scientist to collect water quality data in a Visor handheld computer.

▶ *Alternative input devices: sensors.* Technology forecaster Paul Saffo predicts that the next major breakthroughs will occur as researchers develop—and companies market—inexpensive sensors that allow digital devices to monitor the analog world. Temperature sensors, optical sensors, motion sensors, and other types of sensors already make it possible for computers to track a variety of real-world activities and conditions. But as these technologies mature, more sophisticated devices will serve as eyes, ears, and other types of sense organs for computer networks. In 1997 Saffo wrote in a special anniversary issue of the *Communications of the ACM*:

Two parallel universes currently exist—an everyday analog universe that we inhabit, and a newer digital universe created by humans, but inhabited by digital machines. We visit this digital world by peering through the portholes of our computer screens, and we manipulate with keyboard and mouse much as a nuclear technician works with radioactive material via glovebox and manipulator arms. . . . Now we are handing sensory organs and manipulators to the machines and inviting them to enter into analog reality. The scale of possible surprise this may generate over the next several decades as sensors, lasers, and microprocessors co-evolve is breathtakingly uncertain.

Tomorrow's Software: Evolving Applications and Interfaces

Our goal was bug-free. The new goal is resiliency.
It is much more important to recover from exceptions than to avoid them.

—Bob Frankston, in *Beyond Calculation*

In any economy *infrastructures* are the frameworks that are laid so future economic activity can take advantage of them. Just as the railroads provided the transportation network for the expanding 19th-century American economy, the airline and highway systems have served as the American economic infrastructure for much of this century. In the same way, tomorrow's economy is being shaped by an emerging information infrastructure of computers and networks. Computers and networks are essential parts of the information infrastructure, but they're of little value without software.

In computer research, software continues to be the hardest part. Chapter 12 included discussions of programming technologies, including object-oriented programming languages and visual programming environments. These technologies can help programmers produce more reliable software in less time. But computer scientists aren't even close to developing tools that will allow programmers to produce error-free software quickly.

Still, software technology is advancing rapidly, especially when viewed through the eyes of the user. Twenty years ago the typical computer could be operated only by a highly trained professional, and using a computer was pretty much synonymous with programming a computer; today computers are so easy to use that they're sold at shopping malls and operated by preschoolers. Fifteen years ago documents couldn't easily be transported between computers, or even between different applications on the same computer; today networks can provide seamless communication across platforms and applications, so hardware and software differences are no longer barriers.

The graphical user interface pioneered by Xerox and popularized by Apple and Microsoft has become an industry standard, making it possible for users to move back and forth between computer types almost as easily as drivers can adjust to different brands of cars. (Imagine what would happen if Ford or GM moved the brake pedal to the opposite side of the accelerator in next year's models.) But experts expect user interfaces to continue to evolve for a while before they settle down into the kind of long-lasting standard we're used to in automobiles. Today's *WIMP* (windows, icons, menus, and pointing devices) interface is easier to learn and use than earlier character-based interfaces, but it's not the end of the user interface evolution. Researcher Raj Reddy uses

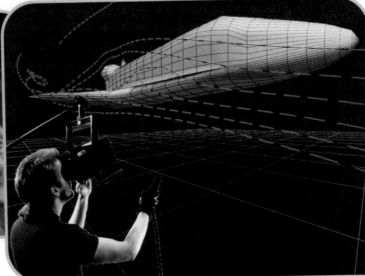

another acronym to describe emerging user interface technologies: *SILK*, for speech, image, language, and knowledge capabilities. SILK incorporates many important software technologies:

In Argonne's CAVE (left), a scientist can interactively study the relationships between the nucleic acids of the molecule. An engineer (right) uses a virtual reality glove to place tracer particles in the air flow over the surface of an aircraft in a virtual wind tunnel; the image behind him in this photo is what he sees in his VR goggles.

▶ *Speech and language.* While we still don't have a language-translating telephone or a foolproof dictation-taking "talkwriter," *speech technology* is rapidly maturing into a practical alternative to keyboard and mouse input. Voice recognition systems are used for security systems, automated voicemail systems, hands-free Web navigation, and other applications. New applications are being developed and marketed every day. With or without speech, *natural-language processing* of English-like commands will be part of future user interfaces. Researchers expect that we'll soon be using programs that read documents as we create them, edit them according to our instructions, and file them based on their content.

▶ *Image.* In the last decade computer graphics have become an integral part of the computing experience. Tomorrow's graphics won't just be still, flat images; they'll include three-dimensional models, animation, and video clips. Today's two-dimensional desktop interfaces will give way to three-dimensional workspace metaphors complete with 3-D animated objects—virtual workspaces unlike anything we use today. Virtual reality (VR) user interfaces will create the illusion that the user is immersed in a world inside the computer—an environment that contains both scenes and the controls to change those scenes.

▶ *Knowledge.* Many experts predict that knowledge will be the most important enhancement to the user interface of the future. Advances in the technology of knowledge—that elusive quality discussed in Chapter 13—will allow engineers to design self-maintaining systems—systems that can diagnose and correct common problems without human intervention. Advances in knowledge will make user interfaces more friendly and forgiving. Intelligent applications will be able to decipher many ambiguous commands and correct common errors as they happen. But more importantly, knowledge will allow software agents to really be of service to users.

Tomorrow's Service: Truly Intelligent Agents

I don't want to sit and move stuff around on my screen all day and look at figures and have it recognize my gestures and listen to my voice. I want to tell it what to do and then go away; I don't want to babysit this computer. I want it to act for me, not with me.

—Esther Dyson, **computer industry analyst and publisher**

At Xerox PARC Alan Kay and his colleagues developed the first user interface based on icons—images that represent tools to be manipulated by users. Their pioneering work helped turn the computer into a productivity tool for millions of people. Today Alan Kay claims future user interfaces will be based on agents rather than tools.

Agents are software programs designed to be managed rather than manipulated. An intelligent software agent can ask questions as well as respond to commands, pay attention to its user's work patterns, serve as a guide and a coach, take on its owner's goals, and use reasoning to fabricate goals of its own.

Many PC applications include *wizards* and other agent-like software entities to guide users through complex tasks and answer questions when problems arise. The Internet is home to a rapidly growing population of bots—software robots that crawl around the Web collecting information, helping consumers make decisions, answering email, and even playing games. But today's wizards, bots, and agents aren't smart enough to manage the many details that a human assistant might juggle.

Tomorrow's agents will be better able to compete with human assistants, though. A well-trained software agent in the future might accomplish these tasks:

- ▶ Remind you that it's time to get the tires rotated on your car, and make an appointment for the rotation.

- ▶ Distribute notes to the other members of your study group or work group, and tell you which members opened those notes.

- ▶ Keep you posted on new articles on subjects that interest you, and know enough about those subjects to be selective without being rigid.

- ▶ Manage your appointments and *keep* track of your communications.

- ▶ Teach you new applications and answer reference questions.

- ▶ Defend your system and your home from viruses, intruders, and other security breaches.

- ▶ Help protect your privacy on and off the Net.

Agents are often portrayed with human characteristics; *2001's* Hal and the computers on TV's *Star Trek* are famous examples. Of course, agents don't need to look or sound human—they just need to possess considerable knowledge and intelligence.

Future agents may possess a degree of sensitivity, too. Researchers at MIT and IBM are developing *affective computers* that can detect the emotional states of their users and respond accordingly. Affective computers use sensors to determine a person's emotional state. Sensors range from simple audiovisual devices to mouse-embedded sensors that work like lie detectors, monitoring pulse or skin resistance. Early research has shown limited success at identifying emotions, but the machines still have much to learn. They can't for example, tell the difference between love and hate, because, from a physiological point of view, they look pretty much the same!

Tomorrow's Way of Life: Transparent Technology

In the first computing revolution, the ratio of people to computers was N-to-1.
In the second revolution, personal computers insisted the ratio be 1-to-1—
one person, one computer. In the third revolution, we are exploring the
impact of having computers everywhere, many per person, 1-to-N.

—**Bob Metcalfe, inventor of Ethernet and founder of 3Com**

The most profound technologies are those that disappear.
They weave themselves into the fabric of everyday life
until they are indistinguishable from it.

—**Mark Weiser, head of the Xerox PARC Computer Science Laboratory**

A wireless network allows this student to connect to the Internet from a quiet spot on campus.

Since Alan Kay coined the term *personal computer* at Xerox PARC, hundreds of millions of personal computers have been sold. Today many researchers think that it's time to move beyond the PC because it commands too much of our attention. According to user interface expert Donald A. Norman, the PC has three main problems:

1 A single device designed to perform many tasks can't do every task in a superior manner.

2 A single machine can't suit every person in the world.

3 The PC business model of yearly upgrades increases the level of complexity in the machines.

At the 2000 Consumer Electronics Show, Sun Microsystems displayed a kitchen of the future. This refrigerator, like the other appliances in the kitchen, is connected to the Internet.

Norman, like other experts, believes we're entering a *post-PC era*. "This will be the generation where the technology disappears into the tool, serving valuable functions but keeping out of the way—the generation of the invisible computer."

Embedded Intelligence

Computers are disappearing into more of our tools all the time. Information appliances, including cell phones, fax machines, and GPS devices, perform their specialized functions while hiding the technological details from their users. Dozens of household appliances and tools have invisible computers. Even our cars are processing megabytes of information as we drive down the road.

Some automobile computers are invisible; others are more obvious. Several companies have introduced dashboard computers that can play CDs, play CD-ROMs, recognize spoken commands, alert the driver to incoming email messages, read those messages aloud, store and retrieve contacts and appointments, dial phone numbers, and recite directions using GPS-based navigation systems. Some include a GPS-based security system that will track the vehicle in the event of theft or other emergency. Others monitor vehicle systems and report problems.

Computers may soon be part of our clothing, too. Most of today's *wearable computers* are strap-on units for active information gatherers. But researchers at MIT and elsewhere are stitching CPUs, keyboards, and touchpads right into the clothes, turning their wearers into wireless Internet nodes. These digital outfits aren't just high-tech fashion statements—when worn with the eyeglass monitors described earlier in the chapter, they might be invaluable for any number of jobs that require both activity and connectivity.

In Japan computer technology has even found its way into the bathroom. A number of Japanese fixture manufacturers sell *smart toilets*—computer-controlled, paperless toilets. Some models automatically collect and store information on blood pressure, pulse, temperature, urine, and weight. The information can be displayed on an LCD display, accumulated for months, and even transmitted by modem to a medical service. Users of these smart toilets get a mini-checkup whenever they visit the bathroom. Body-monitoring features give the toilet an entirely new function—a function that will undoubtedly save lives.

This wearable computer can do just about anything a PC can do without ever leaving your wrist.

Ubiquitous Computers

When computers show up in our toilets, we're clearly entering an era of *ubiquitous computers*—computers everywhere. For several years

Xerox PARC's ubiquitous computers come in three sizes: boards (left), pads (top right), and tabs (bottom right).

researchers at Xerox PARC, Cambridge University, and Olivetti have been experimenting with technology that will make computers even more ubiquitous. A PARC group is working with three sizes of ubiquitous computers: inch-scale *tabs* that are like smart Post-It Notes and badges, foot-scale *pads* that are like smart notebooks and books, and yard-scale *boards* that are like smart bulletin boards and blackboards. Researchers envision a future office with hundreds of these intelligent devices communicating with each other through wireless networks while workers casually move them around their offices.

The best known computer in their futuristic office is the active badge discussed in Chapter 11—a clip-on computerized ID badge first developed at an Olivetti-Cambridge research lab. The active badge continually reports its location to record-keeping databases and to others in the organization. According to PARC's Mark Weiser, in experimental offices equipped with active badges, "doors open only to the right badge wearer, rooms greet people by name, telephone calls can be automatically forwarded to wherever the recipient may be, receptionists actually know where people are, computer terminals retrieve the preferences of whoever is sitting at them, and appointment diaries write themselves."

From Internet to Omninet

Connectivity is a critical part of ubiquitous computing. When computers are embedded in everything, they need to be able to talk to each other—and to us. By connecting embedded computers to the Net, we give them voices and ears. All of these smart, connected devices will certainly change the Internet. As more machines become connected, the Net will evolve from today's loose digital fishnet into a tightly-woven, seamless fabric that surrounds us. In the words of Leonard Kleinrock, the UCLA computer scientist who set up the first ARPANET node three decades ago, "Tech will be everywhere, always there, always on, just the way electricity is there for you." Human communication will be a tiny fraction of the traffic on the Net—the great majority will be machines communicating with other machines on behalf of humans. MIT AI lab director Rodney Brooks says "It won't be that you go onto the Internet—the network will come to you." Brooks is part of MIT's Oxygen, a research project that attempts to make computing as plentiful and ubiquitous as the air we breathe.

Ubiquitous computers offer convenience and efficiency beyond anything that's come before. They also raise serious questions about personal privacy, intimacy, and independence. But we'll face even more serious questions when the streams of information technology and biotechnology converge.

The Day after Tomorrow: Information Technology Meets Biology

Our future is technological; but it will not be a world of gray steel.
Rather our technological future is headed toward a
neo-biological civilization.

—Kevin Kelly, in *Out of Control*

The information age won't last forever. Analysts Stan Davis and Bill Davidson predict in their book *2020 Vision* that a bio-economy will replace the information economy sometime around the year 2020. Whether or not they're right, biotechnology and microtechnology will become more intertwined with information technology in the coming decades. There's no telling exactly what the results will be, but the possibilities are both intriguing and disturbing.

Borrowing from Biology

Ubiquitous computing will require new ways of thinking about, and developing, hardware and software. At the University of California, researchers on a project called Endeavor attempt to chart our course into the digital ocean of the future. According to Professor Randy Katz, the lead investigator of Endeavor, "The supercomplex system of the future has to be able to organize itself so it can be more robust in its behavior, deal with failure, and then pick up the pieces and move on." In other words, the network of the future will be more like a biological system. Neural nets, described in Chapter 13, allow individual computers to learn from experience because their design is inspired by biological nervous systems. Many researchers are experimenting with *genetic algorithms*—algorithms that evolve through many generations, creating survival-of-the-fittest programs. Paul Saffo, director of the Institute for the Future, suggests a biological imperative, too: "The network of today is engineered, and the network of 2050 is grown."

This motor, photographed through an electron microscope, is 250 microns wide. A human hair is included in the picture for comparison purposes.

Microtechnology

The incredible miniaturization achieved in the computer industry is allowing researchers to use microtechnology to develop *micromachines*—machines on the scale of a *millionth* of a meter. Microscopic moving parts are etched in silicon using a process similar to that of manufacturing computer chips. Major universities, corporations (including IBM and AT&T), government labs (including Sandia Labs), and small start-up companies are doing research in what are sometimes called *microelectromechanical systems (MEMS)*. For example, engineers at the University of California at Berkeley have built a motor twice as wide as a human hair that runs on static electricity. Japanese researchers have constructed a micro-car not much bigger than a grain of rice.

So far most applications of microtechnology have been *microsensors*: tiny devices that can detect pressure, temperature, and other environmental qualities. Microsensors are used in cars, planes, and spacecraft, but they show promise in medicine, too. Researchers at Johns Hopkins University have developed a *smart pill* that combines a thermometer with a transmitter so it can broadcast temperatures as it travels through a human digestive tract. This pill is a first step toward other pills that might play more active roles inside our bodies. Scientists speculate that tiny machines may someday be able to roam through the body, locating and destroying cancer cells and invading organisms!

Nanotechnology

If microtechnology is carried to its extreme, it becomes nanotechnology—the manufacture of machines on a scale of a few billionths of a meter. *Nanomachines* would have to be constructed atom by atom using processes drawn from particle physics, biophysics, and molecular biology. Researchers at UCLA, Hewlett-Packard, and other facilities are working on *molecular-scale electronics (moletronics)* that could eventually produce a breed of computers that performs *billions* of times faster than today's fastest machines. Hewlett Packard's Stanley Williams and others are working on technology that may soon allow wires and switches to chemically assemble themselves at the molecular level, eliminating the need to etch circuits onto chips.

Scientists at Yale and Rice universities report they've built a molecular-scale electrical circuit that can be switched on and off—just like their larger silicon-based cousins. The technological breakthrough could herald the era of ubiquitous supercomputing—computers so small they could be woven into the fibers of clothing, using body heat or ambient light for power. More important, many researchers think that molecular circuits could be produced at a fraction of the cost of today's complex microprocessors, because they're built through a purely chemical, or "self-assembly," process, similar to growing a crystal. "If we can truly make this kind of technology manufacturable. . . we'll have computing that's cheap enough to throw away," says Yale scientist Mark Reed, a co-author of the study. IBM scientists have developed a scanning/tunneling microscope that allows them to see and move individual atoms. Using this device, a team of physicists created a tiny switch that relies on the motion of a single atom. Using another approach, biophysicists are studying natural molecular machines like the protein rotor that spins a bacterium's

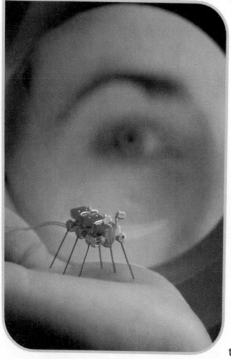

Tiny insect robots like these may be the forerunners of silicon-and-steel artificial life forms.

flagellum tail, hoping to use their findings to create molecular motors. Scientists at MIT are attempting to get E. coli bacteria to respond like circuits. At the same time, geneticists are gradually unlocking the secrets of DNA—biology's self-replicating molecular memory devices. These and other research threads may lead scientists to the breakthrough that will allow them to create atomic assembler devices that can construct nanomachines. Submicron computers, germ-sized robots, self-assembling machines, intelligent clothes, alchemy . . . the possibilities are staggering and the potential risks terrifying.

Artificial Life

For many researchers, the ultimate goal is to create artificial life—synthetic organisms that act like natural living systems. Some artificial life researchers create simple software organisms that exist only in computer memory; many of these organisms are similar to the computer viruses discussed in Chapter 11. Other researchers build colonies of tiny insect robots that communicate with each other and respond to changes in their environment. Artificial life researchers grapple with an array of problems, including the question of definition: Where exactly is the line between a clever machine and a living organism?

Advances in artificial intelligence, robotics, genetics, biotechnology, and microtechnology may someday make the line disappear altogether. Computers and robots will undoubtedly continue to take on more functions that have been traditionally reserved for humans. They may even grow and reproduce using carbon-based genetic technology borrowed from human biology. If they become smart enough to build intelligent machines themselves, almost anything is possible.

This speculation raises questions about the relationship between humans and the machines they create. It's important that we think about those questions while the technology is evolving, because our answers may help us to determine the course of that evolution.

Human Questions for a Computer Age

> The important thing to forecast is not the automobile but the parking problem; not the television but the soap opera.
>
> —Isaac Asimov

> The real question before us lies here: do these instruments further life and its values or not?
>
> —Lewis Mumford, **1934**

In earlier chapters we examined many social and ethical issues related to computer technology, including privacy, security, reliability, and intellectual property. These aren't the only critical issues before us. Before closing we'll briefly raise some other important, and as yet unanswered, questions of the information age.

Will Computers Be Democratic?

> The higher the technology, the higher the freedom. Technology enforces certain solutions: satellite dishes, computers, videos, international telephone lines force pluralism and freedom onto a society.
>
> —Lech Walesa

> The advanced technologies of information are also technologies of disinformation.
>
> —Stewart Brand, in *The Media Lab*

In 1990 a spontaneous protest exploded across computer networks in reaction to the threat to privacy posed by Marketplace, a new CD-ROM product containing consumer information on millions of Americans. The firestorm of protest forced Lotus Development Corporation to cancel distribution of the product. In Santa Monica, California, homeless people used public access terminals in the library to lobby successfully for more access to public showers. In France student organizations used computer networks to rapidly mobilize opposition to tuition increases. In 1999, environmentalists, labor organizations, human rights groups, and a handful of anarchists used the Internet to mobilize massive protests at the World Trade Organization's Seattle meeting. The protests brought many issues surrounding the secretive WTO into the global spotlight for the first time.

Computers are often used to promote the democratic ideals and causes of common people. Many analysts argue that modern computer technology is, by its very nature, a force for equality and democracy. On the other hand, many powerful people and organizations use information technology to increase their wealth and influence.

Will personal computers and the Internet empower ordinary citizens to make better lives for themselves? Or will computer technology produce a society of technocrats and technopeasants? Will computerized polls help elected officials better serve the needs of their constituents? Or will they just give the powerful another tool for staying in power? Will networks revitalize participatory democracy through electronic town meetings? Or will they give tyrants the tools to monitor and control citizens?

Will the Global Village Be a Community?

Progress in commercial information technologies will improve productivity, bring the world closer together, and enhance the quality of life.

—Stan Davis and Bill Davidson, in *2020 Vision*

When machines and computers, profit motives and property rights are considered more important than people, the giant triplets of racism, materialism, and militarism are incapable of being conquered.

—Martin Luther King, Jr.

A typical computer today contains components from dozens of countries. The modern corporation uses computer networks for instant communication among offices scattered around the world; information doesn't stop at international borders as it flows through networks that span the globe. Information technology allows organizations to overcome the age-old barriers of space and time, but questions remain.

In the post–Cold War era, will information technology be used to further peace, harmony, and understanding? Or will the intense competition of the global marketplace simply create new kinds of wars—information wars? Will electronic interconnections provide new opportunities for economically depressed countries? Or will they simply make it easier for information-rich countries to exploit developing nations from a distance? Will information technology be used to promote and preserve diverse communities, cultures, and ecosystems? Or will it undercut traditions, cultures, and roots?

Prometheus brings fire from the heavens to humanity.

Will We Become Information Slaves?

Our inventions are wont to be pretty toys which distract our attention from serious things. They are but improved means to an unimproved end.

—Henry David Thoreau

Computers are useless. They can only give you answers.

—Pablo Picasso

The information age has redefined our environment; it's almost as if the human species has been transplanted into a different world. Even though the change has happened almost overnight, most of us can't imagine going back to a world without computers. Still, the rapid changes raise questions.

Can human bodies and minds adapt to the higher stimulation, faster pace, and constant change of the information age? Will our information-heavy environment cause us to lose touch with the more fundamental human needs? Will we become so dependent on our "pretty toys" that we can't get by without them? Will we lose our sense of purpose and identity as our machines become more intelligent? Or will we learn to balance the demands of the technology with our biological and spiritual needs?

Standing on the Shoulders of Giants

If I have seen farther than other men, it is because
I stood on the shoulders of giants.

—Isaac Newton

When we use computers, we're standing on the shoulders of Charles Babbage, Ada Lovelace, Alan Turing, Grace Hopper, Doug Engelbart, Alan Kay, and hundreds of others who invented the future for us. Because of their foresight and effort we can see farther than those who came before us.

In Greek mythology Prometheus (whose name means "forethought") stole fire from Zeus and gave it to humanity, along with all arts and civilization. Zeus was furious when he discovered what Prometheus had done. He feared that fire would make mortals think they were as great as the gods and that they would abuse its power. Like fire, the computer is a powerful and malleable tool. It can be used to empower or imprison, to explore or exploit, to create or destroy. We can choose. We've been given the tools. It's up to all of us to invent the future.

Borg in the Mirror

Peter Cochrane

Throughout this book we've examined the convergence—the conflu- ence—of technologies. In October, 1999, Forbes ASAP *published a special issue on* The Great Convergence. *In this article abridged from that issue, Peter Cochrane speculates about the next convergence—the coming together of human and machine. Cochrane is the head of research at British Telecommunications a faculty member at the University of Bristol, and the author of* Tips for Time Travelers.

It's easy to imagine a future where information merges onto one global network. In one way or another, the Internet will absorb radio, television, personal computers, telephones, cameras, and so on.

But this is a baby step.

The next real technological advance is a radical symbiosis between humans and machines. The future will be about the cre- ation of networked machinery and digital intelligence to help us deal with a world that's changing faster than our "wet ware" (brains) has evolved to accommodate. And that future demands a subsumption of technology itself into our carbon forms.

Just think of the millions of people with pacemakers, cochlear implants, pain relief modules, and other forms of electronics already embedded in their bodies. Their numbers remind us that we don't just use information technology to communicate, enter- tain, sell, and trade but to sustain life itself.

Right now, at the frontier of this research are paraplegics with chips implanted in their heads that interpret their brain signals, allowing them to control their computers by thinking—and, in the process, pioneering a new communications channel. Experiments with silicon retinal implants have also been encouraging. Early work on the use of silicon tracks to bypass spinal and other mas- sive nervous system damage is also producing positive results. Waiting in the wings is the artificial pancreas. So is the internal pharmacy: Imagine confidently traveling the world knowing you carry a drugstore inside your own body that is ready to dispense, electronically, the right antibiotic on demand.

On the far horizon is the possibility of using silicon brain implants to enhance our memory and computational skills, and even to enable us to directly interface with machines. Impossible? On the contrary, the idea is about as wild as the crystal set radio of 1914 evolving to become the mobile phone of 1984. I remem- ber suggesting in 1996 that chip implants would eradicate the need for keys, passports, drivers' licenses, identity cards, money, bank accounts, and central medical records. Two years later Professor Kevin Warwick at the University of Reading (in the U.K.) had a chip implanted in his arm to open doors automatically, allowing him access to secure buildings and to be tracked by his secretary. I now hear that diplomats are having similar electronic implants to counteract abduction. Obvious extensions would of course include the tagging of prisoners and criminals.

But medical and security purposes aside, the real reason we will invite computers into our brains is that we increasingly face problems far too complex for the human mind and intellect to solve—even to contemplate.

We need a third intelligence to help us cope with a world of growing complexity that has far outstripped our biological evolu- tion. We need to assimilate more information and make decisions faster. A century ago a doctor could have read every published dis- course on every aspect of medicine. The same was true for chemists, physicists, and engineers. Today a doctor could spend every waking hour reading the research papers on urology alone and still not be fully up-to-date. What chance for managers and politicians? Not a lot! We know less and less about more and more. Yet business, government, academia, and many other disci- plines demand that we know ever more.

To cope and thrive in the future we will need to comprehend more but also see patterns between areas of knowledge—from understanding the ramifications of complex drug interactions to the dynamics of global pollution processes to thinking in 10 dimen- sions. The key to survival is not to understand certain things in minute detail but to comprehend everything well enough to make wise decisions. We need help.

Just contemplate the cost of some recent decisions that were made on the basis of a very poor understanding of the issues involved: mad cow disease, nuclear power, the contraceptive pill and thrombosis, genetically modified foods. In each case, what's been missing (and critical) has been our ability to understand what was happening and what was about to happen. The consequences of such ignorance are often tragic. If our brains are insufficient and not up to the task, then we have to create a third intelligence to help.

Before we can create this third intelligence, our machines must be given a range of sensory inputs from our world and the neural ability to create their own perceptions. Right now, a laptop has far more computational power than an ant but nothing of the intelli- gence. To overcome this obstacle, we will have to allow computer chips to become part of us, and allow ourselves to become part of machines.

All of this prompts people to ask: Will machines be able to read our minds? Will we ever tap into the vast resources of a giant machine's "mind"? Will we be able to communicate with machines just by thinking? The answer to all is a guarded yes. In each of these areas we already have evidence that some of this is possible.

But the question that interests me is: Will machines understand and think as we do? Personally, I hope not. We need to increase the diversity, as well as the depth, of thinking and not constrain it by imposing the limited domain of biology.

DISCUSSION QUESTIONS

1. What are *your* answers to the questions posed in the last two paragraphs of this article?
2. Should we "invite computers into our brain?"

Summary   Chapter Review

Predicting the future isn't easy, but it's important. One of the best ways to predict the future of technology for the next decade or two is to examine the work being done in research labs today. Information and communication technology industries generally go through four phases: hardware, software, service, and way of life.

Tomorrow's computers will continue current trends toward smaller, more powerful, faster, more efficient, higher-capacity, cheaper machines. Some new technologies will enhance these trends; others may start new trends. We can expect significant advances in displays, storage devices, processors, and wireless networks. Tomorrow's economy will be shaped by the information infrastructure of computers and networks.

Software reliability will remain elusive, but user interfaces will continue the trend toward ease of use. Today's graphical user interfaces will gradually give way as speech, natural language, 3-D images, animation,

video, artificial intelligence, and even virtual reality become more pervasive.

Perhaps the most important new user interface technology is the intelligent agent. Agents will be managed rather than manipulated by users. They'll carry out users' wishes and anticipate their needs. Most importantly, agents will serve as filters between users and the masses of information on networks.

We're heading into an era of ubiquitous computers—computers that are hardly noticeable because they're everywhere. Embedded computers will improve our everyday tools and, in some cases, give them entirely new functions.

Further into the future, information technology may become intertwined with microtechnology and biotechnology. The results may blur the line between living organisms and intelligent machines. We must be aware of the potential risks and benefits of future technology as we chart our course into the future.

Summary   Chapter Review

Key Terms

active badge, 454
agent, 452
artificial life, 456
bot, 452
information infrastructure, 450

microtechnology, 455
MIPS (millions of instructions per
   second), 448
nanotechnology, 456

optical computer, 449
self-maintaining system, 451
sensor, 450
virtual reality, 451

Review Questions

1. Define or describe each of the key terms listed above. Check your answers using the glossary.
2. What are the four phases of any technology or media business? Describe how each of these applies to two or more forms of modern electronic technology.
3. What trends in computer hardware evolution are likely to continue for the next few years?
4. Describe several new technologies that may produce significant performance improvements in future computers.
5. What did Raj Reddy mean when he said software will evolve from WIMP to SILK?

6. Why is the windows-and-icons GUI likely to be replaced by an agent-based user interface? What will this mean for computer users?
7. The information infrastructure will allow us to customize many of our transactions in an unprecedented way. Explain why, and give several examples.
8. Explain the concept of ubiquitous computers. Give examples of how it might apply in the office of the future and in the home of the future.
9. How might biology, microtechnology, and computer technology become intertwined in the future?

Discussion Questions

1. Some of the most interesting technological ideas are emerging from interdisciplinary labs at MIT, Carnegie-Mellon University, Xerox, and elsewhere—labs where scientists, engineers, artists, and philosophers work

together on projects that break down the traditional intellectual barriers. Why do you think this is so?
2. Millions of computers worldwide are already connected to networks. But unlike highways and railroads

today's computer networks aren't widely available, easy to use, and obviously valuable to the general population. What will need to happen for the information infrastructure to transform our lives the way highways and railroads transformed our ancestors' lives?

3. Arthur C. Clarke and others have suggested that virtual reality will replace TV. Do you agree? If it does, is that a good thing?

4. What kinds of questions might be raised if humans develop biologically based computers? How might the computers change our society?

5. Discuss the questions raised in the section called "Human Questions for a Computer Age." Which of those questions are the most important? Which are hardest to answer?

6. Do you foresee a time when we will share the Earth with truly intelligent beings of our own creation? Why or why not?

Projects

1. Imagine a future in which computers and information technology are forces of evil. Then imagine a future in which computers and information technology are used to further the common good. Write a paper describing both. Whether you use short-story style or essay style, include enough detail so that it's clear how the technology impacts human lives.

2. Write a letter to a long-lost classmate dated 50 years from today. In that letter describe your life during the past 50 years, including the ways computer technology affected it.

Sources & Resources

Books

Most books about the future are extremely perishable because the future continuously turns into the past. Some of the best writing about the future can be found in science fiction, where speculating about the future is a way of life. The books listed here provide several nonfiction views of the future and techniques for exploring the world of tomorrow.

Beyond Calculation: The Next Fifty Years of Computing, by Peter J. Denning and Robert M. Metcalfe (New York: Copernicus, 1997). 1997 marked the 50th anniversary of the transistor and of the Association for Computing Machinery, the premier organization for computer professionals. To mark the occasion, many of the pioneers who helped create the technology wrote articles predicting what the next 50 years might bring. This fascinating book is a collection of 20 speculative articles. Some deal exclusively with technology; others focus on social implications.

Digerati: Encounters with the Cyber Elite, by John Brockman (San Francisco: HardWired, 1996). The fast-paced world of computers and information technology is being shaped by hundreds of thousands of hard-working people, but some of those people have a disproportionate impact on the shaping of our future. This book profiles some of the key writers, academics, systems designers, entrepreneurs, and visionaries of the information age. It's

especially interesting to see what these people say about each other.

The Media Lab: Inventing the Future at MIT, by Stewart Brand (New York: Viking, 1988). This is the book that brought the MIT Media Lab into the public eye. In spite of its age, the book does an admirable job of describing a future radically transformed by the interweaving of the computer, communication, and entertainment industries. It also provides an insightful look at technology researchers in action.

Being Digital, by Nicholas Negroponte (New York: Viking, 1996). The director of the MIT Media Lab wrote thought-provoking columns for *Wired* for many years. This collection of columns provides an optimistic, intelligent vision of a digital future.

When Things Start to Think, by Neil Gershenfeld (New York: Henry Holt and Company, 1999). Another researcher at MIT's Media Lab provides a peek at recent research projects and a glimpse of a future in which computers disappear into everyday objects. As you might expect, Gershenfeld doesn't dwell on the dark side of this emerging technology, but his future visions make for clear, interesting reading.

e-topia: "Urban life, Jim, but not as we know it," by William J. Mitchell (Cambridge, MA: MIT Press, 1999). Mitchell is an expert on architecture and information technology. In this book he outlines his vision of future cities that incorporate virtual as well as physical spaces to support a sustainable way of life.

The Art of the Long View, by Peter Schwartz (New York: Doubleday, 1996). Scenario planning is a particularly useful tool for highlighting the powerful forces that shape the future and choosing strategies that play out well in a variety of possible futures. Schwartz is a master of scenario planning, and this book describes his methodology and provides examples.

21st Century Medicine: RoboSurgery, Wonder Cures, and the Quest for Immortality, by Alexandra Wyke (New York: Plenum Trade, 1997). Some of the most interesting and far-reaching research is happening in the world where digital technology meets biotechnology. This book describes a future in which medicine has been profoundly changed by today's research.

Out of Control: The New Biology of Machines, Social Systems, and the Economic World, by Kevin Kelly (Reading, MA: Addison-Wesley, 1996). Artificial life, artificial intelligence, genetic engineering, virtual reality, and nanotechnology blur the line between the "born" and the "made." Kevin Kelly's powerful, wonderfully readable book explores this line and provides fertile ground for speculation on all kinds of technological, social, and ethical questions.

Taming the Beast: Choice and Control in the Electronic Jungle, by Jason Ohler (Bloomington, IN: Technos Press, 1999). This book examines our relationship with technology with wit, intelligence, common sense, and sound advice. Ohler follows in the tradition of Marshall McLuhan, examining the unseen impact of our media creations on our lives.

The Future Does Not Compute: Transcending the Machines in Our Midst, by Stephen L. Talbott (Sebastopol, CA: O'Reilly & Associates, Inc., 1995). This book by a computer industry veteran is a wake-up call for anyone who blindly accepts computers as benevolent tools. The author raises important questions about the impact of computers on human consciousness and our conscience.

Moths to the Flame: The Seductions of Computer Technology, by Gregory J. E. Rawlins (Cambridge, MA: MIT Press, 1996). Computer science professor Rawlins writes skillfully about our unfolding high-tech future and its impact on our lives. As he writes in the preface, "Our every decision today and for the next twenty years will represent a bet we will be placing against our better natures. Whatever the outcome of those bets, the consequences are likely to be extreme."

Resisting the Virtual Life, edited by James Brook and Iain A. Boal (San Francisco: City Lights Books, 1995). This collection of essays surveys the dark side of computing and information technology: privacy erosion, alienation, technological addiction, oppression, and more.

Silicon Snake Oil, by Cliff Stoll (New York: Doubleday, 1995). Stoll's first book, *The Cuckoo's Egg* (described in Chapter 11), presented the Internet as a worldwide community based on trust. In *Silicon Snake Oil,* Stoll argues that the technology has been oversold and that we need to spend more time unplugged.

The Age of Access: The New Culture of Hypercapitalism Where All of Life is a Paid-for Experience, by Jeremy Rifkin (New York: Penguin Books, 2000). In his latest book, Rifkin argues that we're shifting from an economy based on ownership of physical possessions to one based on paying for experiences. He warns of an approaching era in which giant companies charge us for almost every human experience.

Periodicals

Communications of the ACM: The Next 50 Years, February, 1997 (Volume 40, Number 2). *CACM* is the journal of the premier professional organization for computer scientists. This special 50th-anniversary issue includes articles by leading writers, researchers, and pundits describing their hopes for what technology might bring during the next 50 years. It's an ideal companion to *Beyond Calculation,* described above.

Scientific American. This venerable monthly is the most popular science magazine. It's well known for articles that present scientific and engineering research in articles that are accessible to non-scientists.

Technology Review: MIT's Magazine of Innovation (www.techreview.com). This magazine isn't just another collection of academic research briefs. It's a colorful, engaging periodical that illuminates current technological research and future trends.

Wired (described in Chapter 1) boldly speculates about the future in every issue. The special January 2000 issue is a full-length look at the coming century.

Shift (www.shift.com). This relatively new Canadian magazine covers just about the same beat as Wired. But in recent years Wired has become more conservative, with articles about venture capital and stock options taking up more pages. So far, Shift seems to have a younger, sassier, more irreverant approach to covering the digital culture.

World Wide Web

The World Wide Web is evolving rapidly in amazing ways, but there are still no direct links to the future. The Web links on the *Computer Confluence* page allow you to explore Xerox PARC, the MIT Media Lab, and other organizations dedicated to inventing the future. Other links transport you into speculative discussions about tomorrow's technology and its implications.

The Concise Computer Consumer's Guide

Buying a computer can be an intimidating process, but it doesn't need to be. With the right information, you should have no trouble finding the right system.

Chapter 4 introduced several general principles that apply to just about any personal computer purchase (see Rules of Thumb box, "Computer Consumer Concepts," page 110). But when you're actually ready to buy a system, you'll need more specific information to help you narrow down the myriad of options and choose the system that best meets your needs. The next few pages provide information on each component in a typical computer system; you can use this information to create a profile of an ideal computer system. The CD-ROM includes an interactive Consumer's Guide that can walk you through the process of creating this profile.

Because of the volatile nature of the computer marketplace, the consumer's guides in this book and CD-ROM can't tell you everything you need to know. You'll need more current information to help you turn your ideal system profile into a detailed brand-specific shopping list. The Computer Confluence Web site will point you toward up-to-the-minute consumer-oriented information. Use this Web data along with anything you can glean from magazines, knowledgeable friends, and other sources.

If money were no object, you could purchase a fully loaded, top-of-the-line system with every imaginable peripheral. If, like most of us, you're working with a limited budget, you'll need to be more discriminating. You'll need to figure out exactly which features and components you need, which ones you might want to add later, and which ones you won't need at all. If you have a clear idea of how you're going to use your system, you'll be able to assess the trade-offs involved in choosing features and options. For example, if you're a graphics artist, you'll probably want to put more of your budget into a high-quality monitor if it means scrimping on audio speakers.

When shopping for a computer, there are several questions you need to address:

Is portability important? Portable computers are more expensive than desktop computers of equivalent capabilities. They also aren't as expandable as desktop boxes, so they aren't appropriate for users with highly specialized needs. You have to decide whether the convenience of portability outweighs the additional expense and limited expandability.

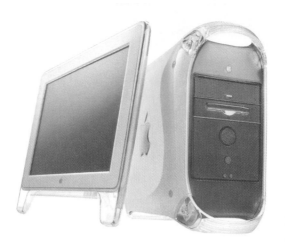

Should you buy a Windows PC or a Macintosh? This is a highly personal decision; you'll probably meet partisans for both camps who will argue with the passion of a religious zealot. The truth is that, while there are still critical differences between the two operating systems, both are capable of serving the needs of most users. If you don't already have a strong preference, check with others in your chosen field to see what they use and why. In general, Windows machines predominate in business, while Macs have loyal followings in publishing, graphics, and multimedia. Consider the kinds of software you'll want to use and find out what's available on each system. Spend some time getting to know both types of systems to see which you prefer.

What is your budget? If you have less than $800 to spend, you'll probably have to get a used computer or an extremely limited system. If you mostly need a word-processing and Web-surfing machine, an older system may be all you need. But most older systems can't run the latest software and have limited expansion options. If you have $800 to $1500 in your computer budget, you can buy a new system with standard capabilities that can handle today's most popular applications. If you can spend more than $1500, you can choose a high-performance system that can run many of the more demanding applications. In general, more expensive computer packages contain higher-quality peripherals as well.

Where do you buy a computer? Many people shop locally at computer specialty stores, superstores, and home electronic stores because of the local service, ease of repairs, and warranty replacements. Others choose mail-order companies for their competitive prices. Mail-order shopping can save money, but it can also mean additional hassles and risks if you don't do your homework or if you choose the wrong company. Leading computer magazines often rate mail-order companies for their service, prices, and reliability. Internet newsgroups can also help you find good deals and businesses with good reputations.

How do you plan to use your computer? Here's a list of computer applications. Which of these applications is most important to you? The applications you choose will determine, to a large degree, what your ideal system will look like.

Desktop Productivity Applications
Word Processing
Spreadsheet
Database
Publishing
Desktop Publishing
Web Publishing

Games
Simulations
Multiplayer gaming
Virtual reality

Communications
Online Service Access
Email
Internet/Web Access
Voice Mail/Fax

Technical Applications
CAD
Mathematical
Statistics
Programming Languages

Financial Applications
Personal Finance/On-line Banking
Accounting

Multimedia/Graphics
Graphic Art
Animation
Video
Music
Presentation Graphics
Multimedia Authoring

CPU

Buy the fastest CPU you can afford. RAM also affects the overall performance of your computer, but it's generally easier to add RAM later than to upgrade a CPU.

Secondary Storage

Most new computers come with a single floppy disk drive, a 2- to 10-gigabyte hard drive, and a CD-ROM or DVD-ROM drive; unless your computing needs are minimal, you probably won't be satisfied with a system that doesn't include these basic components. If you're planning on doing graphic design, digital audio, multimedia authoring, or other storage-intensive jobs, you'll probably also want some kind of removable high-capacity disk drive for transporting and backing up large files, a CD-R drive for creating CD-ROMs, and/or a DVD-RAM drive for reading and writing on high-capacity optical disks.

RAM

Certain applications, especially those that manipulate digital images or audio, demand a great deal of RAM. In general, you should plan on getting a computer with at least 32 megabytes of RAM—more if you will be using memory-intensive applications.

Video Monitor

The quality of the images you can display on your computer is a function not only of the monitor but also of the video adapter inside your system unit. If you plan to make extensive use of intricate color images, you will want a large-screen monitor (17" or greater) capable of supporting a resolution of at least 1024 × 768 pixels, a color depth of 16 million colors, and a noninterlaced refresh rate of at least 75 hertz. If you can afford it, you might consider a space-saving, energy-saving flat-screen monitor. Of course, the video card will have to support your chosen monitor's features and should contain at least 4MB of video RAM.

Input Devices

All computer systems have a keyboard and a pointing device, most commonly a mouse. Many keyboards are now ergonomically designed to reduce the risk of repetitive motion strain. Some users prefer a trackball to the mouse. If you plan to do much graphic design work, consider adding a pressure-sensitive graphics tablet to your system; it's far easier and more accurate to draw with a stylus than a mouse. For serious game playing, a joystick easily beats the mouse. Newer digital joysticks provide superior performance over their analog counterparts and offer more accurate control.

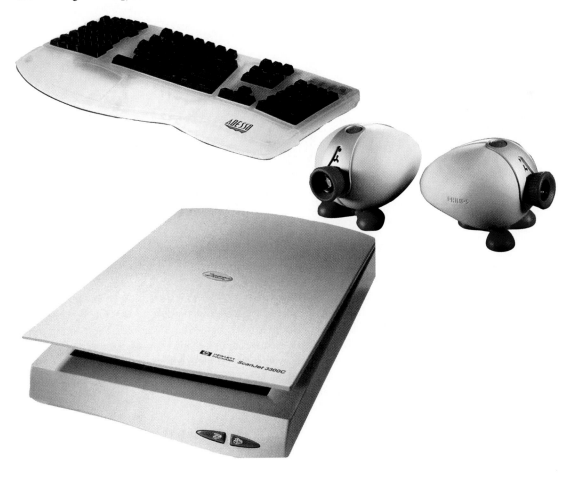

Modem/Communications

Since much Web content is graphics intensive, you shouldn't consider anything less than a 56.6 Kbps modem for Web surfing. In many areas, cable modems and DSL connections can provide high-speed Internet access.

Ports and Slots

Until recently, virtually all PCs had standard serial and parallel ports for adding peripherals and several slots for adding internal devices and boards. Many newer PCs, following in the mouseprints of the Apple iMac, include high-speed, hot-swappable USB and FireWire (IEEE 1394) ports designed to work with the latest peripherals. (FireWire is ideal for, among other things, serious digital video editing because it allows the computer to communicate directly with a digital video camera.)

Some new PCs include older slots and ports alongside the USB and 1394 ports; others are "legacy-free" models with only newer, faster ports. If you're buying all new peripherals, legacy-free machine makes sense; USB and FireWire peripherals are generally better than older models, and there's no reason to pay for ports you'll never use. But if you have a collection of aging peripherals, you'll probably want a machine that supports those peripherals.

Printer

Today's low-cost inkjet printers can produce surprisingly good high-resolution printouts; many are capable of printing impressive color images. Laser printers produce better printouts of text and black-and-white line art at a lower cost per page.

Sound Card/Speakers

All modern PCs and Macintoshes have built-in 16-bit sound cards capable of playing CD-quality audio and MIDI files. Advanced sound cards also supply wave table synthesis and the ability to create and play back studio-quality digital sound samples. These sound cards often contain extensive ROM with megabytes of prerecorded sound samples and expandable RAM banks. No sound system would be complete without a set of amplified, magnetically shielded speakers. The best systems include a separate bass subwoofer for more realistic nondirectional sound.

Software

Most systems come with systems software installed on the hard disk; some come with a number of preinstalled applications programs. Unless your system includes all the software you'll need, you'll have to spend part of your computer budget on software. If your software budget is modest, you may be able to meet most or all of your needs with an inexpensive integrated application such as Microsoft Works or AppleWorks. These all-purpose programs cost much less than more powerful office suites, and they demand much less disk space. Of course, integrated applications and software suites can't handle everybody's software needs. Multimedia work, engineering, and other specialized applications require specialized software. Don't overlook shareware and public domain software if your budget is tight.

Add-ons

There are numerous hardware add-ons that appeal to different special interests. Depending on your needs, you may want to add a flatbed scanner for scanning text and graphics, a digital camera for digitizing real-world images, a MIDI keyboard for playing your own music, or a digital video camera for recording and manipulating full-motion digital video.

One popular type of peripheral is actually another computer—a handheld computer. Devices like the Palm, the Handspring Visor, and the Pocket PC allow you to carry critical information with you when you're away from your desk. You can use one of these handheld PCs to schedule appointments, track tasks, record short notes, do calculations, look up phone numbers, and read files while you're away from your PC. When you return it to its cradle, it can hot-synch with the desktop machine, making sure the most current information is on both computers. The stylus input of these devices is less than ideal for taking notes. But a folding keyboard can make a Palm or Visor into a supremely portable note-taking machine.

Appendix: Correlation Guide to the ACM Code of Ethics and Professional Conduct

There's more to the Information Age than technology. Computers, networks, and digital technology raise all kinds of questions about ethical behavior and the social impact of our use of the new technology. Ethical issues are an important part of any discussion of our emerging information society; that's why discussions of these issues are interwoven into every chapter of this book.

The Association for Computing Machinery (ACM) was born with the computer industry about a half a century ago. The revised ACM Code of Ethics and Professional Conduct is considered by many to be a model code of ethics for the information industry. This 1992 document is reprinted here in its entirety (by permission of the ACM). Alongside each numbered principle you'll find section and page references to related material in *Computer Confluence.*

There's plenty of material for discussion here. For more on the ACM Code and its use, see "Using the ACM Code of Ethics in Decision Making" in the February 1993 issue of *Communications of ACM.* This article can also be downloaded from the Web in PDF format at http://www.acm.org/constitution/p98 anderson.pdf.

ACM CODE OF ETHICS AND PROFESSIONAL CONDUCT (ADOPTED BY ACM COUNCIL OCTOBER 16, 1992)

Commitment to ethical professional conduct is expected of every member (voting members, associate members, and student members) of the Association for Computing Machinery (ACM).

This Code, consisting of 24 imperatives formulated as statements of personal responsibility, identifies the elements of such a commitment. It contains many, but not all, issues professionals are likely to face. Section 1 outlines fundamental ethical considerations, while Section 2 addresses additional, more specific considerations of professional conduct. Statements in Section 3 pertain more specifically to individuals who have a leadership role, whether in the workplace or in a volunteer capacity such as with organizations like ACM. Principles involving compliance with this Code are given in Section 4.

The Code shall be supplemented by a set of Guidelines, which provide explanation to assist members in dealing with the various issues contained in the Code. It is expected that the Guidelines will be changed more frequently than the Code.

The Code and its supplemented Guidelines are intended to serve as a basis for ethical decision making in the conduct of professional work. Secondarily, they may serve as a basis for judging the merit of a formal complaint pertaining to violation of professional ethical standards.

It should be noted that although computing is not mentioned in the imperatives of Section 1, the Code is concerned with how these fundamental imperatives apply to one's conduct as a computing professional. These imperatives are expressed in a general form to emphasize that ethical principles which apply to computer ethics are derived from more general ethical principles.

It is understood that some words and phrases in a code of ethics are subject to varying interpretations, and that any ethical principle may conflict with other ethical principles in specific situations. Questions related to ethical conflicts can best be answered by thoughtful consideration of fundamental principles, rather than reliance on detailed regulations.

1. General Moral Imperatives
2. More Specific Professional Responsibilities
3. Organizational Leadership Imperatives
4. Compliance with the Code

1. General Moral Imperatives

As an ACM member I will . . .

1.1 Contribute to Society and Human Well-Being

This principle concerning the quality of life of all people affirms an obligation to protect fundamental human rights and to respect the diversity of all cultures. An essential aim of computing professionals is to minimize negative consequences of computing systems, including threats to health and safety. When designing or implementing systems, computing professionals must attempt to ensure that the products of their efforts will be used in socially responsible ways, will meet social needs, and will avoid harmful effects to health and welfare.

In addition to a safe social environment, human well-being includes a safe natural environment. Therefore, computing professionals who design and develop systems must be alert to, and make others aware of, any potential damage to the local or global environment.

1.2 Avoid Harm to Others

"Harm" means injury or negative consequences, such as undesirable loss of information, loss of property, property damage, or unwanted environmental impacts. This principle prohibits use of computing technology in ways that result in harm to any of the following: users, the general public, employees, and employers. Harmful actions include intentional destruction or modification of files and programs leading to serious loss of resources or unnecessary expenditure of human resources such as the time and effort required to purge systems of "computer viruses."

Well-intended actions, including those that accomplish assigned duties, may lead to harm unexpectedly. In such an event the responsible person or persons are obligated to undo or mitigate the negative consequences as much as possible. One way to avoid unintentional harm is to carefully consider potential impacts on all those affected by decisions made during design and implementation.

To minimize the possibility of indirectly harming others, computing professionals must minimize malfunctions by following generally accepted standards for system design and testing. Furthermore, it is often necessary to assess the social consequences of systems to project the likelihood of any serious harm to others. If system features are misrepresented to users, coworkers, or supervisors, the individual computing professional is responsible for any resulting injury.

In the work environment the computing professional has the additional obligation to report any signs of system dangers that might result in serious personal or social damage. If one's superiors do not act to curtail or mitigate such dangers, it may be necessary to "blow the whistle" to help correct the problem or reduce the risk. However, capricious or misguided reporting of violations can, itself, be harmful. Before reporting violations, all relevant aspects of the incident must be thoroughly assessed. In particular, the assessment of risk and responsibility must be credible. It is suggested that advice be sought from other computing professionals. See principle 2.5 regarding thorough evaluations.

1.3 Be Honest and Trustworthy

Honesty is an essential component of trust. Without trust an organization cannot function effectively. The honest computing professional will not make deliberately false or deceptive claims about a system or system design, but will instead provide full disclosure of all pertinent system limitations and problems.

A computer professional has a duty to be honest about his or her own qualifications, and about any circumstances that might lead to conflicts of interest.

Membership in volunteer organizations such as ACM may at times place individuals in situations where their statements or actions could be interpreted as carrying the "weight" of a larger group of professionals. An ACM member will exercise care to not misrepresent ACM or positions and policies of ACM or any ACM units.

1.4 Be Fair and Take Action Not to Discriminate

The values of equality, tolerance, respect for others, and the principles of equal justice govern this imperative. Discrimination on the basis of race, sex, religion, age, disability, national origin, or other such factors is an explicit violation of ACM policy and will not be tolerated.

Inequities between different groups of people may result from the use or misuse of information and technology. In a fair society, all individuals would have equal opportunity to participate in, or benefit from, the use of computer resources regardless of race, sex, religion, age, disability, national origin or other such similar factors. However, these ideals do not justify unauthorized use of computer resources nor do they provide an adequate basis for violation of any other ethical imperatives of this code.

1.5 Honor Property Rights Including Copyrights and Patents

Violation of copyrights, patents, trade secrets and the terms of license agreements is prohibited by law in most circumstances. Even when software is not so protected, such violations are contrary to professional behavior. Copies of software should be made only with proper authorization. Unauthorized duplication of materials must not be condoned.

1.6 Give Proper Credit for Intellectual Property

Computing professionals are obligated to protect the integrity of intellectual property. Specifically, one must not take credit for other's ideas or work, even in cases where the work has not been explicitly protected by copyright, patent, etc.

1.7 Respect the Privacy of Others

Computing and communication technology enables the collection and exchange of personal information on a scale unprecedented in the history of civilization. Thus there is increased potential for violating the privacy of individuals and groups. It is the responsibility of professionals to maintain the privacy and integrity of data describing individuals. This includes taking precautions to ensure the accuracy of data, as well as protecting it from unauthorized access or accidental disclosure to inappropriate individuals. Furthermore, procedures must be established to allow individuals to review their records and correct inaccuracies.

This imperative implies that only the necessary amount of personal information be collected in a system, that retention and disposal periods for that information be clearly defined and enforced, and that personal information gathered for a specific purpose not be used for other purposes without consent of the individual(s). These principles apply to electronic communications, including electronic mail, and prohibit procedures that capture or monitor electronic user data, including messages, without the permission of users or bona fide authorization related to system operation and maintenance. User data observed during the normal duties of system operation and maintenance must be treated with strictest confidentiality, except in cases where it is evidence for the violation of law, organizational regulations, or this Code. In these cases, the nature or contents of that information must be disclosed only to proper authorities.

1.8 Honor Confidentiality

The principle of honesty extends to issues of confidentiality of information whenever one has made an explicit promise to honor confidentiality or, implicitly, when private information not directly related to the performance of one's duties becomes available. The ethical concern is to respect all obligations of confidentiality to employers, clients, and users unless discharged from such obligations by requirements of the law or other principles of this Code.

2. More Specific Professional Responsibilities

As an ACM computing professional I will . . .

2.1 Strive to Achieve the Highest Quality, Effectiveness and Dignity in Both the Process and Products of Professional Work

Excellence is perhaps the most important obligation of a professional. The computing professional must strive to achieve quality and to be cognizant of the serious negative consequences that may result from poor quality in a system.

2.2 Acquire and Maintain Professional Competence

Excellence depends on individuals who take responsibility for acquiring and maintaining professional competence. A professional must participate in setting standards for appropriate levels of competence, and strive to achieve those standards. Upgrading technical knowledge and competence can be achieved in several ways: doing independent study; attending seminars, conferences, or courses; and being involved in professional organizations.

2.3 Know and Respect Existing Laws Pertaining to Professional Work

ACM members must obey existing local, state, province, national, and international laws unless there is a compelling ethical basis not to do so. Policies and procedures of the organizations in which one participates must also be obeyed. But compliance must be balanced with the recognition that sometimes existing laws and rules may be immoral or inappropriate and, therefore, must be challenged. Violation of a law or regulation may be ethical when that law or rule has inadequate moral basis or when it conflicts with another law judged to be more important. If one decides to violate a law or rule because it is viewed as unethical, or for any other reason, one must fully accept responsibility for one's actions and for the consequences.

2.4 Accept and Provide Appropriate Professional Review

Quality professional work, especially in the computing profession, depends on professional reviewing and critiquing. Whenever appropriate, individual members should seek and utilize peer review as well as provide critical review of the work of others.

2.5 Give Comprehensive and Thorough Evaluations of Computer Systems and Their Impacts, Including Analysis of Possible Risks

Computer professionals must strive to be perceptive, thorough, and objective when evaluating, recommending, and presenting system descriptions and alternatives. Computer professionals are in a position of special trust, and therefore have a special responsibility to provide objective, credible evaluations to employers, clients, users, and the public. When providing evaluations the professional must also identify any relevant conflicts of interest, as stated in imperative 1.3.

As noted in the discussion of principle 1.2 on avoiding harm, any signs of danger from systems must be reported to those who have opportunity and/or responsibility to resolve them. See the guidelines for imperative 1.2 for more details concerning harm, including the reporting of professional violations.

2.6 Honor Contracts, Agreements, and Assigned Responsibilities

Honoring one's commitments is a matter of integrity and honesty. For the computer professional this includes ensuring that system elements perform as intended. Also, when one contracts for work with another party, one has an obligation to keep that party properly informed about progress toward completing that work.

A computing professional has a responsibility to request a change in any assignment that he or she feels cannot be completed as defined. Only after serious consideration and with full disclosure of risks and concerns to the employer or client, should one accept the assignment. The major underlying principle here is the obligation to accept personal accountability for professional work. On some occasions other ethical principles may take greater priority.

A judgment that a specific assignment should not be performed may not be accepted. Having clearly identified one's concerns and reasons for that judgment, but failing to procure a change in that assignment, one may yet be obligated, by contract or by law, to proceed as directed. The computing professional's ethical judgment should be the final guide in deciding whether or not to proceed. Regardless of the decision, one must accept the responsibility for the consequences.

However, performing assignments "against one's own judgment" does not relieve the professional of responsibility for any negative consequences.

2.7 Improve Public Understanding of Computing and Its Consequences

Computing professionals have a responsibility to share technical knowledge with the public by encouraging understanding of computing, including the impacts of computer systems and their limitations. This imperative implies an obligation to counter any false views related to computing.

2.8 Access Computing and Communication Resources Only When Authorized To Do So

Theft or destruction of tangible and electronic property is prohibited by imperative 1.2—"Avoid harm to others." Trespassing and unauthorized use of a computer or communication system is addressed by this imperative. Trespassing includes accessing communication networks and computer systems, or accounts and/or files associated with those systems, without explicit authorization to do so. Individuals and organizations have the right to restrict access to their systems so long as they do not violate the discrimination principle (see 1.4). No one should enter or use another's computer system, software, or data files without permission. One must always have appropriate approval before using system resources, including communication ports, file space, other system peripherals, and computer time.

3. Organizational Leadership Imperatives

Background Note: This section draws extensively from the draft IFIP Code of Ethics, especially its sections on organizational ethics and international concerns. The ethical obligations of organizations tend to be neglected in most codes of professional conduct, perhaps because these codes are written from the perspective of the individual member. This dilemma is addressed by stating these imperatives from the perspective of the organizational leader. In this context "leader" is viewed as any organizational member who has leadership or educational responsibilities. These imperatives generally may apply to organizations as well as their leaders. In this context "organizations" are corporations, government agencies, and other "employers" as well as volunteer professional organizations.

As an ACM member and an organizational leader, I will . . .

3.1 Articulate Social Responsibilities of Members of an Organizational Unit and Encourage Full Acceptance of those Responsibilities

Because organizations of all kinds have impacts on the public, they must accept responsibilities to society. Organizational procedures and attitudes oriented toward quality and the welfare of society will reduce harm to members of the public, thereby serving public interest and fulfilling social responsibility. Therefore, organizational leaders must encourage full participation in meeting social responsibilities as well as quality performance.

3.2 Manage Personnel and Resources to Design and Build Information Systems that Enhance the Quality of Working Life

Organizational leaders are responsible for ensuring that computer systems enhance, not degrade, the quality of working life. When implementing a computer system, organizations must consider the personal and professional development, physical safety, and human dignity of all workers. Appropriate human-computer ergonomic standards should be considered in system design and in the workplace.

3.3 Acknowledge and Support Proper and Authorized Uses of an Organization's Computing and Communication Resources

Because computer systems can become tools to harm as well as to benefit an organization, the leadership has the responsibility to clearly define appropriate and inappropriate uses of organizational computing resources. While the number and scope of such rules should be minimal, they should be fully enforced when established.

3.4 Ensure that Users and those Who Will Be Affected by a System Have Their Needs Clearly Articulated During the Assessment and Design of Requirements; Later the System Must Be Validated to Meet Requirements

Current system users, potential users and other persons whose lives may be affected by a system must have their needs assessed and incorporated in the statement of requirements. System validation should ensure compliance with those requirements.

3.5 Articulate and Support Policies that Protect the Dignity of Users and Others Affected by a Computing System

Designing or implementing systems that deliberately or inadvertently demean individuals or groups is ethically unacceptable. Computer professionals who are in decision making positions should verify that systems are designed and implemented to protect personal privacy and enhance personal dignity.

3.6 Create Opportunities for Members of the Organization to Learn the Principles and Limitations of Computer Systems

This complements the imperative on public understanding (2.7). Educational opportunities are essential to facilitate optimal participation of all organizational members. Opportunities must be available to all members to help them improve their knowledge and skills in computing, including courses that familiarize them with the consequences and limitations of particular types of systems. In particular, professionals must be made aware of the dangers of building systems around oversimplified models, the improbability of anticipating and designing for every possible operating condition, and other issues related to the complexity of this profession.

4. Compliance with the Code

As an ACM member I will . . .

4.1 Uphold and Promote the Principles of this Code

The future of the computing profession depends on both technical and ethical excellence. Not only is it important for ACM computing professionals to adhere to the principles expressed in this Code, each member should encourage and support adherence by other members.

4.2 Treat Violations of this Code as Inconsistent with Membership in the ACM

Adherence of professionals to a code of ethics is largely a voluntary matter. However, if a member does not follow this code by engaging in gross misconduct, membership in ACM may be terminated.

This Code and the supplemental Guidelines were developed by the Task Force for the Revision of the ACM Code of Ethics and Professional Conduct: Ronald E. Anderson, Chair, Gerald Engel, Donald Gotterbarn, Grace C. Hertlein, Alex Hoffman, Bruce Jawer, Deborah G. Johnson, Doris K. Lidtke, Joyce Currie Little, Dianne Martin, Donn B. Parker, Judith A. Perrolle, and Richard S. Rosenberg. The Task Force was organized by ACM/SIGCAS and funding was provided by the ACM SIG Discretionary Fund. This Code and the supplemental Guidelines were adopted by the ACM Council on October 16, 1992.

Glossary

A

access-control software   Allows user access according to the user's needs. Some users can only open files that are related to their work. Some users are allowed read-only access to files they can see but not change. Also called "remote control" software. *Chapter 11*

account   Monetary category that represents various types of income, expenses, and liabilities. *Chapter 6*

accounting and financial management software   Software especially designed for financial and accounting tasks. The software sets up accounts, keeps track of money flow between accounts, records transactions, adjusts balances in accounts, provides an audit trail, automates routine tasks such as check writing, and produces reports. *Chapter 6*

active badge   A microprocessor-controlled ID badge that broadcasts infrared identification codes every 15 seconds. The badge's code is picked up by a nearby network receiver and transmitted back to a badge-location database that is constantly updated. Used as a security device. *Chapter 11; Chapter 16*

active cell   The cell containing the cursor in a spreadsheet. *Chapter 6*

address   In a spreadsheet, the location of a cell, determined by row number and column number. *Chapter 6*

agent   A software program that can ask questions, respond to commands, pay attention to its user's work patterns, serve as a guide and a coach, take on its owner's goals, and use reasoning to fabricate goals of its own. Typically provides a small cartoonlike character interface. *Chapter 16*

AI   See *artificial intelligence.*

algorithm   A set of step-by-step instructions that, when completed, solves a problem. *Chapter 4; Chapter 12*

alpha testing   Initial testing of a system. Also called "pre-beta testing." *Chapter 12*

analog signal   A continuous wave. *Chapter 9*

Analytical Engine   The first computer, conceived by Charles Babbage. Programmed with punch cards, it included functions of input, output, processing, and storage. *Chapter 1*

animation   The process of simulating motion with a series of still pictures. *Chapter 7*

antivirus program   A vaccine or disinfectant program designed to search for viruses, notify users when they're found, and remove them from infected files. *Chapter 11*

applet   A cross-platform software component. *Chapter 12*

application program (application)   Software tool that allows a computer to be used for specific purposes. *Chapter 1*

application suite (office suite)   A collection of several related application programs that are also sold as separate programs. *Chapter 4*

architecture   Design that determines how individual components of the CPU are put together on the chip. *Chapter 2*

artificial intelligence (AI)   The field of computer science devoted to making computers perceive, reason, and act in ways that have, until now, been reserved for human beings. *Chapter 13*

artificial life   Synthetic organisms that act like natural living systems. *Chapter 16*

ASCII (American Standard Code for Information Interchange)   A code that represents characters as 8-bit codes. Allows the binary computer to work with letters, digits, and special characters. *Chapter 2*

assembler   Translates assembly-language instructions into machine-language instructions. *Chapter 12*

assembly language   A language that is functionally equivalent to machine language but is easier to read, write, and understand. Programmers use alphabetic codes that correspond to the machine's numeric instructions. *Chapter 12*

asynchronous communication   Delayed communication, such as that used for newsgroups and mailing lists, when the sender and the recipients don't have to be logged in at the same time. *Chapter 10*

asynchronous teleconference   An on-line meeting between two or more people in which participants type, post, and read messages at their convenience. *Chapter 9*

attachment (email)   A way to send formatted word processor documents, pictures, and other multimedia files via email. *Chapter 9; Chapter 10*

audio digitizer   Hardware device or software program that captures a sound and stores it as a data file on a disk. *Chapter 7*

audit-control software   Monitors and records computer transactions as they happen so auditors can trace and identify suspicious computer activity after the fact. *Chapter 11*

authoring tool   Used to create multimedia presentations. *Chapter 15*

automated factory   A factory that depends on robots for mechanical tasks and/or computers for tracking inventory, timing the delivery of parts, controlling the quality of production, and other tasks. *Chapter 14*

automated office   An office that uses computers extensively for accomplishing tasks. *Chapter 14*

automatic correction   Catches and corrects common typing errors. *Chapter 5*

automatic footnoting   Word-processing feature that automatically places footnotes where they belong on the page. *Chapter 5*

automatic formatting   Automatically applies formatting to the text. *Chapter 5*

automatic hyphenation   Word-processing feature that automatically divides long words that fall at the ends of lines. *Chapter 5*

automatic link   A link between worksheets in a spreadsheet that ensures that a change in one worksheet is reflected in the other. *Chapter 6*

automatic recalculation   A spreadsheet capability that allows for easy correction of errors and makes it easy to try out different values while searching for solutions. *Chapter 6*

automatic speech recognition   System that uses pattern recognition techniques to analyze digitized voice input. *Chapter 13*

automatic translation   A program that automatically translates one human language into another. *Chapter 13*

automation   The practice of replacing jobs performed by humans with jobs performed by computers and robots. *Chapter 14*

autonomous system   A complex system that can assume almost complete responsibility for a task without human input, verification, or decision making. *Chapter 11*

avatar   A graphical image that ranges from a simple cartoon drawing to a complex three-dimensional model of a human figure. In virtual meeting places, people represent themselves with avatars. Similar to "agent." *Chapter 16*

B

backup   The process of saving data, especially for data recovery. Many systems automatically back up data and software onto disks or tapes. *Chapter 11*

backward compatible   Able to run software written for older CPUs. *Chapter 2*

bandwidth   The quantity of information that can be transmitted through a communication medium in a given amount of time. *Chapter 9*

bar chart   A chart that shows relative values with bars, appropriate when data fall into a few categories. *Chapter 6*

bar-code reader   A reading tool that uses light to read universal product codes, inventory codes, and other codes created out of patterns of variable-width bars. *Chapter 3*

batch processing   Accumulating transactions and feeding them into a computer in large batches. *Chapter 8*

bay   An open area in the system box for disk drives and other peripheral devices. *Chapter 2*

beta testing   Testing of almost-finished software by potential users. *Chapter 12*

binary   A choice of two values, such as yes and no or zero and one. *Chapter 2*

biometrics   Measurements of individual body characteristics, such as a voice print or fingerprint; sometimes used in computer security. *Chapter 11*

bit   Binary digit. The smallest unit of information. A bit can have two values—0 or 1. *Chapter 2*

bit depth (color depth)   The number of bits devoted to each pixel in a color display. *Chapter 7*

bit-mapped (raster) graphics   Painting programs create bit-mapped graphics that are, to the computer, simple maps showing how the pixels on the screen should be represented. *Chapter 7*

bits per second (bps)   A measurement to describe the transmission speed of a modem. *Chapter 9*

booting   Loading the non-ROM part of the operating system into memory. *Chapter 4*

bot   A software robot that exhibits many of the characteristics of an agent. *Chapter 16*

bps   See *bits per second.*

broadband connection   Modem alternatives that have higher bandwidth than standard modem connections. *Chapter 10*

browse   The process of finding information in a database or other data source, such as the World Wide Web. *Chapter 8*

bug   An error in programming. *Chapter 4*

bullet charts   Graphical elements, such as drawings and tables, integrated into a series of charts that list the main points of a presentation. *Chapter 7*

bulletin board system (BBS)   An online version of the bulletin board. *Chapter 9*

bus   Group of wires on a circuit board. Information travels between components through a bus. *Chapter 2*

button (command button)   A hot spot on a screen that responds to mouse clicks. A button can be programmed to perform one of many tasks, such as opening a dialog box or launching an application. *Chapter 7*

byte   Grouping of 8 bits. *Chapter 2*

C

C   One of the most widely-used programming languages today. *Chapter 12*

C++   A variant of the C programming language that supports object-oriented programming. *Chapter 12*

cable modem   Allows Internet connections using the same network of coaxial cables that delivers TV signals. *Chapter 10*

CAD   See *computer-aided design.*

CAI   See *computer-aided instruction.*

CAM   See *computer-aided manufacturing.*

camera-ready   Typeset-quality pages, ready to be photographed and printed. *Chapter 5*

CASE tools   Computer-assisted software engineering tools. Allow analysts and programmers to automate many of the steps involved in turning design specifications into programs. *Chapter 12*

Cathode ray tube (CRT) monitor   A television-style monitor that is used as the output device for many desktop computers. *Chapter 3*

CD-R Compact disk–recordable.   An optical disk on which you can write information, but not remove it. *Chapter 3*

CD-ROM Compact disc—read-only memory.   An optical disk with read-only memory. *Chapter 3*

CD-RW Compact disk–rewritable.   An optical disk that allows writing, erasing, and rewriting. *Chapter 3*

cell   The intersection of a row and a column on the grid of a spreadsheet. *Chapter 6*

centralized database   A database housed in a mainframe computer, accessible only to information-processing personnel. *Chapter 8*

central processing unit (CPU)   Part of the computer that processes information, performs arithmetic calculations, and makes basic decisions based on information values. *Chapter 2*

character-based interface   A user interface based on text characters rather than graphics. *Chapter 4*

chat room   Public real-time teleconference. *Chapter 9*

CIM   See *computer-integrated manufacturing.*

circuit board   Houses the CPU, along with other chips and electronic components in a computer. *Chapter 2*

click   The action of pressing a button on a mouse. *Chapter 3*

client/server database   Client programs in desktop computers send information requests through a network to server databases on mainframes, minicomputers, or desktop computers; the servers process queries and send the requested data back to the client. *Chapter 8*

client/server model   For a local-area network, a hierarchical model in which one or more computers act as dedicated servers and all the remaining computers act as clients. The server fills requests from clients for data and other resources. *Chapter 9*

client/server model   For Internet applications, a client program asks for information, and a server program fields the request and provides the requested information from databases and documents. The client might reside on a personal computer or the host computer, and the server might reside on the same host computer or another host computer elsewhere on the network. *Chapter 10*

clip art   A collection of redrawn images that you can cut out and paste into your own documents. *Chapter 7*

clipboard   A special portion of memory for temporarily holding information for later use. *Chapter 5*

code of ethics   Code of conduct specifically for computer professionals and developed by the ACM (Association for Computing Machinery). *Chapter 11*

coding   Writing a program from an algorithm. *Chapter 12*

color depth (bit depth)   The number of bits devoted to each pixel. *Chapter 7*

columns   Along with rows, comprise the grid of a spreadsheet. *Chapter 6*

command-line interface   User interface that requires the user to type text commands on a command line in order to communicate with the operating system. *Chapter 4*

communication software   Software that allows computers to interact with each other over a phone line or other network. *Chapter 9*

communications satellite   Satellites that match the earth's rotation so they can hang in a stationary position relative to the spinning planet below. *Chapter 9*

compatibility   The ability of a software program to run on a specific computer system. Also, the ability of a hardware device to function with a particular type of computer. *Chapter 4*

compiler   A translator program that compiles a complete translation of a program in a high-level computer language before the program is run for the first time. *Chapter 4; Chapter 12*

component software   Small custom software applications. *Chapter 12*

compression   Making files smaller using special encoding schemes. File compression saves storage space on disk and saves transmission time when files are transferred through networks. *Chapter 10*

computed field   In a database, a field containing formulas similar to spreadsheet formulas; they display values calculated from values in other numeric fields. *Chapter 8*

computer-aided design (CAD)   The use of computers to design products. *Chapter 7*

computer-aided instruction (CAI)   Software programs for teaching that combine drill-and-practice software and tutorial software. *Chapter 15*

computer-aided manufacturing (CAM)   When the design of a product is completed, the numbers are fed to a program that controls the manufacturing of parts. For electronic parts the design translates directly into a template for etching circuits onto chips. *Chapter 7*

computer architecture   Deals with the way hardware and software work together. *Chapter 12*

computer crime   Any crime accomplished through knowledge or use of computer technology. *Chapter 11*

computer-integrated manufacturing (CIM)   The combination of CAD and CAM. *Chapter 7*

computer monitoring   Using computer technology to track, record, and evaluate worker performance, often without the knowledge of the worker. *Chapter 14*

computer science   Focuses on the process of computing through several areas of specialization, including theory, algorithms, data structures, programming concepts and languages, computer architecture, management information systems, artificial intelligence, and software engineering. *Chapter 12*

computer security   Protecting computer systems and the information they contain against unwanted access, damage, modification, or destruction. *Chapter 11*

concurrent processing   A large computer working on several jobs at the same time. The computer uses multiple CPUs to process jobs simultaneously. *Chapter 4*

console cell solver   In spreadsheet software, the long window above the worksheet where typing appears. *Chapter 6*

contract (law)   A type of law that covers trade secrets. *Chapter 11*

control structure   Logical structures that control the order in which instructions are carried out. *Chapter 12*

cookies   Tidbits of information about your session that can be read later; they allow Web sites to remember what they know about you between sessions. *Chapter 10*

copying text   Copying text from one part of a document and duplicating it in another section of the document or in a different document. *Chapter 5*

copy-protected software   Software that prevents a disk from being copied. *Chapter 4*

Copyright (law)   A type of law that traditionally protects forms of literary expression. *Chapter 11*

copyrighted software   Software that is legally protected against duplication. *Chapter 4*

courseware   Educational software. *Chapter 15*

CPU   See *central processing unit.*

CRT   See *cathode ray tube monitor.*

current cell (active cell)   The cell containing the cursor in a spreadsheet. *Chapter 6*

cursor   A line or rectangle, sometimes flashing, that indicates your location on the screen or in a document. *Chapter 3; Chapter 5*

custom application   An application programmed for a specific purpose, typically for a specific client. *Chapter 4*

cut-and-paste   Copying or deleting text from one point and pasting it into another point in the document. *Chapter 5*

cyberspace   A term used to describe the Internet and other on-line networks, especially the virtual communities that form on them. First coined by William Gibson in his novel, *Neuromancer. Chapter 10*

D

data   Information in a form that is workable for the computer. *Chapter 1*

database   A collection of information stored in an organized form in a computer. *Chapter 8*

database management system (DBMS)   A program or system of programs that can manipulate data in a large collection of files (the database), cross-referencing between files as needed. *Chapter 8*

database program A software tool for organizing the storage and retrieval of the information in a database. *Chapter 8*

data compression Reduces the size of a data file so it can be stored in a smaller space. *Chapter 7*

data mining The discovery and extraction of hidden predictive information from large databases. *Chapter 8*

data structure Software construct that determines the logical structure of data. Data structures range from simple numeric lists and tables (arrays) to complex relations at the core of databases. *Chapter 12*

data warehouse An integrated collection of corporate data stored in one location. *Chapter 8*

DBMS See *database management system.*

decision support system (DSS) A computer system that supports managers in decision-making tasks. *Chapter 14*

dedicated (special-purpose) computer Computer that performs specific tasks, such as controlling temperature and humidity in an office building. *Chapter 1*

dedicated (direct) connection A dedicated, direct connection to the Internet through a LAN, with the computer having its own IP address. *Chapter 10*

deleting text Removing text from the document. *Chapter 5*

denial of service attacks A type of computer vandalism that floods popular Websites with bogus traffic that companies can't respond to legitimate customer and client clicks. *Chapter 11*

de-skilling Transforming a job, when it is automated, so that it requires less skill. *Chapter 14*

desktop A visual representation of a desktop in a graphical user interface where the user performs tasks. *Chapter 4*

desktop publishing (DTP) Software used to produce print publications. *Chapter 5*

dialog box In a graphical user interface, a box that allows the user to communicate with the computer. *Chapter 4*

dial-up connection Allows a temporary connection to an Internet host, via a standard serial-line connection, using a modem, standard telephone lines, and terminal emulation software. *Chapter 10*

digital Information made up of discrete units that can be counted. *Chapter 2*

digital camera Captures images the same as a regular camera, but stores bit patterns on disks or other digital storage media instead of using film. *Chapter 3*

digital cash A system for purchasing goods and services on the Internet without using credit cards. *Chapter 10*

digital divide A term that describes the divide between the people who do and do not have access to the Internet. *Chapter 10*

digital image processing software Allows the user to manipulate photographs and other high-resolution images. *Chapter 7*

digital signal A stream of bits. *Chapter 9*

digital video Video that is reduced to a series of numbers and can be edited, stored, and played back without any loss of quality. *Chapter 7*

digitize Converting information into a digital form that can be stored in the computer's memory. *Chapter 3*

digitized sound Sounds recorded and stored in a computer. Computers can play back these sounds. *Chapter 13*

digitized speech Speech recorded and stored in a computer. Computers can play back the speech. *Chapter 13*

direct (dedicated) connection A dedicated, direct connection to the Internet through a LAN, with the computer having its own IP address. *Chapter 9; Chapter 10*

directory A logical container used to group files and other directories. Also called a folder. *Chapter 4*

disinfectant (vaccine) program A program designed to search for viruses, notify users when they're found, and remove them from infected disks or files. *Chapter 11*

disk drive Computer peripheral used to retrieve information from a magnetic disk, and to transfer data to it. *Chapter 3*

diskette (floppy disk) A small, magnetically sensitive, flexible plastic wafer housed in a plastic case, used as a storage device. *Chapter 3*

distance learning Using technology to extend the educational process beyond the walls of a school. *Chapter 15*

distributed computing Integrating all kinds of computers, from mainframes to PCs, into a single, seamless system. *Chapter 14*

distributed database Data strewn out across networks on several different computers. *Chapter 8*

document A data file created with an application. *Chapter 4*

documentation Printed instructions for installing and using software. *Chapter 4*

dot-matrix printer An old-fashioned impact printer that uses pinpoint-size hammers to transfer ink to the page. The printed page is a matrix of tiny dots. *Chapter 3*

download Copying software from an on-line source to a local computer. *Chapter 9*

drag To move the mouse while holding the mouse button down. Used for moving objects, selecting text, drawing, and other tasks. *Chapter 3*

drag-and-drop Editing feature that allows the user to move selected text or an object by dragging it (with the mouse) from one part of the screen to another. *Chapter 5*

drawing software Stores a picture as a collection of lines and shapes. Also stores shapes as shape formulas and text as text. *Chapter 7*

drill-and-practice software Teaching software based on the principles of individualized rate, small steps, and positive feedback. *Chapter 15*

DSL (digital subscriber line) A digital service offered by phone companies. *Chapter 10*

DSS (decision support system) A computer system that supports managers in decision-making tasks. *Chapter 14*

DTP See *desktop publishing.*

DVD-RAM An optical disk which can read, erase, and write data on multi-gigabyte disks. *Chapter 3*

DVD-ROM An optical disk with read-only capability that is the same size as a CD-ROM but holds much more information. *Chapter 3*

E

editing text The process of writing and refining text on the screen. *Chapter 5*

educational simulation Allows students to explore artificial environments that are imaginary or based on reality. Most have the look and feel of a game, but they challenge students to learn through exploration, experimentation, and interaction with other students. *Chapter 15*

edutainment Programs geared toward home markets that combine education and entertainment. *Chapter 15*

electronic commerce (e-commerce) Buying and selling products through a computer network. *Chapter 9; Chapter 14*

electronic cottage A home in which modern technology allows a person to work at home. *Chapter 14*

electronic mail (email) Allows Internet users to send mail messages, data files, and software programs to other Internet users and to users of most commercial networks and on-line services. *Chapter 9*

electronic organizer A specialized database program that automates an address/phone book, an appointment calendar, a to-do list, and miscellaneous notes. Also called a personal information manager (PIM). *Chapter 8*

electronic sweatshop An office where each worker has a single job; computer monitoring is a common practice; wages are low; work conditions are poor; most of the work is mindless keyboarding; and repetitive stress injuries are common. *Chapter 14*

embedded computer Computer that is embedded into a consumer product, such as a wristwatch or game machine, to enhance those products. Also used to control hardware devices. *Chapter 1*

emulation A process that allows programs to run on a noncompatible operating system. *Chapter 4*

encryption Protects transmitted information by scrambling the transmissions. When a user encrypts a message by applying a secret numerical code (encryption key), the message can be transmitted or stored as an indecipherable garble of characters. The message can be read only after it's been reconstructed with a matching key. *Chapter 11*

equation solvers A feature of some spreadsheet programs that determines data values. *Chapter 6*

Ethernet A popular networking architecture developed in 1976 at Xerox. *Chapter 9*

ethics A moral philosophy of right and wrong. Computer ethics involve principles and guidelines to help users focus on the many technology-related dilemmas of our time. *Chapter 11*

equation solver A feature of some spreadsheet programs that determines data values. *Chapter 6*

ergonomics The science of designing work environments that allow people and things to interact efficiently and safely. *Chapter 3*

error message Message from the operating system that lets the user know an error has occurred. *Chapter 4*

expansion slots An area inside the computer's housing that holds special-purpose circuit boards. *Chapter 2*

expert system A software program designed to replicate the decision-making process of a human expert. *Chapter 13*

expert system shell A generic expert system containing human interfaces and inference engines intended to simplify the process of designing an expert system. *Chapter 13*

export data Transmitting records and fields from a database program to another program. *Chapter 8*

extranet A private TCP/IP network designed for outside use by customers, clients, and business partners of an organization. These networks are typically for electronic commerce. *Chapter 10; Chapter 14*

F

facsimile (fax) machine A technology that allows images of paper documents to be transmitted through telephone lines to a destination where they can be printed or displayed on a computer screen. *Chapter 9*

FAQ (frequently asked question) A list that is posted to many newsgroups and mailing lists, so the groups don't get cluttered with the same old questions and answers. *Chapter 10*

fax modem Hardware peripheral that allows a computer to send on-screen documents to a receiving fax machine by translating the document into signals that can be sent over phone wires and decoded by the receiving fax machine. *Chapter 9*

feedback loop In a computer simulation, the user and the computer responding to data from each other. *Chapter 6*

fiber optic cable High-capacity cable that uses light waves to carry information at blinding speeds. *Chapter 9*

field Each discrete chunk of information in a database record. *Chapter 8*

file An organized collection of related information stored in a computer-readable form. *Chapter 2; Chapter 8*

file manager A program that allows users to manipulate files on their computers. *Chapter 8*

file server In a LAN, a computer used as a storehouse for software and data that are shared by several users. *Chapter 9*

fiel transfer protocol (FTP) A communications protocol that allows users anywhere on the Internet to browse through on-line libraries of software and data and transfer copies of those files back to their local machine. *Chapter 10*

filtering software Software that blocks student access to sites with "inappropriate" content. *Chapter 15*

find and replace. See *search and replace*.

find command A command used to locate a particular word, string of characters, or formatting in a document. *Chapter 5*

firewall Guards against unauthorized access to an internal network; keeps internal networks secure while allowing communication with the rest of the Internet. *Chapter 11*

firmware A program, usually for special-purpose computers, stored on a ROM chip so it cannot be altered. *Chapter 1*

flash memory A type of erasable memory chop. *Chapter 16*

floppy disk (diskette) A small, magnetically sensitive, flexible plastic wafer housed in a plastic case, used as a storage device. *Chapter 3*

folder A container for files and other folders. Also called a directory. *Chapter 4*

font A size and style of typeface. *Chapter 5*

footer Block of information that appears at the bottom of every page in a document, displaying repetitive information such as an automatically calculated page number. *Chapter 5*

formula Step-by-step procedure for calculating a number on a spreadsheet. *Chapter 6*

formula bar In spreadsheet software, the long window above the worksheet where typing appears. *Chapter 6*

four generations of computers Designations for major changes in hardware. First-generation computers were built around vacuum tubes. Second-generation computers used transistors. Integrated circuits characterized third-generation computers. The invention of the microprocessor marked the beginning of fourth-generation computers. *Chapter 1*

fourth-generation language (4GL)   Languages have evolved through machine language, assembly language, high-level languages, and into 4GLs. 4GLs use Englishlike phrases and sentences to issue instructions, are nonprocedural, and increase productivity. *Chapter 12*

frame   One still picture in a video or animated sequence. *Chapter 7*

FTP   See *file transfer protocol.*

full-access dial-up connection   Allows a computer connected via modem and phone line to temporarily have full Internet access and an IP address. *Chapter 10*

function   A predefined set of calculations, such as SUM and AVERAGE, in spreadsheet software. *Chapter 6*

G

gateway   A computer connected to two networks that translates communication protocols and transfers information between the two. *Chapter 10*

GB   See *gigabyte.*

geographical information system (GIS)   Combines tables of data with demographic information and displays geographic and demographic data on maps. *Chapter 8*

gigabyte (GB)   Approximately 1000MB. *Chapter 2*

GIGO   Garbage in, garbage out. Valid output requires valid input. *Chapter 6*

GIS   See *geographical information system.*

Global Positioning System (GPS)   A defense department system with 24 satellites that can pinpoint any location on the Earth. *Chapter 9*

grammar and style checker   Component of word-processing software that analyzes each word in context, checking for errors of context, common grammatical errors, and stylistic problems. *Chapter 5*

graphical user interface (GUI)   A user interface based on graphical displays. With a mouse, the user points to icons that represent files, folders, and disks. Documents are displayed in windows. The user selects commands from menus. *Chapter 4*

graphics tablet   A pressure-sensitive touch tablet used as a pointing device. The user presses on the tablet with a stylus. *Chapter 3*

gray-scale graphics   Graphics that allow each pixel to appear as black, white, or one of several shades of gray. *Chapter 7*

gray-scale monitor   Monitor that displays black, white, and shades of gray but no other colors. *Chapter 3*

groupware   Software designed to be used by work groups rather than individuals. *Chapter 5*

groupware   Programs designed to allow several networked users to work on the same documents at the same time. *Chapter 9; Chapter 14*

H

hacker   Soemone who practices unauthorized access to computer systems. *Chapter 11*

hand-held computer   A portable computer small enough to be tucked into a jacket pocket. *Chapter 1*

handwriting recognition software   Software that translates the user's handwritten forms into ASCII characters. *Chapter 3*

hard copy   A paper copy, produced by a printer, of any information that can be displayed on the screen. *Chapter 3*

hard disk   A rigid, magnetically sensitive disk that spins rapidly and continuously inside the computer chassis or in a separate box attached to the computer housing. Used as a storage device. *Chapter 3*

hardware   Physical parts of the computer system. *Chapter 1*

header   Block that appears at the top of every page in a document, displaying repetitive information such as a chapter title. *Chapter 5*

helper application   A program designed to help users present animation, audio, or video. *Chapter 10*

heuristic   A rule of thumb. *Chapter 13*

high-level language   A programming language that falls somewhere between natural human languages and precise machine languages, developed to streamline and simplify the programming process. *Chapter 4; Chapter 12*

high-performance computer   See *super computer.*

home page   The main entry page to a Web site. *Chapter 10*

host system   A computer that provides services to multiple users. *Chapter 9*

HTML   See *hypertext markup language.*

human-centered system   A system designed to retain and enhance human skills rather than take them away. *Chapter 14*

hyperlink   Words or pictures that act as buttons, allowing you to explore the Web with mouse clicks. *Chapter 10*

hypermedia   The combination of text, numbers, graphics, animation, sound effects, music, and other media in hyperlinked documents. *Chapter 7; Chapter 10*

hypertext   An interactive cross-referenced system that allows textual information to be linked in nonsequential ways. A hypertext document contains links that lead quickly to other parts of the document or to related documents. *Chapter 7; Chapter 10*

Hypertext markup language (HTML)   An HTML document is a text file that includes codes that describe the format, layout, and logical structure of a hypermedia document. Most Web pages are created with HTML. *Chapter 10*

I

icon   In a graphical user interface, a picture that represents a file, folder, or disk. *Chapter 4*

idea processor   A word-processing feature that allows the user to organize ideas, drawing them as nodes on a chart with arrows connecting related ideas. *Chapter 5*

identity theft   Use of stolen information to assume the identity of another individual on line. *Chapter 11*

image analysis   The process of identifying objects and shapes in a photograph, drawing, video, or other visual image. *Chapter 13*

impact printer   Printer that forms images by physically striking paper, ribbon, and print hammer together. *Chapter 3*

import data   To move data into a program from another program or source. *Chapter 8*

information   Anything that can be communicated. Some information has value, but some has none. *Chapter 2*

information appliance   Network computer or other internet-capable device used in offices and homes. *Chapter 1*

information economy   An economy based on information-related work. *Chapter 14*

information infrastructure The framework created by computers, networks, and software. *Chapter 16*

information overload The state of being bombarded with too much computer output; a hazard of the automated office. *Chapter 14*

information superhighway The Internet. *Chapter 10*

information system A collection of people, machines, data, and methods organized to accomplish specific functions and to solve specific problems. Programming is part of the larger process of designing, implementing, and managing an information system. *Chapter 12*

information systems manager Responsible for integrating all kinds of computers, from mainframes to PCs, into a single, seamless system in an automated office. *Chapter 14*

inkjet printer A nonimpact printer that sprays ink directly onto paper to produce printed text and graphic images. *Chapter 3*

input Information taken in by the computer. *Chapter 1*

input device Device for accepting input, such as a keyboard. *Chapter 2*

inserting text Adding text at any point in a document. *Chapter 5*

insertion bar Indicates your location in a document. *Chapter 5*

instant messaging A technology that allows an on-line user to create a "buddy list," control who is on the list, and start a conversation with anyone on the list. *Chapter 9*

integrated circuit A chip containing hundreds, thousands, or even millions of transistors. *Chapter 1*

integrated software Software packages that include several applications designed to work well together. *Chapter 4*

intellectual property The results of intellectual activities in the arts, science, and industry. *Chapter 11*

interactive fiction Stories with primitive natural-language interfaces that gave players some control over plot. *Chapter 15*

interacive movie Video-based or animated feature in which one or more characters are controlled by the viewers. *Chapter 15*

interactive multimedia Multimedia that allows the user to take an active part in the experience. *Chapter 7*

interactive processing Interacting with data through terminals, viewing and changing values on line in real time. *Chapter 8*

Interface standards Standards agreed upon by the computer industry to ensure that devices made by one manufacturer can be attached to systems made by other companies. *Chapter 3*

interactive TV Animated features in which one or more of the characters are controlled by the viewers. *Chapter 15*

Internet (Net) A global interconnected network of thousands of networks linking academic, research, government, and commercial institutions, and other organizations and individuals. *Chapter 1; Chapter 10*

Internet appliances Non-PC devices such as set-top boxes that are connected to the Internet. *Chapter 10*

Internet service provider (ISP) A service offering connections to the Internet for users. *Chapter 10*

Internet telephony A program that allows use of a multimedia computer's microphone and speaker to turn the Internet into a toll-free long-distance telephone service. *Chapter 10*

Internet2 An alternative Internet-style network that provides faster network communications for universities and research institutions. *Chapter 10*

internetworking Connecting different types of networks and computer systems. *Chapter 10*

interpreter A program that translates and transmits each programming statement individually. *Chapter 12*

intranet A self-contained intraorganizational network that is designed using the same technology as the Internet. *Chapter 1; Chapter 10; Chapter 14*

J

Java A platform-neutral, object-oriented programming language developed by Sun Microsystems for use on multiplatform networks. *Chapter 4; Chapter 10; Chapter 12*

JavaScript A Web scripting language similar to, but otherwise unrelated to, Java. *Chapter 10; Chapter 12*

joystick A gearshift-like device used as a controller for arcade-style computer games. *Chapter 3*

justification The alignment of text on a line: left justification (smooth left margin and ragged right margin), right justification, full justification (both margins are smooth), and center justification. *Chapter 5*

K

K See *kilobyte*

keyboard Input device, similar to a typewriter keyboard, for entering data and commands into the computer. *Chapter 3*

key field A field that contains data that uniquely identifies the record. *Chapter 8*

kilobyte (K) About 1000 bytes of information. *Chapter 2*

knowledge base A database that contains facts and a system of rules for determining and changing the relationship between those facts. *Chapter 13*

L

label In a spreadsheet, a text entry that provides information on what a column or row represents. *Chapter 6*

LAN See *local area network.*

laptop computer A flat-screen, battery-powered portable computer that you can rest on your lap. *Chapter 1*

laser printer A nonimpact printer that uses a laser beam to create patterns of electrical charges on a rotating drum. The charged patterns attract black toner and transfer it to paper as the drum rotates. *Chapter 3*

LCD See *liquid crystal display monitor.*

line chart A chart that shows trends or relationships over time, or a relative distribution of one variable through another. *Chapter 6*

line printer An impact printer used by mainframes to produce massive printouts. They print characters only, not graphics. *Chapter 3*

Linux A multiple user operating system maintained by volunteers and distributed freely. *Chapter 4*

liquid crystal display (LCD) monitor A flat-panel display monitor typically used for portable computers. *Chapter 3*

local-area network (LAN) A network in which the computers are close to each other, usually in the same building. Typically includes a collection of computers and peripherals; each computer and shared peripheral is an individual node on the network. *Chapter 9*

logic bomb A program designed to attack in response to a particular logical event or sequence of events. A type of software sabotage. *Chapter 11*

logic error An error in the logical structure of a program that causes differences between what you want the program to do and what it actually does. *Chapter 12*

LOGO A computer language developed in the 1960s that created an environment for children. *Chapter 10; Chapter 15*

login name A one-word name that you choose to identify yourself when logging on to get email. *Chapter 9*

M

machine language The language that computers use to process instructions. Machine language uses numeric codes to represent basic computer operations. *Chapter 4; Chapter 12*

machine learning In a game-playing program, if a move pays off, the program is more likely to repeat that move in the future. *Chapter 13*

Mac OS The operating system for the Apple Macintosh computer. *Chapter 4*

macro Custom-designed procedures that you can add to application programs. *Chapter 6*

macro (scripting) language A user-oriented language that allows users to create programs (macros) that automate repetitive tasks. *Chapter 12*

magnetic disk Storage medium with random-access capability, accessed by the computer's disk drive. *Chapter 3*

magnetic-ink character reader Reads numbers printed with magnetic ink on checks. *Chapter 3*

magnetic tape A storage medium used with a tape drive to store large amounts of information in a small space at relatively low cost. *Chapter 3*

magneto-optical (MO) disks A type of removable media that uses a combination of magnetic disk technology and optical disk technology. *Chapter 3*

mailing list An email discussion groups on special-interest topics. A list can be small and local or large and global. Each group has a mailing address that looks like any Internet address. When you send a message to a mailing list address, every subscriber receives a copy, and you receive a copy of every mail message sent by everyone else to the list address. *Chapter 10*

mail merge Produces personalized form letters. When used with a database containing a list of names and addresses, a word processor can quickly generate individually addressed letters and mailing labels. *Chapter 5; Chapter 8*

mainframe computer Expensive, room-size computer, used mostly for large computing jobs. *Chapter 1*

management information systems (MIS) Systems that provide timely, reliable, and useful information to managers in business, industry, and government. MIS specialists apply the theoretical concepts of computer science to real-world, practical business problems. *Chapter 12; Chapter 14*

master pages In desktop publishing, the pages that control the general layout of the document. *Chapter 5*

mathematics processing software Software designed to deal with complex equations and calculations. A mathematics processor allows the user to easily create, manipulate, and solve equations. *Chapter 6*

MB See *megabyte.*

megabyte (MB) Approximately 1000K, or 1 million bytes. *Chapter 2*

memory Stores programs and the data they need to be instantly accessible to the CPU. *Chapter 2*

menu An on-screen list of command choices. *Chapter 4*

menu bar Part of the user interface. A bar that contains menus of choices. *Chapter 4*

menu-driven interface User interface that allows users to choose commands from on-screen lists called menus. *Chapter 4*

microcomputer Small computer made possible by the microprocessor. Now known as a personal computer. *Chapter 1*

microcomputer revolution Period that began in the mid-1970s when several companies introduced small microcomputers that were as powerful as their larger predecessors. *Chapter 1*

microprocessor Critical components of a complete computer, housed on a silicon chip. *Chapter 1*

Microsoft Windows The most popular and powerful PC operating system, uses a graphical user interface. Windows debuted in 1985. *Chapter 4*

microtechnology Technology that allows the development of micromachines, machines on the scale of a millionth of a meter. *Chapter 16*

MIDI (Musical Instrument Digital Interface) A standard interface that allows electronic instruments and computers to communicate with each other and work together. *Chapter 7*

MIPS (millions of instructions per second) A measurement of computer speed. *Chapter 16*

MIS See *management information systems.*

MO See *magneto-optical disks.*

modeling The use of computers to create abstract models of objects, organisms, organizations, and processes. *Chapter 6*

modem Modulator/demodulator. A hardware device that connects a computer's serial port to a telephone line. *Chapter 1; Chapter 9*

module (subprogram) In structured programming, a program is built from smaller programs called modules. *Chapter 12*

monitor Output device that displays text and graphics and receives messages from the computer. *Chapter 3*

monochrome monitor Monitor that displays two colors, usually black and white. *Chapter 3*

monospaced font A font in which all characters are equal width, like a typewriter's characters. *Chapter 5*

morph Video clip in which one image metamorphoses into another. *Chapter 7*

Moore's Law The prediction made in 1965 by Gordon Moore that the power of a silicon chip of the same price would double about every 18 months for at least two decades. *Chapter 1*

mouse A handheld input device that, when moved around on a desktop or table, moves a pointer around the computer screen. *Chapter 3*

moving text Transporting a block of text from one part of a document to another, or from one document to another. *Chapter 5*

MP3 A method of compression that can squeeze a music file to a fraction of its original CD file size with only slight loss of quality. *Chapter 7*

MS-DOS (Microsoft Disk Operating System) A character-based user interface used in the 1980s and early 1990s. Superseded by Windows. *Chapter 4*

multimedia Using some combination of text, graphics, animation, video, music, voice, and sound effects to communicate. *Chapter 7*

multimedia authoring software Enables the creation and editing of multimedia documents. *Chapter 7*

multiprocessing. See *parallel processing.*

multitasking Concurrent processing for personal computers. The user can issue a command that initiates a process and continue working with other applications while the computer follows through on the command. *Chapter 4*

N

nanotechnology The manufacture of machines on a scale of a few billionths of a meter. *Chapter 16*

narrowcasting Provides custom newscasts aimed at narrow groups or individuals. *Chapter 15*

natural language Languages that people speak and write every day. *Chapter 4*

natural-language communication Basically, human speech. In text it poses many software challenges. *Chapter 13*

navigating Moving to different parts of a document. *Chapter 5*

Net (Internet) A global interconnected network of thousands of networks linking academic, research, government, and commercial institutions, and other organizations and individuals. *Chapter 1; Chapter 10*

netiquette Rules of etiquette that apply to Internet communication. *Chapter 10*

network A computer system that links two or more computers. *Chapter 9*

network computer (NC) A computer designed to function as part of a network rather than as a PC. *Chapter 1*

network interface card (NIC) Care that adds an additional serial port to a computer. The port is especially designed for a direct network connection. *Chapter 9*

network license License for multiple copies or removing restrictions on software copying and use at a network site. *Chapter 9*

network operating system (NOS) Server operating system software for a local-area network. *Chapter 9*

network revolution The emergence of networks (clusters of computers linked together for communication and to share resources) and the beginning of the era of interpersonal computing. *Chapter 1*

neural network (neural net) Distributed, parallel computing systems inspired by the structure of the human brain. *Chapter 13*

newsgroup Ongoing teleconferences and public discussion groups on about every imaginable topic. You can check into and out of them whenever you want. All messages are posted on virtual bulletin boards for anyone to read. Newsgroups are organized hierarchically. *Chapter 10*

newsreader A client program that allows you to read newsgroups. Both text-based and graphical newsreaders are available. *Chapter 10*

NIC See *network interface card.*

node Each computer and shared peripheral on a local-area network. *Chapter 9*

nonimpact printer A printer that produces characters without physically striking the page. *Chapter 3*

nonvolatile memory Memory for permanent storage of information. *Chapter 2*

NOS See *network operating system.*

notebook computer Another term for laptop computer. *Chapter 1*

O

object-oriented database Instead of storing records in tables and hierarchies, stores software objects that contain procedures (or instructions) with data. *Chapter 8*

object-oriented (vector) graphics The storage of pictures as collections of lines, shapes, and other objects. *Chapter 7*

object-oriented programming (OOP) In OOP, a program is not a collection of step-by step instructions or procedures; it's a collection of objects. Objects contain both data and instructions and can send and receive messages. *Chapter 12*

OCR See *optical character recognition.*

office suite (application suite) Software bundle containing several application programs that are also sold as separate programs. *Chapter 4*

on line Connected to the computer system and ready to communicate. *Chapter 9*

on-line database A commercial, public, or private database that can be accessed through telecommunication lines. *Chapter 9*

on-line information service A service that allows hundreds of users at a time to send and receive information. America Online is an example. *Chapter 9*

OOP (object-oriented programming) In OOP, a program is not a collection of step-by step instructions or procedures; it's a collection of objects. Objects contain both data and instructions and can send and receive messages. *Chapter 12*

open Loading a file into the application. *Chapter 4*

open source software Software that can be distributed and modified freely by users; Linux is the best-known example. *Chapter 4*

open standards Standards not owned by any company. *Chapter 10*

operating system (OS) A system of programs that perform a variety of technical operations, providing an additional layer of insulation between the user and the bits-and-bytes world of computer hardware. *Chapter 4*

optical character recognition (OCR) Using a wand reader to recognize words and numbers at a POS terminal; locating and identifying printed characters embedded in images. *Chapter 3; Chapter 13*

optical computer A computer that transmits information in light waves rather than electrical pulses. *Chapter 16*

optical disk A high-capacity, highly reliable storage medium. *Chapter 3*

optical disk drive Uses laser beams to read and write bits of information on the surface of an optical disk. *Chapter 3*

optical-mark reader A reading device that uses reflected light to determine the location of pencil marks on standardized test answer sheets and similar forms. *Chapter 3*

OS See *operating system.*

outlining Arranging information into hierarchies or levels of ideas. *Chapter 5*

output Information given out by the computer. *Chapter 1*

output device Device for sending information from the computer, such as a monitor or printer. *Chapter 2*

P

packet switching   The standard technique used to send information over the Internet. A message is broken into packets that travel independently from network to network toward their common destination, where they are reunited. *Chapter 10*

page-description language   A language used by many drawing programs that describes text fonts, illustrations, and other elements of the printed page. *Chapter 7*

page-layout software   In desktop publishing, used to combine various source documents into a coherent, visually appealing publication. *Chapter 5*

painting software   Allows you to paint pixels on the screen with a pointing device. *Chapter 7*

pallete   A collection of colors that are available in drawing software. *Chapter 7*

paperless office   An office of the future in which magnetic and optical archives will replace reference books and file cabinets, electronic communication will replace letters and memos, and digital publications provided through the Internet and on-line services will replace newspapers and other periodicals. *Chapter 14*

paradigm shift   A change in thinking that results in a new way of seeing the world. *Chapter 14*

parallel processing   Using multiple processors to divide jobs into pieces and work simultaneously on the pieces. *Chapter 2*

parsing program (parser)   In translation, a program that analyzes sentence structure and identifies each word according to its part of speech. Another program looks up each word in a translation dictionary and substitutes the appropriate word. *Chapter 13*

password   A string of letters and numbers known only by you and the computer so that the computer can verify your identity. *Chapter 9; Chapter 11*

patent (law)   A type of law that protects inventions. *Chapter 11*

pattern recognition   Identifying recurring patterns in input data with the goal of understanding or categorizing that input. *Chapter 13*

PC   See *personal computer.*

PC card   A credit-card-size card that can be inserted into a slot to expand memory or add a peripheral to a computer; commonly used in portable computers. Once called PCMCIA. *Chapter 2*

PDA   See *personal digital assistant.*

peer-to-peer model   A LAN model that allows every computer on the network to be both client and server. *Chapter 9*

pen-based computer   A keyboardless machine that accepts input from a stylus applied directly to a flat-panel screen. *Chapter 3*

pen scanner   Wireless scanners that can perform optical character recognition. *Chapter 3*

peripheral   Input, output, and secondary storage devices. *Chapter 2*

personal communicator   See *personal digital assistant.*

personal computer (PC)   A small, powerful, relatively low-cost microcomputer. *Chapter 1*

personal digital assistant (PDA)   An antiquated term for a portable computer designed for communication instead of computing, combining a cellular phone, a fax modem, and other communication equipment in a small, wireless box. Now known as a palm-size personal communicator. *Chapter 1; Chapter 9*

personal information manager (PIM)   A specialized database program that automates an address/phone book, an appointment calendar, a to-do list, and miscellaneous notes. Also called an electronic organizer. *Chapter 8*

pie chart   A round pie-shape chart with "slices" that show the relative proportions of the parts to a whole. *Chapter 6*

PIM   See *personal information manager.*

pixel   A picture element (dot) on a computer screen or printout. Groups of pixels compose the images on the monitor and the output of a printout. *Chapter 3; Chapter 7*

platform   The combination of hardware and operating system software upon which application software is built. *Chapter 4*

plotter   An automated drawing tool that produces finely scaled drawings by moving pen and/or paper in response to computer commands. *Chapter 3*

plug-in   Software extensions that add new features. *Chapter 10*

point-of-sale (POS) terminal   A terminal with a wand reader attached, located in a store. The terminal sends information scanned by the wand to a mainframe computer. *Chapter 3*

point size   Measurement of characters, with one point equal to 1/72 inch. *Chapter 5*

port   Socket that allows information to pass in and out. *Chapter 2; Chapter 9*

portable computer   Small computers such as laptops and notebooks that are intended to be used anywhere. *Chapter 1*

Portable Document Format (PDF)   Allows documents of all types to be stored, viewed, or modified on any Windows or Macintosh computer, making it possible for many organizations to reduce paper flow. *Chapter 5*

portal   A Web site designed as a first-stop gateway to the Web. *Chapter 1*

POS   See *point-of-sale terminal.*

PostScipt   A standard page-description language. *Chapter 7*

presentation graphics software   Automates the creation of visual aids for lectures, training sessions, and other presentations. Can include everything from spreadsheet charting programs to animation editing software, but most commonly used for creating and displaying a series of on-screen slides to serve as visual aids for presentations. *Chapter 7*

printer   Output device that produces a paper copy of any information that can be displayed on the screen. *Chapter 3*

processor   Part of the computer that processes information, performs arithmetic calculations, and makes basic decisions based on information values. *Chapter 2*

program   Instructions that tell the hardware what to do to transform input into output. *Chapter 1*

programming   A specialized form of problem solving. The process includes defining the problem; devising, refining, and testing the algorithm; writing the program; and testing and debugging the program. *Chapter 12*

program verification   Techniques that prove the correctness of programs. *Chapter 12*

project management software   Coordinates, schedules, and tracks complex work projects. *Chapter 14*

prompt   Part of the user interface, characters (such as C:\>) that prompt the user to enter information. *Chapter 4*

proportionally spaced font   Fonts that allow more room for wide characters such as W than for narrow characters such as I. *Chapter 5*

protocol   A set of rules for the exchange of data between a terminal and a computer or between two computers. *Chapter 9*

prototype   A limited working system or subsystem which is created to give an idea of how the complete system will work. *Chapter 12*

pseudocode   A cross between a computer language and plain English used for writing algorithms. *Chapter 12*

public domain software Free software that is not copyrighted, offered through World Wide Web sites, electronic bulletin boards, user groups, and other sources. *Chapter 4*

pull-down menu In a graphical user interface, a menu located at the top of the screen and accessed with a mouse or with keyboard shortcuts. *Chapter 4*

pull technology Browsers on client computers pull information from server machines. The browser needs to initiate a request before any information is delivered. *Chapter 10*

push technology Information delivered automatically to a desktop computer. You subscribe to a service and specify the kinds of information you want to receive. Information is pushed to the subscriber through channels. Contrast with pull technology. *Chapter 10*

Q

query An information request. *Chapter 8*

query language A special language for performing queries, more precise than the English language. *Chapter 8*

R

RAM See *random access memory.*

random access Storage method that allows information retrieval without regard to the order in which it was recorded. *Chapter 3*

random access memory (RAM) Memory that stores program instructions and data temporarily. *Chapter 2*

range A rectangular block of cells. *Chapter 6*

raster (bit-mapped) graphics Painting programs create raster graphics that are, to the computer, simple maps showing how the pixels on the screen should be represented. *Chapter 7*

read-only memory (ROM) Memory that includes permanent information only. The computer can only read information from it; it can never write any new information on it. *Chapter 2*

real time When a computer performs tasks immediately. *Chapter 8*

real-time communication Internet communication that allows you to communicate with other users who are logged on at the same time. *Chapter 10*

real-time teleconference An on-line meeting between two or more people in which participants sit at a computer or terminal, watching messages appear on the screen as they're typed by other participants, and typing comments for others to see immediately. *Chapter 9*

record In a database, the information relating to one person, product, or event. *Chapter 8*

reduced matching Compiling profiles by combining information from different database files by looking for a shared unique field. *Chapter 8*

reduced instruction set computer (RISC) Processor designed to omit instructions that are seldom used, for the purpose of increasing speed. *Chapter 2*

regional work center Allows workers to commute to smaller offices closer to their homes. *Chapter 14*

relational database A program that allows files to be related to each other so that changes in one file are reflected in other files automatically. *Chapter 8*

remote access Network access via phone line, TV cable system, or wireless link. *Chapter 9*

remote login Allows users on one system to access other host systems across the network. *Chapter 10*

removable media High-capacity transportable storage devices. *Chapter 3*

repetitive-stress injuries Injuries, such as carpal tunnel syndrome, caused by repeating the same movements over long periods of time. *Chapter 3*

replication Automatic replication of values, labels, and formulas is a feature of spreadsheet software. *Chapter 6*

report A database printout that is an ordered list of selected records and fields in an easy-to-read form. *Chapter 8*

resolution Density of pixels, measured by the number of dots per inch. *Chapter 3; Chapter 7*

right to privacy Freedom from interference into the private sphere of a person's affairs. *Chapter 8*

RISC See *reduced instruction set computer.*

robot A computer-controlled machine designed to perform specific manual tasks. *Chapter 13*

ROM See *read-only memory.*

ROM cartridge A removable permanent storage device often used by home video game machines. *Chapter 2*

rows Along with columns, comprise the grid of a spreadsheet. *Chapter 6*

S

sabotage A malicious attack on work, tools, or business. *Chapter 1*

sans-serif font Fonts without fine lines at the ends of the main strokes of each character. *Chapter 5*

satellite office Allows workers to commute to smaller offices closer to their homes. *Chapter 14*

saving a document Making a disk file of your work for later retrieval. *Chapter 5*

scanner An input device that makes a digital representation of any printed image. *Chapter 3*

scatter chart Discovers a relationship between two variables. *Chapter 6*

scientific visualization software Uses shape, location in space, color, brightness, and motion to help us understand relationships that are invisible to us, providing graphical representation of numerical data. *Chapter 6*

scripting (macro) language A user-oriented language that allows users to create programs (macros) that automate repetitive tasks. *Chapter 12*

scrolling The movement of lines on and off the screen as you move through a document. *Chapter 5*

search Looking for a specific record. *Chapter 8*

search and replace Finding selected words or phrases throughout a document and replacing them with a different word or phrase. *Chapter 5*

search engine A program for locating information on the Web. *Chapter 1; Chapter 10*

search tool See *search engine.*

select (records) Looking for all records that match a set of criteria. *Chapter 8*

selecting text Highlighting text, usually by dragging the cursor across it. *Chapter 5*

self-maintaining system   A system that can diagnose and correct common problems without human intervention. *Chapter 16*

semantics   The underlying meaning of words and phrases. *Chapter 13*

sensing device   Monitors temperature, humidity, pressure, and other physical quantities to provide data used in robotics, environmental climate control, and other applications. *Chapter 3*

sensor   Allows digital devices to monitor the analog world. *Chapter 16*

sequencing software   Software that allows a computer to be used as a tool for musical composition, recording, and editing. *Chapter 7*

sequential access   Storage method that requires the user to retrieve information by zipping through it in the order in which it was recorded. *Chapter 3*

serif font   Fonts embellished with fine lines at the ends of the main strokes of each character. *Chapter 5*

server   A computer especially designed to provide software and other resources to other computers over a network. *Chapter 1*

server   In a local-area network under the client/server model, a high-speed, high-capacity computer containing data and other resources to be shared with client computers. *Chapter 9*

service bureau   A business used by desktop publishers to provide camera-ready pages. *Chapter 5*

set-top box   A special-purpose computer designed to provide Internet access and other services using a standard television set and (usually) a cable TV connection. *Chapter 1*

shareware   Software that is free to try, but must be purchased if kept. *Chapter 4*

shell   A program that puts a graphical face on top of a command line interface such as MS-DOS. *Chapter 4*

silicon chip   Hundreds of transistors packed into an integrated circuit on a piece of silicon. *Chapter 1*

simulation   Creating a computer model of a real-life situation. *Chapter 6*

site license   License for multiple copies or removing restrictions on software copying and use at a network site. *Chapter 9*

slot   Area in the computer's housing for inserting special-purpose circuit boards. *Chapter 2*

smart card   Looks like a standard credit card but uses an embedded microprocessor and memory instead of a magnetic strip. *Chapter 15*

smart weapon   Missiles that use computerized guidance systems to locate their targets. *Chapter 11*

software   Instructions that tell the hardware what to do to transform input into output. *Chapter 1*

software engineering   Attempts to apply engineering principles and techniques to the world of computer software. *Chapter 12*

software license   An agreement allowing the use of a software program on a single machine. *Chapter 4*

software piracy   The illegal duplication of copyrighted software. *Chapter 11*

sound card   A circuit board that allows the PC to accept microphone input, play music and other sound through speakers or headphone, and process sound in a variety of ways. *Chapter 3*

sort   Arranging records in alphabetic or numeric order based on values in one or more fields. *Chapter 8*

source document   In desktop publishing, the articles, chapters, drawings, maps, charts, and photographs that are to appear in the publication. Usually produced with standard word processors and graphics programs. *Chapter 5*

spam   Internet junk mail. *Chapter 10*

special-purpose (dedicated) computer   A computer that performs a specific task, such as controlling temperature and humidity in an office building. *Chapter 1*

speech synthesis   Software that produces synthetic speech. *Chapter 13*

spelling checker   A built-in component of word processors that compares words in a document with words in a disk-based dictionary and flags words not found in the dictionary. *Chapter 5*

spoofing   A process used to steal passwords on line. A spoofer launches a program that mimics a mainframe computer's login screen on an unattended terminal in a public lab. When an unsuspecting person types an ID and password, the program responds with an error message and remembers the secret codes. *Chapter 11*

spreadsheet software   Allows the user to control numbers, manipulating them in various ways. The software can manage budgeting, investment management, business projections, grade books, scientific simulations, checkbooks, financial planning and speculation, and other tasks involving numbers. *Chapter 6*

SQL   A query language available for many different database management systems. More than a query language, SQL also accesses databases from a wide variety of vendors. *Chapter 8*

stack chart   Stacked bars to show how proportions of a whole change over time. *Chapter 6*

statistical analysis software   Specialized software that tests the strength of data relationships, produces graphs showing how two or more variables relate to each other, uncovers trends, and performs other statistical analyses. *Chapter 6*

statistics   The science of analyzing and collecting data. *Chapter 6*

stepwise refinement   Breaking programming problems into smaller problems, and breaking each smaller problem into a subproblem that can be subdivided in the same way. *Chapter 12*

storage device   Long-term repositories for data. Disks and tape drives are examples. *Chapter 2*

structured programming   A technique to make programming easier and more productive. Structured programs are built from smaller programs, called modules or subprograms, that are in turn made of even smaller modules. *Chapter 12*

style sheet   Custom styles for each of the common elements in a document. *Chapter 5*

subnotebook computer   A portable computer, smaller than a notebook or laptop, about the size of a hardbound book. *Chapter 1*

subprogram (module)   In structured programming, a program is built from smaller programs called subprograms. *Chapter 12*

supercomputer   Super fast and super powerful, the fastest and most powerful computer made. *Chapter 1*

syntax   A set of rules for constructing sentences from words. Every language has a syntax. *Chapter 13*

syntax error   Violation of the "grammar rules" of a programming language. *Chapter 12*

synthesized sound   Synthetically generated computer sounds. *Chapter 7*

synthetic speech   Speech generated by computers by converting text into phonetic sounds. *Chapter 13*

system development life cycle   A sequence of steps or phases through which an information system passes between the time the system is conceived and the time it is phased out. *Chapter 12*

systems analyst   The computer professional primarily responsible for developing and managing an information system. *Chapter 12*

system software   Software that handles the details of computing. Includes the operating system and utility programs. *Chapter 4*

T

tape drive   Storage device that uses magnetic tape to store information. *Chapter 3*

tax preparation software   Provides a prefabricated worksheet where the user enters numbers into tax forms. Calculations are performed automatically, and the completed forms can be sent electronically to the IRS. *Chapter 6*

TB   See *terabyte*.

TCP/IP (Transmission Control Protocol/Internet Protocol)   Protocols developed as an experiment in internetworking, now the "language" of the Internet, allowing cross-network communication for almost every type of computer and network. *Chapter 10*

technophobia   The fear of technology. *Chapter 15*

telecommunication   Long-distance electronic communication in a variety of forms. *Chapter 9*

telecommuting   Home information workers, especially those who "commute" by modem. *Chapter 14*

teleconference   An on-line meeting between two or more people. *Chapter 9*

telephony   Allows personal computers to serve as speakerphones, answering machines, and complete voice mail systems. *Chapter 9*

telnet   The protocol that makes remote login through a command line interface possible. *Chapter 10*

template   In desktop publishing, professionally designed empty documents that can be adapted to specific user needs. *Chapter 5*

template   In spreadsheet software, a worksheet that contains labels and formulas but no data values. The template produces instant answers when you fill in the blanks. *Chapter 6*

terabyte (TB)   Approximately 1 million megabytes. *Chapter 2*

terminal   Combination keyboard and screen that transfers information to and from a mainframe computer. *Chapter 1*

terminal emulation   Software that makes your computer act as a dumb terminal—just an input/output device that allows you to send commands to and view information on the host computer. *Chapter 10*

terminal program   Allows a personal computer to function as a character-based terminal, allowing the computer to work with a modem. *Chapter 9*

testing   The process of checking the logic of an algorithm and the performance of a program. *Chapter 12*

text editing   Refining text and correcting errors. *Chapter 5*

text formatting   Controlling the format and style of a document. *Chapter 5*

thesaurus   A synonym finder included with a word processor. *Chapter 5*

3-D modeling software   Allows the user to create three-dimensional objects. The objects can be rotated, stretched, and combined with other model objects to create complex 3-D scenes. *Chapter 7*

timesharing   Technique by which mainframe computers communicate with several users simultaneously. *Chapter 1*

top-down design   A process that starts at the top, with main ideas, and works down to the details. *Chapter 12*

touch pad (trackpad)   A small flat-panel pointing device that is sensitive to light pressure. The user moves the pointer by dragging a finger across the pad. *Chapter 3*

touch screen   Pointing device that responds when the user points to or touches different screen regions. *Chapter 3*

trackball   Pointing device that remains stationary while the user moves a protruding ball to control the pointer on the screen. *Chapter 3*

track point   A small handle that sits in the center of the keyboard, responding to finger pressure by moving the mouse in the direction it is pushed. *Chapter 3*

transistor   Performs the same function as the vacuum tube by transferring electricity across a tiny resistor. *Chapter 1*

Trojan horse   A program that performs a useful task while at the same time carrying out some secret destructive act. A form of software sabotage. *Chapter 11*

Turing test   A way to test machine intelligence. *Chapter 13*

tutorial software   Provides direct instruction in a clearly specified skill or subject. *Chapter 15*

typeface   A style of characters used for printing. *Chapter 5*

U

Undo command   The process of taking back the last operation performed. *Chapter 5*

Unicode   A 65,000-character set for making letters, digits, and special characters fit into the computer's binary circuitry. *Chapter 2*

uninterruptible power supply (UPS)   Protects computers from data loss during power failures. *Chapter 11*

Universal serial bus (USB)   A cross-platform interface that can transmit data faster than the traditional PC serial port. *Chapter 3*

UNIX   An operating system that allows a timesharing computer to communicate with several other computers or terminals at once. UNIX is the most widely available multi-user operating system in use. It is also widely used on Internet hosts. *Chapter 4; Chapter 10*

upgrade   A new and improved version of a software program. *Chapter 4*

upload   The process of posting software on an FTP site or other on-line area so that it's available for others. *Chapter 9*

up-skilling   Increasing the skills required for a job when it is automated. *Chapter 14*

URL (Uniform resource locator)   The address of a Web site. *Chapter 1; Chapter 10*

user interface   The look and feel of the computing experience from a human point of view. *Chapter 4*

utility program   Tools for doing system maintenance and some repairs that are not automatically handled by the operating system. *Chapter 4*

V

vaccine program   A program designed to search for viruses, notify users when they're found, and remove them from infected disks or files. *Chapter 11*

values   The numbers that are the raw material used by spreadsheet software to perform calculations. *Chapter 6*

VDT   See *video display terminal*.

vector (object-oriented) graphics   The storage of pictures as collections of lines, shapes, and other objects. *Chapter 7*

vertical market application A computer application designed specifically for a particular business or industry. *Chapter 4*

video digitizer Converts analog video signals into digital data. *Chapter 7*

video display terminal (VDT) Output device that displays text and graphics and receives messages from the computer. *Chapter 3*

video editing software Software for editing digital video, including titles, sound, and special effect. *Chapter 7*

video teleconference Allows face-to-face communication over long distances by combining video and computer technology. *Chapter 9*

virtual memory Use of part of a computer hard disk as a substitute for RAM. *Chapter 4*

virtual reality Creates the illusion that the user is immersed in a world that exists only inside the computer, an environment that contains both scenes and the controls to change those scenes. *Chapter 4; Chapter 16*

virus Virus software spreads from program to program, or from disk to disk, and uses each infected program or disk to make more copies of itself. A form of software sabotage. *Chapter 11*

visual programming Allows programmers to create large portions of their programs by drawing pictures and pointing to on-screen objects, eliminating much of the coding of traditional programming. *Chapter 12*

voice mail A telephone-based messaging system with many of the features of an electronic mail system. *Chapter 9*

volatile memory Memory such as RAM that loses its contents when it loses electrical power. *Chapter 2*

WAN See *wide area network*.

wand reader A reading device that uses light to read alphabetic and numeric characters written in a specially designed typeface found on sales tags and credit card slips. *Chapter 3*

Web authoring program A WYSIWYG-like page-layout program that allows you to design a Web page, laying out text and graphics exactly the way you want them to look. The program then converts the layout into an HTML document. *Chapter 10*

Web browser An application program that allows you to explore the Web by clicking on hot hyperlinks in Web pages stored on Web sites. *Chapter 1; Chapter 10*

Web casting Delivering of streaming audio or video via the Web. *Chapter 10*

Web page A single document on the World Wide Web (WWW), made up of text and images and interlinked with other documents. *Chapter 1; Chapter 10*

Web server A computer that stores Web content and delivers it on demand to Web browsers. *Chapter 10*

Web site A collection of related Web pages stored on the same server. *Chapter 1; Chapter 10*

"What if?" question A feature of spreadsheet software that allows speculation by providing instant answers to hypothetical questions. *Chapter 6*

wide-area network (WAN) A network that extends over a long distance. Each network site is a node on the network. *Chapter 9*

window In a graphical user interface, a framed area that can be opened, closed, and rearranged with the mouse. Documents are displayed in windows. *Chapter 4*

wireless network Network in which a node has a tiny radio or infrared transmitter connected to its network port so it can send and receive data through the air rather than through cables. *Chapter 9*

wizard A software help technique that walks the user through a complex process. *Chapter 5*

word wrap The process of automatically moving words that will not fit on the current line to the next line in a document. *Chapter 5*

worksheet A spreadsheet document that appears on the screen as a grid of numbered rows and columns. *Chapter 6*

workstation A high-end desktop computer with massive computing power but is less expensive than a minicomputer. Workstations are the most powerful of the desktop computers. *Chapter 1*

World Wide Web (WWW, Web) Part of the Internet, a collection of multimedia documents created by organizations and users worldwide. Documents are linked in a hypertext Web that allows users to explore them with simple mouse clicks. *Chapter 1; Chapter 10*

worm Programs that use computer hosts to reproduce themselves. Worm programs travel independently over computer networks, seeking out uninfected workstations to occupy. A form of software sabotage. *Chapter 11*

WYSIWYG "What you see is what you get." With a word processor, the arrangement of the words on the screen represents a close approximation to the arrangement of words on the printed page. *Chapter 5; Chapter 7*

XML (EXtensible markup language.) A language that allows Web developers to control and display data the way they control text and graphics. Forms, database queries, and other data-intensive operations that can't be completely constructed with standard HTML are much easier with XML. *Chapter 10*

Y2K bug (millennium bug) The international sensation about the two-digit date problem when the year changed from 1999 to 2000. *Chapter 11*

Credits

Chapter 1

p.3   left: Courtesy of International Business Machines Corporation. Unauthorized use not permitted.

p.3   center: University of Minnesota Charles Babbage Institute.

p.3   right: Culver Pictures, Inc.

p.4   Marck Richards/PhotoEdit.

p.5   both: Courtesy of Bay Area Rapid Transit.

p.7   Photograph courtesy of the Hagley Museum and Library, Wilmington, Delaware.

p.8   top: Property of AT&T Archives, reprinted with permission of AT&T.

p.8   bottom: Courtesy of Intel Corporation.

p.9   top left: Robert E. Daemmrich/Tony Stone Images.

p.9   top right: Lonnie Duka/Tony Stone Images.

p.9   bottom: Photo provided courtesy of Proxima Corporation.

p.10   left: ©Steve Chenn/CORBIS.

p.10   right: Christopher Bissell/Tony Stone Images.

p.11   top: Courtesy: LANL-Neg# CN99-144.

p.11   bottom: Courtesy of International Business Machines Corporation. Unauthorized use not permitted.

p.12   left: Courtesy of Apple Computers, Inc.

p.12   right: Courtesy of International Business Machines Corporation. Unauthorized use not permitted.

p.13   top left: Courtesy of Apple Computers, Inc.

p.13   top right: 3COM and the 3COM logo are registered tradmarks. Palm V™ and the Palm V™ logo are trademarks of Palm Computing, Inc., 3COM Corporation or its subsidiaries.

p.13   center: Courtesy of NEC Computer Systems.

p.13   bottom left: Courtesy of International Business Machines Corporation. Unauthorized use not permitted.

p.13   bottom right: Hewlett-Packard Co.

p.14   left: Peter Menzel Photography.

p.14   center: Wheelchair from DEKA/Independence Technology, a Johnson & Johnson Company.

p.14   right: Sony Electronics, Inc.

p.15   all: Time Life Syndication.

p.16   NCSA Media Technology Resources, University of Illinois at Urbana-Champaign.

p.17   Greg Smith/SABA Press Photos, Inc.

p.18   top: Courtesy of International Business Corporation. Unauthorized use not permitted.

p.18   bottom: RCA/Thomson Consumer Electronics.

p.19   top: Courtesy of Adobe Systems, Inc.

p.19   above center: Reprinted by permission from Microsoft Corporation.

p.19   below center: Courtesy of Apple Computers, Inc.

p.19   bottom: Courtesy of Adobe Systems, Inc.

p.22   top: Courtesy of Macromedia.

p.22   above center: Courtesy of OneSeek Com, Inc.

p.22   below center: Courtesy of Caere Corporation.

p.22   bottom: Screenshot reprinted by permission from Microsoft Corporation

p.23   Hank Morgon/Rainbow.

p.24   Wayne R. Billenduke/Tony Stone Images.

p.25   Reprinted by permission of *Newsweek*.

Chapter 2

p.31   Courtesy of International Business Machines Corporation. Unauthorized use not permitted. Y. Karsh/IBM Archives.

p.32   Dell Computer Corporation.

p.36   Photo courtesy of Intel Corporation.

p.39   both: Photo courtesy of Intel Corporation.

p.40   both: Photo courtesy of Intel Corporation.

p.41   left and far left: Courtesy of Apple Computers, Inc.

p.41   right: Photo courtesy of Intel Corporation.

p.41   far right: Hewlett-Packard Company.

p.44   James A. Folts.

p.45   3COM/US Robotics.

p.48   Photo courtesy of Intel Corporation.

p.48   Reprinted by permission of *Forbes ASAP Magazine* ©Forbes, Inc. 1996.

Chapter 3

p.53   Apple Computers, Inc.

p.56   all: Screenshots reprinted by permission from Microsoft Corporation.

p.57   top left: Courtesy of Apple Computers, Inc.

p.57   bottom left: Courtesy of International Business Machines Corporation. Unauthorized use not permitted.

p.57   center and top right: Logitech, Inc.

p.57   bottom right: MicroTouch Systems, Inc.

p.58   top: James A. Folts.

p.58   bottom: Courtesy of C Technologies AB.

p.59   left: Aqcess Technologies, Inc.

p.59   top right: Handspring, Inc.

p.59   bottom right: Walt & Company Communications.

p.62   top left: Walt & Company Communications.

p.62   top center: Earle Palmer Brown.

p.62   top and bottom right: Irez Par Technologies, Inc.

p.62   bottom left: Philips Speech Processing.

p.62   bottom center: Mindstorm Communications.

p.63   top left, bottom left, middle right, bottom right: James A. Folts.

p.63   top right: Shandwick International.

p.65   left: Sony Electronics.

p.65   right: In Focus Systems, Inc.

p.67   top left, center, bottom left: Walt & Company Communications.

p.67   top right: Hewlett-Packard Company.

p.67   middle right: Canon Computer Systems.

p.67   bottom right: Darbe Rotach/CORBIS.

p.69   left: NASA Headquarters.

p.69   top right: Russell D. Curtis/Photo Researchers, Inc.

p.69   bottom right: Ecrix Corporation.

p.70   Courtesy Western Digital Corporation.

p.71   both: Iomega Corporation.

p.74   Mindstorm Communications.

p.75   James A. Folts.

p.76   both: James A. Folts.

p.77   Mindstorm Communications.

p.78   Reprinted by permission of *PC World On-line*.

Chapter 4

p.83   Reuters/Mike Blake/Archive Photos.

p.90   Screenshots reprinted by permission from Microsoft Corporation.

p.92   all: Screenshots reprinted by permission from Microsoft Corporation.

p.93   top: Courtesy of Apple Computers, Inc.

p.93   bottom: Courtesy of Sun Microsystems, Inc.

Index